Honour pricks me on. Yea, but how if honour prick me off when I come on? how then? Can honour set to a leg? No. Or an arm? No. Or take away the grief of a wound? No. Honour hath no skill in surgery, then? No. What is honour? A word. What is that word, honour? Air. A trim reckoning! Who hath it? He that died o' Wednesday. Doth he feel it? No. Doth he hear it? No. 'Tis insensible, then? Yea, to the dead. But will it not live with the living? No. Why? Detraction will not suffer it. Therefore I'll none of it: honour is a mere scutcheon: and so ends my catechism.

FALSTAFF

in Shakespeare's *Henry IV, Part 1*, ACT 5, SC. 1.

PIERRE BERTON'S

WAR of

1812

Being a COMPENDIUM of

THE INVASION OF CANADA

AND

FLAMES ACROSS THE BORDER

ANCHOR CANADA

The Invasion of Canada copyright © 1980 by Pierre Berton Enterprises Ltd.
Flames Across the Border copyright © 1981 by Pierre Berton Enterprises Ltd.
Anchor Canada omnibus edition 2011

This edition contains the complete texts of the original works.

LIBRARY OF CANADA CATALOGUING IN PUBLICATION DATA
is available upon request

ISBN 978-0-385-67648-9

Published in Canada by Anchor Canada,
a division of Random House of Canada Limited

Printed and bound in the United States of America

Visit Random House of Canada Limited's website:
www.randomhouse.ca

10 9 8 7 6 5 4 3 2

The Royal Family

The Mysterious North Klondike

Just Add Water and Stir

Adventures of a Columnist

Fast Fast Fast Relief

The Big Sell

The Comfortable Pew

The Cool, Crazy, Committed
    World of the Sixties

The Smug Minority

The National Dream

The Last Spike

Drifting Home

Hollywood's Canada

My Country

The Dionne Years

The Wild Frontier

The Invasion of Canada

Flames Across the Border

Why We Act Like Canadians

The Promised Land

Vimy

Starting Out

The Arctic Grail

The Great Depression

Niagara: A History of the Falls

My Times: Living with History

1967, The Last Good Year

Picture Books

The New City (with Henri Rossier)

Remember Yesterday

The Great Railway

The Klondike Quest

Pierre Berton's Picture Book of
    Niagara Falls

Winter

The Great Lakes

Seacoasts

Pierre Berton's Canada

Anthologies

Great Canadians

Pierre and Janet Berton's
    Canadian Food Guide

Historic Headlines

Farewell to the Twentieth Century

Worth Repeating

Welcome to the
    Twenty-first Century

Fiction

Masquerade
    (pseudonym Lisa Kroniuk)

Books for Young Readers

The Golden Trail

The Secret World of Og

Adventures in Canadian History
    (22 volumes)

Pierre Berton's War of 1812

The Invasion of Canada, 1812–1813   1

Flames Across the Border, 1813–1814   377

Index to The Invasion of Canada   885

Index to Flames Across the Border   896

The conquest of Canada is in our power. I trust I shall not be deemed presumptive when I state that I verily believe that the militia of Kentucky are alone competent to place Montreal and Upper Canada at your feet.

HENRY CLAY, TO THE UNITED STATES SENATE,

FEBRUARY 22, 1810.

THE
INVASION
OF
CANADA
1812–1813

The Invasion of Canada, 1812-1813

	Maps	5
	Cast of Characters	6
PREVIEW	**Porter Hanks's War**	11
OVERVIEW	**The War of 1812**	16
ONE	**Prelude to Invasion: 1807–1811**	28
	The Road to Tippecanoe	
TWO	**Prelude to Invasion: 1812**	77
	Marching as to War	
THREE	**Michilimackinac**	100
	The Bloodless Victory	
FOUR	**Detroit**	112
	The Disintegration of William Hull	
FIVE	**Chicago**	196
	Horror on Lake Michigan	
SIX	**Queenston Heights**	205
	The End of Isaac Brock	
SEVEN	**Black Rock**	267
	Opéra Bouffe on the Niagara	

EIGHT   **Frenchtown**   276
Massacre at the River Raisin

AFTERVIEW   **The New War**   320
CODA   **William Atherton's War**   328

Sources and Acknowledgements   *332*
Notes   *336*
Select Bibliography   *361*
Index   *885*

Maps

Drawn by Geoffrey Matthews

The Strategic Significance of Michilimackinac   10

American Invasion Strategy, Summer, 1812   14, 15

The Theatre of War   24

American-Indian Battles, 1790–1794   33

Harrison's Purchase   46

Tecumseh's Frontier   56

The Wabash   70

The Battle of Tippecanoe   72

Hull's March to Detroit   93

The Wisconsin-Fox Portage   101

Michilimackinac Island   109

The Detroit Frontier   116

Baynes's Journey to Albany   157

Brock's Passage to Amherstburg   167

The Capture of Detroit   179

Mrs. Simmons's Trek   202

The Niagara Frontier   214

The Battle of Queenston Heights   245

Harrison's Three-Column Drive to the Maumee Rapids   287

American Search and Destroy Missions against the Tribes,
    Autumn, 1812   290

The Battle of Frenchtown   307

Cast of Characters

PRELUDE TO INVASION

British and Canadians

Sir James Craig, Governor General of Canada, 1807–11.

Sir George Prevost, Governor General of the Canadas and commander
of the forces, 1811–15.

Francis Gore, Lieutenant-Governor of Upper Canada, 1806–17. On leave
in England, 1811–15.

Major-General Isaac Brock, Administrator of Upper Canada and
commander of the forces in Upper Canada, 1810–12.

William Claus, Deputy Superintendent, Indian Department, Upper
Canada, 1806–26.

Matthew Elliott, Superintendent of Indian Affairs at Amherstburg,
1796–97; 1808–14.

Robert Dickson (known as **Mascotapah,** the Red-Haired Man), fur
trader. Led Menominee, Winnebago, and Sioux in attack on
Michilimackinac.

Augustus Foster, British Minister Plenipotentiary to America, 1811–12.

Americans

Thomas Jefferson, President, 1801–9.

James Madison, President, 1809–17.

William Eustis, Secretary of War, 1809–12.

William Henry Harrison, Governor, Indiana Territory, 1800–1813.
    Commander of the Army of the Northwest from September,
    1812.

William Hull, Governor, Michigan Territory, 1805–12. Commander of
    the Army of the Northwest, April–August, 1812.

Henry Dearborn, Secretary of War, 1801–9. Senior major-general, U.S.
    Army, 1812–13.

Henry Clay, Speaker of the House of Representatives, November, 1811.
    Leader of the War Hawks.

Indian Leaders

The Prophet. Born Laulewausika; later Tenskwatawa.

Tecumseh, the Prophet's older brother, leader of the Indian Confederacy.

THE DETROIT FRONTIER

Isaac Brock's Command: Summer, 1812

Thomas Bligh St. George, Lieutenant-Colonel; commanding officer,
    Fort Amherstburg.

Henry Procter, Lieutenant-Colonel; succeeded St. George as
    commanding officer, Fort Amherstburg.

J.B. Glegg, Major; Brock's military aide.

John Macdonell, Lieutenant-Colonel; Brock's provincial aide, Acting
    Attorney-General of Upper Canada.

Adam Muir, Major, 41st Regiment.

William Hull's Command: Summer, 1812

Duncan Mc Arthur, Colonel, 1st Regiment, Ohio Volunteers.
James Findlay, Colonel, 2nd Regiment, Ohio Volunteers.
Lewis Cass, Colonel, 3rd Regiment, Ohio Volunteers.
James Miller, Lieutenant-Colonel, 4th U.S. Infantry (regular army).

Henry Procter's Command: Winter, 1812–13

Ebenezer Reynolds, Major, Essex Militia.
Roundhead, Wyandot chief.

William Henry Harrison's Command: Winter, 1812–13

James Winchester, Brigadier-General; commander, left wing, Army of
    the Northwest.
John Allen, Lieutenant-Colonel, 1st Kentucky Rifles.
William Lewis, Lieutenant-Colonel, 5th Regiment, Kentucky
    Volunteers.
Samuel Wells, Lieutenant-Colonel, 17th U.S. Infantry (regular army).

THE NIAGARA FRONTIER

Isaac Brock's Command: Fall, 1812

Christopher Myers, Lieutenant-Colonel; commanding officer, Fort
    George.
Roger Hale Sheaffe, Major-General; second-in-command to Brock.
    Commanded British forces on Brock's death.
Thomas Evans, Brigade Major, Fort George.
John Dennis, Captain, 49th Regiment; commander of flank company
    defending Queenston.
John Williams, Captain, 49th Regiment.
James Crooks, Captain, 1st Lincoln Militia.

William Holcroft, Captain, Royal Artillery.

Frederic Rolette, Lieutenant, Provincial Marine.

Robert Irvine, Second-Lieutenant, Provincial Marine.

John Brant, Mohawk chief.

John Norton, Captain, Indian Department; leader of Mohawks.

Henry Dearborn's Command: Fall, 1812

Stephen Van Rensselaer, Major-General, New York state militia; senior commander on the Niagara frontier.

Solomon Van Rensselaer, Lieutenant-Colonel; cousin and aide-de-camp to Stephen Van Rensselaer.

John Lovett, Major; aide to Stephen and Solomon Van Rensselaer. In charge of artillery at Fort Grey at Battle of Queenston Heights.

William Wadsworth, Brigadier-General, Upper New York State militia.

Alexander Smyth, Brigadier-General, regular army, Niagara frontier. Replaced Stephen Van Rensselaer following Battle of Queenston Heights.

John Chrystie, Lieutenant-Colonel, 13th U.S. Infantry (regular army).

John Fenwick, Lieutenant-Colonel, U.S. Light Artillery.

John E. Wool, Captain, 13th U.S. Infantry.

Winfield Scott, Lieutenant-Colonel, 2nd U.S. Artillery.

Peter B. Porter, Quartermaster General, Upper New York State. Member of the War Hawk faction in Congress.

Jesse D. Elliott, Lieutenant, U.S. Navy.

The Strategic Significance of Michilimackinac

Porter Hanks's War

MICHILIMACKINAC ISLAND, MICHIGAN TERRITORY, U.S.A. *The small hours of a soft July morning in 1812.*

The lake is silent, save for the whisper of waves lapping the shoreline. In the starlight, the island's cliffs stand out darkly against the surrounding flatland. In the fort above the village at the southern tip the American commander, Lieutenant Porter Hanks, lies asleep, ignorant of a war that will tragically affect his future. Napoleon has entered Russia; Wellington is pushing toward Madrid; and in Washington, the die has been cast for invasion. But history has passed Hanks by. It is nine months since he has heard from Washington; for all he knows of the civilized world he might as well be on the moon.

The civilized world ends at the Detroit River, some 350 miles to the southeast as the canoe travels. Mackinac Island is its outpost, a minor Gibraltar lying in the narrows between Lakes Huron and Michigan. Whoever controls it controls the routes to the fur country—the domain of the Nor'Westers beyond Superior and the no man's land of the upper Missouri and Mississippi. It is a prize worth fighting for.

Hanks slumbers on, oblivious of a quiet bustling in the village directly below—of low knockings, whispers, small children's plaints quickly hushed, rustlings, soft footsteps, the creak of cartwheels on grass—slumbers fitfully, his dreams troubled by a growing uneasiness, until the drum roll of reveille wakes him. He suspects something is going to happen. He has been seven years a soldier, knows trouble when he sees it, has watched it paddling by him for a week. An extraordinary number of Indians have been passing the fort, apparently on their way to the British garrison at St. Joseph's Island, forty-five miles to the northeast, just beyond the border. Why? The answers are strangely evasive. The Ottawa and Chippewa chiefs, once so friendly, have turned suspiciously cool. On the British side, it is said, the tribes have gathered by the hundreds from distant frontiers: Sioux from the upper Mississippi, Winnebago from the Wisconsin country, Menominee from the shores of Green Bay.

Hanks peers over the palisades of the fort and gazes down on the village below, a crescent of whitewashed houses, following the curve of a pebbled beach. He sees at once that something is wrong. For the village is not sleeping; it is dead. No curl of smoke rises above the cedar-bark roofs; no human cry echoes across the waters of the lake; no movement ruffles the weeds that edge the roadway.

What is going on? Hanks dispatches his second-in-command, Lieutenant Archibald Darragh, to find out. But he does not need to wait for Darragh's report. Clambering up the slope comes his only other commissioned officer, the surgeon's mate, Sylvester Day, who prefers to live in the village. Dr. Day's breathless report is blunt: British redcoats and Indians have landed at the opposite end of the island. All the villagers have been collected quietly and, for their own safety, herded into an old distillery under the bluff at the west end of town. Three of the most prominent citizens are under guard as hostages.

Hanks reacts instantly to this news: musters his men, stocks his blockhouses with ammunition, charges his field pieces, follows the book. He must know that he is merely playing soldier, for he has fewer than sixty effective troops under his command—men rendered stale by their frontier exile. Presently he becomes aware of a British six-pounder on the forested bluff above, pointing directly into his bastion. Through the spring foliage he can see the flash of British scarlet and—the ultimate horror—the dark forms of their native allies. A single word forms in his mind, a truly terrible word for anyone with frontier experience: massacre—visions of mutilated bodies, decapitated children, disembowelled housewives, scalps bloodying the pickets.

Hanks can fight to the last man and become a posthumous hero. If it were merely the aging troops of Fort St. Joseph that faced him, he might be prepared to do just that. But to the last woman? To the last child? Against an enemy whose savagery is said to be without limits?

A white flag flutters before him. Under its protection a British truce party marches into the fort, accompanied by the three civilian hostages. The parley is brief and to the point. Hanks must surrender. The accompanying phrase "or else" hangs unspoken in the air. The hostages urge him to accept, but it is doubtful whether he needs their counsel. He agrees to everything; the fort and the island will become British. The Americans must take the oath of allegiance to the King or leave. His troops are to be paroled to their homes. Until exchanged they can take no further part in the war.

The war? What war? The date is July 17. A full month has passed since the United States declared war on Great Britain, but this is the first Hanks has heard of it. An invasion force has already crossed the Detroit River into Canada and skirmished with the British, but nobody in Washington, it seems, has grasped the urgency of a speedy warning to the western flank of the American frontier. It is entirely characteristic of this senseless and tragic conflict that it should have its beginnings in this topsy-turvy fashion, with the invaders invaded in a trackless wilderness hundreds of miles from the nerve centres of command.

For its dereliction the American government will pay dear. This bloodless battle is also one of the most significant. The news of the capture of Michilimackinac Island will touch off a chain of events that will frustrate the Americans in their attempt to seize British North America, an enterprise that most of them believe to be, in Thomas Jefferson's much-quoted phrase, "a mere matter of marching."

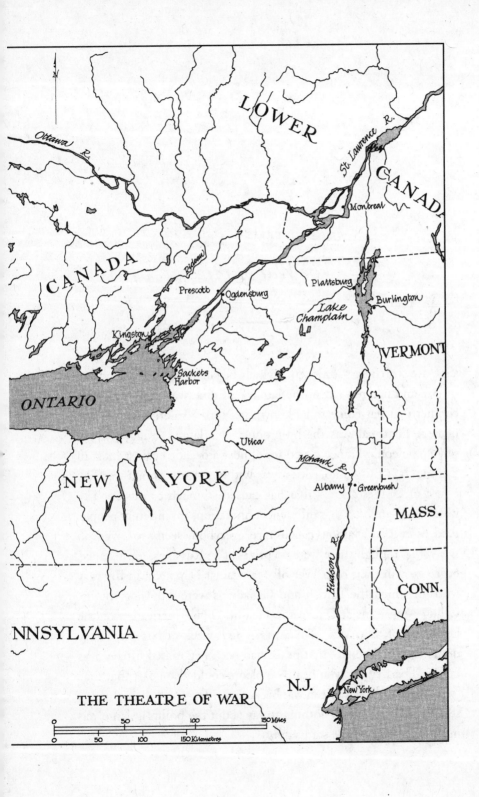

THE THEATRE OF WAR

The War of 1812

———

THE INVASION OF CANADA, which began in the early summer of 1812 and petered out in the late fall of 1814, was part of a larger conflict that has come to be known in North America as the War of 1812. That war was the by-product of a larger struggle, which saw Napoleonic France pitted for almost a decade against most of Europe. It is this complexity, a war within a war within a war, like a nest of Chinese boxes, that has caused so much confusion. The watershed date "1812" has different connotations for different people. And, as in Alice's famous caucus race, everybody seems to have won *something*, though there were no prizes. The Russians, for instance, began to win their own War of 1812 against Napoleon in the very week in which the British and Canadians were repulsing the invading Americans at Queenston Heights. The Americans won the last battle of their War of 1812 in the first week of 1815—a victory diminished by the fact that peace had been negotiated fifteen days before. The British, who beat Napoleon, could also boast that they "won" the North American war because the Treaty of Ghent, which settled the matter, had nothing to say about the points at issue and merely maintained the status quo.

This work deals with the war that Canada won, or to put it more precisely *did not lose*, by successfully repulsing the armies that tried to invade and conquer British North America. The war was fought almost entirely in Upper Canada, whose settlers, most of them Americans, did not invite the war, did not care about the issues, and did not want to fight. They were the victims of a clash between two major powers who, by the accident of geography, found it convenient to settle their differences by doing violence to the body of another. The invasion of Canada was not the first time that two armies have bloodied neutral ground over issues that did not concern the inhabitants; nor has it been the last.

Of all the wars fought by the English-speaking peoples, this was one of the strangest—a war entered into blindly and fought (also blindly) by men out of touch not only with reality but also with their own forces. Washington was separated from the fighting frontier by hundreds of miles of forest, rock, and swamp. The ultimate British authority was an ocean away and the nominal authority a fortnight distant from the real command. Orders could take days, weeks, even months to reach the troops.

Like some other wars, this one began bloodlessly with expressions of civility on both sides and the conviction that it would be over by Christmas. It did not end that way, for horror breeds hatred, and no war (certainly not this one) can be free of atrocity. Nor was it free of bombast. As in most wars, the leaders on both sides were convinced that their cause was just and that the Deity was firmly in their camp, leading them to victory. Slogans about "freedom" and "slavery," "despotism" and "liberty" were batted back and forth across the border like shuttlecocks. Each side believed, or pretended to believe, that the other was held in thrall by a pernicious form of government.

At the outset, it was a gentlemen's war. Officers on opposing sides met for parleys under flags of truce, offered hospitality, exchanged cordialities, murmured the hope that hostilities would quickly end. Belligerents addressed one another in flowery terms. The same men who declared they would never be slaves of the enemy had "the honour to be y'r humble and obedient servant." When Isaac Brock fell at Queenston, the men responsible for his death joined in the general grief. Roger Sheaffe, his successor, expressed in writing his great regret for the wounds suffered by an opposing commander— wounds that put him out of action and helped Sheaffe win the day. "If there be anything at my command that your side of the river cannot furnish, which would be either useful or agreeable . . . I beg you will be so good as to have me apprised of it," he wrote to the enemy. When the first word of the declaration of war reached the British post at Fort George on the Niagara frontier, its officers were entertaining their American opposite numbers at dinner. They insisted that the meal continue as if hostilities had not commenced, then, with much handshaking and expressions of regret, accompanied their guests to their boats. Within a few weeks, the former dinner companions were ripping through one another's homes and fortifications with red-hot cannonballs.

For a war of thirty months' duration, the casualties were not heavy. In those same years many a European battle counted far more dead and wounded in a single day. But for those who did fall, it was a truly terrible war, fought under appalling conditions far from civilization and medical aid. Those victims who were torn to pieces by cannon-balls, their brains often spattering their comrades, might be considered lucky. The wounded endured agonies, banged about in open carts, exposed to blizzards or driving rain, hauled for miles over rutted tracks to the surgeon's table where, with a musket ball clamped between their teeth and when possible a tot of rum warming their bellies, they suffered the horrors of a hasty amputation.

As the war progressed, it grew more vicious. There was savagery on both sides by white frontiersmen as well as Indians, who scalped the fallen sometimes when they were still alive. Men were roasted in flaming buildings, chopped to pieces by tomahawks, sliced open by bayonets, drowned, frozen, or felled by sickness, which took more lives on both sides than all the battles combined. There were times when a third of an army was too ill to fight. The diseases were given vague names like "ague" and "swamp fever," which might mean influenza, pneumonia, malaria, typhus, dysentery, or simply that the combatants were too cold, too weary, or too dispirited to march or even stand. And no wonder: on both sides the armies, especially the citizen soldiers of the militia, were ill equipped for war. Men were forced to trudge through ankle-deep snow and to wade freezing rivers without shoes; to sleep in the open without blankets; to face the Canadian winter lacking mitts and greatcoats, their clothes in tatters, their hands and feet bound in rags, tormented by frostbite in January and insects in June. The military may have seen the war coming, but the politicians were not prepared to pay its price.

At the planning level, the war was marked by incredible bungling. As in so many wars, but especially in this one, the day was often won not by the most brilliant commander, for there were few brilliant commanders, but by the least incompetent. On the American side, where civilian leaders were mixed in with regular army officers, the commands were marked by petty jealousies, vicious infighting, bitter rivalries. On certain memorable occasions, high-ranking officers supposedly fighting the British preferred to fight each other with pistols at dawn. Old soldiers were chosen for command simply because they were old soldiers; they acted like sports heroes long past their prime, weary of the contest, sustained only by the glamour of the past, struggling as much against the ambitions of younger aspirants as against the enemy. Some were chosen capriciously. One general was given an important command solely for political reasons—to get him out of the way.

On the Canadian side, where "democracy" was a wicked word and the army was run autocratically by British professionals, there was little of this. Many of these men, however, were cast-offs from Europe. The officers gained their commissions through purchase, not competence. With certain exceptions, the cream of the British Army was with Wellington, fighting Napoleon's forces on the Iberian Peninsula. Aging veterans made up part of the garrison forces in Canada. Boys of fourteen and fifteen fought with the militia. Lacklustre leadership, incompetent planning, timidity and vacillation were too often the concomitants of command on both sides of the border.

The militia on both sides was a rabble. Hastily summoned and hastily trained when trained at all, they fought sometimes reluctantly, sometimes with gallantry. On the Canadian side these citizen soldiers were drilled about three days in a month. They were called up when needed, placed away from the centre of the line, on the flanks (when the line existed at all), and, after an engagement, sent back to their homes and farms until needed once more. The more patriotic signed up for the duration and became seasoned warriors. The American army was a confusion of regular soldiers, state militia, and federal volunteers recruited from the militia for terms of service that ranged from one month to a year or more.

On both sides men thought nothing of leaving the scene of battle to thresh their grain at harvest time. For most of the men who fought it, then, it was a part-time war. Some refused to fight. In spite of the harsh discipline, men on both sides mutinied. Soldiers were shot for desertion, forced to ride bent saplings, to stand barefoot on sharpened stakes, branded, or flogged almost to death. Neither threats nor pleas could stop thousands of American militiamen from refusing to fight on foreign soil. To the dismay of their commanders, these amateur soldiers took democracy at its face value, electing their own officers and, on occasion, dismissing them. In Upper Canada treason worked its slow poison, even invading the legislature. Farmers were hanged for abetting the enemy; tribunes of the people took refuge on foreign soil to raise squads of traitors; dark suspicions, often unfounded, seeped down the concession roads, causing neighbour to denounce neighbour.

The war, like other wars, brought disaster to thousands and prosperity to thousands more. Prices rose; profits boomed. The border might be in flames, its people at each other's throats, but that did not prevent merchants on both sides from crossing over in the interests of commerce. Americans on the eastern shore of Lake Champlain fed the British troops fighting on the western side. Montreal middlemen grew rich supplying the needs of New England. Pork, beef, and grain from Vermont and other states found their way into the commissariats of Upper Canada. Before the invasion came to an end, two out of every three soldiers fighting for the safety and honour of Canada were subsisting on beef brought in by enemy contractors.

In the Atlantic provinces and the neighbouring New England states, the war scarcely existed. On July 3, 1812, the Lieutenant-Governor of Nova Scotia issued a proclamation announcing that his province and New Brunswick would abstain from predatory warfare against their neighbours and that trade would continue "without Molestation." Between Maine and New Brunswick it was more than business as usual; it was frolic as usual. The border town of St. Stephen, realizing that its American neighbour, Calais, could not obtain fireworks for its Independence Day celebration, obligingly helped out with a gift of gun powder.

But on the fighting frontier it was civil war. There is a story that the man who fired the first cannonball across the river during the battle of Detroit killed his best friend on the American side—a legend, possibly, but perfectly plausible. Almost everyone had a friend or a relative on the other side of the border. Sheaffe, the British general, had a sister Margaret in Boston. William Hull, the defender of Detroit, had a brother Isaac living on the Thames. The border was irrelevant; people crossed it as they would a street. Many owned land or had business interests on the other side. One of these was John Askin of Sandwich, Upper Canada, the venerable fur trader and patriarch (various members of whose extensive family will appear from time to time in these pages). During the war, Askin continued to correspond with his friend and kinsman Elijah Brush, the militia commander at Detroit, who was married to Askin's daughter Adelaide. When the Americans invaded Sandwich and Askin was forced to flee, Brush obligingly detailed some of his men to harvest Askin's crops. When Detroit fell, Brush consigned his personal papers, money, and members of his family to Askin's care. None of this prevented Askin's sons, nephews, and grandsons from taking up arms and killing Americans.

They did so reluctantly, for this was a war that almost nobody wanted. The British, who had been embroiled with Napoleon for seven years, certainly did not want it, did not believe it would occur, and in a clumsy, last-minute effort tried to prevent it. The Canadian settlers, struggling to master a forbidding if fertile wilderness, did not want it either; at best it was an interruption, at worst a tragedy. The majority, whenever possible, did their best to stay out of it. Nor did the mass of the American people want to go to war; a great many, especially in the New England states, sat it out; others fought half-heartedly. Congress, in the words of a Kentucky editor, was "driven, goaded, dragged, forced, kicked" into the conflict by a small, eloquent group that Thomas Jefferson dubbed the War Hawks.

America went to war as a last resort because her leaders felt that the nation's honour had been besmirched to a point where any other action would be unthinkable. In their zeal to conquer Napoleon, the British pushed the Americans too far and dismissed their former colonists with an indifference that bordered on contempt, thus repeating the errors of 1776. In that sense, the War of 1812 was a continuation of the American Revolution.

It began with Napoleon, for without Napoleon there would have been no war. (The President, James Madison, remarked after the fact that had he known Napoleon would be defeated his country would have stayed out of it.) Great Britain, fighting for her life against France, was bent on all-out maritime warfare. If a neutral America, reaping the economic benefits, was bruised a little on the high seas, well, that was unfortunate but necessary. America, in British eyes, was a weak, inconsequential nation that could be pushed around with impunity. In the words of the London *Courier*, "two fifty gun ships would be able to burn, sink and destroy the whole American navy."

This attitude was expressed first in the British policy of boarding American ships and impressing American seamen for service in the Royal Navy on the grounds that they were deserters from British service. At least three thousand and perhaps as many as seven thousand fell victim to this practice, which infuriated the country and was one of the two chief causes of the war.

The other was the equally galling Orders in Council, the last enacted in November, 1807, as an act of reprisal against the French.

With cool disdain for the rights of neutrals as well as for American sea power, the British warned that they would seize on the open ocean any ship that dared sail directly for a Napoleonic port. By 1812 they had captured almost four hundred American vessels, some within sight of the U.S. coast, and played havoc with the American export trade.

There were other irritants, especially in the more volatile southern and western states, where a serious economic depression was blamed, not without reason, on the British blockade. The slump hit the Mississippi Valley in 1808, shortly after Britain proclaimed the Orders in Council. Prices collapsed. Cotton and tobacco could no longer be exported. This, combined with the growing Indian threat to the frontier settlements, was used to bolster the arguments of those seeking an excuse for war. In Kentucky especially—the most hawkish of states—and in Ohio and the territories, it was widely believed that British agents were goading the various tribes to revolt. There was talk of teaching the Indians a lesson, even driving the British out of North America, thereby breaking the fur monopoly, opening the land to settlement, and strengthening the Union. Certain western expansionists also saw the coming war as one of liberation. It was widely believed that most Canadians wanted to become Americans. If they did not, well, that was their destiny.

In the summer of 1812, with three American armies threatening the border strongpoints—Amherstburg, Queenston, Montreal, and Kingston—the early fall of Upper Canada and the subsequent collapse of Quebec seemed certain. In British North America there were some three hundred thousand souls, in the Union to the south, almost eight million. In Upper Canada, three out of five settlers were newly arrived Americans, people of uncertain loyalties, lured from New York, Pennsylvania, and Connecticut by the promise of cheap land. They scarcely thought of themselves as British, though they were forced into a token oath of allegiance, and they certainly did not call themselves Canadian. (That word was reserved for their French-speaking neighbours, many of whom lived on American soil in the vicinity of Detroit.) Surely these people would not oppose an invasion by their compatriots!

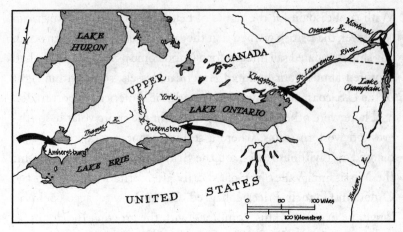

American Invasion Strategy, Summer, 1812

Nor, on the face of it, would they. There is little evidence of any surge of national pride rippling across the grain fields, swamps, and forests of Upper Canada in the early days of the war; quite the opposite. The main emotion was not patriotism but fear: fear of the invaders who could and did loot the farms to feed themselves; fear of the British regulars, whose task it was to stiffen the backbones of the reluctant citizen soldiers; fear of the Indians; fear of losing a harvest, a homestead, and above all a life. Many of the militia had to be goaded into fighting, while large numbers of settlers expressed pro-American sympathies, sometimes openly, more often privately. It is possible, even probable, that without the war the province would eventually have become another state in the Union. The Americans could have had it by osmosis. But the war intervened.

How was it that a tiny population, badly divided, with little claim to any national sentiment, was able to ward off continued attack by a powerful neighbour with vastly greater resources? There are at least three considerations.

First, the British presence. The regulars were few in number but well disciplined. Raw troops were no match for them. And, thanks to Isaac Brock's prescience, the country was better prepared for war than its enemy.

Second, American ineptness, especially in the war's first, crucial year. The United States was not a military nation. Her leaders were antiquated or inexperienced, her soldiers untrained, her government unready for conflict, her state militia reluctant to fight on foreign soil.

Third, and by no means least, the alliance between the Indians and the British, which led to decisive victories in the campaigns of 1812.

History has tended to gloss over the contributions made by the various tribes—and especially by the polyglot army under the leadership of the Shawnee war chief Tecumseh—in the first year of the war. Yet without the presence of the Indians at crucial turning points in the conflict, much of Upper Canada would surely have been in the hands of the Americans by the spring of 1813, if not sooner. British regulars alone could not have stemmed the tide. To shore up the thinly held garrisons the Indians were essential.

They were often a nuisance. Mercurial and unreliable, indifferent to the so-called civilized rules of warfare, difficult, even impossible to control, they came and went as they pleased, consuming vast quantities of scarce provisions. But as guerrillas they were superb. Their very presence was enough to terrify the Americans into submission.

For this, the United States had itself to blame. Jeffersonian policy, stripped of its honeyed verbiage, was to cheat the Indians out of their hunting-grounds. This thinly disguised thievery alienated the tribes in the Northwest, produced the phenomenon of the Shawnee Prophet, led to the inspired leadership of Tecumseh, and eventually drove thousands of native Americans into the arms of the British, leaving America's left flank dangerously exposed in the war that followed.

The only group of Americans who truly thirsted for war, apart from the handful of congressmen known as War Hawks, were Tecumseh's followers. In revenging themselves on the hated Long Knives they hoped to regain the lands from which they had been driven. It was a wistful fantasy, doomed to failure. One of the several ironies of this foolish and unnecessary war is that the warriors who helped save Canada gained nothing except a few American scalps.

The role of the Indians and that of the British regulars was played down in the years following the war. For more than a century it was common cant that the diverse population of Upper Canada—immigrants, settlers, ex-Americans, Loyalists, Britons, Scots, and Irish—closed ranks to defeat the enemy. This belief still lingers, though there is little evidence to support it. Certainly the old Loyalists and their sons rushed to the colours, and in the capital of York the British aristocracy (whose leading ornament was the Reverend Doctor John Strachan) glowed with patriotic fervour. But the mass of the people were at best apathetic and at worst disaffected. Some five hundred of the latter have been officially identified—men and women who either fled to the other side or supported the enemy by word or deed. Who can guess how many more kept prudently silent or worked in secret for the invaders? The reluctance of the militia to do battle when the war went badly suggests that the number was not small.

Traditionally, a common enemy unites a people in a common cause, especially when family farms are overrun, crops despoiled, homesteads gutted, livestock dispersed. But again there is little evidence of a united front against the enemy on the part of the people who suffered these disasters; it is doubtful if they were any angrier at the Americans than at the British and Indians, who actually caused a third of the devastation. The total bill for war losses came to almost a million dollars at a time when a private soldier's daily pay was twenty-five cents. Compensation was not paid until 1824 and never paid in full. None of that helped make the cause universally popular.

Yet, in an odd way, the war did help to change Upper Canada from a loose aggregation of village states into something approaching a political entity. The war, or more properly the *myth* of the war, gave the rootless new settlers a sense of community. In the end, the myth became the reality. In the long run it did not matter who fought or who did not, who supported the cause or who disdained it. As the years went by and memories dimmed, as old scars healed and old grudges evaporated, as aging veterans reminisced and new leaders hyperbolized, the settlers began to believe that they had repelled the invader almost single-handed. For the first time, Upper Canadians shared a common tradition.

It was a tradition founded to a considerable extent on a rejection of American values—a rejection encouraged and enforced by the same pro-British ruling elite who fed the myth of the people's war and who made sure that the province (and eventually all of Canada) would embark on a course markedly different from that of the people to the south. They were, after all, "the enemy," and to be pro-American in post-war Upper Canada was to be considered vaguely traitorous. This attitude affected everything—politics, education, civil liberties, folkways, architecture. It affects us to this day, even those who do not think of themselves as Upper Canadian.

Thus the war that was supposed to attach the British North American colonies to the United States accomplished exactly the opposite. It ensured that Canada would never become a part of the Union to the south. Because of it, an alternative form of democracy grew out of the British colonial oligarchy in the northern half of the continent. The Canadian "way"—so difficult to define except in terms of negatives—has its roots in the invasion of 1812–14, the last American invasion of Canada. There can never be another.

ONE

Prelude to Invasion

1807–1811
The Road to Tippecanoe

———

See our western brothers bleed!
British gold has done the deed.
Child and Mother, Son and Sire,
Beneath the tomahawk expire.

—On the Battle of Tippecanoe,
National Intelligencer, July 11, 1812.

ABOARD THE BRITISH FRIGATE *Melampus*, lying off Hampton
Roads, Chesapeake Bay, Virginia, February, 1807.

The decks are clear of officers, for an entertainment is in progress.
Music. Laughter. The tinkling of glass and silver. Leaning over the
rail is an oddly assorted trio of impressed American seamen. One,
William Ware, is an Indian from Pipe Creek, Maryland, a one-time
wagoner who had served aboard the U.S. frigate *Chesapeake* until he
was impressed, fifteen months ago, by a British boarding party in the
Bay of Biscay. Another, Daniel Martin, is a Negro from Westport,

Massachusetts, impressed at the same time as Ware. The third is a white man, John Strachan, also from Maryland, pressed on board *Melampus* off Cape Finisterre in 1805.

For two years Strachan has been waiting for a chance to escape, and now it has come. Because of the festivities, every boat except the captain's gig has been hoisted in. There is no chance of pursuit. Strachan and his companions leap into the gig and cast off. Somebody hails them: where do they think they're going? They shout back that they are going ashore, and as they pull for land, a hail of musket balls rains upon them. Unharmed, they reach Lowell's Point, haul the boat onto the beach, carefully place the oars on the seats, give three hearty cheers, and dash away to freedom.

It is short lived. At Hampton Roads, the three sign up for service in the American navy aboard *Chesapeake* and soon find themselves at the centre of the "*Chesapeake* incident," which brings America to the very brink of war with Britain.

The date is June 22, 1807. The American frigate is a few hours out of Hampton Roads, bound for the Mediterranean. As she passes a British squadron anchored in American waters, a fifty-gun man-of-war, *Leopard*, the flagship of Vice-Admiral George Berkeley, detaches itself and slips off in pursuit. James Barron, *Chesapeake*'s captain, knows exactly what is happening: the British dander is up; the captain of *Melampus* wants his men back. On the streets and quays of Hampton Roads, where British and American sailors and officers mingle, the presence of known deserters has not gone unnoticed. The Royal Navy has been especially infuriated by one Jenkin Ratford, a British deserter intemperate enough to shout gibes and insults at his former officers. In vain the British have asked for Ratford; the Americans have refused to give him up. Nor will they return the three men who stole the captain's gig from *Melampus*. Now, all four men have thumbed their noses at the British and are safely aboard *Chesapeake*, which is heading out to sea, its lower decks apparently crowded with other British deserters, all well known to the captain but concealed under assumed names. This is too much for Vice-Admiral Berkeley. Off goes an order to every British vessel to stop *Chesapeake* at sea and take the deserters by force. As it happens, Berkeley's own flagship is the one that will essay the task.

Stopped by *Leopard*, Captain Barron cannot believe the British will attack and so makes no attempt to clear *Chesapeake*'s decks for action. A young lieutenant comes aboard, demands the return of the four men—the only ones he can identify since the *Melampus* deserters have not taken false names and Ratford, who is now called Wilson, is easily recognizable from his earlier intemperate encounters. Barron, who has all four hidden below, feigns ignorance. After some fruitless talk, the Englishman leaves. *Leopard*'s captain continues the discussion through a loud hailer. When Barron refuses his demands, Leopard fires a shot across *Chesapeake*'s bow. No reply.

It is too late now for the British to back down. *Leopard* opens fire with her port guns, and a ten-minute cannonade follows. Twenty-one cannonballs tear into *Chesapeake*'s starboard hull. Another shatters her mizzen-mast. Her mainmast topples, her sails are shredded, shrouds cut away, spars splintered. By the time Barron strikes his colours, three of his men are dead and eighteen, including himself, are wounded. The British board the battered frigate but refuse to accept it as a prize. All they want are the three deserters from *Melampus* and the wretched Ratford, whom they will proceed to hang at Halifax to their own great satisfaction and the fury of the American public.

The Americans are in a ferment. The man on the street finds it intolerable that British boarding parties can seize sailors from American ships on the pretext that they are Royal Navy deserters, then force them to serve in the hell hole of a British man-of-war. There is some doubt that the *Melampus* trio *were* impressed (the British insist they volunteered, and certainly two are thoroughgoing rogues), but that evidence is kept secret. To the Americans it is a flagrant attack on national sovereignty. In the words of John Quincy Adams, "No nation can be Independent which suffers her Citizens to be stolen from her at the discretion of the Naval or military officers of another."

But to Britain, impressment is a necessity. Her navy has trebled in size since the war with France began. She cannot man her ships with volunteers. Worse, thousands of British sailors are deserting to American merchantmen, lured by better conditions and better pay—four times as much. Who can blame the British for recapturing bona fide deserters in time of war? Certainly not the British public; they applaud it.

But who is a bona fide deserter? Americans and British speak the same language, look alike, dress alike. British boarding parties, hungry for men, do not always bother with the niceties. They grab whom they can. No one knows how many American seamen have been pressed into British service (the figures run between three and seven thousand), but it takes only a few publicized cases to enrage the American public. Even when a case of mistaken identity is proved and admitted, months elapse before the seaman is returned. Service in the British Navy is like a prison sentence or worse, for as Samuel Johnson once remarked, "no man will be a sailor who has contrivance enough to get himself into jail; for being in a ship is being in jail, with the chance of being drowned." Some American seamen have been known to cut off their hands to avoid impressment; some who refuse to serve are flogged unmercifully by the British; and a few, including the three escapees from *Melampus*, are prepared to risk death to get away.

Their recapture from *Chesapeake* touches off an international incident. Riots break out in New York, where a mob does its best to dismantle a British ship. The British consul is forced to seek police protection while an English diplomat on a tour of the Union finds it prudent to assume an incognito. Public meetings throughout the land denounce the perfidious British. In Quebec, Lieutenant-Colonel Isaac Brock notes that "every American newspaper teems with violent and hostile resolutions against England, and associations are forming in every town for the ostensible purpose of attacking these Provinces."

The future general is right: the country is emotionally ready for war, more so, in fact, than it will be in 1812. But its leaders are not ready. The President, Thomas Jefferson, threatens war but does not mean it—a dangerous posture. "If the English do not give us the satisfaction we demand, we will take Canada which wants to enter the Union," he tells the French minister to Washington. The Frenchman takes these bellicose remarks languidly and reports to Paris that he does not believe that either Jefferson or his foreign secretary, James Madison, wants war. Jefferson bans British war-ships from American waters, enforces an embargo preventing all ships from sailing out of U.S. ports for foreign destinations, and hopes that these threats will force the British to abandon impress-ment. But the British do not yield and the embargo is a failure. The public's ardour for war cools quickly. The crisis passes.

But there is one group of Americans whose ardour does not cool. In the oak and hickory forests of Ohio, in the cornfields along the Maumee and the Wabash, on the banks of the Au Glaize and on the Tippecanoe in Indiana Territory, there is a quickening of the blood, a stirring of old and painful memories of the defeat at Fallen Timbers and the surrender of hunting grounds at Greenville. The war fever, filtering through to the tribes of the Old Northwest, revives the dying hopes of the native Americans for a new conflict in which they will fight side by side with the British against the Long Knives. The Northwest has been at peace since General Anthony Wayne's decisive victory in 1794. But the *Chesapeake* incident acts as a catalyst to animate the tribes and shatter the calm that has prevailed north of the Ohio for more than a decade.

Among the British, the incident produces two oddly contrary reactions. On the one hand it convinces them that America will continue to bluff rather than fight, a conclusion that will lead to calamitous results in 1812. On the other hand they are encouraged to strengthen their defences in Canada against possible invasion. This is Isaac Brock's doing. "It is impossible to view the late hostile meas-ures of the American government towards England, without con-sidering a rupture between the two countries as probable to happen," the young lieutenant-colonel writes, and as the crisis smoulders, he goes on to press for a better trained and expanded militia and for repairs to the fortress of Quebec. He does not easily get his way, but from this time on the prospect of an American invasion is never far

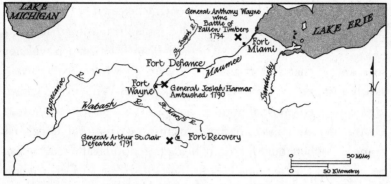

American-Indian Battles, 1790–1794

from that determined and agile mind. When and if the Americans come, Isaac Brock intends to be ready.

———

VINCENNES, INDIANA TERRITORY, August 17, 1807. William Henry Harrison is delivering his gubernatorial message to the legislature.

"The blood rises to my cheek," he cries, "when I reflect on the humiliating, the disgraceful scene, of the crew of an American ship of war mustered on its own deck by a British lieutenant for the purpose of selecting the innocent victims of their own tyranny!"

Harrison's cheeks are sallow, but the blood must rise to them with fair frequency. It rises again as he contemplates the malefactions of British Indian agents, who he is convinced are goading the Indians to violence and murder on the frontier, "for who does not know that the tomahawk and scalping knife of the savage are always employed as instruments of British vengeance. At this moment, fellow citizens, as I sincerely believe, their agents are organizing a combination amongst the Indians within our limits, for the purpose of assassination and murder. . . ."

By British agents Harrison means certain members of the British Indian Department in Upper Canada, especially Thomas McKee, Simon Girty (the "White Indian"), and, worst of all, Matthew

Elliott, the Pennsylvania Irishman who defected to the British during the Revolutionary War and led Indian ambushes that wiped out American detachments. The American frontiersmen will not soon forget that Elliott and Girty watched while the Delaware slowly tortured and burned to death Colonel William Crawford, after wiping out most of his men. So great is the hatred of Elliott in Detroit, it is said, that he hesitates to cross the river from his palatial home in Amherstburg for fear of being tarred and feathered. He has been one of the key members of the British Indian Department; no white man has so much influence with the tribes, especially the Shawnee. At the moment he is under a cloud, dismissed for financial irregularities. Nonetheless he remains a force and will soon be back in the good graces of the British.

But the Governor of Indiana cannot get it into his head that it is not so much British conniving that has caused the Indians to rise up sporadically in defence of their lands as his own policies and those of his political superiors in Washington. Harrison is not a mean or wicked man. His sense of justice is outraged when white juries refuse to convict one of their own for killing a native. The Governor's problem is that he wants to turn the Indians into farmers in order to deprive them of their hunting grounds. That is official government policy, laid down by Thomas Jefferson, who is not a mean or wicked man either but who, in a private letter to Harrison outlining that policy, sounds very much like a hypocrite:

"Our system is to live in perpetual peace with the Indians, to cultivate an affectionate attachment from them by everything just and liberal which we can do for them within the bounds of reason. . . ."

So far so good, despite the qualification. But then:

"When they withdraw themselves to the culture of a small piece of land, they will perceive how useless to them are the extensive forests, and will be willing to pare them off . . . in exchange for necessaries for their farms and families. To promote this . . . we shall push our trading houses, and be glad to see the good and influential individuals among them in debt, because we observe that when these debts go beyond what the individuals can pay, they become willing to lop them off by a cession of lands. . . ."

To this Machiavellian scheme Jefferson appends a chilling warning. Should any tribe refuse the proffered hand and take up the hatchet, he says, it will be driven across the Mississippi and the whole of its lands confiscated.

It all fits neatly with Harrison's own ambitions, which include statehood for Indiana. To become a state the territory needs a population of at least sixty thousand, and there are fewer than half that number living in small settlements connected by trails cut through the jungle of the forest. To attract more people, Harrison requires the lure of cheap land. The Indians have the land. The Governor must secure it for the settlers, one way or another.

The blood rises to Harrison's cheek once more when he recalls how he has been bested by that one-eyed savage known as the Shawnee Prophet. The Prophet has sprung from nowhere and in two years has become more notorious than any other Indian. He seems to have invented a new religion, one tenet of which is the heresy, to the whites, that all Indian lands are held in common and cannot be divided, sold, or bartered away. The ritual includes much mumbo-jumbo—shaking, jerking, and dancing about (derived perhaps from the white sect known as the Shakers, who have helped spark a religious revival on the frontier). It is not confined to any particular tribe—indeed, it has split some tribes—but appears to attract the younger braves who are acting in defiance of their elders. To Harrison, this so-called Prophet is an imposter and a fool who "speaks not the words of the Great Spirit but those of the devil and of the British agents." Harrison sees British agents everywhere, in every wigwam, behind every bush, plotting and conniving.

Yet even Harrison must concede that the Prophet is not quite a fool, for on one memorable occasion he has fooled Harrison, who thought to discredit him by demanding that he produce a miracle.

"Who is this pretended prophet who dares to speak in the name of the Great Creator?" the Governor asked, in a message to the Delaware. "Examine him. . . . Demand of him some proof . . . some miracles. . . . If he is really a prophet, ask him to cause the sun to stand still, the moon to alter its course, the rivers to cease to flow. . . . No longer be imposed on by the arts of an imposter. . . ."

To which the Prophet replied, blandly, that he would accept the challenge and cause the sun to darken. He even named the date and the time—11:32 in the forenoon of June 16, 1806.

The story is told and retold. How the Prophet sent word to Indians for leagues around to assemble on June 16; how the day dawned clear; and how, an hour before the appointed time, the Prophet, gowned in flowing robes, stepped from his wigwam into the circle of onlookers and at exactly 11:32 pointed his finger at the sun.

Slowly the sky darkens; the dark shadow of the moon crosses the solar face; a murmur rises from the assembly. The Prophet waits, then calls out to the Great Spirit to remove his hand from the source of all light. The call is heeded. Pandemonium!

It is too much. Harrison, the soldier-scholar-statesman, outsmarted by an aborigine who managed to learn in advance the date of a solar eclipse! The long, moody features grow moodier. He will continue to call the Prophet a fool, but he knows that he is up against a force beyond his power to control. "This business must be stopped," he tells the head men of the Shawnee. "I will no longer suffer it." But he will have to suffer it, for the chiefs themselves cannot control the Prophet; he has put some of them in fear of their lives. When several of the older Delaware chiefs refused to go along with the new religion, the Prophet had them murdered. His messengers have carried his words to all tribes within a radius of six hundred miles, and the message is always the same: follow me; rid yourself of your old leaders; and (this is Harrison's real concern) don't give up the land.

The Prophet's land policy collides with Harrison's ambition. The tall slender governor with the sombre face and the brooding eyes is no frontier bumpkin or upstart party hack of limited vision. He looks like a scholar and is one. With his long nose and gaunt features he could, in different guise, be mistaken for a Roman priest or an Italian noble in a Renaissance painting. He is slightly out of place here in the wilderness, for he was reared in luxury on a Virginia plantation, trained in Greek and Latin, and has a passion for military history, whose lessons he hopes to absorb.

He has always been a little out of place. He might have made a good doctor, but his medical studies were cut short by a fall in the family fortunes. In the army, where young officers were drinking themselves into early graves, the temperate ensign buried himself in his books. He will not let himself be seen out of control, through drink or through any other vice, for he has the Harrison name to uphold: his father was one of the signers of the Declaration of Independence.

He was a good soldier—he might, someone once said, have been another Washington. He fought with the "mad general," Anthony Wayne, at the Battle of Fallen Timbers, the epic victory over the Indians that won twenty-five thousand square miles of territory for the white men. Now, a soldier no more but with a soldier's bearing and a soldier's outlook, he is, at thirty-nine, a rising politician, living like an aristocrat in the backwoods in his vast brick mansion—the first in the territory—on the outskirts of Vincennes. He calls it Grouseland; with its hand-carved mantels and doors, its four great chimneys, its thirteen rooms and its circular staircase, it has made him proud but property poor.

His problems are only beginning. He has heard from Billy Wells, the Indian commissioner and interpreter at Fort Wayne, that eighty Indians under the Prophet's leadership have gathered at Greenville. Wells, an old frontiersman married to the sister of Little Turtle, the Miami chief, sends a messenger to Greenville to deal with the Prophet and ask him and his supporters to come to Fort Wayne for a parley. The answer is given, not by the Prophet but by his elder brother, a handsome war chief with flashing hazel eyes. It is astonishingly blunt:

"Go back and tell Captain Wells that my fire is kindled on the spot appointed by the Great Spirit above, and if he has anything to communicate to me, *he* must come *here*; and I will expect him in six days from this time."

This is not the way Indians talk to white men. This is the way white men talk to Indians. For the first time an Indian has sent back a message that is stinging in its style and insulting in its content.

William Henry Harrison will hear from the Prophet's brother again and again in the years to come, for he is one of the most extraordinary native North Americans of whom history has record.

His name is Tecumseh, and six years later in the second year of the war, he and Harrison will meet face to face in mortal combat.

———

WASHINGTON, D.C., AUGUST, 1807. Augustus John Foster, aide to the British minister to the United States, has just dispatched a letter to his mother bewailing his "sad disappointment" over the *Chesapeake* affair. It is not the incident itself that disturbs him—like every upper-class Englishman, he is convinced that the Royal Navy acted correctly—but the cruel turn of fate that has forced him to remain in the United States, "a land of swamps and pawnbrokers," and especially in Washington, "a sink of imagination."

Foster, who has spent four years at the British legation, cannot wait to shake Washington's red gumbo from his boots, but the country is in such an uproar that he cannot leave while there is the slightest danger of a rupture between the two nations. Personally, he dismisses the chance of war, cannot conceive that anyone in this ridiculous capital village would have the temerity to challenge the British lion. Still, as he has informed his mother, the Americans keep themselves in a constant ferment: "anything enflames them." He must remain at his post until tempers calm down.

He is an apple-cheeked young aristocrat of twenty-seven with the typical upper-class Englishman's view of Americans. To describe them, in his letters home, he beggars the lexicon of every defamatory epithet. Americans are "consummate rascals," "ragamuffins and adventurers," "the scum of every nation on earth."

"Corruption, Immorality, Irreligion, and, above all, self-interest, have corroded the very pillars on which their Liberty rests."

Clearly, Foster was not bred for America. His father was a Member of Parliament. His mother, an earl's daughter, lives with the Duke and Duchess of Devonshire in an amiable *ménage à trois*. His aunt is married to the Earl of Liverpool. After the London of Mrs. Siddons and Lord Byron, of Turner and Gainsborough, the tiny capital of seven thousand souls must indeed seem a sinkhole. Just seven years old, it has become the butt of jokes—a wretched community of bogs and gullies, broken tree stumps, piles of brushwood and refuse, ponds, potholes, and endless gluelike mud, which mires the carriages on Pennsylvania Avenue and makes sensible communication all but impossible. Paving is non-existent; the streets are mere ruts. Wells are the only source of water; there is no public supply. Petty thieves and burglars abound. Pigs and cattle wander the paths that pass for avenues. The climate is intolerable, the swamps malarial.

Above this morass, each on its separate hillock, rise, incongruously, two jerry-built Greek temples yet unfinished: the Capitol and the Executive Mansion. The columns in the former are so weak they crack under the weight of the visitors' gallery; the latter is still unplastered, its timber already rotting. The roofs of both are so badly constructed that they leak embarrassingly in every rainstorm. Even the politicians hate Washington. Some, if they had their way, would move the seat of government to Philadelphia.

Foster cannot stomach the politicians. Why, there are scarcely five congressmen who look like gentlemen! He treats them all with an amused disdain, which the more perceptive must find maddening. But then, one legislator has actually urinated in his fireplace! Foster relishes that tale. And then there was the business of the caviar that he had his *maitre d'* prepare from Potomac sturgeon. On serving it to his congressional guests, he found them spitting it out by the mouthful, having mistaken it for black raspberry jam. Is this what democracy has wrought? "The excess of democratic ferment in this people is conspicuously evinced by the dregs having got to the top," he reports to Whitehall. It is unthinkable that these grotesque politicians would dare declare war on his country!

Whitehall agrees. The outcry over the *Chesapeake* incident subsides, and by mid-October Foster feels able to escape from the country in which he believes he has sacrificed the four best years of his life. He would not return, he declares, were he to be paid ten thousand pounds a year. But return he will in 1811, a Yankeephobe, singularly blind to the impending war, the wrong man in the wrong place at the wrong time.

Foster's smug views are typical. He is scarcely back in London, reporting the state of affairs in Washington, when the British make a second move to enrage the Americans. Having called Jefferson's bluff, they proceed to tighten their blockade of the French ports. Spencer Perceval's government issues new Orders in Council forbidding neutral ships on pain of seizure to trade with Europe except through Britain. Any vessel that tries to enter any port controlled by Napoleon without first touching at Britain (and paying the required duties and taxes) will be treated as an enemy.

The British are clearly prepared to go beyond the accepted rules for dealing with non-belligerents. They will, if necessary, seize American shipping in the open seas as well as within territorial limits. In no other way can they hope to throttle the French.

In American eyes this is an intolerable return to colonial days. Using the excuse of war, the British are attempting to monopolize the commerce of the world—or so the Americans believe. The Orders represent a clear threat to the fledgling nation. Has the War of Independence been for nothing?

It is clear from Britain's maritime policy that she holds the new union in contempt. To Englishmen, Americans are all uncouth frontiersmen with little breeding and no culture, "less popular and less esteemed among us than the base and bigotted Portuguese, or the ferocious and ignorant Russians," in the words of the *Edinburgh Review*. The British ruling class believes, with Foster, that the Americans will not fight, and, believing that, thinks nothing of goading the former colonists to fury. "America," declares Lord Sidmouth, the Lord Privy Seal, "is no longer a bugbear; there is no terror in her threats."

For the moment, the policy works. In this yeasty winter of 1808—the year of Goethe's *Faust* and Beethoven's Fifth Symphony—America will not go to war over the Orders in Council or the *Chesapeake* affair. The country is badly divided. The Federalist opposition centred largely in the New England states is staunchly opposed to any violent solution. Yet the country's honour has been slighted, her morale badly bruised, and there are some in the Congress who cannot forget the insult and will not let their colleagues forget. They are Republicans, mainly from the southwestern interior and the frontier states. Soon they will be known as the War Hawks, and the time is coming when they will prevail.

FORT AMHERSTBURG, UPPER CANADA, July 11, 1808. One thousand Indian warriors and one hundred chiefs are gathered on the Canadian side of the Detroit River to hear the Lieutenant-Governor of Upper Canada, Francis Gore, cautiously and delicately extend the hand of British friendship. A genial figure, he is in his fortieth year, the smooth face gone slightly to flesh, the cheeks pink from good living. He is careful to play down the possibility of war; that might excite his listeners to premature violence—the last thing the British want. But if war should come, the Indians will be needed.

"I am sure, my Children, that it is quite unnecessary for me to call to your remembrance the faithful assurance with which the King, your Father, has so uniformly complied with all his Engagements and Promises made to your Forefathers and yourselves in former times. . . .

"Nothing is required of you in return for your Great Father's benevolence and religious regard to his promises, but a renewal and faithful observance of the engagements made by your ancestors and yourselves. . . .

"I will not offend you by entertaining the smallest doubt of your readiness on all occasions, when called upon to prove your affectionate attachment to the King, your Great Father. . . .

"I came not to invite you to take up the Hatchet, but I wish to put you on your guard against any attempt that may be made by any enemy whatever to disturb the peace of your Country. . . ."

It is the *Chesapeake* affair that has brought the Lieutenant-Governor to Amherstburg—that and the whisper of a threat from Napoleon that the French may once again take an interest in North America. Since the end of the Revolution, the British have tended to neglect the Indians. Now it is time to mend fences. But the task is complicated: how to regain the affection of the natives, take advantage of their antagonism to the Americans, subtly include them in plans for the defence of Canada, yet at the same time give Washington no cause to believe that British agents are stirring up the tribes to attack? The council at Amherstburg, to which Gore comes late, has been going on for ten days. The public manifestations of friendship and goodwill are innocuous. But who knows what is said to the Indians in private?

Gore cannot even be sure that his listeners will be given an accurate account of what he is saying, for he speaks in English, his remarks interpreted by the superintendent-general of the British Indian Department, William Claus, and his deputy, Matthew Elliott. Elliott has just been reinstated in the key post of Amherstburg, and when the Lieutenant-Governor announces his restoration to favour there are grunts of approval from his audience. In their ritual reply, the Wyandot, senior to all the tribes, express pleasure: "We can place confidence in and rely on him as a man of experience."

It is through Elliott that the government's new Indian policy will be channelled. And he will interpret Whitehall's directives in his own way, according to his prejudices. These are well known: he is pro-Indian, especially pro-Shawnee, and violently anti-American. If war comes it is in Elliott's personal interest that the British win, and not merely for reasons of patriotism. Word has reached him that if the Yankees capture Fort Amherstburg, they intend to kill him and two of his colleagues.

On and off, he has been a member of the Indian Department since the days of the Revolution when he fought with the Shawnee against the Americans. (It remains a secret to the day of his death that he once acted as an emissary for the Americans to try to keep the Shawnee neutral before hostilities began.) Even while out of favour he has acted unofficially for the department, for he is part of that clique, like a band of brothers who follow their own conventions—men who have spent long years with the tribes, who speak the languages fluently, who have lived with Indian women, fathered Indian children, attended Indian councils, fought when necessary on the Indian side. It is a family compact: son often follows father in the service, and the sons are sometimes of mixed blood.

It is toward the Shawnee, especially, that the officers of the Indian Department lean—"that contemptible tribe ... always more insolent and troublesome than any other," in the words of Elliott's nemesis, Captain Hector McLean. It was McLean's observation, in 1799, that "the whole of the Officers of the Department are indeed in some way connected with this tribe either by Marriage or Concubinage." That is certainly true of Elliott, who has fathered two sons by a Shawnee woman and often taken Shawnee chieftains as guests under his roof.

Captain McLean was the cause of Elliott's dismissal, under a cloud, in 1798. The scandal revolved around the traditional British practice of dispensing annual "presents" to the tribes—food, dry goods, tools, weapons. McLean, then in command at the fort, was convinced that Elliott was adding to his departmental pittance by diverting a generous portion of government largess to his own use. How else could he stock his extensive farm with cattle and feed and clothe some fifty servants and slaves? Trapping the slippery Elliott became a minor obsession with McLean. His chance came in the winter of 1797 when he was able to prove that the agent had requisitioned supplies for 534 Indians in a settlement whose total population was only 160. On this evidence Elliott was dismissed.

But now, in 1808, the government, set on a new and more aggressive course, finds it cannot do without him. Elliott's successor, Thomas McKee, son of his old comrade Alexander McKee, is a hopeless drunkard who cannot be depended upon to preside over delicate negotiations. Even before his official reappointment, Elliott has been working for the government without McKee's knowledge, dispatched on a secret mission to sound out the major chiefs in private: to impress upon them "with Delicacy and caution" that England expects their aid in the event of war and to remind them that the Americans are out to steal their lands. And who better than Elliott to invite the Prophet to attend the Amherstburg council? He, of all the Indian agents, knows the family most intimately; his chief clerk is married to the Prophet's sister. So here he is, back in charge again, his honour restored by Gore's convenient fiction that the charges against him were never proved.

A strange creature, this Elliott, Gore must feel—rather ugly and more than a little haughty, swarthy, with small features and a pug nose—a black Donegal Irishman transplanted early into the American wilderness, a rough diamond who has experienced everything, shrunk from nothing. There are Americans who believe that he and Alexander McKee took more scalps after General Arthur St. Clair's disastrous defeat by Little Turtle in 1791 than did the Indians. He cannot read or write; it is an effort for him to put his signature to a document; a clerk accompanies him everywhere to handle his extensive business. He has been a justice of the peace and is now a member of the legislature of Upper Canada, the richest farmer in the region. Though he is in his seventieth year, he will be quite prepared to lead his troops into battle in the war to come.

Elliott had expected the Prophet to travel to Amherstburg for the council, but the Prophet does not appear. In his stead comes his older brother, Tecumthe or Tecumseh, of whom the British have little if any knowledge. Of all the chieftains present at Amherstburg, only this tall catlike Shawnee is in favour of war with the Americans, as Gore, in his letter to his superior, Sir James Craig, the Governor General of the two Canadas, makes clear:

"The Prophet's brother, who is stated to me to be his principal support and who appears to be a very shrewd intelligent man, was at Amherstburg while I was there. He told Colonel Claus and Captain Elliott that they were endeavouring to collect the different Nations to form one settlement on the Wabash about 300 miles

South West of Amherstburg in order to preserve their country from all encroachment. That their intention at present is not to take part in the quarrels of White People: that if the Americans encroach upon them they are resolved to strike—but he added that if their father the King should be in earnest and appear in sufficient force they would hold fast by him."

Tecumseh makes it clear that he does not fully trust the British. The Indians have long memories. They have not forgotten how, when Mad Anthony Wayne defeated them at Fallen Timbers in 1794, the British closed the gates of nearby Fort Miami, and he now reminds Elliott of the number of chiefs who fell as a result. Tecumseh is ready to fight beside the British, but on his own terms. If they are preparing to use him for their own ends (as they are) he is also planning to use them for his.

———

FORT WAYNE ON THE MAUMEE RIVER, September 22, 1809. William Henry Harrison has ridden deep into Indian territory to bargain for land. He is hungry for it. At Vincennes he has felt himself cramped, hemmed in, frustrated in his ambition. The country to the south of the capital is sunken and wet; the sere prairie to the northwest will not be fit for settlement for many years. But just beyond the Indiana border, twenty-one miles to the north along the eastern bank of the Wabash, lie three million acres of farm land, the hunting grounds of the tribes. Harrison means to have it all, has already secured the agreement of the President, James Madison, Jefferson's successor, who makes one stipulation only: get it as cheaply as possible.

The Governor has travelled on horseback for 350 miles on one of those tireless peregrinations for which he is so well fitted, temperamentally as well as physically. He has summoned the chiefs of the affected tribes—the Miami, Delaware, Eel, Potawatomi—to a great council here at Fort Wayne. But he has not summoned the Shawnee, for they are nomads and, in Harrison's view, have no claim to the land.

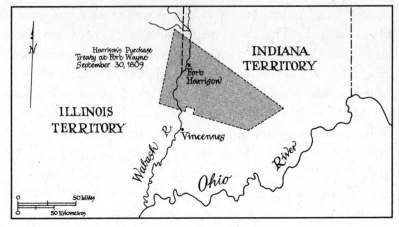

Harrison's Purchase

The council fire is lit. Eleven hundred tribesmen, squatting in a vast circle, listen as Harrison speaks against the murmur of the Maumee. Four sworn interpreters translate his message: the European war has ruined the price of furs, therefore the tribes must adopt a new way of life. The government will buy their lands, pay for them with a permanent annuity. With that income they can purchase domestic animals and become farmers. The Indians, says Harrison, wrongly blame their own poverty and the scarcity of game on the encroachment of white settlers—but that is not the true cause of their misfortunes. The British are to blame! It is they who have urged the wanton destruction of game animals for furs alone.

The chiefs listen, retire, drink Harrison's whiskey, wrangle among themselves. The Potawatomi, who are the poorest and most wretched of the tribes, want to sell; the Delaware waver. But the Miami are inflexible. The British have urged them to hold the lands until they are surveyed and can be sold at the going price of two dollars an acre. Harrison is offering a mere fraction of that sum. Why should they take less?

To counter this recalcitrance, Harrison summons all his histrionic abilities and at the next council fire on the twenty-fifth presents himself in the guise of a patient but much-injured father, betrayed by his own offspring:

"My Children: My Heart is oppressed. If I could have believed that I should have experienced half of the mortification and disappointment which I now feel, I would have entreated your Father the President to have chosen some other Representative to have made known his wishes to you. The proposition which I have made you, I fondly hoped would have been acceptable to all. . . . Is there some evil spirit amongst us?" This evil spirit, Harrison makes clear, is British.

The speech rolls on. Ironically, Harrison is urging tribal solidarity—Tecumseh's crusade—though for very different reasons. War with Great Britain is never far from his mind. The solidarity he proposes must include, also, the white Americans. ("The people upon the other side of the big water would desire nothing better than to set us once more to cut each other's throats.")

He ends with a remarkable pledge:

"This is the first request your new Father has ever made you. It will be the last, he wants no more of your land. Agree to the proposition which I now make you and send on some of your wise men to take him by the hand. He will set your Heart at ease. He will tell you that he will never make another proposition to you to sell your lands."

The palaver lasts for five more days, and in the end Harrison persuades the Miami to give up the idea that the land is worth two dollars an acre. "Their tenaciousness in adhering to this idea," he comments, "is quite astonishing and it required no little pains to get them to abandon it." And, he might have added, no little whiskey. A drunken frolic follows, in which one of the Miami braves is mortally wounded.

Harrison is jubilant. "The compensation given for this cession of lands . . . is as low as it could possibly be made," he writes to Washington. ". . . I think . . . upon the whole that the bargain is a better one for the United States than any that has been made by me for lands south of the Wabash." As soon as the treaty is ratified and a sales office opened "there will be several hundred families along this Tract."

Well may Harrison savour his triumph. The annuities paid the Indians for relinquishing the land are minuscule: the Miami, who get the most, will receive a total of only seven hundred dollars a year. To pay all the annuities forever the government will not have to set aside more than fifty thousand dollars. At two dollars an acre—the price the settlers will pay—the land is potentially worth six million dollars. Thanks to Harrison the government has made an enormous paper profit. No wonder, when his third term of office ends, a grateful legislature recommends him for a fourth, praising his "integrity, patriotism and firm attachment to the general government."

There remains one small cloud on the horizon: Harrison has ignored the Shawnee. By spring the cloud looms larger. The Prophet and his brother Tecumseh, furious with the old chieftains, refuse to concede that any land cession is valid unless approved by all the tribes. The Great Spirit, so the Prophet says, has directed him to collect all the Indians at the mouth of the Tippecanoe, where it joins the Wabash, whereupon one thousand tribesmen forsake their elders and flock to the new settlement, appropriately named Prophet's Town. With the Indians in ferment, Harrison does not dare put surveyors on the newly purchased land. Settlement comes to a standstill. Families flee the frontier. More will leave "unless the rascally prophet is driven from his present position or a fort built somewhere on the Wabash about the upper boundary of the late purchase."

It is not easy to cow the Prophet into submission. Some of the old chiefs have tried, but "this scoundrel does not appear however to be intimidated." In fact, the old chiefs are in fear of their lives. Harrison, determined to threaten his adversary with a show of force, sends for a detachment of regular troops. There is much bustling about with the local militia in Vincennes—constant musterings, parades and reviews—which serves only to increase the panic of the white settlers. Finally, Harrison dispatches his interpreter, James Barron, with a letter intended to convince the Prophet of the folly of taking up arms against the United States:

"Our bluecoats are more numerous than you can count, and our hunting shirts are like leaves of the forests or the grains of sand on the Wabash. Do not think that the red coats can protect you, they are not able to protect themselves, they do not think of going to war with us, if they did in a few moons you would see our flags wave on all the Forts of Canada."

Barron is lucky to escape with his life. The Prophet receives him, surrounded by Indians of different tribes, gazes upon him in silence and contempt for several minutes, then spits out his defiance:

"... You ... are a spy. There is your grave. Look on it!" And points to the spot on which the interpreter is standing.

At this moment, there emerges from the Indian lodges a tall figure in fringed deerskin who takes the frightened Barron under his wing and asks him to state his business. Barron reads Harrison's message, which concludes with a canny invitation: if the Shawnee can prove title to the ceded lands then, of course, they will be returned to the tribe. It is a hollow promise, for there is no title as white men understand the term. But Harrison's message invites the Prophet to come to visit him: if his claim is just, the Governor will personally escort him to the President.

But it is not the Prophet who will lead the delegation to Vincennes. A new warrior is assuming leadership—the tall Indian who again that night saves Barron's life from a group of squaws sent to tomahawk him. Harrison has not yet met him, would not know him to see him, is only now becoming aware of his presence. Someone who has encountered him has described him to the governor as "a bold, active, sensible man, daring in the extreme and capable of any undertaking." He is the Prophet's brother, whom Harrison now sees as "the Moses of the family, really the efficient man"—Tecumseh, the Leaping Panther.

———

VINCENNES, INDIANA TERRITORY, AUGUST 16, 1810. Governor Harrison is seated in an armchair on his estate of Grouseland in the shade of a canopy on the southwest side of the great brick mansion that has all but beggared him. To pay the bills for its construction he has been forced to give up four hundred acres of prime land; but then, some might say, he wants the Shawnee (for whom he is waiting) to give up much more.

The Shawnee have kept him waiting for some days and the Governor is growing impatient. He has made much of this assembly, inviting the town's leading citizens and their ladies, territorial officers and supreme court justices, all arranged like chess pieces on the lawn, in the canopy's shade, guarded by a platoon of soldiers.

If Harrison is nervous, his long features do not reveal it. He operates under a strict maxim—never show fear in front of an Indian. This particular Indian, however, has become uncommonly difficult. Harrison had asked him to come to Vincennes with a small escort, but Tecumseh, who does not take instructions from white men, arrived with more than three hundred armed and painted warriors. That was Saturday. Harrison wanted to start the council on Monday, but Tecumseh would not be hurried. Suspecting treachery, he sent his spies and informers to work through the community, warning of possible trouble. Now it is Thursday; he is coming at last, accompanied by thirty warriors, their faces smeared with vermilion war paint, all armed with tomahawks and clubs.

Tecumseh advances under the curious scrutiny of the dignitaries—a handsome figure, tall for his tribe (at least five foot ten), with an oval rather than an angular face, his complexion light copper, his nose handsome and straight, his mouth "beautifully formed like that of Napoleon." Everyone who has met him notices his eyes, which are a clear, bright hazel under dark brows, and his teeth, which are white and even. He is naked to the waist, his head shaved save for a scalp lock. He walks with a brisk elastic step in spite of a bent leg fractured and imperfectly set after a youthful fall from a pony. There are some who think him the finest specimen of a man they have ever seen, but no authentic likeness exists on paper or canvas, for Tecumseh refuses to have his portrait painted by a white man.

He halts, looks over the assemblage, sees the soldiers, feigns anger, pretends to suspect treachery. He will not go near the canopy, not because he fears the soldiers but because he wishes to place himself on an equal footing with his adversary. He intends to speak as in a council circle, which puts every man on the same level.

The game continues. Harrison's interpreter, Barron, explains that it will be a nuisance to rearrange the seats. Tecumseh disagrees; only the whites need seats, the Indians are accustomed to sitting on the ground: "Houses are made for white men to hold councils in. Indians hold theirs in the open air."

"Your father requests you sit by his side," says Barron, indicating the Governor.

Tecumseh raises an arm, points to the sky.

"*My* father! The Great Spirit is my father! The earth is my mother—and on her bosom I will recline." And so sits cross-legged on the ground, surrounded by his warriors.

The problem is that Tecumseh refuses to act like a Harrison Indian. Nor does he act like a white man. He is unique and knows it. On his endless missions to other tribes, in his dogged attempt to forge an Indian confederacy, it is necessary for him to say only "I am Tecumseh." That is enough to explain his purpose.

This attitude disconcerts Harrison. In his reports to Washington he tries to shrug off Tecumseh: his speeches here at the great council, he says, are "insolent and his pretensions arrogant." Yet he is forced to take him seriously. The talks drag on for days; but when the Shawnee war chief speaks, the Governor listens, for this half-naked man in the deerskin leggings is one of the greatest orators of his time.

His reputation has preceded him. He is known as a consummate performer who can rouse his audience to tears, laughter, fury, action. Even those who cannot understand his words are said to be held by the power of his voice. White men who have heard him speak at past councils have struggled to describe his style: in 1806 at a council at Springfield, Ohio, "the effect of his bitter, burning words . . . was so great on his companions that the whole three hundred warriors could hardly refrain from springing from their seats. Their eyes flashed, and even the most aged, many of whom were smoking, evinced the greatest excitement. The orator appeared in all the power of a fiery and impassioned speaker and actor. Each moment it seemed as though, under the influence of his overpowering eloquence, they would abruptly leave the council and defiantly return to their homes."

Like his physical presence, Tecumseh's oratory is, alas, filtered through the memories of eyewitnesses. Even the best interpreters cannot keep up with his flights of imagery, while the worst garble his eloquence. Occasionally, in the printed record—admittedly imperfect—one hears faintly the echoes of that clear, rich voice, calling across the decades:

"It is true I am Shawnee. My forefathers were warriors. Their son is a warrior. From them I take only my existence. From my tribe I take nothing. I am the maker of my own fortune. And oh! that I might make that of my red people, and of my country, as great as the conceptions of my mind, when I think of the Spirit that rules the universe. . . .

"The way, and the only way, to check and stop this evil, is, for all the red men to unite in claiming a common and equal right in the land; as it was at first; and should be yet; for it never was divided, but belongs to all, for the use of each. That no part has a right to sell, even to each other, much less to strangers who want all and will not do with less. . . .

"Sell a country! Why not sell the air, the clouds and the great sea, as well as the earth? Did not the Great Spirit make them all for the use of his children?"

In this three-hour speech at the great council of Vincennes, Tecumseh threatens to kill any chief who sells land to the white man:

"I now wish you to listen to me. If you do not it will appear as if you wished me to kill all the chiefs that sold you the land. I tell you so because I am authorized by all the tribes to do so. I am the head of them all. I am a Warrior and all the Warriors will meet together in two or three moons from this. Then I will call for those chiefs that sold you the land and shall know what to do with them. If you do not restore the land you will have a hand in killing them."

But from his opening words it is clear that Tecumseh feels that he is not getting through to Harrison:

"Brother, I wish you to listen to me well—I wish to reply to you more explicitly, as I think you do not clearly understand what I before said to you. I will explain again. . . ."

He is like a patient parent, indulging a small unheeding child. But Harrison will never understand, cannot understand. Land is to him private property, circumscribed by fences and surveyors' pins, tied down by documents, deeds, titles. He wants to be fair, but he cannot comprehend this Indian. The land has been bought from its rightful owners and paid for. It is purely a business matter.

Now it is the Governor's turn to speak. He ridicules the idea of a single Indian nation, dismisses the Shawnee claim to ownership of the disputed lands (the Shawnee, he points out, come from farther south), praises the United States above all other nations for a long record of fair dealing.

The Indians listen patiently, waiting for the translations. Not far away on the grass lies the Potawatomi chief Winemac, in fear of his life at Tecumseh's hands, for he is one of those who has agreed to cede the land. He hides in his buckskins a brace of pistols, a gift from the Governor to guard him from assassination. A sergeant and twelve soldiers, originally detailed to guard the assembly, have moved off a distance to escape the searing sun.

The Shawnee translation of Harrison's remarks ends. The Potawatomi translation begins. Suddenly Tecumseh rises and, with violent gestures, starts to shout. Harrison notes, with concern, that Winemac is priming his pistols. John Gibson, the Indiana secretary, who understands the Shawnee tongue, whispers to Lieutenant Jesse Jennings of the 7th Infantry to bring up the guard quickly: "Those fellows mean mischief." Tecumseh's followers leap to their feet, brandishing tomahawks and war clubs. Harrison draws his sword. A Methodist minister runs to the house, seizes a rifle, and prepares to protect the Governor's family. Up runs the twelve-man guard, muskets ready. Harrison motions them to hold their fire, demands to know what Tecumseh is saying. The answer is blunt: the Governor is a liar; everything he has said is false; the United States has cheated the Indians. The angry Harrison banishes Tecumseh and his followers from Grouseland. They leave in a fury, but the following day, his anger spent, Tecumseh apologizes.

What is the meaning of this singular incident? Had Tecumseh planned a massacre, as some believe, only to be faced down by Harrison and his troops? That is unlikely. It is more probable that, hearing the translation of Harrison's words, he briefly lost his remarkable self-possession. It is also possible that it was a carefully staged part of a plan to convince Harrison of Tecumseh's strength and leadership.

Harrison, mollified by the apology, visits Tecumseh at his camp on the outskirts of Vincennes and finds the Shawnee in a totally different mood. The menacing savage has been transformed into a skittish adversary. The two sit together on a bench, Tecumseh talking all the while and edging closer to the governor, who is forced to move over. Tecumseh continues to talk, continues to crowd Harrison, who presently finds himself on the very end of the bench. Harrison at length protests. The Shawnee laughs: how would he like to be pushed right off, as the Indians have been pushed off their lands by white encroachment?

But beneath this burlesque Harrison recognizes a firmness of purpose that makes him apprehensive. As the council proceeds Tecumseh makes it clear that he intends to prevent, by force if necessary, the lands ceded at Fort Wayne from falling into the hands of the whites. His final words are unequivocal:

"I want the present boundary line to continue. Should you cross it I assure you it will be productive of bad consequences."

Harrison has no choice but to halt the surveys of the disputed territory. He will not get his two dollars an acre until the power of the Shawnee brothers is broken forever.

———

WHO ARE THESE SHAWNEE BROTHERS? Harrison may well ask himself. Where have they sprung from? What was it that produced from one Indian tribe and from the same parents the two most compelling native leaders of their time? What has made them rise above their own fellows, their own kin, so that their names are familiar to all the tribes from Michilimackinac to the borders of Florida?

The two do not even look like brothers. If Tecumseh is grudgingly admired, the Prophet is universally despised. To the white romantics one is a "good" Indian, the other "bad"—the noble savage and the rogue native, neat stereotypes in the bosom of a single family. Part of the contrast is physical. Tecumseh is almost too handsome to be true; his younger brother is ugly, awkward, and one-eyed, a handkerchief masking the empty socket, mutilated in childhood by a split arrow. One is a mystic, mercurial and unpredictable, the other a clear-eyed military genius. Yet the two are indivisible, their personalities and philosophies interlocking like pieces of an ivory puzzle.

In looking forward to a new future for the tribes, the brothers are gazing back upon an idyllic past when the vast hunting grounds were open to all. The idea of land held in common springs directly from the Shawnee experience and must have been held by others before them. Always partially nomadic, the Shawnee were deprived of any share of the profits from lands sold to white men in Kentucky. The sedentary Iroquois pocketed the cash while the advancing pressure of settlement forced the Shawnee northward and westward always onto lands occupied by other tribes. For years now they have been hunting over the disputed territory east of the Wabash, but in Harrison's conventional view they do not "own" it because the Miami were there first. Tecumseh's own wanderings underline the Shawnee dilemma. He has no fixed home but has moved northward from settlement to settlement, from Kentucky to Indiana to Ohio to Prophet's Town on the Tippecanoe. Men with such a history must feel the land belongs to all.

Unlike the Prophet, Tecumseh is a warrior. The major influence in his life was his older brother, Cheeseekau, fourteen years his senior and clearly a replacement for his father, who died when Tecumseh was an infant. Cheeseekau taught him to hunt with bow and arrow (nurturing in him a contempt for firearms, which frighten away deer), to fight with a tomahawk, and to develop his scorn and

Tecumseh's Frontier

hatred of the white man, especially white Americans. From the age of fifteen, when he survived his first skirmish at his brother's side against the Kentucky volunteers, he has done battle with American frontiersmen and American soldiers. He has fought in every major engagement, rising to band leader after Cheeseekau's death in the Cherokee war in 1792 and emerging unscathed two years later at the disastrous Battle of Fallen Timbers, when another brother fell to an American musket ball.

Yet his closest companion for fifteen years was a white youth, Stephen Ruddell, who has become a Methodist missionary to the Shawnee. Captured by the tribe during the Revolution and adopted into a Shawnee family, young Ruddell was present on the famous occasion when, at sixteen, Tecumseh impassively watching a white prisoner being consumed by the slow fire of the stake, rose up and in a speech that foreshadowed later eloquence swore he would never again allow such horror in his presence.

It is this mixture of savagery and compassion that baffles men like Harrison. In battle, stripped naked save for a breech cloth, his face daubed with ochre, his tomahawk stained with blood, Tecumseh is demonic. Yet Ruddell remembers that from his boyhood he was "remarkable ... for the dignity and rectitude of his deportment." He does not like to take prisoners in battle, but when he does he treats them with humanity. Nor will he allow the killing of women and children.

Like his younger brother, he has managed to conquer alcohol, not as the result of the mystical experience that transformed the Prophet from an idler and a wastrel into a native messiah but as a simple act of will. Alcohol befuddled his ambition, interfered with the clarity of his vision.

For similar reasons he has managed to free himself from the tyranny of sex. To him, women are inferior creatures; he treats them with courtesy but will not hunt in their company. And like alcohol, they may divert him from his purpose. As a young man he realized his own attraction to the tribal beauties but was determined not to be ensnared. "The handsome are now anxious for me," he told a white acquaintance, "and I am determined to disappoint them."

His first wife, Manete, whom he married at twenty-eight, was a mixed blood, considerably older than he and certainly no beauty. From her as from all his other women he demanded affection and absolute obedience. The day of reckoning came when he asked her to make him a pouch to hold his war paint. She told him she did not know how and offered to find a friend who did. It was the end of the marriage. Tecumseh snatched back the materials, declared that he would save her the trouble, gave her some presents, and banished her forever.

Another wife—the Shawnee are allowed as many as they wish—received a similar rebuff. Tecumseh had killed a turkey and invited friends to dine; he was discomfited to find a few feathers clinging to the fowl when his wife served it. After his guests had gone, he handed her a bundle of clothing and ordered her to leave. Tears, entreaties, promises to do better next time all failed to move him. "I am ashamed of you," said Tecumseh. "We must separate." He did not see her again.

One woman, it is said, intrigued him above all others: Rebecca Galloway, a white girl of sixteen, the daughter of a literate frontiersman at Old Chillicothe, Ohio. She spoke his language, taught him English, introduced him to the Bible, Alexander the Great, Shakespeare's plays (his favourite was *Hamlet*). The passionate Shawnee fell in love; he brought her gifts (a silver comb, a birchbark canoe, furs, venison), called her Star of the Lake, asked for her hand in marriage offering thirty silver brooches as a lure. She was agreeable but made one condition: he must give up the Indian life, adopt white customs and dress. Tecumseh struggled with this dilemma, but his decision was foreordained. He could not bring himself to adopt a course that would cost him the respect of his people. Reluctantly they parted, never to meet again.

Now he is determinedly single. His last wife, White Wing, a Shawnee woman whom he married in 1802, parted from him in 1807. There would be no more women in Tecumseh's life. He is wedded irrevocably to an ideal.

He dreams Pontiac's ancient dream of an Indian confederacy stretching from Florida to Lake Erie—a confederacy strong enough

to resist white pressure. To that end he is prepared to travel astonishing distances preaching to the tribes—to the Kickapoo, Wea,
Creek, Wyandot, Sauk, Fox, Potawatomi, Miami, Choctaw, Osage
and other Indian bands who, like Balkan communities, argue and
squabble among themselves, to their own misfortune and the white
man's benefit. The nucleus of this alliance already exists at the
mouth of the Tippecanoe where the disaffected members of half
a dozen tribes have flocked in response to the mystic summons of
Tecumseh's younger brother.

The Prophet's background is as remarkable as Tecumseh's, though
quite different. Born after his father's death, he was raised by a sister
who clearly favoured his older brother. While Tecumseh was dazzling his fellow tribesmen with his skill as a hunter and, later, his
prowess as a warrior, the future Prophet, born Laulewausika, was
a layabout. He seemed to be a man with no future, no ambition.
Then, with the suddenness of a rocket's flare, he changed, overcome
by a sense of sin. There was talk of a trance, a visit to the Great
Spirit, a vision in which he saw a forked road before him—misery
in one direction, happiness in the other. What brought about this
miraculous transformation that caused him to be as one reborn?
There are only hints, but it is believed in Vincennes that the Shaker
preachers, who were influential in the area (their new home only a
few miles distant), had their effect. The new name that he adopted
to symbolize his reform, Tenskwatawa, is translated as "I am the
door," a phrase used by Jesus, and much of his preaching, which
began in 1805, resembles fundamentalist Christianity. He urges his
followers to give up strong liquor (as he himself did instantly), to
stop beating their wives, to cease intertribal warfare, to renounce
crimes of theft.

But there is something more, which suggests that the Prophet
is in the mainstream of a mystical movement going back to the
Delaware prophet who, in 1762, laid the basis for Pontiac's confederacy. The same movement will go forward to future prophets including the most influential of all, Wovoka of the Paiutes, who in the late
eighties will spread the ritual of the Ghost Dance across the nation.

These native messiahs invariably appear during the death struggles of a threatened culture; their authority is supernatural, their message nostalgic: their people are to return to the old customs and rid themselves of the white man's ways. Tenskwatawa, the Open Door, preaches that his followers must revert to the clothing, the implements, the weapons, the foods that were in use before the Europeans reached North America. Implicit in this philosophy is a rejection of the white man. Harrison has been told, specifically, by two Indian messengers that the Prophet preaches that "the Great Spirit will in a few years destroy every white man in America."

Tecumseh has been fighting white Americans since 1783; how much has he contributed to the Prophet's thoughts? Harrison cannot know, but it is clear to him that at some time in the first decade of the century the two brothers, who like, respect, and listen to one another, have come together in their thinking. The Prophet's followers become Tecumseh's followers; onto the Prophet's religion is grafted the politics of the older brother. It is a dangerous combination; Harrison cannot suffer it much longer, especially with the Indians leaning toward the British. The time is ripe for a preventive war.

———

FORT AMHERSTBURG, UPPER CANADA, November 15, 1810. Matthew Elliott sits in the council circle on the parade ground overlooking the wooded islands in the Detroit River and contemplates his dilemma. With him are the officers of the 100th Regiment, his clerk, George Ironsides (married to one of Tecumseh's sisters), James Girty, an Indian Department interpreter, and some two hundred Potawatomi, Ottawa, Winnebago, Sauk, and Fox. They have come to hear Tecumseh speak, and it is Tecumseh's words that illustrate Elliott's dilemma. The Indian Department has plainly done its work too well.

The Shawnee war chief has in his hands a great belt of wampum—thousands of small coloured shells sewn together—given to his predecessors by the British after the defeat of the French, a talisman, sacred in Indian eyes, symbolizing a treaty of friendship between the British and the natives.

"Father," says Tecumseh, "I have come here with the intention of informing you that we have not forgot (we can never forget) what passed between you English Men and our Ancestors—And also to let you know our present determination. . . .

"Father we have a belt to show you, which was given to our Kings when you laid the French on their back. Here it is, Father; on one end is your hand, on the other, that of the Red people . . . and in the middle the hearts of both. This belt, Father, our great Chiefs have been sitting upon ever since, keeping it concealed. . . . Now the Warriors have taken all the Chiefs and turned their faces toward you, never again to look towards the Americans; and we the Warriors now manage the affairs of our Nation; and we sit at or near the Borders where the Contest will begin.

"Father—It is only five Years ago that I discovered this Belt and took it from under our Kings. You Father have nourished us, and raised us up from Childhood we are now Men, and think ourselves capable of defending our Country, in which cause you have given us active assistance and always advice—We now are determined to defend it ourselves, and after raising you on your feet leave you behind, but expecting you will push towards us what may be necessary to supply our Wants. . . ."

The belt is passed around so that all may examine it. It shows two hands, dark against a white background (the Indian hand darker than the British) outstretched in friendship. As the belt moves round the circle, Tecumseh declares that his followers will never quit their father or let go his hand.

The translation is awkward, but the meaning is clear. The younger warriors who follow the Prophet and his brother have overridden the advice of their elders and are bent on war with the Americans; they want the British to help them. Elliott, it seems, has been too successful in implementing the government's Indian policy. His instructions were to win the tribes over to the British side. Well, he has done that. The difficulty is that in turning the Indians against the Americans and toward the British, he and his colleagues have brought the country to the brink of an Indian war.

Elliott is in a delicate position and knows it. If war should come, the Indians have been told, Elliott will be its messenger. The previous July he had told a Miami chief: "My son, keep your eyes fixed on me; my tomahawk is up now; be you ready but do not strike until I give the signal." The Indians are more than ready. Patience is not among their virtues; how does one keep them keyed up to fight, yet hold them back from action for months, perhaps years? For Elliott, it is an impossible task.

He is an old man, into his seventies, trying to act like a young man. This year he has taken his first legal wife, an Irish girl, Sarah Donovan, half a century his junior. No doubt she sees him as a father, for she married him shortly after the death of her own father, a schoolmaster. But it is no token relationship; she will bear him two sons.

He is wealthy enough to retire, has been for a generation. He is by far the richest farmer in the area, though farmer is scarcely the word for Elliott, who runs three thousand acres as a plantation with a staff of overseers, clerks, and several score slaves, both Indian and Negro. Some of the latter go back thirty years to his raids in Kentucky with Alexander McKee and the Girty brothers. The Indians have made Elliott a fortune. Some of the land on which his handsome home rests was bought directly from the Wyandot and Ottawa tribes in contravention of British government policy (but winked at by his superiors, who have so often winked at his activities).

His mansion, with its neat lawn, ornamented by tree clumps running down to the river, is furnished as few homes are. He has enough flatware and plate to serve one hundred people. His wife has at least fifty dresses and thirteen pairs of kid gloves. He himself owns eleven hats. There are no banks in the Canadas; one's wealth is stored in the attic. In one trunk, Elliott keeps nine hundred pounds' worth of silver plate.

It does not occur to the old man that he can retire. This is his life; he knows no other. He is close to exhaustion, but the job must be done. He dictates a note to his superior, Superintendent William

Claus. Restraint is necessary, of course, he agrees, but—a little wistfully—would it not be proper to keep up "the present spirit of resistance"? Claus sends the note to Gore at York, who passes it on to the ailing governor general, Sir James Craig, at Quebec, who chews over it for months.

Craig is faced with the same dilemma; his own policy has brought about this problem. A distressing possibility confronts him: what if the Indians should attack prematurely and the British be blamed? His conscience tweaks him, and on November 25 he writes to the British *chargé d'affaires* in Washington asking him to warn the American secretary of state that he suspects the Indians are planning to attack the American frontier. That surreptitious message forms one of the strands in the skein of events that will lead to a bloody denouement the following year at Prophet's Town on the Tippecanoe.

As the Governor General attempts to conciliate the Americans at the possible expense of the Indians, his underlings at Amherstburg have been attempting to conciliate the Indians at the possible expense of the Americans. For the traditional dispensation of presents includes a generous supply of hatchets, guns, and ammunition, ostensibly for hunting game but equally serviceable in the kind of frontier skirmish that is already arousing Yankee dander. Within a year the discovery of some of these weapons will fuel the growing American demand for war.

The ceremony follows a time-honoured ritual. Each chief hands Matthew Elliott a small bundle of cedar sticks to the number of his tribe, cut in three lengths to represent men, women, and children. With these, Elliott's clerks determine how the gifts are to be dispersed. Now the presents are brought from the storehouse and heaped around a series of stakes, each of which bears the name of a tribe. Elliott makes a brief speech, calls the chiefs forward, points to the mounds of gifts—bales of blankets and calico cloth, great rolls of tobacco, stacks of combs, scissors, mirrors, needles, copper pots, iron kettles—and weapons. On a signal the young men dart forward, carry the presents to the waiting canoes. Within three minutes the lawn is empty.

This lavish distribution disturbs the new commander of the British forces in Upper Canada, Brigadier-General Isaac Brock. How, he asks Governor General Craig, can the Indians be expected to believe the British are strictly neutral "after giving such manifest indications of a contrary sentiment by the liberal quantity of military stores with which they were dismissed"? Brock is critical of Elliott—"an exceedingly good man and highly respected by the Indians; but having in his youth lived a great deal with them, he has naturally imbibed their feelings and prejudices, and partaking in the wrongs they continually suffer, this sympathy made him neglect the considerations of prudence, which ought to have regulated his conduct." In short, Elliott can help to start an Indian war.

Sir James Craig agrees. He insists that Elliott and his colleagues "use all their influence to dissuade the Indians from their projected plan of hostility, giving them clearly to understand that they must not expect assistance from us."

Many months pass before Elliott is aware of this policy. Sir James is mortally ill with dropsy, his limbs horribly swollen, his energies sapped. Weeks go by before he is able to reply to Elliott's request to maintain "the present spirit of resistance." More weeks drag on before Elliott receives them. The regular mail service from Quebec extends no farther than Kingston and goes only once a fortnight. In the rest of Upper Canada post offices are almost unknown. Letters to York and Amherstburg often travel by way of the United States. It is March, 1811, before Elliott receives Craig's statement of neutrality and the Indians have long since gone to their hunting camps, out of Elliott's reach. He will not be in touch again for months. British policy has done an about-face on paper, but the Indians, goaded to the point of revolt by Harrison's land hunger, are not aware of it. Events are starting to assume a momentum of their own.

———

VINCENNES, INDIANA TERRITORY, July 30, 1811 Once again in the shade of an arbour on his estate of Grouseland, William Henry

Harrison faces his Shawnee adversary in a great council. The stalemate continues over the disputed lands which, with Tecumseh's threat still hanging over the territory, remain unsurveyed. The Governor is convinced that Tecumseh has come to Vincennes to strike a blow for the Indian cause—that here on Harrison's home ground he intends to murder all the neutral chiefs and, if necessary, the Governor himself. He has ignored Harrison's request to come with a small party; three hundred warriors have arrived on the outskirts of Vincennes by land and water.

The town is in a panic; already in the back country some roving bands of Indians have been slaughtering white families encroaching on their territory. Harrison has responded with a show of force. On the day of Tecumseh's arrival, July 27, he pointedly reviews some seven hundred militiamen. He places three infantry companies on duty, moving them about in such a way that the Indians will believe there are five. He shifts his dragoons about the town at night on foot and horseback in order to place Tecumseh's followers in a state of "astonishment and Terror."

Tecumseh strides into the council with 170 warriors, all armed with knives, tomahawks, bows and arrows. Harrison meets him guarded by a force of seventy dragoons. Each man carries a sabre; each has two pistols stuck in his belt. In this warlike atmosphere the council begins, only to be interrupted by a violent downpour.

Harrison is impatient to end it. He is tired of palaver; a plan of action is forming in his mind. If the Indians want war he intends to give it to them, whether Washington condones it or not. He refuses to negotiate further over the new purchase; that, he tells Tecumseh, is up to the President. But if Tecumseh really wants peace, as he claims, then let him turn over to Harrison the Potawatomi braves in his camp who murdered four white men the previous fall.

Tecumseh speaks. His response, even Harrison admits, is artful. He affects to be surprised that the white men should be alarmed at his plans. All he wants to do is to follow the American example and unite the Indian tribes in the same way that the white men united the various states of the Union. The Indians did not complain of *that* union; why should the white men complain when the Indians want to accomplish the same thing? As for the murderers, they are not in his camp, and anyway, should they not be forgiven? He himself has set an example of forgiveness by refusing to take revenge on those who have murdered his people.

Again he makes it clear that he will not allow surveyors to split up the newly purchased territories for sale to white settlers. Harrison responds bluntly: the moon will fall to earth before the President will suffer his people to be murdered, and he would put his warriors in petticoats before he would give up the land fairly acquired from its rightful owners.

There now occurs an oddly chilling incident that illustrates Tecumseh's remarkable self-possession as well as his power over his followers. A Potawatomi leader known as the Deaf Chief because of impaired hearing wishes to challenge Tecumseh's protestations of peace. A friend informs him that as a result Tecumseh has given orders that he is to be killed. The Deaf Chief, undismayed, puts on his war paint, seizes a rifle, tomahawk, war club, and scalping knife, and descends on Tecumseh's camp to find the Shawnee engaged in conversation with Barron, the interpreter. The Deaf Chief rails at him, calls him a coward and an assassin, and then cries out, "Here am I now. Come and kill me!" Tecumseh makes no answer, continues to talk with Barron. The Deaf Chief heaps more insults on him. "You dare not face a warrior!" he screams. Tecumseh, unmoved, keeps up his quiet conversation. The Deaf Chief raves on, calling Tecumseh a slave of the British redcoats. No response; it is as if the Deaf Chief did not exist. At last, exhausted and out of invective, he departs. But that is the last anyone in Vincennes sees of the Deaf Chief, alive or dead.

Tecumseh's zeal and his influence over his people win Harrison's admiration, even as the Governor plans to destroy him:

"The implicit obedience and respect which the followers of Tecumseh pay to him is really astonishing and more than any other circumstance bespeaks him one of those uncommon geniuses, which spring up occasionally to produce revolutions and overturn the established order of things. If it were not for the vicinity of the United States, he would perhaps be the founder of an Empire that would rival in glory that of Mexico or Peru. No difficulties deter him. His activity and industry supply the want of letters. For four years he has been in constant motion. You see him today on the Wabash and in a short time you hear of him on the shores of Lake Erie, or Michigan, or the banks of the Mississippi and wherever he goes he makes an impression favourable to his purpose."

These words are written on August 7, 1811. Harrison can afford to be generous in his estimation of his adversary, for Tecumseh has removed himself from the area. He is off on a six-month tour of the southern United States to try to persuade the tribes—Creek, Choctaw, Osage, and others—to join his confederacy. For the moment he poses no threat, and in his absence Harrison sees his chance. "I hope," he writes to Eustis, the Secretary of War, ". . . before his return that that part of the fabrick, which he considered complete will be demolished and even its foundations rooted up." Now that the brothers are separated it will be easier to tempt the Prophet into battle. As the Deaf Chief discovered, Tecumseh cannot be provoked unless he wishes to be. But "the Prophet is imprudent and audacious . . . deficient in talents and firmness."

The plan that has been forming in Harrison's mind has become a fixation. The confederacy is growing; the British are undoubtedly behind it. It must be smashed before Tecumseh returns, smashed on the enemy's home ground, at Prophet's Town on the banks of the Tippecanoe. Harrison cannot submit to further stalemate. He will march in September.

———

THE BATTLE OF TIPPECANOE is not the glorious victory that Harrison, down through the years, will proclaim. It is not even a battle, more a minor skirmish, and indecisive, for Harrison, in spite of his claims, loses far more men than the Indians. Overblown in the history books, this brief fracas has two significant results: it is the chief means by which Harrison will propel himself into the White House (his followers chanting the slogan "Tippecanoe and Tyler Too"); and, for the Indians, it will be the final incident that provokes them to follow Tecumseh to Canada, there to fight on the British side in the War of 1812.

Tippecanoe is unnecessary. It is fought only because Harrison needs it to further his own ambitions. For while the Governor is writing to Washington branding the Prophet as an aggressor ("I can assure you Sir that there is not an Indian . . . that does not know and acknowledge when asked that he is determined to attack us and wonder at our forbearance"), Tecumseh is warning his brother that he must on no account be goaded into battle.

Harrison means to goad him, but Washington, in the person of Dr. Eustis, the Secretary of War, equivocates. "I have been particularly instructed by the President," the Secretary writes, "to communicate to your excellency his earnest desire that peace may, if possible, be preserved among the Indians, and that to this end every proper measure be adopted. By this it is not intended . . . that the banditti under the prophet should not be attacked and vanquished, provided such a measure should be rendered absolutely necessary."

That is good enough for Harrison. He shores up his position with a series of letters making it clear that such measures *are* absolutely necessary. As soon as Tecumseh is safely out of the way, he informs Eustis that he intends in September to move up to the upper line of the New Purchase (the territory ceded at Fort Wayne) with two companies of regulars, fourteen or fifteen companies of militia, and two troops of dragoons, the latter consisting of about one hundred men. Harrison makes it seem that this is purely a precautionary measure. But "should circumstances render it necessary to break up the Prophet's establishment by force," well then, he adds—preparing Eustis for the inevitable—he can easily get more men to fight, as well as plenty of mounted volunteers from Kentucky, where Indian fighting is a glorious tradition.

The volunteers, in fact, flock to Vincennes. The best known is Joseph Daviess, one of Kentucky's most eloquent lawyers, a brilliant orator, a popular hero, and a mild eccentric, notorious both for his prosecution of Aaron Burr and for his addiction to colourful and often startling costumes. He has a habit of appearing in court wearing a coonskin cap and deerskin leggings and carrying a hunting rifle. In one memorable appearance before the Supreme Court in Washington (the first for any western lawyer) he turned up in ripped corduroy trousers, a threadbare overcoat, and a pair of dilapidated and muddy shoes, and proceeded to down a quantity of bread and cheese while his opponent tried to marshall his case. Now he is hot to do battle in any capacity under the leadership of his hero, Harrison.

"I make free to tell you," he declares, "that I have imagined there were two men in the west who had military talents: And you sir, were the first of the two. . . . I go as a volunteer, leaving to you sir, to dispose of me as you choose. . . ." He arrives along with some sixty others from his state—former army men and Indian fighters—a commanding figure, thirty-seven years old, resplendent in the uniform of the Kentucky mounted volunteers, the plumes in his hat accentuating his six-foot stature. To one eyewitness, it seems "nothing could be more magnificent. He was the very model of a cavalry officer . . . . With his tall, muscular form and face of strong masculine beauty, he would have been the pride of any army, and the thunderbolt of a battlefield."

Harrison and the Indians are moving at cross purposes. On September 25, the Prophet sends off runners from his village on the Tippecanoe with a message of peace for Harrison. At ten o'clock the following morning, the Governor dispatches his troops on his "demonstration of force." They move up the Wabash in shallow flatboats, the regulars in brass-buttoned tailcoats and stove-pipe hats, the citizen soldiers of the militia in deerskin jackets and bearskin caps. When they reach the disputed territory, they build a blockhouse—Fort Harrison—the eloquent Daviess, now a major, chosen to smash a bottle over the new logs. There is much sickness, especially among the regulars, unused to frontier conditions, forced to wade up the Wabash in their skin-tight pantaloons. Shortly, however, the force is augmented by another two hundred and fifty regular soldiers of

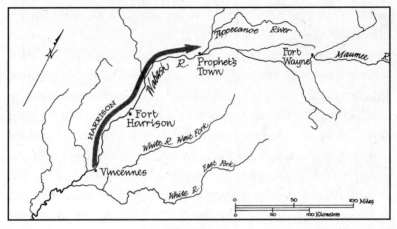

The Wabash

the 4th U.S. Infantry. On October 28 Harrison leaves the new fort and pushes on toward Prophet's Town at the head of one thousand men—a commanding figure in a fringed calico shirt and a beaver hat into which he has jauntily stuck an ostrich feather.

He moves cautiously, expecting Indians behind every tree, suspicious of ambush. Nothing. At two-thirty on the afternoon of November 6, some dozen miles from his objective, he reaches a small wood, halts, draws up his force in battle order, sends scouts forward. There are Indians just ahead, flitting through the trees, but they will not speak to the interpreters.

Back comes Major Daviess, eager for battle, urging an immediate attack against the insolent savages. Why is Harrison vacillating? Have the troops come this far for nothing? The Governor hesitates, mindful of Washington's order that he must try for a peaceful settlement; then, with his men murmuring their eagerness, moves on, yielding "to what appeared to be the general wish." It matters to no one that Prophet's Town is on land that has never been ceded to the United States.

Three Indians approach. Harrison recognizes one: Chief White Horse, principal counsellor to the Prophet. They are conciliatory. They have been trying to reach Harrison, but the messengers have been looking for him on the south side of the river; Harrison has taken the north bank. He assures them that all he seeks is a proper camping ground and they agree to parley on the morrow.

As the town comes into view, Harrison raises his field glass and through it observes the inhabitants running about in apparent terror and confusion behind a breastwork of logs. After some reconnoitring he camps his army about a mile to the northwest among the leafless oaks on a triangle of ground a few feet above the marshy prairie. Here, in the chill of the night, the men slumber, or try to (some have no blankets), in the warmth of huge fires, their loaded guns beside them, bayonets fixed, their coats covering the musket locks to keep them dry. Harrison has dug no trenches, erected no stakes because, he claims later, he has not enough axes.

What are the Indians thinking and planning? No one knows or will ever know, for most of the accounts of the battle come from white men. Those Indian accounts that do exist are second hand and contradictory, filtered through white reports.

Some things are fairly certain: the Indians, not trusting Harrison, expect him to attack and are determined to strike first; the battle, when it comes, is started accidentally when neither side is prepared; and of the several tribes represented at Prophet's Town it is the Winnebago and the Potawatomi and not the Shawnee who are the fiercest in wanting to disobey Tecumseh's orders not to fight.

It is four o'clock, the night still dark and overcast, a light rain rustling the bushes. On the left flank, directly in front of Captain Robert Barton's infantry company, a shivering picket, Private William Brigham, on his knees, his musket on charge, nervously tries to pierce the gloom. He cannot see farther than three feet. Suddenly—footsteps. Brigham raises his musket and almost shoots his fellow picket, William Brown, who has imprudently left his own post in a state of near terror, certain that Indians are lurking in the bushes ahead. His instinct is to flee at once.

"Brigham," he whispers, "let us fire and run . . ."

But Brigham fears a false alarm.

Suddenly something swishes past them. An arrow? Terrified, they turn and dash back toward the camp. Beside them a rifle barks.

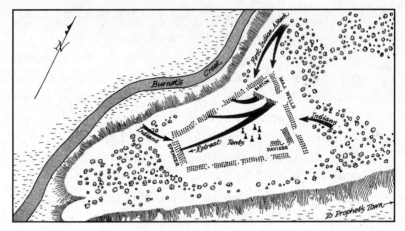

The Battle of Tippecanoe

Another sentry, Stephen Mars, has fired at something moving in the gloom and also dashed toward safety.

In Tent No. 1, Sergeant Montgomery Orr springs awake. Somebody has just rushed past, touching the corner of his tent. He jogs his corporal, David Thompson, awake. Something strikes the tent. Thompson leaps up, seizes his gun as four shots ring out accompanied by a high screaming and yelling. The corporal tumbles back upon the sergeant.

"Corporal Thompson, for God's sake don't give back!" cries Orr, then realizes he is talking to a dead man. He plunges out of the tent, gets a confused impression of a melee—soldiers and Indians firing at each other, Captain Barton trying vainly to form up his men.

Harrison is pulling on his boots when he hears a cacophony of yells and a burst of musketry. One of his officers and two of his men have already been tomahawked and scalped. He calls for his terrified black servant, George, to bring up his favourite mount—a pale grey mare. The boy cannot find her, so Harrison borrows another officer's horse—a black one—and rides into confusion. His men, perfect silhouettes in front of the fires, are falling about him. On the left, Barton's company is already badly mauled. Another has broken. When one of his colonels, mounted on a pale grey mare similar to his missing animal, tumbles to the ground, dead from an Indian musket ball, Harrison realizes that the Indians have mistaken the dead man for himself. An aide rides out on a similar horse; Harrison shoos him back for a black one.

Harrison moves swiftly to reinforce his shattered flank, rides from point to point trying to control the battle. After it is over he will write a careful account, describing the action as if it were a set piece, reconstructing all the movements, making them sound like parade-ground manoeuvres. But at this moment, with the blackened Indians shrieking, the musket fire deafening, the steam rising from fires quickly doused, the clouds of black gun smoke adding to the general overcast, it is impossible for anyone to tell exactly what is happening.

As in every battle, there are moments of horror and moments of heroism.

The Indians are acting in a most un-Indian-like fashion, responding with considerable discipline to signals made by the rattling of deer horns, firing a volley, retreating out of range to reload, advancing again. As Harrison approaches Captain Spier Spencer's company of Kentuckians, known as Yellow Jackets, on the right flank, he can hear the veteran Spencer crying, "Close up, men! Steady! Hold the line!" The Indians have mounted a third attack, so fierce that the balls are shredding the bark from the trees. One strikes Spencer in the head. He continues to shout. Another tears into his thigh, and then another. He calls out for help, and two men rush over, raise him up just as another ball penetrates his body, killing him.

Harrison rides up, sees young John Tipton sighting down a barrel.

"Where's your captain?"

"Dead, sir!"

"Your first-lieutenant?"

"Dead, sir!"

"Your second-lieutenant?"

"Dead, sir!"

"Your ensign?"

"Here, sir!"

Harrison searches about for reinforcements, sees Robb's militia company faltering, rallies them in support of the Yellow Jackets, braces the flank with a company of regulars. A close friend, Thomas Randolph, falls, mortally wounded. Harrison dismounts, bends over his friend, asks if there is anything he can do. Nothing, gasps Randolph, except to look after his child. Harrison keeps that promise.

The impetuous Major Daviess, in charge of the dragoons, is chafing at the rear. He wants to roar into action, but Harrison is holding him back:

"Tell Major Daviess to be patient, he will have an honourable station before the battle is over."

Daviess cannot stand the inaction; he presses Harrison again, gets the same reply, continues to nag. At last the Governor gives in:

"Tell Major Daviess he has heard my opinion twice; he may now use his own discretion."

Daviess has spotted Indians lurking behind some scattered logs seventy-five yards away. Gathering a force of twenty men, he prepares to charge the foe. He has dressed with his customary panache—an unmistakable target, six feet tall, in a white blanket coat that stands out starkly in the gloom. As he leads his men toward the enemy, three balls pierce his body. "I am a dead man," cries Jo Daviess. His followers carry him to the cover of a sycamore tree as the Indians vanish. He has not long to live. "Unfortunately, the Major's gallantry determined him to execute the order with a smaller force than was sufficient," Harrison comments, a little dryly, in his report of the action.

By the time Daviess falls, the entire line is engaged. Daybreak is at hand. As the Indians begin to falter, Harrison determines on a charge from the flanks. This is the climax of the battle. The level of sound is almost unbearable—an ear-splitting mixture of savage yells, shrieks of despair, roar of musketry, agonizing screams, victorious shouts, dying cries mingling in a continuous terrifying uproar that will ring in the ears of the survivors long after the last wound is healed.

Harrison's charge succeeds. The Indians, out of ammunition and arrows, retire across the marshy prairie where horses cannot follow.

The Americans shout cries of triumph, utter prayers of thanks, bind up their wounds, scalp all the dead Indians, kill one who is wounded.

Two days later, they sweep through Prophet's Town, empty save for one aged squaw, on a mission of revenge and plunder. They destroy everything including all the beans and corn that they themselves cannot eat—some three thousand bushels stored up for the winter. In the houses they find British weapons, presents dispensed at Amherstburg the previous year; it confirms their suspicion that British agents have been provoking the Indians to attack (though American weapons distributed by the war department as part of the annuity payments to the tribes are also found). Then they burn all the houses and sheds and take their leave. Thus ends the Battle of Tippecanoe, which has often been called the first battle in the War of 1812.

Harrison has lost almost one-fifth of his force. Thirty-seven white corpses lie sprawled on the battlefield. One hundred and fifty men have been wounded of whom twenty-five will die of their injuries, including the luckless sentry Brigham. No one can be sure how many Indians took part in the skirmish. Nobody knows how many died. Harrison, like most military commanders, overestimates the enemy's losses, declares that the Prophet's casualties run into the hundreds. This is wishful thinking; only thirty-six Indian corpses are found.

The battered army limps back to Vincennes. As soon as Harrison is gone, the Indians, who have retreated across the Wabash, return to the ruins of their village. Although a Kickapoo chief reports to the British that "the Prophet and his people do not appear as a vanquished army," Harrison, intent on beating out some flames of dissent from Kentucky (where Daviess's death is mourned and Harrison's strategy and motives scrutinized), has already launched the long propaganda battle that will convince his countrymen that Tippecanoe was a glorious victory.

What has it accomplished? Its purpose was to teach the Indians a lesson they would never forget, to break Tecumseh's confederacy and the Prophet's power, and to stop the sporadic raids on frontier settlements. But the raids increase in fury. Settlers and soldiers are ambushed. Whole families are wiped out, scalped, mutilated. Farmers abandon their fields and cabins; neighbours club together to build blockhouses; some flee the territory. At Grouseland, Harrison constructs an underground escape tunnel, ships his wife and eight children off to safety in Kentucky, buffers the principal homes of Vincennes with log parapets. Instead of terrifying the Indians, Tippecanoe has stirred them to fury. In March, 1812, both Governor Howard of Missouri Territory and General William Clark, the explorer and superintendent of Indian Affairs, voice the opinion that a formidable combination of Indians are on the warpath, that a bloody war must ensue is almost certain, and that the Prophet is regaining his influence.

Tecumseh returns that same month to Prophet's Town. Later he speaks of his experience:

"I stood upon the ashes of my own home, where my own wigwam had sent up its fires to the Great Spirit, and there I summoned the spirits of the braves who had fallen in their vain attempts to protect their homes from the grasping invader, and as I snuffed up the smell of their blood from the ground I swore once more eternal hatred—the hatred of an avenger."

His mission to the south has failed. The Sauk and Osage tribesmen will not follow him. But his northern confederacy is not shattered as Harrison keeps repeating (and repeating it, is believed). Tecumseh sends runners to the tribes; twelve respond, each sending two leading chiefs and two war chiefs. By May, Tecumseh has six hundred men under his command, making bows and arrows (for they no longer have guns). In Washington, war fever rises on the tales of frontier violence and the legend of Tippecanoe. Tecumseh waits, holds his men back for the right moment. For a while he will pretend neutrality, but when the moment comes, he will lead his confederacy across the border to fight beside the British against the common enemy.

TWO

Prelude to Invasion

1812
Marching as to War

———

We're abused and insulted, our country's degraded
Our rights are infringed both by land and by sea;
Let us rouse up indignant, when those rights are invaded,
And announce to the world, "We're united and free!"

—Anon., circa 1812.

LITTLE YORK, THE MUDDY capital of Upper Canada, February 27, 1812; Brock, in his study, preparing a secret memorandum to that spectacular frontier creature whom the Dakota Sioux call *Mascotapah*, the Red-Haired Man.

His real name is Robert Dickson, and though born a Scot in Dumfriesshire, he is as close to being an Indian as any white can be. His wife is To-to-win, sister to Chief Red Thunder. His domain covers the watershed of the upper Mississippi, some of the finest fur country on the continent, a land of rolling plains, riven by trough-like valleys and speckled with blue lakes, the veinwork of streams

77

teeming with beaver, marten, and otter, the prairie dark with buffalo. He is out there now, somewhere—nobody knows quite where—a white man living like an Indian, exercising all the power of a Sioux chieftain. Brock must find him before the war begins, for Brock is planning the defence of Upper Canada—carefully, meticulously—and the Red-Haired Man is essential to that plan.

Isaac Brock has been preparing for war for five years, ever since the *Chesapeake* affair when, as colonel in charge of the defences of Lower Canada, he forced a grudging administration into allowing him to repair and strengthen the crumbling fortress of Quebec. Now he has power. He is not only a major-general in charge of all the forces in Upper Canada, he is also, in the absence of Francis Gore, the province's administrator, which in colonial terms makes him close to being a dictator, though not close enough for Brock's peace of mind. His years in Canada have been a series of frustrations: frustrations with the civil authorities, whom he views as a nuisance and who prevent him from getting his own way; frustrations with his superior, the new governor general Sir George Prevost, who keeps him on a tight leash lest he do something precipitate and give the Americans cause for war; frustrations with the militia, who are untrained, untidy, undisciplined, and unwilling; frustrations with the civilian population, who seem blithely unaware of the imminence of war; frustrations over money, for he is in debt through no real fault of his own; frustrations, one suspects, over women, for he loves their company but has never been able to bring himself to marry; and finally, frustrations over his posting.

More than anything else, Brock yearns to be with Wellington on the Peninsula, where there is opportunity for active service and its concomitants, glory and promotion. He does not care for Canada, especially this wretched backwater of York with its tiny clique of pseudo-aristocrats, its haggling legislature, and its untutored rabble. In Quebec at least there was sophistication of a sort, and Brock is no rustic: a gourmet, a lover of fine wines, an omnivorous reader, a spirited dancer at society balls, he longs for a larger community.

For all his days in Canada he has been trying to escape his colonial prison. The irony is that this very month the Prince Regent, through Governor General Prevost, has given him leave to depart. Now he cannot go. Duty, with Brock, takes precedence over personal whim. The gentlemen who form the Prince Regent's government may not believe that war is coming, but General Isaac Brock believes it, and "being now placed in a high ostensible situation, and the state of public affairs with the American government indicating a strong presumption of an approaching rupture between the two countries, I beg leave to be allowed to remain in my present command." *Etc. Etc.* Or is it, possibly, more than a strict sense of duty that holds Brock in Canada? Expecting war, does he not also welcome it? May he not now hope to encounter in the colonies what he has longed for on the continent? Glory, honour, adventure all beckon; all these—even death.

His colleagues, friends, subordinates, and adversaries are scarcely aware of the General's inner turmoil. Though his features are not always expressionless—he was once seen to shed a tear at the execution of a soldier—he keeps his frustrations to himself. He is a remarkably handsome man with a fair complexion, a broad forehead, clear eyes of grey blue (one with a slight cast), and sparkling white teeth. His portraits tend to make him look a little feminine—the almond eyes, the sensitive nostrils, the girlish lips—but his bearing belies it; his is a massive figure, big-boned and powerful, almost six feet three in height. He has now, at forty-two, a slight tendency to portliness, and the flush of middle age is on his cheeks; but he is, in his own words, "hard as nails."

He is popular with almost everybody, especially the soldiers who serve him—a courteous, affable officer who makes friends easily and can charm with a smile. But there is also an aloofness about him, induced perhaps by the loneliness of command; on those rare occasions when he does take somebody into his confidence it is likely to be a junior officer of the volunteer army rather than one of his immediate subordinates.

He has no use for democracy. It is an American word, as treasonous in his lexicon as communism will be to a later generation of military authoritarians. Even the modest spoonful of self-determination allowed the settlers of Upper Canada annoys him. He has gone before the legislature this very month to ask that the civilians, who train part time in the militia, be forced to take an oath of allegiance. The militia in his view contains "many doubtful characters." In addition, he wants to suspend the age-old right of habeas corpus. The House of Assembly turns him down on both counts, a decision that, to Brock, smacks of disloyalty: "The great influence which the numerous settlers from the United States possess over the decisions of the lower house is truly alarming, and ought immediately, by every practical means, [to] be diminished." To Brock, the foundations of the colonial superstructure are threatened by treacherous foreign democrats, boring from within, but he cannot convince the Assembly of that.

So he turns to military matters and the secret message to the Red-Haired Man. As a good military commander, Brock has put himself in the boots of his opposite numbers. He is confident that he knows what the Americans will do.

Through their hunger for land they have managed to alienate almost all the tribes on their northwestern frontier. The Indians, then, are the key to American intentions. In other circumstances, it would make sense to hit Canada in the midriff, at Kingston and Montreal, cutting off the supply routes to the upper province, which then must surely fall. But Brock knows that this militarily attractive option is no option at all as long as America's left flank is in flames. The Indians must be subdued, and for that enterprise a very considerable force will be required, drawn principally, Brock believes, from Ohio, whose people are "an enterprising, hardy race, and uncommonly expert on horseback with the rifle." To meet this threat he has already dispatched two hundred regulars to reinforce the garrison at Fort Amherstburg, across from the American military base at Detroit. These will not be enough to counter any American thrust across the Detroit River, but Brock hopes that their presence will stiffen the resolve of the militia, and more important, convince the Indians that Britain means business. For it is on the Indians that the security of Upper Canada depends. If he can rouse the Indians, the United States will be forced to concentrate much of its limited military strength on the northwestern frontier, thereby weakening any proposed thrust along the traditional invasion routes toward Montreal and the St. Lawrence Valley.

Brock views the Indians as a means to an end. His attitude toward them changes with the context. They are "a much injured people" (a slap at American Indian policy), but they are also a "fickle race" (when some insist on remaining neutral). To Brock, as to most white men, Indians are Indians. (It is as if Wellington lumped Lapps with Magyars and Poles with Scots.) He makes little distinction between the tribes; Sioux and Shawnee, Wyandot and Kickapoo are all the same to him—savages, difficult to deal with, inconstant but damned useful to have on your side. Brock means to have as many oddly assorted Indians on his side as he can muster, and that is the substance of his secret communication with the Red-Haired Man.

The Indians, in Brock's assessment, will fight the Americans only if they are convinced the British are winning. If he can seize the island of Mackinac in the far west at the outset of the war, he believes the Indians will take heart. Some will undoubtedly help him attack Detroit (for Brock believes the best defence is offence), and if Detroit falls, more Indians will join the British—perhaps even the Mohawks of the Six Nations, who have been distressingly neutral. The main American invasion, Brock believes, will come at the Niagara border along the neck of land between Lake Ontario and Lake Erie. Anything else will be a diversion.

To put his domino theory into practice, at the outset Brock needs Indians to subdue by their presence, if not their arrows, the defenders of Michilimackinac. He expects the Red-Haired Man to supply them. The secret letter is deliberately couched in euphemisms, and even Brock's immediate superior, the cautious Governor General Prevost, is not aware of it:

CONFIDENTIAL COMMUNICATION TRANSMITTED TO MR. ROBERT DICKSON RESIDING WITH THE INDIANS NEAR THE MISSOURI

Sir,

As it is probable that war may result from the present *state of affairs*, it is very desirable to ascertain the degree of cooperation that you and *your friends* might be able to furnish, in case of such an Emergency taking place. You will be pleased to report with all practicable expedition upon the following matters,

1st. The number of your friends, that might be depended upon.

2. Their disposition toward us.

3. Would they assemble, and march under your orders.

4. State the succours you require, and the most eligible mode, for their conveyance.

5. Can *Equipment* be procured in your *Country*.

6. An immediate direct communication with you, is very much wished for.

7. Can you point out in what manner, that object may be accomplished.

8. Send without loss of time a few *faithful* and *Confidential* Agents—Selected from *your friends*.

9. Will you individually approach the Detroit frontier next spring.

If so, state time and place where *we* may meet. *Memo.* Avoid mentioning names, in your *written communications.*

Almost five months will pass before Brock receives an answer to this memorandum. And when on July 14, at Fort George at the mouth of the Niagara River, an Indian runner finally arrives with a reply from Robert Dickson, it will already be outdated by events. Long before that, the Red-Haired Man and his friends, anticipating Brock, will have departed for the British post at St. Joseph's to prepare for the invasion of the unsuspecting island of Mackinac.

———

WASHINGTON, D.C., MARCH 20, 1812. Spring has come to the capital after an unseasonably cold winter. It is, as one newspaper points out, excellent weather for campaigning; the roads are no longer rivers of mud and slush. Why are the troops not moving north?

At the British legation on Pennsylvania Avenue this bright afternoon, a young officer arrives with dispatches from the British foreign secretary. They tell a familiar tale. In the face of French intransigence, the British government cannot—will not—repeal the Orders in Council that are at the heart of the dispute between the two nations. Lord Wellesley has felt that decision important enough to justify chartering a special ship to rush word of it across the Atlantic.

The Minister Plenipotentiary to America, who must now carry this news to the President, is the same Augustus John Foster who once swore he would not return to Washington for ten thousand pounds a year. Nevertheless, he is back, and no longer in a junior post. His absence from the London social scene since the spring of 1811 has lost him his intended—a priggish young woman named Annabella Milbanke, who will later conclude a loveless and disastrous marriage with Lord Byron. But how could any ambitious young diplomat refuse such a promotion?

How, for that matter, could His Majesty's government have selected Foster to be its eyes, ears, and tongue at this most critical of times? To the clear indications of approaching war Foster's eyes are uncommonly blind, his ears remarkably deaf, and, in his dispatches, his tongue lamentably silent. At thirty-three, with his round, boyish face, he is, to quote one politician, "a pretty young gentleman . . . better calculated for a ballroom or a drawing room, than for a foreign minister."

He spends a good deal of time in ballrooms, drawing rooms, and at dinner tables, entertains as many as two hundred guests at a time and lavishly overspends his expense account (perhaps to counteract the impression conveyed by his juvenile looks, for which, as he complains to his mother, the new Duchess of Devonshire, he is "greatly abused"). He seems to know everybody, rubs shoulders with all the major participants in the dangerous game being played out in the capital this spring, yet manages to miss the significance of what he sees and hears. He dines with the Speaker of the House, Henry Clay, whom he describes as "very warlike," John C. Calhoun, the fiery young congressman from South Carolina, Peter B. Porter, the bellicose leader of the House committee on foreign relations, and other members of the ginger group known as War Hawks, but he does not believe that war will come.

The War Hawks are only a handful, yet they effectively control Congress. Five of them room together in the same boarding house, predictably dubbed the War Mess. Clay is their leader, a brilliant, fervent orator who has been Speaker since the opening of the fall session. Poetically handsome, with fair, tousled hair and a quizzical smile, he is no disinterested chairman. He thinks nothing of leaving his neutral post and invading the floor of the House to speak, sometimes for hours. He has seen to it that his cronies chair the key committees, notably the naval committee and the foreign relations committee. The latter—Peter B. Porter's committee—is packed with Clay supporters. Its majority report, brought down in November, 1811, was unequivocal. Since Britain would not budge on the two major issues threatening peace—the Orders in Council and impressment—therefore "we must now tamely submit and quietly submit or we must resist by those means which God has placed within our reach." In short, a call to war.

At dinner with the President in the still unfinished Executive Mansion, Foster encounters another actor in the drama, the dashing Comte Edouard de Crillon, whose extraordinarily thick legs he cannot help remarking. The following day he invites the count to his own table where they discuss the count's estate in Chile. It is all bunkum, as Foster will presently learn: there is no Chilean estate and no Comte de Crillon, either—only a charlatan named Soubiron, a master at masquerade. This imposter has attached himself to a handsome Irish rascal named John Henry, and the two are in the process of palming off a series of letters that Henry has written while in the pay of Sir James Craig, the former governor general of Canada. It develops that Henry, at his own suggestion, was sent by Craig in 1808 as a spy to Federalist New England to see if anyone within the opposition party there might help force a separation from the Union—in short, to seek and make contact with traitors. Henry, being remarkably unsuccessful, was paid a pittance, but the cunning Soubiron believes that copies of the letters, now more than three years old, are worth a minor fortune.

And so, to James Madison, they appear to be. The President is persuaded to squander the entire secret service fund of $50,000 for documents he believes will discomfit the Federalists, lay some of their leaders open to the charge of treason, and embarrass the British.

Madison's coup backfires. Henry has named no names, mentioned no specifics. The President's enemies quickly discover that the Irishman is not the reformed patriot he pretends to be and that the chief executive has looted the treasury for a batch of worthless paper. But the Henry affair, revealing yet another instance of British perfidy, helps to arouse further public feeling already inflamed by Tippecanoe and its aftermath, by a depression in the southwest brought on by the Orders in Council, and by continuing British high-handedness on the seas—more sailors impressed, more ships seized. "If this event does not produce a war, nothing will do so," Augustus Foster comments after Madison tables the letters on March 9. But war does not come, and this helps shore up Federalist convictions (and Foster's) that for all the Republicans' warlike clamour, the government is bluffing, as it had been after the *Chesapeake* affair. Tragically, the congressional doves do not take the War Hawk movement seriously.

Nor does Foster. He is extraordinarily well informed, for he moves in the highest circles, dining regularly with congressmen, senators, and the President himself. He knows that William Hull, Governor of Michigan Territory, has come to town, hoping (Foster believes) to be made Secretary of War in place of the genial but ineffective incumbent, William Eustis. He knows that a former secretary of war, Henry Dearborn, is also in town, trying to decide whether or not to give up his sinecure as collector of customs in Boston and take over command of the expanding army. He must know that Hull, who is another of his dinner guests, is also pondering the offer of an army command in the northwest. The United States, in short, is acting like a nation preparing for war; the President himself, in Foster's words, is "very warlike," but there is no sense of urgency in the reports he sends to Whitehall. He prefers the company of the President's warm-hearted and unwarlike wife, Dolley, who could not attend his January ball marking the Queen's birthday for political reasons but was forced to gaze on the preparations at a distance, from her bedroom window.

Preparations for war are the responsibility of a trio of old hands—all sixtyish—from the Revolution—Hull, Eustis, and Dearborn. Unlike Clay and his Hawks, these ex-soldiers, none of whom has had experience with staff command, can scarcely be said to be champing at the bit. Hull and Dearborn cannot even make up their minds whether to shoulder the responsibility of leadership. Eustis, a one-time surgeon's assistant, is genial, courteous, and a staunch party man but generally held to be incompetent—an executive unable to divorce himself from detail. Congress has refused to create two assistant secretaries, and so the entire war department of the United States consists of Eustis and eight clerks.

Governor Hull has been invited to the capital to discuss the defence of the northwestern frontier. Brock's assessment has been dead on: the Indians have dictated Washington's strategy; with Tecumseh's followers causing chaos in Indiana and Michigan territories, the United States has no option but to secure its western flank.

Washington believes in Hull. He has a reputation for sound judgement, personal courage, decisive command. During the Revolution he fought with distinction, survived nine battles, received the official thanks of Congress. One gets a fleeting picture of a gallant young field officer in his mid-twenties, rallying his troops on horseback at Bemis Heights, stemming a retreat in the face of Gentleman Johnny Burgoyne's regulars, or helping Mad Anthony Wayne carry the Stony Point fort at bayonet point (a bullet creasing his hat, another clipping his boot).

The President and the Secretary of War listen carefully to Hull's advice. The Governor points out that the United States must secure Lake Erie by reinforcing the tiny fort at Detroit and building warships to command the water routes in order to allow the swift movement of men and supplies. Hull realizes that the Indians hold the key to defeat or victory. A formidable army at Detroit, denying the lake to British transport, can cut the Indians off from the British and perhaps prevent a general uprising of the tribes. And without the Indians, he is convinced, "the British cannot hold Upper Canada."

Eustis goes along with Hull's plan only to discover that no American captain can be found who will take command on Lake Erie. Besides, it costs money to build ships, and Congress is niggardly with naval funds. Hull and Eustis, caught up in the war fever, persuade themselves that it will be enough to march a considerable force north to strengthen Detroit, cow the Indians into neutrality, and convince the British across the river that the natives are under control. Should war come, Detroit will be the springboard for an invasion that will drive the British out of all the country west of Niagara.

Hull declines the command of the army that will reinforce Detroit; he does not wish to give up his post as governor of Michigan Territory. A substitute is found in Colonel Jacob Kingsbury, an old frontier campaigner, aged fifty-seven, who first accepts but then backs out as the result of an attack of gout—an episode that hints at the paucity of leadership material in the American military establishment. Hull is hurriedly called for and told he can keep the governorship if he will accept a commission as brigadier-general in command of the Army of the Northwest.

Finally, Hull agrees. He is to raise an army of twelve hundred volunteers from the Ohio militia (as Brock has predicted) to be augmented by some four hundred regular troops. With this force he is to cut a road through forest and swamp for two hundred miles from Urbana, Ohio, to Detroit and thus secure the frontier.

Henry Dearborn, after cautiously weighing the lifetime post of customs collector against the less secure appointment of Commander-in-Chief of the American Army, finally settles on the latter and is commissioned major-general. He, too, has a plan. If war comes, the main army will attack Montreal by the historic Champlain water route, thus cutting off all of Upper Canada from reinforcements and supplies. At the same time, three columns will strike at Canada from the border points of Detroit, Niagara, and Sackets Harbor. The attack from Detroit will take care of the Indians. The other two, from opposite ends of Lake Ontario, will serve to slice up the upper province, knocking out the major British fortresses at Niagara and Kingston. Dearborn's headquarters will be at Albany, the nerve centre from which roads veer off to the three eastern invasion points. (Detroit is so remote that Dearborn treats it as a separate command.)

On paper all of this makes sense, but it depends on inspired leadership, swift communications, careful timing, well-trained troops, an efficient war department, and a united, enthusiastic nation. None of these conditions exists.

Dearborn leaves the capital early in April for Boston, where he expects, with misplaced optimism, to raise his citizen army. Given the New England governors' violent opposition to war, it is a forlorn hope. Hull, who departs for the Ohio frontier, will have better luck.

In the capital, the war fever grows in the face of British stubbornness. On April 15, Augustus Foster attends a great dinner given by the New Orleans deputies to mark Louisiana's entry into the Union. He is in the best possible position to assess the temper of the Congress, for most of its members are present along with the cabinet. Foster finds himself sandwiched between—of all people—the two leading War Hawks. Henry Clay, on one side, is as militant as ever. The twenty-six-year-old John Calhoun, on the other, is "a man resolved," his tone cool and decided. It all seems very curious to Foster. He decides that a great many people are afraid of being laughed at if they don't fight and thus arrives, quite unconsciously, at the nub of the matter.

Far to the north, in Quebec City, the new governor general of Canada, Sir George Prevost, has no illusions about the future. He warns the British government that he shortly expects a declaration of war from Madison. Foster cannot yet see it. To him, it is merely "a curious state of things." The party grows too noisy for him, and presently he takes his leave, repairing to the Executive Mansion, there to enjoy the more peaceful company of the engaging Dolley Madison.

———

DAYTON, OHIO, April 6, 1812. Duncan McArthur, one of Wayne's old frontier scouts, now General of the Ohio militia, that "enterprising, hardy race" of which Brock has written, is haranguing his citizen soldiers.

"Fellow citizens and soldiers," cries McArthur, "the period has arrived when the country again calls its heroes to arms . . . !" Who, he asks, will not volunteer to fight against perfidious England—"that proud and tyrannical nation, whose injustice prior to 1776, aroused the indignation of our fathers to manly resistance?"

"Their souls could no longer endure slavery," says McArthur. "The HEAVEN protected patriots of Columbia obliged the mighty armies of the tyrant to surrender to American valor. . . ."

He warms to his subject, sneers at Britain's "conquered and degraded troops," gibes at "the haughty spirit of that proud and unprincipled nation," calls for vengeance, justice, victory.

What is going on? Is the country in a state of war? The eager volunteers, harking to their leader's braggadocio, must surely believe that the United States and Britain are at each other's throats. Yet war has not been declared. Few Englishmen believe it likely nor does the majority of Americans. Nonetheless, the call has gone out from Washington for volunteers, and Ohio has been asked to fill its quota. For Duncan McArthur, the original war—the War of Independence—has never ended.

"Could the shades of the departed heroes of the revolution who purchased our freedom with their blood, descend from the valiant mansions of peace, would they not call aloud to arms?" he asks. "And where is that friend to his country who would not obey that call?"

Where indeed? McArthur is preaching to the converted. By May, Ohio's quota of twelve hundred volunteers will be over-subscribed. Sixteen hundred militiamen answer the call. These will form the undisciplined core of the Army of the Northwest, which Brigadier-General William Hull, Governor of Michigan, will lead to Detroit.

The new general joins his troops at Dayton, Ohio, after a journey that has left him weak from cold and fever. In spite of his reputation he is a flabby old soldier, tired of war, hesitant of command, suspicious of the militia who he knows are untrained and suspects are untrustworthy. He has asked for three thousand men; Washington finally allows him two thousand. He does not really want to be a general, but he is determined to save his people from the Indians. A Massachusetts man, he has been Governor of Michigan for seven years and now feels he knows it intimately—every trail, every settlement, every white man, woman, and child, and much of the Canadian border country. He is convinced that the Indians, goaded by the British, are particularly hostile to the Michigan settlers. He sees himself as their protector, their father-figure, and he looks like a stereotype father in a popular illustration, the features distinguished if fleshy, the shock of hair dead white. (He is only fifty-eight, but some of his men believe him closer to seventy.) He chews tobacco unceasingly, a habit that muddies the illusion, especially when he is nervous and his jaws work overtime. There is a soft streak in Hull, no asset in a frontier campaign. As a young man he studied for the ministry, only to give it up for the law, but something of the divinity student remains.

On May 25, Hull parades his troops in the company of Governor Meigs of Ohio, a capable politician with the singular Christian name "Return." The volunteers are an unruly lot, noisy, insubordinate, untrained. Hull is appalled. Their arms are unfit for use; the leather covering the cartridge boxes is rotten; many of the men have no blankets and clothing. No armourers have been provided to repair the weapons, no means have been adopted to furnish the missing clothing, no public stores of arms or supplies exist, and the powder in the magazines is useless. Since the triumph of the Revolution, America has not contemplated an offensive war, or even a defensive one.

For these men, dressed in homespun, armed when armed at all with tomahawks and hunting knives, Hull has prepared the same kind of ringing speech, with its echoes of Tippecanoe, that is being heard in the Twelfth Congress:

"On marching through a wilderness memorable for savage barbarity you will remember the causes by which that barbarity has been heretofore excited. In viewing the ground stained with the blood of your fellow citizens, it will be impossible to suppress the feelings of indignation. Passing by the ruins of a fortress erected in our territory by a foreign nation in times of profound peace, and for the express purpose of exciting the savages to hostility, and supplying them with the means of conducting a barbarous war, must remind you of that system of oppression and injustice which that nation has continually practised, and which the spirit of an indignant people can no longer endure."

Hull and his staff set off to review the troops, a fife and drum corps leading the way. The sound of the drums frightens the pony ridden by one of Hull's staff; it turns about, dashes off in the wrong direction. A second, ridden by Hull's son and aide, Abraham, follows. Soon the General finds his own mount out of control. It gallops after the others, tossing its rider about unmercifully. Encumbered by his ceremonial sword, Hull cannot control the horse; his feet slip out of the stirrups, he loses his balance, his hat flies off, and he is forced to cling to the animal's mane in a most unsoldierly fashion until it slows to a walk. At last the staff regroups, confers, decides not to pass down the ranks in review but rather to have the troops march past. It is not a propitious beginning.

The volunteers have been formed into three regiments. Jeffersonian democracy, which abhors anything resembling a caste system, decrees that they elect their own officers, an arrangement that reinforces Great Britain's contempt for America's amateur army. McArthur is voted colonel of the 1st Regiment of Ohio Volunteers, and it is remarked that he "looks more like a go-ahead soldier than any of his brother officers." A go-ahead soldier on the Ohio frontier, especially an elected one, differs markedly from a go-ahead soldier in Wellington's army. To a later English visitor, McArthur is "dirty and butcher-like, very unlike a soldier in appearance, seeming half-savage and dressed like a backwoodsman; generally considered being only fit for hard knocks and Indian warfare" (which is, of course, exactly the kind of contest that is facing him).

In the volunteer army, officers must act like politicians. More often than not they *are* politicians. McArthur has been a member of the Ohio legislature. The 2nd Regiment of Ohio Volunteers elects a former mayor of Cincinnati, James Findlay, as its colonel. The 3rd votes for Lewis Cass, a stocky, coarse-featured lawyer of flaming ambition who is U.S. marshal for the state. Almost from the outset Hull has his troubles with these three. Cass has little use for him. "Instead of having an able energetic commander, we have a weak old man," he writes to a friend. Hull, on his part, is contemptuous of the militia, whom he found unreliable during the Revolution. Imagine *electing* officers to command!

"Elected officers," he believes, "can never be calculated upon as great disciplinarians. In every station the elected will be unwilling to incur the displeasure of the electors; indeed he will often be found to court their favour by a familiarity and condescension which are totally incompatible with military discipline. The man that votes his officer his commission, instead of being implicitly obedient, as every soldier ought to be, will be disposed to question and consider the propriety of the officer's conduct before he acts. . . ."

Another problem faces Hull. The three militia commanders are full colonels. But James Miller, who will lead the regulars, is only a half-colonel. When Miller protests the injustice of this— if anything, he should outrank the amateurs—Cass, Findlay, and McArthur threaten to quit and disband their regiments unless their rank is maintained. There is nothing that Hull or his superiors in Washington can do about this small-boy petulance. The militia colonels continue to outrank Miller.

The army starts the march north on June 1. A few days later at the frontier community of Urbana, the last outpost of civilization, Hull's suspicions about the militia are reinforced. From this point to Detroit the troops face two hundred miles of wilderness with no pathway, not even an Indian trail to follow. The volunteers turn ugly. They had been promised an advance of fifty dollars each for a year's clothing but have received only sixteen. One unpopular officer is ridden out of camp on a rail, and when the orders come to march, scores refuse to move. Into camp, at this impasse, marches Miller's 4th Infantry Regiment of regulars. These veterans of Tippecanoe prod the wavering volunteers into action, and the troops move out, with McArthur's regiment in the lead, hacking a way through jungle and forest. The following day, three mutinous ringleaders are court-martialled and sentenced to have their heads half shaved and their hands tied and to be marched round the lines with the label "Tory" between their shoulders—a punishment the prisoners consider worse than the death-sentence.

Hull's force is as much a mob as an army. The volunteers mock the General's son Abraham, who, mounted upon a spirited horse, in full uniform and blind drunk, toppled into the Mad River in front of the entire assembly.

"Who got drunk and fell in the Mad River?" somebody calls from the ranks, to which a distant companion answers, "Captain Hull!" and a third echoes, "That's true!"

The jests are needed, for the rain falls incessantly. The newly built road becomes a swamp; wagons are mired and have to be hoisted out by brute strength. The troops keep up their spirits on corn liquor supplied by friendly settlers.

Then, at the brand-new blockhouse on the Scioto named Fort McArthur, a bizarre episode dries up the supply of moonshine. A

Hull's March to Detroit

guard named Peter Vassar lies slumped under a tree, befuddled by drink. He hears a sudden noise, seizes his musket, makes sure it is charged, takes deliberate aim, and shoots another sentry, Joseph England, through the left breast, just missing his heart. Vassar is court-martialled and given a grotesque sentence: both ears are cropped and each cheek branded with the letter M. McArthur issues an order restraining settlers from selling liquor to his men without his written permission. The ban does not extend to his officers.

Thus dispirited, the troops plunge through the pelting rain into the no man's land of the Black Swamp, a labyrinth of deadfalls and ghostly trees behind whose trunks Tecumseh's unseen spies keep watch. A fog of insects clogs the soldiers' nostrils and bloats their faces; a gruel of mud and water rots their boots and swells their ankles. They cannot rest at day's end until they hack out a log breast-work against Indian attack. Strung out for two miles day after day, the human serpent finally wriggles to a halt, blocked by rising water and unbridgeable streams. Hull camps his men in ankle-deep mud, builds a blockhouse, names it Fort Necessity, and there, from ne-cessity, the sodden army waits until the floods ebb. Yet Hull is not cast down. He has more than two thousand rank and file under his command and believes his force superior to any that may oppose it.

Finally the troops move on to the head of navigation on a branch of the Maumee River (also known as the Miami of the Lakes). And here a letter catches up with Hull. It is from Eustis, the Secretary of War, urging him to advance with all possible haste to Detroit, there to await further orders. The letter is dated June 18, but it must have been penned on the morning of that day because it fails to include the one piece of information that is essential to prevent a major blunder: in the afternoon of June 18, the United States has officially declared war on Great Britain.

———

IN WASHINGTON, WHILE HULL'S army trudges through the swamps of Ohio and Robert Dickson's Indians head for St. Joseph's

position, voting a little grudgingly for the various military proposals that have pushed the nation closer to war, but believing almost to the end that commercial retaliation is the answer. James Madison, too, is prepared by spring to go along with war, even though, like his predecessor Jefferson, he has struggled against the idea of involvement in a European conflict. He is a small man, benign of temperament, soft-voiced, distant in his relationships, a scholar, modest and moderate, who owns a single black suit and once lost an election for refusing to supply free whiskey to the voters. His outward composure is sometimes mistaken for weakness; the Federalists think him a pawn of Henry Clay. He is not. Though he dislikes the idea of war, he too comes to believe that his country has no other course. Apart from other considerations, submission would badly damage the Republican Party. Party politics and party unity are important considerations. He is prepared to accept the results of a vote in Congress.

Ironically, during these same weeks the British are preparing to back down. Reports from America are conflicting; Augustus Foster, who is supposed to man their listening post in the capital, continues to believe that the Americans are bluffing; but the oratory in the war congress and Sir George Prevost's warning from Quebec convinces many in Parliament that war is actually possible. Britain responds by dispatching three battalions of regulars to Canada and begins to consider the possibility of a repeal of the Orders in Council. By June, Foster too has changed his mind and reports that the Yankees mean what they say.

The British government, which has been bumbling along, holding a series of sedate hearings into the Orders in Council, now starts to move with uncharacteristic speed. Unfortunately, political affairs have been thrown into disarray by an unprecedented act, the assassination of the Prime Minister, Spencer Perceval, in the lobby of the House of Commons. It is June 16 before the formal motion to repeal the Orders is announced. The move comes too late. There is no Atlantic cable to alert the men of Washington. On June 18, the United States proclaims that a state of war exists between herself and Great Britain. When the news reaches the War Mess on New Jersey Avenue, Calhoun flings his arms about Clay's neck and the two, joined by their fellow Hawks, caper about the table in an approximation of a Shawnee war dance. But would Clay be so boisterous if he could foresee the tragedy that will be visited on his family in less than a year on the frozen banks of the River Raisin?

The news that America is at war brings a more mixed reaction across the nation. The tolling of church bells mingles with the firing of cannon and rockets; flags fly at half-mast while drums beat out the call for recruits; there are parades, cheers, hisses and boos, riots and illuminations depending on the mood of the people, which is divided on both regional and political lines. Five days later, the British motion to repeal the Orders becomes law and the chief reason for the conflict is removed.

At this point, General Hull's army of twenty-two hundred men is in sight of Detroit and within striking distance of the lightly held British fort across the river at Amherstburg. If Hull can capture the fort and disperse his enemies, the route lies open to the capital at York on Toronto Bay. The object is to seize Canada, not necessarily as a permanent prize (although that is in the minds of some) but to hold her hostage to force concessions from the British. Canada, after all, is the only portion of the empire that is open to American attack. Only later in the war, when American defeats are supplanted by American victories, will Madison and his foreign secretary, James Monroe, consider clinging to the conquered nation as part of the Union.

It is a long-held and almost universal belief that Canada is entirely vulnerable, an easy prey to American attack. The campaign, it is thought, will last a few weeks only. The freshman War Hawk, Calhoun, has already declared that "in four weeks from the time that a declaration of war is heard on our frontier the whole of Upper and a part of Lower Canada will be in our possession." Clay's words to the Senate in 1810 are recalled: ". . . the conquest of Canada is in our power. . . ." Felix Grundy, Clay's fellow boarder at the War Mess, declares: "We shall drive the British from our continent," and adds, charitably, that he is "willing to receive the Canadians as adopted brethren."

The general optimism is reflected in the words of Jefferson himself, who writes to a friend at the outset of war that "upon the whole I have known no war entered into under more favourable circumstances . . . we . . . shall strip her [Great Britain] of all her possessions on this continent." The Hawk press reflects these sentiments. In the words of the Kentucky *Gazette*, "Upper and Lower Canada to the very gates of Quebec will fall into the possession of the Yankees the moment the war is started, without much bloodshed, for almost the whole of Upper Canada and a great part of the Lower Province is inhabited by Americans."

At first glance it *does* seem a mere matter of marching. The United States has ten times the military potential of Canada. Congress has authorized a regular force of thirty-five thousand men to serve for five years and undertaken a military call-up of one hundred thousand. But the country is so badly divided that by June only about four thousand regulars have been recruited, bringing the total force to ten thousand, almost half of them untrained recruits and only half available for service in the north. As for the militia, nobody can be sure how many are available or whether they can legally be forced to fight on foreign soil. Like the generals who lead them, few have experience of war.

Even at that, the American forces outnumber the British. In all of British North America there are only forty-five hundred troops, thinly distributed. In Upper Canada a mere fifteen hundred regulars are available to receive the main thrust of the American attack. But as in most wars, the events to follow will be determined not so much by the quality of the men as by the quality of the leadership. The Americans pin their hopes on Hull and Dearborn. Canada is more fortunate. She has Tecumseh, the Leaping Panther, and she also has that impulsive but consummate professional, Major-General Isaac Brock.

THREE

Michilimackinac

The Bloodless Victory

... unless Detroit and
Michilimackinac be both in
our possession at the
commencement of hostilities,
not only Amherstburg but
most probably the whole
country, must be evacuated
as far as Kingston.

—Isaac Brock, February, 1812.

THE WISCONSIN-FOX PORTAGE, Illinois Territory, June 18, 1812.
On the very day that war is declared, Brock's courier catches up
at last with the Red-Haired Man, Robert Dickson. The courier's
name is Francis Rheaume; he and a companion have logged two
thousand miles scouring the plains and valleys seeking their man.
At Fort Dearborn (Chicago), their quest was almost aborted when
the American military commander, Captain Nathan Heald, sniffing

treachery, had them arrested and searched. Heald found nothing; the two men had hidden Brock's letters in the soles of their moccasins. So here they are at last, after three months of travel, standing on the height of land (and also on Brock's letters) where the water in the little streams trickles in two directions—some toward the Gulf of Mexico, the rest north to the Great Lakes.

Dickson reads Brock's message, scrawls an immediate reply. He has, he writes, between two hundred and fifty and three hundred of his "friends" available and would have more but for a hard winter with "an unparalleled scarcity of provisions." His friends are ready to march. He will lead them immediately to the British post at St. Joseph's Island and expects to arrive on the thirtieth of the month.

With his report, Dickson encloses copies of speeches by three of the chiefs who will accompany him. They leave no doubt about the Indians' sympathies: "We live by our English Traders who have always assisted us, and never more so, than this last year, at the risk of

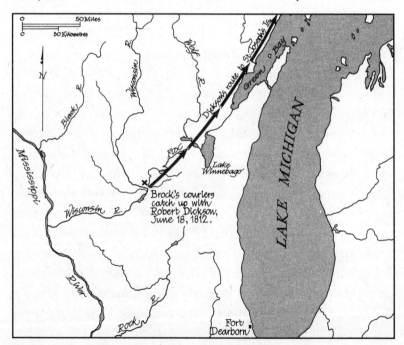

The Wiscosin–Fox Portage

their lives, and we are at all times ready to listen to them on account of the friendship they have always shown us."

The Prophet's message has also penetrated this lonely land: "We have always found our English father the protector of our women and children, but we have for some time past been amused by the songs of the bad Birds from the lower part of the River—they were not songs of truth, and this day we rejoice again in hearing the voice of our English Father, who never deceives us, and we are certain never will." So speaks Wabasha of the Sioux. The others echo his sentiments.

The Indians will follow Dickson anywhere. Here in this land of chiefs and sub-chiefs he is the real chief—their friend, their protector, and in this last harsh winter their saviour. When he arrived the previous August from St. Joseph's Island with his cargo of winter supplies, he found them starving. A disastrous drought had withered their crops and driven away the game. Dickson beggared himself to save his people, distributing all his provisions—ten thousand dollars' worth—among the tribes. He did this out of patriotism as well as humanity, for he knew that American agents were moving about the country, doing their best to influence the Indians. He assumes American hostility toward Britain, but fortunately, as he tells Brock, he is "possessed of the means of frustrating their intentions."

He is a man of commanding presence, a massive and genial six-footer with a flaming shock of red hair and a ruddy face to match. Everybody likes him, for there is an easy sociability about Dickson, a dignity, a sense of honour and principle. Men of every colour trust him. He is of a different breed from Elliott, McKee, and Girty. Highly literate, he is also humane. He has tried to teach the Indians not to kill and scalp when they can take prisoners; the greatest warriors, Dickson tells his people, are those who save their captives rather than destroy them. The infrequent explorers who cross the empty continent are attracted by Dickson. Zebulon Pike, the young army officer who has given his name to the famous peak, writes of his open, frank manner and his encyclopaedic knowledge of the country. Another, William Powell, reports that the Indians reverence and worship Dickson, who is "generous to a fault."

What is he doing out here in this lonely land? Living often in great squalor, existing for weeks on wild rice, corn, and pemmican or sometimes on nothing but melted snow, going for months without hearing his native tongue, trudging for miles on snowshoes or struggling over long portages with back-breaking loads, he is a man never at rest, like the Cut Head Yanktonais, the roving Sioux with whom he travels, knowing no real home but moving ceaselessly along his string of trading posts like a trapper tending a trapline.

His two brothers, who have also emigrated from Dumfriesshire, prefer the civilized life. One is a rising barrister and future politician at Niagara, the other a well-to-do merchant and militia colonel at Queenston. But Robert Dickson has spent twenty years in Indian country. Why? Certainly not for profit, for he has little money; the fur trade is a risky business. Nor for glory, for there is no glory. For power? He could have more in the white man's world. The answer seems to be that he is here, like so many of his countrymen, for the adventure of the frontier, the risks, the dangers, the excitement, and now, perhaps, because after two decades these are his people and this wild, untravelled country is his home. Who else but Dickson has trekked alone across that immense tract—larger than an American state—that lies west of the Mississippi between the Des Moines and the Missouri? He is a man of extraordinary energy and endurance; nowhere else, perhaps, can he feel fulfilled. In the Canadian Northwest, beyond the Great Lakes and the great bay, there are others like him, living among the Indians, exploring the land. Most are Scotsmen.

Dickson likes the Indians for themselves. He is faithful to his Indian wife, prides himself that he is educating his half-Indian children, is angered by the treatment his people receive from American frontiersmen who see the Indian as a dangerous animal to be exterminated. Added to these grievances against the Americans are the strictures enforced against British traders who still insist on flying the Union Jack over American territory. To evade the recent Non-Importation Act, by which the Americans have tried to prevent British traders from bringing goods into the United

States, Dickson has been forced to become a smuggler. So incensed was he over this outrage that he knocked down the customs officer at Michilimackinac who tried to make him pay duty on his trade goods. His patriotism needs no fuelling. He is more than delighted to aid his countrymen.

He loses no time. This very day he dispatches a reply to Brock and sends it to Fort Amherstburg with thirty Menominee warriors. Then, with 130 Sioux, Winnebago, and Menominee, he sets off for St. Joseph's Island at the western entrance to Lake Huron, arriving as promised on the dot of June 30.

St. Joseph's Island, in the words of a young ensign exiled there for satirizing the lieutenant-governor, is "the military Siberia of Upper Canada." It is so remote that its garrison has trouble getting supplies and pay. Quarters are primitive. Rain, snow, and wind pour through the gaps between the blockhouse logs. The troops have shivered all winter for want of greatcoats. They turn out on parade wearing a short covering tailored from blankets intended for the Indians. These blanket coats are not named for St. Joseph's but acquire the phonetic name of the American fortress, forty miles away. As Mackinac or "Mackinaw" coats, created out of necessity, they are destined to become fashionable.

St. Joseph's unpopularity is understandable. Officers almost on arrival begin to think about requesting a transfer. For the troops, the only way out is through desertion. There have been several attempts: in April, 1805, twelve men took off in the garrison's boat; in March, 1810, two privates of the 100th Regiment attempted to escape on foot. Their pursuers found them, one half-dead of cold (he eventually lost both legs), the other a corpse. An investigation uncovered a plan for a mutiny involving a quarter of the garrison.

The fort's commander, Captain Charles Roberts, a twenty-year veteran of the British Army in India and Ceylon, has been in charge since September, 1811. He has, in effect, been pensioned off for garrison duty along with the newly formed 10th Royal Veteran Battalion, a new idea of Brock's for making use of men too old to fight. Brock has been too optimistic about the value of these veterans. In Roberts's words, they are "so debilitated and worn down by unconquerable drunkenness that neither fear of punishment, the love of fame or the honour of their Country can animate them to extraordinary exertions." There are only forty-four of them defending a crumbling blockhouse armed with four ancient and nearly useless six-pound cannon. Roberts himself is experienced, incisive, and eager for action, but he is also mortally ill with a "great debility of the stomach and the bowels."

It is the Indians, then, and the clerks and voyageurs of the North West Company who will form the spearhead of the attack on Michilimackinac. In addition to the members of Dickson's native force, already chafing for action, there are the neighbouring Ottawa and Chippewa tribesmen under John Askin, Jr., a member of the sprawling Askin family, whose patriarch, John, Sr., lives at Sandwich across the river from Detroit. Askin, whose mother is an Ottawa, is interpreter and keeper of the Indian stores at St. Joseph's. His people have blown hot and cold on the subject of war with the Americans. There was a time after the *Chesapeake* incident, when Tecumseh and the Prophet were rallying the tribes, when they were filled with ardour for the old way of life. Sixty, to Askin's astonishment, even refused a gift of rum. But now that ardour has cooled; no one can keep the Indians in a state of animation for long. That is Roberts's problem as the days move on without word from Brock. Dickson's men are becoming restless, but the attack on Mackinac cannot begin without a specific order. If there is going to be a war at all, Roberts wishes it would begin at once.

———

BALTIMORE, MARYLAND, June 18, 1812. John Jacob Astor is hurrying toward Washington, his ample rump rising and falling as he posts his horse. He has come in haste from New York to try to stop the damnfool war. No doubt he feels he has the clout to do just that, but here in Baltimore he learns that he is too late. The war is on—a war that Astor needs as much as he needs a case of smallpox.

He is not a pacifist, merely a businessman. His South West Company straddles the border, the first of the multinational corporations. He has a fortune in trade goods tied up at St. Joseph's on the Canadian side, another fortune in furs at Mackinac on the American side. What will become of these investments? It has apparently not occurred to Astor that the country might actually go to war. As late as February he wrote, in his semi-literate style: "We are happey in the hope of Peace and have not the Smalest Idia of a war with england." He is neither pro-British nor anti-British, merely pro-business, pro-profit. He has been in Canada the past winter, tendering successfully on government bills of specie to support the British army, too preoccupied to sense what is coming. Only at the last moment, as the debates in Congress grow shrill, does he become uneasy and so decides to put his personal prestige on the line and gallop out of New York to reason with the politicians. But now, with war declared, the best he can do is to try to mend his imperilled fortunes.

He determines to get the news as swiftly as possible to his Canadian partners in the South West Company. It does not occur to him that this may be seen as an act approaching treason any more than it occurs to him that his news will travel faster than the official dispatches. The South West Company is owned jointly by Astor and a group of Montreal fur "pedlars," which includes the powerful North West Company. Astor engages in a flurry of letter writing to his agents and partners. Thus the British are apprised of the war before the Americans on the frontier, including General Hull en route to Detroit and Lieutenant Hanks at Michilimackinac, realize it. Brock gets the news on June 26 and immediately dispatches a letter to Roberts at St. Joseph's Island. But a South West Company agent, Toussaint Pothier, based at Amherstburg, has already had a direct communication from Astor. Pothier alerts the garrison, leaps into a canoe, and paddles off at top speed. He beaches his canoe at St. Joseph's on July 3.

Roberts puts his men and Indians on the alert. Lewis Crawford, another South West employee, organizes 140 volunteer voyageurs.

A twelve-day interval of frustration follows. Brock's message, which arrives by canoe on July 8, simply advises that the war is on and that Roberts should act accordingly. Roberts requisitions stores and ammunition from the South West Company (the very stores that concern John Jacob Astor, who will, of course, be paid for them), takes over the North West Company's gunboat *Caledonia*, impresses her crew, and sends off a message by express canoe to the North West Company's post at Fort William, asking for reinforcements.

Just as he is preparing to attack Mackinac, a second express message arrives from Brock on July 12. The impetuous general has had his enthusiasm curbed by his more cautious superior, Sir George Prevost. The Governor General is hoping against hope that the reports of war are premature, that the Americans have come to their senses, that a change of heart, a weakness in resolve, an armistice—anything—is possible. He will not prejudice the slightest chance of peace. Brock orders Roberts to hold still, wait for further orders. The perplexed captain knows he cannot hold the Indians for long—cannot, in fact, afford to. By night they chant war songs, by day they devour his dwindling stock of provisions.

Then, on July 15, to Roberts's immense relief, another dispatch arrives from Brock which, though equivocal, allows him to act. The Major-General, with an ear tuned to Sir George's cautionary instructions and an eye fastened on the deteriorating situation on the border, tells Roberts to "adopt the most prudent measures either of offense or defense which circumstances might point out." Roberts resolves to make the most of these ambiguous instructions. The following morning at ten, to the skirl of fife and the roll of drum—banners waving, Indians whooping—his polyglot army embarks upon the glassy waters of the lake.

Off sails *Caledonia* loaded with two brass cannon, her decks bright with the red tunics of the regulars. Behind her follow ten bateaux or "Mackinac boats" crammed with one hundred and eighty voyageurs, brilliant in their sashes, silk kerchiefs, and capotes. Slipping in and out of the flotilla are seventy painted birchbark canoes containing close to three hundred tribesmen—Dickson, in Indian dress, with his fifty feathered Sioux; their one-time enemies, the Chippewa, with coal-black faces, shaved heads, and bodies daubed with pipe clay; two dozen Winnebago, including the celebrated one-eyed chief, Big Canoe; forty Menominee under their head chief, Tomah; and thirty Ottawa led by Amable Chevalier, the half-white trader whom they recognize as leader.

Ahead lies Mackinac Island, shaped like an aboriginal arrowhead, almost entirely surrounded by 150-foot cliffs of soft grey limestone. The British abandoned it grudgingly following the Revolution, realizing its strategic importance, which is far more significant than that of St. Joseph's. Control of Mackinac means control of the western fur trade. No wonder Roberts has no trouble conscripting the Canadian voyageurs!

They are pulling on their oars like madmen, for they must reach their objective well before dawn. Around midnight, about fifteen miles from the island a birchbark canoe is spotted. Its passenger is an old crony from Mackinac, a Pennsylvania fur trader named Michael Dousman. He has been sent by Hanks, the American commander, to try to find out what is taking place north of the border. Dousman, in spite of the fact that he is an American militia commander, is first and foremost a fur trader, an agent of the South West Company, and an old colleague and occasional partner of the leaders of the voyageurs and Indians. He greets Dickson, Pothier, Askin, and Crawford as old friends and cheerfully tells Roberts everything he needs to know: the strength of the American garrison, its armament (or lack of it), and—most important of all—the fact that no one on the island has been told that America is at war.

Dousman's and Roberts's concerns are identical. In the event of a struggle, they want to protect the civilians on the island from the wrath of the Indians. Dousman agrees to wake the village quietly and to herd everybody into the old distillery at the end of town where they can be guarded by a detachment of regulars. He promises not to warn the garrison.

At three that morning, the British land at a small beach facing the only break in the escarpment at the north end of the island. With the help of Dousman's ox team the voyageurs manage to drag the two six-pounders over boulders and through thickets up to the 300-foot crest that overlooks the fort at the southern tip. Meanwhile, Dousman tiptoes from door to door wakening the inhabitants. He silently herds them to safety, then confronts the bewildered Lieutenant Hanks, who has no course but surrender. The first objective in Brock's carefully programmed campaign to frustrate invasion has been taken without firing a shot.

"It is a circumstance I believe without precedent," Roberts reports to Brock. For the Indians' white leaders he has special praise: their influence with the tribes is such that "as soon as they heard the Capitulation was signed they all returned to their Canoes, and not one drop either of Man's or Animal's blood was Spilt. . . ."

Askin is convinced that Hanks's bloodless surrender has prevented an Indian massacre: "It was a fortunate circumstance that

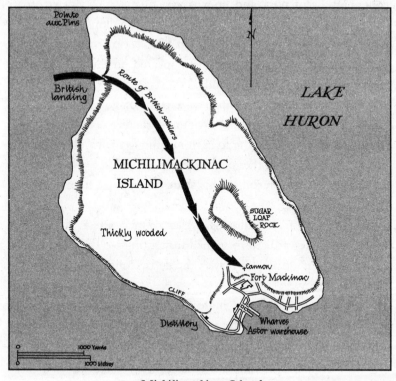

Michilimackinac Island

the Fort Capitulated without firing a Single Gun, for had they done so, I firmly believe not a Soul of them would have been Saved. . . . I never saw so determined a Set of people as the Chippewas & Ottawas were. Since the Capitulation they have not drunk a single drop of Liquor, nor even killed a fowl belonging to any person (a thing never known before) for they generally destroy every thing they meet with."

Dickson's Indians feel cheated out of a fight and complain to the Red-Haired Man, who keeps them firmly under control, explaining that the Americans cannot be killed once they have surrendered. To mollify them, he turns loose a number of cattle, which the Sacs and Foxes chase about the island until the bellowing animals, their flanks bristling with arrows, hurl themselves into the water.

They are further mollified by a distribution of blankets, provisions, and guns taken from the American commissariat, which also contains tons of pork and flour, a vast quantity of vinegar, soap, candles, and—to the delight of everybody–357 gallons of high wines and 253 gallons of whiskey, enough to get every man, white and red, so drunk that had an enemy force appeared on the lake, it might easily have recaptured the island.

These spoils are augmented by a trove of government-owned furs, bringing the total value of captured goods to £10,000, all of it to be distributed, according to custom, among the regulars and volunteers who captured the fort. Every private soldier will eventually receive ten pounds sterling as his share of the prize money, officers considerably more.

The message to the Indians is clear: America is a weak nation and there are rewards to be gained in fighting for the British. The fall of Mackinac gives the British the entire control of the tribes of the Old Northwest.

Porter Hanks and his men are sent off to Detroit under parole: they give their word not to take any further part in the war until they are exchanged for British or Canadian soldiers of equivalent rank captured by the Americans—a device used throughout the conflict to obviate the need for large camps of prisoners fed and clothed at the enemy's expense. The Americans who remain on the island are obliged to take an oath of allegiance to the Crown; otherwise they must return to American territory. Most find it easy to switch sides. They have done it before; a good many were originally British until the island changed hands in 1796.

Curiously, one man is allowed to remain without taking the oath. This is Michael Dousman, Hanks's spy and Roberts's prisoner. Dousman is given surprising leeway for an enemy, being permitted to make business trips to Montreal on the promise that he will not travel through U.S. territory. He is required to post a bond for this purpose but has no trouble raising the money from two prominent Montreal merchants.

Dousman's business in Montreal is almost certainly John Jacob Astor's business. All of Astor's furs are now in enemy territory. But the South West Company is still a multinational enterprise, and Astor has friends in high positions in both countries. Through his Montreal partners he manages to get a passport into Canada. In July he is in Montreal making arrangements for his furs to be forwarded from Mackinac Island (which has not yet fallen). These furs are protected in the articles of capitulation; over the next several months, bales of them arrive in Montreal from Mackinac. Astor's political friends in Washington have alerted the customs inspectors at the border points to pass the furs through, war or no war. Over the next year and a half, the bullet-headed fur magnate manages to get his agents into Canada and to bring shipment after shipment of furs out to the New York market. A single consignment is worth $50,000, and there are many such consignments. For John Jacob Astor and the South West Company, the border has little meaning, and the war is not much more than a nuisance.

FOUR

Detroit

The Disintegration of William Hull

Those Yankee hearts began to ache,
Their blood it did run cold,
To see us marching forward
So courageous and so bold.
Their general sent a flag to us,
For quarter he did call,
Saying, "Stay your hand, brave British boys,
I fear you'll slay us all."

—From "Come All Ye Bold Canadians,"
a campfire ballad of the War of 1812.

ABOARD THE SCHOONER *Cuyahoga Packet*, entering Lake Erie, July 2, 1812. William K. Beall, assistant quartermaster general in William Hull's Army of the Northwest, stretches out on deck, admiring the view, ignorant of the fact that his country has been at war for a fortnight and the vessel will shortly be entering enemy waters.

Beall counts himself lucky. He reclines at his ease while the rest of Hull's tattered army trudges doggedly toward Detroit, spurred on by Eustis's order to move "with all possible speed." Thanks to the *Cuyahoga*'s fortuitous presence at the foot of the Maumee rapids, Hull has been able to relieve his exhausted teams. The schooner is loaded with excess military stores—uniforms, band instruments, entrenching tools, personal luggage—and some thirty sick officers and men, together with three women who have somehow managed to keep up with their husbands on the long trek north.

It is a foolhardy undertaking. War is clearly imminent, even though Eustis, the bumbling secretary, gave no hint of it in his instructions to the General. Hull's own officers have pointed out that the *Cuyahoga* must pass under the British guns at Fort Amherstburg, guarding the narrow river boundary, before she can reach Detroit; but their commander, sublimely unaware of his country's declaration, remains confident that she will get there before the army.

The schooner rolls in Erie's swell. The passengers grow queasy, but not William K. Beall. He is enchanted by the vastness of the lake, has never seen anything like it before. He is a prosperous Kentucky plantation owner whose estate on the Ohio River, not far from Newport, is thirty-six miles square. But this lake! It is hard to conceive of so much fresh water, stretching on beyond the horizon. The only water he has seen since leaving home has flowed sluggishly in the saffron streams veining the dreadful swamps through which the army has just toiled. Beall puts all that out of his mind, basks in the novelty of the heaving deck, opens an appropriate book of poetry—Scott's *Lady of the Lake*—commits three verses to memory, then catnaps as the Cuyahoga sails toward the mouth of the Detroit River.

He wakes as the schooner approaches the village of Amherstburg, nestled outside the British fort (which the Americans call Fort Malden). Again he is charmed by what he sees. The little town seems indifferently built, but the countryside is quite lovely—green meadows and sunny wheat fields rippling in the breeze. This southern fringe of orchards is the garden of Upper Canada, but most of the province beyond remains a wilderness, its great forests of pine and oak, maple and basswood broken here and there by small patches of pioneer civilization, like worn spots on a rug. Vast swamps, dark and terrifying, smother the land. Roads are few and in some seasons impassable, being little more than rivers of rutted mud. Sensible travellers move by water, and it is along the margins of the lakes and the banks of the larger rivers that the main communities such as Amherstburg have sprung up. Between these villages lie smaller settlements. Plots of winter wheat, oats, and rye, fields of corn and root vegetables blur the edges of the forest. Here, along the Detroit River, the fruit trees have been bearing for a decade, and cider has become a staple drink. Beall notes that everything appears to wear "the cheering smiles of peace and plenty."

In the distance an Indian canoe contributes to the picturesqueness of the scene. But as the canoe comes closer it is transformed into a Canadian longboat commanded by an officer of the Provincial Marine, Lieutenant Frederic Rolette, with six seamen, armed with cutlasses and pistols, pulling on the oars.

Rolette calls to the *Cuyahoga*'s captain, Luther Chapin, to lower his mainsails. Chapin is open mouthed. He had expected a friendly hail; now he sees six muskets raised against him. Before he can act, Rolette fires his pistol in the air. Chapin struggles with the sail. Beall and his fellow passengers are in confusion. What is happening? Beall orders the captain to hoist the sail again and press on, but Chapin replies that this is not possible.

Rolette now points his pistol directly at young George Gooding, a second-lieutenant in charge of the soldiers and baggage of the U.S. 4th Infantry Regiment. "Dowse your mainsails!" Rolette orders.

Gooding equivocates. "I have no command here, sir," he shouts. Rolette fires directly at the schooner, the ball whistling past Beall's head. The captain pleads for instructions. "Do as you please," answers the rattled Gooding, whose wife is also on deck. As the mainsails tumble, Frederic Rolette boards the packet.

He is astonished to find the decks jammed with American soldiers. They are not aware that the war has started, but Rolette cannot be sure of that. Nor does he know that all but three are ill and that the muskets and ammunition are out of reach in the hold. All he knows is that he is outnumbered five to one.

This does not dismay him, for he is a seasoned seaman, accustomed to act with boldness and decision. At the age of twenty-nine, this French-speaking Quebecker has a naval record any officer might envy. He has fought in the two greatest sea battles of the era—the Nile and Trafalgar—under the finest commander of his time, Horatio Nelson. He has been wounded five times and, before this newest contest is over, will be wounded again. Now, as William Beall approaches to demand his authority for boarding the schooner, Rolette informs him curtly that an express reached Amherstburg the previous night announcing the commencement of hostilities. Then, losing no time, he orders everybody below decks, posts sentries at the hatches and arms chests with orders to shoot any man who approaches them, orders the helmsman to steer the ship under the water battery at Amherstburg and the band to play "God Save the King."

As the schooner docks at the naval yard, the passengers are released under guard to the open deck and all the baggage is removed. Now the British realize the magnitude of their prize. For here are discovered two trunks belonging to General Hull containing documents of extraordinary value. Hull's aide-de-camp—his son Abraham—has foolishly packed the General's personal papers with his baggage. The astonished British discover that they now possess all the details of the army that opposes them: field states, complete returns of the troops, the names and strengths of the regiments, an incomplete draft of Hull's own memorial of March 6 outlining his strategy, and all his correspondence to and from the Secretary of War. It is a find equal to the breaking of an enemy code. The entire package is dispatched to Brock at York, who immediately grasps its significance and lays his plans.

No one on either side, meanwhile, is quite certain how to behave. Has war actually come? Even the British are reluctant to believe it. William Beall, now a prisoner, doubts it. He is certain that his captors have been wrongly informed, that when Hull demands his return he and his companions will be permitted to go on to Detroit.

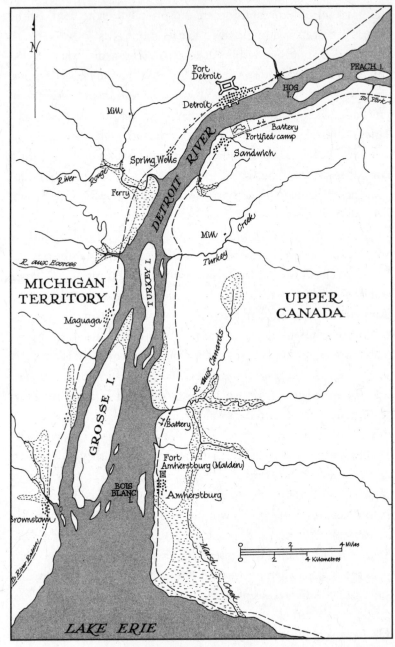

The Detroit Frontier

The British are polite, even hospitable. Lieutenant Edward Dewar, Beall's opposite number in the quartermaster's department at Fort Amherstburg, urges the Americans not to consider themselves prisoners but merely detainees. It is all very unpleasant, Dewar murmurs; he hopes the report of the war may prove incorrect; he hopes the Americans will be able to spend their time in detention as agreeably as possible; if there is any service he and his fellow officers can render to that end, they will be only too pleased to do so; he only wishes the packet could have passed by without interruption; if authentic information arrives that war has not been declared, they will be released at once. And so on.

George Gooding declares he would like to dine ashore and put up at an inn. Dewar gets permission from his commanding officer, Lieutenant-Colonel Thomas Bligh St. George, but points out the C.O.'s fear that the Indians are much enraged at the Americans and advises them to be on guard against attack. The detainees agree to accept billets aboard another ship, *Thames*, where a guard can be stationed. Meanwhile they must be very careful. At this stage of the war, the British are worried at the horrors their native allies may commit on their new enemies. Dewar tells Beall that he fears that the Indians, in a drunken rage, might enter a tavern and murder all the Americans. To underline the danger he tells how an infuriated Indian had recently stepped up behind a man walking with a British officer and tomahawked him. Don't go out into the streets alone, Dewar warns.

Now, having accepted the parole of Beall and his companions that they will not try to escape, Dewar invites them to his home until their accommodation is prepared. On the wharf, a crowd of Indians look them over. In Beall's eyes some appear to rejoice at their capture, while others terrify him with ferocious frowns. Gooding, who fought at Tippecanoe, recognizes some of his former adversaries. Harrison's bitter seed, broadcast on the banks of the Wabash, is already beginning to sprout.

At Dewar's home there is wine, cider, biscuits. It would be improper, says the Lieutenant, to invite the Americans to dine with him, but he accompanies them to Boyle's Inn and Public House, apologizing in his diffident British fashion for its poor quality but explaining that it is the best in town. Following dinner, the men leave the inn and, accompanied by a British officer, stroll through the streets through crowds of Indians who the nervous Beall feels are glaring directly at him. Every white man, however, bows politely to the strangers and one even invites them into his house and pours them several glasses of wine.

Many of these are Americans, lured to Upper Canada by the prospect of free land and low taxes. They have little interest in politics, less in war. In a province of some sixty thousand, they form a clear but powerless majority, having been shut out of all public office by the elite group of British and Loyalist administrators who control the government. This does not unduly concern them, for they are prospering on their free acreage. Democracy may be virtually non-existent in Upper Canada, but so are taxes, since the province is financed by the British treasury. Beall is intrigued to discover that the master of his floating prison, Captain Martin of the *Thames*, owns a well-stocked farm of three hundred acres but pays an annual levy of exactly $1.06¼.

As for the prospect of war, they dismiss it. During their walk through the village, Lieutenant Dewar remarks to Beall that he will be sorry if the two countries cannot adjust their difficulties without violence. Everyone to whom the American speaks echoes that sentiment.

The women, being non-combatants, are sent to the American side; the men remain aboard the *Thames*. Beall estimates that there are at least five hundred Indians in town. On July 4, as the sounds of Independence Day cannonades echo across the water from Detroit, two hundred Sauk warriors arrive, the largest and best-formed men Beall has ever seen, though in his eyes they are as savage and un-cultivated as any other natives.

On the following day, the sound of Hull's bugler blowing reveille reveals that the Army of the Northwest has reached the village of Brownstown, directly across the river, less than a day's march from

Detroit. By nightfall, Amherstburg is in a panic. Women and children run crying toward the vessels at the dockside, loading the decks with trunks of valuables. Indians dash about the streets shouting. Consternation and dismay prevail as the call to arms is sounded. The enemy, in short, is within striking distance of the thinly guarded fort, the sole British bastion on the Detroit frontier. If Hull can seize it in one lightning move, his army can sweep up the valley of the Thames and capture most if not all of Upper Canada.

Beall views it all with mixed feelings. A sensitive and compassionate man who is already starting to pine for his wife Melinda, back in Kentucky, he feels "sensibly for those on both sides who might loose [sic] their lives." Certainly his British hosts have been decent to the point of chivalry; it is difficult to think of them as the enemy. (Could Beall actually shoot at Dewar if he met him on the field?) On the other hand, he is convinced that his day of deliverance is at hand. Surely General Hull will cross the river, crush all resistance at Amherstburg, free him for further service, and, if the campaign is as decisive as everyone expects, return him swiftly to Melinda's arms!

———

THE CRUCIAL DISPATCH TO General Hull, announcing the war, is hidden somewhere in the Cleveland mail. Frustration! Walworth, the postmaster, has written orders to forward it at once by express. But where is it? He can guess what it contains, for the news has already reached Cleveland. A young lawyer, Charles Shaler, stands ready to gallop through swamp and forest to the Rapids of the Maumee and on to Detroit, if need be, once the missing document is found. Nobody, apparently, thinks to send him off at once with a verbal message while others rummage for the official one. Hours pass. Shaler chafes. Then somebody suggests the dispatch might be in the Detroit mail. Reluctantly, the postmaster breaks the law, opens the bags, finds the missing paper.

Off goes Shaler, swimming the unbridged rivers, plunging through the wilderness, vainly seeking a relay steed to replace his gasping horse. Some eighty hours later, on the evening of July I (the *Cuyahoga* has already been dispatched) he reaches the rapids, discovers the army has decamped, gallops after it. He reached Hull's force at two the following morning. The General, half-dressed, reads the dispatch, registers alarm, orders Shaler to keep quiet in the presence of others, calls a council of his officers, orders a boat to take after the *Cuyahoga*. It is too late; she cannot be caught. At dawn the army moves on, Shaler riding with the troops. On reaching Detroit, his much-abused horse drops dead of exhaustion.

The army arrives on July 5, after thirty-five days of struggle through Ohio's swampy wilderness. The soldiers find a primitive settlement of twelve hundred straggling on the outskirts of a log fort. Like their neighbours on both sides of the river, most of the people are French speaking, descendants of families that settled the land a century before and whose strip farms with their narrow river frontage betray their Québécois background. In Hull's view they are "miserable farmers," being descended from voyageurs, traders, soldiers, and artisans—people with no agricultural tradition. They raise apples for cider and gigantic pears for pickling but pay little attention to other forms of agriculture, depending principally on hunting, fishing, and trading with the Indians. In short, they cannot provision his troops—and this is Hull's dilemma: his supply line is two hundred miles long, stretching south along the makeshift trace his men have hacked out of the forests. To secure his position, Hull must have two months' provisions. In Chillicothe, the capital, Ohio's energetic governor, Return Meigs, receives the General's plea, raises a company of ninety-five citizen volunteers, and sends them north through Urbana as escort for a brigade of pack horses, loaded with flour and provisions, and a drove of beef cattle. But to reach Hull, this supply train must eventually follow the road that hugs the southwestern shore of Lake Erie and the Detroit River. That will be dangerous because the British control the water.

Hull's more immediate concern is the fate of the baggage captured aboard the *Cuyahoga*. Have the British actually rifled his personal possessions, discovered his official correspondence? He pens a note to Lieutenant-Colonel St. George, the commander at Fort Amherstburg. Dripping with politeness and studiedly casual, it reads more like an interoffice memorandum than a communication between enemies:

Sir,

Since the arrival of my army at this Encampment . . . I have been informed that a number of discharges of Artillery and of small arms have been made by some of the Militia of the Territory, from this Shore into Sandwich.

I regret to have received such information, the proceeding was [un]authorized by me. I am not disposed to make War on Private Property, or to authorise a wanton attack upon unoffending individuals, I would be happy to learn whether you consider private Property a proper objective of seizure and detention, I allude to the Baggage of Officers particularly. . . .

St. George, in his reply to Hull, outdoes the General in verbal niceties:

Sir,

I am honoured with your letter of this days date; I perfectly coincide with you in opinion respecting private property, and any wanton attack upon unoffending individuals, and am happy to find, what I was certain would be the case, that the aggression in question was unauthorized by you.

In respect to the property of officers not on board a vessel at the time of capture I must be judged by the customs of war in like cases, in justice to the captors, and shall always be ready to meet your wishes . . . when I receive orders . . . from my government. . . .

Which, translated, simply means: go to hell.

The bearer of Hull's letter, under a flag of truce, is Colonel Cass, whose instructions are to spy out the situation at the British fort. Cass takes a good look, reports that rumour has exaggerated the garrison's strength and also the number of Indians. He believes, and will continue to believe, that Fort Amherstburg can be easily taken.

In spite of the suavity of his correspondence, Thomas Bligh St. George is a badly rattled commander. He is an old campaigner, with forty years of service in the British Army, much of it spent in active warfare on the Mediterranean. But he has been a staff officer for the past decade and clearly has difficulty coping with the present crisis. He commands a lightly garrisoned fort, in need of repair and reinforcement. Across the river an army of two thousand sits poised for invasion. Scrambling about in a fever of preparation he is "so harassed for these five days and nights, I can scarcely write." Brock, who receives this communication, is dismayed to discover that Lieutenant-Colonel St. George has let three days slip by before bothering to inform him that Hull's force has reached Detroit.

Fort Amherstburg is in chaos. Indians are coming and going, eating up the supplies; no one can guess their strength from day to day. The same is true of the militia: St. George has no real idea of how many men he commands or whether he has the resources to supply them. The accounts are in disarray, the returns non-existent. He has not enough officers to organize the militia—many of whom are leaving for home or attempting to leave—or enough arms to supply them. Nor does he know how he can pay them.

The little village of Sandwich lies directly across the river from Detroit, upriver from Amherstburg. This, St. George knows, will be Hull's invasion point. He stations some militia units at Sandwich but has little hope that they will be effective. To "encourage" them, in St. George's euphemism, he sends along a detachment of regulars. To supply the wants of his confused and amateur army, St. George is obliged to make use of everything that falls in his way. This includes a brigade of eleven bateaux loaded with supplies that the North West Company has dispatched from Montreal to its post at Fort William at the lakehead. St. George seizes the supplies, impresses the seventy voyageurs.

On the docks and in the streets the Indians are engaged in war dances, leaping and capering before the doors of the inhabitants, who give them presents of whiskey. "I have seen the great Tecumseh," William Beall, still captive aboard the *Thames*, writes in his diary. "He is a very plane man, rather above middle-size, stout built, a noble set of features and an admirable eye. He is always accompanied by Six great chiefs, who never go before him. The women and men all fear that in the event of Genl. Hull's crossing and proving successfull, that the Indians being naturally treacherous will turn against them to murder and destroy them."

Tecumseh's followers have shadowed Hull's army all the way through Michigan Territory, warned by their leader to take no overt action until war is declared and he can bring his federation into alliance with Great Britain. Hull has done his best to neutralize him, sending messengers to a council at Fort Wayne, promising protection and friendship if the Indians stay out of the white man's war.

"Neutral indeed!" cries Tecumseh to the assembled tribes. "Who will protect you while the Long Knives are fighting the British and are away from you? Who will protect you from the attack of your ancient enemies, the western tribes, who may become allies of the British?"

Will a policy of neutrality lead to a restoration of the Indian lands, Tecumseh asks, and as he speaks, takes the emissary's peace pipe and breaks it between his fingers. And later:

"Here is a chance presented to us—yes, a chance such as will never occur again—for us Indians of North America to form ourselves into one great combination and cast our lot with the British in this war. . . ."

Tecumseh leaves Fort Wayne with a large party of Shawnee, Kickapoo, Potawatomi, and Delaware to meet Matthew Elliott at Amherstburg. Hull sends another emissary, urges another council at Brownstown, the Wyandot village directly opposite the British fort. Tecumseh refuses:

"I have taken sides with the King, my father, and I will suffer my bones to bleach upon this shore before I will recross that stream to join in any council of neutrality."

Like the Americans, the Wyandot are split into camps of hawks and doves. They are important to Tecumseh's cause because they are the senior tribe, looked up to by all the others. They are Huron, the remnants of the mighty nation destroyed during the French regime. At a great council held on the parade ground at Fort Amherstburg on July 7, one chief, Roundhead, supports Tecumseh. Another, Walk-in-the-Water, advocates neutrality and crosses back into U.S. territory. But Tecumseh has no intention of letting the Wyandot straddle the fence.

Upriver at Detroit, Hull prepares to invade Canada by landing his army at Sandwich. He attempts to move on July 10 but, to his dismay, discovers that hundreds of militiamen, urged on in some cases by their officers, decline to cross the river. They have not committed themselves to fight on foreign soil.

The next day Hull tries again. Two militia companies refuse to enter the boats. One finally gives in to persuasion; the other stands firm. When Hull demands a list of those who refuse to go, the company commander, a Captain Rupes, hands over the names of his entire command. Hull's adjutant harangues the men. Words like "coward" and "traitor" are thrown at them to no avail. Again the crossing is aborted.

The war has yet to develop beyond the comic opera stage. Across the river at Sandwich an equally reluctant body of citizen soldiers—the militia of Kent and Essex counties, only recently called to service—sits and waits. These young farmers have had little if any training, militia service being mainly an excuse for social carousing. They are not eager to fight, especially in midsummer with the winter wheat ripening in the fields. Patriotism has no meaning for most of them; that is the exclusive property of the Loyalists. The majority are passively pro-American, having moved up from New Jersey, New York, and Pennsylvania. Isolated on the scattered farms and absorbed in the wearisome if profitable task of clearing the land and working the soil, they have as yet no sense of a larger community. Few have ever seen a newspaper; they learn of the war tardily, through handbills. Whether or not Upper Canada becomes another American state they do not really care.

Lieutenant-Colonel St. George, who is convinced that these

unwilling soldiers—most are not even uniformed—will flee to their homes at the first shot, decides to get them out of the way before the attack is launched. Otherwise, their certain rout would throw his entire force into a state of confusion. The only way he can prevent them from melting away to their farms is to march the lot back to the fort and make the most of them; perhaps their backs can be stiffened by the example of the regulars. Even that is doubtful: from his vantage point in the town of Amherstburg William Beall discovers that many of these former Americans express a desire to join Hull as soon as he crosses into Canada.

At last, on July 12, a bright and lovely Sunday, Hull resolves to make the crossing, even though two hundred of his men continue to stand on their constitutional rights. He fears further mutinies if he keeps his troops inactive, and it is also his fancy that the Canadian settlers will feel themselves liberated from the British yoke once he lands and that they and the Indians will stay out of the war.

Hull's landing is unopposed. Colonel Cass is the first to leap from the lead boat, and thus the first American to set foot on Canadian soil. He immediately unfurls the Stars and Stripes while Hull's staff searches about for a headquarters.

Sandwich is a placid little garden village, almost every house set in a small orchard where peaches, grapes, and apples flourish. The conquering general seizes the most imposing residence—a new brick home, built in the Georgian style the year before, its interior still unfinished, belonging to Lieutenant-Colonel François Bâby, a member of a distinguished pioneer fur-trading family. The Bâbys and the Hulls have been on intimate terms, but when James Bâby, a brother and also a militia colonel, protests (his own home not far away is quickly pillaged), all Hull can say is that *circumstances are changed now*, a phrase which Lieutenant-Colonel Bâby will throw back at him a month later.

Hull has scarcely landed when he insists on issuing a proclamation intended to disperse the militia and cow the inhabitants, many of whom are either terrified of his troops or secretly disposed to his cause. Most have fled, but those who remain welcome the invaders as friends, waving white handkerchiefs and flags from the windows and crying out such phrases as "We like the Americans." At Amherstburg, Beall encounters similar sentiments and confides to his journal that many solicit secret interviews with him, and when these are refused "occasionally and slily say 'Success to the Americans and General Hull', 'Let us alone and we will take Malden [Amherstburg] ourselves', et cetera, and many expressions showing their warmth for us and the Americans and their detestation of the British."

Yet Hull cannot resist issuing a bombastic proclamation that seems designed to set the Canadians on edge. He has it printed, rather imperfectly, in Detroit, borrowing the press of a Roman Catholic priest. It is soon the talk of the countryside:

A PROCLAMATION

INHABITANTS OF CANADA! After thirty years of Peace and prosperity, the United States have been driven to Arms. The injuries and aggressions, the insults and indignities of Great Britain have once more left them no alternative but manly resistance or unconditional submission. The army under my Command has invaded your Country and the standard of the United States waves on the territory of Canada. To the peaceful, unoffending inhabitant, It brings neither danger nor difficulty I come to *find* enemies not to *make* them, I come to *protect* you not to *injure* you.

Separated by an immense ocean and an extensive Wilderness from Great Britain you have no participation in her counsels no interest in her conduct. You have felt her Tyranny, you have seen her injustice, but I do not ask *you* to avenge the one or to redress the other. The United States are sufficiently powerful to afford you every security consistent with their rights & your expectations. I tender you the invaluable blessings of Civil, Political, & Religious Liberty, and their necessary result, individual, and general, prosperity: That liberty which gave decision to our counsels and energy to our conduct in our struggle for INDEPENDENCE and which conducted us safely and triumphantly thro' the stormy period of the Revolution. . . .

In the name of my *Country* and by the authority of my Government I promise you protection to your *persons, property, and rights*, Remain at your homes, Pursue your peaceful and customary avocations. Raise not your hands against your brethren, many of your fathers fought for the freedom & *Indepennce* we now enjoy Being children therefore of the same family with us, and heirs to the same Heritage, the arrival of an army of Friends must be hailed by you with a cordial welcome, You will be emancipated from Tyranny and oppression and restored to the dignified status of freemen. . . . If contrary to your own interest & the just expectation of my country, you should take part in the approaching contest, you will be considered and treated as enemies and the horrors, and calamities of war will Stalk before you.

If the barbarous and Savage policy of Great Britain be pursued, and the savages are let loose to murder our Citizens and butcher our women and children, this war, will be a war of extermination.

The first stroke with the Tomahawk the first attempt with the Scalping Knife will be the Signal for one indiscriminate scene of desolation, *No white man found fighting by the Side of an Indian will be taken prisoner* Instant destruction will be his Lot . . .

I doubt not your courage and firmness; I will not doubt your attachment to Liberty. If you tender your services voluntarily they will be accepted readily.

The United State offers you *Peace, Liberty*, and *Security* your choice lies between these, & *War, Slavery, and destruction*, Choose then, but choose wisely; and may he who knows the justice of our cause, and who holds in his hand the fate of Nations, guide you to a result the most compatible, with your rights and interests, your peace and prosperity.

WM. HULL

The General, who is afraid of the Indians, hopes that this document will force his opposite number at Fort Amherstburg to follow the lead of the United States and adopt a policy of native neutrality, at least temporarily. At the very minimum it ought to frighten the settlers and militia into refusing to bear arms. That is its immediate effect. In Brock's phrase, "the disaffected became more audacious, and the wavering more intimidated." The proclamation terrifies the militia. Within three days the force of newly recruited soldiers has been reduced by half as the farm boys desert to their homes.

Yet Hull has overstated his case. These are farmers he is address-ing, not revolutionaries. The colonial authoritarianism touches very few. They do not feel like slaves; they already have enough peace, liberty, and security to satisfy them. This tax-free province is not America at the time of the Boston Tea Party. Why is Hull asking them to free themselves from tyranny? In the words of one, if they had been under real tyranny, "they could at any time have crossed the line to the United States."

Hull has made another error. He threatens that anyone found fighting beside the Indians can expect no quarter. That rankles. *Everybody* will be fighting with the Indians; it will not be a matter of choice. Some of the militiamen who secretly hoped to go over to Hull in the confusion of battle have a change of heart. What is the point of deserting if the Americans intend to kill them on capture?

Precipitate action does not fit the Upper Canadian mood. This is a pioneer society, not a frontier society. No Daniel Boones stalk the Canadian forests, ready to knock off an Injun with a Kentucky rifle or do battle over an imagined slight. The Methodist circuit riders keep the people law abiding and temperate; prosperity keeps them content. The Sabbath is looked on with reverence; card playing and horse racing are considered sinful diversions; the demon rum has yet to become a problem. There is little theft, less violence. Simple pastimes tied to the land—barn raisings, corn huskings, threshing bees—serve as an outlet for the spirited. The new settlers will not volunteer to fight. But most are prepared, if forced, to bear arms for their new country and to march when ordered. In the years that follow some will even come to believe that they were the real sav-iours of Upper Canada.

MONTREAL, LOWER CANADA, July 4, 1812. Sir George Prevost has moved up from his capital at Quebec to be closer to the scene of action. An American army is gathering at Albany, New York, poised to attack Montreal by the traditional invasion route of the Lake Champlain water corridor. If it succeeds, Sir George is perfectly prepared to abandon all of Upper Canada and withdraw to the fortress of Quebec.

At this moment, however, the Captain-General, Governor-in-Chief, Vice-Admiral, Lieutenant-General and Commanding Officer of His Majesty's Forces in Upper Canada, Lower Canada, Nova Scotia, New Brunswick, Cape Breton, Newfoundland and the Bermudas is faced with a crisis on his own doorstep. A riot has broken out at Lachine over the Militia Law, which provides for the drafting of two thousand bachelors for three months' training. Some of the men from the parish at Pointe Claire have refused to go, believing—or pretending to believe—that the act has not been properly passed and the government is simply seizing an excuse to turn young French Canadians into soldiers.

When the army tries force, a mob resists and marches off to Lachine to seize a flotilla of boats in which the draftees hope to escape. The Riot Act is read; shots whistle over the insurgents' heads and are returned; two civilians are killed. Four hundred and fifty soldiers invade the community and begin taking prisoners—so many, indeed, that they are finally released on the promise that they will "implore the pardon of His Excellency the Governor."

His Excellency is a suave diplomat whose forte is conciliation. He has learned that delicate art as governor of St. Lucia and later of Dominica, French-speaking islands in the Caribbean wrested from the mother country by the British but soothed into passivity by a man who has none of the hauteur of a British colonial bureaucrat. Born of a Swiss father and perfectly at home in the French language, Prevost has the exact qualifications needed to win over a race who also consider themselves a conquered people.

Now, before some three hundred insurgents, the Great Conciliator appears and turns on his considerable charm.

"His Excellency expostulated with them as a Father and pointed out to them the danger of their situation in a style truly honourable to his own feelings, assuring them of his forgiveness on delivering up those who had been promoters of the insurrection . . . which they cheerfully agreed to do. . . ."

Thus with the crisis defused and the approving comment of the Montreal *Herald* putting the seal on his actions, the Governor General can turn to graver matters. He is resolved to fight a defensive war only; he does not have the resources to go on the attack, even if he wished to. But he does not wish to. His own natural caution has been sustained by specific instructions from Lord Liverpool, the Secretary of State for War and the Colonies, to do nothing rash.

Rashness is not Sir George's style. He finds it difficult to countenance it in others. Surely the United States will do nothing rash! He is half convinced that the Americans do not actually mean to fight; that some accommodation can be made with them; that the war is not a real war; and that, in any event, it cannot possibly last for more than a few weeks. "Prudent" is a word that slips comfortably into his correspondence. He considers it "prudent and politic to avoid any measure which can in its effect have a tendency to unite the people in the American States," for "whilst disunion prevails among them, their attempts on these provinces will be feeble." Therefore it is important not to anger the enemy. Brock, specifically, is enjoined from "committing any act which may even by construction tend to unite the Eastern and Southern states."

Brock, with his reputation for dash and daring, worries Prevost. The impetuous subordinate is more than a week away by express courier and a month away by post. His audacity is legendary. Prevost has certainly heard the stories. One goes all the way back to Brock's early days, when his regiment, the 49th, was stationed at Bridgetown in Barbados. There was in that company a confirmed braggart and duellist whose practice was to insult fellow officers and finish them off at twelve paces. Brock, when accosted, accepted the challenge but refused to fire at the regulation distance. Instead, he produced a handkerchief and demanded that both men fire across it at point-blank range, thus equalling the odds and making the death of at least one of them a virtual certainty. His adversary panicked, refused to fire, and thus shamed was forced to leave the regiment.

There are other tales: Brock in the saddle, insisting on riding to the very pinnacle of Mount Hillaby, twelve hundred feet above the Caribbean—a feat most horsemen consider impossible; or, in 1803, personally leading an eight-hour chase in an open boat across Lake Ontario to apprehend six deserters, a venture that brought him a reprimand.

To a prudent commander, Brock's presence can be disquieting, even alarming. He is known as a man who believes that "nothing should be impossible to a soldier; the word impossible should not be found in a soldier's dictionary!" Will Brock attempt the impossible in Upper Canada? Prevost is determined that he shall not.

The contrast between the two commanders can be seen in their official portraits. At forty-four, Prevost is a handsome man, his lean face framed by dark sideburns; yet even in his painted likeness there is a furtiveness. The eyes swivel back as if to watch the artist; little furrows crease the brow. There is a slackness of mouth, a hesitancy of stance, none of the knife-edge sharpness that distinguishes the features of his subordinate who, in his portraits, looks off resolutely and serenely into the middle distance.

If Prevost is more diplomat than soldier, Brock is more soldier than diplomat. He remains disdainful of civilians, though he has learned to curb in public the tactlessness that once marked his dealings with the administration in Quebec. Prevost on the other hand has, in less than a year, worked a miracle in Lower Canada by managing to conciliate the French Canadians whose loyalty to the Crown had been placed in jeopardy by the racial arrogance of his predecessor. Under Sir James Craig, the Québécois found themselves shut out of all important government posts.

In contrast to Craig, who believed the French Canadians disloyal, Prevost is convinced they will fight to retain their land. The bombast in Washington prophesying the easy conquest of the Canadas will, he believes, help swell the ranks of the militia. Nonetheless, diplomacy will be needed: "The Canadians in general are grossly ignorant, it will therefore require vigilance and circumspection to prevent the proposed changes from being attended by any circumstance prejudicial to the tranquillity of the colony."

Circumspection Prevost has in quantity; but circumspection does not win wars. In material supplies he is hopelessly deficient. He has no coin with which to pay his troops and will have to persuade the legislature to issue paper money. He is embarrassed that he cannot supply the militia with enough rifles, let alone other equipment. A ship has set out from Bermuda to Halifax with six thousand stands of arms; apparently it has foundered in a storm. The mother country's priorities are Wellington's; she can supply Prevost with little to repel invasion—neither money, nor arms, nor men. He is short of officers; there are only two generals in Lower Canada, himself and Baron Francis de Rottenburg, and in Upper Canada two more: Roger Sheaffe and Isaac Brock.

Brock! In many ways he is worth five generals; Prevost admires and likes him. But—one can see the pursed lips, the furrowed brow—how to keep him in check? Overall British strategy does not envisage the seizure of American territory. Prevost does not wish to provoke the enemy. There is only one way to contain Brock, dictated as much by circumstance as by design, and that is to keep his regular force to a minimum. Upper Canada will get five hundred reinforcements, no more. And Brock must be convinced that these numbers will not "justify offensive operations being undertaken, *unless they were solely calculated to strengthen a defensive attitude.*"

The italics are not Prevost's. But the phrase is one that undoubtedly burns its way into the mind of the military commander of Upper Canada. When the moment comes, he will place the broadest possible interpretation on Sir George Prevost's cautious instructions.

—

SANDWICH, UPPER CANADA, July 23, 1812; with General Hull's Army of the Northwest.

"Why does the army dally?" Robert Lucas asks rhetorically, as he scratches away in his diary. "Why do they not make the Stroke on Maldon [Amherstburg] at once, had proper energy been used, we might have been in Maldon now, we are tampering with them untill they will be able to drive us back across the river. . . ."

Why indeed? Hull's troops are eager to maintain some momentum, have been since the day of the landing when it was expected Hull would sweep down the river to attack the British fort at Amherstburg—a place name that has a sinister connotation for western Americans who have suffered at the hands of the Indians. For this has been the headquarters of Elliott, McKee and Girty, whom the frontiersmen believe were behind the raids on white settlements in the Northwest.

Like his fellow volunteers, Lucas wants to get on with it. Once Fort Amherstburg's guns are silenced, the way to Upper Canada lies wide open. The only other British forts on the western frontier are at the other end of Lake Erie and along the Niagara River. A second American army has been dispatched to attack these strong points. Its task is to cause a diversion, pin down the defending British and prevent reinforcements from reaching Fort Amherstburg.

To Lucas, speed is essential. Amherstburg must be attacked and taken before Brock can divert more men to its defence. Lucas is used to swift, flexible movements, for he has been acting as a scout for Hull. In the General's mixed bag of raw recruits, untrained civilians, professional commanders, and elected leaders, he is a hybrid— general, captain, and private soldier rolled into one. The anomaly springs out of his country's awkward military philosophy, which disdains the idea of a standing army and relies on volunteers for the nation's defence. Lucas had been for some time a brigadier-general in the Ohio state militia. Eager to serve in the regular army, he applied in April for a captain's commission. A few days later, before it came through, McArthur ordered him to transmit from his brigade a proportion of the twelve hundred men required from the state in the coming war. What to do? Lucas, thirsty for action, set an example to his men by enrolling as a private in a volunteer company. To add to the confusion, the men elected his younger brother John as their captain.

Now, at Sandwich, Lucas vents his disgust in his diary: *Why does the army dally?* Hull is not short of supplies, for he has sent McArthur foraging up the Thames, raiding the farms, the barns, and the fields for food and equipment. McArthur and his men, moving without blankets or provisions, living off the land, penetrate sixty miles into the heart of Upper Canada: a land of stump and snake fences; of cabins and shanties of basswood and cedar; of Dutch lofts and clay ovens; of grist mills, fanning mills, and windmills; of chicken hutches, corn cribs, hog pens, and cattle sheds; of pickled pork and pigeon pie and fresh milk kept cool in underground sheds; of oxen hitched in tandem, furrowing the glistening fields, and raw-boned men in homespun linsey-woolsey scything the tawny harvest of midsummer. The raiding party leaves a trail of devastation in its wake, returning in five days with two hundred barrels of flour, four hundred blankets, and wagons loaded with whiskey, salt, cloth, guns, ammunition, household goods, tools—even boats. Grain fields are destroyed, homes ransacked, orchards levelled, corn trampled, fences burned or shattered—actions that enrage the settlers and help to turn them against their former compatriots.

John McGregor, a trader and merchant who has removed his goods to Matthew Dolsen's house and mill on the Thames for safety, loses everything—flour, merchandise, grain, livestock, and boats— and almost loses his life. He and Dolsen are forced to flee when it is learned that McArthur intends to shoot them on sight in the belief that they are rousing the Indians and militia to resistance.

Farmers and townspeople are beggared by the raiders. Jean-Baptiste Beniteau's orchard of sixty fruit trees is destroyed, his fences and pickets reduced to ashes. His neighbour, Jean-Baptiste Ginac, is looted of all his livestock, pork, flour, oats, and corn. Another Jean-Baptiste—Fourneaux—loses 480 bushels of grain, all his cider, as well as his winter's wood supply and furniture. A fourth,

Jean-Baptiste Boismier, a fur trader, sees his entire fortune of 620 skins together with his livestock, tools, utensils, and harvested corn go to the enemy.

Hull's men make no allowance for old friends. Lieutenant-Colonel François Bâby, whose house has become Hull's headquarters, has tried to save some of his chattels by hauling them off to Jean-Baptiste Goyeau's home, three miles distant. But Hull dispatches a party of dragoons with six wagons who remove everything at gunpoint, then, emboldened by conquest, slice up one of Bâby's finest coats with their sabres. Bâby's loss is staggering; he reckons it at 2,678 pounds sterling.

Another raiding party ransacks the estate of the Earl of Selkirk at Baldoon on Lake St. Clair, seizing a thousand pounds' worth of booty, from pewter plates to pitchforks, including the greatest prize of all, more than nine hundred prize Merino sheep, which are ferried across the river to Fort Detroit along with the aged Scot who is their shepherd.

McArthur brushes all complaints aside with the promise that everything will eventually be paid for because, he says, Hull has such a footing in Canada that the British will never be able to drive him out.

And so it appears. At Fort Amherstburg the situation is deteriorating. Militia service works real hardship on those families who depend upon the able-bodied for their livelihood. Hundreds desert. Those who remain loyal—men like Robert Pike of Port Dover or John Williams on the Thames—have no one to harvest their wheat and so lose it all to rot. St. George, the commander at the fort, feels himself obliged to release the oldest and least efficient to return to their farms. Others slip away. On July 8, St. George counts 850 militiamen under his command. A week later the number has dropped to 471. "I expect that in two or three days we shall have very few of them at the post," Matthew Elliott informs his superior, adding that there is no ammunition left in the Indian stores "and, if more Indians come, I really do not know how to act." St. George expects an attack almost hourly, but it does not come. In Robert Lucas's rueful belief,

Hull's dallying has given the British hope. "Our conduct has at least incouraged them much," he notes.

One of the keenest soldiers in Hull's army, Lucas has managed to see more action than most of his followers. As a ranger and scout he has always been in the vanguard of the main army, often in danger. He is one of those natural soldiers, found in every army, who thrive on action. When Hull's boats crossed over to Sandwich, Lucas arranged to switch companies temporarily in order to be one of the first to set foot on Canadian soil because he "could not endure to be behind."

On July 16, Lucas volunteers again: Colonels Cass and Miller are ordered to reconnoitre enemy country up to the River aux Canards, a deep but sluggish stream that winds through the marshes three miles above Amherstburg. Lucas immediately offers to go along. This war will help to make his reputation; one day he will be governor of Ohio and later of Iowa Territory.

Colonel Cass is as eager for glory and for action as Lucas. The bridge at the Canard is held by a detachment of British regulars and Indians—the same Menominee dispatched to Amherstburg from the Wisconsin country the previous month by Robert Dickson. Cass resolves to ford the river upstream and attack in a flanking movement while Miller pins down the sentries. Again Lucas and the rangers are in the vanguard.

Faced with an attack on their rear, the British retire. Cass cannot pursue, for a tributary stream blocks the way. But the British sentries—John Dean and James Hancock of the 41st—stubbornly hold their ground and become the first soldiers to shed their blood on Canadian soil in the War of 1812. Dean, one arm broken by a musket ball, fights on with his bayonet until he is knocked to the ground and disarmed. Hancock, bleeding from at least two wounds, unable to support himself, continues to fight on his knees until he is captured. He dies that night and is scalped by one of the Indians, who sells the trophy to the British—"a good trick for an Indian to make the British Gov. pay for their own Soldiers Scalps," comments Robert Lucas.

This is the first time the Americans have come up against British regulars, that tough, stubborn, hard-drinking, somewhat unimaginative breed whom Wellington has called, not without affection, "the scum of the earth." America, nurtured on the ideal of a free-wheeling grassroots democracy, scorns the British professional as a semi-robot and mercenary, wedded to no political ideal. It is true, certainly, that many a British working man joins for the money: the handsome bounties offered those who transfer from the militia, the prospect of a substantial prize after a successful engagement. But there are other reasons. Wellington believes, not without considerable evidence, that "they have all enlisted for drink." Yet drink is only a symptom; like enlistment, it is a form of escape from the appallingly drab conditions of the British lower classes. The army is composed of men fleeing from a variety of bedevilments—brutal taskmasters, nagging wives, pregnant girl friends, intolerable parents, constables and judges, or simple boredom. Black-sheep sons of well-born families ("gentlemen rankers") rub shoulders with footpads, pickpockets, roustabouts, poachers, smugglers, or plain, resolute English labouring men hungry for adventure in a far-off land, even if that be nothing more glamorous than garrison duty with the 41st in the backwater of Amherstburg.

Wellington's scum are actually in a minority. It is estimated that in a battalion of some three or four hundred men, perhaps fifty are rogues—drunkards, stragglers, potential deserters. A harsh system of discipline keeps them in line. In the summer of 1812, for instance, the 103rd Regiment in Quebec holds thirty-seven courts martial and sentences thirty-one men to a total of 5,725 lashes, of which at least 1,589 are actually laid on the bare back, the others being remitted. (One unfortunate is lashed three hundred times.) But it is the parade-ground drill, hammered into the rankers' subconscious, that trains the men to act automatically—to stand fast as the enemy advances, to hold their fire until ordered, to discharge their muskets in a single shattering volley without flinching, even as the cavalry sweeps down upon the square or hostile bayonets attempt to break the scarlet line. The wounded Dean, now a prisoner of war, and the dying Hancock are products of this system. It simply does not occur to them to desert their posts.

The Americans now hold the bridge that can lead the army to Amherstburg. It appears to Cass and Miller that the entire force should immediately move up to within striking distance of its objective. But Hull dithers. He is going by the book, planning a careful set-piece siege of the British fort. That he will not undertake until his heavy artillery is ready. The fort might be taken by an infantry assault, but the slaughter would be appalling; and that the former divinity student cannot abide. The bridge is abandoned.

He has other concerns. What is happening on the Niagara frontier? It is essential that an American army be in place along that river. Otherwise there is nothing to stop the British from deploying all their resources against him. Eustis and Dearborn have promised a diversion on the Niagara to support his invasion, but communications are such that the General has no way of knowing whether this has been done.

A closer problem torments him. He is certain that Colonel Cass is trying to pressure him for reasons of personal ambition. He feels his authority slipping away; his officers' complaints are beginning to destroy his influence. He calls council after council to try to quell their impatience; it only erodes his command. "They seem to have thought," he will later argue, "that when a council of war was called, it was to be governed by the laws of a town meeting."

He is determined not to advance until there is "an absolute certainty of success." How long will it take to prepare the cannon? Two days? Two weeks? After each meeting, the time stretches. Hull fears defeat. Defeat will mean starvation for the troops and, worse, devastation by the Indians. The militia fear the Indians. At the bridge over the Canard and also at Turkey Creek and Petite Coté, where desultory skirmishing continues almost daily, Dickson's Menominee and Tecumseh's followers terrify the raw recruits. One regular officer writes to the New York *Gazette*:

"Had it not been for the dastardly conduct of the drafted Ohio militia who composed one half of the party and who took to their heels when they evidently had the advantage, the whole of the Indians would have been killed or taken. The officers endeavoured to rally them and said they would be fired at by their own party if they did not stand. They replied that they would rather be killed by them than by the damned Indians."

There is savagery on both sides. The first Indian scalp is taken by Captain William McCullough of the Rangers, who describes in a letter to his wife how he tore it from the corpse's head with his teeth.

Word of these skirmishes reaches William K. Beall and his fellow prisoners aboard the *Thames*, docked at Amherstburg. It fuels their hope for speedy deliverance. On the night of the encounter at the Canard bridge, Beall learns that Hull's army is camped within reach. Glorious news! But instead of seeing American soldiers marching into town he is greeted by a more macabre spectacle: Thomas McKee of the Indian Department (the perennial drunkard whom Elliott has replaced) arrives at the head of about fifty Indians, all naked except for their breech cloths. McKee, who is also dressed as a native, halts opposite the gaping prisoners and hoists a fresh scalp, fastened to a long pole, which he shakes exultantly, all the time taunting the prisoners with savage cries.

For this spectacle, "which would have chilled the frigid blood of a Laplander or . . . crimsoned the tawny cheek of an unrelenting Turk," Beall abuses everything British, from the King on down. His fury is misplaced, for the scalp is undoubtedly that of the unfortunate British sentry Hancock.

Beall and his fellow prisoners have other concerns. Where is Hull? What can be keeping him? Gone now is the optimism, the good humour, the gallantry of those first days in captivity. Beall no longer sees the British as gentlemen but as monsters. And he is desperately homesick. His nights are troubled by visions of his young wife, far away on their estate of Beallmont in Kentucky. "In my sleep the air drawn figure of my Melinda often rises to my view: beautious as an Angel, gentle as the spring, smiling on me with enchanted tenderness and yealding to my fond embrace. In dreams, with rapturous fondness, I have pressed her to my bosom, felt her soft touch, heard the sweet accents of her voice, and gazed upon her lovely countenance till every sense was lost in extacy and love."

These visions are rendered more poignant by Beall's disillusionment with his general: "The British officers and soldiers begin to laugh at Hull. . . . He is now the object of their jest and ridicule instead of being as he was formerly their terror and greatest fear."

Even as Beall is committing these thoughts to paper, on July 26, Hull, at Sandwich, is shaken by an alarming piece of intelligence. A ship, the *Salina*, flying British colours, is brought about by a shot from the shore. Aboard is a group of American citizens and soldiers, led by Lieutenant Porter Hanks, the former commander at Michilimackinac, paroled by his adversary, Roberts. Now, for the first time, Hull learns of Mackinac's fall. It is a major disaster. "I can scarcely conceive of the impression made by the fall of Mackanac," Colonel Cass writes to a relative. For the western anchor on the American frontier has come unstuck, releasing, in Hull's phrase, "the northern hive of Indians," who will shortly come "swarming down in every direction."

Hull feels himself surrounded by Indians. He reasons that there must be two or three thousand Ottawa, Chippewa, and Sioux at his rear, advancing from Mackinac. On his left are the Iroquois of the Grand Valley. They are still neutral, as far as he knows, but he also has news that Brock has sent a detachment to try to bring them into the fight—a task rendered less difficult by the news of Mackinac's fall. In front of him, at Amherstburg, lies another potent force: hundreds more Indians led by the great Tecumseh. Hull fears these more than he does the handful of British regulars.

Within the fort, by the end of the month William Beall and the other American officers have lost all hope of rescue. "I can scarcely think that Genl. H. will be defeated," Beall writes, "but appearances justify such a belief. I am confident that he will not take Malden, though 300 men could do it. . . . Why does he not, by taking Malden, silence and drive the Indians away who infest the Country and secure a safe communication with the States, and safety to our Frontiers. Heaven only knows. I for a Harrison, a Daviess or a Wells."

YORK, UPPER CANADA, July 28, 1812. Isaac Brock, administrator of Upper Canada, resplendent in military crimson and gold, is opening the legislature and managing to mask the emotions of contempt, frustration, and even despair that boil up within him.

> *... when invaded by an Enemy whose avowed object is the entire Conquest of this Province, the voice of Loyalty as well as of interest calls aloud to every Person in the Sphere in which he is placed, to defend his Country.*
>
> *Our Militia have heard that voice and have obeyed it, they have evinced by the promptitude and Loyalty of their Conduct, that they are worthy of the King whom they serve, and of the Constitution which they enjoy ...*

This is hokum, and Brock knows it. He has already written a private note to Prevost declaring his belief that it seems impossible "to animate the militia to a proper sense of duty" and that he almost despairs of doing anything with them. Worse, at Long Point on Lake Erie, where he has attempted to muster five hundred men to march to the relief of Fort Amherstburg, there has been open mutiny. The men have refused to march under Lieutenant-Colonel Thomas Talbot, the eccentric and domineering Irish aristocrat who controls some sixty thousand acres of land in the area. One reason for the mutiny has been the wives' fear of being left alone to the mercy of the neutral Iroquois at the Grand River. Another has been the inflammatory speeches made to them by pro-American civilian dissidents. A third, one suspects, has been Talbot himself, a curious specimen, tyrannical in his control over the settlers—a man who once lived in luxury but who now dresses in homespun, bakes his own bread, labours like a peasant, drinks like a toper, and affects a harsh mode of life which, in the words of a former lieutenant-governor, "might suit a Republic but is not fitted to a Monarchical Government."

In spite of this disaffection, Brock continues the charade:

. . . it affords me particular satisfaction, that while I address You as Legislators, I speak to men who in the day of danger, will be ready to assist, not only with their Counsel, but with their Arms . . .

He does not believe it, and his private correspondence reflects his dismay and cynicism. The people and their leaders appear convinced that the war is lost: ". . . a full belief possesses them that this Province must inevitably succumb. . . . Legislators, magistrates, militia officers, all have imbibed the idea, and are so sluggish and indifferent in their respective offices that the artful and active scoundrel is allowed to parade the country without interruption and commit all imaginable mischief."

The artful and active scoundrels include a big, ginger-haired blacksmith named Andrew Westbrook and a land surveyor from Montreal named Simon Z. Watson. Westbrook, a recent arrival from the United States, has enthusiastically espoused Hull's cause, helped distribute his proclamation, and volunteered to fight with the Detroit militia. Watson, "a desperate character" in Brock's view, is a bitter enemy of Thomas Talbot, and thus of the government, because of a longstanding rivalry over land fees and speculation. Created a temporary colonel by Hull, he has "vowed the most bitter vengeance against the first characters of the Province." There are other dissidents, such as John Beamer, a justice of the peace, who has chaired a meeting in Norfolk County urging the militia not to fight.

But Brock plays all this down:

A few Traitors have already joined the Enemy. . . . Yet the General Spirit of Loyalty which appears to pervade the Inhabitants of this Province, is such as to authorize a just expectation that their efforts to mislead and deceive, will be unavailing . . .

In private he reports:

"A petition has already been carried to Genl. Hull signed by many inhabitants about Westminster inviting him to advance with a promise to join him—What in the name of heaven can be done with such a vile population?"

Yet who can blame the mass of the people? The nature of the colonial aristocracy denies them a say in their own destiny, even though they are required to swear allegiance to the King, George III, who being certifiably insane is king in name only, the real monarch being his son, the Prince Regent, known to the irreverent masses as Prinny. The province is administered by the Prince Regent's appointee, Francis Gore, and in his absence by Isaac Brock, who also commands the army and the militia and is thus a near dictator. He sits at the head of a seven-man council, which, being appointed for life, can be said to be almost as conservative as the mad king himself, and a fourteen-man assembly, elected by freeholders, whose members serve for four years—or less, at the governor's pleasure. Anyone who dares speak disrespectfully of the King, the government, or its officers is treading perilously close to sedition.

The Church of England clergy, the military, and the leading officeholders form a ruling elite, the legacy of the first lieutenant-governor, John Graves Simcoe, who was convinced that a landed aristocracy, conservative in its attitudes and British in its antecedents, was the only way to combat the twin viruses of democracy and republicanism creeping across the border. The tight little group that forms the apex of the social triangle in Upper Canada, entrenched by nepotism and by an educational system that ignores the masses, will shortly become known as the Family Compact. It does not tolerate opposition.

The "vile population" wants to be left alone. Militia service deprives the farms of their greatest asset, able-bodied men. Loyalists and the sons of the Loyalists—men like John Beverley Robinson, or the Ryersons of Norfolk County—will flock to the colours because their whole heritage represents a rejection of American values. And there are others who see in war a chance for adventure or escape. But these are in a minority. Brock is determined to rally the rest by Draconian methods, if need be. He wants to suspend habeas corpus and establish martial law but finds that in spite of his impressive authority he has little hope of either. The legislature will not vote for the first, and if he attempts the second "I am told the instant the law is promulgated the Militia will disperse. . . ."

He is convinced that the legislators, expecting an American victory, are fearful of taking any overt action that might displease the conquerors. "I really believe it is with some cause that they dread the vengeance of the democratic party, they are such a set of unrelenting villains."

Pinned down at York by his civilian duties, he has taken what action he can to stiffen the defence at Fort Amherstburg, dispatching a younger and more energetic officer, Lieutenant-Colonel Henry Procter, to take over from the confused and harassed St. George.

Amherstburg is vital. If Hull seizes it—as he seems likely to do—he can sweep up the Thames or turn eastward to attack the British rear at Fort George on the Niagara and link up with the second American army already forming along that gorge. Brock *must* maintain a strong defence on the Niagara, yet his force at Amherstburg is distressingly thin. His only immediate solution is to move some men from Fort George to Fort Erie, a mid-point between the two bastions. From there they can be dispatched swiftly in either direction, depending upon the threat. Fortunately, he commands the Lakes.

He has also sent detachments down the valley of the Thames, recalling the militia from the harvest fields, attempting to waken the countryside to action, and distributing a proclamation of his own designed to counter Hull's. In this paper battle with the enemy, Brock, conjuring up the spectre of Napoleon, shows that he is no stranger to the art of magniloquence:

> . . . it is but too obvious that once estranged from the powerful protection of the United Kingdom you must be reannexed to the dominion of France, from which the Provinces of Canada were wrested by the Arms of Great Britain, at a vast expense of blood and treasure, from no other motive than to *relieve* her ungrateful children from the oppression of a cruel neighbor: this restitution of Canada to the Empire of France was the stipulated reward for

the aid offered to the revolted Colonies, now the United States; The debt is still due, and there can be no doubt but that the pledge has been renewed. . . . Are you prepared Inhabitants of Upper Canada to becoming willing subjects or rather slaves to the Despot who rules the nations of Europe with a rod of Iron? If not, arise in a Body, exert your energies, co-operate cordially with the King's regular Forces to repel the invader, and do not give cause to your children when groaning under the oppression of a foreign Master to reproach you with having too easily parted with the richest Inheritance on Earth—a participation in the name, character and freedom of Britons . . .

In his proclamation, Brock praises "the brave bands of Natives who inhabit this Colony," but the ink is scarcely dry on the paper when he learns that one brave band—the Iroquois of the Grand Valley—remains totally uninterested in fighting the Americans. Brock is infuriated. Their conduct is "ungrateful and infamous . . . mortifying." He would like to see them all expelled from their land. By refusing to take sides, the Iroquois "afford the Militia a plausible pretext for staying at home—They do not like leaving their families within the power of the Indians. . . ."

> *Honourable Gentlemen of the Legislative Council and Gentlemen of the House of Assembly.*
>
> *We are engaged in an awful and eventful Contest. By unanimity and despatch in our Councils, and by vigour in our Operations, we may teach the Enemy this lesson—that a Country defended by Free men, enthusiastically devoted to the cause of their King and Constitution, can never be Conquered.*

Brock's closing words have a hollow ring. According to inviolable ritual, they will be parroted back to him twice: first by the Speaker of the Council and on the following day by the Speaker of the House, while Brock frets. He yearns to be at Amherstburg in the thick of things, away from the stuffy corridors of York and in sight of the enemy. Words are not his long suit, though in his loneliness he has become a voracious reader, devouring Plutarch's *Lives*, Hume's *Essays*, Pope's *Homer*, and dozens of military volumes. It is even said that much of his proclamation is the work of his friend Mr. Justice William Dummer Powell. Action is his forte, and it is action he craves. On the Iberian peninsula, Wellington has just won the battle of Salamanca and is basking in the approbation of Francisco Goya, the irascible Spanish court painter who has somehow got through the lines to commence an equestrian portrait of the victor. But it is thirteen years since Brock has seen real action (setting aside the naval attack on Copenhagen when he was sequestered aboard one of Nelson's ships, *Ganges*). He is not likely to forget that October afternoon at Egmont-op-Zee when death whispered to him as a musket ball, happily near spent, buried itself in his silk cravat, knocking him insensible from his horse. He was a lieutenant-colonel of the 49th then, a regiment that he had thoroughly shaken up, transforming it (in the Duke of York's opinion) from one of the worst to one of the best in the service. Now a whole country needs shaking up. Defeatism, timidity, irresolution, and treason stalk the land. It is Brock's task to achieve another miracle, and he cannot accomplish that in the dust and gumbo of provincial York. Duty calls. Immortality beckons. A new October awaits.

———

AUGUST 5, 1812. At the River aux Ecorces, on the American side of the Detroit, Robert Lucas the scout lies hidden in the bushes, waiting for the dawn, watched by unseen eyes. Two fellow rangers lie beside him along with the ranger captain McCullough, who has the dubious distinction of being the only American thus far to take an Indian scalp.

The four men lie on the left flank of an armed body sent across the river by Hull to make contact with the wagon train of supplies, which he desperately needs to feed his army. The supply train, under the command of a young Chillicothe lawyer, Captain Henry Brush, has reached the Rapids of the Maumee and is moving on to the River Raisin after a gruelling march through dense thickets and treacherous mires. But Brush does not dare continue to Detroit without an escort, for his cattle train and pack animals must pass within cannon shot of Fort Amherstburg. Hull has answered his plea by dispatching two hundred Ohio volunteers under Major Thomas Van Horne. Some of these are the same men who refused to cross the river in July; Van Horne has picked them up at Detroit along with their company commander, the recalcitrant Captain Rupes, who, astonishingly, is still in charge, having been re-elected by democratic vote after a court martial ordered him cashiered.

Dawn breaks. McCullough and his scouts rise and mount their horses, making a wide reconnaissance sweep around the detachment. They scent trouble, noting tracks on the road and trails in the grass— evidence that a party of Indians has been watching them during the night. Out on the river, a faint splish-splash penetrates the shroud of mist that hangs over the water. Oars! Hull's army cannot remain long on Canadian soil unless its supply lines are secured. The British, who control the river, intend that this shall not be.

The detachment moves, McCullough, Robert Lucas, and Van Horne's black servant riding out in front. Lucas continues to eye the river. Is a British force crossing over from Fort Amherstburg? The mist frustrates his view.

They ride through the Wyandot village of Maguaga. It is deserted, the houses empty. Tecumseh and Matthew Elliott have preceded them and persuaded the wavering Walk-in-the-Water to cross to British territory with his followers. Brock's assessment has been correct: news of the victory at Michilimackinac has tipped the scales, and the tribe wants to be on the winning side.

The road forks around a corn field. Lucas and a companion take the right fork; McCullough takes the left and rides into an ambush. Lucas hears a volley of shots, but before he can reach him, the scalper is himself scalped, tomahawked, riddled with musket balls. The rear guard is in a panic, but the Indians have already vanished into the tall corn.

Shaken, the detachment moves on, leaving three corpses under a cover of bark and ignoring a Frenchman's warning that a large force of Indians is waiting for them at Brownstown. The Americans do not trust the French settlers, some of whom are pro-British and seek to confuse them with false reports.

The war party moves in double file. Between the files, mounted men escort the mail—a packet of personal letters written by Hull's soldiers to their families and friends, many of them critical of their general, and, more significantly, Hull's official dispatches to Washington, revealing both his plans and his pessimism.

Brownstown village lies ahead, but Brownstown Creek must first be crossed. The only practical ford lies in a narrow defile with thick bushes on the right and fields of tall corn on the opposite bank and on the left. It is the perfect spot for an ambush; Lucas recognizes the danger and rides along the right column warning the men to see that their muskets are freshly primed. Tecumseh has recognized it, too. He and his followers are flat on their bellies directly ahead—twenty-four Shawnee and Ottawa and one white man, Matthew Elliott's son Alexander.

As Tecumseh silently waits, the American files close up to cross the creek. Then, at a range of no more than twenty-five yards, the Indians rise out of the corn, their high-pitched war cries mingling with the explosion of their weapons. Lucas's horse is shot, topples sideways against another wounded animal, pitches its rider onto the ground, his musket flying from his hand. Weaponless, Lucas tries with little success to rally the men. The odds are twenty to one in favour of the Americans, but the Indians are shouting so wildly that Van Horne believes himself outnumbered. It is scarcely necessary to order a retreat; his men fling down their weapons, scatter the mail, and plunge headlong back the way they came, actually outrunning their pursuers, who follow them for three miles before giving up the chase. Robert Lucas, covering the retreat as best he can, is the last man to escape.

The Battle of Brownstown, as it will be called, represents a serious setback for Hull. Van Horne has lost eighteen men killed and twenty wounded. Some seventy are missing, many hiding in the bushes; the following day, most straggle back. Worse than the loss of seven officers is the abandoning of the mail. This will raise Brock's spirits, for here, in letters home, is strong evidence of the discontent and illness in the ranks, of a lack of confidence in the leadership, and, even more important, Hull's letter of August 4 to the Secretary of War, outlining the critical situation of his army, pleading for another two thousand men, and expressing his deep-seated fear of the Indians who he believes will shortly be swarming down from Mackinac Island.

At Brownstown, meanwhile, a strong detachment of the British 41st accompanied by militia and civilian volunteers under Major Adam Muir has crossed the river, too late to take part in the skirmish but prepared to frustrate any further attempt by Hull to open the supply line. The men have waited all night, unable to light a fire, shivering in the damp, without blankets or provisions. Now they are exposed to a spectacle calculated to make them shudder further.

The Indians hold a young American captive and are intent on killing him. Muir does his best to intervene, offers a barrel of rum and articles of clothing if the prisoner's life is spared. But then a series of piercing cries issues from the forest—the funeral convoy of a young chief, Blue Jacket, the only casualty among Tecumseh's followers. Four tribesmen carry in the body. Thomas Verchères de Boucherville, a citizen volunteer and experienced fur trader from Amherstburg, realizes there is no hope for the American, for the Indians are intent on avenging their chief. They place his corpse at the captive's feet and he, too, seems to understand his fate.

The American turns pale, looks about him, asks in a low voice if it is possible that the English allow such acts of barbarity. The cries of the Indians drown out the response.

The oldest Potawatomi chief raises his hatchet over the prisoner; a group of Indian women draw near. At the chief's signal, one plunges a butcher knife into the victim's head; a second stabs him in the side while the chief dispatches him with a tomahawk. Tecumseh, who would surely have prevented the execution, is not present.

The white witnesses including Alexander Elliott (himself in Indian dress) are stunned. They feel impotent, knowing that these dark allies hold the keys to British success. Young Thomas de Boucherville, the fur trader, who will never shake the incident from his memory, puts their dilemma into words:

"We all stood around overcome by an acute sense of shame. We felt implicated in some way in this murder . . . and yet, under the circumstances what could we do? The life of that man undoubtedly belonged to the inhuman chief. The government had desperate need of these Indian allies. Our garrison was weak and these warriors were numerous enough to impose their will upon us. If we were to rebuke them in this crisis . . . they would withdraw from the conflict, and retire to their own country on the Missouri whence they had come to join us."

De Boucherville is coming to realize what others will soon grasp—that the British are, in a subtle way, as much prisoners of the Indians as the young American whose tomahawked corpse lies stretched out before them.

———

SANDWICH, UPPER CANADA, August 6, 1812. In his headquarters in François Bâby's half-finished mansion, General Hull continues to vacillate. He has promised his impatient officers that he will attack the fort whether the artillery is ready or not. Now he has second thoughts. In Washington he allowed himself to be talked out of his original proposal: that America take steps to control the water routes. Now he himself is paying the price for that negligence. He cannot float his artillery downriver in the teeth of British gunboats. But his enemies can cross the river at will to harass his supply lines and herd Walk-in-the-Water's Wyandot followers into Canada to reinforce Fort Amherstburg.

He seriously considers retreat but backs off after a stormy meeting with Colonel McArthur. He broods, changes his mind, calls a council of his commanders, finally agrees to adopt their plan of attacking

Fort Amherstburg. He will move against it at the head of his troops "and in whatever manner the affair may terminate, I will never reflect on you, gentlemen."

Dazzling news! Robert Lucas, back from the debacle at Brownstown, is exultant: the long faces of his comrades have been replaced by smiles. A wave of good cheer surges over the camp. The sick rise from their beds and seize their muskets; the wounded urge the surgeons to pronounce them fit for duty. Orders are issued for five days' rations, three to be cooked—pork the staple fare. Ammunition and whiskey (twelve barrels) are loaded into wagons, axes, picks, and spades requisitioned, cannon placed on floating batteries. All unnecessary tents, baggage, and boats are sent back to Detroit.

Then, on the afternoon of August 7, hard on the heels of the news from Brownstown, comes an express rider with dispatches for Hull from two American commanders on the Niagara frontier. Boats loaded with British troops have been seen crossing Lake Erie and heading for Amherstburg; more British regulars accompanied by Canadian militia and Indians are en route from Niagara by boat to the fort. Since the British control the lakes, there is nothing the Americans can do to stop them.

Hull is badly rattled. What is happening? Washington's overall strategy was to pin down the British forces on the Niagara frontier by a series of attacks that would leave Fort Amherstburg lightly held. Now the British are taking troops from Fort George and Fort Erie, leaving that frontier exposed to attack. That may be of some comfort to his colleagues on the Niagara River, but it is disastrous for Hull; it is impossible for him "to express the disappointment which this information occasioned." What he does not know is that Prevost has sent an emissary to discuss an immediate armistice with General Henry Dearborn, the American commander-in-chief. Brock does not know this, either, but things are so quiet on the Niagara frontier that he feels justified in taking a gamble; he will reduce his forces there to a minimum in order to bolster his defence at Amherstburg and frustrate any attack by General Hull.

Both commanders—Hull at Sandwich, Brock at York—are suffering from bouts of gloom and frustration. Half blinded by the myopia of war, each believes his own position to be untenable, his adversary's superior. Brock, thwarted by timid civilians and a lukewarm militia, expects Hull to attack his weak garrison at Fort Amherstburg at any moment. He is desperate to reinforce it but despairs of holding it against greater numbers. Hull, isolated on Canadian soil, is convinced that Brock's combined force is not only stronger but also growing at an alarming rate.

Unlike Brock, Hull is no gambler. He feels doomed by bad fortune: the supposedly friendly Indians turning their coats and crowding into Amherstburg; the blocking of his supply train; now a fresh onslaught of fighting men. The General sees himself and his troops suddenly trapped in an unfriendly country, their backs to the river, their food running out, surrounded by Indians, facing Brock's regulars and Tecumseh's braves. Irresolution at last gives way to decision, but a decision tainted with panic. He must get his army back onto American soil, with the barrier of the river between him and his enemies—to Detroit at the very least, and perhaps all the way to the Maumee.

He sends again for his officers and breaks the news. It is his responsibility, and his alone, he declares, to decide the ultimate fate of the army. "Well, General," says the swarthy McArthur, "if it is your opinion, it must be so, but I must beg leave to decline giving any further opinion as to the movements of the army."

Hull suggests, hesitantly, that the army might be well advised to withdraw as far as the Maumee. Cass retorts that if he does that, every man in the Ohio militia will leave him. That puts an end to it: the army will withdraw across the river to Detroit, but no farther.

Lewis Cass is beside himself. In his eyes, Hull's decision is both fatal and unaccountable; he cannot fathom it. Coming after a series of timid, irresolute, and indecisive measures, this final about-face has dispirited the troops and destroyed the last vestige of confidence they may have had in their commander. Cass is undoubtedly right; far better if Hull had never crossed the river in the first place—at least until his supply lines were secure. A sense of aston-ishment, mingled with a feeling of disgrace, ripples through the camp. Robert Lucas feels it: the orders to cross the river under cover of darkness are, he thinks, especially dastardly. But cross the army must, and when night falls the men slink into their boats. By the following morning there is scarcely an American soldier left on Canadian soil.

WHILE BROCK IS ADVANCING toward the Detroit frontier, intent on attack, his superior, Sir George Prevost, is doing his best to wind down the war. He informs Lord Liverpool that although his policy of conciliation has not prevented hostilities, he is determined to do nothing to exacerbate the situation by aggressive action:

". . . Your Lordship may rest assured that unless the safety of the Provinces entrusted to my charge should require them, no measures shall be adopted by me to impede a speedy return to those accus-tomed relations of amity and goodwill which it is the mutual interest of both countries to cherish and preserve."

Sir George, who has never believed in the reality of the war, is now convinced it will reach a swift conclusion. Augustus Foster has written from Halifax, en route home from Washington, with the news that Britain has revoked the hated Orders in Council. American ships may now trade with continental Europe without fear of seizure. Madison in June made it clear that the Orders were America's chief reason for going to war. Surely, then, with Britain backing off, he will come to his senses and halt the invasion.

Sir George sees no reason to wait for the President. Why not suspend hostilities at once—at least temporarily? Why spill blood senselessly if the war is, in effect, over?

On August 2, he dispatches his aide, Lieutenant-Colonel Edward Baynes, with a flag of truce to treat with Major-General Henry Dearborn, the U.S. commander, at his headquarters at Greenbush, across the river from Albany, New York.

The American in charge of the overall prosecution of the war in the north has not seen military service for two decades. A ponderous, flabby figure, weighing two hundred and fifty pounds, with a face to match, Dearborn does not look like a general, nor does he act like one. He is a tired sixty-one. His soldiers call him Granny.

His reputation, like Hull's, rests on the memory of another time. As a Revolutionary major he fought at Bunker Hill, then struggled, feverish and half-starved, with Arnold through the wintry forests of Maine to attack Quebec, was captured and exchanged to fight again—against Burgoyne at Saratoga, at Monmouth Court House in '78, with General John Sullivan against the Indians in '79, at Yorktown in '81. A successful and influential Massachusetts politician in the post-war era, Secretary of War for eight years in Jefferson's cabinet, he is now an old soldier who was slowly fading away in his political sinecure until the call to arms restored him to command.

The American strategy, to attack Canada simultaneously at Detroit, Niagara, Kingston, and Montreal, is faltering. Given the lack of men and supplies it is hardly likely that these thrusts can occur together. It is assumed, without anybody quite saying so, that Dearborn will co-ordinate them, but General Dearborn does not appear to understand.

Strategically, the major attack ought to be made upon Montreal. A lightning thrust would sever the water connection between the Canadas, deprive the upper province of supplies and reinforcements, and, in the end, cause it to wither away and surrender without a fight. The problem is that the New Englanders, whose co-operation is essential, do not want to fight, while the southerners and westerners in Kentucky, Tennessee, South Carolina, and Ohio are eager for battle. There is also the necessity of securing America's western flank from the menace of the Indians. Thus, the American command pins its initial hopes on Hull's army while the forces on Lake Champlain remain stagnant.

To describe Dearborn's prosecution of the war as leisurely is to understate that officer's proclivity for sluggish movement. He has spent three months in New England, attempting in his bumbling fashion to stir the people to belligerence with scarcely any success. The governors of Massachusetts and Connecticut are particularly obdurate. When Dearborn asks Caleb Strong to call out fourteen companies of artillery and twenty-seven of infantry for the defence of his Massachusetts ports and harbours, Governor Strong declares that the seacoast does not need defending since the government of Nova Scotia has "by proclamation, forbid[den] any incursions or depredations upon our territories." Governor John Cotton Smith of Connecticut points out that the Constitution "has ordained that Congress may provide for calling forth the militia *to execute the laws of the Union, suppress insurrections, and repel invasions.*" Since there has been neither insurrection nor invasion, he argues, no such emergency exists. Of course, Governor Smith adds, the militia stands ready to repel any invasion should one take place. Clearly, he believes that will never happen.

Dearborn dawdles. Eustis tries to prod him into returning to his base at Albany to get on with the invasion of Canada, but Eustis is not much of a prodder. "Being possessed of a full view of the intentions of government," he starts out—then adds a phrase scarcely calculated to propel a man of Dearborn's temperament into action; "take your time," he finishes, and Dearborn does just that.

It is an odd coincidence that the Secretary of War and his predecessor, Dearborn, are both medical men, former physicians trained to caution, sceptical of haste, wary of precipitate moves that might cause a patient's death. One of Dearborn's tasks is to create diversions at Kingston and at Niagara to take the pressure off Hull; but when Hull crosses the Detroit River, Dearborn is still in Boston. "I begin to feel that I may be censured for not moving," he remarks in what must be the understatement of the war, but he doubts the wisdom of leaving. To which Eustis responds: "Go to Albany or the Lake. The troops shall come to you as fast as the season will admit, and the blow must be struck. Congress must not meet without a victory to announce to them." Dearborn ponders this for a week before making up his mind, then finally sets off, reaching Greenbush on July 26, where some twelve hundred unorganized troops await him.

His letters to Washington betray his indecision ("I have been in a very unpleasant situation, being at a loss to determine whether or not I ought to leave the seacoast"). He is woefully out of touch with his command, has no idea who runs his commissary and ordnance departments, is not even sure how far his authority extends, although this has been spelled out for him. In a remarkable letter he asks Eustis: "Who is to have command of the operations in Upper Canada? I take it for granted that my command does not extend to that distant quarter." These are the words of a man trying to wriggle out of responsibility, a man for whom the only secure action is no action at all. He has been ordered to keep the British occupied while Hull advances. But he does nothing.

This, then, is the character of the commander who is to receive an offer of truce brought to his headquarters by the personable Lieutenant-Colonel Baynes.

It takes Baynes six days to reach Albany from Montreal. An experienced officer with thirty years' service behind him, he keeps his eyes open, recording, in the pigeon-holes of his mind, troop dispositions, the state of preparedness of soldiers, the morale of the countryside. At Plattsburg he is greeted cordially by the ranking major-general, a fanner named Moore, who gets him a room at the inn. Baynes notes that the militia have no uniforms, the only distinguishing badge being a cockade in their hats, and that they do not appear to have made any progress in the first rudiments of military drill. All the officers at Plattsburg express approval of Baynes's mission and one of them, a Major Clarke, is ordered to accompany him by boat to Burlington near the southern end of Lake Champlain. From this point on Baynes proceeds with more difficulty; the commander at Burlington is not enchanted by the spectacle of an enemy officer coolly looking over his force. But Baynes finally persuades him to let him proceed to Albany, 150 miles to the south.

For Lieutenant-Colonel Baynes the journey is salutary. He fails to see any military preparation but forms a strong opinion of the mood of the people, which he reports to Prevost:

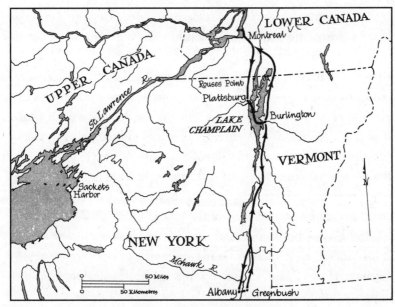

Baynes's Journey to Albany

"My appearance travelling thro' the country in uniform excited very great curiosity and anxiety. The Inns where the coach stopt were instantly crowded with the curious and inquisitive. I did not hear a single individual express a wish but for the speedy accommodation of existing differences and deprecating the war, in several instances these statements were expressed in strong and violent language and on Major Clarke endeavouring to check it, it produced a contrary effect. The universal sentiment of this part of the country appears decidedly adverse to war. I experienced everywhere respect and attention."

On the evening of August 8, Baynes reaches Albany and goes immediately to Dearborn's headquarters at nearby Greenbush. The American commander receives him with great affability, says he personally wants an armistice on honourable terms, and admits that "the burden of command at his time of life was not a desirable charge." Baynes finds him in good health but shrewdly concludes that he "does not appear to possess the energy of mind or activity of body requisite for the important station he fills."

An agreement of sorts is quickly concluded. Dearborn explains that his instructions do not allow him to sign an armistice, but he can issue orders for a temporary cessation of hostilities. The two men agree that should Washington countermand this order, four days' notice will be given before hostilities are resumed. Under this arrangement, the troops will act only on the defensive until a final decision is reached. To Dearborn, the procrastinator, this agreement has the great advantage of allowing him to recruit his forces and build up his supplies without fear of attack. "It is mutually understood that . . . no obstructions are to be attempted, on either side, to the passage of stores, to the frontier posts."

And Hull, who is desperate for both supplies and men? Hull is not included, specifically at Dearborn's request: "I could not include General Hull . . . he having received his orders directly from the department of war."

Thus is concluded a kind of truce, in which both sides are allowed to prepare for battle without actually engaging in one.

These arrangements completed, Lieutenant-Colonel Baynes prepares to take his leave. There is a brief altercation over the use of Indians in the war. Dearborn, in strong language, attacks the British for using native warriors, implying that the Americans are free from reproach in this area. Baynes retorts that Hull's captured dispatches make it clear that he has been doing his best to persuade the Indians to fight for the Americans. That ends the argument. But Baynes has misread Hull's intentions. At Madison's insistence, the Americans use the Indians as scouts only. Hull's efforts have been designed only to keep the Indians neutral.

With great difficulty, Baynes convinces Dearborn to allow him to return to Montreal by a different route along the eastern shores of Lake Champlain; it allows him to size up American strength and assess the mood of the New Englanders.

The little coach clip-clops its way through Vermont's beguiling scenery, rattling down crooked clay roads and over rustic bridges, past stone mills perched above gurgling rivers, through neat, shaded villages hugging the sloping shoreline—a peaceful, pastoral land of farms, wayside inns, and the occasional classical courthouse, as yet untouched by battle. The war seems very far away and, Baynes notes, the people almost totally unprepared. The militia do not impress him.

"The men are independent in their habits and principles, their officers ignorant and totally uninformed in every thing relating to the possession of arms and possess no influence over the militia but in proportion as they court it by popular and familiar intercourse." A few, he notes, are prepared to march on Montreal; the rest just want to go home. More than half of them are absent with or without leave, and nobody seems able to control them.

Recruiting for the regular army, he reports to Prevost, is proceeding very slowly, even though the term of service is only five years and the bounty pay for signing up very liberal:

"There appears to exist in the United States the greatest contempt and repugnance to the restraint and discipline of a military life and few gentlemen of respectability are willing to become officers but prefer the militia where they obtain high rank without serving."

As the coach moves on along the maple-shaded roads, Baynes is subjected to a series of minor astonishments. He learns that one militia general is a farmer, another a sawmill keeper, a third a millwright. The coach pulls up at a tavern. Out comes the innkeeper to take the reins and water the horses. Baynes's sense of military decorum is severely shaken when he discovers that this servitor is a colonel and second-in-command of the entire Vermont militia. The gap between the British and the American attitudes toward their military is obviously wider than Baynes suspected, and he has more than a little trouble absorbing it. He concludes that of all the officers he has observed there is only one with any real military talent—the same commander at Burlington who vigorously opposed his presence in the United States.

As for the American people, they "have a very high and overrated opinion of their military prowess, conceiving it to be in their power to pillage Montreal and to march to Quebec whenever they think proper. The siege of the fortress alone they consider as a task of difficulty. From the actual state of the American forces assembled on

Lake Champlain, I do not think there exists any intention of invading this part of the province."

As Baynes moves back to Canada, Dearborn dispatches a note to Hull, dated August 9, explaining what has happened and suggesting that the General of the Army of the Northwest make his own decision as to whether he should join in the truce. (Hull has just withdrawn from his beachhead at Sandwich, but Dearborn has no knowledge of that.) Reinforcements are, of course, out of the question. "The removal of any troops from Niagara to Detroit, while the present agreement continues, would be improper and incompatible with the true interest of the agreement."

Thus does Dearborn relieve himself of the responsibility of reinforcing Hull or of creating the promised diversion along the Niagara frontier that might prevent Brock from reinforcing Amherstburg. Communications being what they are, Hull cannot know this. And by the time Dearborn's letter reaches him, it will not matter.

———

BROWNSTOWN, MICHIGAN TERRITORY, August 9, 1812. Thomas Verchères de Boucherville, the fur trader and Amherstburg storekeeper, is weary of waiting. On and off for four days he and his comrades have been on the alert on the American side of the river, expecting to surprise another of Hull's armed escorts seeking to bring in the wagon train of supplies held up at the River Raisin. But the Americans do not come and finally Major Muir gives the order to embark for the Canadian shore.

The men are clambering into the boats when from the woods there issues a series of piercing cries. In a few minutes Tecumseh's scouts come bounding out of the thickets to report that a detachment of Long Knives has been spotted upriver "like the mosquitoes of the swamp in number." This is no minor force of the kind that was routed a few days before; Hull has sent six hundred men including two hundred regulars, supported by cavalry and cannon. He is determined that this time the supply train will get through.

Muir puts into action a plan proposed by Tecumseh: his troops will march to a ravine near the Indian village of Maguaga, three miles upriver from Brownstown, and there lie in wait. Their orders are to charge with the bayonet as soon as the first volley of musket balls is fired. The Indians will conceal themselves in the corn fields on the right and the left, securing the flanks.

De Boucherville and his companions, having no uniforms, stick sprigs of basswood into their caps for identification and set out along the muddy track for Maguaga. Soon an odour, sickly sweet, assails their nostrils, and a horrifying spectacle comes into view at the turn of the trail—the battlefield of the previous week. De Boucherville shudders and is seized with revulsion as he sees displayed before him the corpses of the cavalrymen, already decomposed and impaled on stakes by Tecumseh's men, who have left the cadavers in full view to terrify the Americans. Gnawed and mangled by crows and animals, the rotting bodies give off an indescribable stench.

At almost the same moment, James Dalliba, a young American artillery officer in Lieutenant-Colonel Miller's advancing force, sees the bloated and scalped carcass of the luckless ranger captain, McCullough, lying beside the road under its covering of bark.

Marching with the British is an Amherstburg acquaintance of de Boucherville, young John Richardson, a member of the wide-spread Askin family (John, Senior, is his grandfather). Richardson, not yet turned sixteen, is a gentleman volunteer in the 41st and a future novelist—one of Canada's first. He will never forget this silent march to Maguaga; thirty years later it remains vividly in his mind:

"No other sound than the measured step of the troops interrupted the solitude of the scene, rendered more imposing by the wild appearance of the warriors, whose bodies, stained and painted in the most frightful manner for the occasion, glided by us with almost noiseless velocity . . . some painted white, some black, others half black, half red; half black, half white; all with their hair plastered in such a way as to resemble the bristling quills of the porcupine, with no other covering than a cloth around their loins, yet armed to the teeth with rifles, tomahawks, war-clubs, spears, bows, arrows and scalping knives. Uttering no sound, intent only on reaching the enemy unperceived, they might have passed for the spectres of those wilds, the ruthless demons which War had unchained for the punishment and oppression of man."

Screened by the forest, the two forces move blindly towards one another, neither side knowing when or where the clash will take place but all sensing that within minutes men will fall and some will die. Most have had no experience of battle; many have had no military training; save for Miller's Tippecanoe veterans, few have fired a musket at a living human.

At Maguaga, the British and Canadians take up their position behind a low rise, each man hugging the ground as he would a friend. De Boucherville finds himself next to another acquaintance, Jean-Baptiste Bâby, whose family home at Sandwich has been seized by Hull. Nervous, he asks Bâby for a pinch of snuff "to keep me in countenance a little." A moment later comes the sound of an enemy drum, the stroke wavering slightly as if the drummer, too, fears whatever lies ahead.

The British remain concealed, waiting for the signal. Suddenly an American officer, brilliant in blue and gold, riding a superb horse, his hat covered by a three-foot plume, appears on an eminence. A shot rings out; the American falls dead at his horse's feet, and the battle is joined.

Confusion! A melee of painted bodies, scarlet tunics, snorting horses, flying tomahawks, splintered foliage, black musket smoke. On the left, Tecumseh leads his men forward in an attempt to turn the American flank. Five hundred yards to the right, another group of Indians, trying a similar manoeuvre, is forced back. To the British volunteers all Indians look alike; they believe the retreating natives to be part of the advancing enemy and fire on them. Ally battles ally as the skirmish grows hotter.

"Take care, de Boucherville!" cries an officer on the left. "The Kentuckians are aiming at you." Even as he speaks a ball strikes him in the head, and he falls into de Boucherville's arms. "Well, old fellow," thinks the volunteer to himself, "you came out of that all right." But a moment later he is hit in the thigh by a musket ball.

Muir, the British commander, seeing an American taking deliberate aim at him, hastily raises his short rifle and lays it across the shoulders of a fellow officer, Lieutenant Charles Sutherland. Both adversaries fire at the same time. The American drops dead; his rifle balll enters Sutherland's cheek, comes out the back of his neck and passes through Muir's shoulder. (Sutherland's wound is not mortal, but he will shortly die of loss of blood as a result of brushing his teeth before it is properly healed.)

Now occurs one of those maddening misunderstandings that frustrate the best-laid plans. Brock's reinforcements from the Niagara frontier, hustled across the river by Procter, arrive on the scene, sixty strong, just as Muir's bugler, by pre-arrangement, sounds the bayonet charge.

The new troops, confused, take this as a signal to retreat, and the British centre begins to break. Muir receives a second wound in the leg but carries on.

By now the American six-pounder is in action spraying grape-shot, its initial discharge so terrifying Lieutenant-Colonel Miller's horse that it throws the American commander to the ground. Tecumseh's warriors rush forward to take his scalp but are forced back. Miller remounts, cries for a cavalry charge. But the cavalry fails to respond, and the main advance is made by foot soldiers. The smoke is now so dense that no one can see for more than twenty paces.

Tecumseh is making a strategic withdrawal toward the west, drawing the American fire away from the retiring British and forcing Miller to divide his forces. The manoeuvre slows down the American advance, allows the British to reach the boats they have concealed on the beach and make their escape out of range of the American muskets.

Miller draws his men up in line and utters the obligatory words of commendation:

"My brave fellows! You have done well! Every man has done his duty. I give you my hearty thanks for your conduct this day; you have gained my highest esteem; you have gained fresh honor to yourselves and to the American Arms; your fellow soldiers will love you and your country will reward you. . . ."

With this accolade ringing in their ears, the Americans move through the woods, seeking the dead and the wounded. Hidden in a cedar swamp under a gigantic deadfall lie three men—Thomas Verchères de Boucherville, his friend Jean-Baptiste Berthe (another member of the Askin family and a civilian volunteer), and a regular soldier. Caught in the crossfire between the British rear and the advancing Americans, they have run into the woods to escape the shower of musket balls. It is now four in the afternoon, but they cannot leave their soggy retreat for the enemy is only a few feet away. Finally, at ten, under cover of a violent thunderstorm, they crawl out of the water onto a drier knoll, guided by lightning flashes, and here they crouch, soaked through, for the rest of the night, while the rain beats down on them and a violent gale, wrenching the branches from the trees, puts them in as much danger as the battle itself.

De Boucherville's wound is bleeding but painless. He cakes earth over it as he has seen the Indians do, binding it with a towel brought along for just such a misfortune, and considers his plight. Only a few days before he was at dinner with some guests when he heard a drummer parading the streets of Amherstburg, beating the call to arms. With his friend Berthe and several others he answered the summons for volunteers, not pausing to finish his meal but taking care to bury all his money, secretly, in his backyard. Now here he is, wounded, wet, and miserable, waiting for the dawn.

At first light, he and his two companions set out for the river, watching all the time for the enemy. They reach it at four o'clock, gather some planks and strands of basswood from a deserted Indian village, construct a crude raft, and cross to an island in midstream. Here they do their utmost to attract attention, wiping their muskets dry and firing them off, making flags of their shirts and waving them on long poles. Eventually a boat rescues them. On the dockside are friends, officers, natives, civilians, all cheering. They had given de Boucherville and Berthe up for dead.

De Boucherville stumbles home, flops onto a sofa, falls into a dead sleep. When he wakes he is astonished to find an Indian by his bedside. It is Tecumseh himself, who has been sitting silently for hours waiting for him to wake.

A surgeon removes the ball from de Boucherville's thigh but cannot extract a quantity of shot. Tecumseh fetches a Shawnee healer, who prescribes a herbal remedy. In ten days the wound is healed, de Boucherville is back behind the counter of his store, and the Battle of Maguaga is a memory to be savoured in the retelling for the remainder of his days.

Hull, in his message to Washington, treats the battle as a stunning victory. It is scarcely that, for it has failed in its purpose of opening his line of supply. Captain Brush's wagon train still cannot get through, and Lieutenant-Colonel Miller, even in victory, cannot help. In the heat of the battle his troops have thrown away their knapsacks and are without rations, forced to lie all night in the open in the same driving thunderstorm that poured down on de Boucherville. Miller himself is tottering with fatigue, ague, and two wounds; he has been on and off the sick list for weeks. He sends to Hull for reinforcements and provisions in order to move on. Colonel McArthur arrives with a fleet of bateaux bringing two barrels of flour, one of pork, and considerable whiskey, all of which the troops devour in a single breakfast. The wounded are loaded into bateaux for the return voyage. But the British, who have control of the river, seize twelve boats, capture some fifty Americans, and recapture two of their own men held as prisoners.

At sunset an express arrives from Hull: because he cannot spare further reinforcements, Miller and his men are ordered to return to Detroit without completing their mission. They make their way to the river in the driving rain, soaking wet, shoeless, sleeping that night as best they can in dripping blankets. They reach Detroit at noon on August 11. Brush and the supply train remain pinned down at the River Raisin.

Miller has lost eighteen men killed and some sixty wounded. The British casualties are fewer: six killed, twenty-one wounded. But

Hull writes to Eustis that "the victory was complete in every part of the line," and that is the way the history books will record it.

———

ISAAC BROCK HAS NO time for democratic chatter. He prorogues the legislature on August 5 and, with the consent of his appointed council, declares martial law. He has decided on a mighty gamble: he will gather what troops he can, speed post-haste to Amherstburg at their head, and, if that fort has not fallen, provoke Hull into a fight, then try to get back to the Niagara frontier before the Americans attack. He is taking a long chance, but he has little choice. Off he goes, moving swiftly southwest through the province, calling for volunteers to accompany him to Amherstburg. Five hundred rush to apply, "principally the sons of Veterans, whom His Majesty's munificence settled in this country." He can take only half that number. The York Volunteers will become Brock's favourite militia unit, including among its officers such names as Ridout, Jarvis, and Robinson, all of them scions of the tight Upper Canada aristocracy, trained at the Reverend John Strachan's famous school at Cornwall. The war will entrench them in the Family Compact.

Brock reaches Port Dover on the north shore of Lake Erie on August 8, where he hopes enough boats have been commandeered to move his entire force to Amherstburg. The British have the immense advantage of being able to move troops swiftly by water in contrast to the Americans' slow drive through the wilderness. But at Dover, Brock finds that not nearly enough boats have been provided, while those available are leaky, uncaulked, dilapidated. A day is required to make ten of them ready, and these are in such bad shape that the men grow exhausted from constant bailing.

The flotilla can move no faster than the slowest vessel, the hundred-ton schooner *Nancy*, which must be manhandled over the narrow neck of the Long Point peninsula—a backbreaking task that requires the energy of all the boat crews—and later dragged by ropes onto the beach at Port Talbot. Here the troops take refuge from the same thunderstorm that is drenching the Americans after the battle of Maguaga.

All that day the men, joined by sixty volunteers from the village of Queenston on the Niagara, lie in the boats or on the sand as the rain pelts down.

Yet they remain in good spirits. Brock notes it: "In no instance have I witnessed greater cheerfulness and constancy than were displayed by these Troops under the fatigue of a long journey in Boats and during extremely bad Weather . . . their conduct throughout excited my admiration."

The admiration is mutual. At one point Brock's own boat strikes a sunken rock. His boat crew goes to work with oars and poles. When they fail to push her free, the General, in full uniform, leaps over the side, waist deep in water. In an instant the others follow and soon have the boat afloat. Brock climbs aboard, opens his liquor case, gives every man a glass of spirits. The news of this act, spreading from boat to boat, animates the force.

On August 11, the weather again turns capricious. The wind drops. The men, wet and exhausted from lack of sleep, are forced to row in relays for hours. Then a sudden squall forces the flotilla once more in to shore. That night the weather clears, and the impatient general makes another attempt to get underway, this time in the

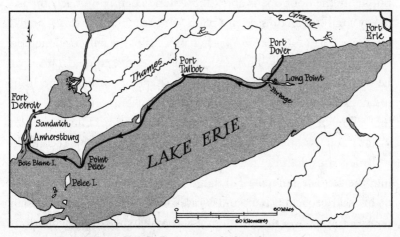

Brock's Passage to Amherstburg

dark, his boat leading with a lantern in the stern. They sail all night, the boats too crowded for the men to lie down. The following day they hear that Hull has re-crossed the river to Detroit and that there has been a skirmish (Maguaga) on the American side. At Point Pelee that afternoon, some of the men boil their pork; others drop exhausted onto the beach. Early next morning they set off again and at eight in the forenoon straggle into Amherstburg, exhausted from rowing, their faces peeling from sunburn.

Brock has preceded them. Unable to rest, the General and a vanguard of troops have departed the previous afternoon and reached their objective shortly before midnight on August 13. Lieutenant-Colonel Procter and Matthew Elliott are waiting on the quayside. Across the water from Bois Blanc Island comes the rattle of musketry. It startles Brock. When Elliott explains that the Indians, bivouacked on the island, are expressing their joy at the arrival of reinforcements, the General expresses concern over the waste of ammunition: "Do, pray, Elliott, fully explain my wishes and motives, and tell the Indians that I will speak to them to-morrow on this subject."

Midnight has passed. But before Brock can sleep he must read the dispatches and mail captured at Brownstown. He sits in Elliott's study with his aide, Major J.B. Glegg, the yellow light from tallow candles flickering across a desk strewn with maps and papers. Suddenly the door opens and Elliott stands before him accompanied by a tall Indian dressed in a plain suit of tanned deerskin, fringed at the seams, and wearing leather moccasins heavily ornamented with porcupine quills. This is clearly a leader of stature. In his nose he wears three silver ornaments in the shape of coronets, and from his neck is hung, on a string of coloured wampum, a large silver medallion of George III. The Indian is beaming. Glegg gets an instant impression of energy and decision. This must be Tecumseh.

Brock rises, hand outstretched to his ally. The contrast is striking: the British general—fair, large-limbed, blue-eyed, impeccable in his scarlet jacket, blue-and-white riding trousers, and Hessian boots—towers over the lithe figure of the Shawnee. Brief salutations follow. Brock explains about the waste of ammunition. Tecumseh agrees. Each man has taken the other's measure and both are impressed. Brock will write to Lord Liverpool that "a more sagacious and gallant Warrior does not I believe exist. He was the admiration of every one who conversed with him. . . ." Tecumseh's comment, delivered to his followers, is blunter. "This," says Tecumseh, "is a *man!*"

Brock calls a council of his officers, asks for a military appreciation. Tecumseh urges an immediate attack on Detroit, unrolls a strip of elm bark, pulls his scalping knife from his belt, and proceeds to scratch out an accurate map of the fort and its surroundings.

Brock points out that the British and Indians will be outnumbered by the Americans: "We are committed to a war in which the enemy will always surpass us in numbers, equipment and resources." One by one his officers are polled. One by one they opt for caution: a crossing is too dangerous to attempt. Lieutenant-Colonel Henry Procter, who will one day clash with Tecumseh over tactics, is particularly cautious. Only one man, Colonel Robert Nichol, the diminutive ex-storekeeper who has just been named quartermaster general of the militia, supports Brock. Nichol has lived in Detroit, knows every cranny of town and fort, boasts that he can lead the troops to any point that Brock wants to attack. He and the commander are old friends, their acquaintance going back to 1804 when Brock commanded at Fort Erie and Nichol ran a general store. Nichol's sudden appointment to field rank has offended some of the political higher-ups, but Brock knows his man. It is said that Nichol would follow his general into Vesuvius if need be.

At this midnight council the contrast between Brock and Hull is starkly clear. Brock listens carefully to his subordinates' reservations, then speaks: nothing, he says, can be gained by delay. "I have decided on crossing, and now, gentlemen, instead of any further advice, I entreat of you to give me your cordial and hearty support."

The following morning, standing beneath a great oak on the outskirts of the fort, he addresses several hundred Indians representing more than a dozen tribes on both sides of the border. (Even the recalcitrant Iroquois are here, though only thirty in number.) He has come, says Brock, to battle the Long Knives who have invaded the country of the King, their father. The Long Knives are trying to force both the British and the Indians from their lands. If the Indians will make common cause with the British, the combined forces will soon drive the enemy back to the boundaries of Indian territory.

Tecumseh rises to reply. This polyglot assembly is of his making—the closest he will ever get to achieving the confederacy of which he dreams. The hazel eyes flash, the oval face darkens as he conjures up the memory of Tippecanoe:

"They suddenly came against us with a great force while I was absent, and destroyed our village and slew our warriors."

All the bitterness against the land-hunger of the frontier settlers is revived:

"They came to us hungry and cut off the hands of our brothers who gave them corn. We gave them rivers of fish and they poisoned our fountains. We gave them forest-clad mountains and valleys full of game and in return what did they give our warriors and our women? Rum and trinkets and a grave!"

Brock does not intend to reveal the details of his attack plan to such a large assembly. The oratory finished, he invites Tecumseh and a few older chiefs to meet at Elliott's house. Here, through interpreters, he explains his strategy as the chiefs nod approval. The General is concerned, however, about alcohol: can Tecumseh prevent his followers from drinking to excess? The Shawnee replies that before his people left the Wabash they promised to abstain from all spirits until they had humbled the Long Knives. Brock responds with satisfaction: "If this resolution be persevered in, you must conquer."

He has one further act of diplomacy before he leaves for Sandwich. He issues a general order intended to heal the wounds caused by Hull's divisive proclamation:

"The major-general cannot avoid expressing his surprise at the numerous desertions which have occurred from the ranks of the militia, to which circumstance the long stay of the enemy on this side of the river must in great measure be ascribed. He is willing to believe that their conduct proceeded from an anxiety to get in their harvest, and not from any predilection for the principles or government of the United States."

This pretty fiction serves its purpose of uniting the people behind him. Hull has deserted them: Brock, by implication, has promised an amnesty. As he rides that same afternoon past the ripening apple trees to Sandwich he knows he is passing through friendly country.

———

DETROIT, MICHIGAN TERRITORY, AUGUST 12, 1812. Colonel Lewis Cass is seething with frustration over what he conceives to be the inadequacies and follies of his commander. He can contain himself no longer and finds a temporary outlet for his anger in a letter to his brother-in-law:

"Our situation is become critical. If things get worse, you will have a letter from me giving you a particular statement of this business. As bad as you may think of our situation it is still worse than you believe. I cannot descend into particulars for fear this should fall into the hands of the enemy."

From the outset he has thought of Hull as a weak old man. Now other, more sinister epithets begin to form in his mind. Cass is contemplating something very close to treason, a word he will shortly apply to his commanding officer.

His style is as blunt as his body. He has powerful arms and legs and a trunk like an ox. Nobody would call him handsome. Long, unruly hair dominates a coarse face. A later official portrait shows him scowling blackly at the artist, one hand thrust into his tunic, Napoleon-fashion. At thirty, he has the resonant voice of a frontier lawyer, toughened on the court circuit, his endurance tested by years spent on horseback on old Indian trails or on pitching flatboats in wilderness rivers, arguing and pleading in primitive courthouses where the judge, on occasion, has been known to descend from the bench to wrestle a pugnacious spectator into submission.

He is an ambitious man, Cass. He has been a member of the Ohio House, a state marshal, a brigadier-general in the militia. He loves the military life, likes to wear splendid uniforms (his officer's plume is the highest of any), insists on parading his men whenever the opportunity allows, believes in regular, arduous drilling. For all that he is popular, for his is the easy camaraderie of the circuit court. He mixes freely with his men, who respect him in spite of a certain humourlessness. Unlike Hull, Cass conveys an air of absolute conviction; he *knows* he is right; and the fact that Hull, in Cass's view, is wrong drives him to distraction. In spite of his ponderous appearance he has all the nervous energy of a tomcat—not the kind of man to sit quietly by and watch the enemy preparing for an assault.

Cass's disillusionment with Hull is shared by his fellow officers and has filtered down through the ranks. On this same day (the very day on which Wellington's forces enter Madrid), the scout Robert Lucas is writing to a friend in Portsmouth, Ohio, in much the same vein:

"Never was there a more Patriotic army . . . neither was there ever an army that had it more completely in their power to have accomplished every object of their Desire than the Present, And must now be sunk into Disgrace for want of a General at their head—

"Never was there officers . . . more united than our Patriotic Colonels . . . to promote the Public good neither was there ever men of talents as they are so shamefully opposed by an imbesile or Treacherous Commander as they have been. . . . Would to God Either of our Colonels had the command, if they had, we might yet wipe off the foul stain that has been brought upon us. . . ."

The army is close to mutiny. A round robin is circulating among the troops urging that Hull be replaced by McArthur. Cass, Findlay, and McArthur meet with Miller and offer to depose Hull if he will take command. Miller refuses but agrees to unite with the others to oppose Hull and give the command to McArthur. McArthur, who has already said privately that Hull will not do, also refuses—nobody wants to bell the cat. All three turn to Cass, who agrees to write secretly to Governor Meigs of Ohio, urging him to march at once with two thousand men. The assumption is that Meigs will depose Hull.

"From causes not fit to be put on paper but which I trust I shall live to communicate to you, this army has been reduced to a critical and alarming situation," Cass writes. When he finishes the letter, he, McArthur, Gaylor (the Quartermaster General), and Elijah Brush of the Michigan state militia all affix their signatures to a cryptic postscript:

"Since the other side of this letter was written, new circumstances have arisen. The British force is opposite, and our situation has nearly reached its crisis. Believe all the bearer will tell you. Believe it, however it may astonish you; as much as if told by one of us. Even a c———is talked of by the———! The bearer will supply the vacancy. On you we depend."

The missing words are "capitulation" and "commanding officer." The signature of Lieutenant-Colonel Miller, the career officer, is conspicuously absent.

Hull by this time knows of the incipient plot against him but hesitates to arrest the ringleaders, fearing perhaps a general uprising. He has, however, the perfect excuse for ridding himself temporarily of the leading malcontents. Captain Henry Brush, still pinned down at the River Raisin, has discovered a back-door route to Detroit; it is twice as long as the river road but hidden from Fort Amherstburg. When he asks again for an escort for his supply train, Hull is only too pleased to dispatch both Cass and McArthur with 350 men for this task. They leave Detroit at noon on August 14.

The General has, of course, weakened his own garrison in spite of strong evidence that the British, now directly across the river at Sandwich, are planning an attack. What is in Hull's mind? Has he already given up? He has in his possession a letter, intercepted from a British courier, written by Lieutenant-Colonel Procter to Captain Roberts at Michilimackinac, informing him that the British force facing Detroit is so strong that he need send no more than five thousand Indians to support it!

It is a sobering revelation. Brock and Tecumseh face Hull across the river; now at his rear he sees another horde of painted savages.

He cannot know that the letter is a fake, purposely planted by Brock and Procter, who already have an insight into his troubled state of mind through captured documents. There are only a few hundred Indians at Mackinac, and on August 12 they are in no condition to go anywhere, being "as drunk as Ten Thousand Devils" in the words of John Askin, Jr. But Brock well knows that the threat of the Indians is as valuable as their presence and a good deal less expensive.

Many months later, when his peers sit in judgement upon him, Hull will swear to his firm belief that the British had no intention of attacking Detroit. He believes their conduct of the war will be entirely defensive. He has put himself in Prevost's shoes but certainly not in those of Isaac Brock who, contrary to all instructions, is preparing to invade the United States.

Brock is completing the secret construction of a battery directly across from Detroit—one long eighteen-pound gun, two long twelve-pounders, and a couple of mortars—hidden for the moment behind a building and a screen of oak. Lieutenant James Dalliba of Hull's ordnance department suspects what is going on. Dalliba, who has twenty-eight heavy guns and has constructed his own battery in the centre of town, asks Hull if he may open fire.

"Sir, if you will give permission, I will clear the enemy on the opposite shore from the lower batteries."

Dalliba will not soon forget Hull's reply:

"Mr. Dalliba, I will make an agreement with the enemy that if they will never fire on me I will never fire on them," and rides off, remarking that "those who live in glass houses must take care how they throw stones."

The following morning, to the army's astonishment, Hull has a large marquee, striped red and blue, pitched in the centre of camp, just south of the walls of the fort. It is a measure of the army's low morale and lack of confidence in their general that many believe Hull is in league with the British and that the coloured tent is intended as a signal.

In a barrack room, a court of inquiry under the ailing Lieutenant-Colonel Miller is investigating Porter Hanks's surrender of Mackinac. Hanks has asked for a hearing to clear his name. But part way through the testimony an officer looking out onto the river spies

174
—
PIERRE
BERTON'S
WAR OF
1812

a boat crossing from the opposite shore under a white flag. Miller adjourns the hearing. It will never be reopened.

Up the bank come Brock's two aides, Major J.B. Glegg and Lieutenant-Colonel John Macdonell, with a message for Hull. They are blindfolded and confined to a house in the town near the fort while Hull ponders Brock's ultimatum:

"The force at my disposal authorizes me to require of you the immediate surrender of Fort Detroit. . . ."

The force at his disposal! Brock has at most thirteen hundred men; Hull has more than two thousand. Brock is proposing to attack a fortified position with an inferior force, an adventure that Hull, in declining Amherstburg, has said would require odds of two to one.

But Brock has studied his man, knows his vulnerable spot:

"It is far from my intention to join in a war of extermination; but you must be aware that the numerous body of Indians who have attached themselves to my troops will be beyond my control the moment the contest commences. . . . Lieutenant-Colonel M'Donnell and major Glegg are fully authorised to conclude any arrangement that may lead to prevent the unnecessary effusion of blood."

What Brock is threatening is a war of extermination—a bloody battle in which, if necessary, he is quite prepared to accept the slaughter of prisoners and of innocent civilians, including women and children. He is, in short, contemplating total war more than a century before the phrase comes into common use. The war is starting to escalate as all wars must; a zeal for victory clouds compassion; the end begins to justify the means.

Like other commanders, Brock salves his conscience with the excuse that he cannot control his native allies; nonetheless he is quite happy, in fact eager, to use them. It is sophistry to say they have "attached themselves" to his troops; he and his colleagues have actively and consistently enlisted their support. The Americans are equally hypocritical; they pompously upbraid the British for waging uncivilized warfare, but their own men take scalps indiscriminately. The conflict, which began so softly and civilly, is beginning to brutalize both sides. The same men who censure the Indians for dismembering non-combatants with tomahawks are quite prepared to blow the limbs off soldiers and civilians alike with twenty-four-pound cannonballs. Though it may offer some comfort to the attacker, the range of the weapon makes little difference to its victim.

Hull mulls over Brock's extraordinary document for more than three hours while the General's two aides fidget behind their blindfolds. At last he summons up an answer:

"... I have no other reply than to inform you, that I am prepared to meet any force which may be at your disposal, and any consequences which may result from any exertion of it you may think proper to make."

At about three that afternoon, Major Josiah Snelling of Miller's 4th Infantry steps out onto the street to see the General's son and aide, Captain Abraham Hull, heading off with his father's reply in his pocket. The little village is alive with people running toward the fort carrying their family possessions or burying their valuables. Snelling picks up his glass and sees that the British across the river are chopping down the oaks and removing the building that masks their battery. He forms up his men, marches them through the gates of the fort, and, on Hull's orders, mans the ramparts.

Hull's back seems to have stiffened.

"The British have demanded the place," he says. "If they want it they must fight for it."

He sends a messenger to recall the party under Cass and McArthur, who have become entangled in a swamp some twenty-five miles away. The troops in Detroit, knowing their force to be superior, are astonished at what they consider the insolence of the British.

The boat carrying Brock's aides has no sooner reached the Canadian shore than the cannonade commences. Hundreds of pounds of cast iron hurtle across the mile-wide river, tearing into walls and trees and plunging through rooftops but doing little damage. James Dalliba with his battery of seven twenty-four-pounders replies immediately to the first British volley. He stands on the ramparts until he sees the smoke and flash of the British cannon, then shouts "Down!" allowing his men to drop behind the parapet before the shot strikes.

The British are aiming directly at his battery, attempting to put it out of action.

A large pear tree near Dalliba's battery is blocking the guns and giving the British a point to aim at. Dalliba orders a young Michigan volunteer, John Miller, to cut it down. As he is hacking away, a cannonball finishes the job for him. Miller turns and shouts across the water: "Send us another, John Bull; you can cut faster than I can!"

The artillery duel continues until well after dark. The people scramble after every burst, ducking behind doors, clinging to walls, until they become used to the flash and roar. In the doorway of a house by the river a *Canadien* stands unconcerned, puffing on his pipe, as the hot metal screams by him until a shell fragment tears the stem from his mouth. Infuriated, he seizes his musket, wades out into the river, and fires back at the British battery until his ammunition is exhausted.

A mortar shell, its fuse burning brightly, falls upon the house of Augustus Langdon on Woodward Avenue. It tears its way through the roof, continues through the upper storey and into the dining room, dropping directly upon the table around which Langdon and his family are sitting. It rips through the table, continues through the floor and into the cellar as the family dashes for safety. They are no sooner clear than the shell explodes with such power that it tears the roof away.

Hull's brigade major, Thomas Jesup, reports that two British warships are anchored in midstream just opposite Spring Wells, two miles from the fort, and that the British appear to be collecting boats for an invasion. At sundown, Hull sends Major Snelling to Spring Wells to report on the British movements. Snelling reports that the *Queen Charlotte* is anchored in the river but can be dislodged by one of the fort's twenty-four-pounders. Hull shakes his head, finds reasons why the gun can't be moved. Something odd is happening to the commander. To Jesup he seems pale and very much confused.

At ten that evening the cannonade ceases. Quiet descends upon the American camp. The night is clear, the sky tinselled with stars, the river glittering in the moonlight. At eleven, General Hull, fully clothed, his boots still laced, slumps down in the piazza of the barracks and tries to sleep. Even as he slumbers, Tecumseh and his Indians are slipping into their canoes and silently crossing to the American side.

SANDWICH, UPPER CANADA, AUGUST 16, 1812. Dawn.

The moment is at hand. Brock's couriers have scoured the countryside, roused the militia from the farms, emptied the mills and harvest fields. Now these raw troops gather on the shore at McKee's Point, four hundred strong, waiting their turn to enter the boats and cross to the enemy side. Three hundred have been issued the cast-off crimson tunics of the 41st to deceive Hull into believing that Brock's force of regular soldiers is double its actual strength.

The Indians are already across, lurking in the forest, ready to attack Hull's flank and rear should he resist the crossing. Thomas Verchères de Boucherville has watched their war dance the night before; he finds it an extraordinary spectacle—six hundred figures, leaping in the firelight, naked except for their breech cloths, some daubed in vermilion, others in blue clay, and still others tattooed with black and white from head to foot. Even to de Boucherville, with his years of experience in the fur trade, the scene is macabre— frightful and horrifying beyond expression. It occurs to him that a stranger from Europe witnessing it for the first time would believe he was standing at the very entrance to Hell "with the gates thrown open to let the damned out for an hour's recreation on earth!"

But on this calm and beautiful Sunday morning, a different spectacle presents itself. A soft August sun is just rising as the troops climb into the boats and push out into the river, their crimson jackets almost perfectly reflected in the glassy waters. Behind them, the green meadows and ripening orchards are tinted with the dawn light; ahead, in the lead boat, stands the glittering figure of their general. Charles Askin thinks it the handsomest sight he has ever

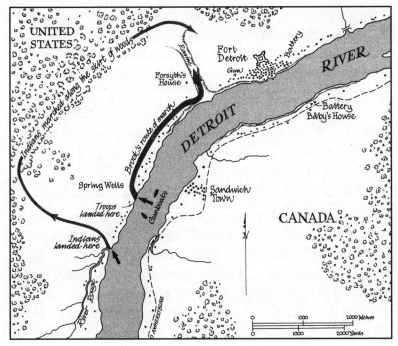

The Capture of Detroit

seen, even though in a few hours he may well be fighting his own brother-in-law. Already cannonballs and mortar bombs are screaming overhead.

On the far bank, pocked and riven by springs (hence the name Spring Wells), the figure of Tecumseh can be discerned, astride a white mustang, surrounded by his chiefs. The enemy is not in sight and the troops land without incident or opposition.

Brock's plan is to outwait Hull, draw him out of his fort, and do battle in the open where, he believes, his regulars can devastate the wavering American militia. But now an Indian scout rides in with word that enemy horsemen have been spotted three miles to the rear. This is the detachment, 350 strong, that Hull has sent to the River Raisin and recalled to reinforce Detroit. Brock's position suddenly becomes precarious. His men are caught between a strong fortification and an advancing column in their rear. Without hesitation Brock changes his plans and decides to attack immediately.

He draws up his troops in column, doubling the distance between the sections to make his diminutive force seem larger. His route to Detroit hugs the river bank at his right, protected by the guns of the *Queen Charlotte* and the *Hunter* (Frederic Rolette's command) and by the battery at Sandwich. On his left, slipping through the corn fields and the woods, are Tecumseh's Indians. To many of the militia this is familiar territory. Charles Askin, marching with the 2nd Brigade, greets and waves to old friends along the road, many of whom seem happy to see him.

At the town gate, the forward troops can spot two long guns—twenty-four-pounders—positioned so that they can enfilade the road. A single round shot, properly placed, is capable of knocking down a file of twenty-five men like dominoes. American gunners stand beside their weapons with matches burning. William McCay, who has come up from Queenston as a volunteer and is marching with Captain Hatt's company just behind the British 41st, screws up his courage, expecting to be fired upon at any moment. Young John Richardson, the future novelist, cannot help a sinking feeling in the pit of his stomach that he and his comrades are marching directly into the jaws of death, for the road "is as bad as any cul-de-sac."

Brock, at the head of the line, rides impassively forward, a brilliant target in his cocked hat and gold epaulettes. His old friend, little Colonel Nichol, trots up to remonstrate with his commander:

"Pardon me, General, but I cannot forbear entreating you not to expose yourself thus. If we lose you, we lose all; let me pray you to allow the troops to pass on, led by their own officers."

To which Brock replies: "Master Nichol, I duly appreciate the advice you give me, but I feel that in addition to their sense of loyalty and duty, many here follow me from a feeling of personal regard, and I will never ask them to go where I do not lead them."

Why have the guns not fired? There is a host of explanations after the fact. One is that Hull refuses to give the order for reasons of cowardice or treason. Another, more plausible, is that the British are still out of effective range and the American artillery commander is waiting until they draw closer so that his grape-shot—a large number of musket balls packed in canvas bags—can mow down the column.

If so, Brock outwits him, for suddenly, the British wheel to the left through an orchard and into a ravine protected from the enemy guns. John Richardson, for one, breathes more freely. Brock, meanwhile, commandeers William Forsyth's farmhouse as a headquarters, then climbs up the bank to reconnoitre his position.

The town of Detroit, a huddle of some three hundred houses, lies before him. Its population, three-quarters French-speaking, is inured to siege and plunder. It has been transferred three times by treaty, twice besieged by Indians, burned to the ground only a few years previously. It is enclosed on three sides by a wooden stockade of fourteen-foot pickets. Entrance can be gained only by three massive gates. On the high ground to the northeast, covering three acres, sprawls the fort, built originally by the British, repaired by the Americans. The parapet is eleven feet high, twelve feet thick. A ditch, six feet deep and twelve feet across, together with a double row of pickets, each twice the height of a man, surrounds the whole. It is heavily armed with long guns, howitzers, and mortars. Most of the troops are quartered outside the walls.

The American position seems impregnable, but Brock has a secret weapon—psychology. Hull has already been led to believe that three hundred militiamen are regulars. Now Tecumseh and his Indians are ordered to march in single file across an open space, out of range but in full view of the garrison. The spectacle has some of the quality of a vaudeville turn. The Indians lope across the meadow, vanish into the forest, circle back and repeat the manoeuvre three times. Hull's officers, who cannot tell one Indian from another, count fifteen hundred painted savages, screeching and waving tomahawks. Hull is convinced he is outnumbered.

Brock is still scrutinizing his objective, all alone, some fifty yards in front of his own troops, when an American officer suddenly appears, waving a white flag and bearing a note from his general. The American commander, it seems, is on the verge of giving up without a fight.

INSIDE THE PALISADE, William Hull appears on the edge of nervous collapse. Except for Colonel Findlay, he has no battalion commanders to fall back on. Cass and McArthur have not yet returned. Miller is too ill to stand up. Hull's son and aide, Abraham, is not only drunk but has picked a fight with a senior officer, in his father's presence, and challenged him to a duel. A dozen Michigan volunteers on picket duty at the rear of the fort have allowed themselves to be captured by Tecumseh's Indians. Elijah Brush, in charge of the Michigan militia, believes that if attack comes his men will flee. The fort itself is so jammed with soldiers, civilians, and cattle, all seeking refuge from the bombardment, that it is difficult to manoeuvre.

The cannonade has unnerved Hull. He saw blood enough in his Revolutionary days, but now he is transfixed by a spectacle so horrifying that it reduces him to jelly. Lieutenant Porter Hanks, relieved for the moment of appearing at his court of inquiry, has come into the fort to visit an old friend and is standing in the doorway of the officers' mess with several others when a sixteen-pound cannonball comes bouncing over the parapet and skipping across the open space. It strikes Hanks in the midriff, cutting him in two, then tears both legs off Cass's surgeon's mate, Dr. James Reynolds, instantly killing him and mangling a second man with the appropriately grisly name of Blood.

A second cannonball dispatches two more soldiers. Blood and brains spatter the walls and the gowns of some women who have sought refuge nearby. One drops senseless to the ground; others begin to scream. Hull cannot be sure from a distance who is dead, but a frightful thought crosses his mind: can it be his own buxom daughter, Betsey? It is more than possible. She and her child have taken refuge in the fort with most of the civilians, all of whom Hull knows as well as his own family.

Something very odd is happening to Hull: he is becoming catatonic; his brain, overloaded by too much information, refuses to function. It has happened before to better commanders when events crowded in too quickly, to Washington at the Battle of Brandywine, for one, and it will happen again—to Napoleon at Waterloo, to Stonewall Jackson at White Oak Swamp, to Douglas MacArthur at Manila.

Hull's brigade major, Jesup, finds his commander half-seated, half-crouched on an old tent that is lying on the ground, his back to the ramparts under the curtain of the fort that faces the enemy. Save for the movement of his jaws he seems comatose. He is chewing tobacco at a furious rate, filling his mouth with it, absently adding quid after quid, sometimes removing a piece, rolling it between his fingers and then replacing it, so that his hands run with spittle while the brown juice dribbles from the corners of his mouth, staining his neckcloth, his beard, his cravat, his vest. He chews as if the fate of the army depended upon the movement of his jaws, rubbing the lower half of his face from time to time until it, too, is stained dark brown. Jesup, who has reconnoitred the British position, asks for permission to move up some artillery and attack their flank with dragoons. Hull nods, but he is clearly not in control. All he can say, as much to himself as to Jesup, is that a cannonball has killed four men.

It is the future as much as the present that renders him numb. A procession of ghastly possibilities crowds his mind; his troops deserting pell-mell to the enemy; the women and children starving through a long siege; cannon fire dismembering more innocent bystanders; and finally—the ultimate horror—the Indians released by Brock and Tecumseh, bent on revenge for Tippecanoe and all that came before it, ravaging, raping, burning, killing. He sees his daughter scalped, his grandchild mutilated, his friends and neighbours butchered. He believes himself outnumbered and outmanoeuvred, his plea for reinforcements unheeded. Sooner or later, he is convinced, defeat is inevitable. If he postpones it, the blood of innocent people will be on his hands. If he accepts it now, before the battle is joined, he can save hundreds of lives. He can, of course, fight on to the last man and go into the history books as a hero. But can he live with himself, however briefly, if he takes the hero's course?

There is another thought, too, a guilty thought, lurking like a vagrant in the darker recesses of that agitated mind. The memory of the notorious proclamation has returned to haunt him. He himself has threatened no quarter to any of the enemy who fight beside the Indians. Can he or his charges, then, expect mercy in a prolonged struggle? Might the enemy not use his own words to justify their allies' revenge?

The shells continue to scream above his head and explode. Six men are now dead, several more wounded, the fort in a turmoil. Hull determines to ask for a cease-fire and a parley with Brock, scrawls a note, hands it to his son, asks him to have Major Snelling take it across the river. (Incredibly, it does not occur to him that Brock may be with his troops outside the palisade.) At the same time he orders a white tablecloth hung out of a window where Dixon, the British artillery commander on the Canadian shore, can see it. He will not fight to the last man; in the future metropolis of Detroit there will be no Hull Boulevard, no Avenue of the Martyrs.

Abraham Hull ties a handkerchief to a pike and gives it to Snelling, who declares he'll be damned if he'll disgrace his country by taking it out of the fort. Young Hull takes it himself and crosses the river, only to discover that Brock is on the American side. When he returns, Snelling is persuaded to seek out the British general.

Outside the fort, Jesup, seeking to take command of the dragoons to meet Brock's expected attack, finds the whole line breaking up, the men marching back toward the fort by platoons. Baffled, he asks what on earth is going on. An officer riding by tells him: "Look to the fort!" Jesup for the first time sees the white flag.

He rides back, accosts Hull, demands to know if surrender is being considered. Hull's reply is unintelligible. Jesup urges Hull to hold out at least until McArthur and Cass return. But all Hull can exclaim is, "My God, what shall I do with these women and children?"

Hull has ordered the Ohio volunteers to retreat into the fort. Their commander, Colonel Findlay, now rides up in a rage and asks, "What the hell am I ordered here for?" Hull replies, in a trembling voice, that several men have been killed and that he believes he can obtain better terms from Brock if he capitulates now than if he waits for a storm or a siege.

"Terms!" shouts Findlay. "Damnation! We can beat them on the plain. I did not come here to capitulate; I came here to fight!"

He seeks out the ailing Miller.

"The General talks of surrender," says Findlay. "Let us put him under arrest."

But Lieutenant-Colonel Miller, a regular officer, is no mutineer:

"Colonel Findlay, I am a soldier; I shall obey my superior officer."

By now the shelling has ceased. Hidden in the ravine, Brock's men are enjoying breakfast provided by William Forsyth, one of 120 British males who refused to change their allegiance when Detroit became an American community in 1796. Forsyth's house lies in the ravine, and its owner, who has been plundered by Hull, is glad to open his doors to Brock's officers and the contents of pantry and cellar to his troops, who manage in this brief period to consume twenty-four gallons of brandy, fifteen gallons of madeira and nine of port.

In the midst of this unexpected revel, some of the men spot Brock's two aides, Glegg and Macdonell, moving toward the fort with a flag of truce. A buzz of excitement: is it all to be over so quickly? Some—especially the younger officers—hope against hope that Hull will not give in. They thirst for glory and for promotion, which can only be gained in the smoke of battle and (a thought swiftly banished) the death or incapacity of their superiors. In this they resemble Tecumseh's young men, who have flocked to his side also seeking glory and hoping, some of them, to gain precedence over the older chiefs who try to dissuade them from rashness. But most of Brock's followers breathe a little more freely. Charles Askin, a seasoned son of the frontier, wishes for a ceasefire for the sake of the women and children who, he believes, will be massacred by the Indians once the action commences.

Hull wants a truce, has asked for three days. Brock gives him three hours: after that he will attack.

After this no-nonsense ultimatum it becomes clear that Hull is prepared for a full surrender. He will give up everything—the fort, its contents, all the ordnance, all supplies, all the troops, even those commanded by the absent Cass and McArthur and by Captain Henry Brush at the River Raisin. *Everything.* When Hull tries tentatively to make some provision for those Canadian deserters who have come over to his side, Macdonell replies with a curt "Totally inadmissible." Hull makes no further remonstrance. The surrender details he leaves to Elijah Brush and Miller, actually to Brush alone, since Miller, trembling with ague, is now prostrate on the ground. But sick or not, he is in no mood to sign any surrender document and does so only reluctantly.

Two more signatures are required—those of Hull and Brock. The British general now rides into the fort accompanied by a fife and drum corps playing "The British Grenadiers" and by his advance guard, which includes John Beverley Robinson, the future chief justice of Upper Canada, Samuel Peters Jarvis, whose family will give its name to one of Toronto's best-known streets, and two members of the Askin family, Charles and his fifteen-year-old nephew, John Richardson. Askin, for one, has never felt so proud as at this moment.

The advance guard, however, has advanced a little too quickly. The articles of surrender stipulate that the Americans must leave the fort before the British enter. A confused melee follows. The American soldiers are in a turmoil, some crying openly, a few of the officers breaking their swords and some of the soldiers their muskets rather than surrender them. Others cry "Treason!" and "Treachery!" and heap curses and imprecations on their general's head. One of the Ohio volunteers tries to stab Macdonell before the advance guard moves back across the drawbridge.

Within the fort, Abraham Hull wakens in his quarters from a sound sleep, doubtless brought on by his earlier inebriation, to discover enemy soldiers entering the fort. He breaks through a window and, hatless, rushes up to a British officer to demand his business there with his "redcoat rascals." The officer raises his sword and is about to run him through when an American runs up to explain that the General's son is temporarily deranged.

Finally the tangle is straightened out. The Americans stack their arms and move out of the fort. The 4th Regiment of regulars, its members in despair and in tears, gives up its colours, sewn by a group of Boston ladies and carried through the Battle of Tippecanoe. Charles Askin, watching them shamble past, wonders at the legend of their invincibility. To him they look like the poorest set of soldiers he has seen in a long time, their situation and their ragged clothing making them appear as sick men.

Now the British and Canadians officially enter the fort, the regulars in the lead, followed first by the uniformed militia, then by those not in uniform and, bringing up the rear, Tecumseh's followers led by the chiefs and the officers of the British Indian Department, themselves dressed and painted as Indians.

Down comes the Stars and Stripes. A bluejacket from one of the gunboats has tied a Union Jack around his body in preparation for this moment. It is hoisted high to the cheers of the troops. John Richardson, whose musket is taller than himself, is one of those chosen to mount the first guard at the flagstaff. He struts up and down his post, peacock proud, casting his eyes down at the vanquished Americans on the esplanade below the fort. Almost at this moment, in Kentucky, Henry Clay is predicting the fall of Fort Amherstburg and the speedy conquest of Upper Canada.

As the flag goes up, the Indians pour through the town, cheering, yelling, firing off their guns and seizing American horses. There is looting but no savagery; Tecumseh keeps his promise to Brock that his people will not molest the prisoners. As the two ride together through the fort, the general seems larger than life in his black cocked hat—his crimson uniform and gilt epaulettes contrasting sharply with the fringed buckskin of his lither Shawnee ally. It is a moment for legend: a story will soon spring up that Brock has torn off his military sash and presented it to Tecumseh. If so, Tecumseh is not seen to wear it. Perhaps, as some say, he has turned it over to Roundhead, who as senior member of the senior tribe of Wyandot is held by the Shawnee to be more deserving. Perhaps Tecumseh feels the gaudy silk is too much out of character for the plain deerskin garb that, in a kind of reverse vanity, he has made his trademark. Perhaps. The incident becomes part of the myth of Tecumseh, the myth of Brock.

Brock has one more symbolic act to perform. He goes directly to the guardroom to release John Dean, the British regular who struggled to hold the bridge during the first engagement at the River aux Canards. He releases him personally, shakes his hand, and in the presence of his men, his voice breaking a little with emotion, tells Dean he is an honour to his military calling.

These and other formalities observed, he turns the command of the captured territory over to Lieutenant-Colonel Procter and prepares to leave for York, where he will be hailed as the saviour of the province. In just nineteen days he has met the legislature, arranged the public affairs of Upper Canada, travelled three hundred miles to invade the invader, captured an entire army and a territory as large as the one he governs. Now he must hurry back to the capital and return the bulk of his troops as swiftly as possible to the sensitive Niagara frontier, under threat of imminent attack.

On this triumphant journey across the lake he makes a remark to a captain of the York Volunteers, Peter Robinson, that is both self-revealing and prophetic.

"If this war lasts, I am afraid I shall do some foolish thing," says General Brock, "for I know myself, there is no want of courage in my nature—I hope I shall not get into a scrape."

———

ONCE THE SURRENDER IS accomplished, Hull emerges from his catatonic state like a man coming out of an anaesthetic. Scarcely able to speak or act that morning, he is now both lucid and serene. "I have done what my conscience directed," he declares. "I have saved Detroit and the Territory from the horrors of an Indian massacre." He knows that his country will censure him (though he cannot yet comprehend the magnitude of that censure), knows that he has "sacrificed a reputation dearer to me than life," but he is by no means downcast. A prisoner of the British, he no longer carries on his shoulders the crushing burden of command. As his former friend Lieutenant-Colonel Bâby remarks to him in his captivity—echoing Hull's own brittle comment of the previous month—*"Well, General, circumstances are changed now indeed."*

Of his surrender, Hull says, "My heart approves the act." His colleagues are of a different mind. McArthur and Cass, trotting to the relief of Detroit, their exhausted and famished troops riding two to a horse after a forced march of twenty-four miles, have heard the cannonade cease at 10 A.M. and are convinced that Hull has repulsed the British. The astonishing sight of the Union Jack flying over the fort changes their minds, and they move back several miles. Their men have had nothing to eat for forty-eight hours except green pumpkins and unripe corn garnered in the fields. Now they spy an ox by the roadside, slaughter and roast it. In the midst of this feast they are accosted by two British officers bearing a flag of truce who inform them that by the terms of their commander's surrender they are all prisoners.

"Traitor!" cries Cass. "He has disgraced his country," and seizing his sword from its sheath proceeds to break it in two.

It does not, apparently, occur to either of these commanders, so eager now to have at the enemy, that they might make their way back to Urbana without much fear of pursuit. Tired and dispirited, they meekly lay down their weapons and are marched into captivity.

Captain Henry Brush, at the River Raisin, is an officer of different mettle. When Matthew Elliott's son William, a militia captain, arrives to inform him of the surrender, Brush denounces the document of capitulation as a forgery, calls Elliott an imposter and spy, places him under arrest, and with all of his men except the sick decamps to the Rapids of the Maumee and thence through the Black Swamp to Urbana, where his followers disperse in small groups to their homes in Chillicothe. Tecumseh gives chase with three hundred mounted Indians, but Brush's men are too far in the lead to be captured. It makes little difference: the war still has rules of a sort, and under the terms of the surrender document, the United States officially recognizes Brush's men as prisoners. They cannot fight again until they are exchanged for an equal number of captured British.

Hull, who is worth thirty privates in a prisoner exchange, is shipped off to Quebec with his officers and the regular troops of Miller's 4th Infantry. Some of these men, hungry and emaciated, do not survive the journey. One regular, the enterprising Robert Lucas, has no intention of making it. The instant the British flag replaces the Stars and Stripes over the fort, he slips out of his uniform, hides his sword in his brother's trunk, and disguised as a civilian volunteer boards the vessel that is taking the Ohio militia on parole to Cleveland. Twenty years from now the Democratic party of Ohio will nominate him for governor over his only rival—Colonel James Findlay, his fellow prisoner.

Tecumseh knows many of the American prisoners by sight and greets them in Detroit without apparent rancour. This is his supreme moment. One of the militia engineers, Lieutenant George Ryerson (older brother of the great educator, Egerton) sees the buckskin-clad Shawnee chief shortly after the surrender, sitting with his brother, the Prophet, smoking his pipe "with his face perfectly calm, but with the greatest satisfaction beaming in his eye."

Now, in the aftermath of the bloodless victory, a number of tales are added to the legend of Tecumseh.

There is, for instance, the story of Father Gabriel Richard, the priest of Ste Anne's parish, who refuses to take the oath of allegiance to the British Crown because, he says, he has already sworn an oath to support the American Constitution. Procter, whom Brock has left in charge, imprisons the priest at Sandwich. When Tecumseh insists upon his release, Procter snubs him. Tecumseh swiftly assembles his followers, warns Procter that he will return to the Wabash if the priest is not freed. The Colonel gives in. It is the first but not the last time that he will clash with the Shawnee.

There are other tales: Tecumseh is speaking to his followers at the River Raisin when he feels a tug at his jacket, looks down, sees a small white girl. When he continues to speak, she tugs again: "Come to our house, there are bad Indians there."

He stops at once, follows her, seizes his tomahawk, drops the leader with one blow and, as the others move to attack, shouts out: "Dogs! I am Tecumseh!" The Indians retreat. Tecumseh, entering the house, finds British officers present. "You are worse than dogs to break faith with your prisoners!" he cries, and the British apologize for not having restrained the Indians. They offer to place a guard on the house, but that is not necessary, the child's mother tells them. So long as Tecumseh is near she feels safe.

Another incident occurs about the same time. Tecumseh's followers are ravenous. The game has fled; the settlers are short of supplies. Near the River Raisin, Tecumseh approaches a boy working with two oxen.

"My friend," says Tecumseh, "I must have these oxen. My young men are very hungry. They have nothing to eat."

The youth remonstrates. His father is ill. The oxen are their only farm animals. Without them they will die.

"We are the conquerors," Tecumseh says, "and everything we want is ours. I *must* have the oxen, but I will not be so mean as to rob you of them. I will pay you one hundred dollars for them, and that is more than they are worth."

He has his interpreter write out an order on Matthew Elliott for that sum, then takes the beasts, which his men roast and eat. But Elliott will not pay: Hull, after all, has stolen quantities of Canadian cattle, not to mention a herd of fine Merino sheep. When Tecumseh hears this he drops everything, takes the boy to Elliott, insists on payment. The Shawnee's anger rises when Elliott remains stubborn:

"You can do what you please, but before Tecumseh and his warriors came to fight the battles of the great King they had enough to eat, for which they only had to thank the Master of Life and their good rifles. Their hunting grounds supply them with enough food, and to them they can return."

"Well," Elliott responds, "if I *must* pay, I will."

"Give me hard money," says Tecumseh, "not rag money."

Elliott counts out one hundred dollars in coin. Tecumseh gives it to the boy, then turns to Elliott.

"Give me one dollar more," he says.

Elliott grudgingly hands him an extra coin.

"Here," says Tecumseh to the boy, "take that. It will pay you for the time you have lost getting your money."

There are many such tales growing out of the victory at Detroit. The Americans believe Tecumseh to be a brigadier-general in the British Army. He is not, but he dines with the officers at the victory dinner in Amherstburg, ignoring the wine in which the toasts are drunk yet displaying excellent table manners while his less temperate followers whoop it up in the streets of Detroit.

When news of Prevost's armistice reaches him, he is enraged. The action confirms his suspicions that the British are not interested in prosecuting the war to its fullest. If they will not fight, then the Indians will. Already the tribes are investing the American wilderness blockhouses—Fort Harrison, Fort Wayne, Fort Madison. Tecumseh leaves them to it and heads south on a new journey, attempting once again to rally new tribes to his banner.

For the British, if not for the Indians, the results of Detroit's surrender are staggering. Upper Canada, badly supplied and even worse armed, now has an additional cache of 2,500 captured muskets, thirty-nine pieces of heavy ordnance, forty barrels of gunpowder, a sixteen-gun brig, *Adams* (immediately renamed *Detroit*), a great many smaller craft, and Henry Brush's baggage train of one hundred pack animals and three hundred cattle, provisions and stores. The prize money to be distributed among the troops is reckoned at $200,000, an enormous sum considering that a private's net pay amounts to about four shillings, or one dollar, a week.

As a result of the victory at Detroit, every private soldier receives prize money of more than four pounds—at least twenty weeks' net pay. The amount increases according to rank and unit. Sergeants of the 41st Foot receive about eight pounds, captains, such as Adam Muir, forty pounds. General Brock is due two hundred and sixteen pounds. One luckless private bearing the Biblical name of Shadrach

Byfield is left off the list by mistake and does not receive his share until May of 1843.

More significant is the fact that Brock has rolled back the American frontier to the Ohio River, the line that the Indians themselves hold to be the border between white territories and their own lands. Most of Michigan Territory is, for practical purposes, in British hands. A council of tribal leaders called by the U.S. government at Piqua, Ohio, for the express purpose of maintaining native neutrality collapses with the news of Hull's surrender. Many Indians, such as the Mohawk of the Grand Valley, who have been reluctant to fight on either side, are now firmly and enthusiastically committed to the British. The same can be said for all the population of Upper Canada, once so lukewarm and defeatist, now fired to enthusiasm by Brock's stunning victory. In Montreal and Quebec, the spectacle of Hull's tattered and ravaged followers provokes a wave of patriotic ardour.

The General, who has to this point treated the militia with great delicacy, reveals an iron fist. Now he has the power and the prestige to enforce the oath of allegiance among the citizen soldiers and to prosecute anybody, militiaman or civilian, for sedition, treason, or desertion.

In Canada Brock is the man of the hour, but in America the very word "Hull" is used as a derogatory epithet. In their shame and despair, Americans of all political stripes—civilians, soldiers, politicians—lash out blindly at the General, who is almost universally considered to be a traitor and a coward. On his drooping shoulders will be laid all the guilt for his country's singular lack of foresight and for its military naïveté. Forgotten now are Hull's own words of advice about the need for controlling the Lakes before attempting to invade Canada. Ignored is Major-General Dearborn's dereliction in refusing to supply Hull with the reinforcements for which he pleaded or launching the diversionary attacks at Niagara and Kingston, which were key elements in American strategy.

Hull is to be made the scapegoat for Dearborn's paralysis and Washington's bumbling. When he is at last exchanged (and Prevost is anxious to release him because he believes Hull's return will cause dissension in America), he faces a court martial that is a travesty of a trial. Here he comes up against his old adversaries, McArthur, Cass, Findlay, Miller. But his lawyer is not permitted to cross-examine these officers or to examine other witnesses; the old general, un-schooled in law, must perform that task himself.

Though his papers were burned on their way from Detroit to Buffalo after the surrender, he is not allowed to examine copies at Washington. The court is packed against him: Henry Dearborn is the presiding judge. He is unlikely to be sympathetic, for if the court acquits Hull of the twin charges of cowardice and treason, Dearborn himself and his superiors in Washington must be held culpable for the scandal at Detroit.

The charge of treason is withdrawn on the grounds that it is beyond the court's jurisdiction. Three months later, when the weary process is at last completed and Hull is found guilty of cowardice, the court adds a rider saying that it does not believe him to be guilty of treason. There is more to this than simple justice, for the charge is based entirely on the loss of the *Cuyahoga* and all Hull's baggage before he knew war was declared. That misfortune cannot be laid at the ill-starred general's door but at that of Dr. Eustis, the Secretary of War, who was scandalously remiss in informing his outposts of the outbreak of hostilities.

Hull, officially branded as a coward, is sentenced to be shot. The President, taking into account the General's Revolutionary gallantry and perhaps also pricked by a guilty conscience, pardons him. Hull spends the rest of his life attempting to vindicate his actions. It is an irony of war that had he refused to surrender, had he gone down to defeat, his fort and town shattered by cannon fire, his friends and neighbours ravaged by the misfortunes of battle, his soldiers dead to the last man, the civilians burned out, bombed out, and inevit-ably scalped, the tired old general would have swept into the history books as a gallant martyr, his name enshrined on bridges, schools, main streets, and public buildings. (There is also the possibility that he might have beaten Brock, though somehow one doubts it.) But for the rest of their lives the very soldiers who, because of him, can go back whole to the comfort of their homesteads, and the civilians who are now able to pick up the strings of their existence, only briefly tangled, will loathe and curse the name of William Hull who, on his deathbed at the age of seventy-two, will continue to insist that he took the only proper, decent, and courageous course on that bright August Sunday in 1812.

FIVE

Chicago

Horror on Lake Michigan

The wretchedness of that night who can tell! the despondency
that filled the hearts of all, not so much in regard to the present
as from apprehension for the future, who . . . can comprehend? . . .
Alas, where were their comrades—friends, nay, brothers of yester-
day? Where was the brave, the noble-hearted Wells . . . the manly
Sergeant Nixon . . . the faithful Corporal Green—and nearly two-
thirds of the privates of the detachment?
          —From *Wau-nan-gee,* by John Richardson.

FORT DEARBORN, ILLINOIS TERRITORY, August 15, 1812. Billy
Wells has blackened his face in the fashion of a Miami warrior. It is
a sign that he expects to be killed before sundown.

He has come to escort the garrison and the people of Chicago
from the protection of the fort to the dubious security of Fort Wayne
on the Maumee. It is not his doing; the move has been explicitly
ordered by General Hull, who is himself only a day away from defeat
and disgrace. Billy Wells has greater reason than Hull for pessimism;
his blackened face betrays it.

Billy Wells is that curious frontier creature, a white man who thinks like an Indian—citizen of a shadow world, half civilized, half savage, claimed by two races, not wholly accepted by either. His story is not unusual. Captured by the Miami as a child, raised as a young warrior, he grew to manhood as an Indian, took the name of Black Snake, married the sister of the great war chief Little Turtle, became a leader of his adoptive people. As the years drifted by, the memories of his childhood—he is a descendant of a prominent Kentucky family—began to blur. Did he dream them? Was he really white? In the successful attacks on the Maumee against Harmar in 1790 and St. Clair in 1791 he fought with tomahawk and war club by the side of his brother-in-law. In that last battle—the greatest defeat inflicted on any American force by Indians in pre-Custer days—he butchered several white soldiers. But when the grisly work was done, old memories returned, and Billy Wells was haunted by a nagging guilt. Was it possible that he had actually killed some of his own kinsmen? Guilt became obsession. The call of blood defeated the bonds of friendship. Wells could no longer remain an Indian: he must leave his wife, his children, his old crony Little Turtle and return to his own people. There was a legendary leave-taking: "We have long been friends [to Little Turtle]; we are friends yet, until the sun stands so high [pointing to the sky] in the heavens; from that time we are enemies and may kill one another."

Billy Wells joined General Anthony Wayne, advancing down the Maumee, became chief of Wayne's scouts, fought on the white side in the Battle of Fallen Timbers. The battle over, his wife and family rejoined him. Billy Wells was appointed government agent and interpreter at Fort Wayne; Little Turtle, rendered docile by defeat, continued as his friend and confidant.

Yet no one can be quite sure of Billy Wells, who, like Matthew Elliott, prospers from his government and Indian connections. William Henry Harrison does not trust him, believes him to be secretly conniving with his former people. Tecumseh despises him and Little Turtle as turncoats. Billy Wells is history's captive, and today he will become history's victim.

As the heavy stockade gate swings open, he leads a forlorn group down the road that will become Michigan Avenue in the Chicago of the future. He has brought along an escort of thirty Miami warriors to lead to safety the entire population of the fort and the adjacent village of Chicago—some hundred soldiers and civilians. Half of his Miami escort rides beside him. Directly behind is Captain Nathan Heald, commander of the fort (the same man who, the previous spring, intercepted Brock's couriers to Robert Dickson), with his wife Rebekah, who is Billy Wells's niece, and his garrison of regular soldiers. A wagon train follows with the women and children of the settlement, the younger children riding in one of the covered carts. The Chicago militia and the remainder of Wells's Miami bring up the rear.

Why are these people leaving the sturdy protection of an armed stockade and venturing into hostile Indian territory? Simply because General Hull, dismayed by the loss of Michilimackinac, has decided to evacuate the area. He has instructed Heald to destroy all arms and distribute the supplies, provisions, food, and blankets among the neighbouring Indians. The gesture, designed to placate the natives, has the opposite effect, especially as Heald decides to destroy all the garrison's liquor as well as its arms. Since whiskey and guns are what the Indians desire most, the deliberate destruction of these prizes has put them in an ugly mood. Moreover, one of Tecumseh's runners has arrived with news of Hull's crumbling position at Detroit. The momentum of British success and American failure has got their blood up. Just ahead, concealed behind a ridge of sand dunes, lurks a war party of six hundred Potawatomi, the tribe so prominent at the Battle of Tippecanoe.

Billy Wells's trained eye spots the ambush. He gallops back to warn Heald, swings his hat in a circle to indicate that the force is surrounded, then leads a bayonet charge up the bank.

It is a tragic error of judgement, bold but foolhardy, for it leaves the wagon train unprotected. Heald's two junior officers, together with twelve newly recruited militiamen and a handful of regulars, fight furiously with bayonet and musket butt but are quickly subdued by the superior force of Indians. Only one white civilian, John Kinzie, the Chicago trader, survives, spared, perhaps, by the same Indians with whom he is accustomed to do business. At the wagon train, the soldiers' wives, armed with their husbands' swords, fight as fiercely as the men. Two are hacked to pieces: a Mrs. Corbin, wife of a private, who has vowed never to be taken prisoner, and Mrs. Heald's black slave, Cicely, who is cut down with her infant son.

Within the wagons, where the younger children are huddled, there is greater horror. One young Indian slips in and slaughters twelve single-handed, slicing their heads from their bodies in a fury of blood lust.

Billy Wells, a musket ball in his breast, his horse wounded and faltering, hears the clamour at the wagons and attempts to turn back in a last effort to save the women and children. As he does so, the horse stumbles, and he is hurled to the ground, one leg caught under the animal's body. The Indians are bearing down, and Billy Wells knows that his hour has come. He continues to fire, killing at least one man. As he does so, he calls out to his niece Rebekah, bidding her goodbye. An Indian takes deliberate aim. Billy Wells looks him square in the eye, signals him to shoot.

A short distance away, Heald's sergeant, Hayes, is engaged in a death struggle with a Potawatomi warrior. Their muskets have been discharged; there is no time to reload. The Indian rushes at Hayes, brandishing his tomahawk. As the blow falls, the sergeant drives his bayonet up to the socket into his enemy's breast. They die together.

Walter Jordan, one of Wells's men, has a miraculous escape. One ball takes the feather off his cap, another the epaulette from his shoulder, a third the handle from his sword. He surrenders to the Indians and is recognized by a chief:

"Jordan, I know you. You gave me tobacco at Fort Wayne. We won't kill you, but come and see what we will do to your captain." He leads him to where Wells's body lies, cuts off the head, and places it on a long pole. Another cuts out the heart and divides it among the chiefs, who eat it raw, hoping thereby to absorb some of Wells's courage.

Heald, wounded in arm and thigh, abandoned by Wells's escort of Miami, half his force of regulars dead, all his officers casualties, decides to surrender. He approaches the Potawatomi chief, Black Bird, promises a ransom of one hundred dollars for everyone left alive if the Indians will agree not to kill the prisoners. Black Bird accepts; the soldiers lay down their arms and are marched back past the naked and headless bodies of the women and children. Heald, thinking he recognizes the torso of his wife, briefly repents the surrender, then is overjoyed to find that she is alive at the fort, weeping among a group of Indian women, saved apparently by the intervention of a friendly chief, Black Partridge.

Black Bird does not keep his promise. One of the wounded soldiers, Sergeant Thomas Burns of the militia, is killed almost immediately by the squaws. His is a more fortunate fate than that of five of his comrades who are tortured to death that night, their cries breaking the silence over the great lake and sending shivers through the survivors.

More than half the band that left the fort in the morning are dead by the following day. The remainder, twenty-nine soldiers, seven women, and six children, are captives of the Indians, destined to be distributed among the various villages in the area. Thus begins their long travail.

The Healds' captivity is short-lived. After a few days, with Michigan now in British hands, most of the Indians take off to attack Fort Wayne, and Heald is able to buy his way to St. Joseph's Island in British territory, where Captain Roberts sends them home under parole. At Detroit, Mrs. Heald's "inimitable grace and fulness of contour" together with her "magnificence of person and brilliancy of character" make a lasting impression on the fifteen-year-old John Richardson, who, at the end of his life, gives her a certain immortality by making her the heroine of his novel *Wau-nan-gee*.

Others are less fortunate. That winter one captive freezes to death on the trail; two more, who cannot keep up, are tomahawked; nine exist as slaves for almost a year before they are ransomed through the efforts of the red-headed trader, Robert Dickson.

The family of John Needs, one of Heald's regular soldiers, manages to survive the massacre only to die in captivity. The Needs' only child, crying with hunger, so annoys the Indians that they tie it to a tree to perish from starvation. Needs also dies of cold and hunger. His wife expires the following January.

The family of the murdered Sergeant Burns is shattered. One grown son is killed in the fighting; two small children are victims of the wagon massacre. A nine-year-old daughter, though scalped, succeeds in freeing herself. She, her mother, and an infant in arms survive for two years among the Indians before being ransomed by a white trader. For the rest of her life the scalped girl is marked by a small bald spot on the top of her head.

In the fate of the Lee family are all the ingredients of a nineteenth-century frontier novel. All its members except the mother and an infant daughter are killed in the fighting. The two survivors are taken by Black Partridge to his camp. Here the baby falls ill and Black Partridge falls in love—with Mrs. Lee. In order to win her hand he determines to save the infant's life. He takes her back to Chicago where a newly arrived French trader named Du Pin prescribes for her and cures her. Learning of Black Partridge's romantic intentions, Du Pin ransoms Mrs. Lee, then marries her himself.

These stories pale before the long odyssey of Mrs. John Simmons, whose husband also perishes during the defence of the wagons. Believing that the Indians delight in tormenting prisoners who show any emotion, this remarkable woman resolves to preserve the life of her six-month-old child by suppressing all outward manifestations of grief, even when she is led past a row of small, mutilated corpses which includes that of her two-year-old boy, David. Faced with this grisly spectacle, she neither blinks an eye nor sheds a tear, nor will she during the long months of her captivity.

Her Indian owners set out for Green Bay on the western shore of Lake Michigan. Mrs. Simmons, carrying her baby, trudges the entire distance, working as a servant in the evenings, gathering wood and building fires. When the village is at last reached, she is insulted, kicked, and abused. The following day she is forced to run the gauntlet between a double line of men and women wielding sticks and clubs. Wrapping the infant in a blanket and shielding it in her arms, she races down the long line, emerging bruised and bleeding but with her child unharmed.

She is given over to an Indian "mother," who feeds her, bathes her wounds, allows her to rest. She needs such sustenance, for a worse ordeal faces her—a long tribal peregrination back around the lake. Somehow Mrs. Simmons, lightly clad, suffering from cold, fatigue, and malnutrition, manages to carry her child for the entire six hundred miles and survive. She has walked with the Indians from Green Bay back to Chicago, then around the entire eastern shore of the lake to Michilimackinac. But a second, even more terrible trek faces her—a three-hundred-mile journey through the snow to Detroit, where the Indians intend to ransom her. Ragged and starving, she exists on roots and acorns found beneath the snows. Her child, now a year old, has grown much heavier. Her own strength is waning. Only the prospect of release sustains her.

Yet even after her successful ransom her ordeal is not over. The route to her home near Piqua, Ohio, is long and hard. By March of 1813 she reaches Fort Meigs on the Maumee. Here she manages to secure passage in a government wagon, part of a supply train that

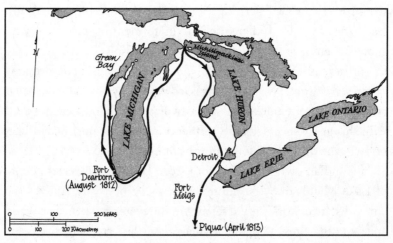

Mrs. Simmons's Trek

winds its way through swampy roads, depositing her, in mid-April, four miles from her father's farm.

Mother and child walk the remaining distance to find that the family, which has long since given her up for dead, has taken refuge in a blockhouse against Indian marauders. Here, safe at last, she breaks down and for several months cannot contain her tears. In August, she has further reason to weep. Her sister and brother-in-law, working in a nearby flax field, are surprised by Indians, shot, tomahawked, and scalped in front of their four horrified children. Such, in part, is the legacy of Tippecanoe and all that preceded it.

To these tales of horror and heroism must be added a bizarre coda:

It is October, 1816; the war has been over for two years. Two workmen helping to rebuild Fort Dearborn are travelling by skiff up the north branch of the Illinois, searching out suitable timber, probing deep into the wilderness, far from human habitation. Suddenly they hear the cries of Indian women and, above that gabble, the sound of English words. They spy, half-hidden in the underbrush, an Indian hut and then a white man, standing on the bank, who pleads with them to stop and talk, for he has heard no English for four years. This is the tale he tells:

He is one of Heald's force of soldiers, badly wounded in the battle with the Potawatomi and saved by an aging Indian woman, to whom he has previously been kind. She prevents her people from scalping him and, with the help of her three daughters, moves him across the river, hides him in the undergrowth, and tends his wounds until he is well enough to be moved.

The four women secure a piece of timber from the ruined fort, tie him to it, and tow the makeshift raft forty miles northward to the shores of a small lake. And here all five live together. He marries his benefactor, Indian fashion. When she dies he takes the two older daughters as his wives. Since that day they have been living here together in the wilderness.

The workmen return to Chicago to report their strange discovery. Next day, the army surgeon accompanies them upriver with a boatload of presents for the quartet, only to discover that the women are on the point of spiriting their joint husband away, deeper into the wild. He, for his part, has made no objection; indeed, he has decided to take their younger sister as his third common-law wife.

The doctor examines his wounds. They have healed; but one leg is shorter than the other, and one arm is useless. Does he wish to return to his own kind? The old soldier shakes his head: not as long as his harem will live with him and care for him, he says. He is already preparing to move further from civilization, further into the unpopulated forest. Perhaps he will visit the fort some day, he remarks, but only if the soldiers solemnly promise not to make fun of his little teenaged bride.

But he does not come. No white man ever sees or hears of him again. He and his little family melt away into the recesses of the coniferous jungle that clothes the territory. No pen records his odyssey; no stone marks his grave; nor can anyone recall his name. Like so many others he is the faceless victim of a war not of his making; and, again like so many others, he has managed to come to terms with his fate and in that process to survive and even prosper in his fashion, a creature of the wild, at once its prisoner and its conqueror, master and servant of all he surveys, monarch of an empty empire.

SIX

Queenston Heights

The End of Isaac Brock

No tongue shall blazon forth their fame—
The cheers that stir that sacred hill
Are but the promptings of the will
That conquered then, that conquers still
And generations shall thrill
At Brock's remembered name.

—Anon.

LEWISTON, NEW YORK, AUGUST 15, 1812; with the United States Army of the Centre.

Major John Lovett, who is more poet than soldier, leaps out of his quarters to the roar of musket fire on the heights above the Niagara River, flings himself onto his horse, and dashes off. The cries of his commanding officer, Major-General Stephen Van Rensselaer, echo behind him: *Come back! Come back!* But Lovett gallops on. Later, the General will tell him that he fully expected he was about to run away, never to be seen again; but this is mere badinage, for the two are old friends. Lovett serves the American commander officially as military aide and secretary; he is also confidant, political ally, and something of a court jester—an antidote against the loneliness and burden of command. To Lovett, soldiering is a new experience, war is something of a lark, the sound of musketry exciting.

As the Major gallops for the cliffs, he realizes that two other riders are close behind him. Both are high-ranking officers. Lieutenant-Colonel Solomon Van Rensselaer is the General's aide-de-camp, kinsman, and friend. Brigadier-General William Wadsworth of the Upper New York State militia has been in charge of recruiting for the coming thrust against Queenston—a difficult and thankless task, given the mood of the region.

As they run their horses up the broken rock of the precipice (the worst terrain Lovett has ever known), the musket fire increases. They burst out of a copse into open land; a soldier runs up crying, "General, do ride into that hollow, for the balls fly dreadfully here!" but they gallop in, seeking to discover the cause of the gunfire. One of the guards posted on the cliff starts to explain just as a ball fans his face. He leaps behind a great oak, pulling his arms close in to his body to make himself invisible, and then, seeing the ludicrousness of his position, grins ruefully, causing Lovett to burst out laughing. General Wadsworth maintains a straight face and is careful to present his breast to the enemy at all times, for he does not intend, he says, "that a Wadsworth should be shot through the back." A few minutes later the skirmish ends inconclusively. It has been caused, significantly, by the attempts of two Americans to desert to the Canadian side of the Niagara River by boat.

That evening, Lovett takes pains to write his friend and confidant, John Alexander of Albany, a breathless account of the incident "principally for the purpose of enabling you to meet the *lye* should any fool or scoundrel manufacture one, out of what little did actually take place." He does not want it "conjured up as to another *Sackett's Harbor Battle.*" Lies there have been and rumours aplenty, including one monstrous falsehood, heard during the army's march north through Utica, that the American post at Sackets Harbor had been attacked and blockaded by the British—a piece of fiction that caused the General to abandon his route to the Niagara River and march to the relief of the town, only to find that nothing untoward had taken place.

Now, Stephen Van Rensselaer has set up his headquarters at Lewiston, concentrating his forces here, directly across from the Canadian village of Queenston. This very day, Dr. Eustis, the Secretary of War, has sent an order to Van Rensselaer's superior, General Dearborn, at Albany: "Considering the urgency of a diversion in favour of General Hull under the circumstances attending his situation, the President thinks it proper that not a moment should be lost in gaining possession of the British posts at Niagara and Kingston, or at least the former, and proceeding in co-operation with General Hull in securing Upper Canada." Both Eustis and Dearborn cling to the fancy that Hull has been victorious in Upper Canada and that Fort Amherstburg has already fallen.

In Lewiston, General Van Rensselaer is under no such illusion, though he will not learn of Hull's situation for several days. There is not much he can do to aid Hull. It is all very well for Eustis to talk of an attack on the Niagara frontier; it is quite a different matter to put his strategy into practice. The British control not only the far shore but also the Niagara River and the two lakes. Van Rensselaer has less than a thousand men to guard a front of thirty-six miles. One-third of his force is too ill to fight. None has been paid. His men lie in the open without tents or covering. Ammunition is low; there are scarcely ten rounds per soldier. There are no heavy ordnance, no gunners, no engineers, scarcely any medical supplies.

And even if, through some miracle of logistics, these deficiencies were rectified, it is questionable whether the state militia will agree to fight on foreign soil. On July 22, a humiliating incident at Ogdensburg made the General wary of his civilian soldiers. Across the St. Lawrence at Prescott lay a British gunboat. The General's aide and cousin, Solomon, had planned a daring raid to capture her; he and 120 men would row silently upriver at three in the morning, cross to the Canadian shore, seize the wharf buildings, and attack the ship simultaneously from land and water. At two, everything was in readiness; four hundred men were paraded and volunteers called for, but when only sixty-six agreed to go, the expedition had to be aborted.

If the troops are reluctant, their militia leaders, with the exception of Solomon Van Rensselaer, are inexperienced. Wadsworth, the militia general, knows so little of war that he has pleaded to be released from his assignment of assembling volunteers: "I confess myself ignorant of even the minor details of the duty you have assigned to me, and I am apprehensive that I may not only expose myself but my Government," he tells the Governor of New York.

Stephen Van Rensselaer is himself a militiaman without campaign experience. When the crunch comes, colleagues in the regular forces will refuse to co-operate with him. The irony is that the General is totally and unequivocally opposed to a war that he now intends, as a matter of honour, to prosecute to the fullest—even at the risk of his own reputation. He is a leading Federalist politician, a candidate for governor with a strong following in New York State, and that is precisely why he is here at the head of a thousand men, very much against his will.

For his appointment he has his political rival to thank—the iron-jawed incumbent, Governor Daniel D. Tompkins, an able administrator and machine politician who is up for re-election the coming spring. As the Republican standard-bearer, Tompkins is as interested in getting his Federalist opponent out of the way as he is in prosecuting the war, and there is little doubt that Stephen Van Rensselaer will be a formidable rival.

He is the head of one of the first families in New York, and in his name one hears the ring of history. He is the eighth and last patroon of the feudal estate of Rensselaerwyck on the outskirts of Albany, a vast domain close to twelve hundred square miles in size and after almost two centuries still in the hands of the original family. A relic of the early Dutch immigration to America, the General is a Harvard graduate, a farmer, a millionaire, a philanthropist, and, more from a sense of duty than from ambition, a politician. He has served in the state assembly, in the state senate, and as lieutenant-governor of New York. Though he is entitled to feudal tithes, he does not collect them. He is liberal enough to vote against his own class in favour of extending the suffrage. His military training and experience as a militia general are all but non-existent, but that does not bother Governor Tompkins. By appointing his rival to the command of the army on the state's northern frontier he has everything to gain and nothing to lose—except, possibly, the war.

Politically, it is a masterstroke. Stephen Van Rensselaer can scarcely refuse the post; if he does he will be discredited in the eyes of the voters. If he accepts, he ends Federalist opposition to the war in New York State. If he blunders, he will undoubtedly be relieved of his command, and that will work against him in the political contest to come. If he performs brilliantly he will not be able to relinquish command and so will pose no political threat.

He accepts—but under one condition: he insists that his cousin Solomon be his aide-de-camp. For Solomon, in the words of his friend Lovett, "is all formed for war." Unlike the General, with his pert and amiable Dutch features, the Lieutenant-Colonel looks like a soldier—"the handsomest officer I ever beheld," in the words of a contemporary. The son of a Revolutionary general, ensign at seventeen, he fought with distinction under Wayne at Fallen Timbers. (Though seriously wounded, he took command of his shattered force and for his gallantry was promoted to major.) For most of the intervening years since leaving the regular army at the century's turn he has been adjutant-general for the state of New York. Now thirty-eight, he is ten years younger than his commanding officer.

The two cousins with Lovett form a close triumvirate—"our little family," Lovett calls it. They can rely on no other counsel than their own, for their politics render them suspect, especially to such fire-breathing War Hawks as Peter B. Porter, chairman of the House committee on foreign relations, who has been appointed quartermaster general for the state of New York. (Porter and his brother are themselves in the contracting and provisioning business and thus in a position to profit from supplying the army, but no one worries about that; the phrase "conflict of interest" has yet to enter the language.) In Albany, Governor Tompkins and General Dearborn show no great eagerness to assist the beleaguered force along the Niagara. Solomon, for one, is convinced that his political enemies are deliberately trying to sabotage him.

Lovett is determined to keep a careful record of everything that happens (or does not happen)—"the history of every occurrence that can possibly be tortured into a lie"—in the event of later distortions or misunderstandings. He does so in a series of breathless letters to his friend John Alexander, scribbling away at night, even though exhausted from his unaccustomed soldiering. He has neither stamina nor time to scrawl out a sentence to his wife, Nancy; that duty he leaves to his friend: "Tell my good wife, I have not another moment to write, that I am neither homesick, crop-sick, war sick, nor sick of my Wife," he writes. And again: "Don't let my wife get alarmed" and "Don't forget my Wife and Children, nor suffer them to be lonely. Keep their spirits up" and so on. It does not seem to occur to Lovett that the best way to keep up the family spirits might be to send off a letter in his own hand. But then Mrs. Lovett, herself a general's daughter, prefers to relay her own messages to her husband through their chosen intermediary, Alexander.

To Alexander, Lovett pours out his own pessimism and despair, which he shares with his two friends, the Van Rensselaer cousins. The war, to him, is foolish:

"If any man wants to see folly triumphant, let him come here, let him view friends by friends stretched for hundreds of miles on these two shores, all loving and beloved; all desirous of harmony; all wounded by being coerced, by a hand unseen, to cut throats. The People must awaken, they will wake from such destructive lethargy and stupor. . . .

"What might not the good spirit of this great People effect, if properly directed. History while recording our folly, will dress her pages in mourning, the showers of Posterity's tears will fall in vain; for the sponge of time can never wipe this blot from the American Name. . . ."

And yet, when the men under his friends' command refuse to leave the boundaries of the state to attack the British gunboat on the opposite shore, he is "mortified almost to death." For John Lovett is torn by conflicting emotions. He hates the idea of the war but badly wants to win it. He adjures his friend Alexander not to breathe a word about the defections of the militia lest the news cause further defections. He worries about Hull, hoping against hope that he can hold out, but expecting the worst. His despair over the outbreak of war is accompanied by a despair over his general's inability to strike a decisive blow against the enemy. To him, this war is "the Ominous Gathering of folly and madness," yet he deplores the lack of two thousand disciplined troops who, he has been told, are necessary for a successful attack on Fort George, the British post at the Niagara's mouth.

He is a lawyer by profession, a *bon vivant* by inclination, a satirical poet, a dinner wit, an amateur politician. He is good with juries, bad with law, for he cannot abide long hours spent with dusty tomes in murky libraries. He is restless, always seeking something new, changing employment frequently. It is doubtful, however, that he ever expected to become a soldier.

"I am not a soldier," he tells his friend the General when he seeks to employ him. To which Stephen Van Rensselaer replies, "It is not your *sword*, but your *pen* I want."

Now, in spite of himself, in spite of his hatred of war and bloodshed, in spite of his aching back and his head cold, in spite of long hours spent in the saddle and damp days on the hard ground, he discovers that he is actually enjoying the experience. It is for him a kind of testing, and his letters bubble with the novelty of it all.

"If flying through air, water, mud, brush, over hills, dales, meadows, swamps, on wheels or horseback, and getting a man's ears gnawed off with mosquitoes and gallinippers make a *Soldier*, then I have seen service for—one week," he boasts. And he revels in the tale of how he and his two friends, shipwrecked in a thunderstorm near Sackets Harbor, sought refuge in an abandoned house where he went to sleep in a large Dutch oven, aided by a sergeant of the guard who laid him on a large board and pushed him into its mouth "like a pig on a wooden shovel."

He worships the Van Rensselaer cousins (after all he is employed as a propagandist):

"One thing I can with great truth say; nothing but General Stephen Van Rensselaer's having the command of this campaign could have saved the service from confusion; the State from disgrace, and the cause from perdition; and nothing could have been more fortunate for the General than the man he has at his elbow, for Solomon in *fact* and *truth* does know everything which appertains to the economy of a camp—Stop:—Away we must all march, at beat of drum, and hear an old Irish clergyman preach to us, Amen. I have become a perfect machine; go just where I'm ordered."

———

LEWISTON, NEW YORK, AUGUST 16, 1812. Consternation in the American camp! Excitement—then relief. A red-coated British officer gallops through, carrying a flag of truce. Hull may be in trouble on the Detroit frontier. (He is, at this very moment, signing the articles of surrender.) But here on the Niagara the danger of a British attack, which all have feared, is over.

Major John Lovett cannot contain his delight at this unexpected reprieve. "Huzza! Huzza!" he writes in his journal, ". . . an Express from the Governor General of Canada to Gen. Dearborn proposing an Armistice!!!!" The news is so astonishing, so cheering, that he slashes four exclamation marks against it.

The following night, at midnight, there is a further hullabaloo as more riders gallop in from Albany bearing letters from Dearborn "enclosing a sort of three legged armistice between some sort of an Adjutant General on behalf of the governor general of Canada and the said Gen. Dearborn." Now the camp is in a ferment as messages crisscross the river: "There is nothing but flag after flag, letter after letter."

A truce, however brief, will allow the Americans to buy time, desperately needed, and to reinforce the Niagara frontier, desperately undermanned, that stretches thirty-six miles along the river that cuts through the neck of land separating Lake Erie from Lake Ontario. At the southern end, the British Fort Erie faces the two American towns of Buffalo, a lively village of five hundred, and its trading rival, Black Rock. At the northern end, Fort George on the British side and Fort Niagara on the American bristle at each other across the entrance into Lake Ontario. The great falls, whose thunder can be heard for miles, lie at midpoint. Below the gorge that cuts through the Niagara escarpment are the hamlet of Lewiston, on the American side, where Van Rensselaer's army is quartered, and the Canadian village of Queenston, a partially fortified community, overshadowed physically by the heights to the south and economically by the village of Newark (later Niagara-on-the-Lake) on the outskirts of Fort George.

At Lewiston, the river can be crossed in ten minutes, and a musket ball fired from one village to the other still has the power to kill. For some time the Americans have been convinced that the British mean to attack across the river. It is widely believed that they have three thousand men in the field and another thousand on call. As is so often the case in war, both sides overestimate the forces opposite them; Brock has only four hundred regulars and eight hundred militia, most of the latter having returned to their harvest.

New York State is totally unprepared for war. The arms are of varying calibres; no single cartridge will suit them. Few bayonets are available. When Governor Tompkins tries to get supplies for the militia from the regular army, he is frustrated by red tape. From Bloomfield comes word from one general that "if Gen. Brock should attack . . . a single hour would expend all our ammunition." From Brownville, another general reports that the inhabitants of the St. Lawrence colony are fleeing south. From Buffalo, Peter B. Porter describes a state bordering on anarchy—alarm, panic, distrust of officers, military unpreparedness. If Hull is beaten at Detroit only a miracle can save Van Rensselaer's forces from ignoble defeat.

Now, when least expected, the miracle has happened and the army has been given breathing space.

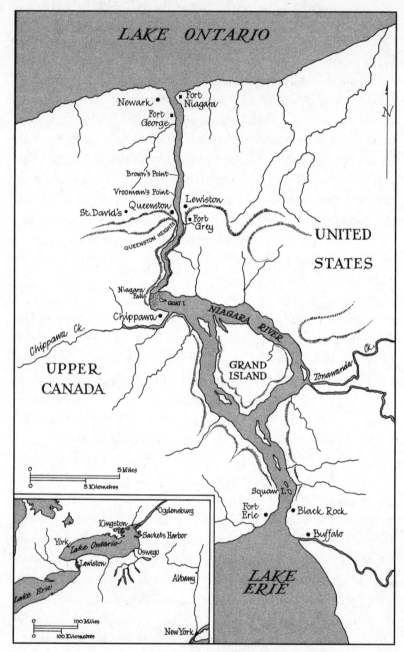

LAKE ONTARIO

Newark • ■ Fort Niagara

Fort George ■

Brown's Point

Vrooman's Point

Queenston • Lewiston •

St. David's • ■ Fort Grey

QUEENSTON HEIGHTS

UNITED

STATES

Niagara Falls

GOAT I.

Chippawa • NIAGARA RIVER

Chippawa Ck.

UPPER
CANADA

GRAND
ISLAND

Tonawanda Ck.

Squaw I.

Fort Erie • • Black Rock

• Buffalo

LAKE
ERIE

N

5 Miles

5 Kilometres

Ogdensburg

Kingston • • Sackets Harbor

York • Lake Ontario

• Lewiston

Oswego

Albany

New York

Lake Erie

100 Miles

100 Kilometres

The Niagara Frontier

Lieutenant-Colonel Solomon Van Rensselaer, the old campaigner, immediately grasps the significance of the projected armistice, but he faces serious problems. All the heavy cannon and supplies he needs are far away at Oswego at the eastern end of Lake Ontario. The roads are mired; supplies can only be moved by water. At present the British control the lake, but perhaps the terms of the truce can be broadened to give the Americans an advantage.

The agreement with Dearborn is specific: the British will not allow any facility for moving men and supplies that did not exist before it was signed. In short, the Americans cannot use the lake as a common highway. Solomon is determined to force his enemies to give way; the security of the Army of the Centre depends upon it.

He goes straight to his cousin, the General.

"Our situation," he reminds him, "is critical and embarrassing, *something* must be done, we must have cannon and military stores from Oswego. I shall make a powerful effort to procure the use of the waters, and I shall take such ground as will make it impossible for me to recede. If I do not succeed, then Lovett must cross over and carry Gen. Dearborn's orders into effect."

"Van," says Lovett, "you may as well give that up, you will not succeed."

"If I do not," retorts his friend, "it will not be my fault."

He dons full military dress and crosses to the British fort. Three officers are there to meet him: Brock's deputy, Major-General Roger Sheaffe, Lieutenant-Colonel Christopher Myers, commanding the garrison, and the brigade major, Thomas Evans. Sheaffe agrees readily to the American's proposal that no further troops should move from the district to reinforce Brock at Amherstburg; the Americans do not know that most of the needed troops have already been dispatched. But when Van Rensselaer proposes the use of all navigable waters as a common highway, Sheaffe raps out a curt "Inadmissible!" The Colonel insists. Again the General refuses. Whereupon Solomon Van Rensselaer engages in Yankee bluff.

"There can be no armistice," he declares; "our negotiation is at an end. General Van Rensselaer will take the responsibility on himself to prevent your detaching troops from this district."

The British officers leap to their feet. Sheaffe grips the hilt of his sword.

"Sir," says he, "you take high ground!"

Solomon Van Rensselaer also rises to his feet, gripping his sword. "I do, sir, and will maintain it." Turns to Sheaffe and speaks directly: "You do not dare detach the troops."

Silence. The General paces the room. Finally: "Be seated and excuse me." Withdraws with his aides. Returns after a few minutes: "Sir, from amicable considerations, I grant you the use of the waters."

It is a prodigious miscalculation, but it is Prevost's as much as Sheaffe's. The British general has his orders from his cautious and over-optimistic superior. Brock, contemplating an all-out offensive across the Niagara River, is still in the dark at Detroit.

The truce, which officially begins on August 20, can be cancelled by either side on four days' notice. It ends on September 8 after President Madison informs Dearborn that the United States has no intention of ending the war unless the British also revoke their practice of impressing American sailors. By that time Van Rensselaer's army has been reinforced from Oswego with six regiments of regulars, five of militia, a battalion of riflemen, several batteries of heavy cannon and, in Brock's rueful words, "a prodigious quantity of Pork and Flower." As Lovett puts it, "we worked John Bull in the little Armistice treaty and got more than we expected." Not only has Lewiston been reinforced, but the balance of power on Lake Ontario has also been tilted. General Van Rensselaer, taking advantage of the truce, has shot off an express to Ogdensburg on the St. Lawrence to dispatch nine vessels to Sackets Harbor, a move that will aid the American naval commander, Captain Isaac Chauncey, in his attack on the Upper Canadian capital of York the following year.

In spite of his diplomatic coup, Solomon Van Rensselaer is not a happy man. Somehow, at the height of the negotiations with the British, he has managed to hold a secret and astonishing conversation with Sheaffe's brigade major, Evans, in which he has confided to his enemy his own disillusionment with the government at

Washington, his hope that the war will speedily end, and his belief that the majority of Americans are opposed to any conflict. Solomon feels himself the plaything of remorseless fate—surrounded by political enemies, forced into a war he cannot condone, nudged towards a battle he feels he cannot win, separated from a loving wife whose protracted silence dismays him, and, worst of all, crushed by the memory of a family tragedy that he cannot wipe from his mind.

The vision of a sunlit clover lot near the family farm at Bethlehem, New York, is never far from his thoughts: his six-year-old son, Van Vechten, romps in the field with an older brother. Suddenly a musket shot rings out; the boy drops, shot through the ear, his brain a pulp. The senseless tragedy is the work of an escaped lunatic, and there is nothing anybody can do. Even revenge is futile, and Solomon Van Rensselaer is not a vengeful man. Again and again in his dreams and nightmares, he sees himself picking up the small bleeding corpse and struggling back across the field to his white-faced wife, Harriet.

It is she who worries him. The incident occurred on May 29, not long before he was forced to leave his family to take up arms. Why has she not written? Has the tragedy deranged her? Since leaving home he has sent her at least a dozen letters but has received no answer. "Why under the Heavens is the reason you do not write me?" he asks on August 21. Silence. A fortnight later he asks a political friend in Albany to tell him the truth: "The recollection of that late overwhelming event at home, I fear has been too much for her" No doubt it has. But what he apparently does not know, and will not know until the affair at Queenston is over, is that Harriet is in the final stages of pregnancy and about to present him with a new son.

His unhappy state of mind is further agitated by his political opponents, "who even pursue me to this quarter of the Globe." The chief of these is Henry Clay's supporter Peter B. Porter, who, in Solomon's opinion, has with some Republican friends been causing "confusion and distrust among the Troops on this Frontier to answer party purposes against the Commander." The Lieutenant-Colonel blames Porter, as quartermaster general of the army, for "speculating and attending to mischief and his private affairs" when the army is in such want of supplies. The camp is short of surgical instruments, lint, bandages, hospital stores.

In Solomon's view, Porter is "an abominable scoundrel." He makes so little attempt to hide that opinion that Porter eventually challenges him to a duel. Solomon chooses Lovett as his second, but when his cousin, the General, hears of the affair he threatens to court-martial both antagonists. Their job, he points out, is to fight the British, not each other. Yet this quarrel reveals only the tip of an iceberg of dissension, which in the end will force the Van Rensselaers into rash action. For after the truce ends on September 8, Porter and his hawkish friends begin to whisper that the General is a coward and a traitor who does not really want to attack the heights of Queenston.

———

WITH ISAAC BROCK, ABOARD the schooner *Chippewa*, Lake Ontario, August 23, 1812.

Euphoric after his capture of Detroit, the General is hastening back to his capital at York when a provincial schooner, *Lady Prevost*, approaches and fires a seventeen-gun salute. The ceremony over, her commander comes aboard and presents Brock with a dispatch—his first intimation of the armistice that Prevost and Dearborn have concluded on the Niagara frontier.

The General's elation dissolves. He is stunned, mortified, disillusioned. He had planned to continue the relentless momentum of his victory, to roll up the entire New York frontier from Buffalo to Sackets Harbor, to hammer at the Americans while they were still off balance and poorly supplied. Now his hands are tied by Prevost, and he cannot conceal his bitterness. He does not share his superior's optimism that the armistice is the first step towards a permanent cessation of hostilities. He is convinced that the sharp Yankees are buying time to reinforce their own position, that John Bull has been gulled by Brother Jonathan.

What he desires most of all is a quick victory, one that will allow him to leave the stifling colonial atmosphere of the Canadas and return to Europe to serve under Wellington and to visit with his several brothers, to whom he writes regularly. Indeed, on the very day of Detroit's fall, while plagued by a score of problems, he has managed to send them a brief dispatch: "Rejoice at my good fortune, and join me in prayers to Heaven," adding, somewhat cryptically, "Let me hear that you are all *united* and happy."

For there has been a family falling out, which disturbs him mightily. It springs from the collapse of the banking firm of which his brother William was senior partner, a financial blow that has all but beggared the family, including the General himself. Years before, his brother advanced him three thousand pounds with which to purchase his commission in the 49th. William Brock, who has no close relatives except his brothers, had no intention that the money should be paid back; nonetheless, it remains on the books of the bankrupt firm as a debt, and the assignees are clamouring for it, even threatening legal action. Brock has pledged his entire civil salary as governor of Upper Canada—one thousand pounds a year—to pay off the debt ("Depend on my exercising the utmost economy. . . . Did it depend on myself, how willingly would I live on bread and water"). Typically, he is less concerned about this loss than about the estrangement between William Brock and his brother Irving, also connected with the firm.

On September 3, after stopping at York en route to Kingston (he is never still in these last days), he finds time aboard ship to write a longer letter, making use of the example of his recent victory to heal the family rift: "Let me know, my dearest brothers, that you are all again united. The want of union was nearly losing this province, without even a struggle, and be assured that it operates in the same degree in regard to families."

In spite of the depressing news of Prevost's armistice, he cannot conceal his ecstasy over the bloodless victory at Detroit. He knows he has taken a desperate gamble, but "the state of the province admitted of nothing but desperate remedies." He is irked that his enemies should attribute his success to blind luck. He believes in careful preparation, not luck. His victory has proceeded from "a cool calculation of *pours* and *contres*" and it is his alone, for he crossed the river against the advice of the more conservative Procter, who now commands at Detroit, and other advisers. "I have," he exults, "exceeded beyond expectation."

The best news is that as general he will receive the largest share of the Detroit prize money. The value of captured articles is now reckoned at between thirty and forty thousand pounds and may go higher. He does not want it for himself, but if it will enable him to contribute to the comfort and happiness of his nearly destitute family, he will "esteem it my highest reward." At the moment of victory, "when I returned Heaven thanks for my amazing success, I thought of you all; you appeared to me happy—your late sorrows forgotten; and I felt as if you acknowledged that the many benefits, which for a series of years I received from you, were not unworthily bestowed."

His brothers will, he believes, be able to see the colours of the U.S. 4th Regiment, which he expects his aide, Major Glegg, will bring to England. He doubts, however, that his fellow countrymen will hold the trophy in much esteem. "Nothing is prized," he writes acidly, "that is not acquired with blood."

In Canada he is a national hero, and he knows it. The plaudits pour in. The Chief Justice of Lower Canada hastens to send his congratulations "in common with every other subject of his majesty in British North America." General Alexander Maitland, the honorary colonel of the 49th, dispatches a gushing note from across the Atlantic, which Brock never receives. His old friend Justice William Dummer Powell cannot contain himself: "There is something so fabulous in the report of a handful of troops supported by a few raw militia leaving their strong post to invade an enemy of double numbers in his own fortress, and making them all prisoners without the loss of a man, that . . . it seems to me the people of England will be incredulous . . ." He can hardly wait to get the news in person from Brock when he reaches Kingston.

Brock himself is a little stunned by the adulation. He has received so many letters hailing his victory that he begins "to attach to it more importance than I was at first inclined." If the English take the same view as the Canadians, then "I cannot fail of meeting reward, and escaping the horror of being placed high on a shelf, never to be taken down."

He reaches Kingston on September 4, to be greeted by an artillery salute and a formal address of congratulation from the populace. As he has done at York a few days before, he replies with tact, praising the York and Lincoln regiments of militia, now at Queenston, whose presence, he declares (stretching the truth more than a little), induced him to undertake the expedition that brought about the fall of Detroit.

He praises everybody—citizens, soldiers, magistrates, officers, militia—for he intends to squeeze every possible advantage out of his victory, uniting Canadians against the invader. The change in attitude is startling; he notes privately that "the militia have been inspired . . . the disaffected are silenced." People are calling him the Saviour of Upper Canada. It is an accurate title, and in more ways than one, for he has saved the province not only from the Americans but also from itself.

He cannot rest. Back he goes across the lake to Fort George on the Niagara to study the situation along the frontier. Lieutenant-Colonel Baynes has already written to him of his meeting with Dearborn, describing the mood at Albany where the Americans are convinced that the British are weak and their own resources superior, exaggerations that are both "absurd and extravagant." But Baynes has urged Prevost to send more reinforcements to Niagara, so that if matters come to a head the British force will be superior.

Brock reaches Fort George on September 6, chagrined to discover how heavily the Americans have been reinforced during the armistice, due to end in two days. He expects an immediate attack. "The enemy will either turn my left flank which he may easily accomplish during a calm night or attempt to force his way across under cover of his Artillery." He sends at once to Procter at Amherstburg and Lieutenant-Colonel John Vincent at Kingston asking for more troops.

There is one bright spot, the result again of the victory at Detroit: three hundred Mohawk Indians are on the ground and another two hundred on their way under the controversial John Norton of the Indian Department. Born a Scotsman, now an adopted Mohawk chief, Norton sees himself the successor of the great Joseph Brant and the arch-rival of William Claus, his superior in the service.

Brock has mixed feelings about Norton's followers, who have cast aside their neutrality only as a result of British victories. Any form of neutrality is, to Brock, little short of treason. He cannot forgive the Mohawk, cannot understand why they would not wish to fight for the British, cannot grasp the truth—that the quarrel is not really theirs, that its outcome cannot help them. Now, he notes, "they appear ashamed of themselves, and promise to whipe [*sic*] away the disgrace into which they have fallen by their late conduct." It is doubtful whether the Indians feel any sense of disgrace; they have simply been following a foreign policy of their own, which is to reap the benefits of fighting on the winning side.

Brock is a little dubious of their value: "They may serve to intimidate; otherwise expect no essential service from this degenerate race." Has he forgotten so quickly that the great value of the Indians at Michilimackinac and Detroit was not to fight but to terrify? In his account to Prevost of the capture of Detroit, he has mentioned both Elliott and McKee by name but not Tecumseh, without whose presence the state of affairs on the Canadian frontier might easily have been reversed. For Tecumseh and the Indians are also the Saviours of Upper Canada.

But Brock urgently needs to bolster the loyalty of the Indians on the western frontier in Michigan Territory, which the British hold. That loyalty has been badly shaken by Sir George Prevost's armistice; the natives, who have been suspicious of British intentions since the gates of the fort were closed to them after the Battle of Fallen Timbers, are growing uneasy again. Brock has ordered Procter to dispatch a force to invest Fort Wayne on the Maumee—the kind of aggressive move that is totally opposed to Prevost's wishes and intentions. He explains to Prevost that he has done this with the hope of preserving the lives of the garrison from an Indian massacre. This humanitarian motive is overshadowed by a more realistic if cynical objective. Brock wants to preserve the Indians' allegiance, to keep the native warriors active and at the same time demonstrate an aggressive policy on the part of the British against the Long Knives. If Tecumseh's followers desert him "the consequences must be fatal," and to preserve their loyalty he has pledged his word that England will enter into no negotiation with the United States in which the interest of the Indians is not consulted. He reminds Prevost of this and Prevost reminds Whitehall. The Governor General, who seems to believe that peace is just around the corner, revives the old British dream of an Indian buffer state—a kind of native no man's land—separating British North America from the Union to the south.

But Prevost still believes that the path to peace lies in being as inoffensive as possible with the enemy. He wants to evacuate Detroit and indeed all of Michigan Territory—a possibility that appalls Brock, for he knows that it would cause the Indians to desert the British cause and make terms with the Americans. "I cannot conceive of a connexion so likely to lead to more awful consequences," he tells Prevost.

The Governor General backs down, but relations between the two men are becoming increasingly strained. Brock is prepared to attack across the Niagara River, is, in fact, eager to attack, convinced that he can sweep the Americans from the frontier and make himself master of Upper New York State, even though "my success would be transient." But Prevost has him shackled. Even after the armistice ends on September 8 Sir George clings to the wistful fancy that the Americans will come to terms if only the British do nothing to annoy them. This is fatuous. American honour has been sullied, and nothing will satisfy it but blood. It is psychologically impossible for the Americans to break off the war after the ignominy of Detroit. Thus far the only bright spot in America's abysmal war effort has been the defeat and destruction of the British frigate *Guerrière* by the *Constitution* off the Grand Banks on August 19.

This naval encounter by two isolated ships will have little effect on the outcome of the war, but it does buoy up America's flagging spirits and makes a national hero of the *Constitution*'s commander, Isaac Hull, at the very moment when his uncle William has become a national scapegoat.

Sir George makes one telling point in his instructions to his frustrated general: since the British are not interested in waging a campaign of conquest against the United States but only in containing the war with as little fuss as possible while battling their real enemy, Napoleon, it surely makes sense to let the enemy take the offensive "having ascertained by experience, our ability in the Canadas to resist the attack of a tumultuary force."

There is a growing testiness in Prevost's correspondence with Brock—more than a hint that he is prepared, if necessary, to write off the Niagara frontier. Sir George berates Brock obliquely for weakening the line of communication along the St. Lawrence between Cornwall and Kingston: by moving troops from those points to Niagara he has encouraged predatory raids by the enemy. Between the lines can be seen Prevost's fear of giving his impetuous subordinate too many troops lest he make an overt move that will upset the fine balance with which Prevost still hopes to conciliate the Americans.

But Brock has not been a soldier for the best part of three decades without learning to obey orders: "I have implicitly followed Your Excellency's instructions, and abstained, under great temptation and provocation, from every act of hostility." To his brother Savery he pours out his frustrations: "I am really placed in a most awkward predicament. . . . My instructions oblige me to adopt defensive measures, and I have evinced greater forbearance than was ever practised on any former occasion. It is thought that, without the aid of the sword, the American people may be brought to a full sense of their own interests. I firmly believe that I could at this moment sweep everything before me from Fort Niagara to Buffalo. . . ."

At last he has some officers he can trust. These come not from the 41st, which he finds wretchedly officered, but from his old regiment, the 49th, six companies of which he has brought to Fort George from Kingston: "Although the regiment has been ten years in this country drinking rum without bounds, it is still respectable...."

Many U.S. regulars, tired of service, are deserting to him; more, he believes, would do so if the opportunity offered. Those deserters who do not drown in the swirling river report a state of poor morale on the opposite side. They complain of bad food, scanty pay, continual sickness, and they are jealous of the militia, which they believe to be better fed and better treated. Brock disdains the American militia. He sees them as an undisciplined rabble of "enraged democrats . . . who . . . die very fast."

His enemies cannot help but admire him. Years later, Winfield Scott will recall how the Canadian commander of a small provincial vessel made a landing on the Erie shore and plundered several farm families of their table silver, beds, and other possessions. The indignant Brock seized the vessel, sent her back under a flag of truce with all the property that had not been destroyed and the money for the remainder. "Such conduct could not fail to win all noble hearts on both sides of the line."

But Brock has not the temperament for the kind of bloodless warfare that has been his lot since hostilities began. He is impatient for action and, since he cannot initiate it, hopes and expects the Americans will. He is convinced (correctly) that the Americans will have to make a move soon to keep their restless and undisciplined militia in line. To warn of attack he has ordered a line of beacon signals along the frontier. Now he can only sit and wait. His sword has yet to be raised in combat, and this clearly irks as much as it puzzles him:

"It is certainly something singular that we should be upwards of two months in a state of warfare, and that along this widely extended frontier not a single death, either natural or by the sword, should have occurred among the troops under my command, and we have not been altogether idle, nor has a single desertion taken place."

Who, in Europe, can take this bloodless colonial fracas seriously? On September 9, the day after Prevost's armistice ends, Napoleon launches and, at great cost, wins the Battle of Borodino, thus opening the way to Moscow. The casualties on that day exceed eighty thousand—a figure greater than the entire population of Upper Canada. On the Niagara frontier, two tiny, untrained armies face each other across the boiling river, each afraid to make the first move, each expecting the other to launch an attack.

Brock is certain that something decisive will happen before the month's end. "I say decisive, because if I should be beaten, the province is inevitably gone; and should I be victorious, I do not imagine the gentry from the other side will be anxious to return to the charge."

In short, he will either be confirmed as the Saviour of Upper Canada or there will be no Upper Canada. And whatever happens, Brock is convinced, this brief and not very bloody war will come to a swift conclusion. There are, of course, other possibilities, both glorious and at the same time tragic, but these he does not consider.

———

IN LEWISTON, DURING THESE same weeks, General Stephen Van Rensselaer finds himself pushed to the brink of a battle for which he is inadequately prepared by a series of circumstances over which he has little control. Events pile up, one upon another, like ocean breakers, driving him unwillingly towards a foreign shore.

On August 27 the camp is subjected to a dreadful spectacle: across the river for more than half a mile straggle the remnants of Hull's defeated army, ragged, shoeless, dispirited, the wounded groaning in open carts, the whole prodded onward by their British captors.

"The sensations this scene produced in our camp were inexpressible," Lovett writes his friend. "Mortification, indignation, fearful apprehension, suspicion, jealousy, dismay, rage, madness." The effect on Van Rensselaer's force is twofold: the militia is cowed by this demonstration of British invincibility while the Hawks among the officers salivate for action.

"Alarm pervades the country and distrust among the troops," the General writes to Governor Tompkins. Like Hull's beaten soldiers, many of his own are without shoes; all are clamouring for pay. "While we are thus growing daily weaker, our enemy is growing stronger." The British are reinforcing the high ground above Queenston, pouring in men and ordnance and fortifying every prominent point from Fort Erie to Fort George.

Governor Tompkins, who is thunderstruck by the disaster, receives another letter from his political ally, the belligerent quartermaster general, Peter B. Porter:

"Three days ago we witnessed a sight which made my heart sick within me, and the emotions it excited throughout the whole of our troops along the line . . . are not to be described. The heroes of Tippecanoe, with the garrisons of Detroit and Michilimackinac . . . were marched like cattle from Fort Erie to Fort George, guarded by General Brock's regular troops with all the parade and pomp of British insolence, and we were incapacitated by the armistice and our own weakness from giving them the relief which they seemed anxiously to expect, and could only look on and sicken at the sight. . . .

". . . This miserable and timid system of defense must be abandoned or the nation is ruined and disgraced. Make a bold push at any one point and you will find your enemy. . . .

"The public mind in this quarter is wrought up almost to a state of madness. Jealousy and distrust begin to prevail toward the general officers, occasioned perhaps by the rash and imprudent expressions on politics of some of the persons attached to them, but principally to the surrender of Detroit, which among the common people is almost universally ascribed to treachery. . . ."

On September 7, a day before the armistice ends, Major Lovett, the General's eloquent aide, comes to the conclusion that "we must either fight or run. . . . There are some pretty strong reasons to believe that Brock is attempting to *Hull* us. . . ." Yet nobody on the American side can guess Brock's intentions or even estimate the true strength of his force because it is impossible to persuade a single man to risk his neck by acting as a spy on the Canadian shore. Van Rensselaer must resort to the timeworn artifice of sending officers across under flags of truce to treat with the enemy on various pretexts while peering about at the fortifications.

At Albany, General Dearborn's resolve is wavering. As late as mid-August he stated his belief that Montreal and all of Upper Canada would fall to the Americans before winter. Now Hull's defeat has shaken him. He still insists that he will attack Niagara, Kingston, and Montreal, but his purpose is circumscribed by a hedgerow of "ifs." *If* the governors of the neighbouring states will supply enough reinforcements quickly; *if* the Quartermaster General can get him sufficient supplies, ammunition, and guns, then "I am persuaded we may act with effect." *If* he can muster some five thousand regulars and additional militia, he will push on to Montreal to support Van Rensselaer's offensive on the Niagara, hoping to cut communications between the two Canadas, "but whether I shall be able to effect anything or not depends on so many contingencies as to leave all in doubt."

He has dispatched some five thousand troops to Plattsburg on Lake Champlain and another two thousand (all militia) to Sackets Harbor and expects to have an army of seven thousand on the Niagara, including three thousand regulars. Unfortunately Brigadier-General Wadsworth, the New York militia commander, who has grossly overestimated Brock's forces, has warned him that anything fewer than ten thousand will not do.

In his reports to Washington, Dearborn manages to be gloomy and optimistic in the space of a single sentence: "I fear . . . that we shall meet with additional misfortunes on the borders of Upper Canada . . . but if we redouble our exertions and inspire a due degree of firmness and spirit in the country, all will ultimately go well."

He is an old man, indecisive, inexperienced, out of his depth, querulous and uninformed ("Will the militia consent to go into Canada?"), the victim of his country's military myopia, the prisoner of its bureaucratic confusion. Hampered by lack of supplies, lack of men, lack of money, he tells Eustis: "I have never found official duties so unceasing, perplexing and fatiguing as at this place" and then adds a sympathetic postscript: "I presume you are not on a bed of roses."

At Lewiston, while Dearborn vacillates, Peter B. Porter chafes for action. He and his cronies mount a whispering campaign against Van Rensselaer's command. The General's aide, Solomon, is convinced that "they have so far succeeded in the Camp and the Country that in the former it is only whispered, but in the Latter it is openly said, that Gen. Van Rensselaer is a traitor to his Country and the Surrender of the Army when it crosses the River is the price of his Infamy." As a result, "he cannot enforce the Subordination which is so necessary to the safety and glory of the Troops he Commands."

Reluctantly, Solomon writes to Morgan Lewis, a former Republican governor of New York and now the state's quartermaster general, suggesting that another commander—somebody of the same politics as the government—replace his cousin on the frontier. Nothing comes of it.

The General expects a British attack imminently and prepares to defend against it. He decides to maintain Fort Niagara, opposite Fort George, decrepit though it is, removes the roof from a stone building, sets up a battery of two twelve-pound cannon in its upper storey, establishes a second battery of three eighteen-pounders a mile upriver across from a similar British emplacement, builds a new communications road back of the river and beyond enemy fire, and co-opts an additional five hundred men stationed at Buffalo to strengthen his own force.

The British are also active. Gazing across the narrow river, General Van Rensselaer can see the *Royal George* arrive with two hundred gunners. He has learned that one hundred smaller boats loaded with stores for the enemy fort have passed up the St. Lawrence together with two regiments of troops. The situation, he admits, is critical, but "a retrograde movement of this army upon the back of that disaster which has befallen the one at Detroit would stamp a stigma upon the national character which time could never wipe away." He will hold out against superior strength until he is reinforced. There is no evidence that he contemplates an attack. It is the British who will attack, or so the General believes.

But the British do not attack, and the promised reinforcements do not arrive. In Van Rensselaer's army of two thousand, on September 22, one hundred and forty-nine are too sick to fight, including his cousin Solomon. The weather is dreadful; raw winds and cold rains harass the troops, soaking such blankets and tents as are available.

After suffering for six days with fever, Solomon attempts to return to duty, suffers a relapse, is bled thrice and doctored with enough salts, jalap, castor oil, and calomel to render an ordinary man insensible. It takes him another week to recover from the doctors' ministrations. By contrast Lovett, the amateur soldier, is in splendid condition, "hardened almost to the hide, muscles and houghs of an ox" and clearly having the time of his life:

"We are every few days, deluged in water, such storms of rain and wind I think I never experienced, the cloth of my Tent is mere sieve stuff; every third night I get wet as a Muskrat. But in the worst of it I sing, in proper tune: 'No burning heats by day, Nor blasts of evening air, Shall take my health away, If God be with me there.' . . . I feel safe; for I feel myself in duty. I am glad I came. . . ."

In Albany, General Dearborn continues to promise that money, men, and provisions are on the way, albeit tardily ("a strange fatality seems to have pervaded the whole arrangement" is the way he puts it), and urges aggressive action. His letter to Stephen Van Rensselaer bubbles with enthusiasm: on the western frontier, General Harrison is marching to the relief of Detroit with a new Army of the Northwest, six or seven thousand strong; two thousand more troops are stationed at Sackets Harbor; the American navy is operating in Lake Ontario. "In fact we have nothing to fear and much to hope."

Everything, however, depends on what happens on the Niagara River: *"By putting on the best face that your situation admits, the enemy may be induced to delay an attack until you will be able to meet him and carry the war into Canada. At all events, we must calculate on possessing Upper Canada before winter sets in."* Dearborn underlines this passage as if, by a pen stroke, he can will his ragtag army into victory.

At the end of September, the longed-for reinforcements arrive, including seventeen hundred soldiers under the command of one of the more curious specimens of American generalship, Brigadier-General Alexander Smyth. Smyth is bombastic, egotistical, jealous of his prerogatives. A regular officer, he disdains the militia and has no intention of co-operating with his nominal commander, Stephen Van Rensselaer. Though he knows nothing of the country and has only just arrived, he takes it upon himself to advise the General that the best place for a crossing of the Niagara would be above the falls and not below them. He has therefore decided not to take his troops to Lewiston but to encamp them near Buffalo, thus splitting the American force. Nor does he report personally to Van Rensselaer. He says he is too busy.

By now, General Stephen Van Rensselaer has, in the words of his cousin Solomon, "resolved to gratify his own inclinations and those of his army" and commence operations. The British show no inclination to attack. Dearborn has demanded action. For better or for worse, Stephen is determined that he shall have it.

If numbers mean anything, his chances for success are excellent. He now has some eight thousand troops under his command, half of them regulars, of whom forty-two hundred are encamped at Lewiston. (The remainder are at Fort Niagara and either at Buffalo or, in the case of some two thousand Pennsylvania volunteers, en route to Buffalo.) To counter this force Brock has about one thousand regular troops, some six hundred militia, and a reserve of perhaps six hundred militia and Indians, strung out thinly from Fort Erie to Fort George. The bulk of his strength he must keep on his wings to prevent the Americans from turning one of his flanks and attacking his rear. Thus his centre at Queenston is comparatively weak.

Yet numbers do not tell the whole story. Morale, sickness, discipline, determination—all these Van Rensselaer must take into account. By his own count he has only seventeen hundred *effective* militia men at Lewiston. The state of his army is such that he knows he must act swiftly, if at all:

"Our best troops are raw, many of them dejected by the distress their families suffer by their absence, and many have not necessary clothing. We are in a cold country, the season is far advanced and unusually inclement; we are half deluged by rain. The blow must be struck soon or all the toil and expense of the campaign will go for nothing, and worse than nothing, for the whole will be tinged with dishonor."

The key word is "dishonor." It creeps like a fog through the sodden tents of the military, blinding all to reality. It hangs like a weight over the council chambers in Albany and Washington. Stephen Van Rensselaer feels its pressure spurring him to action, *any* action. No purpose now in disputing the war and its causes, no sense in further recriminations or I-told-you-so's. Detroit must be avenged! "The national character is degraded, and the disgrace will remain, corroding the public feeling and spirit until another campaign, unless it be instantly wiped away by a brilliant close of this." The words might have sprung from the lips of Porter, the War Hawk; they are actually those of Van Rensselaer, the Federalist and pacifist.

He knows that with his present force at Lewiston it would be rash to attempt an attack. But Smyth has arrived with an almost equal number and that is enough. He plans a two-pronged assault: Smyth's regulars will cross the river near Newark and storm Fort George from the rear while he leads the militia from Lewiston to carry the heights above Queenston. This will divide the thinly spread British forces, cut their line of communications, drive their shipping from the mouth of the Niagara River (which will become an American waterway), provide the troops with warm and extensive winter quarters, act as a springboard for the following season's campaign, and—certainly not least—"wipe away part of the score of our past disgrace."

The scheme is plausible, but it depends on the co-operation of Brigadier-General Smyth; and Smyth has no intention of co-operating. He acts almost as if Van Rensselaer did not exist. The Commander invites him to a council of officers to plan the attack. Smyth does not reply. The General writes again, more explicitly. Still no reply. Several days pass. Nothing. A fellow officer now informs Van Rensselaer that he has seen Smyth, who is unable to name the day when he can come to Lewiston for a council. The General thereupon sends a direct order to Smyth to bring his command "with all possible dispatch." Silence.

In no other army would such insubordination be tolerated, but America is not yet a military nation. The amiable Van Rensselaer does not court-martial his recalcitrant underling; he simply proceeds without him. He has already told Dearborn that it would be rash to attack Queenston with the militiamen under his command at Lewiston. Now, with Smyth's regulars apparently out of the picture, he determines to do just that.

He has very little choice for, at this juncture, an incident occurs near Black Rock that reduces his options.

———

BLACK ROCK, NEW YORK, October 8, 1812. Lieutenant Jesse Elliott of the U.S. Navy, a veteran of the 1807 attack on *Chesapeake* (and said to be a nephew of Matthew Elliott), supervising the construction of three ships of war for service in Lake Erie, finds himself tempted by the sight of two British ships, newly anchored under the guns of Fort Erie. One is the North West Company's two-gun schooner *Caledonia*, which Captain Roberts impressed into service during the successful attack on Michilimackinac. The other is a former American brig, *Adams*, mounting six guns, captured at Detroit and renamed for that city by the British. Elliott conceives a daring plan: if he can capture both vessels and add them to the fleet under construction, the balance of power will shift to the American side on Lake Erie.

He needs seamen. Fortunately some ninety American sailors are on the march from Albany. Elliott sends a hurry-up call, selects fifty for the job. Isaac Roach, a young artillery adjutant (and a future mayor of Philadelphia), offers fifty more men from his own regiment. There is a scramble to volunteer. The battalion commander, Winfield Scott, then on the threshold of what will be a long and glorious career, warns his men that they can expect a hard fight, but this only excites them further. When Roach, a mere second-lieutenant, orders "Volunteers to the front: March!" the entire battalion steps forward. Officers senior to Roach attempt to resign their commissions in order to serve under him. Men are so eager for battle that Roach finds he must select ten more than his quota.

The attack is made in two longboats, each carrying about fifty armed men, who must track their craft against the rapid current of the Niagara to the mouth of Buffalo Creek—difficult work. Here the men are forced to wade into the freezing water to their shoulders to haul the empty longboats over the bar at the creek's mouth in order to enter Lake Erie. It is past midnight; the troops, soaking wet, with a chill sleet falling about them, must now row for three hours up the lake "and not allowed to even laugh to keep ourselves warm."

At three they come silently upon their unsuspecting quarry. A fire in the caboose of *Detroit* gives them a light to steer by. Roach and Elliott, in the lead boat, head straight for the vessel. Sailing Master George Watts and Captain Nathan Towson of Winfield Scott's regiment take their boat under the stern of *Caledonia*. It is not possible to achieve complete surprise for the sleet has ended, the night is calm, the lake glassy. Two volleys of musket fire pour into the lead boat from the deck of *Detroit*, whose captain is the same Lieutenant Frederic Rolette who captured *Cuyahoga* at the start of the war. Rolette and his crew are quickly overpowered as Elliott manages to loose the topsails in an attempt to get the ship underway. Suddenly a British cannon opens up; a heavy ball whizzes twenty feet above the heads of the boarding party ("John Bull always aims too high," says Roach), ricochets onto the opposite shore where half of Winfield Scott's men are lined up to watch the action and tears an arm off a Major Cuyler of the New York militia, knocking him from his horse, mortally wounded. Roach, with a bundle of lighted candles in his hand, touches off *Detroit*'s six-pound deck guns in reply.

Aboard *Caledonia*, the commander, a young Scot, Second-Lieutenant Robert Irvine, roused from his bed, has thrown himself down the gangway, calling on his inexperienced crew of a dozen men to follow him and discharging his blunderbuss into the attackers. He has time only for a second charge before he is felled by a cutlass stroke, but he has managed to kill or wound several of the boarding party. Watts and Towson get *Caledonia* underway— thus distracting the enemy fire from *Detroit*, whose attackers are axing through her cables—and sail her across the river, where she anchors under the protection of the American batteries at Black Rock. She is a considerable prize, being loaded with pork destined for Amherstburg, a rich cargo of furs, and a good many American prisoners captured at Michilimackinac and Detroit who now find themselves free men again.

Elliott and Roach, still facing a concentrated fire from Fort Erie, drift down the river, unable to manoeuvre *Detroit*. A half mile below Black Rock she grounds on the British side of Squaw Island. Exposed to enemy fire, the Americans abandon ship, taking the captured Lieutenant Rolette and his men and all but three American prisoners of war who had been held in the hold.

A seesaw battle ensues for the shattered *Detroit*. A British detachment crosses the river, seizes her, attempts to pull her off the shoal. This is too much for Winfield Scott, who dispatches another party to land on the northeast shore of Squaw Island and drive the British away. The Americans do their best to warp *Detroit* into open water, but she has lost her anchor and the British fire is so hot they are forced to abandon the attempt. They strip her of armament and supplies and burn her to the water line, thus denying her to the enemy.

It is a considerable blow to the British. The Americans have captured four cannon, two hundred muskets, and so much pork that Procter's men at Amherstburg will be forced on to half rations. But the real effect of the loss of one ship and the seizure of another will not be felt until the following year at the Battle of Lake Erie.

Brock, who gallops directly to the scene as soon as he receives the news, instantly sees the danger. The event, he tells Prevost, "may reduce us to incalculable distress. The enemy is making every effort to gain a naval superiority on both lakes, which, if they accomplish, I do not see how we can retain the country." Brock cannot resist a small gibe at Prevost's continuing policy of caution: "Three vessels are fitting out for war on the other side of Squaw Island, which I would have attempted to destroy but for Your Excellency's instructions to forbear. Now such a force is collected for their protection as would render any operation against them very hazardous."

Jesse Elliott's bold adventure has another equally far-reaching result. The only American victory on the frontier, its success will goad the Americans into premature attack. The newspapers seize upon it thirstily. The Buffalo *Gazette* headlines it as a GALLANT AND DARING EXPLOIT. Congress publicly thanks Elliott and presents him with a sword. A thrill runs through the nation. At Lewiston, General Van Rensselaer is presented with an ultimatum from his troops, who are now hot for action—or claim to be. The General is warned that if he does not take the offensive immediately, they will all go home. With Smyth sulking in his tent at Buffalo, Van Rensselaer decides to abandon his two-pronged attack and launch a single assault upon Queenston on October 11. What follows is high farce.

He has planned to cross the river at night in thirteen boats, each capable of carrying twenty-five men. Lieutenant-Colonel John Fenwick's artillery will come up from Niagara to support the attack, and it is hoped that Smyth will send further reinforcements. The crossing will be made from the old ferry landing directly opposite the heights of Queenston where the river is a tumult of eddies and whirlpools; thus experienced boatmen are mandatory. The best man for the job is one Lieutenant Sims, who is sent ahead in the darkness while the troops follow in wagons.

Now an extraordinary incident takes place which defies explanation. Sims, by accident or design, passes the embarkation point, lands his boat far upriver where it cannot be found, then, perhaps through panic at his error or perhaps from cowardice, abandons his boat and is not seen again. In the growing drizzle, the troops wait in vain for him to return. Solomon Van Rensselaer, roused from his sickbed to command the assault and shaking with fever, waits with them. Nothing can be done because, for reasons unexplained, the oars for all the boats are with the wretched Sims.

The troops wait all night as the storm rises in fury. (It will continue for twenty-eight hours, deluging the camp.) Finally, as daylight breaks, they are marched back to camp, the boats half-concealed in the rushes. Van Rensselaer calls a council, hoping that the incident will dampen the spirits of his eager officers. On the contrary, they are even keener to attack. Lieutenant-Colonel John Chrystie, newly arrived on the scene, has already reported that his officers and men are "full of ardor and anxious to give their country proof of their patriotism." Everybody, the General discovers, seems to "have gained new heat from the recent miscarriage." Events not of his making have him in their grasp. A friend in Albany, the Federalist congressman Abraham Van Vechten, realizes this and in a letter (delivered too late) warns Solomon that "the General's reputation forbids rashness. To shun the Enemy improperly would be censurable—but to seek him under manifest disadvantages would be madness." The time has long passed, however, when the General can accept such cool advice. The pressure on him is so great that he realizes that "my refusal to act might involve me in suspicion and the service in disgrace."

As his aide and friend John Lovett describes it, "the impetuosity of not only men but his first officers became such that he was absolutely compelled to go to battle or risk such consequences as no man could endure." It is not possible to wait, even though there is no proper plan of attack. He must strike the blow at once, this very night.

———

FORT GEORGE, UPPER CANADA, October 11, 1812. As Brock's brigade major, Thomas Evans, rises from his dinner at the officers' mess, his commander hands him an alarming note. It comes from Captain James Dennis, commanding one of the flank companies of the 49th at Queenston. Dennis's detachment is in a state of mutiny. The men have threatened to shoot their officers.

"Evans," says Brock, "you will proceed early in the morning and investigate this business, and march as prisoners in here half a dozen of the most culpable and I will make an example of them."

There can be little doubt what that example will be. Years before, Brock literally pounced on Fort George and in a few minutes seized and shackled a group of mutineers plotting to shoot their commander, Roger Sheaffe. The ringleaders were taken to Quebec, court-martialled, and shot by a firing squad in the presence of the entire company, a demonstration that shook everyone including Brock himself, who was seen to wipe the tears from his eyes as the order was executed.

Brock has a second instruction for Major Evans:

"You can also cross the river and tell Van Rensselaer I expect he will immediately exchange the prisoners taken in the *Detroit* and *Caledonia* for an equal number of Americans I released after the capture of Detroit."

Thus, on the very eve of the most famous battle on Canadian soil, a British officer will enter and reconnoitre the enemy camp.

Evans reaches Queenston the following morning to find the guardhouse gutted and Dennis in a state of alarm. The two repair to Dennis's quarters in the largest home in the village, a handsome stone edifice on the high bank above the river, built by the best-known trader on the frontier, the late Robert Hamilton. It is owned now by his son Alexander, sheriff of Queenston, member of the Legislative Council, and a lieutenant-colonel in the militia. Alexander is another of the many grandsons of John Askin of Amherstburg.

Just as Evans is about to leave the Hamilton house to arrest the ringleaders of the mutiny, he hears a scatter of musket fire from the opposite shore. A ball whizzes through the room, passing directly between the two officers. Evans is outraged and demands to know the meaning of "such unusual insolence." Dennis replies that sporadic firing has been going on for some days, making it hazardous to use the door on the river side of the building.

Evans decides to cross the river at once, musket balls or no, and orders Dennis to corral the prisoners for his return. Then, with the balls still hurtling past his ears, he walks over to the home of a militia captain, Thomas Dickson, the brother of Robert, the Red-Haired Man, and—such are the close-knit relationships of the frontier trade—a cousin of the late Robert Hamilton.

Evans asks Mrs. Dickson for a white kerchief to serve as a flag of truce and invites Dickson to join him in the river crossing. Mrs. Dickson expostulates. Others in the house join her: the venture is far too dangerous; the enemy is in a temper; they will no longer respect a white flag.

At this, Evans seizes Dickson by one hand, takes the flag in the other, descends the steep steps to a canoe at the water's edge, and starts off across the two-hundred-yard stream in an unceasing shower of musket balls. The canoe, battered by the eddies and filling with water, becomes unmanageable and seems about to founder when the American fire suddenly ceases and the two men are able to reach the far shore.

As Evans is about to leap to the ground, an American with a bayonet stops him. The Major asks to see the Adjutant-General, Solomon Van Rensselaer, but is told that Solomon is too ill to receive him. He replies that he carries an important message from Brock and is prepared to see either the General himself or somebody deputized by him. Eventually, Major Lovett appears, and Evans presents his request about the prisoner exchange. Lovett's reply is abrupt and curiously evasive. Nothing can be done, he says, "till the day after tomorrow."

Evans is instantly on the alert. What have the Americans planned for the morrow? When he presses his case, Lovett remains evasive. Evans urges him to consult the General. Lovett agrees and goes off.

It appears to Evans that Lovett is trying to delay his return to the Canadian side—it is already past midday. Lovett does not come back for two hours. He explains that the prisoners have been sent on to Albany and cannot quickly be brought back, but all will be settled "the day after tomorrow."

This constant harping on the morrow confirms Evans in his suspicions that the enemy is planning an immediate attack. Now he is anxious to get away and report to Brock. He has kept his eyes open and notices that the Americans' numbers have been "prodigiously swelled by a horde of half-savage troops from Kentucky, Ohio, and Tennessee." (The prevailing British opinion is that the American militia and volunteers consist of uncivilized wild men.) Even more significant, Evans spots more than a dozen boats half-hidden in fissures in the bank and partially covered with brush. This convinces him that "an attack on our shores could not be prudently delayed for a single day."

He and Dickson paddle swiftly to their own shore. Dickson's first task is to remove his family from their house on the river bank, clearly the site of any future battle. Evans, meanwhile, rushes to warn the 49th flank companies and the militia stationed at Queenston. It is now past three. Fort George is six miles away. Every man will be needed to defend the town, including the mutinous prisoners. On his own responsibility, Evans liberates them "on the specious plea of their offence proceeding from a too free indulgence in drink," appealing to their loyalty and courage, which he has no doubt will be tested by the following day.

Then, after making sure a fresh supply of ammunition has been distributed and "infusing all the spirit and animation in my power to impart," the harried brigade major sets off at a gallop for Fort George, alerting the various posts along the route to the coming danger. He reaches the fort at six, having been exposed for thirteen hours "to wet feet and extreme heat without refreshment of any kind." He is so exhausted he cannot speak. He takes some food, recovers his breath, and is ushered into the dining room before Brock and his senior officers.

At first they do not believe him, charge him with overreaction, offer to place bets against his predictions of an attack on the following day. Brock himself appears doubtful, then changes his mind as Evans talks on. With a grave face he asks Evans to follow him into his office where he questions him carefully on the day's occurrences. At last he is convinced. The two men return to the dining room where the General issues orders calling in all the militia in the neighbourhood that very evening; others in outlying districts are told to report as swiftly as possible. He thanks Evans, who is ordered to make all necessary preparations at headquarters to meet the coming assault. Brock then returns to his office to work late into the night.

Evans toils until eleven, then slumps onto a mattress. A few hours later, his slumber is disturbed by the rumble of distant guns.

———

LEWISTON, NEW YORK, October 13, 1812. At 3 A.M. General Stephen Van Rensselaer opens the attack on Queenston, after some unfortunate skirmishing between his regular and militia officers on the touchy subject of seniority. Lieutenant-Colonel Winfield Scott refuses to serve under Solomon Van Rensselaer, who has been deputed to lead the first wave. Lieutenant-Colonel John Chrystie, another regular, also demurs. A solution is worked out that gives Chrystie a command equal to but separate from Solomon's. Chrystie will command the three hundred regular troops during the crossing; Solomon will be in charge of an equal number of militiamen picked carefully from the best-drilled battalions. Not all of the regulars are as touchy as Scott and Chrystie. Lieutenant-Colonel John Fenwick is so anxious to get into the battle that he drops his rank and puts himself under the command of the militia.

Stephen Van Rensselaer's attack plan and his preparations for the assault are both faulty. He has already lost the advantage of surprise; now he proposes to make the first crossing with only a handful of bateaux: two large boats, each holding eighty men, and a dozen smaller ones, each holding twenty-five. His initial attack force, which will cross in two waves, consists of some six hundred men, half of them militia. A few miles upriver are more boats, which could easily be floated down, but the General does not take advantage of these, believing that once the boats are emptied on the opposite shore they can quickly return for reinforcements. Half a dozen trips may serve to ferry the entire force across the river. It is a serious miscalculation.

Nor does Stephen Van Rensselaer think to make use of Jesse Elliott's bluejackets at Black Rock, men who might be considered experienced boatmen. His own militia, of course, know this part of the river well; they have been staring across it, sometimes navigating it under flags of truce, for some six weeks. But those who have just joined his force from Buffalo, Black Rock, and Fort Niagara are strangers to the area.

There are other problems. Van Rensselaer has failed to distribute enough ammunition. He has not insisted strongly enough on making use of Smyth's regular forces at Buffalo. Nobody has thought to find boats large enough to transport heavy field pieces across the river; the bateaux cannot handle cannon or caissons. Nor have the various commands been assigned to specific objectives. The orders are general: get across, seize the village, gain the heights.

It is still dark when the first boats push off in the teeth of a chill, sleety drizzle. To oppose the landing, the British have fewer than three hundred men in and about Queenston. But the defenders are on the alert. John Lovett, who has been placed in charge of the American battery at Fort Grey on the heights above Lewiston, notes that the Canadian shore is an incessant blaze of musketry and that his friend Solomon lands in what seems to be a sheet of fire. His own guns—eighteen-pounders—open up to cover the attack, aided by two six-pounders and a mortar on the Lewiston shore, the cannonballs and shells whistling over the heads of the troops in the bateaux.

At that moment, the British open fire. Half-way up the heights, in an arrow-shaped emplacement known as a redan, a single cannon begins to lob eighteen-pound balls down on the boats. Darkness is banished as bombs burst and muskets flash. At Brown's Point, half-way between Queenston and Fort George, young Lieutenant John Beverley Robinson of the York Volunteers (the future chief justice) sees all of the village lit by gun fire.

In one of the boats approaching the shore sits the oldest volunteer in the American army, an extraordinary Kentucky frontiersman named Samuel Stubbs, sixty-two years old and scarcely five feet in height, gripping the rifle with which, in just three months, he has killed forty-five deer. Peering into the gloom illuminated now by the flash of cannon, Stubbs sees the opposite shore lined with redcoats "as thick as bees upon a sugar maple." In a few minutes he is ashore under heavy fire, "the damned redcoats cutting us up like slain venison," his companions dropping "like wild pigeons" while the musket balls whistle around him "like a northwest wind through a dry cane break."

Colonel Van Rensselaer's attack force has dwindled. Three of the boats, including the two largest containing almost two hundred men, have drifted downriver and turned back. On the bank above, Captain Dennis with forty-six British regulars and a handful of militia is keeping up a withering fire. Solomon Van Rensselaer is no sooner out of his boat than a ball strikes him in the right thigh. As he thrusts forward, waving his men on, a second ball enters his thigh—the British are purposely firing low to inflict maximum damage. As the Colonel continues to stumble forward, a third shot penetrates his calf and a fourth mangles his heel, but he does not stop. Two more strike him in the leg and thigh. Weak from loss of blood, his men pinned down by the killing fire, he totters back with the remnant of his force to the shelter of the steep bank above the river and looks around weakly for his fellow commander. Where is Chrystie? He is supposed to be in charge of the regulars. But Chrystie is nowhere to be seen.

Chrystie's boat has lost an oarlock and is drifting helplessly downstream while one of his officers attempts to hold an oar in place. None of these regulars is familiar with the river; all are dependent upon a pilot to guide them. But as they come under musket fire from the Canadian bank the pilot, groaning in terror, turns about and makes for the American side. Chrystie, wounded in the hand by grape-shot, struggles with him to no avail. The boat lands several hundred yards below the embarkation point, to which Chrystie and the others must return on foot.

In Solomon Van Rensselaer's later opinion, this is the turning point of the battle. Chrystie's return and the heavy fire from the opposite shore "damped the hitherto irrepressible ardor of the militia." The very men who the previous day were so eager to do battle— hoping, perhaps, that a quick victory would allow them to return to their homes—now remember that they are not required to fight on foreign soil. One militia major suddenly loses his zest for combat and discovers that he is too ill to lead his detachment across the river.

At the embarkation point, Chrystie finds chaos. No one, apparently, has been put in charge of directing the boats or the boatmen, most of whom have forsaken their duty. Some are already returning without orders or permission, landing wherever convenient, leaving the boats where they touch the shore. Others are leaping into bateaux on their own, crossing over, then abandoning the craft to drift downriver. Many are swiftly taken prisoner by the British. Charles Askin, lying abed in the Hamilton house suffering from boils, hears that some of the militia have cheerfully given themselves up in the belief that they will be allowed to go home as the militia captured at Detroit were. When told they will be taken to Quebec, they are distressed. Askin believes that had they known of this very few would have put a foot on the Canadian shore.

As Chrystie struggles to collect the missing bateaux, his fellow commander, Lieutenant-Colonel Fenwick, in charge of the second assault wave, arrives only to learn that he cannot cross for lack of boats. Exposed to a spray of grape- and canister-shot, Fenwick herds his men back into the shelter of the ravine until he manages to secure enough craft to move the second wave out onto the river. The crossing is a disaster. Lieutenant John Ball of the 49th directs the fire of one of his little three-pounders, known as "grasshoppers," against the bateaux. One is knocked out of the water with a loss of fifteen men. Three others, holding some eighty men, drift into a hollow just below the Hamilton house. All are slaughtered or taken prisoner, Fenwick among them. Terribly wounded in the eye, the right side, and the thigh, he counts nine additional bullet holes in his cloak.

None of the regular commanders has yet been able to cross the narrow Niagara. On the opposite shore under the sheltering bank, Solomon Van Rensselaer, growing weaker from his wounds, is attempting to rally his followers, still pinned down by the cannon fire from the gun in the redan and the muskets of Captain Dennis's small force on the bank above. Captain John E. Wool, a young officer of the 13th Infantry, approaches with a plan. Unless something is done, and done quickly, he says, all will be prisoners. The key to victory or defeat is the gun in the redan. It must be seized. Its capture could

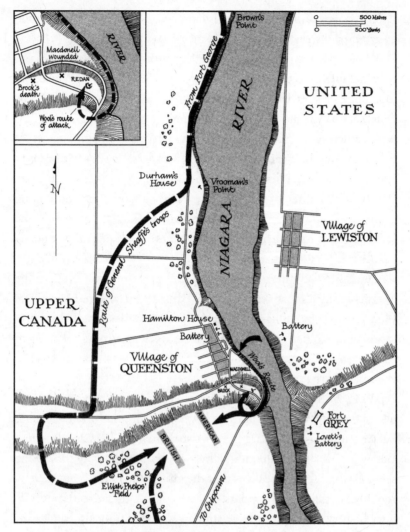

The Battle of Queenston Heights

signal a turning point in the battle that would relieve the attackers while the fire could be redirected, with dreadful effect, among the defenders. But how can it be silenced? A frontal attack is out of the question, a flanking attack impossible, for the heights are known to be unscalable from the river side. Or are they? Young Captain Wool has heard of a fisherman's path upriver leading to the heights above the gun emplacement. He believes he can bring an attacking force up the slopes and now asks Solomon Van Rensselaer's permission to attempt the feat.

Wool is twenty-three, a lithe, light youth of little experience but considerable ambition. One day he will be a general. The fact that he has been shot through the buttocks does not dampen his enthusiasm. With his bleeding commander's permission, he sets off with sixty men and officers, moving undetected through a screen of bushes below the river bank. Solomon Van Rensselaer's last order to him is to shoot the first man in the company who tries to turn tail. Then, as Wool departs, the Colonel slumps to the ground among a pile of dead and wounded, a borrowed greatcoat concealing the seriousness of his injuries from his wet and shivering force. Shortly afterwards he is evacuated.

Captain Wool, meanwhile, finds the path and gazes up at the heights rising almost vertically more than three hundred feet above him. Creased by gullies, blocked by projecting ledges of shale and sandstone, tangled with shrubs, vines, trees and roots clinging to the clefts, they look forbidding, but the Americans manage to claw their way to the crest.

Wool, buttocks smarting from his embarrassing wound, looks about. An empty plateau, bordered by maples and basswood, stretches before him. But where are the British? Their shelters are deserted. Below, to his right, half-hidden by a screen of yellowing foliage, he sees a flash of scarlet, realizes that the gun in the redan is guarded by the merest handful of regulars. Brock, who is a great reader of military history, must surely have studied Wolfe's famous secret ascent to the Plains of Abraham, yet, like the vanquished Montcalm, he has been assured that the heights are safe. He has brought his men down to reinforce the village, an error that will cost him dear. Wool's men, gazing down at the red-coated figures manning the big gun, cannot fail to see the tall officer with the cocked hat in their midst. It is the General himself. A few minutes later, when all are assembled, their young commander gives the order to charge.

AT FORT GEORGE, BROCK has awakened in the dark to the distant booming of cannon. What is happening? Is it a feint near Queenston or a major attack? He is inclined to the former possibility, for he has anticipated Van Rensselaer's original strategy and does not know of Smyth's obstinacy. Brock is up in an instant, dressed, and on his grey horse Alfred, dashing out the main gate, waiting for no one, not even his two aides, who are themselves hurriedly pulling on their boots. Later someone will spread a story about Brock stopping for a stirrup cup of coffee from the hands of Sophia Shaw, a general's daughter, said to be his fiancée. It is not convincing. On this dark morning, with the wind gusting sleet into his face and the southern sky lit by flashes of cannon, he will stop for nobody.

As he hurries through the mud toward Queenston, he encounters young Samuel Jarvis, a subaltern in his favourite militia unit, the York Volunteers. Jarvis, galloping so fast in the opposite direction that he cannot stop in time, finally reins his horse, wheels about, tells his general that the enemy has landed in force at the main Queenston dock. Jarvis's mission ought not to be necessary because of Brock's system of signal fires, but in the heat of battle nobody has remembered to light them.

Brock gallops on in the pre-dawn murk, past harvested grain fields, soft meadows, luxuriant orchards, the trees still heavy with fruit. The York Volunteers, stationed at Brown's Point, are already moving toward Queenston. Brock dashes past, waving them on. A few minutes later his two aides also gallop by. John Beverley Robinson, marching with his company, recognizes John Macdonell, Brock's provincial aide and his own senior in the York legal firm to which the young volunteer is articled. Brock has reason to be proud of the York militia, who answered his call to arms with alacrity, accompanied him on the embarkation to Amherstburg, were present at Detroit's downfall, and are now here on the Niagara frontier after six hundred miles of travel by boat and on foot.

A few minutes after Brock passes, Robinson and his comrades encounter groups of American prisoners staggering toward Fort George under guard. The road is lined with groaning men suffering from wounds of all descriptions, some, unable to walk, crawling toward nearby farmhouses, seeking shelter. It is the first time that these volunteers have actually witnessed the grisly by-products of battle, and the sight sickens them. But it also convinces them, wrongly, that the engagement is all but over.

Dawn is breaking, a few red streaks tinting the sullen storm clouds, a fog rising from the hissing river as Brock, spattered with mud from boots to collar, gallops through Queenston to the cheers of the men of his old regiment, the 49th. The village consists of about twenty scattered houses separated by orchards, small gardens, stone walls, snake fences. Above hangs the brooding escarpment, the margin of a prehistoric glacial lake. Brock does not slacken his pace but spurs Alfred up the incline to the redan, where eight gunners are sweating over their eighteen-pounder.

From this vantage point the General has an overview of the engagement. The panorama of Niagara stretches out below him—one of the world's natural wonders now half-obscured by black musket and cannon smoke. Directly below he can see Captain Dennis's small force pinning down the Americans crouching under the riverbank at the landing dock. Enemy shells are pouring into the village from John Lovett's battery on the Lewiston heights, but Dennis is holding. A company of light infantry occupies the crest directly above the redan. Unable to see Wool's men scaling the cliffs, Brock orders it down to reinforce Dennis. Across the swirling river, at the rear of the village of Lewiston, the General glimpses battalion upon battalion of American troops in reserve. On the American shore several regiments are preparing to embark. At last Brock realizes that this is no feint.

He instantly dispatches messages to Fort George and to Chippawa to the south asking for reinforcements. Some of the shells from the eighteen-pounder in the redan are exploding short of their target, and Brock tells one of the gunners to use a longer fuse. As he does so, the General hears a ragged cheer from the unguarded crest above and, looking up, sees Wool's men charging down upon him, bayonets glittering in the wan light of dawn. He and the gunners have time for one swift action: they hammer a ramrod into the touchhole of the eighteen-pounder and break it off, thus effectively spiking it. Then, leading Alfred by the neck reins, for he has no time to remount, the Commander-in-Chief and Administrator of Upper Canada scuttles ingloriously down the hillside with his men.

In an instant the odds have changed. Until Wool's surprise attack, the British were in charge of the battle. Dennis had taken one hundred and fifty prisoners; the gun in the redan was playing havoc with the enemy; Brock's forces controlled the heights. Now Dennis is retreating through the village and Wool's band is being reinforced by a steady stream of Americans.

Brock takes shelter at the far end of the town in the garden of the Hamilton house. It would be prudent, perhaps, to wait for the reinforcements, but Brock is not prudent, not used to waiting. As he conceives it, hesitation will lose him the battle: once the Americans consolidate their position in the village and on the heights they will be almost impossible to dislodge.

It is this that spurs him to renewed action—the conviction that he must counterattack while the enemy is still off balance, before more Americans can cross the river and scale the heights. For Brock believes that whoever controls the heights controls Upper Canada: they dominate the river, could turn it into an American waterway; they cover the road to Fort Erie; possession of the high ground and the village will slice the thin British forces in two, give the Americans warm winter quarters, allow them to build up their invading army for the spring campaign. If the heights are lost the province is lost.

He has managed to rally some two hundred men from the 49th and the militia. "Follow me, boys," he cries, as he wheels his horse back toward the foot of the ridge. He reaches a stone wall, takes cover behind it, dismounts. "Take a breath, boys," he says; "you will need it in a few moments." They give him a cheer for that.

He has stripped the village of its defenders, including Captain Dennis, bleeding from several wounds but still on his feet. He sends some men under Captain John Williams in a flanking movement to attack Wool's left. Then he vaults the stone fence and, leading

Alfred by the bridle, heads up the slope at a fast pace, intent on retaking the gun in the redan.

His men, struggling to keep up, slide and stumble on a slippery footing of wet leaves. Above him, through the trees, Wool's men can be seen reinforcing the gun emplacement. There is a confused skirmish; the battle seesaws; the Americans are driven almost to the lip of the precipice. Someone starts to wave a white handkerchief. Wool tears it away, orders a charge. The British are beaten back, and later some will remember Brock's cry, "This is the first time I have ever seen the 49th turn their backs!"

The sun, emerging briefly from the clouds, glistens on the crimson maples, on the Persian carpet of yellow leaves, on the epaulettes of the tall general, sword in hand, rallying his men for a final charge. It makes a gallant spectacle: the Saviour of Upper Canada, brilliant in his scarlet coat, buttons gleaming, plumed hat marking him unmistakably as a leader, a gap opening up between him and his gasping followers.

Does he realize that he is a target? No doubt he does—he has already been shot in the hand—but that is a matter of indifference. Leaders in Brock's army are supposed to lead. The spectacle of England's greatest hero, Horatio Nelson, standing boldly on deck in full dress uniform, is still green in British memory. The parallels are worthy of notice. The two heroes share similar strengths and flaws: disdain for the enemy, courage, vanity, ambition, tactical brilliance, innovative minds, impetuosity. Both have the common touch, are loved by their men, whom they, in turn, admire, and are idealized by the citizens of the countries they are called upon to protect. And both, by their actions, are marked for spectacular death. They seem, indeed, to court it. Brock's nemesis steps out from behind a clump of bushes and when the General is thirty paces from him draws a bead with his long border rifle and buries a bullet in his chest, the hole equidistant from the two rows of gilt buttons on the crimson tunic. George Jarvis, a fifteen-year-old gentleman volunteer in the 49th, rushes over. "Are you much hurt, sir?" he asks. There is no answer, for Brock is dead. A grisly spectacle follows as a cannonball slices another soldier in two and the severed corpse falls upon the stricken commander.

The gallant charge has been futile. Brock's men retreat down the hill, carrying their general's body, finding shelter at last under the stone wall of the Hamilton garden at the far end of the village. Here they are joined by the two companies of York Volunteers, whom Brock passed on his gallop to Queenston. These men, arriving on the dead run, catch their breath as American cannon fire pours down upon them from the artillery post on the opposite heights. A cannon-ball slices off one man's leg, skips on, cripples another in the calf. Then, led by young John Macdonell, the dead general's aide, the augmented force makes one more attempt to recapture the heights.

Impulsively, Macdonell decides to follow Brock's example. Possessed of a brilliant legal mind—he was prosecuting criminal cases at sixteen and has been acting attorney-general of the province for a year—he has little experience in soldiering. Quick of temper and a little arrogant, he reveres his dead commander and, in the words of his fellow aide Major Glegg, determines "to accompany him to the regions of eternal bliss." Macdonell calls for a second frontal attack on the redan. Seventy volunteers follow him up the heights to join the remainder of the 49th under Captain John Williams taking cover in the woods. Together, Williams and Macdonell form up their men and prepare to attack.

"Charge them home and they cannot stand you!" cries Williams. The men of the 49th, shouting "Revenge the General!" (for he was *their* general), sweep forward. Wool, reinforced by several hundred more men, is waiting for them, his followers concealed behind logs and bushes.

As Macdonell on horseback waves his men on, his steed, struck by a musket ball, rears and wheels about. Another ball strikes Macdonell in the back, and he tumbles to the ground, fatally wounded. Williams, on the right flank, also falls, half scalped by a bullet. As Captain Cameron rushes forward to assist his fallen colonel, a ball strikes him in the elbow and he too drops. Macdonell, in terrible pain, crawls toward his closest friend, Lieutenant Archibald McLean of the York Volunteers, crying, "Help me!" McLean attempts to lead him away and is hit by a ball in the thigh. Dismayed by these losses, the men fall back, bringing their wounded with them. Dennis is bleeding from five wounds. Williams, horribly mangled, survives, but Macdonell is doomed.

Everything that Brock feared has happened. The Americans occupy both the village and the heights and are sending over reinforcements, now that they have unopposed possession of the river. The British have retreated again to the outskirts of the village. All of their big guns, except for one at Vrooman's Point, have been silenced. At ten o'clock on this dark October morning, Upper Canada lies in peril.

———

AT THIS POINT, ALL General Van Rensselaer's forces should be across the river, but so many of his boats have been destroyed or abandoned that he is hard put to reinforce his bridgehead. He has no more than a thousand men on the Canadian side, and of these two hundred are useless. Stunned by their first experience of warfare, the militiamen cower beneath the bank; no power, it seems, no exhortation to glory or country, no threat of punishment can move them.

The General crosses at noon with his captain of engineers, whose job it is to help the troops on the heights. Unfortunately all the entrenching tools have been left at Lewiston; conditions are such that they will never arrive. The General sends the touchy Winfield Scott to the top of the ridge to take over from the wounded Wool, then prepares to return to the American shore. As he does so, a rabble of militiamen leaps into the boat with him.

During this lull, Winfield Scott works furiously with the engineers to prepare a defence of the high ground. The Americans know that British reinforcements are on their way from both Chippawa and Fort George; an American-born militiaman has deserted with that information. Scott would like to attack the Chippawa force, cutting it off from the main army, but has not enough men for the job; nor can he get more. His little force is diminishing. Whole squads of militia slink away into the woods or the brush above the bluffs. Scott posts his remaining men along the ridge with their backs to the village, his left flank resting on the edge of the bluff, his right in a copse of trees and bushes.

He realizes his danger. Ammunition is running out. He has managed to get a six-pound gun across the river in a larger boat, but there are only a few rounds available for it. In the distance he can see a long column of red-coated regulars marching up the road from Fort George under Brock's successor, Major-General Roger Sheaffe.

Now Scott becomes aware of an odd spectacle. Dashing back and forth along the ragged line of the militia is a man in civilian clothes, waving a naked sword, swearing profusely, and exhorting the men to form and fight to the death. This is Brigadier-General William Wadsworth of the New York militia, who has the reputation of being the most eloquently profane officer in the army. He has come across the river on his own, without orders, to try to instil some fighting spirit into his citizen soldiers.

Scott is nonplussed. Wadsworth outranks him, but he is not a regular. Scott cannot—*will* not—serve under him.

"General Wadsworth," he says, "since you are in command I propose to confine my orders strictly to the regular troops here!"

To which the militia general replies, quite sensibly and amiably:

"That's all damned nonsense, sir! You are a regular officer, you know professionally what should be done! Continue your command, sir, I am here simply for the honor of my country and that of the New York Militia!"

And off he rushes to raise some volunteers for the firing line.

Scott desperately needs to get the eighteen-pound cannon at the redan into action to protect his rear and cover the landing of the reinforcements that his general has promised him. But Brock has spiked it well: Scott's men cannot drive or drill the ramrod out. The Lieutenant-Colonel scrambles down the hillside to help, but as he does so a terrifying sound pierces the air. It is the screaming war-whoop of the Mohawk Indians, led by John Norton and his Indian friend, the young chief John Brant. They come swooping out of the woods and hurtling across the fields, brandishing their tomahawks, driving in Scott's pickets and forcing the trembling troops back. Only Scott's own presence and voice prevent a general rout. The Indians retire into the woods at the first volley, then work their way around toward the American left. No American soldier has fallen during this brief attack, but the damage is done, for the cries of the Indians have carried across the river and sent a chill through the militiamen on the far side.

Almost at the same time, two British guns have opened up in the garden of the Hamilton house, effectively barring passage across the river. Scott knows that his chances of getting reinforcements before the final battle are slim. He can see the men he needs—hundreds of them, even thousands, lined up on the far bank like spectators at a prizefight. For all the good they can do him, they might as well be back at their farms, where at this moment most of them fervently wish they were.

General Van Rensselaer is helpless. He has promised reinforcements and ammunition to the defenders on the heights but can supply neither. He has sent to Brigadier-General Smyth asking for more men, but Smyth again declines. And he cannot budge the troops at the embarkation point. They have been milling about for some hours in the drizzle, watching the boats return with terribly wounded men (and sometimes with deserters), watching other boats founder in the frothing stream, and now, with the screams of the Indians echoing down from the heights, they have no stomach for battle.

The General, riding a borrowed horse, with Major Lovett at his side, moves through the sulking soldiers, urging them to enter the boats. No one budges. One of their commanders, a Lieutenant-Colonel Bloom, returns from the heights wounded, mounts his horse and, still bleeding, exhorts, swears, prays. The troops refuse to advance. A local judge, Peck by name, appears from somewhere, a large cocked hat on his head, a long sword dangling from his broad belt, preaching and praying to no avail. The troops have broken ranks and assumed the role of witnesses to the coming batttle, and there is nothing, under the Constitution, that their officers can do.

Frustrated to fury and despair, Van Rensselaer starts to compose a note to General Wadsworth:

"I have passed through my camp; not a regiment, not a company is willing to join you. Save yourselves by a retreat if you can. Boats will be sent to receive you."

The promise is hollow. The terrified boatmen refuse to recross the river.

———

AT NEWARK, EARLY THAT morning, Captain James Crooks of the 1st Lincoln Militia, a Canadian unit, notes the inclement weather and decides against turning out. All that summer at daybreak the militiamen have paraded on one of the village streets, protected by intervening buildings from the eyes of the enemy in order to conceal their paucity. The wind and the sleet convince Captain Crooks that for once his subordinates can handle the parade. He turns over in his blankets, is starting to doze off again when a knock comes at his window and a guard reports that the Yankees have crossed the river at Queenston. Crooks is startled; this is the first he has heard of it. Even now he cannot hear the sound of the guns because of the gale blowing off the lake.

The orders are to rendezvous at the fort. Crooks leaps from his bed, pulls on his uniform, orders his men to form up, noting with pleasure the enthusiasm with which each unit outdoes the others to see which can reach the bastion first. Once there, the men stack their arms and wait. No one knows exactly what is happening, but the word is out that General Brock has already left for Queenston.

At the fort's gate, Crooks runs into the artillery commander, Captain William Holcroft, who tells him he is about to open fire on Fort Niagara across the river but is short of men. Crooks supplies him with several including Solomon Vrooman, who is sent to man the twenty-four-pounder on a point a mile away. Vrooman's big gun, which is never out of action, does incalculable damage and is one reason for the American militia's refusal to cross the river. From this day on, the emplacement will be known as Vrooman's Point.

At the naval yards, Crooks encounters Captain James Richardson, who is thunderstruck at the news of the attack. His ship, at dock loaded with gunpowder, is within point-blank range of the American battery, nine hundred yards across the water. He makes haste to unload his explosive cargo and send it to the fort. This proves fortunate; the powder in the fort's magazine, which has not seen use since the Revolutionary War, is so old it cannot propel shot more than half-way across the river.

A deafening artillery battle follows. The Americans heat their cannonballs until they glow red, then fire them into the village and the fort, burning the courthouse, the jail, and fifteen other buildings until, at last, their batteries are reduced by British cannon.

In the meantime Brock's express has arrived from Queenston with orders for 130 militiamen to march immediately to the relief of the heights. Captain Crooks is anxious to lead his men, but an older brother in the same company is the senior of the two. Crooks manages to talk him into staying behind, assembles men from five flank companies, forms them into a reinforcement detachment, and marches them off toward the scene of battle. A mile out of Newark he is told of Brock's death, tries to keep the news from his men, fails, is surprised to find it has little immediate effect. At Brown's Point, he passes one of the York Volunteers, who asks him where he is going. When he answers, "To Queenston," the officer tells him he is mad: if he goes any farther all his people will be taken prisoner; the General is dead; his force is completely routed; his aide is mortally wounded; four hundred Yankees are on his flank, moving through the woods to attack Newark. Crooks replies that he has his orders and will keep going. He tells his men to load their muskets and marches on. Shortly afterward he encounters a second officer who repeats almost word for word what he has heard a few minutes before. Crooks ignores him.

About a mile from town he halts his men at a house owned by a farmer named Durham. It is filled with American and British wounded, including the dying Macdonell. The troops are hungry, having missed their breakfast. He sends them foraging in a nearby garden to dig potatoes. Soon every pot and kettle in the house is bubbling on the fire, but before the potatoes can be eaten General Sheaffe arrives with the remainder of the 41st Regiment and orders the militia to fall in. Off they march to battle, still hungry.

Sheaffe, a cautious commander, has no intention of repeating Brock's frontal assault, has planned instead a wide flanking movement to reach the plateau above the village, where Wool's Americans are preparing for battle. His force will veer off to the right before entering the village, make a half circle around the heights, and ascend under cover of the forest by way of an old road two miles west of Queenston. Here Sheaffe expects to be joined by the second detachment that Brock ordered from Chippawa. In this way he can keep his line of march out of range of the American battery on the heights above Lewiston while the Indians, who have preceded him, act as a screen to prevent the enemy patrols from intercepting him as he forms up for battle.

Meanwhile, Captain Holcroft of the Royal Artillery has, at great risk, managed to trundle two light guns through the village, across a ravine, and into the garden of the Hamilton house, guided by Captain Alexander Hamilton, who knows every corner of the ground. It is these guns that Winfield Scott hears, effectively blocking the river passage, as Norton and his Mohawks harass his forward positions.

The Indians, screening Sheaffe's force, continue to harry the Americans. They pour out of the woods, whooping and firing their muskets, then vanish into the trees, preventing Scott from consolidating his position, driving in the pickets and flank patrols to inhibit contact with the advancing British, and forcing the Americans into a tighter position on the heights. Their nominal chief is John Brant, the eighteen-year-old son of the late Joseph Brant, the greatest of the Mohawk chieftains, whose portrait by Romney will later grace every Canadian school book. But the real leader is the theatrical Norton, a strapping six-foot Scot who thinks of himself as an Indian and aspires to the mantle of his late mentor. He is more Indian than most Indians, has indeed convinced many British leaders (including the English parliamentarian and abolitionist William Wilberforce) that he is a Cherokee. He wears his black hair in a long tail held in place by a scarlet handkerchief into which he has stuck an ostrich feather. Now, brandishing a tomahawk, his face painted for battle, he whoops his way through the woods, terrifying the American militia and confusing the regulars.

Directly behind the woods on the brow of the heights, hidden by the scarlet foliage and protected by the Mohawks, Roger Sheaffe forms up his troops on Elijah Phelps's ploughed field. He is in no hurry. He controls the road to Chippawa and is waiting for Captain Richard Bullock to join him with another 150 men from the south. Captain Dennis of the 49th has already joined his company, his body caked with blood. Exhausted and wounded as a result of the battle at the river's edge, he refuses to leave the field until the day is won. Now he stands with the others, waiting for the order to advance, while the American gunners pour down fire from across the river. For the unblooded militia the next hour is the longest they have known, as a rain of eighteen-pound balls and smaller shot drops about them.

At about four o'clock, just as Bullock comes up on the right flank, Sheaffe orders his men to advance in line. He has close to one thousand troops in all. The enemy has almost that number—or *had* almost that number, but now many of the American militia, with the war cries of the Indians echoing in their ears, have fled into the woods or down the cliff toward the river. When Scott counts his dwindling band he is shocked to discover that it numbers fewer than three hundred. In the distance he sees the scarlet line of British regulars, marching in perfect order, the Indians on one flank, the militia slightly behind, two three-pound grasshopper guns firing.

Van Rensselaer's despairing note has just reached Wadsworth: reinforcement is not possible. The Americans call a hurried council and agree to a strategic withdrawal.

Now the battle is joined. James Crooks, advancing with his militia detachment, has been in many hailstorms but none, he thinks wryly, where the stones fly thick as the bullets on this October afternoon. Little scenes illuminate the battle and remain with him for the rest of his days: the sight of an Indian tomahawking a York militiaman in the belief that he is one of the enemy. The sight of the Americans' lone six-pounder, abandoned, with the slow match still burning (he turns it about and some of his men fire several rounds across the river). The bizarre spectacle of Captain Robert Runchey's platoon of black troops—escaped slaves who have volunteered at Newark— advancing on the flank of the Indians. The sight of a companion, his knuckles disabled by a musket ball at the very moment of pulling the trigger. Crooks seizes the weapon and fires off all its spare am- munition, saving the final round for a man in a small skiff in the river whom he takes to be an American fleeing the battle. Fortunately he misses; it is one of his own officers crossing over with a flag of truce to demand General Van Rensselaer's surrender.

Scott's regulars are attempting to cover the American withdrawal. The Colonel himself leaps up on a fallen tree and literally makes a stump speech, calling on his men to die with their muskets in their hands to redeem the shame of Hull's surrender. They cheer him and face the British, but the advance continues with all the precision of a parade-ground manoeuvre, which, of course, it is. The Americans are trapped between the cliff edge on their left and the cannon fire from Holcroft's guns in the village below them on their right.

As the Indians whoop forward once more—the British and Canadian militia advancing behind with fixed bayonets—the American line wavers, then breaks. The troops rush toward the cliffs, some tumbling down the hill, clinging to bushes and outcroppings, others, crazed with fear, leaping to their deaths on the rocks below. Scores crowd the beach under the shoulder of the mountain, waiting for boats that will never come. Others, badly mangled, drown in the roaring river.

The three ranking Americans, Scott, Wadsworth, and Chrystie, carried downward by the rush of escaping men, now decide that only a quick surrender will save the entire force from being butchered by the Indians. The problem is how to get a truce party across to the

British lines. Two couriers, each carrying a white flag, have tried. The Indians have killed both.

At last Winfield Scott determines to go himself.

There are no white handkerchiefs left among the company, but Totten, the engineering officer, has a white cravat, which Scott ties to his sword point. He will rely on his formidable height and his splendid uniform to suggest authority. These attributes, however, are of little value, for Scott is almost immediately attacked and seized by young Brant and another Indian, who spring from a covert and struggle with him. The American's life is saved by the timely appearance of John Beverley Robinson and his friend Samuel Jarvis of the York Volunteers, who free him and escort him to Sheaffe.

The British general accepts Scott's surrender and calls for his bugler to sound the ceasefire. The Mohawk pay no attention. Enraged at the death of two of their chiefs, they are intent on exterminating all the Americans huddled under the bluff. Scott, seeing his men's predicament, hotly demands to be returned to share their fate. Sheaffe persuades the future conqueror of Mexico to have patience. He himself is appalled at the carnage, and after the battle is over some of his men will remember their general flinging off his hat, plunging his sword into the ground in a fury, and demanding that his men halt the slaughter or he, Sheaffe, will immediately give up his command and go home. A few minutes later the firing ceases and the battle is over. It is half-past four. The struggle has raged for more than twelve hours.

Now, to Scott's mortification and despair, some five hundred militiamen appear from hiding places in the crevices along the cliffs and raise their hands in surrender.

The British have taken 925 prisoners including a brigadier-general, five lieutenant-colonels, and sixty-seven other officers. One prisoner is allowed to go free—the diminutive sextuagenarian Samuel Stubbs of Boonsboro, Kentucky. Stubbs, expecting to be killed and scalped, discovers that the British look on him as an oddity, as if he had been born with two heads. A British officer takes one look at Stubbs and lets him go. "Old daddy," he says, "your age and odd appearance induce me now to set you at liberty, return home to your family and think no more of invading us!" Stubbs promises cheerfully to give up fighting, but "I didn't mean so for I was determined I wouldn't give up the chase so, but at 'um again." And so he will be—all the way from the attack on Fort York to the final bloody battle of New Orleans, where in his sixty-sixth year, he is responsible for the deaths of several British officers.

In addition, the Americans suffer some 250 casualties. These include the badly mangled Solomon Van Rensselaer, who will eventually recover, and John Lovett, who, though not hit by ball or shrapnel, is incapacitated for life. What began as a lark has for him ended as tragedy. For Lovett, the conversationalist and wit, the world has gone silent. Placed in charge of the big guns on the heights above Lewiston, he has been rendered permanently deaf.

British casualties, by contrast, are light.

"God, man," says the staff surgeon, Dr. Thorne, to James Crooks as the battle ends, "there does not seem to be any of you killed."

"Well, Doctor," replies the Captain, "it is well it is so but go into that guard house and you'll find plenty to do for your saws. . . ."

The British have lost only fourteen killed and seventy-seven wounded, but there is one loss that cannot be measured and by its nature evens the score at the Battle of Queenston Heights. Isaac Brock is gone. There is no one to fill his shoes.

———

ALL OF CANADA IS stunned by Brock's loss. His own soldiers, the men of the 49th who were with him in Holland and at Copenhagen, are prostrated by the news. Of all the scenes of sorrow and despair that day, the most affecting is the one reported by Lieutenant Driscoll of the 100th Regiment, who had come up from Fort Erie to help direct artillery fire against the American battery at Black Rock. At two that afternoon Driscoll looks up to see a provincial dragoon gallop up, dishevelled, without sword or helmet, his horse bathed in foam, his own body spattered with mud.

One of Brock's veterans, a man named Clibborn, speaks up:

"Horse and man jaded, sir; depend upon it, he brings bad news."

Driscoll sends the veteran across to discover what message the dragoon has brought. The soldier doubles over to the rider but returns at a funereal pace, and Driscoll realizes that something dreadful has occurred. He calls out:

"What news, Clibborn? What news, man? Speak out."

Clibborn walks slowly toward the battery, which is still maintaining a brisk fire at the Americans across the river. Musket balls plough into the ground around him; he does not seem to see them. He cannot speak, can only shake his head. At last he slumps down on the gun platform, his features dead white, his face a mask of sorrow.

Driscoll cannot stand the silence, shakes Clibborn by the shoulder:

"For heaven's sake, tell us what you know."

Clibborn answers at last, almost choking:

"The General is killed; the enemy has possession of Queenston Heights."

At those words, every man in the battery becomes paralysed. The guns cease firing. These are men of the 49th, all of whom have served under Brock in Europe; they are shattered by the news. Some weep openly. Others mourn in silence. Several begin to curse in frustration. The sound of enemy cheers, drifting across the river, rouses them to their duty. In a helpless rage over the death of their general, they become demonic, loading, traversing, and firing the heavy guns as if they were light field pieces, flinging round after round across the river in an attempt to avenge their former chief.

All over the province, similar expressions of grief are manifest. Glegg, Brock's military aide, calls it "a public calamity." Young George Ridout of the York Volunteers writes to his brother that "were it not for the death of General Brock and Macdonell our victory would have been glorious . . . but in losing our man . . . is an irreparable loss." Like many others, Ridout is convinced that Brock was the only man capable of leading the divided province. Samuel Jarvis crosses the lake to bring the news of the tragedy to York where "the thrill of dismay . . . was something indescribable."

In Quebec, an old friend, Anne Ilbert, who once volunteered to embroider some handkerchiefs for the bachelor general so the laundresses wouldn't steal them, writes to an acquaintance that "the conquest of half the United States would not repay us for his loss ... by the faces of the people here you would judge that we had lost everything, so general is the regret everyone feels for this brave man, the victory is completely swallowed up in it." She fears for the future, wonders what the troops will do under another commander, suspects that Upper Canada will fall to the Americans before winter's end. "This is the first real horror of war we have experienced. God send it may not lead to a train of others."

Prevost, when he learns of his general's death, is so badly shaken that he can scarcely hold the pen with which to report the tragedy to Sir John Sherbrooke in Halifax. Yet he mentions the matter only briefly in that letter. And later, when a dispatch reaches him quoting the Prince Regent at some length on Brock's heroism and ability, he publishes in the Quebec *Gazette* the first non-committal sentence only, omitting phrases about "an able and meritorious officer ... who ... displayed qualities admirably adapted to awe the disloyal, to reconcile the wavering, and animate the great mass of the inhabitants against successive attempts by the enemy to invade the province...."

Meanwhile, Sheaffe concludes an immediate armistice with the Americans, "the most ruinous policy that ever was or could have been adopted for the country," to quote a nineteen-year-old subaltern, William Hamilton Merritt, the future builder of the Welland Canal. Brock, who has been knighted for the capture of Detroit (posthumously, as it develops), would certainly have pursued Van Rensselaer's badly shaken force across the river to attack Fort Niagara and seize the northern half of New York state, but Sheaffe is a more cautious commander—Prevost's kind of general.

Brock's body, brought back to Newark, lies in state for three days. His funeral, in George Ridout's words, is "the grandest and most solemn that I have ever witnessed or that has been seen in Upper Canada." Brock's casket and Macdonell's are borne through a double line of Indians and militia—five thousand men resting on reversed arms. The twin coffins are buried in the York bastion of the fort. Guns boom every minute during the procession while across the river, at both Niagara and Lewiston, the Americans fire a salute to their old enemy. Sheaffe, on hearing the American guns, is overcome and says in a choked voice to one of his officers that "noble minded as General Brock was, he would have ordered the same had a like disaster befallen the Enemy."

Upper Canada is numb, its people drawn closer by a common tragedy that few outsiders can comprehend. In the United States, attention is quickly diverted by another naval skirmish in which the American frigate *Wasp*, having incapacitated and captured the British sloop of war *Frolic*, is herself taken by the enemy.

Europe is far more interested in the fate of Moscow, under attack by Napoleon, who at the very moment of the naval skirmish on October 18 is preparing to withdraw his army from the charred and deserted Russian capital. This bitter decision, still unknown to most of the world, marks the beginning of the end of the war with France. Had Madison foreseen it, the invasion of Canada, scarcely yet underway, would never have been attempted.

With Brock's burial, the myth takes over from the man. The following day, the Kingston *Gazette* reports "the last words of the dying Hero."

> General Brock, watchful as he was brave, soon appeared in the midst of his faithful troops, ever obedient to his call, and whom [he] loved with the adoration of a father; but, alas! whilst collecting, arranging, forming, and cheering his brave followers, that great commander gloriously fell when preparing for victory— *"Push on brave York Volunteers,"* being then near him, they were the last words of the dying Hero—Inhabitants of Upper Canada, in the day of battle *remember BROCK*.

If Brock ever uttered these words it could only have been when he passed the York Volunteers on the road to Queenston. It was the

49th, his old battalion, that surrounded him at the moment of his fall. Nor do dead men utter school-book slogans. Nonetheless, the gallant injunction passes into common parlance to become almost as well known as "Don't give up the ship," uttered in the same war by an American naval commander whose men, on his death, did give up the ship. The phrase will be used in future years to support a further myth—that the Canadian militia really won the war. In December, the York *Gazette* gushes that "it must afford infinite satisfaction to every Loyal Bosom that on every occasion, the Militia of the Province has distinguished itself with an alacrity & spirit worthy of Veteran Troops." It is not an assessment with which the dead general would have agreed, but it is a fancy that will not die. John Strachan, future bishop of Toronto, leader of the Family Compact and mentor of the young officers who formed the backbone of the York Volunteers, helps to keep it green. In Strachan's belief, the militia "without the assistance of men or arms except a handful of regular troops" repelled the invasion.

The picture of Brock storming the heights at Queenston, urging on the brave York Volunteers, and saving Canada in the process is the one that will remain with the fledgling nation. He is the first Canadian war hero, an Englishman who hated the provincial confines of the Canadas, who looked with disdain on the civilian leaders, who despised democracy, the militia, and the Indians, and who could hardly wait to shake the Canadian mud from his boots and bid goodbye forever to York, Fort George, Quebec, and all the stuffy garrison towns between. None of this matters.

His monument will be erected on the ridge, not far from where he fell, by the leaders of a colonial aristocracy intent on shoring up power against republican and democratic trends seeping across the border. This Tuscan pillar, 135 feet high, becomes the symbol of that power—of the British way of life: the Loyalist way as opposed to the Yankee way. In 1840, a disaffected Irish Canadian named Benjamin Lett, one of William Lyon Mackenzie's followers in his failed rebellion against an elitist autocracy, determines on one last act of defiance and chooses the obvious site: he blows up Brock's monument.

The Family Compact cannot do without its symbol, mounts a long public campaign, raises fifty thousand dollars, builds a more splendid monument, half as high again as its predecessor—taller, it is said, than any in the world save for Wren's pillar marking London's Great Fire. John Beverley Robinson, Strachan's protégé and the Compact's chief justice, is on hand, of course, at the dedication, and so is his successor and fellow subaltern in the Brave York Volunteers, Mr. Justice Archibald McLean. Robinson's spectacular career dates from Queenston Heights when, a mere law student of twenty-one, he is named acting attorney-general of the province to replace the mortally wounded Macdonell. ("I had as much thought of being made Bey of Tunis," he recalled.) By Confederation the field on which he and McLean did battle has become, in the words of the *Canadian Monthly*, "one of Canada's sacred places" and the battle, in the description of the Canadian nationalist George Denison, is "Canada's glorious Thermopylae."

So Brock in death is as valuable to the ruling class as Brock in life. He will not be remembered for his real contribution to the country: his military prescience, his careful preparation for war during the years of peace, his astonishing bloodless capture of an American stronghold. When Canadians hear his name, as they often will over the years, the picture that will form in their minds will be of that final impetuous dash, splendidly heroic but tragically foolish, up the slippery heights of Queenston on a gloomy October morning.

SEVEN

Black Rock

Opéra Bouffe on the Niagara

*Hearts of War! Tomorrow will
be memorable in the annals
of the United States.*
> —Brigadier-General Alexander Smyth,
> November 29, 1812.

BUFFALO, NEW YORK, November 17, 1812. Brigadier-General Alexander Smyth is putting the finishing touches to a proclamation, which, like Hull's, will return to haunt him.

"*Soldiers!*" he writes, underlining the word. "You are amply prepared for war. You are superior in number to the enemy. Your personal strength and activity are greater. Your weapons are longer. The regular soldiers of the enemy are generally old men, whose best years have been spent in the sickly climate of the West Indies. They will not be able to stand before you when you charge with the bayonet.

"You have seen Indians, such as those hired by the British to murder women and children, and kill and scalp the wounded. You have seen their dances and grimaces, and heard their yells. Can you fear *them*? No. You hold them in the utmost contempt."

Smyth warms to his task. Having stiffened the backs of the regular troops he will now imbue the recalcitrant militia with a fighting spirit:

"VOLUNTEERS!" he prints in large, bold capitals. "I esteem your generous and patriotic motives. You have made sacrifices on the altar of your country. You will not suffer the enemies of your fame to mislead you from the path of duty and honor, and deprive you of the esteem of a grateful country. You will shun the *eternal infamy* that awaits the man, who having come within sight of the enemy, *basely* shrinks in the moment of trial.

"SOLDIERS OF EVERY CORPS! It is in your power to retrieve the honor of your country; and to cover yourselves with glory. Every man who performs a gallant action, shall have his name made known to the nation. Rewards and honors await the brave. Infamy and contempt are reserved for cowards. Companions in arms! You came to vanquish a valiant foe. I know the choice you will make. Come on my heroes! And when you attack the enemy's batteries, let your rallying word be *'The cannon lost at Detroit—or death.'*"

Out it goes among the troops and civilians, most of whom greet it with derision. To this Smyth is absolutely oblivious, for he is a prisoner of his ego. The word "vanity" hardly does justice to his own concept of himself. He is wholly self-centred. His actions and words, which others find bizarre and ridiculous, are to him the justifiable responses of a supreme commander who sees himself as the saviour of the nation. The newspapers scoff at him as "Alexander the Great" and "Napoleon II." Smyth is the kind of general who takes that satire as a compliment.

If words were bullets and exclamation points cannonballs, Smyth might cow the enemy through the force of his verbiage. A master of the purple passage, he bombards his own countrymen with high-flown phrases:

Men of New York: The present is the hour of renown. Have you not a wish for fame? Would you not choose to be one of those who, imitating the heroes whom Montgomery led, have in spite of the seasons, visited the tomb of the chief and conquered the country where he lies? Yes—You desire your share of fame. Then seize the present moment. If you do not, you will regret it. . . .

Advance, then, to our aid. I will wait for you a few days. I cannot give you the day of my departure. But come on, come in companies, half companies, pairs or singly. I will organize you for a short tour. Ride to this place, if the distance is far, and send back your horses. But remember that every man who accompanies us places himself under my command, and shall submit to the salutary restraints of discipline.

Smyth is now in total charge of the Niagara campaign. Stephen Van Rensselaer has resigned in his favour. (He will run for governor in the spring, to be beaten by the craftier Tompkins.) His cousin Solomon is recovering from his wounds and dandling his new son on his lap; he will not fight again. Smyth, who never came face to face with either, reigns supreme.

On paper, the new commander's qualifications seem suitable enough. He is an Irishman whose father, a parish rector, brought him to Virginia at the age of ten. A member of his state's bar, he has also been an elected representative in the lower house. As the colonel of a rifle regiment, he was ordered to Washington in 1811 "to prepare a system of discipline for the army." Within eighteen days of the declaration of war he was promoted to inspector general and ordered to the Niagara frontier.

"I must not be defeated," he declares on taking over from Van Rensselaer; and he enters into a flurry of boat building, for he intends, he says, to land more than four thousand men on the Canadian shore. This is bombast: more than half his force is in no condition to fight. The bulk of the regulars are raw recruits who have never fired a musket. The militia continue to desert—one hundred in a single night. Hundreds more clog the hospitals suffering from measles, dysentery, grippe. The cemetery behind the camp, where men are buried four to a grave, has expanded to two acres. The ill-clothed army has not yet been paid; two regular regiments and one militia company have already mutinied on this account; the captain of another volunteer company warns that his men will not cross the river until they receive pay and clothing allowances. The troops of Fort Niagara are starving for want of bread, and there is considerable doubt whether the eighteen hundred Pennsylvania volunteers due to arrive in mid-November will agree to fight on foreign soil.

Nonetheless, on November 9 the General announces that he will invade Canada in fifteen days. So loudly does he boast about his intentions that the British are well prepared for any attack; on November 17 they launch a heavy bombardment of Smyth's head-quarters at Black Rock, burning the east barrack, exploding the magazine, and destroying a quantity of the furs captured from *Caledonia*. Just as the Quartermaster General, Peter B. Porter, is sitting down to dinner, a twenty-four-pound cannonball crashes through the roof of his home, a disaster not calculated to improve a digestion already thrown out of kilter by Smyth's bizarre and inconclusive orders. Another cannonade begins at dawn on the twenty-first opposite Fort Niagara. The British pour two thousand rounds of red-hot shot into the American fort, which replies in kind. Buildings burn; guns blow up; men die; nothing is settled.

On November 25, Smyth issues orders for the entire army to be ready to march "at a moment's warning." Two days later he musters forty-five hundred men at Black Rock for the impending invasion.

"Tell the brave men under your command not to be impatient," he writes to Porter, who is in charge of the New York volunteers. "See what harm impatience did at Queenston. Let them be firm, and they will succeed."

At three on the morning of the twenty-eighth, Smyth sends an advance force of some four hundred men across the river to destroy the bridge at Frenchman's Creek (thus cutting British communications between Fort Erie and Chippawa) and to silence the battery upstream. The British are waiting. Boats are lost, destroyed, driven off. In the darkness there is confusion on both sides, with men mistaking enemies for friends and friends for enemies. In spite of this the Americans seize the battery and spike its guns while a second force reaches the bridge, only to discover that they have left their axes in the boats and cannot destroy it before the British counter-attack. In the end some of the advance party are captured for lack of boats in which to escape. The remainder cross to the safety of the American camp with little accomplished.

An incredible spectacle greets the British next morning. Lining their own shore in increasing numbers, they watch the American attempt at embarkation as if it were a sideshow. Smyth himself does not appear but leaves the arrangements to his subordinates. The operation moves so ponderously that the afternoon shadows are lengthening before all the troops are in the boats. Some have been forced to sit in their craft for hours, shivering in the late November weather—a light snow is falling and the river is running with ice.

The only logical explanation for an action that defies logic is that Smyth is attempting to terrify the British into surrendering through what General Sheaffe calls "an ostentatious display" of his force. If so, it does not work. When Smyth sends a message across to Lieutenant-Colonel Cecil Bisshopp, urging him to surrender to "spare the effusion of blood," Bisshopp curtly declines.

Late in the afternoon, with the entire force prepared at last to cross the river, the General finally makes an official appearance and issues an amazing order. "Disembark and dine!" he cries. At this point the troops are on the edge of rebellion. Several, reduced to impotent fury, pointedly break their muskets.

Smyth returns to his paper war:

> Tomorrow at 8 o'clock, all the corps of Army will be at the Navy yards, ready to embark. Before 9 the embarkation will take place. The General will be on board. Neither rain, snow, or frost will prevent the embarkation.
>
> It will be made with more order and silence than yesterday; boats will be alloted to the brave volunteers. . . .
>
> The cavalry will scour the fields from Black Rock to the bridge & suffer no idle spectators.

While embarking the music will play martial airs. *Yankee Doodle* will be the signal to get underway. . . .

When we pull for the opposite shore, every exertion will be made. The landing will be effected in despite of cannon, The whole army has seen that cannon is to be little dreaded.

The information brought by Captain Gibson assures us of victory. . . .

Smyth's council of officers is aghast. Surely, with the British alerted, the General does not propose a daylight frontal assault from the identical embarkation point on a strongly fortified position! But Smyth declines to change his plans.

Next morning, however, the troops, who arrive at the navy yard promptly at eight, are sent into the nearby woods to build fires and keep warm. Smyth's staff has managed overnight to knock some sense into their commander. The departure time is changed to three the following morning. The troops will not cross directly but will slip quietly down the river, hoping to avoid the enemy cannon, and will land above Chippawa, attack its garrison and, if successful, march through Queenston to Fort George.

In the dark hours of the following morning, the wet and exhausted men are once more herded down to the boats. As before, the embarkation proceeds in fits and starts; when dawn arrives the boats are still not fully loaded. Now Smyth discovers that instead of three thousand men he has fewer than fifteen hundred in the boats, many of these so ill they cannot stand a day's march. The Pennsylvania volunteers have not even arrived on the ground; they are, it develops, perfectly prepared to fight on foreign soil but not under General Smyth. Other troops, lingering on the shore, sullenly refuse to embark.

Out in midstream, about a quarter of a mile from shore, Peter B. Porter has been waiting impatiently in a scout boat to lead the flotilla downriver to the invasion point. Hours pass. On the shore, the confusion grows. In his quarters, General Smyth is holding a council with his regular officers to which the militia commanders have not been invited. At last a message is sent out to Porter: the troops are to disembark. The invasion of Canada is to be abandoned for the present. Smyth does not intend to stir until he has three thousand men fit for action. The regulars will go into winter quarters; the volunteers are dismissed to their homes.

This intelligence provokes a scene of the wildest fury. Officers break their swords in rage; ordinary soldiers batter their muskets to pieces against tree trunks. The mass of the militia runs amok, firing off their weapons in all directions, some shouting aloud in frustration, others cheering in delight. Some of the volunteers offer to fight under Porter, promising to capture Fort Erie if Smyth will give them four cannon. The embattled commander turns the request aside.

Roused to a passion, the troops try to murder their general. Musket balls whiz through his tent, almost killing an aide who has his belt and cap shot off. Smyth doubles his guard, moves his headquarters repeatedly to protect his life.

Porter is outraged by Smyth's posturing. Some of the other officers are calling the General a traitor. Porter merely attacks him as a coward but puts that word into the public record in the Buffalo *Gazette* (which is forced, briefly, to cease publication, so great are the disturbances). A duel follows on Grand Island; shots are exchanged; both men's marksmanship is lamentable; unmarked, they shake hands, but the bitterness continues.

Smyth is the object of intense execration. Governor Tompkins's censure is blunt: "Believing that there was some courage and virtue left in the world, I did not, indeed could not, anticipate such a scene of gasconading and of subsequent imbecility and folly as Genl. Smith [*sic*] has exhibited. To compare the events of the recent campaign with those of the days of the Revolution, is almost enough to convince one, that the race of brave men and able commanders will before many years become extinct."

Smyth's career is finished. With his life in danger from both his officers and his men, he slips away to his home in Virginia where, within three months, the army drops him from its rolls.

Dearborn is aghast. He has sent four thousand troops to Niagara: how is it that not much more than a thousand were in a condition to cross the river? He himself has kept such a low profile that the firestorm of public disgust and fury with the losses of Hull, Van Rensselaer, and Smyth sweeps past him. Yet as the senior commander he is as culpable as any, and so is his fellow physician, the myopic secretary of war Dr. Eustis.

At Lake Champlain Dearborn has the largest force of all under arms, including seven regular army regiments with supporting artillery and dragoons. But these have been infected by the same virus as the others. Dearborn's overall strategy is to attack Montreal simultaneously with Smyth's invasion on the Niagara. On November 8, he informs Eustis that he is about to join the army under General Bloomfield at Plattsburg to march on Lower Canada. An attack of rheumatism delays him. On November 19, when he finally arrives, he finds Bloomfield too ill to lead his troops. Illness, indeed, has all but incapacitated his army, a third of which is unfit for duty. An epidemic of measles has raged through the camps. A neglect of proper sanitary measures has reduced one regiment from nine hundred to two hundred able-bodied men. Typhus, accompanied by pneumonia, has killed two hundred at Burlington. Fifteen per cent of Dearborn's entire force has died from one of these several afflictions.

Dearborn takes command of his depleted invasion force. Two separate and independent advance columns, numbering about 650 men, are dispatched north to surprise the British outposts at the border. They advance by different roads, run into one another in the dark, each mistaking the other for the enemy. A brisk skirmish follows until daylight, when, exhausted and dispirited by their error, they retreat with twenty casualties, a number that is shortly augmented by forty deaths from disease contracted during the expedition. Meanwhile Dearborn manages to get three thousand militia men as far as Rouse's Point at the northern end of Lake Champlain. When two-thirds refuse to cross the border, Dearborn gives up, slinks back to Plattsburg, and returns to Albany as quietly as possible. The news of Smyth's humiliation provides the final blow. Dearborn offers to surrender his command "to any gentleman whose talents and popularity will command the confidence of the Government and the country." But it will be another six months before his government, and a new and more aggressive secretary of war, get around to relieving him.

EIGHT

Frenchtown

Massacre at the River Raisin

The Battle's o'er, the din is past!
Night's mantle on the field is cast,
The moon with Sad and pensive beam
Hangs sorrowing o'er the bloody Stream . . .
Oh! Pitying Moon! Withdraw thy light
And leave the world in murkiest night!
For I have seen too much of Death
Too much of this dark fatal heath . . .
> —From "A Night View of the Battle of the Raisin,
> January 22nd, 1813" (written on the field
> by Ensign William O. Butler).

GEORGETOWN, KENTUCKY, AUGUST 16, 1812. Henry Clay is addressing two thousand eager Kentucky militiamen who have volunteered to march into Canada under the banner of William Henry Harrison to reinforce Hull's Army of the Northwest. The dark eyes flash, the sonorous voice rolls over the raw troops as he exhorts them to victory. More than most Americans, Clay is telling them, they have a twofold responsibility—to uphold the honour of their state as well as that of their country:

"Kentuckians are famed for their bravery—you have the double character of Americans and Kentuckians to support!"

This is more than posturing. Kentucky is a world unto itself, as different from Maine and New York as Scotland from Spain. No frustrated general will need to prod the Kentuckians across the Canadian border; they will, if necessary, swim the Detroit River to get at the British. When, the previous May, the Governor called for volunteers to fill Kentucky's quota of fifty-five hundred men, he found he had too many on his hands. Clay at the time wrote to the Secretary of State that he was almost alarmed at the enthusiasm displayed by his people.

Now, on the very day of Hull's defeat, Clay fires up the troops, who confidently believe that the American forces are already half-way across Canada. And why not? Kentucky has been told only what it wants to hear. The newspaper stories from the frontier have been highly optimistic. Editors and orators have bolstered the state's heroic image of itself. In these exhortations can be heard echoes of the Revolution. "Rise in the majesty of freedom," the Governor, Charles Scott, has pleaded; "regard as enemies the enemies of your country. Remember the Spirit of '76."

The troops who are to march off through the wilderness of Michigan and into Canada expect the briefest of wars—a few weeks of adventure, a few moments of glory (swords glistening, bugles calling, drums beating, opponents fleeing), then home to the family farm with the plaudits of the nation and the cheers of their neigh-bours ringing in their ears.

Most have signed on for six months only, convinced that the war cannot last even that long. On this warm August day, standing in ragged, undisciplined lines, basking in Clay's oratory, they do not contemplate November. They wear light shoes and open shirts of linen and cotton: no coats, no blankets. Not one in twenty is pre-pared for winter. The war department has lists of goods needed for the campaign, but no one has paid much attention to that. The army is without a commissariat; private contractors, whose desire for profit often outweighs their patriotism, have been hired to handle all supplies. As for the Congress, it has not been able to screw up enough courage to adopt new taxes to finance the war; the unpopular resolution has been postponed, and Clay and his Hawks, eager to get on with the fighting, have gone along with the delay without a whimper.

Every able-bodied man in Kentucky, it seems, wants to fight. Six congressmen don uniforms. One, Samuel Hopkins, becomes a major-general; two are happy to serve as privates. Clay remains behind to fight the war in Congress, but his brother-in-law, Nathaniel Hart, goes as a captain, and so does John Allen, the second most eminent lawyer in the state. Thomas Smith, editor of the Kentucky *Gazette*, inflamed by the optimistic reports in his own newspaper, quits his desk and signs up to fight the British and the Indians. Dr. John M. Scott, a militia colonel and an old campaigner, insists on his right to command a regiment even though he is desperately ill; his friends expect (rightly) that he will not return alive. By the end of the year there will be more than eleven thousand Kentuckians in the army.

Most of these will be in the volunteer forces, for the people of Kentucky are confident that the war will be fought to a speedy conclusion by citizen soldiers enrolled for a single, decisive campaign. Regulars are sneered at as hired mercenaries who cannot compete for valour or initiative with a volunteer who has a direct interest in the outcome of the struggle.

The idea of individual initiative is deeply ingrained in the Kentucky character. They are a hardy, adventurous people, confident to the point of ebullience, optimistic to the point of naïveté—romantic, touchy, proud, often cruel. Not for them the effete pastimes of settled New England. Their main entertainments are shooting, fighting, drinking, duelling, horse racing. Every Kentucky boy is raised with a rifle. An old state law provides that every white male over sixteen must kill a certain number of crows and squirrels each year. Instead of raffles, Kentuckians hold shooting contests to pick winners. The very word "Kentuck" can cause a shiver of fear in the Mississippi River towns, where their reputation is more terrifying than that of the Indians. As scrappers they are as fearless as they are ferocious, gouging, biting, kicking, scratching. Kentuckians like to boast that they are "half horse and half alligator tipped with snapping turtle." A future congressman, Michael Taul, is elected captain of his militia company not because he has any military training—he has none—but because he has beaten his opponent, William Jones, in a particularly vicious encounter—a "hard fight," in Taul's words, "fist and skull, biting and gouging, etc."

Kentucky lies on the old Indian frontier, and though its Indian wars are history, bloody memories remain. Youths are raised on tales of British and Indian raiders killing, scalping, and ravaging during the Revolution. Tippecanoe has revived a legacy of fear and hatred. The reports of British weapons found at Prophet's Town confirm the people of the state in their belief that John Bull is again behind the Indian troubles.

Tippecanoe is seen as the real beginning of the war. "War we now have," the Kentucky *Gazette* exulted when news of the battle reached Lexington. The shedding of Kentucky blood on the banks of the Wabash fuelled the latent desire for revenge, so that when war was declared Kentucky indulged in a delirium of celebration. Towns were illuminated, cannon and muskets discharged in the villages. And in the larger towns, Senator John Pope, the one Kentucky member of the Twelfth Congress to vote against the war, was hanged in effigy.

On the Fourth of July, the state wallowed in patriotic oratory. At a public celebration in Lexington no fewer than eighteen toasts were drunk, the celebrants raising their glasses to "Our volunteers—Ready to avenge the wrongs and vindicate the right of their country—the spirit of Montgomery will lead them to victory on the Plains of Abraham." Little wonder that a Boston merchant travelling through Kentucky a little later described its people as "the most patriotic . . . I have ever seen or heard of."

This yeasty nationalism springs out of Kentucky's burgeoning economy. It has become the most populous state west of the

Alleghenies. In two decades its population has leaped from 73,000 to more than 406,000. Log cabins have given way to handsome brick houses. Frontier outposts have become cities. But all this prosperity depends on a sea-going trade—a trade now threatened by Great Britain's maritime strictures. The opposite side of the coin of nationalism is a consuming hatred of Great Britain. Henry Clay is its voice.

What Clay wants, Clay is determined to get; and Henry Clay wants William Henry Harrison to command the army going north to subdue the Indians and to reinforce General Hull at Detroit. The Hero of Tippecanoe is by all odds the most popular military leader in the state. Every Kentuckian, it seems, wants to serve under him; but the Secretary of War has long since chosen James Winchester of Tennessee to take command. Now an active campaign, spearheaded by Clay and orchestrated with all the cunning of a political *coup d'état*, is mounted to force the government's hand and replace Winchester with Harrison. In this enterprise, Clay has Harrison's willing cooperation. The Hero of Tippecanoe himself tours the state, rousing martial feeling, fuelling the clamour for his appointment.

Early in August a caucus of influential Kentucky politicians, including Scott, the retiring governor, Isaac Shelby, the governor-elect, and several of the War Hawks, agrees to appoint Harrison a brevet (honorary) major-general in the Kentucky militia. He accepts command of two regiments of infantry and one of mounted rifles (under Clay's young congressional colleague, Richard M. Johnson) which have already left to join General Winchester in Cincinnati. But Clay wants more. Harrison outranks Winchester, but Winchester is a regular army man. It is important that there be no ambiguity about who is in charge. Once more he puts pressure on James Monroe, the Secretary of State, rising to heights of hyperbole, which, even for Henry Clay, are more than a little florid:

"If you will carry your recollection back to the Age of the Crusades and of some of the most distinguished leaders of those expeditions, you will have a picture of the enthusiasm existing in this country for the expedition to Canada and for Harrison as the commander."

Up to this point, James Monroe has fancied himself for the post of commander-in-chief of the Army of the Northwest. The cabinet, in fact, has been seriously considering his appointment. But now, with Clay and his cronies in full cry, the Secretary's military ambitions are dashed. The pressure is too great. Harrison it will be.

———

AS THE CABINET VACILLATES over the choice of a commander for the new northwest army, Harrison marches to Cincinnati at the head of his troops. He is convinced that he can persuade Winchester to allow him to take command of all the forces for the relief of Detroit. On August 26, he receives the dreadful news of Hull's surrender. Two days later, he reaches Winchester's camp at Cincinnati and immediately assumes command of all the Kentucky militia, leaving Winchester in charge of the regulars. Stiff little notes pass between the generals' tents. Harrison insists that he, as a major-general, outranks Winchester. Winchester objects, points out that Harrison is only a political appointee, but when Harrison persists, Winchester at last gives in: Harrison can assume command under his own responsibility. Winchester returns to Lexington to continue recruiting.

The new commander has some twenty-one hundred men at Cincinnati; an equal number are on their way to join him. They inspire mixed feelings. The Kentuckians, in his opinion "are perhaps the best materials for forming an army the world has produced. But no equal number of men was ever collected who knew so little of military discipline." It is a shrewd assessment.

He has neither time nor personnel to instruct his raw recruits in the art of soldiering. He is, in fact, short of almost everything—of food, clothing, equipment, weapons, ammunition, flints, swords. His only ordnance piece is an ancient cast-iron four-pounder. Autumn is fast approaching with its chilling rain and sleet. He must hack new roads through forest and swamp, build blockhouses and magazines, all the time watched and harassed by the Indians on his flank.

And he must move immediately, for word has come that the British and the Indians are planning an attack on Fort Wayne, the forward outpost on the Maumee. Three hundred Indians are laying siege to the fort, a British column is moving south, houses have been burned, crops and livestock destroyed. The commander, James Rhea, has some eighty men with whom to withstand the siege but is himself nervous and frequently drunk. Harrison's first task is to relieve the fort.

That same day he dispatches all his available troops on that mission. He joins them at Dayton on September I. Here are more cheers for Harrison and a salute of cannon, marred only by the tragic incompetence of the gunners. During the salute one man is seriously wounded, another has both hands blown off. And here Harrison receives a blow of a different kind: the government has officially confirmed his commission, but only as brigadier-general. Winchester now outranks him.

He does not give up. In another letter to Washington, he subtly advances his cause: "The backwoodsmen are a singular people. . . . From their affection and an attachment everything may be expected but I will venture to say that they never did nor never will perform anything brilliant under a stranger."

The message, though self-serving, is undoubtedly true. Winchester is unpopular largely because he is a stranger. Harrison is a known hero. All along his route of march, volunteers have flocked to his banner. At Piqua, en route to Fort Wayne, he makes from the tail-board of a camp wagon one of those tough little stump speeches for which he is famous. He is planning a forced march on half-rations, and some of the Ohio militia are hesitating. To them Harrison declares that "if there is any man under my command who lacks the patriotism to rush to the rescue, he, by paying back the money received from the government, shall receive a discharge. I do not wish to command such. . . ." Only one man makes this choice. His comrades are given a permit to escort him part of the way home. They hoist him onto a rail and with a crowd following duck him several times in the river.

Harrison, at the head of three thousand men, reaches Fort Wayne on September 12. The fort is relieved without a shot being fired though not entirely bloodlessly, since during the march one man has been shot and killed in error by one of the guards. The bodies of two sentinels, killed by the Indians and buried within the palisade, are disinterred and brought out to be buried with full military honours. The troops, many of whom have never seen a dead man, stand by in awe. William Northcutt, a young dragoon in Captain William Garrard's company of "Bourbon Blues" (made up of men from Bourbon County, Kentucky, all uniformed in blue broadcloth), cannot help shedding tears as the corpses are brought out through the gate, even though the men are complete strangers. But before his term of service is over, Northcutt becomes so hardened that he could, if necessary, sleep on a corpse, and it occurs to him as the war grows nastier that "the man that thinks about dying in a Battle is not fit to be there and will do no good for his country. . . ."

Harrison is determined to crush all Indian resistance. Columns of cavalry fan out to destroy all Indian villages within sixty miles. The ailing Colonel John Scott insists on leading the attack on the Elkhart River in Indiana Territory, though his officers urge him not to go. But he mounts his horse, crying out: "As long as I am able to mount you, none but myself shall lead my regiment. . . ." It is the death of him. Exhausted, after a protracted march of three days and nights, he is scarcely able to return to camp. Shortly afterwards he is carried home in a litter where, the second day after arrival, he expires.

Harrison's policy of search and destroy makes no distinction between neutral and hostile tribes. His intention is to turn the frontier country into a wasteland, denying both food and shelter to the natives. Mounted columns, one led by Harrison himself, burn several hundred houses, ravage the corn fields, destroy crops of beans, pumpkins, potatoes, and melons, ransack the graves and scatter the bones. The Potawatomi and Miami flee to British protection at Brownstown and Amherstburg and wait for revenge.

On September 18, General Winchester arrives at Fort Wayne to take command of the Army of the Northwest. The troops are in an ugly mood. They do not wish to be commanded by a regular officer, fearing perhaps (without much evidence) that Winchester will be a greater disciplinarian than Harrison.

Winchester's ordeal has only begun. As he moves slowly north, the Kentuckians under his command refuse his orders, torment him with pranks and practical jokes, and are generally obstreperous. He cannot even visit the latrine without suffering some indignity. At one camp, they skin a porcupine and place the skin on a pole over the latrine pit; the General applies his buttocks to the hide with painful results. At another, they employ a trick that must go back to Caesar's army: sawing a pole partially through so that it fails to support the General's weight at a critical moment. The next morning, William Northcutt of the Bourbon Blues, passing Winchester's tent, notes with amusement the General's uniform, drying out, high on a pole.

What has Winchester done to deserve this? His only crime is to be less popular than Harrison. He does suffer by comparison, for Harrison at forty is vigorous, decisive, totally confident, while Winchester, at sixty, is inclined to fussiness, a little ponderous, and not entirely sure of himself. (He did not have to relinquish command to Harrison during that first encounter at Cincinnati.) Like Hull, he appears to the young recruits to be older than his years (Northcutt thinks him at least seventy)–a plump, greying figure who has to be helped to mount and dismount his horse. Worst of all, Winchester fears his own troops and places a bodyguard around his quarters day and night.

Like so many others, he is a leftover from another war, his reputation resting on the exploits of his youth—on those memorable years in the mid-seventies when America struggled for her independence and young James Winchester, at twenty-four, was promoted in the field for his gallantry, wounded in action, captured, exchanged, recaptured and exchanged again to fight as a captain at York town. All that is long behind him, as are his years as an Indian fighter in North Carolina. Honours he has had: brigadier-general in the North Carolina militia; Speaker of the state senate of Tennessee; master of a vast Tennessee estate, surmounted by the great stone mansion known as Cragfont; father of fourteen children, four of them born out of wedlock but rendered legitimate by a tardy marriage. A kindly, sedentary man, fond of rich, easy living, known for his humanity. But no Harrison.

He lacks Harrison's style, has not Harrison's way with men, cannot bring himself to mingle with the troops in Harrison's easy, offhand manner. It is impossible to think of Winchester, dressed in a simple hunting shirt, making a stump speech to the Kentucky volunteers; it is equally impossible to believe that anyone would saw through a log in Harrison's latrine.

The murmurings against Winchester are not confined to the men. A group of officers, led by Henry Clay's congressional colleague Captain Sam McKee, is drawing up a petition, apparently with Harrison's blessing, urging that the command be taken from Winchester. The rebels get cold feet, temporize, delay, and are relieved at last of the charge of mutiny by a war department order authorizing Harrison to assume command of the Army of the Northwest.

———

OLD FORT DEFIANCE, OHIO, October 2, 1812. It is close to midnight when William Henry Harrison, accompanied by a strong escort, gallops into camp, summoned by a frantic note from General Winchester warning that a combined force of British redcoats and Indians is marching south. Winchester's intelligence is accurate but out of date. The British, believing themselves outnumbered, have already withdrawn.

Now Harrison breaks the news that he is in full command of the new Army of the Northwest, charged with the task of subduing the Indians in his path, relieving Detroit, and invading Canada. Winchester is crestfallen. Convinced that Harrison has secretly connived against him, he seriously considers resigning, then thinks better of it and decides to hang on until Fort Amherstburg is captured. Harrison determines to mollify him by giving him command of the army's left flank and naming in his honour the new fort being built not far from the ruins of the old: Fort Winchester.

The troops are unaware of Harrison's presence. Half starved, inadequately clothed, they have lost the will to fight. A delegation of Kentucky officers wakes Harrison to warn him that one regiment intends to quit and go home. All attempts to dissuade them have been met with insults.

Early the next morning, Harrison acts. He orders Winchester to beat the alarm instead of the customary drum roll for reveille. The Kentuckians pour out of their tents, form a hollow square, and, as Winchester introduces them to their new commander, holler their enthusiasm.

Harrison knows exactly what to say. He tells them they can go home if they wish to, "but if my fellow soldiers from Kentucky, so famed for patriotism, refuse to bear the hardships incident to war ... where shall I look for men who will go with me?"

Cheers and shouts greet these words and continue as the General reveals that two hundred wagons loaded with biscuit, flour, and bacon are on their way; some supplies, indeed, have already arrived. This kills all talk of desertion. One Kentuckian writes home that "Harrison, *with a look,* can awe and convince ... where some would be refractory . . . All are afraid and unwilling to meet with his censure."

Harrison has been given authority to requisition funds and supplies, to protect the northwestern frontier, and after retaking Detroit to penetrate Upper Canada "as far as the force under your command will in your judgment justify." For this purpose he expects to have ten thousand troops.

His strategy is to move the army to the foot of the Rapids of the Maumee in three columns. Winchester, protecting his left flank, will march from the new fort along the route of the Maumee. A central force of twelve hundred men will follow Hull's road to the same rendezvous. The right division, under Harrison himself, is proceeding from Wooster, Ohio, by way of the Upper Sandusky.

But Winchester is pinned down at the newly constructed fort

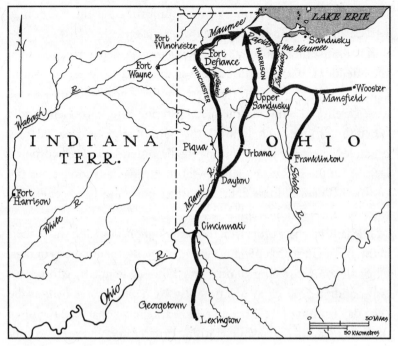

Harrison's Three-Column Drive to the Maumee Rapids

that bears his name. He dare not move without supplies, and the promised supplies are not forthcoming. Harrison has ordered Brigadier-General Edward Tupper's mounted brigade to dash to the foot of the Rapids of the Maumee to harvest several hundred acres of corn for the famished troops. But the scalping of a ranger not two hundred yards from the camp has the men in such a panic that only a handful will follow. The mission is abandoned.

On October 8, the day after Tupper's fiasco, Frederick Jacob of the 17th Regiment is caught asleep at his post, and Winchester, faced with growing insubordination, decides to make an example of him. A court martial sentences Jacob to be shot. The following morning Winchester's entire force, reduced now to eighteen hundred, forms a hollow square to witness the execution. Drums roll, the chaplain prays, the prisoner is led to the post, blindfolded, made to kneel. The troops fall silent, waiting for the volley. Then, at the last instant, a reprieve arrives. The General has judged the wretched guard "not to be of sound mind," a verdict which if unjustified at the outset may well be applicable in the days following the ordeal.

There are other punishments: "riding the wooden horse," in which the offender is placed astride a bent sapling and subjected to a series of tossings and joltings to the great amusement of the troops, or a dozen well-laid blows on the bare posterior with a wooden paddle bored full of holes to help break the skin. In spite of these salutary examples, the army is murmuring its discontent over the continued lack of supplies. Rations remain short, Harrison's promises to the contrary. There is little flour, almost no salt, and the beef—what there is of it—is deplorable.

Disdaining strict orders, men wander out of camp and waste their ammunition in search of game, many barefoot, their clothes in rags. They sleep on frozen ground, some without blankets. More than two hundred are sick at one time. By November, three or four die each day from typhus. Civilian contractors reap a harvest; the price of hogs goes sky high while clothing ordered for the troops comes in sizes so small it seems to have been designed for small boys. Materials are shoddy, delays calculated. One contractor's profit, it is said, amounts to $ 100,000.

Nothing seems to be going right. In late September, the new governor of Kentucky, Isaac Shelby, has ordered two thousand mounted thirty-day volunteers—"the most respectable citizens that perhaps were ever embodied from this or any other State in the Union"—to march under Major-General Samuel Hopkins, one of Clay's congressional War Hawks, against the Indians of Indiana and Illinois territories. Shelby does not wait for war department authorization or equipment. The men, whipped to a high pitch of enthusiasm, bring their own arms and blankets. The quota of volunteers is exceeded; twelve hundred disappointed Kentuckians have to be sent home.

The euphoria does not last. By October 14, after two hard weeks in the saddle, the volunteers are dispirited. They cannot find any Indians, their rations dwindle away, they become hopelessly lost. At this point, their unseen quarry fires the tall prairie grass, threatening all with a painful death.

Hopkins's choice is retreat or mutiny, a situation that leaves the Governor aghast. What has happened to Kentucky's élan? ". . . the flower of Kentucky are now returning home deeply mortified by the disappointment." On mature consideration, Shelby decides to put the blame on "secret plotting."

There is worse to come. A note of uncertainty begins to creep into Harrison's dispatches to Washington: "If the fall should be very dry, I will retake Detroit before the winter sets in; but if we should have much rain, it will be necessary to wait at the Rapids until the Margin of the Lake is sufficiently frozen to bear the army and its baggage."

"The one bright ray amid the gloom of incompetency" (to quote John Gibson, acting governor of Illinois Territory) is the news of Captain Zachary Taylor's successful defence of Fort Harrison—a desperate struggle in which a handful of soldiers and civilians, many of them ill, withstood repeated attacks by Miami and Wea warriors until relief arrived. It is the first land victory for the United States, and it wins for Taylor the first brevet commission ever awarded by the U.S. government. Nor will the moment of glory be forgotten. One day, Brevet Major Taylor will become twelfth president of the United States.

The news from the Niagara frontier banishes this brief euphoria. Another army defeated! A third bogged down. By October 22, Harrison finds he can no longer set a firm date for the attack on Detroit. There are no supplies of any kind in Michigan Territory; the farms along the Raisin have been ravaged. He will require one million rations at the Rapids of the Maumee before he can start a campaign; but the fall rains have already begun and he cannot move his supplies, let alone his artillery. By early November, the roads are in desperate condition and horses, attempting to struggle through morass and swamp, are dying by the hundreds.

The army switches to flatboats, but just as these are launched the temperature falls and the boats are frozen fast along the Sandusky, Au Glaize, and St. Mary's rivers. By early December, Harrison despairs of reaching the rapids at all and makes plans to shelter his force in huts on the Au Glaize. He suggests that Shelby prepare the

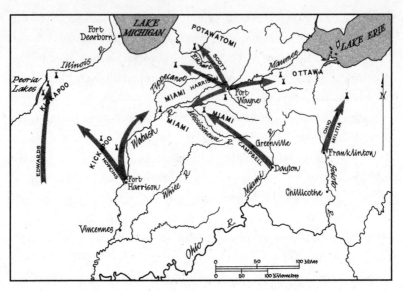

American Search and Destroy Missions against the Tribes, Autumn, 1812

public for a postponement in the campaign by disbanding all the volunteer troops except those needed for guard and escort duty. But Washington will have none of it. The Union has suffered two mortifying failures at Detroit and Queenston; it will not accept a third.

The setbacks continue. Hopkins's failure has left Harrison's left flank open to Indian attack. He decides to forestall further Indian raids on Winchester's line of communications by striking at the Miami villages along the Mississinewa, a tributary of the Wabash in Indiana Territory. On November 25, Lieutenant-Colonel John Campbell and six hundred cavalry and infantry set out to do the job. The result is disastrous.

In spite of Campbell's attempts at secrecy, the Miami are forewarned. They leave their villages, wait until the troops are exhausted, then launch a night attack, destroying a hundred horses, killing eight men, wounding forty-eight. A false report is spread that the dreaded Tecumseh is on the way at the head of a large force. Campbell's dejected band beats a hasty retreat.

It is bitterly cold; provisions are almost gone; the wounded are dying from gangrene, the rest suffer from frostbite. A relief party finally brings them into Greenville, where it is found that three hundred men—half of Campbell's force—are disabled. One mounted regiment is so ravaged it is disbanded. Harrison has lost the core of his cavalry without any corresponding loss among the Indians. The General decides to put a bold front on the episode: he announces that the expedition has been a complete success. He has learned something from the experience of Tippecanoe.

By December 10, Harrison has managed to get his cannon to Upper Sandusky, but at appalling cost. He has one thousand horses, hauling and pulling; most are so exhausted they must be destroyed, at a cost of half a million dollars. Wagons are often abandoned, their contents lost or destroyed. The teamsters, scraped up from frontier settlements, are utterly irresponsible. "I did not make sufficient allowance for the imbecility and inexperience of public agents and the villainy of the contractors," Harrison writes ruefully to the acting secretary of war, James Monroe, who has replaced the discredited Dr. Eustis.

Winchester's left wing is still pinned down near the junction of the Maumee and the Au Glaize, waiting for supplies. It is impossible to get them through the Black Swamp that lies between the Sandusky and the Maumee. William Atherton, a diminutive twenty-one-year-old soldier in Winchester's army who is keeping an account of his adventures, writes that he now sees "nothing but hunger and cold and nakedness staring us in the face." The troops have been out of flour for a fortnight and are existing on bad beef, pork, and hickory nuts. Sickness and death have reduced Winchester's effective force to eleven hundred. Daily funerals cast a pall over the camps, ravaged by the effects of bad sanitation and drainage (Winchester is forced to move the site five times) and the growing realization that there is no chance of invading Canada this year.

On Christmas Eve, another soldier, Elias Darnell, confides to his journal that "obstacles had emerged in the path to victory, which must have appeared insurmountable to every person endowed with common sense. The distance to Canada, the unpreparedness of the army, the scarcity of provisions, and the badness of the weather, show that Malden cannot be taken in the remaining part of our time. . . . Our sufferings at this place have been greater than if we had been in a severe battle. More than one hundred lives . . . lost owing to our bad accommodations! The sufferings of about three hundred sick at a time, who are exposed to the cold ground, and deprived of every nourishment, are sufficient proofs of our wretched condition! The camp has become a loathsome place. . . ."

On Christmas Day, Winchester receives an order from Harrison. He is to move to the Rapids of the Maumee as soon as he receives two days' rations. There he will be joined by the right wing of the army. Two days later, a supply of salt, flour, and clothing arrives. Winchester, eager to be off, sets about building sleds, since his boats are useless. On December 29, he is ready. The troops are exuberant—anything to be rid of this pestilential camp! But Darnell realizes what they are facing:

"We are now about commencing one of the most serious marches ever performed by the Americans. Destitute, in a measure, of clothes, shoes and provisions, the most essential articles necessary for the existence and preservation of the human species in this world and more particularly in this cold climate. Three sleds are prepared for each company, each to be pulled by a packhorse, which has been without food for two weeks except brush, and will not be better fed while in our service. . . ."

The following day, the troops set off for the Maumee rapids. Few armies have presented such a ragtag appearance. In spite of the midwinter weather, scarcely one possesses a greatcoat or cloak. Only a lucky few have any woollen garments. They remain dressed in the clothes they wore when they left Kentucky, their cotton shirts torn, patched, and ragged, hanging to their knees, their trousers also of cotton. Their matted hair falls uncombed over their cheeks. Their slouch hats have long since been worn bare. Those who own blankets wrap them about their bodies as protection from the blizzards, holding them in place by broad belts of leather into which are thrust axes and knives. The officers are scarcely distinguishable from the men. They carry swords or rifles instead of long guns and a dagger—often an expensive one, hand-carved—in place of a knife.

Now these men must become beasts of burden, for the horses are not fit to pull the weight. Harnessed five to a sleigh, they haul their equipment through snow and water for the next eleven days. The sleighs, it develops, are badly made—too light to carry the loads, not large enough to cross the half-frozen streams. Provisions and men are soon soaked through. But if the days are bad, the nights are a horror. Knee-deep snow must be cleared away before a camp can be made. Fire must be struck from flint on steel. The wet wood, often enough, refuses to burn. So cold that they cannot always prepare a bed for themselves, the Kentuckians topple down on piles of brush before the smoky fires and sleep in their steaming garments.

Then, on the third day, a message arrives from Harrison: *turn back!* The General has picked up another rumour that the redoubtable Tecumseh and several hundred Indians are in the area. He advises—does not order—Winchester not to proceed. With the Indians at his rear and no certainty of provisions at the rapids, any further movement toward Canada this winter would be foolhardy.

But James Winchester is in no mood to retreat. He is a man who has suddenly been released from three months of dreadful frustration—frustration over inactivity and boredom, frustration over insubordination, frustration over sickness and starvation, and, perhaps most significant, frustration over his own changing role as the leader of his men. Now at least he is on the move; it must seem to him some sort of progress; it is action of a sort, and at the end—who knows? More action, perhaps, even glory . . . vindication. He has no stomach to turn in his tracks and retreat to that "loathsome place," nor do his men. And so he moves on to tragedy.

———

AT FORT AMHERSTBURG, Lieutenant-Colonel Procter has concluded that the Americans have gone into winter quarters. His Indian spies have observed no movement around Winchester's camp for several weeks, and he is convinced that Harrison has decided to hold off any attempt to recapture Detroit until spring. It is just as well, for he has only a skeleton force of soldiers and a handful of Indians.

The Indians concern Procter. He cannot control them, cannot depend on them, does not like them. One moment they are hot for battle, the next they have vanished into the forest. Nor can he be sure where their loyalties lie. Matthew Elliott's eldest son, Alexander, has been killed and scalped by one group of Indians who pretended to be defecting to the British but who were actually acting as scouts for Winchester. Brock called them "a fickle race"; Procter would certainly agree with that. Neither has been able to understand that the Indians' loyalty is not to the British or to the Americans but to their own kind. They will support the British only as long as they believe it suits their own purpose. But the British, too, can be fickle; no tribesman, be he Potawatomi, Wyandot, Shawnee, or Miami, can ever quite trust the British after the betrayal at Fallen Timbers in 1794.

Nor do the British trust them—certainly not when it comes to observing the so-called rules of warfare, which are, of course, white European rules. Tecumseh is the only chief who can restrain his followers from killing and torturing prisoners and ravaging women and children. Angered by Prevost's armistice and ailing from a wound received at Brownstown, Tecumseh has headed south to try to draw the Creeks and Choctaws to his confederacy. His brother, the Prophet, has returned to the Wabash.

Procter needs to keep the Indians active, hence his attempt to capture Fort Wayne with a combined force of natives and regulars. The attempt failed, though it helped to slow Harrison's advance. Now he is under orders from Prevost to refrain from all such offensive warfare. His only task is defence against the invader.

He must tread a line delicately, for the Indians' loyalty depends on a show of British resolution. As Brock once said, "it is of primary importance that the confidence and goodwill of the Indians should be preserved and that whatsoever can tend to produce a contrary effect should be carefully avoided." That is the rub. The only way the confidence and goodwill of the Indians can be preserved is to attack the Americans, kill as many as possible, and let the braves have their way with the rest. Procter is not unmindful of how the news of the victory at Queenston has raised native morale—or of how the armistice has lowered it.

Prevost, as usual, believes that the British have overextended themselves on the Detroit frontier. Only Brock's sturdy opposition prevented the Governor General from ordering the evacuation of all captured American territory to allow the release of troops to the Niagara frontier. But Brock understood that such a show of weakness would cause the Indians to consider making terms with the enemy.

Brock's strategy, which Procter has inherited, has been to let the Americans keep the tribes in a state of ferment. The policy has succeeded. Harrison's attempt to subdue the Indians on the northwestern frontier has delayed his advance until midwinter and caused widespread indignation among the natives. Some six thousand have been displaced, nineteen villages ravaged, seven hundred lodges burned, thousands of bushels of corn destroyed. Savagery is not the exclusive trait of the red man. The Kentuckians take scalps whenever they can, nor are women and children safe from the army. Governor Meigs had no sooner called out the Ohio militia in the early fall than they launched an unprovoked attack on an Indian village near Mansfield, burning all the houses and shooting several of the inhabitants.

The worst attacks have been against the villages on the Peoria lakes, destroyed without opposition by a force of rangers and volunteers under Governor Ninian Edwards of Illinois Territory. One specific foray will not soon be forgotten: a mounted party under a captain named Judy came upon an Indian couple on the open prairie. When the man tried to surrender, Judy shot him through the body. Chanting his death song, the Indian killed one of Judy's men and was in turn riddled with bullets. A little later the same group captured and killed a starving Indian child.

In their rage and avarice, Edwards's followers scalp and mutilate the bodies of the fallen and ransack Indian graves for plunder. Small wonder that the Potawatomi chief Black Bird, in a later discussion with Claus, the Canadian Indian superintendent, cries out in fury, "The way they treat our killed and the remains of those that are in their graves to the west make our people mad when they meet the Big Knives. Whenever they get any of our people into their hands they cut them like meat into small pieces."

All that fall the Indians continue to concern Procter. They have been devouring his provisions at an alarming rate. The white leadership is shaky. At seventy, Matthew Elliott can scarcely sit a horse, and McKee is worn down by drink. Tecumseh's restraining hand is absent. Procter has some hope of reorganizing the tribes around Amherstburg into a raiding party under Colonel William Caldwell, a veteran of Butler's Rangers during the Revolution. Caldwell possesses enormous influence among the Wyandot, whom he has persuaded to adopt the British cause.

Meanwhile, Procter solves part of his supply problem by dispatching most of the Indians under Elliott to the Rapids of the Maumee, where several hundred acres of corn are waiting to be harvested—the same corn that Harrison has been trying vainly to seize. Elliott may be old and infirm, but he has lost none of his frontier cunning. He has sent Indian spies into Ohio who report that Winchester is again advancing. Elliott dispatches couriers to the villages of the Ottawa and the Potawatomi in Michigan Territory and to the Miami at the ravaged villages of the Mississinewa in Indiana. War parties begin to trickle into Amherstburg; within a month the native force has increased from three hundred to almost eight hundred braves, all stirred to a fever by the depredations of Harrison's army.

Winchester's army, meanwhile, is advancing toward the rapids. He arrives on January 11; Procter learns of this two days later. The British commander moves swiftly, calling out the militia, assembling the Indians. It is his intention to scorch the earth (whatever is not already scorched) along the Detroit frontier to deny the Americans provisions and shelter. The following day he dispatches Major Ebenezer Reynolds of the Essex militia with two flank companies and a band of Potawatomi to the little village of Frenchtown on the River Raisin. Reynolds's orders are to destroy the village and all its supplies and to remove the French-speaking settlers—forcibly, if necessary—to Canadian soil.

It is not a pleasant task. Who wants his home destroyed, his property removed, and his cattle driven off and killed by Indians? The settlers have worked hard to improve their farms, which lie on both sides of the narrow, low-banked river. Their town, a simple row of some twenty dwelling houses, squatting on the north bank three miles from the mouth, is not designed as a fort. Its only protection is a fence made of split pickets to secure the yards and gardens. The villagers are in a panic; as Reynolds and his men move in, a delegation slips away, heading for the Rapids of the Maumee to plead with Winchester for help. They carry with them a note for Harrison from Isaac Day, a long-time Detroit citizen, who writes that "five hundred true and brave Americans can secure the District of Erie—A timely approach of our armies will secure us from being forced to prison and the whole place from being burned by savage fury." Day has scarcely sent off this letter when he is seized and jailed. If Winchester is to act at all to save the settlement, he must act at once.

———

RAPIDS OF THE MAUMEE, January 17, 1813. Winchester and his senior officers sit in council. Should they go to the relief of Frenchtown? For almost four days word has been coming back of Indian outrages and British high-handedness. Everything is being removed from the village—cattle, carrioles, sleighs, grain, foodstuffs. Citizens such as Isaac Day, suspected of pro-American feelings, have been bundled off to confinement across the river. Winchester's information is that the British force is ridiculously small: between forty and fifty militia and perhaps a hundred Indians. It is, however, building rapidly. If the Americans move quickly, Day's note has told them, they can provision themselves at Frenchtown by securing three thousand barrels of flour and much grain. That possibility must seem as tempting as the succour of the villagers.

Lieutenant-Colonel John Allen rises—a graceful, commanding presence, perhaps the most popular man in Winchester's army,
certainly the most distinguished, the most eloquent. A handsome
Kentuckian, tall, sandy-haired, blue-eyed, close friend and boyhood
companion of the lamented Jo Daviess (Tippecanoe's victim), next
to Clay the state's greatest orator, leading lawyer, state senator,
onetime candidate for governor. When he speaks all listen, for Allen
commands as much respect as, if not more than, his general.

He is fed up with inactivity—weary of slow movements that get
nowhere, as he complains in one of his letters to his wife, Jane,
herself the daughter of a general. He hungers for action; now he
sees his chance.

Winchester's forces, he points out, have three choices: they can
withdraw—an ignominy which, piled upon other American setbacks,
is unthinkable. They can wait here at the Maumee rapids for the rest
of Harrison's force, but if they do that they will give the British time
to build strength. Or they can go to the aid of the beleaguered inhabitants of Frenchtown, secure the desperately needed food at the
settlement, strike a decisive blow against the British, open the road
to Detroit, and—certainly not least—cover themselves with glory.

The council does not need much convincing, nor does Winchester.
Why wait for Harrison, who is sixty-five miles away? A victory over
the British—*any* victory—can make Winchester a national hero.
His men, he knows, are as eager to move as he is. The term of the
six-month volunteers will end in February; they have refused to
re-enlist. All want one brief taste of glory before returning home.
They have just received a welcome shipment of woollen underwear,
and their morale, reduced by long weeks of inactivity and hunger,
has risen again. And there is *food* at Frenchtown! Winchester, who
has already written to General Perkins at Lower Sandusky asking
for reinforcements for a proposed advance, now dispatches a second
letter to Harrison announcing his intention to send a detachment
to relieve Frenchtown and hold it.

One of Harrison's many frustrations during this exhausting fall
and winter has been a collapse of communications. His letter to

Winchester, urging him to abandon his march to the rapids, arrived too late. Winchester's reply, announcing his intention to move ahead to the rapids, does not reach him until the force is actually at its destination. It is carried by an eighteen-year-old Kentucky volunteer named Leslie Combs, who, with a single guide, crosses one hundred miles of trackless forest through snow so deep that the two men dare not lie down for fear of suffocation and are forced to sleep standing up. Exhausted, ill, and starving, the pair reach Fort McArthur on January 9. Harrison, at Upper Sandusky, gets Winchester's letter two days later.

Five days pass during which time Harrison has no idea of Winchester's position or intentions. Then on the night of the sixteenth he hears from Perkins at Lower Sandusky that Winchester has reached the rapids and wants reinforcements, apparently contemplating an attack.

The news alarms him—if it were in his power he would call Winchester off. He sets off at once for Lower Sandusky, travelling so swiftly that his aide's horse drops dead of exhaustion. There he immediately dispatches a detachment of artillery, guarded by three hundred infantrymen, to Winchester's aid. The camp at the rapids is only thirty-six miles away, but the roads are choked with drifting snow, and the party moves slowly.

Two days later, on January 18, he receives confirmation of Winchester's intention to send a detachment to relieve Frenchtown. Now Harrison is thoroughly alarmed. The proposed move is "opposed to a principle by which I have ever been governed in Indian warfare, i.e. never to make a detachment but under the most urgent circumstances." He orders two more regiments to march to the rapids and sets off himself, with General Perkins, in a sleigh. Its slowness annoys him. He seizes his servant's horse, rides on alone. Darkness falls; the horse stumbles into a frozen swamp; the ice gives way; Harrison manages to free himself and pushes on through the night on foot.

Winchester, meanwhile, has already ordered Lieutenant-Colonel William Lewis and 450 troops to attack the enemy at Frenchtown on the Raisin. Off goes Lewis, with three days' provisions, followed a few hours later by a second force of one hundred Kentuckians under the eager Lieutenant-Colonel Allen. They rendezvous at Presqu'Isle, a French-Canadian village on the south side of the Maumee, twenty miles from the rapids, eighteen from the Raisin. Elias Darnell is overwhelmed, as are his comrades, by this first contact with anything remotely resembling civilization:

"The sight of this village filled each heart with emotions of cheerfulness and joy; for we had been nearly five months in the wilderness, exposed to every inconvenience, and excluded from everything that had the appearance of a civilized country."

The inhabitants pour out of their homes, waving white flags, shouting greetings. The troops are in high spirits; they know that some will be corpses on the morrow, but with the eternal optimism of all soldiers, most hew to the conviction that they will survive. Nonetheless, those who can write have sent letters home to wives, parents, or friends. One such is Captain James Price, commander of the Jessamine Blues, who writes rather formally to his wife, Susan, at Nicholasville, Kentucky, that "on the event of battle I have believed it proper to address you these lines."

It is his two-year-old son that concerns Captain Price rather than his three daughters who, he feels, are his wife's responsibility: "Teach my boy to love truth," he writes, "to speak truth at all times. . . . He must be taught to bear in mind that 'an honest man is the noblest work of God'; he must be rigidly honest in his dealings. . . . Never allow him to run about on Sabbath days, fishing. Teach my son the habits of industry. . . . Industry leads to virtue. . . . Not a day must be lost in teaching him how to work. . . . It may be possible I may fall in battle and my only boy must know that his father, next to God, loves his country, and is now risking his life in defending that country against a barbarous and cruel enemy. . . . Pray for me that you may be with me once more."

The following morning, January 18, as the Kentucky soldiers march along the frozen lake toward their objective, they meet refugees from Frenchtown. What kind of artillery do the British have, the troops want to know. "Two pieces about large enough to kill a mouse," is the reply. From Frenchtown comes word that the British are waiting. Lewis forms up his troops on the ice, and as they come in sight of the settlement, the lone British howitzer opens up. "Fire away with your mouse cannon!" some of the men cry, and as the long drum roll sounds the charge, they cross the slippery Raisin, clamber up the bank, leap the village pickets, and drive the British back toward the forest.

Later, one of the French residents tells Elias Darnell that he has watched an old Wyandot—one of those who took part in the rout of Tupper's Ohio militia at the rapids—smoking his pipe as the Americans come into sight. "I suppose Ohio men come," he says. "We give them another chase." Then as the American line stampedes through the village he cries, "Kentuck, by God!" and joins in the general retreat.

The battle rages from 3 P.M. to dark. John Allen forces the British left wing back into the forest. The British make a stand behind a chain of enclosed lots and small clusters of houses, where piles of brush and deadfalls bar the way. The American centre under Major George Madison (a future governor of Kentucky) and the left under Major Benjamin Graves now go into action, and the British and Indians fall back, contesting every foot. When dusk falls they have been driven two miles from the village, and the Americans are in firm possession.

Lewis's triumphant account of the victory is sent immediately by express rider to Winchester, who receives it at dawn. The camp at the rapids is ecstatic. Harking back to Henry Clay's speech of August 16, Lewis reports that "both officers and soldiers supported the double character of Americans and Kentuckyans." The state's honour has been vindicated. The soldiers at both French town and the rapids now feel they are unbeatable, that they will roll right on to Detroit, cross the river, capture Amherstburg. General Simon Perkins, after the fact, will write dryly: "I fancy they were too much impressed with the opinion that Kentucky bravery could not fall before [such] a foe as Indians and Canadians."

The troops on the Raisin are dangerously exposed. Yet their eagerness for battle is such that Winchester would be hard put to withdraw them even if he wished to—even Harrison will admit that. But Winchester does not wish to. Caught up in the general intoxication of victory, seeing himself and his army as the saviours of his country's honour, he takes what troops he can spare—fewer than three hundred—and marches off to Frenchtown.

There is another force drawing him and his men toward the little village—an attraction quite as powerful as the prospect of fame and glory: Frenchtown, at this moment, is close to paradise. Here on the vine-clad banks of *la Rivière au Raisin* is luxury: fresh apples, cider by the barrel, sugar, butter, whiskey, and more—houses with roofs, warm beds, hearth sides with crackling fires, the soft presence of women. When Winchester arrives late on the twentieth, Lewis's men have already sampled these delights. Billeted in no particular order in the homes of the enthusiastic settlers, they are already drunk and quarrelsome, wandering about town late into the night. There is some vague talk of entrenching the position, but it is only talk. The men are weary from fighting, unruly from drink, and in no mood to take orders.

The village is surrounded on three sides by a palisade constructed of eight-foot logs, split and sharpened at the ends. These pickets, which do not come all the way down to the river bank, enclose a compact community of log and shingle houses, interspersed with orchards, gardens, barns, and outbuildings. The whole space forms a rectangle two hundred yards along the river and three hundred deep.

On the right of the village, downriver, lies an open meadow with a number of detached houses. Here Lieutenant-Colonel Samuel Wells, brother to the slain scout Billy Wells and a veteran of Tippecanoe, encamps his regulars. Winchester demurs: the regulars would be better placed within the palisade. But Wells insists on his prerogatives: military etiquette determines that the regular troops should *always* be on the right of the militia. Winchester does not argue. Wells's men are exposed, but he expects to find a better campground for them on the following day.

Leaving Wells in charge of the main camp, the General and his staff, including his teenaged son, take up quarters on the south side of the river in the home of Colonel Francis Navarre, a local trader. It is a handsome building, the logs covered with clapboard, the whole shaded by pear trees originally brought from Normandy. Winchester is given a spacious guest room at the front of the house, warmed by a fireplace. It is now Wells's turn to demur. He believes the General and his officers should be as close as possible to the troops on the far side of the river in case of sudden attack. The British fort is only eighteen miles away.

But James Winchester has made up his mind. For twenty years as a wealthy plantation owner he has enjoyed the creature comforts of a sedentary life. For five months without complaint he has slept out in the elements, enduring the privations with his troops, existing on dreadful food—when there was food at all—drinking, sometimes, stagnant water scooped out of wagon tracks. Later, he will argue that there was no house in Frenchtown; he would have had to move some of the wounded. But this is palpably false.

A strange lassitude has fallen over the General and his troops. The sudden euphoric victory, the almost magical appearance of food, drink, warmth, and shelter—the stuff of their dreams for these past weeks—has given them a dreamlike confidence. There is talk of moving the camp to a better position, and on the following day the General and some of his officers ride out to look over the ground. Nothing comes of it. It does not apparently occur to them that it might be a good idea to put the river between themselves and the British.

Wells leaves camp that morning claiming that he has baggage to collect at the rapids. Winchester, who believes that Wells has lost faith in him, sends a note with him to Harrison, detailing his situation. It reflects his sense of security: his patrols have detected no British in the vicinity; he does not believe any attack will take place for several days. His own intentions are far from clear. Later that night, Captain Nathaniel Hart, Harrison's emissary, rides in with the news that Harrison has arrived at the Maumee rapids and that reinforcements are on the way. This adds to the general complacency.

It is an axiom of war that from time to time even the best of generals suffer from a common failing—a refusal to believe their own intelligence reports. Psychological blinkers narrow their vision; they decline to accept any evidence that fails to support their own appreciation of the situation. Winchester seems deaf to all suggestions that the British are massing for an attack. On the morning of the twenty-first, he sends Navarre's son Peter and four of his brothers to scout toward the mouth of the Detroit River. En route, they intercept Joseph Bordeau, Peter's future father-in-law, crossing on the ice from the British side. Bordeau, who has escaped from Amherstburg, brings positive news that the British, with a large body of Indians, will be at the Raisin some time after dark. But "Jocko" La Salle, a voluble and genial French Canadian—and a possible British plant—convinces Winchester that this news must be in error. Winchester and his officers, "regaling themselves with whiskey and loaf sugar" as Elias Darnell believes, dismiss Peter Navarre with a laugh.

That afternoon, a second scout confirms the story, but again Winchester is deaf. Later in the evening, one of Lewis's ensigns learns from a tavern keeper that he has been talking to two British officers about an impending attack. But Lewis does not take the report seriously.

Some of Winchester's field officers expect that a council will be called that night, but no word comes from the General. Though Winchester has issued vague orders about strengthening the camp, little has been done. Nor does he issue the ammunition, stored at Navarre's house. Wells's detachment is down to ten rounds per man.

It is bitterly cold. The snow lies deep. Nobody has the heart to send pickets out onto the roads leading into the settlement. William Atherton notices that most of the men act as if they were perfectly secure, some wandering about town until late into the night. Atherton himself feels little anxiety, although he has reason to believe the situation is perilous. He sleeps soundly until awakened by the cry "To arms! to arms!" the thundering of cannon, the roar of muskets, and the discordant yells of attacking Indians.

AMHERSTBURG, UPPER CANADA, January 19, 1813. It is long past midnight. From the windows of Draper's tavern comes the sound of music and merriment, laughter and dancing. The young people of the town and the officers of the garrison have combined to hold a ball to celebrate the birthday of Queen Charlotte, the consort of the mad old king of England. Suddenly the music stops and in walks Procter's deputy, Lieutenant-Colonel St. George, equipped for the field. His voice, long accustomed to command, drowns the chatter.

"My boys," says the Colonel, "you must prepare to dance to a different tune; the enemy is upon us and we are going to surprise them. We shall take the route about four in the morning, so get ready at once."

Procter has just received word of the British defeat at the Raisin. The Americans, he knows, are in an exposed position and their numbers are not large. He determines to scrape up as many men as possible and attack at once. This swift and aggressive decision is not characteristic of Procter, a methodical, cautious officer who tends to follow the book. It was Procter, after all, who strongly opposed Brock's sally against Detroit. Now Brock's example—or perhaps Brock's ghost—impels him to precipitate action. The moves are Procter's, but the spirit behind them is that of his late commander.

He plans swiftly. He will send a detachment under Captain James Askin to garrison Detroit. He will leave Fort Amherstburg virtually defenceless, manned only by the sick and least effective members of the militia under Lieutenant-Colonel Jean-Baptiste Bâby. The remainder—every possible man who can be called into service, including provincial seamen from the gunboats—will be sent across the river. In all, he counts 597 able men and more than five hundred Indians—Potawatomi displaced from their homes by Harrison, with bitter memories of Tippecanoe; Miami, victims of the recent attacks at Mississinewa; and Chief Roundhead's Wyandot, formerly of Brownstown.

The first detachment leaves immediately, dragging three three-pound cannon and three small howitzers on sleighs. John Richardson, the future novelist, is young enough at fifteen to find the scene romantic—the troops moving in a thin line across the frozen river under cliffs of rugged ice, their weapons, polished to a high gloss, glittering in the winter sunlight.

Lieutenant Frederic Rolette, back in action again after the prisoner exchange that followed the battle of Queenston Heights and fresh from his losing struggle to regain the gunboat *Detroit* from the Americans, has charge of one of the guns. He is suffering from such a splitting headache that Major Reynolds urges him to go back. Rolette looks insulted, produces a heavy bandanna. "Look here," he says, "tie this tight around my head." Reynolds rolls it into a thick band and does so. "I am better already," says Rolette and pushes on.

The following day the rest of Procter's forces cross the river, rest that night at Brownstown, and prepare to move early next morning. As darkness falls, John Richardson's favourite brother, Robert, aged fourteen, a midshipman in the Provincial Marine, sneaks into camp. His father, an army surgeon, has given him strict orders to stay out of trouble on the Canadian side, but he is determined to see action and attaches himself to one of the gun crews.

In the morning, Procter moves his force of one thousand to Rocky River, twelve miles from Brownstown, six miles from the American camp. Two hours before dawn on the following day they rise, march the intervening distance, and silently descend upon the enemy.

The camp at Frenchtown is asleep, the drum roll just sounding reveille. This, surely, is the moment for attack, while the men are still in their blankets, drowsy, brushing the slumber from their eyes, without weapons in their hands. But the ghost of Isaac Brock has departed. Procter goes by the book, which insists that an infantry charge be supported by cannon. Precious moments slip by, and the army's momentum slows as he places his pieces. A sharp-eyed Kentucky guard spots the movement. A rifle explodes, and the leading grenadier of the 41st, a man named Gates, drops dead: a bullet has literally gone in one ear and out the other. Surprise is lost. The battle begins. Procter's caution will cost the lives of scores of good men.

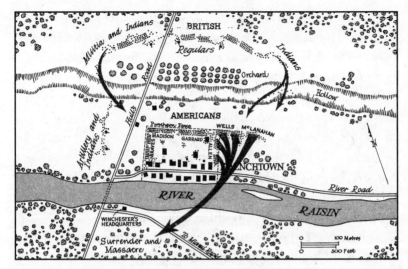

The Battle of Frenchtown

It is still dark. The British and Canadians can see flashes of musketry several hundred yards to the front but nothing else. Slowly, in the pre-dawn murk, a blurred line of figures takes shape, standing out in front of the village. They fire a volley at this welcome target, but the line stands fast. They fire again without effect. Who are these supermen who do not fall when the muskets roar? Dawn provides the answer: they have been aiming, not at their enemies, but at a line of wooden pickets that protects them.

A second problem frustrates them. Procter has placed one of his three-pounders directly in front of his centre, so that the American fire aimed at the gun plays upon the men behind it while the gunners themselves are in jeopardy from their own men in the rear.

A British musket ball strikes Frederic Rolette in the head. The tightly rolled silk bandanna saves his life. The ball is caught in the fold and flattens against his skull, increasing his headache and causing a goose egg but no further damage.

The fire grows hotter. Behind the palisades the Americans can easily pick out targets against the lightening sky. When the British abandon a three-pounder twenty yards from the fence, the Kentuckians leap over the puncheons to capture it. But Rolette's mate, Second-Lieutenant Robert Irvine, the same man who tried to beat off the attack on *Caledonia*, seizes the drag rope and hauls it back to the British line just as a musket ball shreds his heel.

Private Shadrach Byfield, whose name was left off the list for prize money after the fall of Detroit, is fighting in Adam Muir's company of the 41st when the man on his left falls dead. It is light enough now to see the enemy, and he spots a Kentuckian coming through the palisades. "There's a man!" cries Byfield to a friend. "I'll have a shot at him." As he pulls the trigger, a ball strikes him under the left ear and he topples to the ground, cutting his friend's leg with his bayonet in the process. He is only twenty-three, a Wiltshire man who joined the British army at eighteen—the third in his family to enlist—an action that caused his poor mother to fall into a speechless fit from which she never recovered. Now he believes his last moment has come. "Byfield is dead!" his friend cries out, and Shadrach Byfield replies, in some wonder, "I believe I be." An age-old question flashes across his mind, a question that must occur to every soldier the instant he falls in battle. "Is this death?" he asks himself. *Is this how men die?*

But he is not dead. He raises his head and begins to creep off on his hands and knees. "Byfield," calls a sergeant, "shall I take you to the doctor?" But Shadrach Byfield at twenty-three is an old soldier. "Never mind me, go and help the men," he says, and makes his way to a barn to have his wound dressed. Here he encounters a spectacle so affecting that he can never forget it—a young midshipman, wounded in the knee, crying in pain for his mother, convinced he is going to die.

At the palisade, John Richardson feels as if he were sleep-walking. The early call and the six-mile march have exhausted him. Even as the balls begin to whistle about his head he continues to feel drowsy. He tries to fire his musket, finds it will not respond; someone the night before has stolen his flintlock and replaced it with a damaged part. The infantry manual lists twelve separate drill movements for firing a Brown Bess musket and Richardson goes through all of them without effect, but all he gets is a flash in the pan. He finds a bit of wire, tries to fix his weapon, fires again, gets another flash. He feels more frustration than fear at being fired upon by an unseen foe and not being able to fire back, even though he later comes to realize that if he had fired fifty rounds not one of them would have had any effect on the pickets (and probably not on the enemy, either, for the musket is a wretchedly inaccurate weapon).

To his horror, Richardson notes that the American sharpshooters are picking off the wounded British and Canadians as they try to crawl to safety and that some are making use of the tomahawk and scalping knife. He is still struggling vainly with his useless weapon when he hears his name called. Somebody shouts that his brother has been wounded—young Robert's right leg was shattered as he applied a match to a gun. Now, in great pain, Robert begs to be carried off, not to the staff section where his father is caring for the wounded, but to another part of the field so that he may escape his parent's wrath. And there Shadrach Byfield is witness to his suffering.

On the left of the British line, Richardson can hear the war-whoops of the Indians who, with the help of the Canadian militia, are driving directly through the open field in which Lieutenant-Colonel Wells insisted on placing the regulars of the 17th U.S. Infantry. Wells is still at the Maumee. His second-in-command, Major McClanahan, cannot hold his unprotected position. The troops fall back to the frozen Raisin, and the American right flank is turned.

The Americans are in full flight across the river with Caldwell and his Indians under Roundhead, Split Log, and Walk-in-the-Water in hot pursuit. One of the Wyandot overtakes an American officer and is about to tomahawk him when Caldwell intercedes, makes him prisoner, takes him to the rear. The Kentuckian, catching him off guard, draws his knife and slits Caldwell's throat from ear to ear, but the wound is shallow and Caldwell, who is as tough as his Indian followers, catches his assailant's arm, pulls the dagger from his throat, and plunges it again and again into his prisoner's body until he is dead. Caldwell survives.

But where, when all this is going on, is the General?

Winchester has awakened to the sound of musket fire and how-itzer bombs exploding. He runs to the barn, borrows a horse from his host (who, fearing British retribution, is glad to be rid of him), dashes into action. His two battalion commanders, Lewis and Allen, join him, and the three attempt to rally the fleeing men under the bank of the Raisin. It is too late; the troops, pursued by the Indians, are in a panic. Lewis has sent two companies to the right flank to reinforce the regulars, but these too are in retreat.

The three officers withdraw across the river and attempt a second rally behind the fences on the south side. It is futile. The men dash past into a narrow lane leading to the main road. This is suicide, for the Indians are ahead of them and behind them, on both sides of the lane. One hundred men are shot, tomahawked, scalped. Winchester attempts a third rally in an orchard about a mile and a half from the village. It also fails.

The right flank is in full retreat, the men throwing away their weapons in panic. The Potawatomi are in no mood to offer quarter. Lieutenant Ashton Garrett tries to form up a group of fifteen men but finding some sixty Indians running along both sides and in front with their arms at the trail decides instead to surrender. The Indians order Garrett and his men to ground their arms; then, securing all the weapons, they coolly shoot and scalp every one except Garrett himself.

John Allen, shot in the thigh during his attempts to stem the retreat, limps on for two miles until he can go no farther. Exhausted and in pain, he slumps onto a log, resigned to his fate. One of the Potawatomi chiefs, seeing his officer's uniform, determines to capture and ransom him, but just as he signals that intention a second Indian moves in. Allen dispatches him with a swipe of his sword. The other shoots the Colonel dead and scalps him.

Winchester and Lewis are more fortunate. They fall into the hands of Roundhead, the principal chief of the Wyandot, who, after stripping the General of his cocked hat, coat, and epaulettes, takes the two officers and Winchester's seventeen-year-old son by a circuitous route back behind the British lines. The battle for the village is still raging, but Winchester, noting Procter's artillery, dazed by the rout and despairing of any reinforcements from Harrison, has given up hope. As the Indians return with as many as eight or nine scalps hanging from their belts, he asks to see Procter. The British commander is blunt:

"Some of your troops, sir, are defending themselves from the fort in a state of desperation—had you not better surrender them?"

"I have no authority to do so," replies Winchester, shivering in the cold in his silk shirt. "My command has devolved upon the senior officer in the fort, as you are pleased to call it."

Procter now makes the classic answer—Brock's threat at Detroit, Roberts's at Mackinac: if there is no surrender he will be forced to set the town on fire; if he is forced to attack, he cannot be responsible for the conduct of the Indians or the lives of the Americans; if Winchester will surrender, he will be responsible for both. Winchester repeats that he is no longer in command but will recommend surrender to his people.

The command of the American forces still fighting inside the palisade has devolved on Major George Madison, a forty-nine-year-old veteran of the Revolution and of St. Clair's defeat at the hands of the Indians in 1791 and for twenty years keeper of public accounts for the state of Kentucky. At this moment he is concerned about the possession of an empty barn 150 yards from the palisade. If the enemy seizes that building, they will hold a commanding position overlooking the defenders. Madison calls for a volunteer to fire the barn, and a young ensign, William O. Butler, steps forward, seizes a blazing stick of firewood, vaults the fence, and dashes toward the barn under direct fire from the British and Indians on both sides.

Butler reaches the barn, flings the burning brand into a pile of hay, races back through a hail of musket balls, has almost reached the safety of his own lines when he realizes that the hay has not caught. Back he goes, re-enters the barn, fans the hay into a roaring blaze, outstrips the Indians trying to head him off, and with his clothes ripped by passing musket balls tumbles across the pickets and comes to a full stop, standing upright, trying to catch his breath. It is then that a musket ball strikes him full in the chest. Fortunately, it is spent, and Butler survives. Like his commander, George Madison, he will one day run for governor of Kentucky.

Now comes a lull in the fighting. Of the sixteen British gunners, thirteen are casualties; the remainder are too numb with cold to fire their weapons. Moreover, their ammunition is low; a wagon bearing additional rounds has been shot up and its driver killed by Kentucky riflemen. Procter has withdrawn his forces into the woods, waiting for the Indians to return from the chase before resuming the attack. The defenders seize this interlude to devour some breakfast. This is the moment when Winchester agrees to attempt a surrender.

The Americans, seeing a flag of truce, believe that Procter is asking for a respite to bury his dead. It does not occur to any that surrender is being proposed. When he learns the truth, George Madison is mortified; yet he knows his position is hopeless, for he has only a third of a keg of cartridges left. The reserve supply remains at the Navarre house across the river. He insists, however, on conditions.

"It has been customary for the Indians to massacre the wounded and prisoners after a surrender," he tells Procter. "I shall therefore not agree to any capitulation which General Winchester may direct, unless the safety and protection of all the prisoners shall be stipulated."

Procter stamps his foot:

"Sir, do *you* mean to dictate for *me*?"

"I mean to dictate for myself," Madison coolly replies. "We prefer to sell our lives as dearly as possible rather than be massacred in cold blood."

Procter agrees, but not in writing. Private property, he promises, will be respected; sleighs will be sent the following morning for the American sick and wounded; the disabled will be protected by a proper guard.

Thus the battle ends. Some of the troops plead with their officers not to surrender, saying they would rather die in action. Many are reduced to tears. Others, in a rage, throw down their guns with such force as to shiver the stocks from the barrels. Some joke and laugh. One stands on a stile block and shouts to the English, "You have taken the greatest set of game cocks that ever came from Kentuck." But the general feeling is one of despair. Atherton notes that news of the surrender is "like a shock of lightning from one end of the lines to the other." To Thomas P. Dudley, another Lexington volunteer, "the mortification at the thought of surrender, the Spartan band who fought like heroes, the tears shed, the wringing of hands, the swelling of hearts, indeed, the scene beggars description."

Only thirty-three men have managed to escape. McClanahan, Wells's second-in-command is one. Private John J. Brice is another; he gets away by pulling off his shoes and running through the snow in his stocking feet in order to leave tracks resembling those of an Indian in moccasins and so becomes the first man to report the defeat and surrender to Harrison.

Winchester's loss is appalling. Two hundred Kentuckians are dead or wounded, another seven hundred are prisoners of the British, and the worst is yet to come. The blow to American morale, already bruised by the losses at Mackinac, Detroit, and Queenston, is overwhelming. As for Harrison, the Battle of Frenchtown has wrecked his plans. His left wing has been shattered, his advance on Detroit halted indefinitely. He must now withdraw up the Maumee, out of reach of the enemy. The idea of a swift victory over Canada is gone forever.

———

FRENCHTOWN, MICHIGAN TERRITORY, January 23, 1813. William Atherton wakes at dawn, the wound in his shoulder throbbing. He cannot escape a feeling of dread that has tormented his sleep. An ominous stillness hangs over the village where the American wounded are still hived. Procter, fearing an imminent attack from Harrison, has long since dragged his own wounded off on sleds, and since there are not enough of these for the Americans, he has promised to return early in the morning to take them all to Amherstburg.

No one points to the illogic of this. If Procter fears Harrison's early arrival, why would he return for the wounded? If he doesn't fear it, why has he departed, taking everybody with him except one officer, Major Reynolds, and three interpreters? Actually, Harrison, learning of the disaster, has withdrawn his relief force. In the chorus of recriminations that will follow, nobody apparently bothers to ask why. With Procter's forces off balance and Fort Amherstburg virtually defenceless, he might easily have snatched victory from defeat. But he contents himself with putting all the blame on Winchester.

The camp at Frenchtown is uneasy. Some time in the dark hours of the night, Reynolds and the interpreters have slipped away. Atherton's fears have been further aroused by an Indian, apparently a chief, who speaks fluent English and who came into his quarters the evening before, seemingly trying to gain information about Harrison's movements. Just as he left, the Indian made an oddly chilling remark: "I am afraid," he said, "some of the mischievous boys will do some mischief before morning."

The sun has been up for no more than an hour when Atherton's fears are realized. Without warning, the door of the house in which he and some of the wounded are being cared for is forced open, and an Indian, his face smeared with red and black paint, appears waving a tomahawk, followed by several others. Their purpose is loot: they begin to strip the clothing and blankets from the wounded, groaning on the floor. Atherton, near the door, manages to slip out of the room, only to come face to face with one of the most savage-looking natives he has ever seen. This creature's face is painted jet black. Half a bushel of feathers are fastened to his scalp lock, an immense tomahawk gleams in his right hand, a scalping knife hangs from his belt. He seizes Atherton by the collar, propels him out the front door, leads him through the gate and down the river for a hundred yards to the home of Jean-Baptiste Jerome, where several wounded officers have spent the night. The building has also done duty as a tavern, and the Indians are ransacking the cellars for whiskey.

In front of the house Atherton sees a scarecrow figure, bleeding, barefoot, clad only in a shirt and drawers. This is Captain Nathaniel Hart, commander of the Lexington Light Infantry, inspector of the North West Army, the emissary whom Harrison sent to Winchester the night before the battle. He is twenty-eight and wealthy, having made a fortune in hemp. Now he is pleading for his life. The previous night, Hart, badly wounded in the knee, was visited by an old friend, Matthew Elliott's son William, a militia captain who was once cared for in the Hart home in Lexington during a bout of illness. Hart has Elliott's assurance that he will send his personal sleigh for him in the morning and convey him to his home in Amherstburg. In fact, Elliott has assured all the wounded in Jerome's house that they are in no danger. The promise is hollow; they are all in deadly peril. Some are already dying under the tomahawk blows of the Indians.

Hart turns to an Indian he recognizes—the same English-speaking chief whom Atherton encountered the evening before—and reminds him of Elliott's promise.

"Elliott has deceived you," the Indian replies. "He does not intend to fulfill his promise."

"If you will agree to take me, I will give you a horse or a hundred dollars," Hart declares. "You shall have it on our arrival at Malden."

"I cannot take you."

"Why?"

"You are too badly wounded."

"Then," asks Captain Hart, "what do you intend to do with us?"

"Boys," says the Indian, "you are all to be killed."

Hart maintains his composure, utters a brief prayer. Atherton expects at any moment to feel the blow of a tomahawk. Now follows a scene of pure horror: Captain Paschal Hickman, General William Hull's son-in-law, emerges from Jerome's house, dragged by an Indian who throws him face down into the snow. Hickman, who has already been tomahawked, chokes to death in his own blood as Atherton watches in terror, then, taking advantage of the confusion, turns from the spectacle and begins to edge slowly away, hoping not to be seen.

Albert Ammerman, another unwilling witness to the butchery, crouches on a log, guarded by his Indian captor. A private in the 1st Regiment of Kentucky Volunteers, he has been wounded in the thigh but is doing his best to conceal his injury, for he knows it is the Indians' practice to kill all who cannot walk. Now he watches helplessly while the Indians loot the houses, strip the clothes from the wounded, tomahawk and scalp their prey, and set fire to the buildings. Some, still alive, force their heads out of the windows, half-enveloped in smoke and flames, seeking rescue. But there is no rescue.

Ammerman is marched off at last toward Brownstown with some other prisoners. After limping about half a mile, they are overtaken. One Indian has Captain Hart in custody and is engaged in a violent argument with another, apparently over the reward that Hart has offered for his safe conduct to Amherstburg. As Ammerman watches, the two take aim at each other as if to end the quarrel. But they do not fire. Instead they turn upon their prisoner, pull him from his horse, knock him down with a war-club, tomahawk him, scalp him, strip him of his remaining clothing, money, and effects. Ammerman (who will shortly be ransomed in Detroit) notes that Hart, during these final moments, refrains from making any pleas and appears, to the end, perfectly calm. The news of his death, when it finally filters through to Lexington three months later, will cause a particular shiver of despair and fury in Kentucky. For this mangled and naked corpse, thrown like carrion onto the side of the road, was once the brother-in-law of Speaker Henry Clay.

Back at Frenchtown, little William Atherton (he is only five foot five) is trying to reach a small log building some distance from the scene of horror. He edges toward it, is a few steps from it, when a Potawatomi seizes him and asks where he is wounded. Atherton places a hand on his shoulder. The Indian feels it, finds it is not serious, determines that Atherton shall be his prize, perhaps for later ransom. He wraps his new possession in a blanket, gives him a hat, takes him to the back door of one of the houses, and puts the wounded Kentuckian in charge of all his plunder.

Atherton is flabbergasted. For almost an hour he has expected certain death. Now he lives in the faint hope that his life may be spared. He experiences "one of those sudden transitions of mind impossible to be either conceived or expressed, except by those whose unhappy lot it has been, to be placed in like circumstances."

As the house blazes behind him, Atherton watches his fellow prisoners being dragged away to Brownstown. For the first time, perhaps, he has been made aware of the value a man places on his own life. He sees members of his own company, old acquaintances, so badly wounded they can scarcely be moved in their beds, suddenly leap up, hearing that the Indians will tomahawk all who cannot depart on foot. They hobble past him on sticks but, being unable to keep up, are soon butchered.

After two hours, Atherton's captor returns with an army pack horse and a great deal of plunder. The Potawatomi hands his prisoner the bridle, and the two set off on the road to Brownstown, bordered now by a ghastly hedgerow of mutilated corpses.

They halt for the night at Sandy Creek, where a number of Potawatomi are encamped. Here, around a roaring fire of fence rails, the Indians feed their captives gruel. And here another grisly scene takes place. An Indian walks up to Private Charles Searls and proposes to exchange his moccasins for the soldier's shoes. The exchange effected, a brief conversation follows, the Indian asking how many men Harrison has with him. The name of the Hero of Tippecanoe seems to drive him into a sudden rage. His anger rising, he calls Searls a "Madison," raises his tomahawk, strikes him a deep blow on the shoulder.

Searls, bleeding profusely, clutches the weapon embedded in his flesh and tries to resist, whereupon a surgeon's mate, Gustavus Bower, tells him his fate is inevitable. Searls closes his eyes, the blow falls again, and Bower is drenched with brains and blood. Not long after, three more men are indiscriminately dispatched.

When Atherton asks his captor if the Indians intend to kill all the prisoners, the Indian nods. Atherton tries to eat, has no stomach for it, even though he has had little nourishment for three days. Then he realizes his captor does not understand English and hope returns.

The march resumes with many alarms. Atherton is in daily fear of his life, sleeping with a kerchief tied around his head in the belief that the Indians will want to steal it before tomahawking him in his sleep, thus giving him some warning. But they do not kill him. His captor, whose brother has been killed at the River Raisin, has other plans. It is the custom of the Potawatomi, among others, to adopt healthy captives into the families of those who have lost sons in the same engagement. It is some time before Atherton realizes that his enemies do not intend to kill or ransom him. On the contrary, they are determined to turn him into an Indian. For the rest of his life, if they have their way, he will live as a savage in the forest.

From Frenchtown, Dr. John Todd, surgeon for the 5th Regiment of Kentucky Volunteers who has been left in charge of the wounded, is conveyed to the British camp where he again encounters Captain William Elliott. The two met the previous evening when Todd was a witness to the discussions between Elliott and Hart. Now Todd urges Elliott to send his sleigh back to the Raisin where some of the badly wounded, including his friend Hart, may yet be saved. But Elliott, who has lived all his life with the Indians and is half Shawnee, knows it is too late and says so. When Todd presses the case, Elliott remarks that charity begins at home, that the British and Canadian wounded must be cared for first, that when sleighs are available they will be sent to Frenchtown. He adds, in some exasperation, that it is impossible to restrain the Indians and tries to explain that they are simply seeking revenge for their own losses. Tippecanoe is only fourteen months in the past, Mississinewa less than two.

Along the frozen shores of the River Raisin a great stillness has fallen. The cold is numbing; nothing moves. Those few settlers who still remain in Frenchtown do not venture outside their doors.

In the little orchard across the river, along the narrow lane that leads from the Navarre home and beside the Detroit River road, the bodies of the Americans lie, unshriven and unburied. The Potawatomi have made it known that any white man who dares to touch the remains of any of the hated Harrison men will meet a similar fate.

The naked corpses lie strewn for miles along the roadside in the grotesque attitudes of men who, in a sudden flash, realize their last moment has come. In death they bear a gruesome similarity, for each skull is disfigured by a frozen smear of fleshy pulp where the scalp has been.

Here, contorted in death, lies the flower of Kentucky: Captain Hart and Captain Hickman; Lieutenant-Colonel John Allen; Captain John Woolfolk, Winchester's aide-de-camp, who offered one thousand dollars to anyone who would purchase him but was tomahawked in spite of it; Captain John Simpson, Henry Clay's fellow congressman and supporter; Ensign Levi Wells, the son of Lieutenant-Colonel Sam Wells of the 4th Infantry; Allen Darnell, whose brother looks helplessly on as he is shot and scalped because he cannot keep up with the others; and Ebenezer Blythe, a surgeon's mate, tomahawked in the act of offering ransom. And here, like a discarded doll, is the cadaver of young Captain Price of the Jessamine Blues whose last letter home gave instructions for the upbringing of his two-year-old son.

A few days after the battle, the French inhabitants, emerging at last from their homes, are treated to a ghastly spectacle. Trotting along the roadway come droves of hogs that have been feeding off the corpses and are now carrying off the remains—whole arms and legs, skulls, bits of torso and entrails clamped between their greedy jaws. The hogs, too, are victims of the war, for they seem now to be as demented as the men who fight it, "rendered mad," according to one opinion, "by so profuse a diet of Christian flesh."

The war, which began so gently, has turned ugly, as all wars must. The mannerly days are over. New emotions—hatred, fury, a thirst for revenge, a nagging sense of guilt—distort the tempers of the neighbours who live on both sides of the embattled border. And it is not over. Peace is still two years away. The blood has only begun to flow.

The New War

WITH THE BATTLE OF Frenchtown, the campaign of 1812 ended. It was too cold to fight. The war was postponed until spring, when it would become a new war with new leaders and new followers. The six-month volunteers from Kentucky, Ohio, Pennsylvania and other states went back to their farms, refusing to enlist for another term of service. Harrison withdrew up the Maumee to start work on a new outpost, Fort Meigs. Along the Niagara River the American regulars moved back ten miles while others went into winter quarters at Sackets Harbor, Burlington, and Greenville. The only American fighting men in Canada were the prisoners of war at Quebec.

It was as if both Canada and the United States were starting from scratch. America had a new secretary of war, John Armstrong. Most of the old commanders—Brock, Hull, Van Rensselaer, Smyth, Winchester—were gone. Dearborn's days were numbered as were Sheaffe's. Only two major leaders remained from the early days of 1812, Tecumseh and Harrison, old adversaries fated to meet face to face at the Thames in the autumn of 1813.

Now Canada had time to breathe. With Napoleon's army fleeing Russia, some of the pressure was off Great Britain. A detachment of reinforcements was dispatched to Bermuda, there to wait until the ice cleared in the St. Lawrence. The United States, too, had time to rethink its strategy—or lack of it—and to plan more carefully for the future.

It was not the war that the Americans, inspired and goaded by the eloquence of Henry Clay and his colleagues, had set out to fight and certainly not the glamorous adventure that Harrison's volunteers expected. The post-Revolutionary euphoria, which envisaged the citizen soldiers of a democratic nation marching off to sure victory over a handful of robot-like mercenaries and enslaved farmers, had dissipated. America had learned the lessons that most nations relearn at the start of every war—that valour is ephemeral, that the heroes of one war are the scapegoats of the next, that command is for the young, the vigorous, the imaginative, the professional. Nor does enthusiasm and patriotism alone win battles: untrained volunteers, no matter how fervent, cannot stand up to seasoned regulars, drilled to stand fast in moments of panic and to follow orders without question. It was time for the United States to drop its amateur standing now that it intended to do what its founding fathers had not prepared for—aggressive warfare.

It was clear that possession of the water held the key to victory. Britain, by seizing Michilimackinac and Detroit, both commanding narrow channels, effectively controlled all easy transit to the northwest and thus to the fur trade. Two other strong points, Kingston and Montreal, commanded the entrance to Lake Ontario and the St. Lawrence lifeline to the sea. And so, as winter gave way to spring, the ring of hammers on the Lakes announced a different kind of contest as both sides engaged in a shipbuilding race.

Immediately after Hull's defeat, Madison and Eustis had awoken to the fact that the disgraced commander's original proposals had been right. And so to Sackets Harbor that winter—the only available harbour at the eastern end of Lake Ontario—a new commander, Captain Isaac Chauncey, quickly dubbed a commodore, was dispatched with 700 seamen and marines and 140 ships' carpenters to help construct two fighting ships, each of thirty-two guns. Jesse Elliott, hero of the previous summer's attack, had added the captured *Caledonia* to the vessels he was already building. Brock had rightly seen that event as a serious and significant loss. At Erie, Pennsylvania, two twenty-gun brigs and several gunboats were also under construction. With Elliott's warships these formed the backbone of the fleet with which Oliver Hazard Perry would in the summer of 1813 seize control of the lake from the British, thus opening up Amherstburg and the valley of the Thames to American attack.

The British were also building ships—one big vessel at the protected harbour of Kingston, another at York, wide open to attack, a split decision that proved costly when Chauncey's fleet appeared off the capital in April. At Amherstburg a smaller vessel was under construction. But the British suffered from a lack of supplies, of mechanics, and, most important, of trained seamen. Already, following some skirmishing outside Kingston Harbour in November, control of Lake Ontario was in doubt. Was it possible that the upstart Americans could outsail, outmanoeuvre, and outfight the greatest maritime power in the world? On the Atlantic, in single engagements—the *United States* versus the *Macedonian* in October, the *Constitution* versus the *Java* in December—the Americans were the winners. After a season of reverses on land, these victories, though not significant in military terms, gave the country hope.

British strategy remained the same: to stay on the defensive. An attempt would be made to dislodge Harrison from his threatening position at Fort Meigs on the Maumee, but with Brock gone there was no hint of offensive warfare. The Americans planned to open the campaign with attacks on both Kingston and York to destroy the new warships, then to seize Fort George at the mouth of the Niagara and march on Fort Erie. By spring Dearborn had watered down this plan, eliminating Kingston, which was held to be too strong for an attack.

The United States remained deeply divided over the war. Following Napoleon's disastrous retreat from Moscow, the Russian minister in Washington proposed to Madison (now serving his second term as the result of the November election) that his emperor, Alexander I, mediate between the two belligerents. After all, with the Orders in Council out of the way the only real impediment to peace was the matter of impressment, and with the war in Europe apparently winding down, that would soon be of academic interest. Madison agreed, but before the issue could be negotiated, Alexander, to England's fury, made a separate peace with Napoleon. Russia, the British felt, like America before her had stabbed them in the back. And so the war went on.

The New England states continued, in effect, to be at peace with their neighbours in Britain's Atlantic colonies. But across the nation a new and savage emotion, which since the beginning of history has acted as a unifying force among peoples, was beginning to be felt. The contempt and disdain once felt for the British had been transformed into rage. Procter was the villain; his officers were seen as monsters. Harrison's troops, especially, thirsted for revenge and would get it finally when autumn reddened the leaves in the valley of the Thames.

In Kentucky, the failure at the Raisin cut deep. When the news reached Lexington, Governor Shelby was attending a theatrical performance. He hurried out as whispers of the defeat rippled from row to row. People began to leave, some in tears, all distressed, until by the play's third act the house was empty. Scarcely a family in the state was not touched in some way by the tragedy at Frenchtown. The idea of a swift victory was shattered. For hundreds of families, weeping over lost sons and lost illusions, the war that at the outset seemed almost like a sporting event had become a horror. Some did not learn for months whether their men were alive, dead, or in prison. Some never knew.

Captain Paschal Hickman's mother did not recover from the blow. "Sorely distressed about the massacre," in the words of her husband, ". . . she pined away and died on June 9, 1813."

Captain Hart's widow, Anna, suffered a similar end. Prostrated over her husband's fate, she was sent by relatives to New Orleans and then to New York in the hope that a change of scene would lighten her grief. It failed. She set out again for Lexington but could go no farther than Philadelphia, where she died at twenty-seven.

Lieutenant-Colonel Allen's widow, Jane, hoped against hope that her husband was not dead but a captive of the Indians. For eight years she watched and waited at her home on the Lexington-Louisville road, keeping the shutters open each night that he might see the candle she kept burning there. At last, with all hope extinguished, she, too, wasted away from grief. In February, 1821, she died.

It was not only in Kentucky that the tragedy struck home. All of America was dumbfounded. In the town of Erie, Pennsylvania, the citizens at a public meeting resolved to wear black crêpe on their arms and in their hats for ninety days out of respect for those who "gloriously fell in the field defending the only free government on earth." In Kentucky, a new slogan arose and was used to stimulate recruiting: *Remember the Raisin!* Nine counties were named in honour of nine officers slain on its frozen banks. Now the government's war loan, only two-thirds subscribed, was taken up in a new wave of patriotic fervour, partly as a result of the efforts of John Jacob Astor, whose own patriotism had been called in question as the result of his actions of the previous summer.

Lieutenant-Colonel Procter, the subject of almost universal excoriation in America, brushed off the massacre at the Raisin as he would an annoying insect. In his dispatch to Sheaffe he simply wrote that "the zeal and courage of the Indian Department never were more conspicuous than on this occasion, the Indian warriors fought with their usual courage." In a later report he referred to the massacre briefly and with regret but stated that the Kentucky soldiers too killed the wounded and took scalps; all perfectly true. That, however, scarcely justified the General Order issued at Quebec on February 8, which was enough to make the American prisoners grind their teeth:

On this occasion, the Gallantry of Colonel Procter was most nobly displayed in his humane and unwearied exertions in securing the vanquished from the revenge of the Indian warriors.

That was not the view of some of Procter's people. Dr. Robert Richardson, two of whose sons fought at the Raisin, was outraged by the massacre and wrote to his father-in-law, John Askin, "We have not heard the last of this shameful transaction. I wish to god it could be contradicted."

Crowded into a small wood yard at Amherstburg, without tents, blankets, or fires, unprotected from rain and snow, Procter's prisoners shivered in their thin clothing for almost two days before being moved to a chilly warehouse. Eventually, they were marched five hundred miles by a roundabout route through the back country to Fort George, where the regulars were sent to Quebec City and the volunteers paroled to their homes under the guarantee that they would not take up arms against Great Britain or her allies until exchanged in the regular way.

Allies? When one Kentuckian sarcastically asked a British officer who Great Britain's allies were, the reply was evasive and shame-faced: Britain's allies, said the officer, were well known; he did not wish to continue the discussion. Nor did Henry Procter want to talk about the massacre, half convincing himself that it had never happened. In Detroit, when a group of citizens asked for an inquiry into the killing of the prisoners, he flew into a rage and demanded firm evidence that any such atrocity had occurred. Like Brock before him, Procter was a virtual prisoner of the Indians, whose American captives languished that spring in the villages of the Potawatomi. His own force, badly mauled at Frenchtown, was smaller than Harrison's on the Maumee. Indian support was essential to even the odds, and he knew that he would not get it if he tried to interfere with time-honoured rituals. He refused to bow to demands that the Indians release all their captives to him, agreeing to ransom them but for no more than five dollars a head—an empty gesture when the going rate in Detroit started at ten dollars and ran as high as eighty.

The Indians scattered that spring to their hunting-grounds. Tecumseh was still in the south, pursuing his proposal to weld the tribes into a new confederacy. The British saw eye to eye with his plan for an Indian state north of the Ohio; it would act as a buffer between the two English-speaking nations on the North American continent and make future wars unattractive. The idea had long been at the core of British Indian policy.

But the Indians were soon ignored. In the official dispatches they got short shrift. The names of white officers who acted with conspicuous gallantry were invariably recorded, those of the Indian chieftains never. Even the name of Tecumseh, after Brock's initial report, vanishes from the record. Yet these painted tribesmen helped save Canada's hide in 1812:

At Michilimackinac and Detroit, their presence was decisive. In each case the threat of an Indian attack broke the morale of the defenders and brought about unconditional surrender.

At the River aux Canards and Turkey Creek, Tecumseh's warriors, acting as a screen, contributed to Hull's decision not to attack Fort Amherstburg. At Brownstown and Maguaga, the same mixed group of tribesmen was essential to the British success in preventing Captain Brush's supply train from getting through to Detroit.

At Queenston Heights, the Mohawk advance guard so terrified Scott's militiamen that hundreds fled to the woods before the battle was joined, while the forward American scouts were prevented from probing the strength and position of Sheaffe's forces. The war-whoops of Norton's followers, echoing across the gorge, sent a chill through thousands more, confirming them in their refusal to cross the river.

And at Frenchtown, the Wyandot and Potawatomi turned Winchester's right flank and caused the surrender of his entire force.

Perhaps if Brock and Tecumseh had lived, the Indian claims might have received greater consideration. Brock's attitude to the tribes was ambivalent, but he believed in keeping his promises; his dispatches to Prevost underline his concern for the Indian position. But with Brock gone, Tecumseh's death at the Thames in the fall of 1813 (the Indians fighting on after Procter and the British fled) meant an end to Shawnee aspirations for a native confederacy.

It was among the white settlers in Upper Canada that a new confederacy was taking shape. There the war was no longer looked on with indifference. In the muddy capital of York a new leader was about to emerge in the person of the Reverend Dr. John Strachan, perhaps the most significant and influential Canadian of his time, a product of the War of 1812. In December of that first war year Strachan presided over the formation of the Loyal and Patriotic Society of Upper Canada, organized to provide winter clothing for the militia and, later, to help their families and others who had suffered from the war. The directors of the Loyal and Patriotic Society included Strachan's proteges and the elite of York—the tight ruling group that would soon be known as the Family Compact.

Thus the key words in Upper Canada were "loyalty" and "patriotism"—loyalty to the British way of life as opposed to American "radical" democracy and republicanism. Brock—the man who wanted to establish martial law and abandon habeas corpus—represented these virtues. Canonized by the same caste that organized the Loyal and Patriotic Society, he came to represent Canadian order as opposed to American anarchy—"peace, order and good government" rather than the more hedonistic "life, liberty and the pursuit of happiness." Had not Upper Canada been saved from the invader by appointed leaders who ruled autocratically? In America, the politicians became generals; in British North America, the opposite held true.

This attitude—that the British way is preferable to the American; that certain sensitive positions are better filled by appointment than by election; that order imposed from above has advantages over grassroots democracy (for which read "licence" or "anarchy"); that a ruling elite often knows better than the body politic—flourished as a result of an invasion repelled. Out of it, shaped by an emerging nationalism and tempered by rebellion, grew that special form of state paternalism that makes the Canadian way of life significantly different from the more individualistic American way. Thus, in a psychological as well as in a political sense, we are Canadians and not Americans because of a foolish war that scarcely anyone wanted or needed, but which, once launched, none knew how to stop.

William Atherton's War

———

MICHIGAN TERRITORY, APRIL, 1813. *To William Atherton, captive of the Potawatomi, home seems to be on another planet. Adopted into a Potawatomi family to replace a son killed at Frenchtown, he now lives as an Indian, wears Indian buckskin, hews to Indian customs. He hunts with bow and arrow, engages in the corn dance, sleeps in a wigwam, exists on boiled corn and bristly hogmeat. He neither hears nor speaks English.*

His one contact with civilization is a tattered Lexington newspaper, found among the Indians' effects. This is his sole comfort: he reads and re-reads it, clinging to the brittle pages as a reminder that somewhere beyond the brooding, snow-covered forests there really is another world—a world he once took for granted but which comes back to him now as if in a dream. Will he ever see it again? As winter gives way to spring, Atherton gives way to despair, stealing out of camp for moments of solitude when he can think of home and weep without being discovered.

In May, the Indians head for Detroit. On the way, they encounter another band which has just captured a young American surgeon in battle. What battle? Atherton has no way of knowing that an American fleet has captured York and that the British have badly mauled Harrison's army during the siege of Fort Meigs on the Maumee. The two men converse eagerly in the first English that Atherton has heard in three months; then the other departs, Atherton believes to his death.

They reach Amherstburg, but Atherton has no hope of escape. With his long swarthy face and his matted brown hair, uncut for months, he is just another Indian to the British, who fail to notice his blue eyes. When the band moves across to Spring Wells to draw rations at the British commissary, Atherton's Indian father learns, with delight, that his new son can write. He has him double the original number of family members on the chit, thus increasing the handout of provisions. Again, the British do not realize that Atherton is white.

He loses track of time. Crawling with vermin, half-starved, with no hope of escape from the family that nurtures but also guards him, he throws himself on their mercy and pleads to be ransomed. To his surprise, his Indian father agrees, albeit reluctantly. It is clear that Atherton has become part of the family, more a son than a captive. They cannot refuse him, even though it means losing him. Eventually, in Detroit, they find a man who will give a pony for him. Atherton bids his Indian parents goodbye—not without sorrow, for they have, in their fashion, been kind—and becomes a prisoner of war. All that summer he is lodged in a British guardhouse, almost naked, sleeping on the floor with a log for a pillow, wondering about the course of the war.

Fort George is assaulted and taken by the Americans. At Stoney Creek, a British force captures two American generals who mistake them for friends in the darkness. The Caughnawagas trounce the Americans at Beaver Dams, the battle that makes a heroine of Laura Secord. Of these triumphs and defeats Atherton knows nothing. Only when his captors return from the unsuccessful British siege of Fort Stephenson at Lower Sandusky, their faces peppered with small shot, does he have an inkling that beyond the guardhouse walls, all along the border, men are still fighting and dying.

Summer gives way to fall. On September 10, Atherton and his fellow prisoners can hear the rumble of heavy guns reverberating across Lake Erie. Clearly, a naval battle is raging, but his captors refuse details. At last a private soldier whispers the truth: Oliver Hazard Perry has met the enemy and they are his. The British fleet is obliterated. Erie is an American lake.

The victory touches off a major retreat. The British pack up hastily in the face of Harrison's advancing army. Atherton can hardly wait for the Kentucky forces to arrive and free him, but that is not to be. The prisoners are hurried across to the Canadian shore and herded up the Thames Valley to Burlington, then on to York, Kingston, Montreal.

It seems as if the entire city has turned out to stare at them—verminous, shaggy, half-starved after a journey of nine hundred miles. As Atherton trudges down the cobbled streets he notices the doors and windows crammed with curious women. In the jail they are given a little "Yankee beef," taunted with the fact that it has been purchased by the British from Americans trading with the enemy.

Two weeks later they are sent to Quebec City. Here, for the first time, Atherton learns that Harrison has captured Fort Amherstburg, rolled up the Thames, won the Battle of Moravian Town, and presided over the death of his enemy, Tecumseh.

The Kentuckians' reputation has preceded them. The Quebeckers think of them as a species of wildman—savage forest creatures, half-human, half-beast. They crowd to the jail, peering at the captives as they would at animals in a zoo, astonished, even disappointed, to find they do not live up to their billing. One man gazes at them for some minutes, then delivers the general verdict: "Why, they look just like other people."

Beyond the prison, the war rages on. The two-pronged American attack designed to seize Montreal fizzles out at Châteauguay and Crysler's Farm, but Atherton is only dimly aware of it. Fall turns to winter, with both sides once again deadlocked along the border. As the spring campaign opens, a more cheerful piece of news reaches Quebec: there is to be a general prisoner exchange. Eventually Atherton is released and sent back across the border, only a few weeks before the war's bloodiest battle at Lundy's Lane. In Pittsburgh he encounters a group of vaguely familiar men— British prisoners of war. Who are they? Where has he seen them before? He remembers: these are the soldiers who were once his guards when he was a captive in Detroit. It all seems a long time ago.

Atherton reaches his home at Shelbyville, Kentucky, on June 20, 1814, almost two years to the day since war was first declared. The invasion goes on. The battles of Chippawa and Lundy's Lane, the long siege of Fort

Erie, and the naval encounter on Lake Champlain all lie ahead. But Atherton is out of it. He has had enough, will not fight again.

His story is not unique. Eighty or ninety Kentuckians have been captured by the Potawatomi braves, and of these a good number have been adopted into Indian families. Timothy Mallory has all his hair shaved off except for a scalp lock, his face painted half black, half red, his ears pierced for rings. John Davenport is painted, adorned with earrings, bracelets, and a silver band wound round his shaved skull. "We make an Indian out of you," one of his captors promises, "and by'n by you have squaw, by'n by you have a gun and horse and go hunting."

Both these men live as Indians for several months and like Atherton, who prefers his treatment by the Indians to that of the British (he finds them "brave, generous, hospitable, kind and . . . honest"), are surprised to discover that their Indian families are genuinely fond of them, that the women go out of their way to protect them when the braves indulge in drinking bouts, and that when at last they are ransomed, the Indians are clearly reluctant to part with them.

No one knows exactly how many Kentucky volunteers are held captive by the natives, adopted into families that have lost sons in the battle. No one knows exactly how many have escaped or been ransomed. It is possible, even probable, that as the war rolls on there are some Kentuckians who have gone entirely native, taken Indian wives and removed themselves from white society.

There is irony in this; but then it has been a war of irony and paradox—a war fought over a grievance that was removed before the fighting began; a war that all claimed to have won except the real victors, who, being Indians, were really losers; a war designed to seize by force a nation that could have been attached by stealth. Are there in the forests of Michigan among the Potawatomi—those veterans of Tippecanoe— certain warriors of lighter skin and alien background? If so, that is the final irony. Ever since Jefferson's day it has been official American policy to try to turn the Indians into white men. Who can blame the Indians if, in their last, desperate, doomed resistance, they should manage in some measure to turn the tables?

Sources and Acknowledgements

This work is based largely on primary sources—official documents and correspondence, military reports and records, public speeches, private letters, diaries, journals, memoirs, and contemporary newspaper accounts. I have as well made a reconnaissance of those battlefields whose sites have not been obliterated by the advance of civilization.

As every lawyer knows, witnesses to any event rarely agree; thus it has often been necessary to compare various conflicting reports to arrive at an approximation of the truth. Confused recollections of even minor skirmishes are not easy to untangle. Each participant sees the engagement from his own point of view. Opposing generals invariably underestimate their own strength and overestimate that of the enemy, seeking in a variety of ways to shape their reports to make themselves seem brilliant. The memories of junior officers and common soldiers are distorted by the heat of the moment and often clouded by the passage of time. Fortunately, in almost every case there is such a richness of material available on the events of 1812–13 (much of the human detail ignored by historians) that it is possible to arrive at a reasonably clear and accurate account of what occurred, not only tactically and politically but also in the hearts and minds of the participants.

For each incident I have had to ask myself these questions: was the narrator—diarist, officer, soldier, correspondent, memoirist—

present at the event described? How soon after the event did he set down his account of what happened? How competent was he as a witness? Can some of his statements be cross-checked against those of others to assess his credibility? A memoir written thirty years after the events, obviously, cannot be considered as reliable as one scribbled down on the spot.

Students of the war may be surprised that I have set aside John Richardson's famous account of the death of the young American captive after the battle of Brownstown (page 149) in favour of a less well known description by Thomas Vercheres de Boucherville. Richardson, after all, belongs to the pantheon of early Canadian novelists; de Boucherville was only a fur trader and storekeeper. The two versions were both set down many years after the event and differ considerably in detail, Richardson's being the more dramatic. But a close reading of his account reveals that the future novelist, who was only fifteen at the time, was not actually present at the scene he describes while de Boucherville was. De Boucherville was also twelve years older and experienced in Indian customs. There can be no doubt that his version is the more reliable.

For the leading British, American, and Canadian figures in the war, a wealth of easily authenticated biographical and background material is available. But for the Indians, with two exceptions, there is very little. This was really their war; for them the stakes were higher, the victories more significant, the defeats more devastating. One would have liked to know more about Roundhead, Walk-in-the-Water, Black Bird, Little Turtle, and all the other shadowy tribesmen who appear briefly and often violently on the stage. History, alas, ignores them. They have come down to us as faceless "savages," brandishing their tomahawks, shouting their war cries, scalping their victims, melting into the forests.

Only Tecumseh and to some degree his brother, the Prophet, stand out as individuals—flesh-and-blood figures with human strengths, human weaknesses, and human emotions. Here, nevertheless, one must tread cautiously, for so much of their story—especially that of their early years—is overlaid with legend. It was Charles Goltz who recently revealed in his superb doctoral dissertation on the Shawnee brothers that one widely accepted tale of Tecumseh's early years was pure myth.

Most of his biographers have tried to explain Tecumseh's hatred of the white man with an anecdote about his father's death. As the story goes, the father was killed by a group of white hunters when he refused to act as their guide and died in the arms of his son, denouncing the faithlessness of white men. There is much detail: the mother at the graveside urging the young Shawnee to seek eternal revenge; Tecumseh's yearly visits to the scene to renew his pledge; and so on. But, as Goltz discovered, this web of convincing evidence was the invention of an Indiana woman who, in 1823, entered it in a fiction contest sponsored by the *New York Mirror*. The following year a Canadian magazine reprinted the tale, and it became accepted as history.

In compiling and sifting all this mountain of material I have again depended upon the extraordinary energy and wise counsel of the indefatigable Barbara Sears, for whom the term "research assistant" is scarcely adequate. I cannot praise her labours too highly. She and I wish to thank a number of people and institutions who helped make this work possible.

First, the Metropolitan Library of Toronto, with special thanks to Edith Firth and her staff at the Canadian History Department, to Michael Pearson and the staff of the History Department, and to Norma Dainard, Keith Alcock, and the staff of the newspaper section. Thanks also to Robert Fraser of the editorial staff of the *Dictionary of Canadian Biography*.

Second, the Public Archives of Canada, with special thanks to the staff of the manuscript division, to Patricia Kennedy of the Pre-Confederation Archives, to Peter Bower, Gordon Dodds, Bruce Wilson, and Brian Driscoll of British Archives, and to Glenn T. Wright and Grace Campbell of the Public Records Division; the Ontario Archives; the Library of Congress Manuscript Division; the Filson Club of Kentucky; and Peter Burroughs of Dalhousie University.

Third, the U.S. National Archives, Washington; the Buffalo Historical Society (Art Detmers); the Chatham Kent Museum (Mary Creasey); the Historical Society of Pennsylvania; the Indiana State Library; the Kentucky Historical Society; the Wisconsin Historical Society; the Lundy's Lane Historical Society; the Niagara Historical Society; the Niagara Parks Commission's Fort Erie staff; Parks Canada's staff at Fort George and Fort Malden; Robert S. Allen and Elizabeth Vincent at Parks Canada, Ottawa; the Public Record Office, London, England; the Tennessee State Museum; Esther Summers; Bob Green; Paul Romney; and Professor H.N. Muller.

I am especially grateful for the useful comments and suggestions made by Janice Tyrwhitt, Charles Templeton, Roger Hall, Elsa Franklin, Janet Berton, and Leslie Hannon, who read the manuscript at various stages. The several versions were typed by Ennis Armstrong, Catherine Black, and Lynne McCartney. I was rescued from certain grammatical imbecilities by my wife, Janet, and from various textual inconsistencies by my editor Janet Craig, for whose unsparing eye and great common sense I am specially grateful. The errors that remain are mine.

Kleinburg, Ontario
March, 1980

Notes

Abbreviations used:

ASPFR	American State Papers, Foreign Relations
ASPIA	American State Papers, Indian Affairs
ASPMA	American State Papers, Military Affairs
LC	Library of Congress
MTPL	Metropolitan Toronto Public Library
PAC	Public Archives of Canada
PAO	Public Archives of Ontario
SN	Secretary of the Navy
SW	Secretary of War
USNA	United States National Archives

PREVIEW: PORTER HANKS'S WAR

p.12 l.12   Brannan, pp. 34–35, Hanks to SW, 4 Aug. 1812.

p.12 l.27   Ibid.; May, p. 14.

p.13 l.16   Brannan, pp. 34–35, Hanks to SW, 4 Aug. 1812.

p.13 l.19   Ibid.

p.13 l.31   Jefferson, VI: 75–76, Jefferson to Duane, 4 Aug. 1812.

OVERVIEW

p.18 l.5   Bonney, p. 269, Sheaffe to Stephen Van Rensselaer, 16 Oct. 1812.

p.18 l.13   Kirby, p. 157.

p.21 l.1   PAC, RG 8, vol. 1219, p. 274, Prevost to Bathurst, 27 Aug. 1814.

p.21 l.5   PAC, MG 24 A57, vol. 19, Sherbrooke proclamation, 3 July 1812.

p.21 l.31   Quaife, *Askin Papers*, p. 709, [Askin] to McGill, 17 July 1812; p. 729, Brush to Askin, 11 Aug. 1812; p. 729, Brush to Askin, 24 Aug. 1812.

p.22 l.8   Quoted in Perkins, *Prologue*, p. 415.

p.22 l.33   Perkins, *Prologue*, pp. 90–93.

p.26 l.12   PAO, Register of persons connected with high treason during the War of 1812 with the U.S.A.

p.26 l.23   PAC, RG 19 E5(a), vol. 3739, file 2, n.d. General abstract, claims for damages; *Upper Canada Gazette*, supplement, 3 June 1824.

PRELUDE TO INVASION: 1807–1811

p.29 l.12   U.S. Congress, ASPFR, III: 17, Barron to SN, 7 April 1807.

p.30 l.21   Ibid., 18, Barron to SN, 23 June 1807, and enclosures; p. 19, return of dead and wounded; p. 19, Hunt to Gordon, 23 June 1807; p. 19, Smith, Smith and Brooker to Gordon, 23 June 1807; p. 21, L.W. Tazewell, report of court of inquiry; Steel, pp. 245–49.

p.30 l.28   Steel, pp. 250–52.

p.30 l.32   Quoted in Perkins, *Prologue*, p. 428.

p.31 l.30   Cruikshank, "Some Unpublished Letters," p. 19, Brock to Dunn, 17 July 1807.

p.32 l.5   Quoted in Burt, p. 243.

p.32 l.22   Burt, pp. 242–46.

p.32 l.33   Tupper, p. 64, Brock to Gordon, 6 Sept. 1807.

p.33 l.9   Harrison, I: 235, Harrison speech, 17 Aug. 1807.

p.33 l.18   Ibid., p. 236.

p.34 l.19   Ibid., p. 234.

p.35 l.6   Jefferson, IV: 472, Jefferson to Harrison, 27 Feb. 1803

p.35 l.20   Harrison, I: 251, Harrison to the Shawanese, Aug. 1807.

p.36 l.3   Ibid., pp. 183–84, Harrison to the Delawares, early 1806.

p.36 l.22   Ibid., p. 251, Harrison to the Shawanese, Aug. 1807.

p.37 l.34   Randall, pp. 462–63.

p.38 l.11   LC, Foster MSS, Foster to his mother, 31 July 1807.

p.38 l.32   Ibid., Foster to his mother, 20 Sept. 1806.

p.38 l.16   Foster, *Two Duchesses*, p. 228, Foster to his mother, 30 June 1805.

p.38 l.25   LC, Foster MSS, Foster to his mother, 16 July 1807.

p.38 l.30   Foster, *Two Duchesses*, p. 233, Foster to his mother, 30 July 1805.

p.38 l.31   Ibid., p. 240, Foster to his mother, 22 Feb. 1805.

p.38 l.33   Ibid., p. 233, Foster to his mother, 30 July 1805.

p.38 l.33   Ibid., p. 247, Foster to his mother, Nov. 1805.

p.39 l.31   LC, Foster MSS, Journal.

p.40 l.30   Quoted in Perkins, *Prologue*, p. 7

p.40 l.35   Quoted in Perkins, *Prologue*, p. 187.

p.42 l.3   PAC, RG 10, vol. 11, Gore's speech, 11 July 1808.

p.42 l.25   PAC, RG 10, vol. 11, Indian reply, 13 July 1808.

p.43 l.13   Horsman, *Expansion*, p. 146.

p.43 l.16   Ibid.

p.43 l.30   Allen, p. 63.

p.44 l.5   Horsman, "British Indian Policy," pp. 53, 56.

p.45 l.6   PAC, RG 10, vol. 11, Gore to Craig, 27 July 1808.

p.45 l.32   Goltz.

p.46 l.11   Harrison, I: 365, Journal, 4 Oct. 1809.

p.47 l.8   Ibid., p. 367.

p.47 l.21   Ibid., p. 368.

p.47 l.26   Ibid., p. 389, Harrison to SW, 3 Nov. 1809.

p.47 l.28   Ibid., p. 376, Journal, 22 Sept. 1809.

p.47 l.35   Ibid., p. 389, Harrison to SW, 3 Nov. 1809.

p.48 l.10   Cleaves, p. 68.

p.48 l.23   Harrison, I: 419, Harrison to SW, 25 April 1810.

p.48 l.26   Ibid., p. 450, Harrison to SW, 25 July 1810.

p.49 l.4   Ibid., p. 448, Harrison to the Prophet, 19 July 1810.

p.49 l.8   Ibid., pp. 448–49.

p.49 l.26   Ibid., p. 456, Harrison to SW, 6 Aug. 1810.

p.49 l.27   Ibid.

p.50 l.20   Tucker, *Tecumseh*, p. 159.

p.50 l.25   Hatch, p. 113.

p.51 l.2   Tucker, *Tecumseh*, p. 160; Drake, pp. 125–26.

p.51 l.13   Tucker, *Tecumseh*, pp. 161, 348.

p.51 l.21   Harrison, I: 460, Harrison to SW, 22 Aug. 1810.

p.52 l.3   Hatch, pp. 99–100.

p.52 l.21   Klinck, p. 73.

p.52 l.24   Tucker, *Tecumseh*, pp. 163, 348.

p.52 l.33   Harrison, I: 466, Tecumseh's speech, 20 Aug. 1810.

p.53 l.3   Ibid., p. 463.

p.53 l.14   Ibid., p. 459, Harrison to SW, 22 Aug. 1810.

p.53 l.28   Cleaves, p. 74.

p.53 l.35   Harrison, I: 461, Harrison to SW, 22 Aug. 1810.

p.54 l.2   Ibid., pp. 461, 468.

p.54 l.19   Tucker, *Tecumseh*, pp. 166, 349.

p.54 l.26   Harrison, I: 469, Tecumseh's speech, 21 Aug. 1810.

p.57 l.21   Draper MSS, Tecumseh Papers, 2YY, p. 120, Ruddell's account of Tecumseh.

p.57 l.35   Ibid., 12YY, 1821, Drake's notes on conversation with Anthony Shane.

p.58 l.8   Ibid.

p.58 l.16   Ibid.

p.58 l.29   Tucker, *Tecumseh*, pp. 77–80; Randall, p. 455.

p.58 l.33   Draper MSS, Tecumseh Papers, 12YY, 1821, Drake's notes on conversation with Anthony Shane.

p.60 l.10   Harrison, I: 239, Wells to Harrison, 20 Aug. 1807.

p.61 l.23   PAC, CO 42/351/42, Elliott to Claus, 16 Nov. 1810, encl. Tecumseh's speech, 15 Nov. 1810.

p.62 l.7   Harrison, I: 447, Harrison to SW, 18 June 1810.

p.63 l.3   PAC, CO 42/351/ Elliott to Claus, 16 Nov. 1810.

p.63 l.12   Quoted in Goltz, Craig to Moirier, 25 Nov. 1811.

p.63 l.34   Weld, pp. 192–96.

p.64 l.12   Tupper, pp. 94–96, Brock to Craig, 27 Feb. 1811.

p.64 l.16   "Collections of Papers," pp. 280–81, Craig to Gore, 2 Feb. 1811.

p.65 l.18   Harrison, I: 546, Harrison to SW, 6 Aug. 1811.

p.66 l.11   Dawson, p. 184.

p.66 l.29   Drake, pp. 142–43.

p.67 l.8   Harrison, I: 549, Harrison to SW, 7 Aug. 1811.

p.67 l.21   Ibid.

p.68 l.8   Harrison, I: 527, Harrison to SW, 2 July 1811.

p.68 l.20   Ibid., p. 536, SW to Harrison, 20 July 1811.

p.68 l.33   Ibid., p. 550, Harrison to SW, 7 Aug. 1811.

p.69 l.14   Ibid., p. 558, Daviess to Harrison, 24 Aug. 1811.

p.69 l.22   "Jo Daviess," p. 355.

p.70 l.16   Harrison, I: 620, Harrison to SW, 18 Nov. 1811.

p.72 l.2   Ibid., p. 703, statement of William Brigham.

p.72 l.10   Ibid., p. 702, statement of Sergeant Orr.

p.73 l.3   Ibid., pp. 691–92, Harrison to Dr. John Scott, Dec. 1811.

p.73 l.26   Cleaves, pp. 100–101.

p.73 l.35   Ibid., p. 101.

p.74 l.6   Ibid.

p.74 l.15   Lossing, *Field-book*, p. 205.

p.74 l.21   Harrison, I: 703, statement of William Brigham.

p.74 l.26   Ibid., p. 624, Harrison to SW, 18 Nov. 1811.

p.74 l.33   Ibid., p. 702; Walker, pp. 24–25.

p.75 l.28   Cruikshank, *Documents Relating to the Invasion*, p. 6, Elliott to Brock, 12 Jan. 1812.

p.76 l.13   U.S. Congress, ASPIA, I: 808, opinions of Gov. Howard and Gen. Clark, 3 March 1812.

p.76 l.22   Tucker, *Tecumseh*, p. 230.

p.81 l.4	Ibid., p. 95, Brock to Craig, 27 Feb. 1811.
p.81 l.5	Ibid., p. 195, Brock to Prevost, 3 July 1812.
p.81 l.23	Ibid., pp. 123–30, Brock to Prevost, 2 Dec. 1811.
p.82 l.18	Wood, I: 423, ? to Dickson, 27 Feb. 1812.
p.82 l.29	Caffrey, p. 142.
p.83 l.6	Ibid.
p.83 l.23	Quoted in Perkins, *Prologue*, p. 275.
p.83 l.29	LC, Foster MSS, Foster to his mother, 2 Jan. 1812.
p.83 l.33	Ibid., Journal, 15 April 1812.
p.84 l.18	Quoted in Brown, p. 55.
p.84 l.22	LC, Foster MSS, Journal, 29 and 30 Jan. 1812.
p.84 l.23	Ibid., Journal, 31 Jan. 1812.
p.84 l.33	U.S. Congress, ASPFR, III. 546–47, Craig to Henry, 6 Feb. 1809.
p.85 l.4	Morison, pp. 271–72.
p.85 l.15	Quoted in Cruikshank, *Political Adventures*, p. 126.
p.85 l.26	LC, Foster MSS, Journal, 19 Feb. 1812.
p.85 l.33	Ibid.
p.86 l.3	Ibid., Journal, 20 Jan. 1812, 5 Feb. 1812.
p.87 l.2	Cruikshank, *Documents Relating to the Invasion*, p. 22, Hull to SW, 6 March 1812.
p.87 l.25	Mahon, p. 44.
p.88 l.4	USNA, M221/43, Dearborn to SW, 28 July 1812.
p.88 l.21	LC, Foster MSS, Journal, 15 April 1812.
p.88 l.24	Foster, *Two Duchesses*, p. 360, Foster to his mother, 18 April 1812.
p.88 l.28	PAC, CO 42/146/120, Prevost to Liverpool, 3 April 1812.
p.88 l.32	LC, Foster MSS, Journal, 15 April 1812.
p.89 l.15	Quoted in Cramer, p. 128.
p.89 l.27	Ibid.
p.90 l.26	Hull, *Memoirs*, p. 34.
p.91 l.7	McAfee, p. 51.
p.91 l.19	Cramer, p. 130.
p.91 l.26	Ibid.
p.91 l.31	Cruikshank, "General Hull's Invasion," p. 216.
p.92 l.6	Hull, *Report*, p. 136.
p.92 l.16	Ibid., Hull's defence, p. 57.
p.92 l.22	USNA, M221/47/M341, McArthur, Cass, Findley to SW, 18 July 1812; M221/45/ H271, Miller to SW, 12 June 1812.
p.93 l.6	Hull, *Report*, pp. 124–25; USNA, M221/44/H275, Hull to SW, 18 June 1812.
p.93 l.13	Quaife, *War*, pp. 187–88.
p.94 l.8	Ibid., pp. 208–9; Walker, pp. 46–47.
p.94 l.26	Hull, *Memoirs*, p. 35.
p.95 l.4	Quoted in Perkins, *Prologue*, p. 434.

p.95 l.18   Quoted in Perkins, *Prologue*, pp. 433–34.

p.96 l.9   Brown, p. 52.

p.96 l.24   Tucker, *Tecumseh*, p. 114.

p.96 l.35   Quoted in Perkins, *Prologue*, p. 433.

p.98 l.4   Green, *Washington*, p. 56.

p.98 l.32   Quoted in Perkins, *Prologue*, p. 427.

p.99 l.2   Quoted in Pratt, *Expansionists*, pp. 51, 140.

p.99 l.7   Ibid., p. 153.

p.99 l.12   *Kentucky Gazette*, 3 Sept. 1811.

MICHILIMACKINAC

p.101 l.2   Quoted in Cruikshank, "General Hull's Invasion," p. 247.

p.101 l.13   Wood, I: 424, Dickson to ?, 18 June 1812.

p.102 l.8   Ibid., p. 425, speech of Wabasha.

p.102 l.21   Ibid., pp. 426–27, statement of Robert Dickson.

p.102 l.33   Pike, I: 64–65.

p.102 l.35   Powell, p. 157.

p.104 l.4   Quoted in Chalou, p. 72, *Louisiana Gazette*, 6 June 1812.

p.104 l.13   Vincent.

p.104 l.29   Ibid.

p.105 l.4   Wood, I: 440, Roberts to Clegg, 29 July 1812.

p.105 l.8   PAC, RG 8, vol. 789, p. 109, D. Mitchell note, 13 June 1813.

p.105 l.22   Quaife, *Askin Papers*, p. 569, John Askin Jr. to his father, 1 Sept. 1807.

p.105 l.35   Porter, p. 258.

p.106 l.9   Quoted in Porter, p. 249.

p.106 l.25   Ibid., p. 258.

p.106 l.33   Wood, I: 448, observations of Toussaint Pothier.

p.106 l.35   Ibid., p. 430, Roberts to Brock, 12 July 1812.

p.107 l.3   Ibid.

p.107 l.10   Ibid., p. 429, Roberts to Brock, 12 July 1812.

p.107 l.25   PAC, RG 8, vol. 676, p. 183, Roberts to Adjutant General, 17 July 1812; Wood, I: 433, Roberts to Brock, 17 July 1812.

p.108 l.6   Wood, I: pp. 432–34, Roberts to Baynes, 17 July 1812; pp. 436–37, John Askin Jr. to Claus, 18 July 1812; pp. 450–51, observations of Toussaint Pothier; Kellogg, pp. 135–36; Grignon, pp. 268–69.

p.108 l.27   Kellogg, pp. 138–39.

p.109 l.13   Wood, I: 434, Roberts to Brock, 17 July 1812.

p.110 l.7   Ibid., pp. 436–37, John Askin Jr. to Claus, 18 July 1812.

p.110 l.13   Dobbins, p. 303.

p.110 l.20   Wood, I: 442, return of provisions, 30 July 1812; Quaife, *Askin Papers*, p. 730, John Askin Jr. to his father, 16 Sept. 1812.

p.110 l.26   Wood, III, part I, p. 7, General Order, Montreal, 29 May 1814.

p.*111 l.12*   PAC, RG 8, vol.91, 15 Jan. 1816, proceedings of inquiry; Cook, p. 29.

p.*111 l.19*   Porter, p. 263.

p.*111 l.23*   Ibid., p. 262.

p.*111 l.27*   Ibid., pp. 263–71.

DETROIT

p.*113 l.28*   Beall, p. 786.

p.*114 l.12*   Ibid., p. 787.

p.*114 l.32*   Ibid.

p.*117 l.25*   Ibid., p. 788.

p.*117 l.28*   Ibid., p. 789.

p.*118 l.32*   Ibid., pp. 789–90.

p.*119 l.12*   Ibid., p. 791.

p.*120 l.1*   Lossing, *Field-book*, p. 258.

p.*120 l.7*   Hull, *Memoirs*, p. 76.

p.*120 l.25*   Williams, p. 12, Hull to Meigs, 11 July 1812.

p.*120 l.29*   Ibid., pp. 13–14.

p.*121 l.16*   Cruikshank, *Documents Relating to the Invasion*, pp. 40–41, Hull to St. George, 6 July 1812.

p.*121 l.30*   Ibid., p. 41, St. George to Hull, 6 July 1812.

p.*122 l.11*   Ibid., p. 47, St. George to Brock, 8 July 1812.

p.*122 l.14*   Ibid., p. 74, Brock to Prevost, 20 July 1812.

p.*122 l.27*   Ibid., p. 45, St. George to Brock, 8 July 1812.

p.*122 l.33*   Ibid., p. 46.

p.*123 l.8*   Beall, p. 793.

p.*123 l.25*   Tucker, *Tecumseh*, p. 243.

p.*123 l.33*   Drake, p. 163.

p.*124 l.7*   Tucker, *Tecumseh*, p. 245.

p.*124 l.19*   Lucas, *Journal*, p. 27.

p.*125 l.7*   Cruikshank, *Documents Relating to the Invasion*, p. 51, St. George to Brock, 10 July 1812; p. 61, St. George to Brock, 15 July 1812.

p.*125 l.10*   Beall, p. 795.

p.*125 l.20*   Lossing, *Field-book*, p. 262; Woodford, p. 59.

p.*125 l.31*   Cruikshank, *Documents Relating to the Invasion*, p. 214, Cochran to his mother, 13 Sept. 1812.

p.*126 l.2*   Hatch, p. 28.

p.*126 l.9*   Beall, p. 795.

p.*127 l.33*   Cruikshank, *Documents Relating to the Invasion*, pp. 58-60.

p.*128 l.3*   Ibid., p. 157, Brock to Prevost, 17 Aug. 1812.

p.*128 l.5*   Ibid., pp. 62–63, Elliott to Claus, 15 July 1812.

p.*128 l.13*   Smith, p. 83.

p.*129 l.25*   *Montreal Herald*, 4 July 1812.

p.130 l.7   Ibid.

p.130 l.24   Tupper, p. 201, Prevost to Brock, 10 July 1812.

p.130 l.27   Ibid., p. 201.

p.131 l.5   Ibid., pp. 5-6.

p.131 l.9   Nursey, p. 30.

p.131 l.11   Tupper, pp. 25–26.

p.131 l.15   Ibid., p. 258.

p.131 l.35   PAC, CO 42/146/42, Prevost to Liverpool, 3 March 1812.

p.132 l.6   Ibid.

p.132 l.13   PAC, CO 42/147/18, Prevost to Liverpool, 25 July 1812.

p.132 l.28   Tupper, pp. 200–201, Prevost to Brock, 10 July 1812.

p.133 l.7   Lucas, *Journal*, p. 174.

p.134 l.4   Ibid., pp. v and vi.

p.134 l.29   PAC, RG 19, E5(a), vol. 3746, no. 423.

p.134 l.32   PAC, RG 19, E5(a), vol. 3728, no. 147.

p.134 l.33   Ibid., no. 156.

p.134 l.35   Ibid., no. 137.

p.135 l.2   Ibid., no. 171.

p.135 l.11   PAC, RG 19, E5(a), vol. 3752, no. 1196.

p.135 l.17   PAC, RG 19, E5(a), vol. 3751, no. 1072; Hull, *Report*, p. 152.

p.135 l.21   PAC, RG 19, E5(a), vol. 3746, no. 423.

p.135 l.27   PAC, RG 19, E5(a), vol. 3728, nos. 44 and 51.

p.135 l.31   Cruikshank, *Documents Relating to the Invasion*, p. 49, Dixon to Bruyères, 8 July 1812; p. 61, St. George to Brock, 15 July 1812.

p.135 l.34   Ibid., p. 63, Elliott to Claus, 15 July 1812.

p.136 l.2   Lucas, *Journal*, p. 42.

p.136 l.10   Ibid., p. 28.

p.136 l.34   Ibid., p. 36.

p.137 l.11   Quoted in Oman, p. 42.

p.137 l.29   PAC, RG 8, vol. 165, return of regimental courts martial, 103rd Regt., 22 April to 10 Oct. 1812.

p.138 l.10   Hull, *Report*, Hull's defence, pp. 44–45.

p.138 l.24   Ibid., p. 57.

p.138 l.26   Ibid., p. 45.

p.139 l.5   Cruikshank, *Documents Relating to the Invasion*, p. 76.

p.139 l.6   Richardson, *Richardson's War*, p. 32.

p.139 l.23   Beall, p. 799.

p.140 l.2   Ibid., p. 800.

p.140 l.6   Ibid., p. 802.

p.140 l.15   Hull, *Report*, p. 135.

p.140 l.18   Cruikshank, *Documents Relating to the Invasion*, pp. 185–86, Hull to SW, 26 Aug. 1812.

p.140 l.35   Beall, p. 805.

p.141 l.13   Cruikshank, *Documents Relating to the Invasion*, pp. 195–96, Brock, speech on opening legislature.

p.141 l.17   Ibid., p. 75, Brock to Prevost, 20 July 1812.

p.141 l.23   Ibid., p. 93, Talbot to Brock, 27 July 1812.

p.141 l.32   Quoted in Hamil, p. 46.

p.142 l.3   Cruikshank, *Documents Relating to the Invasion*, p. 196, Brock, speech on opening the legislature.

p.142 l.12   Cruikshank, *Documentary History*, III: 152, Brock to Baynes, 29 July 1812.

p.142 l.18   Ibid., p. 146, Brock to Prevost, 26 July 1812.

p.142 l.22   Ibid.

p.142 l.31   Cruikshank, *Documents Relating to the Invasion*, p. 196, Brock, speech on opening the legislature.

p.143 l.2   Ibid., pp. 119–20, Brock to Baynes, 4 Aug. 1812.

p.144 l.3   Ibid., p. 119.

p.144 l.8   Cruikshank, *Documentary History*, III: 152, Brock to Baynes, 29 July 1812.

p.145 l.11   Cruikshank, *Documents Relating to the Invasion*, p. 82, Brock, proclamation, 22 July 1812.

p.145 l.21   Ibid., p. 120, Brock to Baynes, 4 Aug. 1812.

p.145 l.29   Ibid., p. 197, Brock, speech on opening the legislature.

p.148 l.33   Lucas, *Journal*, pp. 46–51.

p.150 l.14   Quaife, *War*, pp. 92–93.

p.151 l.3   Hull, *Report*, p. 57.

p.151 l.6   Lucas, *Journal*, p. 52.

p.151 l.8   Quaife, *War*, p. 277.

p.151 l.13   Ibid.

p.151 l.29   Hull, *Memoirs*, p. 61.

p.152 l.25   Hull, *Report*, p. 58.

p.152 l.28   Hull, *Memoirs*, p. 64.

p.152 l.34   Cruikshank, *Documents Relating to the Invasion*, p. 219, Cass to SW, 10 Sept. 1812.

p.153 l.3   Hatch, p. 35.

p.153 l.4   Lucas, *Journal*, p. 105.

p.153 l.17   PAC, CO 42/147/80, Prevost to Liverpool, 5 Aug. 1812.

p.153 l.21   Ibid.

p.153 l.32   Ibid.

p.155 l.8   U.S. Congress, ASPMA, I: 323, Strong to Eustis, 5 Aug. 1812.

p.155 l.15   Ibid., pp. 325–26, Smith to Eustis, 2 July 1812.

p.155 l.21   Cruikshank, *Documents Relating to the Invasion*, p. 40, SW to Dearborn, 26 June 1812.

p.155 l.30   USNA, M221/43, Dearborn to SW, 13 July 1812.

p.155 l.33   Quoted in Adams, VI: 308, Eustis to Dearborn, 9 July 1812.

344

p.156 l.3	USNA, M221/43, Dearborn to SW, 13 July 1812.
p.156 l.9	Ibid., Dearborn to SW, 28 July 1812.
p.157 l.10	PAC, RG 8, vol. 677, pp. 31–32, Baynes to Prevost, 12 Aug. 1812, encl. report.
p.157 l.18	Ibid., p. 30.
p.158 l.11	Cruikshank, *Documents Relating to the Invasion*, p. 128, Dearborn to SW, 9 Aug. 1812.
p.158 l.15	Ibid., p. 127.
p.159 l.7	PAC, RG 8, vol. 677, pp. 33–34, Baynes to Prevost, 12 Aug. 1812, encl. report.
p.159 l.17	Ibid., p. 35.
p.160 l.3	Ibid., p. 37.
p.160 l.11	Cruikshank, *Documents Relating to the Invasion*, p. 129, Dearborn to Hull, 9 Aug. 1812.
p.160 l.32	Quaife, *War*, p. 94.
p.161 l.20	Quaife, "Brownstown," p. 74.
p.162 l.5	Richardson, *Richardson's War*, p. 34.
p.162 l.17	Quaife, *War*, p. 96.
p.162 l.19	Ibid.
p.163 l.2	Ibid., p. 97.
p.163 l.8	Richardson, *Richardson's War*, p. 37.
p.163 l.10	Ibid.
p.163 l.17	Quaife, *War*, p. 97.
p.163 l.25	Ibid.; Quaife, "Brownstown," p. 75.
p.164 l.3	Quaife, "Brownstown," p. 77.
p.165 l.10	Quaife, *War*, pp. 103–5.
p.165 l.12	Cruikshank, *Documents Relating to the Invasion*, pp. 139–41, Hull to SW, 13 Aug. 1812.
p.165 l.24	Hull, *Report*, pp. 107–8.
p.165 l.26	Pearkes, p. 459.
p.166 l.2	Cruikshank, *Documents Relating to the Invasion*, p. 136, Procter to Brock, 11 Aug. 1812; p. 141, return of killed and wounded at Maguaga; p. 140, Hull to SW, 13 Aug. 1812.
p.166 l.5	Ibid., p. 195, Brock to Liverpool, 29 Aug. 1812, enclosure A.
p.166 l.13	Ibid., p. 192.
p.166 l.27	Ibid., pp. 130–31, Macdonald to Cameron, 10 Aug. 1812; Wood, 533, Askin Journal.
p.167 l.2	Wood, I: 535, Askin Journal; Pearkes, p. 459.
p.167 l.10	Cruikshank, *Documents Relating to the Invasion*, p. 193, Brock to Liverpool, 29 Aug. 1812.
p.167 l.17	Tupper, p. 259.
p.168 l.8	Wood, I: 534–35, Askin Journal; p. 548, McCay Diary.
p.168 l.18	Tupper, p. 243.

p.168 l.30	Ibid.
p.169 l.4	Cruikshank, *Documents Relating to the Invasion*, p. 192, Brock to Liverpool, 29 Aug. 1812.
p.169 l.5	Tupper, p. 262.
p.169 l.13	Tucker, *Tecumseh*, p. 264.
p.169 l.30	Tupper, pp. 260–61.
p.170 l.4	Nursey, p. 118; Tupper, p. 244.
p.170 l.17	Tucker, *Tecumseh*, p. 265; Nursey, pp. 118–19.
p.170 l.27	Tupper, p. 245.
p.171 l.2	Cruikshank, *Documents Relating to the Invasion*, p. 142, District General Order, 14 Aug. 1812.
p.171 l.16	Hull, *Report*, p. 135.
p.172 l.25	Lucas, *Journal*, pp. 59–60.
p.172 l.34	Cramer, p. 132; Van Deusen, p. 579.
p.173 l.11	Cruikshank, *Documents Relating to the Invasion*, p. 137, Cass to Meigs, 12 Aug. 1812; p. 219, Cass to SW, 10 Sept. 1812.
p.173 l.12	Ibid., p. 138.
p.174 l.1	Lossing, *Field-book*, p. 285.
p.174 l.4	Quaife, *Askin Papers*, p. 730, John Askin Jr. to John Askin Sr., 16 Sept. 1812.
p.174 l.8	Hull, *Report*, Hull's defence, p. 85.
p.174 l.25	Richardson, *Richardson's War*, pp. 49–51; Hull, *Report*, p. 82.
p.174 l.31	Lucas, *Journal*, p. 62.
p.175 l.19	Cruikshank, *Documents Relating to the Invasion*, p. 144, Brock to Hull, 15 Aug. 1812.
p.176 l.11	Ibid., pp. 144–45, Hull to Brock, 15 Aug. 1812.
p.176 l.20	Hull, *Report*, pp. 35–36.
p.176 l.23	Ibid., p. 150.
p.176 l.35	Lossing, *Field-book*, p. 287.
p.177 l.7	Ibid.
p.177 l.15	Witherell, p. 304.
p.177 l.23	Ibid., p. 303.
p.177 l.27	Hull, *Report*, p. 89.
p.177 l.31	Ibid., pp. 36–37.
p.177 l.33	Ibid., p. 89.
p.178 l.13	Lossing, *Field-book*, p. 285; Byfield, p. 65.
p.178 l.25	Quaife, *War*, p. 108.
p.179 l.2	Wood, I: 536.
p.179 l.16	Cruikshank, *Documents Relating to the Invasion*, p. 158, Brock to Prevost, 17 Aug. 1812; p. 187, Hull to SW, 26 Aug. 1812; pp. 219–20, Cass to SW, 10 Sept. 1812.
p.180 l.9	Wood, I: 536.
p.180 l.17	Ibid., p. 550, McCay Diary, 16 Aug. 1812.

p.180 l.20   Richardson, *Richardson's War*, p. 55.

p.180 l.31   Tupper, p. 260.

p.180 l.33   Clarke, p. 455.

p.181 l.2   Ibid., p. 456.

p.181 l.5   Richardson, *Richardson's War*, p. 55.

p.181 l.30   Cruikshank, "General Hull's Invasion," p. 281.

p.182 l.6   Hull, *Report*, pp. 90–91; Clarke, p. 450.

p.182 l.8   Hull, *Report*, p. 163.

p.182 l.10   Ibid.

p.182 l.23   Hatch, p. 42.

p.182 l.27   Lucas, *Journal*, pp. 63–64; Hatch, p. 42; Lossing, *Field-book*, p. 288.

p.183 l.20   Hull, *Report*, pp. 39–40, 93.

p.184 l.15   Lossing, *Field-book*, p. 289.

p.184 l.20   Hull, *Report*, p. 99.

p.184 l.22   Ibid., pp. 37–39, 99

p.184 l.27   Ibid., p. 92.

p.184 l.32   Ibid.

p.185 l.10   Ibid., p. 45; Lossing, *Field-book*, p. 289.

p.185 l.19   PAC, RG 19 E5(a), vol. 3749, no. 754.

p.185 l.33   Wood, I: 537, Askin Journal.

p.185 l.35   Cruikshank, "General Hull's Invasion," p. 284.

p.186 l.8   Hull, *Report*, p. 99.

p.186 l.12   Ibid., pp. 39, 109.

p.186 l.21   Wood, I: 538, Askin Journal.

p.186 l.30   Cruikshank, "General Hull's Invasion," p. 285; Lucas, *Journal*, pp. 67–68; Walker, 16 Aug. 1812; Woodford, pp. 70–71; Hull, *Report*, p. 46.

p.187 l.2   Clarke, p. 453.

p.187 l.10   Wood, I: 538, Askin Journal; Walker, 16 Aug. 1812.

p.187 l.18   Richardson, *Richardson's War*, pp. 57–58.

p.187 l.22   Ibid., p. 58.

p.187 l.24   Cruikshank, "General Hull's Invasion," p. 290.

p.188 l.3   Wood, I: 540–41, Askin Journal; Tupper, p. 290, Nichol to Brock, 25 Aug. 1812; Kosche, pp. 56–58; James, I: 291–92.

p.188 l.11   Richardson, *Richardson's War*, p. 58.

p.188 l.26   Tupper, p. 262.

p.188 l.30   Hull, *Report*, p. 103.

p.189 l.2   Lossing, "Hull's Surrender," p. 20.

p.189 l.7   Cruikshank, *Documents Relating to the Invasion*, p. 214, Cochran to his mother, 13 Sept. 1812.

p.189 l.8   Lossing, "Hull's Surrender," p. 20.

p.189 l.21   Woodford, pp. 70–71.

p.190 l.4   Williams, pp. 33–35.

p.190 l.13   Lucas, *Journal*, pp. 68–71.

p.*190 l.22*   Read, p. 158.

p.*190 l.33*   Tucker, *Tecumseh*, p. 274; Draper MSS, Tecumseh Papers, 5YY, p. 57.

p.*191 l.10*   Drake, p. 227.

p.*192 l.7*   Witherell, pp. 315–17.

p.*192 l.12*   Tucker, *Tecumseh*, p. 273.

p.*192 l.29*   PAC, CO 42/150/112, Prevost to Bathurst, encl. return of ordnance; Cruikshank, "General Hull's Invasion," pp. 286–87.

p.*193 l.2*   PAO, Hiram Walker Museum Collection, 20–287.

p.*194 l.6*   Hull, *Memoirs, passim*.; Hull, *Report, passim*.

CHICAGO

p.*196 l.12*   Kirkland, p. 84.

p.*196 l.17*   Quaife, *Chicago*, p. 216, Hull to Heald, 29 July 1812.

p.*198 l.13*   Ibid., p. 225.

p.*198 l.23*   Ibid., p. 216.

p.*199 l.11*   Ibid., pp. 226–29.

p.*199 l.20*   Ibid., p. 228.

p.*199 l.31*   Kirkland, p. 69.

p.*200 l.11*   Quaife, *Chicago*, pp. 229–30.

p.*200 l.22*   Ibid., pp. 232–34.

p.*200 l.27*   Ibid., pp. 241–42.

p.*200 l.29*   Richardson, *Wau-nan-gee*, p. 126.

p.*201 l.5*   Quaife, *Chicago*, pp. 235–36.

p.*201 l.12*   Ibid., p. 252.

p.*201 l.21*   Ibid., pp. 254–55.

p.*203 l.10*   Ibid., pp. 247–51.

p.*204 l.20*   Ibid., pp. 261–62.

QUEENSTON HEIGHTS

p.*206 l.24*   Bonney, p. 207.

p.*206 l.32*   Ibid.

p.*207 l.14*   USNA, M6/5, SW to Dearborn, 15 Aug. 1812.

p.*207 l.27*   Bonney, p. 204; Van Rensselaer, p. 10.

p.*208 l.4*   Bonney, pp. 198–99, Stephen Van Rensselaer to Tompkins, 23 July 1812; p. 199, Lovett to Alexander, 23 July 1812.

p.*208 l.11*   Quoted in Irwin, p. 148.

p.*209 l.18*   Bonney, p. 209, Lovett to Alexander, n.d.

p.*209 l.20*   Ibid., p. 211.

p.*209 l.29*   Ibid., p. 209.

p.*210 l.5*   Ibid., p. 247, Solomon Van Rensselaer to his wife, 10 Oct. 1812.

p.*210 l.8*   Ibid., p. 207, Lovett to Alexander, 16 Aug. 1812.

p.210 *l.15*   Ibid., p. 200, Lovett to Alexander, 23 July 1812.

p.210 *l.16*   Ibid., p. 230, Lovett to Alexander, 8 Sept. 1812.

p.210 *l.17*   Ibid., p. 229, Lovett to Alexander, 6 Sept. 1812.

p.210 *l.35*   Ibid., pp. 202–3, Lovett to Alexander, 29 July 1812.

p.211 *l.3*   Ibid., p. 202, Lovett to Alexander, 29 July 1812.

p.211 *l.7*   Ibid., p. 200, Lovett to Alexander, 23 July 1812.

p.211 *l.11*   Ibid., p. 203, Lovett to Alexander, 29 July 1812.

p.211 *l.14*   Ibid., p. 206, Lovett to Alexander, 14 Aug. 1812.

p.211 *l.23*   Ibid., p. 196.

p.211 *l.32*   Ibid., p. 196, Lovett to Alexander, 20 July 1812.

p.212 *l.2*   Ibid., p. 201.

p.212 *l.13*   Ibid., p. 208, Lovett to Alexander, 16 Aug. 1812.

p.212 *l.24*   Ibid., p. 208, Lovett to Alexander, 16 Aug. 1812.

p.212 *l.29*   Ibid., p. 209, Lovett to [Alexander], 17 Aug. 1812.

p.212 *l.30*   Ibid., p. 209.

p.213 *l.26*   Irwin, p. 149.

p.213 *l.28*   Quoted in Irwin, p. 149, Hall to Tompkins, 9 July 1812.

p.213 *l.30*   Ibid., p. 149, Brown to Tompkins, 25 June 1812.

p.213 *l.32*   Cruikshank, *Documentary History*, III: 223–24, Porter to Tompkins, 30 Aug. 1812.

p.215 *l.21*   Bonney, p. 210.

p.216 *l.9*   Ibid., pp. 210–11.

p.216 *l.22*   Wood, I: 587, Brock to Prevost, 7 Sept. 1812.

p.216 *l.23*   Bonney, p. 229, Lovett to Alexander, 6 Sept. 1812.

p.217 *l.2*   Wood, I: 598, Evans report, 19 Aug. 1812.

p.217 *l.16*   Bonney, pp. 224–25, Solomon Van Rensselaer to his wife, 1 Sept. 1812; p. 228, Harriet Van Rensselaer to her husband, 6 Sept. 1812.

p.217 *l.24*   Ibid., p. 211, Solomon Van Rensselaer to his wife, 21 Aug. 1812, p. 227, Solomon Van Rensselaer to Van Vechten, 5 Sept. 1812.

p.217 *l.29*   Ibid., p. 247, Solomon Van Rensselaer to his wife, 10 Oct. 1812.

p.217 *l.33*   Ibid., p. 231, Solomon Van Rensselaer to Lewis, 11 Sept. 1812.

p.218 *l.1*   Ibid.

p.218 *l.3*   Ibid., p. 227, Solomon Van Rensselaer to Van Vechten, 5 Sept. 1812.

p.218 *l.7*   Ibid., p. 231, Solomon Van Rensselaer to Lewis, 11 Sept. 1812.

p.218 *l.12*   Ibid.

p.218 *l.20*   Tupper, p. 293.

p.218 *l.22*   Ibid.

p.219 *l.6*   Ibid., p. 280, Brock to his brothers, 16 Aug. 1812.

p.219 *l.17*   Ibid., pp. 110-11, Brock to Savery Brock, 7 Oct. 1811; pp. 112–13, Brock to Irving Brock, 30 Oct. 1811.

p.219 *l.20*   Ibid., p. 113, Brock to Irving Brock, 30 Oct. 1811.

p.219 *l.29*   Ibid., pp. 284–85, Brock to his brothers, 3 Sept. 1812.

p.220 *l.15*   Ibid.

p.220 l.20   Ibid., p. 286, Brock to his brothers, 3 Sept. 1812.

p.220 l.24   Ibid., p. 287, Sewell to Brock, 3 Sept. 1812.

p.220 l.26   Ibid., p. 287, Maitland to Brock, 8 Oct. 1812.

p.220 l.32   Ibid., p. 285, Powell to Brock, 27 Aug. 1812.

p.221 l.4   Ibid., p. 284, Brock to his brothers, 3 Sept. 1812.

p.221 l.14   Ibid., p. 301.

p.221 l.16   Ibid., p. 285, Brock to his brothers, 3 Sept. 1812.

p.221 l.25   Ibid., p. 300, Baynes to Brock, 13 Aug. 1812.

p.221 l.27   Ibid., p. 299.

p.221 l.33   Wood, I: 587, Brock to Prevost, 7 Sept. 1812.

p.221 l.35   Ibid., pp. 586–87.

p.222 l.15   Ibid., p. 587.

p.222 l.20   Ibid.

p.223 l.1   Cruikshank, *Documentary History*, III: 271–73, Brock to Procter, 17 Sept. 1812; Wood, I: 593, Brock to Prevost, 18 Sept. 1812.

p.223 l.6   Wood, I: 593, Brock to Prevost, 18 Sept. 1812.

p.223 l.10   Ibid., p. 593; Cruikshank, *Documentary History*, IV: 36–37, Prevost to Bathurst, 5 Oct. 1812.

p.223 l.20   Wood, I: 596, Brock to Prevost, 28 Sept. 1812.

p.223 l.27   Tupper, p. 316, Brock to Savery Brock, 18 Sept. 1812.

p.224 l.12   Ibid., p. 325, Prevost to Brock, 25 Sept. 1812.

p.224 l.18   Ibid.

p.224 l.25   Ibid., p. 314, Brock to Prevost, 18 Sept. 1812.

p.224 l.32   Ibid., pp. 315–16, Brock to Savery Brock, *18* Sept. 1812.

p.225 l.2   Ibid., p. 316.

p.225 l.8   Wood, I: 588–89, Brock to Prevost, 13 Sept. 1812.

p.225 l.10   Tupper, p. 316, Brock to Savery Brock, 18 Sept. 1812.

p.225 l.18   PAC, RG 8, vol. 677, p. 131, note signed "Winfield Scott," Nov. 1863.

p.225 l.24   Wood, I: 588–89, Brock to Prevost, 18 Sept. 1812.

p.225 l.32   Tupper, p. 317, Brock to Savery Brock, 18 Sept. 1812.

p.226 l.10   Ibid., pp. 316–17.

p.226 l.27   Bonney, p. 221, Lovett to Van Vechten, 28 Aug. 1812.

p.227 l.2   Cruikshank, *Documentary History*, III: 227, Stephen Van Rensselaer to Tompkins, 31 Aug. 1812.

p.227 l.6   Tompkins, III. 105, Tompkins to Porter, 9 Sept. 1812.

p.227 l.27   Cruikshank, *Documentary History*, III: 223–24, Porter to Tompkins, 30 Aug. 1812.

p.227 l.31   Bonney, p. 228, Lovett to Alexander, 6 Sept. 1812.

p.227 l.34   Ibid., p. 239, Lovett to Van Vechten, 8 Sept. 1812.

p.228 l.11   USNA, M221/43/D130, Dearborn to SW, 15 Aug. 1812.

p.228 l.16   USNA, M221/43/D154, Dearborn to SW, 22 Aug. 1812.

p.228 l.20   USNA, M221/43, Dearborn to SW, 14 Sept. 1812.

p.228 l.24   USNA, M221/43/D145, encl. Wadsworth, 26 Aug. 1812 (extract).

p.228 l.28	USNA, M221/43/D146, Dearborn to SW, 4 Sept. 1812.
p.228 l.31	USNA, M221/43/D158, Dearborn to SW, 8 Sept. 1812.
p.228 l.35	USNA, M221/43, Dearborn to SW, 14 Sept. 1812.
p.229 l.10	Bonney, p. 231, Solomon Van Rensselaer to Lewis, 11 Sept. 1812.
p.229 l.14	Ibid.
p.229 l.24	Cruikshank, *Documentary History*, III: 264–65, Stephen Van Rensselaer to Tompkins, 15 Sept. 1812.
p.229 l.32	Bonney, p. 233, Stephen Van Rensselaer to Dearborn, 17 Sept. 1812; p. 236, Stephen Van Rensselaer to Tompkins, 17 Sept. 1812.
p.230 l.4	Ibid., p. 237, Lovett to Alexander, 22 Sept. 1812; p. 242, Lovett to Alexander, 6 Oct. 1812.
p.230 l.10	Ibid., pp. 242–43, Lovett to Alexander, 6 Oct. 1812.
p.230 l.12	Ibid., p. 228, Lovett to Alexander, 6 Sept. 1812.
p.230 l.18	Ibid., p. 243, Lovett to Alexander, 6 Oct. 1812.
p.230 l.21	Cruikshank, *Documentary History*, III: 295–96, Dearborn to Stephen Van Rensselaer, 26 Sept. 1812.
p.230 l.27	Ibid., p. 296.
p.230 l.32	Ibid.
p.231 l.11	Ibid., p. 300, Smyth to Stephen Van Rensselaer, 29 Sept. 1812.
p.231 l.14	Van Rensselaer, p. 18.
p.231 l.31	Cruikshank, *Documentary History*, IV: 41, Stephen Van Rensselaer to Dearborn, 8 Oct. 1812.
p.232 l.4	Ibid.
p.232 l.13	Ibid.
p.232 l.27	Ibid., p. 42.
p.232 l.31	Bonney, p. 242, Stephen Van Rensselaer to Smyth, 5 Oct. 1812.
p.232 l.32	Ibid., p. 242, Stephen Van Rensselaer to Smyth, 6 Oct. 1812.
p.232 l.35	Cruikshank, *Documentary History*, IV: 79, Stephen Van Rensselaer to Eustis, 14 Oct. 1812.
p.233 l.2	Severance, p. 218.
p.233 l.8	Cruikshank, *Documentary History*, IV: 41, Stephen Van Rensselaer to Dearborn, 8 Oct. 1812.
p.233 l.30	Cruikshank, *Documentary History*, IV: 45, Elliott to SN, 9 Oct. 1812.
p.234 l.1	Roach, p. 132.
p.234 l.4	Ibid., pp. 132–33.
p.234 l.12	Ibid., p. 134.
p.234 l.30	Ibid., pp. 134–35; Cruikshank, *Documentary History*, IV: 52, Hall to Stephen Van Rensselaer, 10 Oct. 1812; p. 54, inquiry on loss of Detroit.
p.235 l.9	Richardson, *Richardson's War*, pp. 50–51.
p.235 l.34	Wood, I: 601–3, Brock to Prevost, 11 Oct. 1812; Cruikshank, *Documentary History*, IV: 60–62, quoting *Buffalo Gazette*, 13 Oct. 1812.

p.235 l.24 Cruikshank, *Documentary History*, IV: 60–62, quoting *Buffalo Gazette*, 13 Oct. 1812, pp. 45–47, Elliott to SN, 9 Oct. 1812, 10 Oct. 1812; Elliott, pp. 51–53.

p.235 l.34 Wood, I: 601–3, Brock to Prevost, 11 Oct. 1812.

p.236 l.4 Ibid.

p.236 l.35 Cruikshank, *Documentary History*, IV: 80–81, Stephen Van Rensselaer to Eustis, 14 Oct. 1812; Van Rensselaer, pp. 21–23.

p.237 l.6 Bonney, p. 249

p.237 l.9 Cruikshank, *Documentary History*, IV: 60, Fenwick to Stephen Van Rensselaer, undated.

p.237 l.10 Ibid., p. 81, Stephen VanRensselaer to Eustis, 14 Oct. 1812.

p.237 l.15 Bonney, p. 251, Van Vechten to Solomon Van Rensselaer, 12 Oct. 1812.

p.237 l.18 Cruikshank, *Documentary History*, IV: 81, Stephen Van Rensselaer to Eustis, 14 Oct. 1812.

p.237 l.22 Bonney, p. 271, Lovett to VanVechten, 21 Oct. 1812.

p.238 l.4 PAC, MG 24 F70, Thomas Evans to ?, 15 Oct. 1812.

p.241 l.2 Ibid.

p.241 l.8 Scott, pp. 56–57.

p.241 l.9 Cruikshank, *Documentary History*, IV: 96, Chrystie to Cushing, 22 Feb. 1813.

p.241 l.10 Ibid., p. 96; p. 81, Stephen Van Rensselaer to Eustis, 14 Oct. 1812.

p.241 l.16 Scott, pp. 56–57; Elliott, p. 57; Cruikshank, *Documentary History*, IV: 96, Chrystie to Cushing, 22 Feb. 1813.

p.241 l.26 Bonney, p. 279, Lovett to Alexander, 4 Nov. 1812; Cruikshank, *Documentary History*, IV:93, Col. Meade's statement, 18 Nov. 1812.

p.241 l.16 Bonney, p. 266, Lovett to Alexander, 14 Oct. 1812.

p.241 l.26 Cruikshank, *Documentary History*, IV: 103, (J.B. Robinson] to ?, 14 Oct. 1812.

p.243 l.2 Stubbs, pp. 24–25.

p.243 l.16 Bonney, p. 266, Lovett to Alexander, 14 Oct. 1812.

p.243 l.27 Cruikshank, *Documentary History*, IV: 96–97, Chrystie to Cushing, 22 Feb. 1813.

p.243 l.30 Van Rensselaer, pp. 28–29.

p.243 l.35 Ibid., p. 29.

p.244 l.7 Cruikshank, *Documentary History*, IV: 98, Chrystie to Cushing, 22 Feb. 1813.

p.244 l.13 Cruikshank, "Letters of 1812," pp. 45–47, C. Askin to J. Askin, 14 Oct. 1812.

p.244 l.19 Cruikshank, *Documentary History*, IV: 98, Chrystie to Cushing, 22 Feb. 1813.

p.244 l.26 Bonney, pp. 275–76, Lovett to Alexander, 2 Nov. 1812.

p.246 l.2 Ibid., p. 272, Wool to Solomon Van Rensselaer, 23 Oct. 1812; pp. 267–68, Lovett to Alexander, 14 Oct. 1812; Crooks, p. 40.

p.246 l.33	Bonney, p. 272, Wool to Solomon Van Rensselaer, 23 Oct. 1812.
p.247 l.18	Nursey, pp. 158–59.
p.247 l.28	Robinson, p. 34, Robinson to ?, 14 Oct. 1812.
p.248 l.5	Ibid., p. 104.
p.248 l.30	Wood, I: 605–8, Sheaffe to Prevost, 13 Oct. 1812.
p.249 l.28	Cruikshank, *Documentary History*, IV: 116, Jarvis narrative.
p.249 l.31	Ibid.
p.250 l.8	Fortescue, p. 540.
p.250 l.10	Elliott, p. 61.
p.250 l.33	Canadian War Museum, Brock uniform; Elliott, p. 61; Kosche, pp. 33–56.
p.250 l.34	Cruikshank, *Documentary History*, IV: 116, Jarvis narrative.
p.251 l.2	Robinson, p. 35, Robinson to ?, 14 Oct. 1812.
p.251 l.11	Ibid., p. 36.
p.251 l.24	Cruikshank, *Documentary History*, IV: 105, [J.B. Robinson] to ?, 14 Oct. 1812.
p.251 l.25	Ibid., p. 116, Jarvis narrative.
p.251 l.31	Ibid. p. 115, McLean narrative, from *Quebec Mercury*, 27 Oct. 1812.
p.251 l.32	Robinson, pp. 36–37, Robinson to ?, 14 Oct. 1812.
p.251 l.34	Cruikshank, *Documentary History*, IV: 115, McLean narrative, from *Quebec Mercury*, 27 Oct. 1812.
p.252 l.1	Ibid., p. 115.
p.252 l.2	Ibid.
p.252 l.26	Cruikshank, *Documentary History*, IV: 101, Chrystie to Cushing, 22 Feb. 1813.
p.253 l.27	Elliott, pp. 63–64.
p.253 l.32	Scott, pp. 59–60.
p.254 l.4	Ibid., p. 60; Wood, III, part 2, p. 560, Merritt Journal.
p.254 l.15	Elliott, p. 65.
p.254 l.21	Fortescue, p. 54.
p.255 l.1	Bonney, p. 267, Lovett to Van Vechten, 14 Oct. 1812.
p.255 l.6	Scott, p. 60.
p.255 l.20	Crooks, pp. 32–33.
p.256 l.10	Ibid., pp. 33–34.
p.256 l.33	Ibid., p. 34.
p.257 l.24	Zaslow, pp. 39–40.
p.257 l.30	Norton, pp. 306–8.
p.258 l.2	Johnston, p. 101–2.
p.258 l.10	Wood, III, part 2, p. 561, Merritt Journal.
p.258 l.16	Crooks, p. 36.
p.258 l.20	Ibid.
p.258 l.28	Elliott, p. 65.
p.259 l.1	Crooks, p. 37.

p.259 l.15	Ibid.
p.259 l.19	Elliott, p. 66.
p.259 l.35	Cruikshank, *Documentary History*, IV: 102–3, Chrystie to Cushing, 22 Feb. 1813; Scott, pp. 60–61; Robinson, pp. 37–38, Robinson to ?, 14 Oct. 1812.
p.260 l.3	Scott, pp. 61–62.
p.260 l.12	Elliott, p. 67; Scott, p. 62.
p.260 l.19	Scott, pp. 62–63.
p.260 l.24	Zaslow, p. 43.
p.260 l.28	Elliott, p. 67.
p.260 l.30	Cruikshank, *Documentary History*, IV: 74, return, 15 Oct. 1812.
p.261 l.7	Stubbs, pp. 25–29.
p.261 l.14	Bonney, p. 268, Lovett to Alexander, 14 Oct. 1812; p. 274, Lovett to Alexander, 25 Oct. 1812; Van Rensselaer, p. 24.
p.261 l.19	Crooks, p. 37.
p.261 l.23	Cruikshank, *Documentary History*, IV: 74, return, 15 Oct. 1812.
p.261 l.32	Ryerson, pp. 368–71.
p.262 l.28	Cruikshank, *Documentary History*, IV: 83, Glegg to Brock, 14 Oct. 1812.
p.262 l.32	Ibid., p. 146, Ridout to his brother, 21 Oct. 1812.
p.262 l.35	Nursey, p. 213.
p.263 l.11	MTPL, S135, Sandham Col., Ilbert to Taylor, 22 Oct. 1812.
p.263 l.14	PAC, MG 24 B16, Cochran MSS, Cochran to Stewart, 25 Oct. 1812.
p.263 l.15	Cruikshank, *Documentary History*, IV: 148, Prevost to Bathurst, 21 Oct. 1812.
p.263 l.22	Tupper, pp. 338–39; PAC, CO 42/147/233, 8 Dec. 1812, (Bathurst) to Prevost; Cruikshank, *Documentary History*, V, General Order, 10 March 1813.
p.263 l.25	Wood, III, part 2, p. 564, Merritt Journal.
p.263 l.35	Cruikshank, *Documentary History*, IV: 147.
p.264 l.8	Bonney, p. 274, Lovett to Alexander, 25 Oct. 1812.
p.264 l.32	*Kingston Gazette*, 24 Oct. 1812.
p.265 l.11	*York Gazette*, 12 Dec. 1812.
p.265 l.16	Loyal and Patriotic Society, *Report*, p. 365, Appendix no. 1, 22 Nov. 1812 (sermon).
p.266 l.12	PAO, Tupper MSS, Robinson to Tupper, 15 April 1846.
p.266 l.14	*Canadian Monthly*, July 1874.
p.266 l.16	Quoted in Berger, p. 97.

BLACK ROCK

p.268 l.19	Severance, p. 228.
p.269 l.11	Cruikshank, *Documentary History*, IV: 194, Smyth's proclamation, 10 Nov. 1812.

p.269 l.26   Severance, p. 222, Smyth to Dearborn, 30 Oct. 1812.

p.269 l.28   Ibid.

p.269 l.34   Ibid., pp. 223–24, Smyth to Dearborn, 9 Nov. 1812; Cruikshank, *Documentary History*, IV: 249, statement of David Harvey.

p.270 l.7   Severance, p. 225, Smyth to Dearborn, 9 Nov. 1812.

p.270 l.9   Ibid., p. 225.

p.270 l.17   Lossing, *Field-book*, p. 426.

p.270 l.21   Cruikshank, *Documentary History*, IV: 227–28, Myers to Sheaffe, 22 [Nov.] 1812; pp. 233–35, McFeeley to Smyth, n.d.

p.270 l.23   Severance, p. 231.

p.270 l.28   Ibid., p. 232, Smyth to Porter [27 Nov. 1812].

p.271 l.6   Cruikshank, *Documentary History*, IV: 253–56, Bisshopp to Sheaffe, 1 Dec. 1812; pp. 260–63, Winder to Smyth, 7 Dec. 1812.

p.271 l.14   Severance, p. 233.

p.271 l.17   Cruikshank, *Documentary History*, IV: 252, Sheaffe to Prevost, 30 Nov. 1812.

p.271 l.20   Ibid., p. 250, Smyth to Bisshopp, 28 Nov. 1812; p. 251, Bisshopp's reply, n.d.

p.271 l.23   Severance, p. 233.

p.272 l.7   Ibid., p. 234, Smyth to his "Hearts of War," 29 Nov. 1812.

p.272 l.26   Ibid., pp. 237–38, Smyth to McClure and others, 3 Dec. 1812.

p.272 l.28   Ibid., pp. 237–38; Lossing, *Field-book*, pp. 430–31.

p.273 l.13   Lossing, *Field-book*, p. 431.

p.273 l.17   *York Gazette*, 12 Dec. 1812, deposition of Bill Sherman, dated 3 Dec. 1812.

p.273 l.22   Severance, pp. 240–41, Porter to *Buffalo Gazette*, 8 Dec. 1812; *York Gazette*, 12 Dec. 1812, deposition of Bill Sherman.

p.273 l.24   *Buffalo Gazette*, 15 Dec. 1812.

p.273 l.32   Severance, p. 243, Tompkins to Fleming, 2 Jan. 1813.

p.274 l.14   USNA, M221/43/D227, Dearborn to SW, 8 Nov. 1812.

p.274 l.16   USNA, M221/43/D254, Dearborn to SW, 24 Nov. 1812.

p.274 l.20   Mann, p. 39; USNA, M221/43/ D262, Dearborn to SW, 11 Dec. 1812.

p.274 l.34   USNA, M221/43/254, Dearborn to SW, 24 Nov. 1812.

p.275 l.3   USNA, M221/43/D262, Dearborn to SW, 11 Dec. 1812.

FRENCHTOWN

p.277 l.5   Clay, p. 715, speech, 16 Aug. 1812.

p.277 l.14   Ibid., p. 697, Clay to Monroe, 29 July 1812.

p.277 l.23   Quoted in Mason, p. 84.

p.278 l.1   Ibid., p. 86.

p.279 l.6   Cruikshank, "Harrison and Procter," p. 151.

p.279 l.10   Hammack, p. 27.

p.279 l.20   Quoted in Hammack, p. 11.

p.279 l.31   Ibid., 7 July 1812.

p.279 l.33   Ibid., p. 21.

p.280 l.3   *Niles Register,* 30 Nov. 1811; Mason, p. 79.

p.280 l.23   Harrison, II: 91, Gibson to Hargrove, 20 Aug. 1812.

p.280 l.35   Clay, p. 720, Clay to Monroe, 25 Aug. 1812.

p.281 l.2   Cruikshank, "Harrison and Procter," p. 130.

p.281 l.9   Harrison, II: 99, Harrison to SW, 28 Aug. 1812.

p.281 l.16   Cleaves, p. 117; Harrison, II: 98–99, Harrison to SW, 28 Aug. 1812.

p.281 l.18   Winchester, *Historical Details,* pp. 9-10; DeWitt, p. 90.

p.281 l.19   Ibid.

p.281 l.21   Ibid.

p.281 l.28   Harrison, II: 100, Harrison to SW, 28 Aug. 1812.

p.281 l.32   Ibid.; ibid., pp. 103–4, Harrison to SW, 29 Aug. 1812.

p.282 l.3   Ibid., pp. 103–4.

p.282 l.13   Darnell, 1 Sept. 1812.

p.282 l.15   Harrison, II: 92, SW to Harrison, 22 Aug. 1812; DeWitt, p. 90.

p.282 l.21   Harrison, II: 110, Harrison to SW, 3 Sept. 1812.

p.282 l.32   Cleaves, p. 119.

p.282 l.35   Darnell, 5 Sept. 1812.

p.283 l.16   Northcutt, p. 170.

p.283 l.18   Harrison, II: 143–47, Harrison to SW, 21 Sept. 1812.

p.283 l.22   Ibid., pp. 143–44.

p.283 l.32   Ibid., pp. 143–47.

p.284 l.3   DeWitt, p. 401.

p.284 l.10   Northcutt, p. 176.

p.284 l.15   Ibid.

p.284 l.23   Ibid., p. 177.

p.285 l.16   Winchester, *Historical Details,* pp. 71–72, Eve to Garrard, 22 Nov. 1814.

p.285 l.18   Ibid.; Harrison, II: 136–37, SW to Harrison, 17 Sept. 1812.

p.285 l.23   Cruikshank, "Harrison and Procter," pp. 133–34.

p.285 l.25   Ibid.

p.285 l.32   Winchester, *Historical Details,* p. 13.

p.286 l.2   Cruikshank, "Harrison and Procter," p. 134; Harrison, II: 160–61, Harrison to Winchester, 4 Oct. 1812

p.286 l.6   Cruikshank, "Harrison and Procter," p. 134.

p.286 l.16   Quoted in Cleaves, p. 126.

p.286 l.23   Ibid.

p.286 l.27   Harrison, II: 136–37, SW to Harrison, 17 Sept. 1812.

p.286 l.34   Ibid., pp. 156–57, Harrison to SW, 27 Sept. 1812.

p.287 l.7   Ibid., pp. 167–72, Tupper to Harrison, 12 Oct. 1812.

p.288 l.2   Darnell, pp. 27–28, 9 Oct. 1812.

p.288 l.18   Lossing, *Field-book,* p. 348; Cleaves, p. 127.

p.288 l.20   Harrison, II: 184, Harrison to Eustis, 22 Oct. 1814.

p.288 l.24   Ibid., pp. 153–54, Shelby to Harrison, 26 Sept. 1812.

p.288 l.35   Ibid., pp. 192–93, Shelby to Harrison, 1 Nov. 1812.

p.289 l.4   Ibid., p. 192.

p.289 l.5   Ibid., p. 201, Shelby to Harrison, 7 Nov. 1812.

p.289 l.10   Ibid., p. 177, Harrison to SW, 13 Oct. 1812.

p.289 l.11   Ibid., p. 133, Gibson to Hargrove, 12 Sept. 1812.

p.289 l.16   Ibid., pp. 124–28, Taylor to Harrison, 10 Sept. 1812.

p.289 l.27   Ibid., p. 242, Harrison to SW, 12 Dec. 1812; pp. 182–84, Harrison to SW, 22 Oct. 1812.

p.289 l.30   Ibid., p. 241, Harrison to SW, 12 Dec. 1812.

p.289 l.33   Ibid., p. 238, Bodley to Harrison, 11 Dec. 1812; p. 241, Harrison to SW, 12 Dec. 1812.

p.290 l.2   Cruikshank, "Harrison and Procter," p. 134.

p.290 l.15   Harrison, II: 228, Harrison to Campbell, 25 Nov. 1812; pp. 253–65, Campbell to Harrison, 25 Dec. 1812.

p.291 l.2   Ibid., p. 261, Campbell to Harrison, 25 Dec. 1812.

p.291 l.6   Ibid., pp. 288–90, General Orders, 2 Jan. 1813.

p.291 l.15   Ibid., p. 243, Harrison to SW, 12 Dec. 1812.

p.291 l.24   Atherton, p. 19.

p.292 l.7   Darnell, p. 40.

p.292 l.11   Winchester, *Historical Details*, p. 21.

p.292 l.23   Darnell, p. 41, 29 Dec. 1812.

p.293 l.1   Richardson, *Richardson's War*, p. 140.

p.293 l.4   Atherton, p. 27.

p.293 l.14   Winchester, *Historical Details*, p. 23.

p.294 l.1   Cruikshank, "Harrison and Procter," p. 152.

p.294 l.10   Cruikshank, "Harrison and Procter," p. 140.

p.294 l.35   Cruikshank, *Documentary History*, III: 272, Brock to Procter, 17 Sept. 1812.

p.295 l.18   Chalou, p. 163.

p.295 l.23   Cruikshank, "Harrison and Procter," p. 143.

p.295 l.32   Ibid., p. 141.

p.296 l.5   Cruikshank, *Documentary History*, VI: 242, Black Bird to Claus, 15 July 1813.

p.296 l.9   PAC, RG 8, vol. 677, pp. 163–65, Procter to Sheaffe, 30 Oct. 1812.

p.296 l.19   PAC, RG 8, vol. 677, pp. 176–77, Elliott to Claus, 28 Oct. 1812.

p.296 l.24   PAC, RG 8, vol. 677, p. 181, Elliott to St. George, 11 Nov. 1812; Chalou, pp. 207–8.

p.296 l.27   PAC, RG 8, vol. 677, p. 182, Ironside to Claus, 13 Nov. 1812; Chalou, pp. 207–8.

p.296 l.29   Wood, II: 5, Procter to Sheaffe, 13 Jan. 1813.

p.297 l.3   Cruikshank, "Harrison and Procter," p. 153.

p.297 l.17 Harrison, II: 308, Day to Harrison, 12 Jan. 1813.

p.297 l.18 Ibid., p. 314, Winchester to Harrison, 17 Jan. 1813.

p.298 l.12 Mason, p. 89.

p.298 l.32 DeWitt, p. 95; Harrison, II: 336, Harrison to SW, 26 Jan. 1813.

p.298 l.33 Harrison, II: 314, Winchester to Harrison, 17 Jan. 1813.

p.299 l.9 Lossing, *Field-book*, p. 350.

p.299 l.15 Harrison, II: 335, Harrison to SW, 26 Jan. 1813.

p.299 l.18 Ibid., p. 336; Cruikshank, "Harrison and Procter," p. 155.

p.299 l.20 Cruikshank, "Harrison and Procter," p. 155; Harrison, II: 331–32, Harrison to SW, 18 Jan. 1813.

p.299 l.24 Harrison, II: 314, Winchester to Harrison, 17 Jan. 1813; p. 336, Harrison to SW, 26 Jan. 1813.

p.299 l.28 Ibid., p. 337, Harrison to SW, 26 Jan. 1813.

p.299 l.33 Cleaves, p. 139.

p.300 l.1 Harrison, II: 314, Winchester to Harrison, 17 Jan. 1813.

p.300 l.11 Darnell, p. 46.

p.300 l.32 Quoted in Clift, p. 160, Price to his wife, 16 Jan. 1813.

p.301 l.5 Dudley, p. 1.

p.301 l.15 Darnell, p. 47.

p.301 l.26 Cruikshank, "Harrison and Procter," p. 154.

p.301 l.29 Harrison, II: 319, Lewis to Winchester, 20 Jan. 1813.

p.301 l.35 "Correspondence," Perkins to Meigs, 28 Jan. 1813.

p.302 l.4 Harrison, II: 330, Harrison to Meigs, 24 Jan. 1813.

p.302 l.17 Atherton, pp. 40, 42; Darnell, p. 50; Cruikshank, "Harrison and Procter," p. 156; "Correspondence," p. 102, Whittlesey to his wife, 25 Jan. 1813.

p.302 l.33 Lossing, *Field-book*, p. 353; DeWitt, p. 98.

p.303 l.9 Lossing, *Field-book*, pp. 353–54.

p.303 l.18 DeWitt, pp. 98–99.

p.303 l.24 Harrison, II: 339, McClanahan to Harrison, 26 Jan. 1813.

p.303 l.28 Winchester, *Historical Details*, pp. 32–33.

p.303 l.30 Ibid.

p.304 l.15 Lossing, *Field-book*, p. 354; Harrison, II: 340, McClanahan to Harrison, 26 Jan. 1813.

p.304 l.16 Darnell, pp. 50–51.

p.304 l.19 Ibid., p. 51; Lossing, *Field-book*, p. 354.

p.304 l.22 Darnell, pp. 51–52.

p.304 l.27 Harrison, II: 339, McClanahan to Harrison, 26 Jan. 1813.

p.304 l.35 Atherton, p. 42.

p.305 l.11 Coffin, p. 203.

p.305 l.31 Wood, II: 10, return of those in action on 22 Jan. 1813.

p.306 l.4 Richardson, *Richardson's War*, p. 134.

p.306 l.12 Coffin, p. 205.

p.306 l.19 Richardson, *Richardson's War*, pp. 137–38.

p.306 l.23 Wood, II: 7, Procter to Sheaffe, 25 Jan. 1813; Richardson, *Richardson's War*, p. 134.

p.306 l.31 Ibid., pp. 134–35.

p.306 l.33 Coffin, p. 204.

p.307 l.8 Richardson, *Richardson's War*, Richardson to his uncle, 4 Feb. 1813.

p.307 l.12 Coffin, p. 204.

p.307 l.16 Coffin, p. 205.

p.308 l.3 Richardson, *Richardson's War*, pp. 137–38.

p.308 l.18 Byfield, p. 73.

p.308 l.26 Ibid., p. 74.

p.309 l.5 Richardson, *Richardson's War*, Richardson to his uncle, 4 Feb. 1813.

p.309 l.14 Ibid., pp. 137–38.

p.309 l.32 Ibid., pp. 139–40.

p.310 l.2 LC, Harrison MSS, 22 Aug. 1818, sworn statement of Francis Navarre.

p.310 l.13 Atherton, pp. 44–45; Harrison, II: 340, McClanahan to Harrison, 26 Jan. 1813.

p.310 l.21 McAfee, p. 214; Lossing, *Field-book*, p. 355; U.S. Congress, *Barbarities*, pp. 150–51, statement of Ashton Garrett, 13 April 1813.

p.310 l.28 Atherton, pp. 48–49.

p.310 l.33 Winchester, *Historical Details*, p. 37; Lossing, *Field-book*, p. 356; Richardson, p. 135.

p.311 l.15 Winchester, *Historical Details*, p. 38.

p.312 l.2 Hammack, pp. 51–52.

p.312 l.13 Atherton, p. 53.

p.312 l.26 Ibid.

p.312 l.30 Ibid., pp. 53–54.

p.312 l.34 Ibid., p. 52.

p.313 l.1 Ibid., p. 54.

p.313 l.4 Ibid., p. 52.

p.313 l.7 Dudley, p. 2.

p.313 l.13 *History of Pike County*.

p.314 l.15 Atherton, pp. 57–60.

p.314 l.30 Ibid., pp. 61–62.

p.315 l.5 U.S. Congress, *Barbarities*, p. 142, Todd to Bledsoe, 2 May 1813; Lossing, *Field-book*, p. 358; Atherton, p. 55.

p.315 l.7 U.S. Congress, *Barbarities*, p. 142, statement of John Todd, 2 May 1813.

p.315 l.22 Atherton, p. 63.

p.315 l.31 Ibid., p. 64.

p.316 l.5 U.S. Congress, *Barbarities*, pp. 148–50, statement of Albert Ammerman, 21 April 1813.

p.316 l.17 Ibid., pp. 149–50.

p.316 l.35 Atherton, p. 65.

p.317 l.26 U.S. Congress, *Barbarities,* pp. 140–41, statement of Gustavus Bower, 24 April 1813.

p.317 l.27 Ibid., p. 140.

p.317 l.31 Atherton, p. 70.

p.318 l.21 U.S. Congress, *Barbarities*, pp. 143–44, statement of John Todd, 2 May 1813.

p.318 l.30 Ibid., p. 131, statement of Alexis Labadie, 6 Feb. 1813.

p.319 l.5 *Niles Register,* 10 April 1813, Ensign Baker's statement, 25 Feb. 1813.

p.319 l.9 Darnell, p. 62.

p.319 l.10 U.S. Congress, *Barbarities*, p. 152, statement of Charles Bradford, 29 April 1813; Atherton, pp. 67–68; Dudley, n.p.

p.319 l.21 U.S. Congress, *Barbarities*, p. 130, statement of Alexis Labadie, 6 Feb. 1813.

AFTERVIEW

p.321 l.34 Mahan, I: 362.

p.323 l.24 *Niles Register,* 13 Feb. 1813.

p.323 l.32 Quoted in Clift, p. 151.

p.324 l.2 Dunn, p. 31.

p.324 l.8 Clift, p. 115.

p.324 l.14 Brannan, p. 135, report of Erie meeting, 20 Feb. 1813.

p.324 l.15 Clift.

p.324 l.26 Wood, II: 8, Procter to Sheaffe, 25 Jan. 1813.

p.324 l.28 PAC RG 8, vol. 678, pp. 61–63, Procter to Sheaffe, 1 Feb. 1813.

p.324 l.34 PAC RG 8, vol. 1170, General Order, 8 Feb. 1813.

p.325 l.5 Quaife, *Askin Papers,* p. 570, Richardson to J. Askin, 7 Feb. 1813.

p.325 l.9 McAfee, p. 222; Witherell, p. 307; Winchester, *Historical Details,* p. 45.

p.325 l.18 McAfee, p. 223.

p.325 l.22 Ibid., p. 225.

p.325 l.30 Beal, p. 338.

CODA: WILLIAM ATHERTON'S WAR

p.331 l.34 Atherton, pp. 77–146, *passim.*

Select Bibliography

UNPUBLISHED MANUSCRIPT MATERIAL

Public Archives of Canada:
RG 8, "C" series *passim.*, British Military Records.
RG 10, vol. II, Indian Affairs.
CO 42, vols. 143–149 (Lower Canada); vols. 351–354 (Upper Canada).
  Colonial Office, original correspondence, Secretary of State.
RG 19 E5(a), Department of Finance, War of 1812 Losses, vols. 3728–3768
  passim.
FO 5, vols. 84–86. Foreign Office, General Correspondence, United States
  of America, series II.
MG 24 A9 Prevost Papers.
MG 24 A57 Sherbrooke Papers.
MG 24 B15 Cochran Papers.
MG 24 F70 Evans Papers.

Library of Congress:
Harrison Papers.
Augustus Foster Papers.

U.S. National Archives:
RG 107 Records of the office of the Secretary of War.
  M6, reel 5, Letters sent by the Secretary of War.
  M221, reels 42–49, Letters received by the Secretary of War.

Wisconsin Historical Society:
Draper MSS, Tecumseh Papers.

Public Archives of Ontario:
Tupper Papers.
Hiram Walker Museum Collection.

Metropolitan Toronto Public Library:
Alfred Sandham Collection.

PUBLISHED PRIMARY SOURCES

Armstrong, John. *Notices of the War of 1812*, 2 vols., vol. I. New York: G. Dearborn, 1836.

Atherton, William. *Narrative of the Suffering & Defeat of the North-western Army under General Winchester.* . . . Frankfort, Ky., 1842.

Beall, William K. "Journal of William K. Beall," *American Historical Review*, vol. 17 (1912).

Bonney, Catharina V.R. *A Legacy of Historical Gleanings.* . . . 2nd ed., vol. I. Albany, N.Y., 1875.

Boylen, J.C. (ed.). "Strategy of Brock Saved Upper Canada: Candid Comments of a U.S. Officer Who Crossed at Queenston," *Ontario History*, vol. 58 (1966).

Brannan, John (ed.). *Official Letters of the Military and Naval Officers of the United States, during the War with Great Britain in the Years 1812, 13, 14, & 15.* Washington: Way and Gideon, 1823.

[Brenton, E.B.] *Some Account of the Public Life of the Late Lieutenant-General Sir George Prevost, Bart, Particularly of His Services in the Canadas.* . . . London: Cadell, 1823.

Byfield, Shadrach. "Narrative," *Magazine of History*, extra no. 11, 1910.

Claus, William. "Diary," *Michigan Pioneer and Historical Collections*, vol. 23, 1895.

"Collections of Papers on File in the Dominion Archives at Ottawa, Canada, Pertaining to Michigan As Found in the Colonial Office Records," *Michigan Pioneer and Historical Collections*, vol. 25, 1896.

"Correspondence Relating to the War of 1812," *Western Reserve Historical Society*, Tract no. 92.

[Clay, Henry.] *The Papers of Henry Clay*, vol. I, edited by James Hopkins. Lexington, Ky.: University of Kentucky Press, 1959.

Coyne, James H. (ed.). "The Talbot Papers," *Royal Society of Canada Transactions*, ser. 3, sect. 2, vols. I and III, 1909.

Crooks, James. "Recollections of the War of 1812," *Women's Canadian Historical Society of Toronto*, Transaction no. 13 (1913/14).

Cruikshank, E.A. (ed.). "Campaigns of 1812–14: Contemporary Narratives . . . ," *Niagara Historical Society Publications*, no. 9 (1902).

—— (ed.). *The Documentary History of the Campaign upon the Niagara Frontier 1812–1814.* 9 vols. Welland: Lundy's Lane Historical Society, 1902–1908.

—— (ed.). *Documents Relating to the Invasion of Canada and the Surrender of Detroit,* Canadian Archives Publications, no. 7. Ottawa: Government Printing Bureau, 1912.

—— (ed.). "Letters of 1812 from the Dominion Archives," *Niagara Historical Society Publications,* no. 23 (n.d.).

—— (ed.). "Some Unpublished Letters of General Brock," *Ontario Historical Society Papers and Records,* vol. 13 (1915).

Darnell, Elias. *A Journal Containing an Accurate and Interesting Account of the Hardships . . . of . . . Kentucky Volunteers and Regulars Commanded by General Winchester in the Years 1812–1813. . . .* Philadelphia: Lippincott, Grambo, 1854.

Dobbins, Daniel and Dobbins, William. "The Dobbins Papers," *Buffalo Historical Society Publications,* vol. 8 (1905).

Douglas, John. *Medical Topography of Upper Canada.* London: Burgess and Hill, 1819.

Dudley, Thomas. "Battle and Massacre at Frenchtown, Michigan, January 1813," *Western Reserve Historical Society,* Tract no. 1, 1870.

Edgar, Matilda. *Ten Years of Upper Canada in Peace and War, 1805–1815; Being the Ridout Letters. . . .* Toronto: W. Briggs, 1890.

Foster, Vere (ed.). *The Two Duchesses.* London: Blackie, 1898.

[Harrison, William Henry.] *Messages and Letters,* 2 vols., edited by Logan Esarey. Indiana Historical Collections, vols. 8 and 9. Indianapolis: Indiana Historical Commission, 1922.

Grignon, Augustin. "Seventy-two Years' Recollections of Wisconsin," *State Historical Society of Wisconsin Collections,* vol. 3 (1856).

Hatch, William S. *A Chapter in the History of the War of 1812 in the Northwest. . . .* Cincinnati: Miami Printing & Publishing, 1872.

Heriot, George. *Travels through the Canadas. . . .* London: Richard Phillips, 1807; reprinted, Toronto: Coles, 1971.

Hull, William. *Memoirs of the Campaign of the North Western Army of the United States, A.D. 1812. . . .* Boston: True and Greene, 1824.

[Hull, William.] *Report of the Trial of Brigadier-General William Hull* . . . New York: Eastburn, Kirk, 1814.

[Jefferson, Thomas.] *The Writings of Thomas Jefferson,* vols. IV and VI, edited by H.A. Washington. New York: Riker, Thorrie, 1854.

Kingston Gazette, 1812.

[Kinzie, John.] "John Kinzie's Narrative of the Fort Dearborn Massacre," edited by Mentor L. Williams, *Journal of the Illinois State Historical Society,* vol. 46 (1953).

Klinck, Carl F. (ed.). *Tecumseh: Fact and Fiction in Early Records.* Englewood Cliffs, N.J.: Prentice-Hall, 1961.

Lajeunesse, Ernest J. (ed.). *The Windsor Border Region.* Toronto: University of Toronto Press, 1960.

[Larrabee, Charles.] "Lt. Charles Larrabee's Account of the Battle of Tippecanoe," edited by Florence G. Watts, *Indiana Magazine of History,* vol. 57 (1961).

Loyal and Patriotic Society of Upper Canada. *The Report of the . . . Society . . . with an Appendix, and a List of Subscribers and Benefactors.* Montreal: W. Gray, 1817.

[Lucas, Robert.] *The Robert Lucas Journal of the War of 1812 during the Campaign under General William Hull,* edited by John C. Parish. Iowa City: Iowa State Historical Society, 1906.

Mann, James. *Medical Sketches of the Campaigns of 1812, 13, 14.* Dedham, Mass., 1816.

Melish, John. *Travels through the United States of America. . . .* Philadelphia: T. & G. Palmer, 1812.

Montreal Herald, 1812.

Niles Weekly Register, 1811-12.

[Northcutt, William B.] "War of 1812 Diary of William B. Northcutt," edited by G. Glenn Clift, *Register of the Kentucky Historical Society,* April, 1958.

[Norton, John.] *The Journal of Major John Norton,* edited by Carl Klinck and James J. Talman. Toronto: Champlain Society, 1970.

Palmer, T.H. (ed.). *The Historical Register of the United States,* 4 vols., vol. 1. Philadelphia: G. Palmer, 1814.

[Pike, Zebulon.] *The Journals of Zebulon Montgomery Pike,* edited by Donald Jackson. Norman, Okla.: University of Oklahoma Press, 1966.

[Powell, William.] "William Powell's Recollections," intro. by Lyman C. Draper, *State Historical Society of Wisconsin Proceedings,* 1912.

Quaife, Milo M. *Chicago and the Old Northwest 1673–1835, A Study of the Evolution of the Northwestern Frontier together with a History of Fort Dearborn.* Chicago: University of Chicago Press, 1913.

—— (ed.). *The John Askin Papers, 1796–1820,* 2 vols., vol. II. Detroit: Detroit Library Commission, 1931.

—— (ed.). *War on the Detroit: The Chronicles of Thomas Verchères de Boucherville, and The Capitulation by an Ohio Volunteer.* Chicago: Lakeside Press, 1940.

Richardson, John. *Eight Years in Canada.* Montreal: H.H. Cunningham, 1847.

[Richardson, John.] *Richardson's War of 1812* . . . , edited by Alexander C. Cassel-man. Toronto: Historical Publishing, 1902.

[Richardson, John.] *The Letters Veritas* . . . Montreal: W. Gray, 1815.

Roach, Isaac. "Journal of Major Isaac Roach, 1812–1824," *Pennsylvania Magazine of History and Biography,* vol. 17 (1893).

Schultz, Christian. *Travels on an Inland Voyage through the States* . . . New York: I. Riley, 1810.

Scott, Winfield. *Memoirs of Lieut.-General Scott, Written by Himself,* 2 vols., vol. I. New York: Sheldon, 1864.

Severance, Frank H. "The Case of Brig.-Gen. Alexander Smyth, As Shown by His Own Writings . . . ," *Buffalo Historical Society Publications,* vol. 18 (1914).

[Sheaffe, Roger Hale.] "Documents Relating to the War of 1812: the Letter-book of Gen. Sir Roger Hale Sheaffe," *Buffalo Historical Society Publications,* vol. 17 (1913).

Smith, Michael. *A Geographical View of the Province of Upper Canada* . . . , 3rd. ed. rev. Trenton, N.J.: Moore & Lake, 1813.

Stubbs, Samuel. *A Compendious Account of the Late War, to Which Is Added, The Curious Adventures of Corporal Samuel Stubbs.* . . . Boston: 1817; reprinted, *Magazine of History,* extra no. 152, 1929.

[Tompkins, Daniel D.] *Public Papers of Daniel D. Tompkins* . . . , 3 vols., edited by Hugh Hastings. Albany: J.B. Lyon, 1898–1902.

Tupper, Ferdinand Brock. *The Life and Correspondence of Major-General Sir Isaac Brock, K.B.* . . . , 2nd ed. rev. London: Simpkin, Marshall, 1847.

United States Congress. *American State Papers: Military Affairs, vol. I.* Washington: Gales and Seaton, 1832.

—— *American State Papers: Indian Affairs,* vol. I. Washington: Gales and Seaton, 1832.

—— *American State Papers: Foreign Relations,* vol. 3. Washington: Gales and Seaton, 1832.

United States Congress, House of Representatives. Barbarities of the Enemy Exposed in a Report. . . . Troy, N.Y.: Francis Adancourt, 1813.

Van Horne, James. *Narrative of the Captivity and Sufferings of James Van Horne*. Middlebury, Conn.: 1817.

Van Rensselaer, Solomon. *A Narrative of the Affair of Queenstown, in the War of 1812*. New York: Leavitt, Lord, 1836.

Verchères de Boucherville, Thomas, *see* Quaife, Milo M., *War on the Detroit*.

Walker, Adam. *A Journal of Two Campaigns of the 4th Regiment of U.S. Infantry. . . .* Keene, N.H.: Sentinal Press, 1816.

Weld, Isaac. *Travels through the States of North America and the Provinces of Upper and Lower Canada during the Years 1795, 1796 and 1797*, 3rd. ed. London: 1800.

Whickar, J. Wesley (ed.). "Shabonee's Account of Tippecanoe," *Indiana Magazine of History*, vol. 17 (1921).

Williams, Samuel. "Expedition of Captain Henry Brush with Supplies for General Hull 1812," *Ohio Valley Historical Series*, no. 2 (1870).

[Winchester, James.] *Historical Details Having Relation to the Campaign of the North-Western Army under Generals Harrison and Winchester. . . .* Lexington, Ky.: Worsley and Smith, 1818.

Winchester, James. "Papers and Orderly Book of Brigadier General James Winchester," *Michigan Pioneer and Historical Society Collections*, vol. 31 (1902).

Witherell, B.F. "Reminiscences of the North-west," *State Historical Society of Wisconsin Collections*, vol. 3 (1856).

Wood, William C.H. (ed.). *Select British Documents of the Canadian War of 1812*, Champlain Society, vols. 13–15, 17. Toronto: The Society, 1920–28.

York [Upper Canada] *Gazette*, 1811–12.

SECONDARY SOURCES

Adams, Henry. *A History of the United States of America during the Administrations of Thomas Jefferson and James Madison*. New York: Charles Scribner's Sons, 1889–91.

Allen, Robert S. "The British Indian Department and the Frontier in North America, 1755–1830," *Canadian Historic Sites: Occasional Papers in Archeology and History*, no. 14 (1975).

Babcock, Louis L. *The War of 1812 on the Niagara Frontier*. Buffalo: Buffalo Historical Society, 1927.

Bailey, John R. *Mackinac, Formerly Michilimackinac*. Lansing, Mich.: 1895.

Bayles, G.H. "Tecumseh and the Bayles Family Tradition," *Register of the Kentucky Historical Society*, October, 1948.

Bayliss, Joseph and Estelle. *Historic St. Joseph Island*. Cedar Rapids, Ia.: Torch Press, 1938.

Beal, Vernon L. "John McDonnell and the Ransoming of American Captives after the River Raisin Massacre", *Michigan History*, vol. 35 (1951).

Beard, Reed. *The Battle of Tippccanoc*, 4th ed. Chicago: Hammond Press, 1911.

Beasley, David R. *The Canadian Don Quixote: The Life and Works of Major John Richardson, Canada's First Novelist*. Erin, Ont.: Porcupine's Quill, 1977

Beirne, Francis F. *The War of 1812*. New York: Dutton, 1949.

Berger, Carl. *The Sense of Power: Studies in the Ideas of Canadian Imperialism, 1867–1914*. Toronto: University of Toronto Press, 1970.

Bishop, Levi. "The Battle of Brownstown," *Michigan Pioneer and Historical Collections*, vol. 6 (1884).

—— "The Battle of Monguagon," *Michigan Pioneer and Historical Collections*, vol. 6 (1884).

Botsford, David P. "The History of Bois Blanc Island," *Ontario Historical Society Papers and Records*, vol. 47 (1955).

Brett-James, Anthony. *Life in Wellington's Army*. London: Allen and Unwin, 1972.

Brown, Roger Hamilton. *The Republic in Peril: 1812*. New York: Columbia University Press, 1964.

Burt, Alfred L. *The United States, Great Britain, and British North America from the Revolution to the Establishment of Peace after the War of 1812*. New Haven: Yale University Press, 1940.

Caffrey, Kate. *The Twilight's Last Gleaming: The British against America, 1812–1815*. New York: Stein and Day, 1977.

Calder-Marshall, Arthur. *The Two Duchesses*. London: Hutchinson, 1978.

Campbell, Maria. *Revolutionary Services and Civil Life of General William Hull*... New York: D. Appleton, 1848.

Carnochan, Janet. "Sir Isaac Brock," *Niagara Historical Society Publications*, no. 15 (1907)

Chalou, George C. "The Red Pawns Go to War: British-American Indian Relations, 1810–1815." Ph.D. dissertation, University of Indiana, 1971.

Clark, Jerry E. *The Shawnee*. Lexington, Ky.: University Press of Kentucky, 1978.

Clark, S.D. *The Social Development of Canada: An Introductory Study with Select Documents*. Toronto: University of Toronto Press, 1942.

Clarke, James F. "History of the Campaign of 1812, and Surrender of the Post of Detroit," in Maria Campbell, *Revolutionary Services and Civil Life of General William Hull.* ... New York: D. Appleton, 1848.

Cleary, Francis. "Defence of Essex during the War of 1812," *Ontario Historical Society Papers and Records*, vol. 10 (1913).

Cleaves, Freeman. *Old Tippecanoe: William Henry Harrison and His Time.* New York: Charles Scribner's Sons, 1939; reprinted, New York: Kennikat Press, 1969.

Clift, G. Glenn. *Remember the Raisin! Kentucky and Kentuckians in the Battles and Massacre at Frenchtown, Michigan Territory.* Frankfort, Ky.: Kentucky Historical Society, 1961.

Coffin, William F. *1812: The War, and Its Moral: A Canadian Chronicle.* Montreal: J. Lovell, 1864.

Coleman, Christopher. "The Ohio Valley in the Preliminaries of the War of 1812," *Mississippi Valley Historical Review*, vol. 7 (1920).

Coles, Harry L. *The War of 1812.* Chicago: University of Chicago Press, 1965.

Cook, Samuel F. *Mackinaw in History.* Lansing, Mich.: R. Smith, 1895.

Craick, W.A. "The Story of Brock's Monument," unpublished manuscript, Baldwin Room, Metropolitan Toronto Public Library.

Craig, G.M. *Upper Canada: The Formative Years, 1784–1841.* Toronto: McClelland and Stewart, 1963.

Cramer, C.H. "Duncan McArthur: The Military Phase," *Ohio State Archeologi-cal and Historical Quarterly*, vol. 46 (1937).

Cruikshank, E.A. *The Battle of Queenston Heights*, 3rd ed. rev. Welland: Tribune, 1904.

—— "The 'Chesapeake' Crisis As It Affected Upper Canada," *Ontario Historical Society Papers and Records*, vol. 24 (1927).

—— "The Contest for the Command of Lake Erie in 1812–13," *Royal Canadian Institute Transactions*, vol. 6 (1899).

—— "The Contest for the Command of Lake Ontario in 1812 and 1813," *Royal Society of Canada Transactions*, ser. 3, sect. 2, vol. 10 (1916).

—— "From Isle aux Noix to Chateauguay," *Royal Society of Canada Transactions*, ser. 3, sect. 2, vol. 7 (1913).

—— "Harrison and Procter: the River Raisin," *Royal Society of Canada Transactions*, ser. 3, sect. 2, vol. 4 (1910).

—— "General Hull's Invasion of Canada in 1812," *Royal Society of Canada Transactions*, ser. 3, sect. 2, vol. 1 (1907).

—— *The Political Adventures of John Henry.* Toronto: Macmillan, 1936.

—— "Robert Dickson, the Indian Trader," *State Historical Society of Wisconsin Collections*, vol. 12 (1892).

Currie, J.G. "The Battle of Queenston Heights," *Niagara Historical Society Publications*, no.4 (1898).

Dawson, Moses. *A Historical Narrative of the Civil and Military Services of Major-General William H. Harrison* . . . Cincinnati, 1824.

Dewitt, John H. "General James Winchester, 1752–1826," *Tennessee Historical Magazine*, vol. 1 (1915).

Dictionary of American Biography, 22 vols. New York: Charles Scribner's Sons, 1928–58.

Dictionary of Canadian Biography, vol. IX: 1861–70. Toronto: University of Toronto Press, 1976.

Dictionary of National Biography, 22 vols. Oxford: Oxford University Press, 1885–1900.

Douglas, R. Alan. "Weapons of the War of 1812," *Michigan History*, vol. 47 (1963).

Drake, Benjamin. *Life of Tecumseh and of His Brother the Prophet, with a Historical Sketch of the Shawanoe Indians*. Cincinnati: E. Morgan, 1841.

Dunn, C. Frank. "Captain Nathaniel G.S. Hart," *Filson Club Quarterly*, vol. 24 (1950).

Eaton, Clement. *Henry Clay and the Art of American Politics*. Boston: Little, Brown, 1957.

Edgar, Matilda. *General Brock*. Toronto: Morang, 1904.

Egan, Clifford L. "The Origins of the War of 1812: Three Decades of Historical Writing," *Military Affairs*, vol. 38 (1974).

Elliott, Charles W. *Winfield Scott: The Soldier and the Man*. New York: Macmillan, 1937.

Ermatinger, Charles O. *The Talbot Regime, or, The First Half Century of the Talbot Settlement*. St. Thomas: Municipal World, 1904.

Erney, Richard A. "The Public Life of Henry Dearborn." Ph.D. dissertation, Columbia University, 1957.

Farmer, Silas. *The History of Detroit and Michigan*. . . . Detroit: Silas Farmer, 1884.

Farr, Finis. *Chicago: A Personal History of America's Most American City*. New York: Arlington House, 1973.

Forester, C.S. *The Age of Fighting Sail: The Story of the Naval War of 1812*. Garden City, N.Y.: Doubleday, 1956.

Fortescue, Sir John W. *A History of the British Army*, 13 vols., vol. VIII. London: Macmillan, 1917.

Gilpin, Alec. *The War of 1812 in the Old Northwest*. Toronto: Ryerson Press; East Lansing, Mich.: Michigan State University Press, 1958.

Glover, Richard. *Peninsula Preparation: The Reform of the British Army, 1795–1809*. Cambridge: Cambridge University Press, 1963.

Goltz, Charles H. "Tecumseh and the Northwest Indian Confederacy." Ph.D. dissertation, University of Western Ontario, 1973.

Goodman, Warren H. "The Origins of the War of 1812: A Survey of Changing Interpretations," *Mississippi Valley Historical Review*, vol. 28 (1941).

Green, Constance McLaughlin. *Washington*, vol. 1, *Village and Capital, 1800–1878*. Princeton: Princeton University Press, 1962.

Green, Thomas Marshall. *Historic Families of Kentucky* . . . Cincinnati: Robert Clarke, 1889.

Gurd, Norman S. *The Story of Tecumseh*. Toronto: W. Briggs, 1912.

Hacker, Louis M. "Western Land Hunger and the War of 1812 . . . ," *Mississippi Valley Historical Review*, vol. 10 (1924).

Hall, Ellery L. "Canadian Annexation Sentiment in Kentucky Prior to the War of 1812," *Register of the Kentucky Historical Society*, October, 1930.

Hamil, Fred Coyne. *Lake Erie Baron*. Toronto: Macmillan, 1955.

Hammack, James W., Jr. *Kentucky and the Second American Revolution: The War of 1812*. Lexington, Ky.: University of Kentucky Press, 1976.

Hare, John S. "Military Punishments in the War of 1812," *Journal of the American Military Institute*, vol. 4 (1940).

Hatzenbuehler, Ronald L. "The War Hawks and the Question of Congressional Leadership in 1812," *Pacific Historical Review*, vol. 45 (1976).

——"Party Unity and the Decision for War in the House of Representatives, 1812," *William and Mary Quarterly*, 3rd ser., vol. 29 (1972).

Havighurst, Walter. *Three Flags at the Straits: The Forts of Mackinac*. Englewood Cliffs, N.J.: Prentice-Hall, 1966.

Heaton, Herbert. "Non-importation, 1806–1812," *Journal of Economic History*, vol. 1 (1941).

Higginson, T.B. (ed.). *Major Richardson's Major General Sir Isaac Brock and the 41st Regiment*. Burks Falls: Old Rectory Press, 1976.

History of Pike County, Missouri. Des Moines, Ia.: Mills & Co., 1883.

Hitsman, J. Mackay. *The Incredible War of 1812: A Military History*. Toronto: University of Toronto Press, 1965.

—— "Sir George Prevost's Conduct of the Canadian War of 1812," *Canadian Historical Association Report*, 1962.

—— "Spying at Sackets Harbor, 1813," *Inland Seas*, vol. 15 (1959).

Hodge, Frederick W. (ed.). *Handbook of American Indians North of Mexico*, 2 vols. Washington: Smithsonian Institution, Bureau of American

Ethnology, Bulletin no. 30, 1906; reprinted, New York: Pageant Books, 1959.

Horsman, Reginald. "British Indian Policy in the Northwest, 1807–1812," *Mississippi Valley Historical Review*, vol. 45 (1958).

——— *The Causes of the War of 1812*. Philadelphia: University of Pennsylvania Press, 1962.

——— *Expansion and American Indian Policy, 1783–1812*. East Lansing, Mich.: Michigan State University Press, 1967.

——— *Matthew Elliott, British Indian Agent*. Detroit: Wayne State University Press, 1964.

——— *The War of 1812*. New York: Knopf, 1969.

——— "Western War Aims, 1811–12," *Indiana Magazine of History*, vol. 53 (1957).

Irving, L. Homfray. *Officers of the British Forces in Canada during the War of 1812–15*. Welland: Tribune Print, for Canadian Military Institute, 1908.

Irwin, Ray. *Daniel D. Tompkins: Governor of New York and Vice President of the United States*. New York: New York Historical Society, 1968.

Jacobs, James R. *The Beginning of the US. Army, 1783–1812*. Princeton: Princeton University Press, 1947.

James, William. *A Full and Correct Account of the Military Occurrences of the Late War between Great Britain and the United States of America*, vol. 1, London, 1818.

"Jo Daviess of Kentucky," *Harper's New Monthly Magazine*, vol. 21, August, 1860.

Johnston, C.M. "William Claus and John Norton: A Struggle for Power in Old Ontario," *Ontario History*, vol. 57 (1965).

Jones, Robert Leslie. *A History of Agriculture in Ontario, 1613–1880*. Toronto: University of Toronto Press, 1946.

Keegan, John. *The Face of Battle*. London: Jonathan Cape, 1976.

Kellogg, Louise P. "The Capture of Mackinac in 1812," *State Historical Society of Wisconsin Proceedings*, 1912.

Kelton, Dwight H. *Annals of Fort Mackinac*. Detroit: Detroit Free Press, 1888.

Ketchum, William. *An Authentic and Comprehensive History of Buffalo*. vol. II. Buffalo: Rockwell, Baker & Hill, 1864–65.

Kirby, William. *Annals of Niagara*. Welland: Lundy's Lane Historical Society Publications, 1896.

Kirkland, Joseph. *The Story of Chicago*. Chicago: Dibble, 1892.

Koke, Richard J. "The Britons Who Fought on the Canadian Frontier: Uniforms of the War of 1812," *New York Historical Society Quarterly*, vol. 45 (1961).

Kosche, Ludwig. "Relics of Brock: An Investigation," *Archivaria*, no. 9, Winter 1979–80.

Lamb, W. Kaye. *The Hero of Upper Canada*. Toronto: Rous and Mann, 1962.

Lossing, Benson J. *The Pictorial Field-book of the War of 1812 . . .* New York: Harper and Brothers, 1868.

—— "Hull's Surrender of Detroit," *Potter's American Monthly*, August, 1875.

Lower, Arthur R.M. *Canadians in the Making: A Social History of Canada*. Toronto: Longmans, Green, 1958.

Lucas, Sir Charles P. *The Canadian War of 1812*. Oxford: Clarendon Press, 1906.

McAfee, Robert. *History of the Late War in the Western Country. . . .* Lexington, Ky.: Worsley and Smith, 1816.

Macmillan Dictionary of Canadian Biography, 4th ed., edited by W. Stewart Wallace and W.A. McKay. Toronto: Macmillan, 1978.

Mahan, Alfred T. *Sea Power in Its Relations to the War of 1812*, 2 vols., vol. 1. Boston: Little, Brown, 1905.

Mahon, John K. *The War of 1812*. Gainesville: University of Florida Press, 1972.

Marshall, Humphrey. *The History of Kentucky . . .* Frankfort, Ky.: G.S. Robinson, 1824.

Mason, Philip P. (ed.). *After Tippecanoe: Some Aspects of the War of 1812*. Toronto: Ryerson; East Lansing, Mich.: Michigan State University Press, 1963.

May, George S. *War 1812*. [Lansing?]: Mackinac Island State Park Commission, 1962.

Mayo, Bernard. *Henry Clay, Spokesman of the New West*. Boston: Houghton Mifflin, 1937.

Morgan, Henry J. *Sketches of Celebrated Canadians. . . .* Quebec: Hunter, Rose, 1862.

Morison, Samuel Eliot. *By Land and Sea*. New York: Knopf, 1954.

Muller, H.N. "A Traitorous and Diabolic Traffic': The Commerce of the Champlain-Richelieu Corridor during the War of 1812," *Vermont History*, vol. 44 (1976).

—— "Smuggling into Canada: How the Champlain Valley Defied Jefferson's Embargo," *Vermont History*, vol. 38 (1970).

Murray, John M. "John Norton," *Ontario Historical Society Papers and Records*, vol. 37 (1945).

Naylor, Isaac. "The Battle of Tippecanoe," *Indiana Magazine of History*, vol. 2 (1906).

Nursey, Walter R. *The Story of Sir Isaac Brock*, 4th ed. rev. Toronto: McClelland and Stewart, 1923.

Oman, Sir Charles. *Wellington's Army, 1809–1814*. London: Edward and Arnold, 1913.

Pearkes, G.R. "Detroit and Miami," *Canadian Defence Quarterly*, vol. 11 (1934).

Perkins, Bradford. *Castlereagh and Adams: England and the United States, 1812–1823*. Berkeley: University of California Press, 1964.

—— *Prologue to War: England and the United States, 1805–1812*. Berkeley: University of California Press, 1961.

Petersen, Eugene T. *Mackinac Island: Its History in Pictures*. Mackinac Island, Mich.: Mackinac Island State Park Commission, 1973.

Pirtle, Alfred. *The Battle of Tippecanoe*. Louisville: J.P. Morton, 1900.

Porter, Kenneth W. *John Jacob Astor, Businessman*. Cambridge, Mass.: Harvard University Press, 1931.

Pratt, Julius. *Expansionists of 1812*. New York: Macmillan, 1925.

—— "Western Aims in the War of 1812," *Mississippi Valley Historical Review*, vol. 12 (1925).

Quaife, Milo M. "The Story of Brownstown," *Burton Historical Collection Leaflets*, vol. 4 (1926).

Randall, E.O. "Tecumseh the Shawnee Chief," *Ohio Archeological and Historical Society Publications*, vol. 15 (1906).

Read, David B. *Life and Times of Major-General Sir Isaac Brock, K B.* Toronto: W. Briggs, 1894.

Redway, Jacques W. "General Van Rensselaer and the Niagara Frontier," *New York State Historical Association Proceedings*, vol.8 (1909).

Richardson, John. *Wau-nan-gee, or the Massacre at Chicago*. New York: H. Long, 1852.

Risjord, Norman K. "1812: Conservatives, War Hawks and the Nation's Honor," *William and Mary Quarterly*, 3rd ser., vol. 18 (1961).

Robinson, Sir Charles W. *Life of Sir John Beverley Robinson, Bart., C.B., D.C.L. . . .* Toronto: Morang, 1904.

Ryerson, Adolphus Egerton. *The Loyalists of America and Their Times, from 1620 to 1816*, 2 vols., 2nd ed. Toronto: W. Briggs, 1880.

Sapio, Victor A. *Pennsylvania and the War of 1812*. Lexington, Ky.: University Press of Kentucky, 1970.

Shortt, Adam. "The Economic Effect of the War of 1812 on Upper Canada," *Ontario Historical Society Papers and Records*, vol. 10 (1913).

—— "Life of the Settler in Western Canada before the War of 1812," Dept. of History and Political and Economic Science, Queen's University, *Bulletin*, no. 12 (1914).

Slocum, Charles E. "The Origin, Description and Service of Fort Winchester," *Ohio Archeological and Historical Society Publications*, vol. 9 (1901).

Smelser, Marshall. "Tecumseh, Harrison and the War of 1812," *Indiana Magazine of History*, vol. 65 (1969).

Stagg, J.C.A. "James Madison and the Malcontents: The Political Origins of the War of 1812," *William and Mary Quarterly*, 3rd ser., vol. 33 (1976).

Stanley, George F.G. "The Indians in the War of 1812," *Canadian Historical Review*, vol. 31 (1950).

—— "The Significance of the Six Nations Participation in the War of 1812," *Ontario History*, vol.55 (1963).

Steel, Anthony. "More Light on the Chesapeake," *Mariner's Mirror*, vol. 39 (1953).

Taylor, George R. "Agrarian Discontent in the Mississippi Valley Preceding the War of 1812," *Journal of Political Economy*, vol. 39 (1931).

—— "Prices in the Mississippi Valley Preceding the War of 1812," *Journal of Economic and Business History*, vol. 3 (1930).

Tohill, Louis A. "Robert Dickson, Fur Trader on the Upper Mississippi," *North Dakota Historical Quarterly*, vol. 3 (1928).

Tucker, Glenn. *Poltroons and Patriots: A Popular Account of the War of 1812*, 2 vols., vol. 1. Indianapolis: Bobbs-Merrill, 1954.

—— *Tecumseh: Vision of Glory*. Indianapolis: Bobbs-Merrill, 1956.

Turner, Wesley B. "The Career of Isaac Brock in Canada." Ph.D. dissertation, University of Toronto, 1961.

Upton, Emory. *The Military Policy of the United States*. Washington: Government Printing Office, 1907.

Van Deusen, John G. "Court Martial of General William Hull," *Michigan History Magazine*, vol. 12 (1928).

—— "Detroit Campaign of General William Hull," *Michigan History Magazine*, vol. 12 (1928).

Vincent, Elizabeth. "Fort St. Joseph: A History." Unpublished manuscript, Parks Canada, Ottawa.

Walden, Keith. "Isaac Brock: Man and Myth; A Study of the Militia of the War of 1812 in Upper Canada." M.A. thesis, Carleton University, Ottawa, 1972.

Widder, Keith R. *Reveille till Taps: Soldier Life at Fort Mackinac, 1780–1895*. N.p.: Mackinac Island State Park Commission, 1972.

Wilkinson-Latham, Robert. *British Artillery on Land and Sea, 1790–1820*. Newton Abott: David and Charles, 1973.

Wilson, Bruce. "The Enterprises of Robert Hamilton." Ph.D. dissertation, University of Toronto, 1978.

Wilson, Samuel M. "Kentucky's Part in the War of 1812," *Register of the Kentucky Historical Society*, vol. 29.

Wiltse, Charles. *John C. Calhoun, Nationalist*. Indianapolis: Bobbs-Merrill, 1944.

Wise, S.F. and Brown, R. Craig. *Canada Views the United States: Nineteenth Century Political Attitudes*. Toronto: Macmillan, 1967.

Woodford, Frank B. *Lewis Cass, the Last Jeffersonian*. 1950. Reprinted New York: Octagon Books, 1973.

Young, James S. *The Washington Community, 1800–1828*. New York: Columbia University Press, 1966.

Zaslow, Morris and Turner, Wesley B. (eds.). *The Defended Border: Upper Canada and the War of 1812*. Toronto: Macmillan, 1964.

FLAMES ACROSS THE BORDER

1813-1814

Flames Across the Border, 1813-1814

	Maps	*381*
	Cast of Characters	*383*
PREVIEW	**New Brunswick Goes to War**	389
OVERVIEW	**The All-Canadian War**	394
ONE	**The Capture of Little York** April 26–May 2, 1813	405
TWO	**Stalemate on the Niagara Peninsula** May 27–August 1, 1813	434
THREE	*The Northwest Campaign: 1* **The Siege of Fort Meigs** April 12–May 8, 1813	474
FOUR	*The Northwest Campaign: 2* **The Contest for Lake Erie** June–September, 1813	503
FIVE	*The Northwest Campaign: 3* **Retreat on the Thames** September 14–October 5, 1813	553
SIX	**The Assault on Montreal** October 4–November 12, 1813	590

SEVEN   **The Niagara in Flames**   627
November–December, 1813

EIGHT   **Marking Time**   653
January–June, 1814

NINE   **The Struggle for the Fur Country**   686
May–September, 1814

TEN   **The Last Invasion**   701
July–November, 1814

ELEVEN   **The Burning of Washington**   750
August, 1814

TWELVE   **The Battle of Lake Champlain**   764
September, 1814

THIRTEEN   **Ghent**   790
August–December, 1814

AFTERVIEW   **The Legacy**   810

Aftermath   *817*
Author's Note and Acknowledgements   *824*
Notes   *827*
Select Bibliography   *865*
Index   *896*

Maps

Drawn by Geoffrey Matthews

The Theatre of War, 1813-1814	392–3
Changing U.S. Strategy, Winter, 1813	404
The Capture of Little York	416–7
The Capture of Fort George	437
The Niagara Peninsula, 1813	443
The Battle of Stoney Creek	448
The Battle of Beaver Dams	459
The Northwest Frontier	476
The Battle of Fort Meigs	491
Action on Lake Erie, Summer, 1813	506
Presque Isle	508
The Battle of Lake Erie: 12:15 p.m.	536
The Battle of Lake Erie: 2:40 p.m.	545
The Battle of Lake Erie: 3:00 p.m.	547
Procter Withdraws	561
Retreat Up the Thames, September 27–October 5, 1813	563
The Battle of the Thames	579
Lake Ontario, October, 1813	591
Wade Hampton's Movements, September–October, 1813	595
The Battle of Châteauguay: Phase 1	604
The Battle of Châteauguay: Phase 2	607

Wilkinson Moves on Montreal,   612–13
    October 31–November 11, 1813

The Battle of Crysler's Farm: Phase 1   618

The Battle of Crysler's Farm: Phase 2   621

British Infantry Tactics at Crysler's Farm   622

The Niagara Frontier, December, 1813   629

Lake Huron, Summer, 1814   698

The Battle of Chippawa   708

The Battle of Lundy's Lane: Phase 1   721

The Battle of Lundy's Lane: Phase 2   725

The Siege of Fort Erie   738

The British March on Washington, August 19–24, 1814   753

Lake Champlain, 1814   765

Macdonough at Anchor, Plattsburgh Bay, September, 1814   769

The Battle of Lake Champlain   782

Plattsburgh, September 11, 1814   787

382
—

Cast of Characters

On the British–Canadian side

William Adams, Admiralty lawyer; commissioner at Ghent peace talks, 1814.

William Allan, York merchant; Major, 3rd Regiment, York Militia.

Robert Heriot Barclay, Commandant, British naval forces, Lake Erie, 1813.

Lord Bathurst, Secretary for War and the Colonies.

Cecil Bisshopp, Lieutenant-Colonel; Inspecting Field Officer of Militia, Upper Canada; led attack on Black Rock, 1813.

Shadrach Byfield, Private, Light Company, 1st Battalion, 41st Regiment.

Viscount Castlereagh, Foreign Secretary

George Cockburn, Rear-Admiral; second-in-command, British fleet off American east coast.

Francis De Rottenburg, Major-General; Commander-in-Chief and Administrator, Upper Canada, 1813, succeeding Major-General Roger Sheaffe.

Charles-Michel de Salaberry, Lieutenant-Colonel, Canadian Voltigeurs.

Robert Dickson, fur trader; Assistant Superintendent of Indian Affairs, Michigan Territory, 1813–15.

George Downie, Commandant, British naval forces, Lake Champlain, 1814.

Gordon Drummond, Lieutenant-General; Commander-in-Chief and Administrator, Upper Canada, 1814, succeeding Francis De Rottenburg.

Dominique Ducharme, Captain, Indian Department.

Matthew Elliott, Superintendent, Indian Department, Amherstburg.

James FitzGibbon, Captain, 49th Regiment.

James Gambier, Rear-Admiral; British commissioner at Ghent peace
talks, 1814.

Henry Goulburn, British politician; commissioner at Ghent peace talks,
1814.

George Gleig, Lieutenant, 85th Regiment, attack on Washington, 1814.

John Harvey, Lieutenant-Colonel; deputy adjutant-general, British
forces in Canada.

Lord Liverpool, Prime Minister, 1812-27.

George Macdonell, Lieutenant-Colonel, 2nd Battalion, Select Embodied
Militia.

Robert McDouall, Lieutenant-Colonel, Royal Newfoundland
Regiment; aide to Sir George Prevost, 1813; commander at
Michilimackinac, 1814.

William Hamilton Merritt, Captain; commander, Provincial Dragoons.

Sir George Prevost, Governor General and Commander-in-Chief of His
Majesty's forces in Canada, the Atlantic Colonies, and Bermuda.

Henry Procter, Major-General; commander, Right Division, Detroit
frontier, 1813.

Phineas Riall, Major-General; commander, Right Division, Niagara
frontier, 1814.

John Richardson, gentleman volunteer, 1st Battalion, 41st Regiment.

John Beverley Robinson, Acting Attorney General, Upper Canada.

Robert Ross, Major-General; commander of army attacking
Washington, August, 1814.

Sir Roger Hale Sheaffe, Major-General; Commander-in-Chief and
Administrator, Upper Canada, October 1812–June 1813.

John Strachan, Anglican minister; chaplain of Fort York.

Tecumseh, Shawnee war chief; leader of the Indian confederacy.

John Vincent, Major-General; commander, Centre Division, Niagara
frontier, 1813.

James Lucas Yeo, Commodore; commander-in-chief, naval forces on the
Great Lakes.

John Quincy Adams, American ambassador to Russia; commissioner at
Ghent peace talks, 1814.

John Armstrong, Secretary of War, 1813–14.

James Bayard, Senator; commissioner at Ghent peace talks, 1814.

John Boyd, Brigadier-General; succeeded Morgan Lewis as commander
at Fort George, 1813; commanded at Battle of Crysler's Farm.

Jacob Brown, Major-General; commander on Niagara frontier, 1814,
succeeding James Wilkinson.

Cyrenius Chapin, Buffalo surgeon; commander of partisan irregulars,
Niagara frontier, 1813.

Isaac Chauncey, Commodore; commander of naval forces on the Great
Lakes.

Henry Clay, Speaker of the House; commissioner at Ghent peace talks, 1814.

George Croghan, Major, later Lieutenant-Colonel; commander at Fort
Stephenson, 1813; led attack on Michilimackinac, 1814.

Henry Dearborn, Major-General; commander of Army of the North to
July, 1813.

David Bates Douglass, 2nd-Lieutenant, artillery, Fort Erie.

Jesse Elliott, Lieutenant; second-in-command, naval forces, Lake Erie.

Edmund Gaines, Brigadier-General and Adjutant General; commander
at Fort Erie, summer, 1814.

Albert Gallatin, Secretary of the Treasury; commissioner at Ghent peace
talks, 1814.

William Henry Harrison, Major-General; former governor of Indiana
Territory; commander of the Army of the Northwest.

Wade Hampton, Major-General; commander of the army on Lake
Champlain, 1813.

Jarvis Hanks, drummer boy, 11th Infantry.

George Izard, Major-General; operated on Lake Champlain and
Niagara frontier, 1814.

Thomas Jesup, Major, 19th Infantry, at Chippawa and Lundy's Lane.

Richard Johnson, Congressman; Colonel, Kentucky regiment of
mounted rifles, Battle of the Thames, 1813.

Morgan Lewis, Major-General, Niagara frontier, succeeding Zebulon
    Pike as Dearborn's second-in-command to June 1813; second-in-
    command to James Wilkinson, autumn, 1813.

George McClure, Brigadier-General, New York Militia; commander at
    Fort George, late autumn, 1813.

Thomas Macdonough, Commodore, naval forces, Lake Champlain, 1814.

Alexander Macomb, Brigadier-General; commander of army at
    Plattsburgh, September, 1814.

James Madison, President, 1809–17.

Benajah Mallory, Major, Canadian Volunteers; former member Upper
    Canadian legislature; traitor. Succeeded Joseph Willcocks in
    command.

Abraham Markle, Major, Canadian Volunteers; former member Upper
    Canadian legislature; traitor.

James Monroe, Secretary of State, 1811–15. Replaced John Armstrong as
    Secretary of War, autumn, 1814.

Oliver Hazard Perry, Commodore, naval forces, Lake Erie, 1813.

Zebulon Montgomery Pike, Brigadier-General; second-in-command to
    Dearborn at York, 1813.

Peter Buell Porter, Congressman; Quartermaster General, later Major-
    General, New York Militia, Niagara frontier, 1813–14.

Eleazar Ripley, Brigadier-General under Jacob Brown, Niagara frontier,
    1814.

Jonathan Russell, American ambassador to Sweden; commissioner at
    Ghent peace talks, 1814.

Winfield Scott, Colonel and Adjutant-General, Niagara frontier, 1813;
    Brigadier-General under Jacob Brown, Niagara frontier, 1814.

Tobias Stansbury, Brigadier-General; commander of Maryland Militia,
    Bladensburg, August, 1814.

James Wilkinson, Major-General; commander, Army of the North, 1813,
    succeeding General Dearborn.

Joseph Willcocks, Lieutenant-Colonel, Canadian Volunteers; former
    member Upper Canadian legislature; traitor.

William Winder, Brigadier-General; captured at Stoney Creek, 1813;
    commander of Washington defences, 1814.

Eleazer Wood, Captain, Engineers, siege of Fort Meigs, 1813; Colonel and aide to Jacob Brown, Niagara frontier, 1814.

New Brunswick Goes to War

MADAWASKA RIVER, LOWER CANADA, MARCH 5, 1813

The cold has become unbearable. The temperature stands at twenty-seven below, Fahrenheit. A northeaster, sweeping down the frozen expanse of Lake Temiscouata, cuts like a scythe through the greatcoats of the soldiers, bent double in the teeth of the gale. The snow is frozen hard as sand. Only the squeak of the toboggans, the rasp of the snowshoes, and the whine of the wind breaks the white silence. It has been like this for the best part of a fortnight, ever since the regiment left Saint John, and it is growing worse.

The light company of the 104th—the New Brunswick Regiment—shuffles forward, single file, following the winding course of the Madawaska. This is the rearguard, the last of six companies, each spread out a day apart, trudging through the Canadian winter toward Lower Canada to help resist the next American invasion. In this silent, hostile forest there is no sign of settlement, no tinkle of sleighbells, no welcoming pillar of smoke— only the sullen pines, half crushed beneath their burden of snow. Even the birds are silent; it is too cold for song.

Lieutenant John Le Couteur gasps forward on his snowshoes, the wind cutting off his breath. In spite of layers of flannel and fur, the cold seems to reach to the very core of his body. He is temporarily in charge, for his captain has taken a party on ahead to prepare huts and firewood. Perhaps there will be shelter at the day's end, but Le Couteur remembers the previous evening when the men's hands were so numb they could scarcely work, let alone singe a piece of salt pork over a sputtering flame.

As he leads his squad around a bend in the river, he is alarmed to see that the forward elements have stopped, causing the centre and rear to bunch up. In this weather it is death to halt. He steps out of the line, flounders through the deep snow beside the track, and moves up the column, noting that every man he passes is rubbing snow into frostbitten cheeks. His own nose is frozen, but he cannot attend to that. He must get Private Reuben Rogers onto a toboggan and under a pile of blankets: the soldier's entire body is an ulcerated mass from frostbite, as if he had been plunged into a vat of boiling water. That done, he gets the column moving again.

It is slow going. Le Couteur knows that the men in the lead suffer most and must be replaced every four or five minutes if they are to survive. By the time the company reaches the huddle of huts, 90 men out of 105 are suffering from frostbite. The roughly constructed quarters are overcrowded—jammed with shivering troops because the company ahead has been forced back across the lake by the gale. That night Le Couteur finds it impossible to keep warm. One man who tries gets too close to the fire and burns his feet.

The next morning, both companies set off across the Grand Portage between Lake Temiscouata and Rivière du Loup (leaving poor Rogers behind with a corporal). They force their way through a spectral landscape—burned country, where the skeleton pines rise out of the twelve-foot drifts like ghosts. Here are weary hills to climb and dangerous, ice-sheathed slopes down which to manoeuvre runaway toboggans. Sleep that night is not possible, for a high wind turns the pine thatch on one hut to tinder dryness. When it catches fire, officers and men turn out, thigh deep in the snow, freezing their feet as they struggle to put out the flames.

After these adversities, all that follows is anticlimax. As the men trudge off, dragging their toboggans, Le Couteur realizes with a sense of relief that the wilderness is almost behind them. Presently he hears the music of distant sleighbells breaking the interminable silence. A horse and cutter appears, loaded with rum and provisions from the commissariat in Quebec. The village of St. André is not far off, and here the men from New Brunswick and Nova Scotia—sons of Loyalists and British soldiers—view for the first time the great sweep of the St. Lawrence. A road of beaten snow leads upriver to the capital; on this hard surface it is not difficult to march twenty miles in a day.

A fortnight later, the entire regiment is in Quebec City, basking in the praise of the Governor General. But the march is not over. Now the New Brunswickers set off for Montreal with Le Couteur pushing on ahead to report their speedy arrival to Major-General Francis De Rottenburg. Are the troops in good wind? the General asks. In excellent wind, replies the proud lieutenant. Then, says the General, they can push on another two hundred miles to Kingston.

"They think we are like the children of Israel," one of the soldiers cries when he hears that news. "We must march forty years before we halt!"

On they go, sweating now in the spring sun, wading to their hips in icy freshets, but never faltering until, on April 12, an extraordinary spectacle greets them. The town of Kingston lies before them and beyond, a familiar sight to any Maritimer: the masts and spars of tall ships.

"The sea! The sea!" the men cry out. "The ships! The ships!"

A flood of sensations overcomes Le Couteur: astonishment . . . delight . . . wonder. Here is an entire squadron of warships frozen on the bosom of the lake! He had not expected to find men-of-war so far inland.

The date is April 12. In just fifty-two days, close to six hundred troops have marched more than seven hundred miles, most of it on snowshoes, under the worst possible conditions without losing a man (for the frost-bitten Private Rogers is about to rejoin his company). This remarkable trek has helped to tip the scales of war. Directly across the lake, at Sackets Harbor, an American army, poised to invade Canada, waits for the ice to break. Its target was Kingston. But now, with reinforcements pouring in—their numbers blown out of all proportion by rumour—that target has been changed. The Americans will attack York instead. The lifeline that links the two Canadas will not be severed.

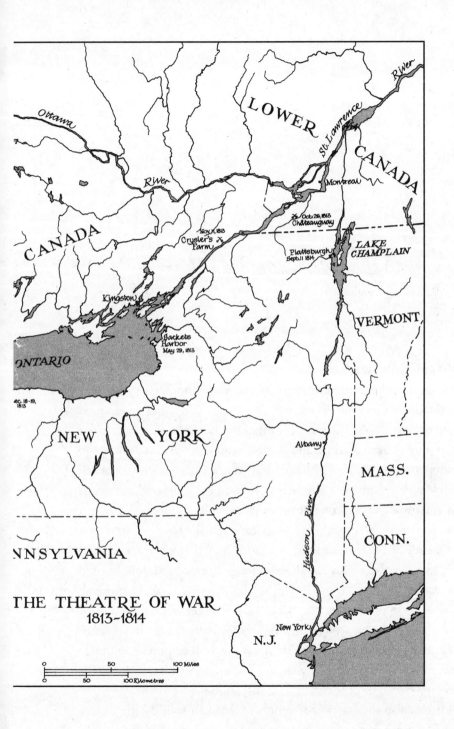

LOWER

CANADA

River

St. Lawrence

River

Ottawa

Montreal

CANADA

River

26 Oct.26,1813
Châteauguay

Nov.11,1813
Crysler's
Farm

Plattsburgh
Sept.11 1814

LAKE
CHAMPLAIN

Kingston

Sackets
Harbor
May 29, 1813

VERMONT

ONTARIO

ec.18-19,
1813

NEW   YORK

Albany

MASS.

CONN.

Hudson River

NNSYLVANIA

THE THEATRE OF WAR
1813–1814

New York

N.J.

0   50   100 Miles
0   50   100 Kilometres

The All-Canadian War

———

THE BORDER WAR OF 1812 was a singular conflict. Geography, climate, weather, language, and propinquity combined to make it distinctively Canadian. It was a seasonal war: campaigns were timed with one eye on the calendar, the other on the thermometer. It was a stop-and-go war: seeding and harvest often took priority over siege and attack. It was a neighbours' war (but no less vicious for that): men fought their own kin; others refused to fight; trade between enemies was frowned on but never successfully suppressed. It was a pinch-penny war: in 1813, the Americans actually tried to run it on a budget of $1,480,000 a month—a parsimony that greatly frustrated the campaign of that year. It was a long-distance war, fought on a thousand-mile front from the Upper Mississippi to Lake Champlain; yet the total number of combatants never exceeded the combined casualties in the greatest of the Napoleonic battles. Finally, it was an incendiary war in which private homes as well as public buildings and military fortifications went up in flames, fuelling a desire for revenge that transcended strategy and politics.

It was also the last war fought on Canadian soil. By the end of the first campaign in January, 1813, Canada had successfully resisted all attempts at invasion. As a result, the morale of the United States was at its lowest ebb. The government of James Madison, which had hurled its armies at the Canadian border to chastise Great Britain for her arrogance on the high seas, had learned that the conquest of British North America was not, after all, "a mere matter of marching."

Thomas Jefferson's thoughtless phrase left a sour taste in the mouths of those who had survived the triple disasters of Detroit, Queenston Heights, and Frenchtown. These prisoners of war were the only Americans left in Canada when the campaign begun in 1812 ended in massacre at Frenchtown in the wilderness of Michigan territory.

Three armies captured! Outbluffed in August by the British general Isaac Brock, the Americans at Detroit gave up without firing a shot, their commander doomed to face a court martial for cowardice. At Queenston, in October, Canada lost her hero-general but won a re-sounding victory when the New York militia refused to cross the river or hid in the underbrush waiting to surrender. And at Frenchtown, in January, on the frozen banks of the River Raisin, when the flower of Kentucky fell to the scalping knives of the Potawatomi, the rem-nants of another army were herded across the border to captivity.

Now it was too cold to fight, especially for those southerners who marched blithely north in their thin linsey-woolsey blouses, expecting to be home before the leaves deserted the maples. In Europe, the remnants of Napoleon's Grande Armée on its winter retreat from Moscow continued to skirmish with Cossack guer-rillas, but on the Canadian border the combatants simply sat it out. Except for Frenchtown, campaigns ended in December not to resume until spring.

In the defence of British North America, the weather was as important an ally as the Indians and the British regulars, who bore the brunt of the fighting. The invaders could not move until the ice left the lakes. A forward thrust late in the season could mean, if not disaster, at least stalemate. No American was prepared to sit out the winter on hostile ground in hastily built huts or thin tents.

Even on friendly soil, conditions were such that officers deserted their own troops.

This was a wilderness war, much of it fought in such isolation that the combatants had no idea of events in the outer world. On the western flank in the first months of 1813, the soldiers and fur traders who formed the militia would have had no clear picture of the war in Europe: the decimation of the Grande Armée in its retreat from Moscow; the defection of Prussia from the Napoleonic cause; the resurgence of an anti-French coalition, which was already signalling the downfall of Bonaparte. In wintertime, the news could take four months or longer to reach the captured bastion of Michilimackinac Island at the western end of Lake Huron.

There were further anomalies. The War of 1812 was not the only war in which both sides spoke the same language, but it was one of the few in which tens of thousands on both sides violently opposed it, sat it out, or maintained both friendly and commercial relations with the so-called enemy. The absence of a language barrier made desertion attractive, espionage easy, subterfuge possible. In the dark it was difficult to distinguish friend from foe. Spies and planted decoys crossed and re-crossed the border with information for opposing generals, some of it authentic, some of it intended to deceive.

The Atlantic provinces took little part in the war, having made a pact with their American neighbours to continue business as usual. The New England states, especially Vermont and Massachusetts, were so opposed to "Mr. Madison's war" that they refused to send troops or lend money to the government. In 1814, they even considered secession.

Thousands of state militia, especially those from New York and Pennsylvania, thought so little of the conflict that they stood on their constitutional rights and refused to cross the border at crucial moments during the campaign. America's Founding Fathers had never contemplated an offensive war; the state militia, in the law's strictest interpretation, could be used only in the defence of the Union.

In Upper Canada, where three out of five settlers were recent arrivals from the United States, there was at best apathy, at worst treason. The Loyalists, who made up a fifth of the population, were keen to fight, as were the sons of British immigrants, army officers, upper-class merchants, and civil servants. But the farmers, desperate to harvest their crops, scorned by the ruling elite, virtually disenfranchised by the colonial autocracy, felt no such compunction. Much of the despair felt at the beginning of the conflict had been wiped out by Brock's successes. But most yeomen (as they were officially called) simply wanted to be left alone.

If propinquity encouraged understanding, distance exaggerated differences. Kentucky was hawkish from the beginning, but by February, 1813, its zeal had turned to rage. Henry Procter, the victor at Frenchtown on the River Raisin, had recrossed the Detroit River hurriedly, expecting a counter-attack and leaving his wounded prisoners, Kentuckians all, to the savagery of his Indian allies. The resultant massacre brought the state to the boiling point. *"Remember the Raisin!"* became a recruiting cry. Few of the new soldiers, thirsting for revenge, knew what a Canadian looked like. Many lumped them with the Indians. As for the Canadians, they thought of Kentuckians as wild beasts.

Although President Madison had disavowed any territorial ambitions at the war's outset, most Kentuckians and not a few others saw the invasion of Canada as a war of conquest. That was not the war's original purpose. America only wanted to teach the British a lesson by attacking their North American colonies. The Napoleonic war had strained British-American relations to the breaking point. Determined to throttle Bonaparte, Great Britain thought nothing of enforcing her blockade of European ports by stopping and searching American ships in mid-ocean. Desperately short of seamen, she insisted that every man born an Englishman must serve as one. By impressing from U.S. ships any sailor she considered British—and at cannon point if necessary—she succeeded in enraging all Americans.

"Honour" was a word much used in 1812. The British were still treating the United States as a colony. The Americans, in honour, could not accept that. The British, in honour, could not back down. The War of 1812 was to be called, with some truth, the Second War of

Independence. Britain finally gave in on the matter of the blockade, but the news did not reach Washington before war was declared. By then it was too late; the war fever, once whipped up, would not subside. Madison announced that hostilities would continue as long as the British insisted on impressing seamen from American vessels. "Impressment" became a war cry. The Americans, Madison insisted, would *never* give in on impressment. Nor would Great Britain, mistress of the seas. Honour would not allow it.

Because the United States could not carry the war to the heart of Britain, she did the next best thing and attacked Canada. And so this war for maritime rights was fought mainly on land and on fresh water by men who were largely untrained and often reluctant, led by officers who were often incompetent and usually myopic.

As the campaign of 1813 approached, the American regular forces outnumbered the British seventeen thousand to seven thousand. This was illusory; many of the so-called regulars in the U.S. armies were untrained recruits. In addition, the British had an additional force of at least two thousand Indians at Detroit and on the Niagara frontier, the best and most constant under the command of the brilliant Shawnee war chief, Tecumseh. The Americans had not, as yet, used Indians in battle.

Both sides could also call upon large reserves of citizen soldiers— the militia, always an uncertain factor in battle. The American militia draftees and volunteers were generally called up for short terms—as little as sixty days, as much as a year. With the exception of the Kentuckians, most refused to continue in service beyond their designated term.

In Canada, the Sedentary Militia, largely untrained and incompetent, was available as an auxiliary arm in time of crisis. All fit males between eighteen and sixty were obliged to serve in it when circumstances required. The Incorporated Militia of Upper Canada consisted of volunteers serving for the duration and made up of young men attracted by patriotism, a sense of adventure, or the bounty of eight dollars paid to every man on enlistment. In Lower Canada, a similar body, the Select Embodied Militia, composed of men from eighteen to twenty-five, was drawn by lot to serve for a maximum of two years. These were paid and trained as regulars. There were, in addition, regular units recruited in Canada such as the Glengarry Light Infantry (or Fencibles) and the Provincial Corps of Light Infantry, better known as Canadian Voltigeurs. When properly trained, these men fought as bravely and as efficiently as the British regulars. At Châteauguay they stood off an entire American army, unaided.

At the senior levels, on both sides of the border, there was extraordinary incompetence. Many of the British regular officers were Wellington's cast-offs, who had reached their rank through the indefensible practice of purchasing promotion. In British military eyes, the Canadian war had a low priority. As a British Army surgeon, William "Tiger" Dunlop observed, "any man whom The Duke deemed unfit for the Peninsula was considered quite good enough for the Canadian market."

As for the American army, at the start of the war Winfield Scott, a future commanding general, remembered that "the old officers had, very generally, sunk into either sloth, ignorance, or habits of intemperate drinking." Regimental leaders were chosen for their political influence.

Federalists, who opposed the government, were excluded from command and "the selection from those communities consisted mostly of coarse and ignorant men," while in others, educated men were passed over in favour of "swaggerers, dependants, decayed gentlemen . . . utterly unfit for any military purpose whatever." Although some of the worst of these choices had been put out to pasture after the disasters of 1812 and eight new brigadier-generals created, Scott's blunt critique still held true in 1813.

To a visitor from another milieu, the European style of battle transferred to Canada must have seemed incongruous, even comic. Such a one was the celebrated Sauk chief, Black Hawk, who was contemptuous of the white man's mode of fighting. As he explained it to his astonished comrades: "Instead of stealing upon each other and taking every advantage to *kill the enemy* and *save our own people*, as we do (which, with us, is considered good policy in a war chief), they march out, in open daylight, and fight regardless of the number of warriors they may lose." The observant Black Hawk then gave a witty account of the self-serving dispatches and General Orders that opposing commanders used to justify their blunders and make defeat seem like victory:

> After the battle is over, they retire to feast and drink wine, as if nothing had happened; after which, they make a *statement in writing* of what they have done—*each party claiming the victory!* and neither giving an account of half the number that have been killed on their own side. They all fought like braves, but would not do to *lead a war party* with us. . . . Those chiefs would do to *paddle* a canoe, but not *steer* it. . . .

The regular troops on both sides were trained to fight the kind of European set-piece battle that raised Black Hawk's eyebrows. In 1812, parade-ground drill and army tactics were identical. The basic infantry weapon was the awkward, muzzle-loading Brown Bess musket, a notoriously inaccurate weapon scarcely able to hit a barn door at one hundred feet—and not meant to. The little one-ounce ball, wobbling down the unrifled barrel, could fly off in any direction. This did not matter, for the soldier did not aim his musket; he pointed it in the direction of the enemy line, fired it only when ordered. The effect of several hundred men, marching in line, shoulders touching, each firing in unison, reloading, and advancing behind a spray of shot—the file closers filling the gaps as soon as a man dropped—could disconcert all but the best-trained troops. The noise alone was terrifying, for the musket's roar makes the crack of a modern rifle sound like a popgun. And, in those days before smokeless powder, the battlefield was obscured by thick greyish white clouds shortly after the first volleys were loosed.

A well-trained soldier could fire off five rounds in a minute if on his own, or two or three a minute if firing in unison—a singular tribute to the persistence of the drill sergeants, for the loading of the Brown Bess was an awkward business, although the army drill manual reduced it to eighteen swift, economical motions. The weapon was fired when the firelock struck the flint, in the fashion of a modern cigarette lighter. (The larger locks on heavy cannon worked on the identical principle.) In practice, since the musket was a short-range weapon, an advancing line rarely fired more than two or three volleys; after that the bayonet was used—the British, especially, considered it the basic infantry weapon. The rifle was slower firing but more accurate and probably more effective in bush warfare.

The regulars who fought in line were not the neat-looking soldiers of the war paintings. Their uniforms were patched, tattered, sometimes hanging in shreds. Some had no uniforms. The phrase "literally naked" appears again and again in the official correspondence of both armies from commanders complaining that their men have neither shoes, tunics, nor pantaloons. Sanitation was primitive, sickness widespread. Men sometimes went a year without being paid, and hundreds deserted for that reason alone.

In battle after battle, the combatants on both sides were at least half drunk. Physicians believed that a daily issue of spirits was essential to the good health of the troops who, in spite of it, suffered and often died from measles, malaria, typhus, typhoid, influenza, and a variety of diseases that went under the vague collective names of "ague" or "lake fever." The British were given a daily glass of strong Jamaica rum. The Americans were fed a quarter-pint of raw whiskey. Many a teenaged farm boy got his first taste of spirits in the army, and many were corrupted by it. An era of drunkenness, which led to the temperance movement in mid-century, was surely a legacy of the war. Much of the looting in the wake of battle was initiated by men seeking hard liquor.

The lack of hospital supplies and proper food helped to bolster the sick list. In Canada, almost every item the army needed, from rum to new uniforms, came by ship from overseas. Every scrap of canvas, every yard of rope, every anchor, cannonball, bolt, cable, rivet came across the ocean by sail to Montreal. From there it was trundled by sleigh in winter or flatboat in summer to Kingston,

York, Fort George, or Amherstburg. Troops on the Niagara peninsula, a thousand miles from the sea, were fed on pork from Ireland,
flour from England, grog from the West Indies. Upper Canada was
joined to the lower province by the most tenuous of supply lines—
the St. Lawrence route. If the Americans could cut that lifeline at
Kingston, the upper province would certainly wither and fall. That
was the basic American strategy in 1812—a strategy foiled by Brock
and Tecumseh. With the new campaign awaiting only the opening
of the lakes, it remained the American strategy in 1813.

Three new armies threatened Canada. The Army of the North at
Plattsburgh on Lake Champlain, only fifty miles south of Montreal,
forced the British to keep the bulk of their troops in Lower Canada to
meet the threat. The Army of the Center, at Sackets Harbor, Oswego,
and the Niagara River, threatened Kingston, Fort George, and York.
The Army of the Northwest, under William Henry Harrison, secure
behind the ramparts of Fort Meigs on the Maumee, was poised to
retake Detroit, cross the river, and threaten Fort Amherstburg and
the valley of the Thames.

John Armstrong, the new American Secretary of War, worked
out the strategy. In order to field enough men to cut the Canadian
lifeline he planned to move the Plattsburgh army secretly to Sackets
Harbor. There, the combined forces under Major-General Henry
Dearborn would, with the co-operation of the newly built American
fleet, sweep across the lake and capture Kingston. Harrison, on the
American left flank, was ordered to create enough diversions to
prevent British reinforcements being sent east to resist the American
thrust. But he was told not to attack Canada until a second American
fleet, under construction on Lake Erie, was ready to seize control of
the waters. The Americans had learned an expensive lesson in 1812:
he who controls the lakes controls the war.

On both Lake Erie and Lake Ontario, the two sides were engaged
all winter in a frantic shipbuilding contest. The British were hammering together two big frigates for Lake Ontario, one at Kingston,
another at York. The Americans were rushing their Lake Ontario
fleet to completion at Sackets Harbor. The British had another big

ship on the ways at Amherstburg, preparing for the coming struggle for Lake Erie. The Americans, who had had no vessels on Erie in 1812, were building an entire fleet at Black Rock and at Presque Isle.

Time was of the essence. The side that got its ships into the water first could control the lake. So delicate was the balance of power that whoever managed to destroy one or more enemy vessels might easily gain naval superiority.

If Kingston were to be captured, the British supply line to Upper Canada cut, and the fleet in the harbour destroyed, the war was as good as over. With undisputed control of Lake Ontario, the Americans could easily invade the upper province, then mount an attack down the St. Lawrence to seize Montreal. And yet, as spring approached both Commodore Isaac Chauncey and Major-General Dearborn began to have second thoughts about the projected attack on Kingston. Dearborn became convinced that between six and eight thousand troops were guarding the Canadian stronghold, including three thousand regulars. This was a monumental overestimate. The regulars did not exceed nine hundred and were supported by only a handful of militia. Yet such was Dearborn's apprehension that he daily expected an attack on his base at Sackets Harbor. Chauncey, while disputing Dearborn's figures, believed that the British knew of the American plans and would be prepared for any attack. This extraordinary failure of nerve set the tone for the campaign to follow.

Somehow, the two cautious commanders managed to persuade themselves that an attack on York would be just as effective and more certain of success. In short, they decided to lop off a branch of the tree rather than attack the trunk—a total reversal of the original American plan, which had insisted on the capture of Kingston before any assault on York or Fort George.

Still, there was *something* to be gained at York, for the Americans had no corner on myopia. Instead of concentrating their activities at Kingston, the British had foolishly decided to build one of their big ships at York's unprotected harbour. That ship, *Isaac Brock*, and one or two smaller vessels, would be the object of the combined naval

Changing U.S. Strategy, Winter, 1813

and military assault on the Upper Canadian capital. If the ships at York could be captured intact and transferred to the American navy, Chauncey would have control of the lake. After that, the main British bastion on the Niagara—Fort George—could be seized, the peninsula rolled up, and, finally, Kingston invaded.

Both commanders succeeded in convincing the Secretary of War and each other that this strategy would be the most effective for the spring of 1813. Both waited impatiently for the ice to break in the lakes. On April 18, Sackets Harbor was open, freeing the fleet, but a week went by before the ships set sail. Finally, on the evening of April 26, after a rough passage, the invasion force appeared off the Scarborough bluffs not far from Little York. The campaign of 1813 was under way.

ONE

The Capture of Little York

April 26–May 2, 1813

While its left wing holds fast on the Lake Erie front, the main American army, under Major-General Dearborn, embarks at Sackets Harbor to attack York, the capital of Upper Canada. Its purpose is twofold: to seize the two large warships in Toronto harbour, add them to its fleet, and thus gain naval superiority on Lake Ontario; and to destroy the garrison troops. That accomplished, the American command is convinced that Fort George, and later Kingston, will fall before a combined land and water attack, and Upper Canada will be out of the war.

YORK, UPPER CANADA, APRIL 26, 1813

The Reverend Dr. John Strachan, schoolmaster, missionary, and chaplain of the York garrison, is in the act of drafting a letter to his mentor, the Reverend James Brown, professor at Glasgow University.

"I have just received a letter from my Brother sealed with black," Strachan has written. "My mother . . . is no more. . . . My mind is strong to bear misfortune tho it sometimes recoils upon itself. My heart would break before a Spectator knew I was much affected. I think that I can bear calamity better than others. . . ."

Calamity of another kind is lying just beyond the eastern bluffs, but the stoical clergyman is not aware of it. Having unburdened himself, he changes the subject, suggests publication of a joint volume of sermons, then suddenly breaks off, blotting the paper, as an express rider, galloping through the muddy streets, shouts out his news.

". . . I am interrupted," Strachan writes. "An express has come in to tell us that the enemy's Flotilla is within a few miles steering for this place all is hurry, and confusion, and I do not know, when I shall be able to finish this. . . ."

But finish it he will, some six weeks later, making a fair copy of the blotted draft, which he carefully saves, as he saves everything—his letters, first and final copies, poems, manuscripts, journals, sermons, and polemics—for the Reverend Doctor rejoices in the conviction that he is marked for posterity. In that he is right, for coming events will help propel him into a position of leadership. John Strachan will shortly become the most powerful man in Upper Canada aside from the Governor himself, the acknowledged leader of the ruling elite soon to be known as the Family Compact.

Before he puts his pen aside, Strachan adds one more sentence: "I am not afraid, but our Commandant is weak."

It is a revealing remark by a man who prides himself on having conquered all emotions, or at least their outward manifestations—fear, passion, grief—and who sees himself also as a military expert, an armchair general. He has pronounced views on almost everything, thinks nothing of dispatching long letters of military advice to professional soldiers. An amateur tactician, he is an opponent of the defensive strategy prescribed by the British war office and carried out by the cautious and conciliatory commander-in-chief, Sir George Prevost, Governor General of Canada.

"Defensive warfare will ruin the country," declares Strachan. Did not Isaac Brock, his dead hero, believe that offence was the best defence? In the pugnacious clergyman's view, Major-General Sir

Roger Hale Sheaffe, Brock's successor in charge of the forces of Upper Canada, is weak and vacillating. As for the navy, its officers are "the greatest cowards who ever lived." Strachan reserves his praise for the civilian soldiers who make up the militia, especially the York Volunteers, who number among their officers a commendable sprinkling of his own proteges. In Strachan's view, the militia "are capable of doing more than the bravest Veterans."

This is bunkum. The militia fought bravely enough at Queenston Heights; but many are badly trained—in many cases not trained at all—and have a dismaying habit of quitting their duty for the harvest fields.

Yet such are Strachan's persuasive powers that he will one day convince the country, against all evidence, that these civilians are the saviours of Upper Canada. It is an attractive myth, powerful enough to unite a province. A century after the war, it will still be believed.

Strachan, then, is the catalyst that will make this grubby little war appear as a great national enterprise, in which an aroused and loyal populace almost single-handedly repulses a corrupt and despotic invader. Even before war threatened, he understood his duty: to save Upper Canada from the Americans. For in Strachan's eyes they are "vain and rapacious and without honor," obsessed with "licentious liberty."

That is also the view of the Loyalists, those American Tories who moved into Canada after the Revolution and who must continue to justify that decision by rejecting all republican and democratic values. Strachan believes as implicitly in the British colonial system as he believes in the Church of England. A cornerstone of his faith is the partnership of Church and State, especially in matters of education—a useful tool to combat republicanism. He both despises and fears the incursion of Methodism, an alien cult from below the border, "filling the country with the most deplorable fanaticism." He is equally aghast at the number of American settlers pouring into the province from the border states, bringing with them—in his view—an irreligious and materialistic way of life.

He is a man of many convictions. If the stocky figure in clergy-man's black, moving across the mud-spattered cobbles of Little York seeking more news of the Yankee fleet, is subject to doubts, he keeps them concealed behind a dour mask. At thirty-five he is not unhand-some—a black Scot with a straight nose, a firm cleft chin, and droop-ing eyes—a little sad, a little haughty. He is beyond argument the most energetic man in town, if not in the province, and, as events are about to prove, one of the most courageous. He teaches the chosen in his own grammar school, runs his parish, presides at weddings, funer-als, christenings, and military parades, pokes his nose regularly into government, and manages a prodigious literary output: textbooks, newspaper articles, sermons, an emigrant's guide, moral essays, and an effusion of indifferent poetry—sonnets, quatrains, lyrics, odes—even an autobiography, set down at the age of twenty-two.

The war has hardened his attitudes. To him it is a just war, one that Christians can prosecute with vigour and a clear conscience: "The justice of our cause is . . . indeed half the victory."

He is not alone in this conviction. Aboard the tall ships lurking outside the harbour, bristling with cannon, other men, equally pur-poseful, are preparing for bloody combat; and their leaders are as certain as John Strachan that their cause is just and that the God of battles stands resolutely in their ranks.

ABOARD U.S.S. *MADISON,*

OFF YORK, UPPER CANADA, APRIL 26, 1813

In his cabin on the American flagship, Zebulon Montgomery Pike, the American army's newest brigadier-general, scratches out a letter to his wife, knowing it may be his last.

"We are now standing on and off the harbor of York which we shall attack at daylight in the morning: I shall dedicate these last moments to you, my love. . . . I have no new injunction, no new charge to give you, nor no new idea to communicate. . . . Should I fall, defend my memory and only believe, had I lived, I would have aspired to deeds worthy of your husband. . . ."

Throughout his military life Pike has aspired to deeds of glory that will bring him everlasting renown. Yet, in spite of a flaming ambition, the laurel has eluded him. Although he has been a soldier for nineteen of his thirty-four years, his only action has been an inglorious skirmish on the Canadian border the previous November, stumbling about in the dark through unknown country, his troops shooting at their own men.

He yearns for his nation's accolade. If he cannot get it in life, he is perfectly prepared to accept a hero's death. He has already written to his father, another old soldier, that he hopes to be "the happy mortal destined to turn the scale of war." If not, "may my fall be like Wolfe's—to sleep in the arms of victory."

Although he is a good officer he is better known as an explorer, in spite of the fact that his explorations have been inept and his published journals badly written, unrevealing, and inaccurate to the point of dishonesty. Twice hopelessly lost, captured and held prisoner by the Spanish, he has achieved a certain notoriety for a peak in the Rockies which bears his name, even though he did not discover it, did not climb it, did not come within fifteen miles of it. Even that dubious expedition was overshadowed by the journey of Lewis and Clark, of whom Brigadier-General Pike is more than a little jealous.

Qualities that in a civilian might be considered flaws have made him an effective commander. He is bold, even impulsive. Having eloped with his cousin, to the fury of her wealthy father, he dramatically declared, "Whilst I have breath I will never be the slave to any." Serenely confident in his own ability, he feels destined for greatness. Almost pathologically patriotic, he is a stickler for discipline and morality, lecturing his soldiers on the evils of drink and debauchery.

He is loyal to his friends and heroes, notably his long-time patron, Major-General James Wilkinson, undoubtedly the greatest rogue ever to wear two stars, a man despised and distrusted by almost every other officer save Pike. This commendable if foolhardy fealty has frustrated Pike's ambitions. In spite of years of politicking, promotion has been maddeningly slow. The war is his opportunity. "If we go into Canada," he wrote to Wilkinson, "you will hear of my fame or of my death. For I am determined to seek the 'Bubble' even in the cannon's mouth."

Who knows what the morrow may hold? Further promotion, perhaps. Pike has been chosen to lead the troops in the attack on York, for his commanding general, Henry Dearborn, is ill, or pretends to be. An indecisive, grotesque pudding of a man, who looks and acts far older than his sixty years, Dearborn longs for retirement. He scarcely inspires confidence in his troops, who call him Granny. At 250 pounds, he is so gross that he has trouble getting about and must be trundled in a two-wheeled device, later to be copied by midwestern farmers and dubbed a "dearborn."

The fleet stands off the bluffs to the east of the Don River— fourteen sail in all, jammed with fourteen hundred troops. Six hundred are crowded aboard *Madison*, many seasick, all weary of close quarters. Now, after four days of fits and starts, the troops learn that the attack will be made on the Upper Canadian capital and not, as some believed, on Fort George, at the Niagara's mouth, or on Kingston.

Pike's orders to his officers are explicit: any man who fires his musket or quits his post is to be instantly put to death. The bayonet is to be used in preference to the bullet. Plunderers of private property will be shot, but public stores may be looted with impunity. The honour of the American army is at stake; the country cannot suffer another defeat; "the disgraces which have recently tarnished our arms" must be wiped clean. Honour—that most precious of all human commodities—must finally be satisfied.

LITTLE YORK, APRIL 26, 1813

As General Pike seals the letter to his wife, Mrs. Grant Powell, dressed in her finest gown, waits nervously in her drawing room on Front Street for the guests she has invited to supper. They are more than fashionably late. The clock ticks off the minutes; finally, one woman arrives; nobody else. What can it all mean? Is Mrs. Powell being snubbed? No; the news is not quite that bad. Her father-in-law, Mr. Justice William Dummer Powell, arrives breathlessly with the explanation: the American fleet has been sighted; he and all other able-bodied men have been called on to bear arms—everyone between the ages of sixteen and sixty, and even some outside that span. Young Allan MacNab, a mere fourteen but big for his age, has shouldered a musket; so has John Basil, the ancient doorkeeper of the Legislative Council.

Justice Powell, in common with John Strachan, most government officials, British officers, and common soldiers, is convinced that the attack can be repulsed. Major-General Sheaffe may be a weak commander in Strachan's belief, but at least he is in town, having postponed his departure for Fort George because of a hunch that the Americans are coming. Also, by good fortune, two companies of the British 8th Regiment, known as the King's, just happen to be passing through York.

Now, as John Strachan leaves his house to seek more details and Mrs. Powell ruefully cancels her supper party, the farmers begin to straggle in, weapons on their shoulders. Some have had militia training. Lieutenant Ely Playter has just reached his farmhouse on Yonge Street after a day at the garrison when he is routed out again, with his brother George, by Major William Allan, a leading merchant now second-in-command of the York Volunteers. Wartime speculation in flour, pork, and rum will make Allan wealthy. The events of this week will help make him powerful as well.

York is a community of fewer than a thousand souls. Now it is abuzz. People rush about, hiding valuables, burying treasure, exchanging news, gawking at soldiers.

Donald McLean, Clerk of the House of Assembly, who has exchanged gown for musket, hurries to the home of the absent inspector general and squirrels away all of the public papers.

The Chief Justice, Thomas Scott, and his fellow jurist, Powell, both members of the province's executive council, hurry to the home of Prideaux Selby, the Receiver General. Selby is on his deathbed, insensible to all the events of this and future nights. He is beyond help, but the three thousand pounds of public money in his keeping is not. The pair convinces Selby's daughter that this fund must be concealed. She hides most of it in an iron chest but secretes a small sum in another container with some public documents, which she takes to Donald McLean's. The Americans, it is reckoned, will not credit the Clerk of the Assembly with having so much cash.

Major-General Sir Roger Sheaffe cannot be sure where the main attack will come. To resist the invaders he has three hundred regulars, three hundred militia, perhaps one hundred Indians. Most are in the main garrison, close to the Governor's house commanding the entrance to the harbour west of the town. But Sheaffe cannot be certain the enemy will land there. He has had to divide his force, quartering a company of regulars and some militia at the eastern end of the settlement. Until he has a clearer idea of the enemy's intention he must protect both entrances to Toronto harbour, hoping to move swiftly to repulse the landing. He will need resolute troops, but the militia are not all as eager as John Strachan believes. Some have been murmuring their discontent for days, planning to go back to their farms as soon as their pay arrives.

When Ely Playter reaches the garrison he finds a whirlwind of activity. Patrols and pickets are being dispatched in all directions for the security of the community. Playter is given a job at once: he is to take two men and search out Major James Givins of the Indian Department. The tribesmen—Chippewa and Mississauga—will be needed on the morrow.

Playter finds Givins with General Sheaffe at the Governor's house. Here there is no sense of panic. Some will affect to remember the Major-General's forthright remark on this night—that "it would be a breakfast spell to drive every damned Yankee into the lake." Now Sheaffe tells Playter that nothing can be done until dawn. At first light, Playter is to take some Indians and patrol eastward to try to spot a possible enemy landing at that end of the town. Until then, Sheaffe says, he might as well snatch some sleep. At that the lieutenant-farmer gratefully stretches out on the floor of the Governor's dining room and slumbers peacefully until cockcrow.

John Strachan is up at four and astride his horse, galloping westward toward the garrison. The American fleet has come into view, and Strachan cannot stand to be on the perimeter of the action. He must be at the centre, for it is power he seeks—he makes no bones about that—and as the events of the next few days will show, he knows how to seize it. Not for nothing has he educated the sons of the elite, first in Cornwall, now at York. His avowed plan is to place these young men in positions of influence. The weak lower house—the House of Assembly—the only elected body in the province, is composed, in his view, of "ignorant clowns." He blames that on "the spirit of levelling that seems to pervade the province," a dangerous Yankee idea. But when he gets his pupils into the assembly, then "I shall have more in my power." Already his chief protege, John Beverley Robinson, a solemn twenty-one-year-old of good Loyalist stock who fought at Queenston, has been named acting attorney general.

Strachan understands the road to power, knows how to cultivate the aristocracy, how to make the most of opportunity. He has married into power: his pretty little wife, Ann, is the widow of Andrew McGill, brother of James, one of Montreal's leading fur merchants whose name will one day be enshrined on a famous university. The McGill connection has opened doors to Montreal's ruling merchant class. A Doctor of Divinity degree, for which Strachan has actively lobbied, adds to his stature. Strachan, the elitist, knows how to make the most of his fellow elitists, for although "there are no distinctions of rank in this country no people are so fond of them. If a fellow gets a commission in the militia however low he will not speak to you under the title of Captain." But everybody speaks to the Reverend Doctor Strachan.

The Reverend Doctor gazes out onto the lake. He counts fourteen sail, the ships in line, flagship in the van, others behind towing assault craft. As he gallops to the water's edge, he sees the fleet drop anchor. He raises his spyglass, observes the decks thickly covered with troops, some already clambering into the boats. A question forms on the lips of the amateur tactician: Where are *our* men? Why are there no troops rushing to the invasion point to repel them? It is a question that Dr. Strachan, protector of York, will ask again when the battle is done, for he has set his sights on the Major-General himself. Roger Sheaffe's days as Administrator of Upper Canada are numbered.

The whole town has watched the fleet round Gibraltar Point, hesitate, then move on, the morning clear and sunny, no trace of haze, a brisk east wind filling the sails. Ely Playter has already seen it. Rising from the dining-room floor of the Governor's house, he is off with his Indian scouts, galloping seven miles toward the east to make sure no Americans have landed on the far borders of the town. Satisfied, he and his men double back toward the garrison. As they do, they hear the guns start to fire.

Major-General Sheaffe faces a dilemma, though his features do not betray it. Even his detractors—and he has many—will remark on his absolute coolness in the events that follow. He is a bulky man, a little ponderous, less impulsive than his former commander, Brock, in whose shadow he languishes. It grates on Sheaffe that the dead hero should get the credit for the victory at Queenston. After all, Brock was losing the battle when he incautiously dashed up the heights to his death. The day was saved by Sheaffe's careful flanking movement, but men like Strachan have made Brock the symbol of Canadian resistance to the invader.

Yet Sheaffe admired, indeed loved, Brock, who once saved him from demotion. Years before, Sheaffe was so hated by his men for his harsh discipline that they plotted to kill him. As Brock put it, "he possesses little knowledge of Mankind." The mutiny was nipped, and Sheaffe, at Brock's urging, was kept in his post at Fort George—a good officer if not a great one who, as his superior predicted, learned from his experience.

He has no wish to fight the Americans, has, in fact, asked to be posted elsewhere, for they are his former countrymen. The Revolution split his family: Roger Hale Sheaffe stayed loyal to the Crown, but his sister remained in Boston until her death. Though

New England wants no part of this war, it does not sit easily with Sheaffe that he may be responsible for the deaths of men who know his family.

But he has no time for reflection as the American fleet glides past the garrison. Where do they intend to land? His force is so thin he cannot guess or gamble. The only men he can depend on are his three hundred regulars—the two companies of the King's (one at the far end of town), a few members of the Newfoundland Fencibles, and a handful of Glengarry Light Infantry. The Indians are unpredictable, most of the militia useless.

One mile to the west of the garrison, opposite a small clearing— the site of an old French fort—the enemy ships attempt to anchor. This is the intended landing place. It is a military axiom that an amphibious landing must be halted at the water's edge before the enemy can establish a beachhead. The Americans will have to come ashore in waves, sending the boats back for more troops after the first have leaped over the side. In the initial minutes, then, Sheaffe's force will outnumber the invaders. Now is the time to rush every available man through the woods that separate the garrison from the landing point, with orders to hurl the Americans back.

Sheaffe will not gamble. Already he has waited overlong. Now he dispatches his troops piecemeal: Major Givins and the Indians first, to oppose the landing, then a company of Glengarries to support them. He would like to send the militia, but not being disciplined they are still straggling in and have yet to form up in the ravine near the garrison. In their place he sends the grenadier company of the King's, under its elegant captain, Neal McNeale, and the Newfoundland Fencibles. He sends for the second company of the King's, beyond the eastern end of town. Then, when the militia is finally formed, he dispatches them under their adjutant general, Aeneas Shaw, to protect his right flank along the Dundas road. Sheaffe also has two six-pounders at his disposal, but he does not believe these can be trundled through the woods and so does not commit them.

At this point, things begin to go wrong for Roger Sheaffe. Shaw is supposed to know every foot of the ground between the garrison

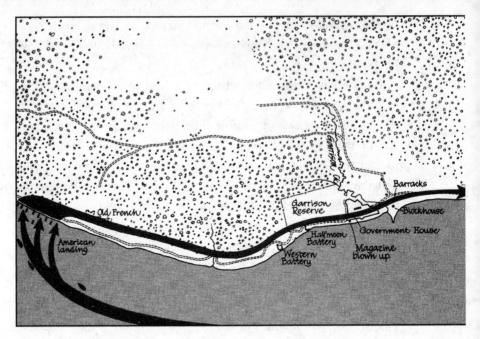

The Capture of Little York

and the old fort, but somehow—nobody can explain how—he takes the Glengarries with him on his flanking movement. They lose their way, retrace their steps along a maze of paths, and arrive late at the landing. By this time the American advance troops are ashore, the green-clad riflemen threading their way into the woods, cutting down the tardy defenders.

———

General Pike cannot stand the inaction. From his position on the foredeck of *Madison* he can see Captain Benjamin Forsyth's rifle corps pulling for the Canadian shore. A stiff east wind blows them past the chosen landing place and, as the soldiers struggle with the oars, the painted forms of Givins's Indians emerge from the woods and open fire.

"Rest on your oars," says Forsyth in a low voice as the musket balls rattle into the boats. "Prime!"

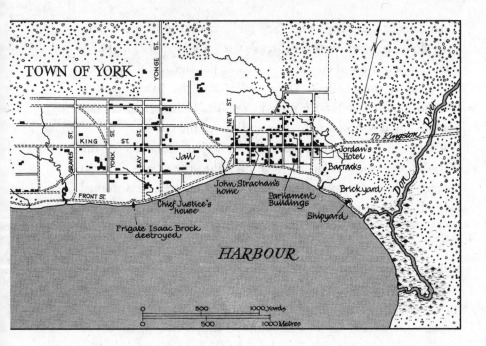

His men shake black powder from horn to pan, ram in their cartridges, return the fire.

This is Pike's moment. The glory he seeks lies directly ahead; the Indians are already scattering into the woods.

"By God!" cries the General, "I can't stand here any longer."

Turns to his staff: "Come, jump into the boat."

Off he goes, surrounded by his suite, directly toward the centre of the fray, a square, serene figure in blue and an obvious target for the balls that whistle around his head but leave him untouched.

Forsyth's men are ashore, seeking the protection of the woods, the natural habitat of American sharpshooters, hiding behind trees and logs, covering the main landing of the infantry, skirmishing with the redcoats.

Pike wades ashore with his men, forms the infantry into platoons under the high bank, orders them to scale the incline and charge across the field with the bayonet. At this moment, Neal McNeale's grenadiers pour out of the forest and down the bank, forcing the

Americans to the water's edge. Several light-draft schooners move in at close range to spray the British with grape-shot. The heavy balls, bursting from their sacs, do terrible damage. Neal McNeale falls dead; so does Donald McLean, Clerk of the Assembly, who saved the public accounts the night before. The Indians, their morale shattered by the shower of grape, vanish from the scene.

Caught in a crossfire between the naval barrage and Forsyth's sharpshooters, the regulars stumble back into the woods. Used to the broad plains and open warfare of Europe, they are unaccustomed to frontier skirmishing; in their scarlet jackets they make easy targets for the riflemen concealed between logs and trees.

"Show us our enemy! Show us our enemy!" they cry, but disciplined for a different kind of battle, they disdain the natural protection of the forest and drop like grouse on a highland shoot. Of 119 grenadiers, only 30 survive the ordeal. Two, it is believed, fall through the rotting ice of a deep pond, which will be known to future generations as Grenadier Pond. Another, both legs shattered, survives in the woods for more than three days by drinking water from a muddy pool, only to expire as he is rescued.

Yet it does not occur to the grenadiers to retreat, any more than it occurs to them to seek cover until, after a futile attempt to dislodge the Americans, their surviving officers lead them back toward the Western Battery that guards the lake road. By now the din in the woods is deafening—the shouts of the combatants, the warwhoops of the Indians, the roar of cannon and musket, and above all this the piercing notes of Forsyth's bugler indicating success.

The naval guns continue to pour a hail of grape and canister shot into the woods as Pike forms his men into columns and, with the fife and drum corps playing "Yankee Doodle," marches them toward York through the woods along the road that hugs the lake.

Ely Playter, back from his reconnaissance at the eastern end of town, arrives just as the first of the retreating British stagger out of the woods. Above the sound of music he can hear the cheers of the American sailors as six ships, beating against a brisk east wind, move up toward the Western Battery. Here Sheaffe intends to make a stand. It will not be easy, for the battery is already jammed with men, all jostling each other and harassing the gunners who are doing their best to return the fire from the lake. The six American vessels can throw more than two hundred pounds of iron at the battery in a single volley. The twelve British gunners, working largely with old, condemned cannon whose trunnions have broken off, have scarcely one-third the firepower. Pike's men have managed to haul two field guns through the woods—a feat that Sheaffe believed impossible. Now they advance upon the battery, arms at the trail.

Before the Americans can fling themselves at the battery, a dreadful accident brutally shatters the defenders' morale. In the cramped quarters, somebody jostles one of the gunners. Behind him is a portable wooden magazine, crammed with cartridges and powder. A spark from a gunner's slow match falls into the box, causing an explosion, killing more than a dozen men, scorching others horribly, and tearing away the gun platform.

A twelve-year-old boy, Patrick Finan, standing at the garrison gate, sees the maimed and burned men emerge, faces coal black, hair frizzled, clothing charred. He will never forget the spectacle or the unbearable odour of roasting flesh. One man is brought out in a wheelbarrow, so badly battered that Finan thinks every bone in his body must be broken. He lies in a heap, shaking with every movement, his legs dangling from his body as if held by the merest thread, his shrieks adding to the hullabaloo.

John Strachan has not been still all this time. He has galloped back to town, left his horse at home to prevent its capture, hastened back to the garrison on foot, encountered the stream of wounded emerging from the woods, and helped some of them reach medical aid. Now he experiences the shock of the explosion and thinks an enemy ship has been blown up. A glance at the carnage of the battery and the fleeing militiamen disabuses him. He decides to head back to town to see to the safety of his wife and the other women.

The regulars, meanwhile, are struggling to remount the big gun. The militia are fleeing. Nobody seems to know exactly what is to be done. The General himself is not at the battery. Outnumbered, he has decided that the town cannot be defended and is laying plans to save his regulars and deny the public stores to the enemy.

Pike's force advances with little opposition, seizes the Western Battery, moves on to the so-called Halfmoon Battery, which, being unarmed, is no battery at all, and pushes on along the lake toward Government House and the garrison.

The retreating militia have lost all semblance of order. Many are already across the creek that separates Government House from the blockhouse and barracks on the eastern bank. But Ely Playter and several others cling to the right bank, having exchanged their officer's swords for muskets. Up comes Major Allan, who orders them to rally the militia and make a stand, but the fire from the ships is so hot that all seek the protection of the garrison battery. A further attempt is made to form the militia in a small hollow, but when the citizen soldiers see the beaten regulars retreating they refuse orders.

Playter realizes that the garrison is about to be evacuated. He does not know that Sheaffe and his officers have already decided to pull out and blow up the main magazine on the waterfront below Government House. Within this underground fort are at least two hundred barrels of gunpowder—perhaps five hundred—together with a vast quantity of cartridges, shells, round shot. Sheaffe, concerned only with saving his regulars, gives little attention to the straggling militia, several dozen of whom are within a whisper of the magazine.

The fuse is burning. Playter and his men have already been ordered to march off. But the young farmer has left his coat in his quarters. He runs to retrieve it, warning another straggler, a cook named Mrs. Chapman, to make haste away as the Americans are coming. Somebody else is inside the post—Matthias Saunders, struggling to remove a portable magazine from behind one of the twelve-pound guns. He, too, is unaware that the magazine is about to blow.

Zebulon Montgomery Pike is within four hundred yards of the garrison, having halted his column and ordered his men to hug the ground while he brings up the six-pounder and the howitzer which his gunners have dragged through the mud and stumps. He is on the verge of victory and knows it. At any moment he expects to see a white flag rise from the blockhouse ahead. When that happens he will have the honour of receiving the sword of the ranking British general and accepting the surrender of close to a thousand men. It will be the first victory of American arms after ten months of bitter defeat. For lesser exploits in this disappointing war men of lower rank have received ceremonial swords and the thanks of Congress, their names toasted the breadth of the land, their profiles engraved on medals of solid gold. How sweet the prospect!

He sits down on a stump, awaiting the final attack. One of his men has captured a Canadian militia sergeant, and the Brigadier-General with his two aides, Lieutenant Donald Fraser and Captain John Nicholson, prepares to question him.

At this instant the ground shakes and the world turns dazzling white. A prodigious roar splits the ears of the attackers as a gigantic cloud spurts from the blazing magazine to blossom in the sky. From this vast canopy there bursts in all directions an eruption of debris—great chunks of masonry, broken beams, gigantic boulders, rocks and stones of every size. This terrifying hail pours down upon the attackers, covering the ground for a thousand feet in every direction, killing or maiming more than a hundred men, striking off arms and legs, crushing chests, decapitating bodies.

Ely Playter, who has retrieved his coat and reached the barrack gate, has an appalling close-up view. Miraculously, he is untouched. He sees huge boulders dropping all around him, some skipping across the ground, others burying themselves in the mud. He sees Matthias Saunders's leg smashed to a pulp. He sees a boulder kill the horse of Sheaffe's aide, Captain Robert Loring. He sees the oldest volunteer of all, the doorkeeper of the legislature, John Basil, struck twice in head and knee. The British casualties run to forty, most of them militia. But the Americans suffer more than five times that number. Their General is among the dying.

Zebulon Pike lies prostrate among his mangled followers. A huge boulder has crushed his ribs, torn a large hole in his back. His aide and pupil, Nicholson, is dead. So is the unfortunate Canadian sergeant.

Pike's wounds are mortal and he knows it. How ignominious—to be killed by a falling rock! Not for him the gallant death, waving his sword in the teeth of the fray, achieving the instant martyrdom of a Nelson or a Brock. Time only for a few gasping phrases for the history books: "Push on, my brave fellows, and avenge your general!"

As the surgeons carry him from the field, the troops give a sudden huzza. The General turns his head at that. Someone tells him that the Union Jack has been hauled down from the shattered fort and the Stars and Stripes is going up. He manages a wan smile. The Americans have won the battle of Little York, yet somehow, in spite of the cheering, Pike's victory is not quite the triumph that Washington hoped for. The two warships in the harbour will not bolster the American fleet on Lake Ontario. One is in flames; the other has got away. And the British regulars, who ought to have surrendered, have slipped out of the bag before the noose can be pulled tight. The British army escapes to fight another day, and Brigadier-General Zebulon Montgomery Pike, expiring aboard *Madison*, his head pillowed on the captured British flag, will go down in history not as a military hero but only as one who accidentally gave his name to a mountain that somebody before him discovered and somebody after him climbed.

———

John Strachan, en route from the garrison to his home, hears the explosion of the magazine just as he enters the town. He hastens to his house, finds his wife in a state of terror, bundles her and the children off to a friend's home some distance out of town, then rushes back toward the garrison. In a ravine he finds Sheaffe and the regular troops preparing to leave. Later, Strachan will demand to know why the Major-General did not seize this moment to counter-attack. But Sheaffe, a good half mile from the scene, has no way of knowing the havoc the explosion has wreaked on the enemy. With his cause lost, the most sensible thing he can do is burn the naval stores and the big vessel *Isaac Brock*, under construction in the harbour, and retire with his men to reinforce Kingston.

Young Patrick Finan, still dazed by the spectacle of two magazine explosions, has joined in the retreat with his family. The two-week journey by foot, horseback, and finally canoe is no pleasure trip. The spring snows have just melted; a heavy rain pelts down; the Kingston road is a river of mud; and the settlers en route are hostile. On the way out of town, the Finans meet several recent arrivals from below the border who are cheered by the American success. Young Finan is shocked, but the atmosphere does not dissipate as the troops move eastward. Believing the Americans have won the war, many a settler does not hesitate to avow his disloyalty. And when the Finan family begs for transport, the farmers, who have purposely concealed their horses and wagons in the woods, insist they have none.

In York, the command of the militia devolves upon Lieutenant-Colonel William Chewett, the sixty-year-old surveyor general, and his second-in-command, Major William Allan, the merchant. This pair has been detailed by Sheaffe to deal with the enemy. But Strachan, who turns up just as the arrangements are completed, has no intention of being left out. He volunteers his services, and in the days to come, the clergyman and not the officers will be chief negotiator for the people of Little York.

Ely Playter, meanwhile, struggles to catch up to the bands of militia retreating from the shattered garrison. Breathless after escaping from the explosion, he looks over his shoulder to see the first American skirmishers breaching the line of wooden pickets on the edge of the ditch protecting the Governor's house. A few spent musket balls sizzle his way, to no effect. Now, as the militia are halted, Playter watches while a small group heads back toward the garrison with a white flag. A few moments later the negotiators return; they have been told to come back in fifteen minutes.

Playter marches toward town with the militia. An infantry captain gallops up, asks for help to fire the marine stores and the brig *Isaac Brock*. (The *Duke of Gloucester* was, by good fortune, out of the harbour when the attack came.) When the dockyard is safely ablaze they repair to Jordan's Tavern, where some of Playter's friends are surprised to find him alive.

Though grateful to be in one piece, the young farmer is exhausted by the day's events. He heads up Yonge Street to the family farmhouse, plagued by fears of the unknown, apprehensive of the enemy's intentions. How will the Americans treat him and his friends? He is almost too tired to care. When he reaches his home he flops on his cot and sleeps like a dead man.

———

At the home of the Commissary, George Crookshank, on Front Street near the western edge of the town, an acrimonious argument is taking place between the Americans and the militia negotiators. The invaders are furious at the burning of one vessel and the escape of another. The major object of the expedition—to change the delicate balance of naval power on the lake—has been frustrated in the most dishonourable fashion, *after* the white flag of surrender has gone up. The Americans, who expected to deal with Sheaffe and his regulars, are mortified to find that the real army is out of reach and they must treat with amateur soldiers and a clergyman.

Strachan, who is rapidly assuming the leadership of the York negotiators, replies with spirit to the American representatives— Colonel George Mitchell of the 3rd Artillery and Major William King of the 15th Infantry. He and his associates knew nothing of the burning of the ship, he argues, and cannot be held responsible. He puts the blame on the retreating regulars. When the Americans castigate Sheaffe, the Canadians, who will never forgive the General for deserting them, agree. At last a surrender document is worked out. Strachan is not happy with it but must accept it, having no bargaining power.

Under its terms, all arms and public stores are to be given up to the Americans; the militia will not be made prisoners but will be paroled and thus neutralized for the remainder of the war unless exchanged. The officers are to be imprisoned. Private property will be respected.

King and Mitchell go back to the American lines to have the document ratified. They do not return. A junior officer arrives in their stead, arrests Major Allan, takes his sword, marches him off in the centre of a column of soldiers.

But now a black-clad figure dashes into the heart of the column, protesting this breach of the traditional white flag. It is Strachan. He catches up with Allan and marches proudly with him through town. Strachan the martyr? Not entirely; his clerical habit gives him a certain invulnerability. Yet it is an act of considerable courage, and the people of York will not forget it. In standing up to the enemy, John Strachan has given them back a little of their bruised pride.

Allan is held, but Strachan is not. With the terms of surrender still unsigned, those of the militia who can be found are imprisoned in the garrison. Their officers are freed under parole until the morning. Benjamin Forsyth's riflemen are appointed to patrol the town, a decision that strikes fear into the inhabitants, for this is the corps which, in Strachan's view, "bears the worst character in the American army."

Yet the looting on this night is comparatively light. Some Americans invade the House of Assembly and plunder the office of the late clerk, Donald McLean. Houses vacated by terrified women fleeing to the open country are also a target. With her husband absent, Mrs. James Givins, the wife of the Indian Department leader, and her seven children are driven from her home by plunderers who strip it of all valuables—furniture, curtains, bedsheets, liquor, everything from a silver toast rack to an English saddle. And when Judge Powell takes the distressed woman to General Dearborn to complain, the American commander replies that he cannot protect her. To the Americans, the officers of the British Indian Department are pariahs; the scalps taken at Frenchtown earlier in the year have not been forgotten.

The home of Powell's son, Grant, acting superintendent of the Marine Department, is also looted. Mrs. Powell, his American-born wife, her supper party aborted on the previous evening, had fled to a neighbour's. Now she returns to discover Americans in her house, one of them munching on a piece of loaf sugar. A spirited argument follows, with the soldier, a six-footer, getting much the worst of it.

Go home, says Mrs. Powell, *and mind your own business.*

"I guess I wish I could," replies the soldier, miserably.

Mrs. Powell relents a little, asks where he lives.

"Down to Stillwater, New York," he tells her. "I've one of Major Bleecker's farms."

At which Mrs. Powell bursts into laughter, for Major Bleecker is her father.

As the night deepens, silence falls over the occupied town. Only in the garrison hospital, guarded by five hundred American soldiers, is there activity. Here, scores of desperately wounded men from both sides scream without let-up into the darkness. An American surgeon's mate, Dr. William Beaumont, records their cries:

Oh Dear! Oh Dear! Oh, my God, my God! Do, Doctor! Doctor! Do cut off my leg, my arm, my head to relieve me from misery! I can't live! I can't live!

Beaumont has seen death, but this macabre scene rends his heart—the men groaning and screaming, the surgeons, "wading in blood," severing limbs with knife and saw or trepanning shattered skulls. The most hardened assassin, the cruellest savage, thinks Beaumont, would be shocked at the spectacle. For forty-eight hours, without food or sleep, the young doctor cuts and slashes, sickened by the carnage of war.

In his eyes these mashed and mangled men are no longer friends or enemies, only fellow creatures. Nobody, he thinks, can view such a spectacle without the blood chilling in his veins; none can behold it without agonizing sympathy.

LITTLE YORK, APRIL 28, 1812

John Strachan is in a state of high dudgeon. The indignity suffered by William Allan is too much; worse, the terms of capitulation have yet to be ratified.

At the home of Prideaux Selby, the dying receiver general, the outraged clergyman encounters William King, the American infantry major who prepared the surrender document the previous day. Strachan goes for King, charges him with breaking his promise to have the document ratified, cries *Deception!* The American retreats a little before this blast, apologizes, urges Strachan to see his superior officer, Colonel Cromwell Pearce who, with Pike dead and Dearborn still aboard *Madison,* is the ranking American officer on shore.

Strachan hurries to the garrison, tackles Pearce in his quarters, demands action. Pearce says he can do nothing but agrees to order rations for the militia, who have been held all night in the blockhouse without food or medicine. Now the militant clergyman demands to be taken out to meet Dearborn himself; but before a boat can be arranged the General lands, accompanied by the Commodore of the fleet, the corpulent Isaac Chauncey.

Dearborn is in a bad humour, clearly nonplussed by the presumption of this cleric badgering him over minor details of a surrender the General considers a *fait accompli.* Strachan brandishes the articles of capitulation; Dearborn glances at the document without comment. Strachan persists: when will Dearborn parole the officers and men of the militia? When will he allow the townspeople to care for their own sick and wounded? Dearborn's irritation grows. Who are the conquered here? Who the conqueror? Who is this strange civilian with the thick Scots burr who seems to think he can deal with generals? He tells Strachan, harshly, that the Americans have been given a false return of the captured officers, then warns him away. *Keep off,* he orders Strachan; *don't follow me around.* He has more important business to attend.

Strachan will not be diverted. He turns to Chauncey, looses a diatribe at him: this is a new mode of treating people in a public character, he says. He, Strachan, has transacted business with greater men than Dearborn without being insulted. Perhaps the delay in signing the surrender document is intentional: to give the riflemen a chance to loot with impunity before the pledges regarding private property are signed. Well, he, Strachan, will not be duped or insulted. Either the document is signed at once or it will not be signed at all: there will be *no* capitulation! Let the Americans do their worst!

With that he turns on his heel and walks back to the garrison, where the other members of the surrender committee await him.

These brusque tactics are successful. Dearborn, in a better humour, appears, rereads the surrender terms, and ratifies them. The militia are paroled. The community begins to return to something resembling normality. But the public funds so carefully concealed must be given up; if not, the Americans threaten to burn the town.

The Americans get the paper money from the home of Donald McLean, but not the gold. Major Allan's wife and Mrs. Prideaux Selby have worked out a plan to save it. They persuade Selby's chief clerk, Billy Roe, to dress up as an old market woman, complete with sunbonnet and voluminous skirts. The gold goes into a keg, is loaded onto a one-horse wagon and covered with vegetables. Roe in his disguise drives slowly out toward the Don River, crosses it, passes the American guards without incident, and buries the treasure.

In the farmhouse on Yonge Street, Ely Playter is awakened by a friend, Joel Beman, who, believing him killed, has arrived to look after the Playter family. Playter dispatches his wife and children to Newmarket in Beman's wagon, then with his brother George walks back toward town, picking up fragments of news from passersby and friends. He has no intention of giving his parole to the Americans and the following day packs up his valuables and hides them. He and his brother take refuge in the woods and watch helplessly as looters break down his door and pillage his possessions—his sword, a set of razors, a powder horn, a shot pouch, a box of jewellery, clothing.

The next day—Friday, April 30—on William Allan's advice he agrees at last to go to the garrison, sign his parole, and get a pass from the enemy.

The town is pillaged—"dismal" is Playter's word. The garrison buildings are shattered. The Council Office is stripped bare, every window broken. The legislative building, a low, one-storey brick structure with two wings, one for each house, is ablaze. Nobody knows who set the fire. The Americans are blamed but without any hard evidence. The best guess is that the culprits are individual American sailors, who wear no military uniform; they have discovered a human scalp in the building and have, presumably, used this example of British infamy as an excuse to fire the entire structure.

The scalp (it may be only a wig) is presented to Commodore Chauncey, who sends it on to the Secretary of the Navy with the undocumented charge that it was found hanging over the Speaker's mace in the main chamber. The following day the Americans burn what remains of the Governor's house and other buildings at the fort. These are the only fires, but the myth that "the Americans burned the capital" gathers credence in the years that follow.

Little York is scarcely a cohesive community. The upper class is united in its opposition to the American invasion, but scores of ordinary citizens welcome it, or at least accept it. For every man concealing himself to escape parole there seems to be another eager to sign a paper that will take him out of the war. A number openly join the enemy; some are actually aboard *Madison* or at the garrison giving information to Dearborn. When it becomes clear that the Americans intend to evacuate the town, panic seizes the disaffected, some of whom urge the American officers to hold on to York and give them protection, promising to help the invaders and complaining of "the further exposure to the fury and persecution of the royalists."

Suspicion and sedition go hand in hand, as neighbour breaks with neighbour over idle remarks or disloyal outbursts. In Michael Dye's tavern in Markham Township, Alfred Barrett offers a toast: "Success to the American fleet!" His cronies, John Lyon and Simeon Morton, raise their glasses in agreement. George Cutter overhears them and notes as well a conversation between two others who agree that it is foolish to support the government of Upper Canada—the country, they say, really belongs to the United States, and they both hope the Americans will win. On Cutter's evidence, and that of others, all four men will find themselves in the York jail, charged with sedition.

Elijah Bentley, an Anabaptist preacher who has pleaded with Dearborn to arrange a parole for his son, tells a friend that he has seen more liberty during those few hours with Dearborn than he had seen in the whole of the province: why, the men in the American army were allowed to answer their own officers back! For these remarks and others, Bentley too will be jailed.

The Americans also make themselves popular with many of the farmers by distributing a quantity of farm implements, which had been sent out from Britain intended for the settlers but as a result of bureaucratic inertia had never been distributed.

John Finch, who has been given some iron and ploughshares, encounters a fellow farmer, Henry Mulholland, and upbraids him for taking part in the attempt to repulse the invaders. Finch grows bolder: the British government, he declares, is austere and tyrannical. He would rather see his sons serve in hell than in a British garrison. He hopes the American fleet will destroy York "and all the damned crew." Henry Mulholland stores all this in his mind and, when the time comes, informs upon Finch who, with more than two dozen others, finds himself under indictment.

But one does not need to be disaffected to applaud the distribution of farm equipment. Many are convinced that the ruling class was reserving all this largesse for its friends. Before the fleet departs, the American soldiers also distribute to destitute families all the peas, flour, and bread they cannot load on board the ships.

Dr. Strachan is not to be seduced by this generosity. His church has been looted; anarchy of a sort prevails. Once again the resolute clergyman goes after the hard-pressed Dearborn. All the American general wants to do now, as April gives way to May, is to get out of York. There is no advantage in holding the town. The brig in the harbour is destroyed. More significantly, all the public stores destined for the Detroit frontier have been captured. All the armament and equipment for the British squadron on Lake Erie and the new ship under construction at Amherstburg—cables, cordage, canvas, tools, guns, ammunition—have been seized and cannot be replaced. This is a considerable loss and will badly cripple the British Right Division, which holds Detroit and most of Michigan Territory, for it can affect the balance of naval power on Lake Erie where the

Americans are constructing a fleet of their own. If the Americans can win Lake Erie, Detroit will be regained and the entire right wing of the British Army will be in peril.

Dearborn is embarrassed by the continued looting, which makes a mockery of the terms of surrender (but not so embarrassed that he can resist the offer of a private soldier to purchase for one hundred dollars the gold snuff box, set with diamonds, looted from the effects of Major-General Sheaffe). He realizes that he cannot control his own troops and wants nothing more than to leave as soon as the fleet is ready. He is only too happy to turn the civilian control of the town back to the magistrates and rid himself of the importunate Dr. Strachan and his friends.

Control does not return easily. On May 1, as the fleet makes ready to sail, Strachan surprises two looters, rushes impetuously at them demanding that they cease, and almost receives a bullet for his pains. An officer appears and forestalls Strachan's murder. That night, most of the Americans board their ships, leaving the town to deal with its own disaffected.

Commodore Chauncey, riding out a storm that keeps the American troops trapped and seasick on board the fleet for the best part of the week, is convinced that "we may consider the upper province as conquered." Although the troops that attacked York are now reduced through injury, illness, and death to one thousand effectives, reinforcements are on the way. Dearborn expects six hundred men to join him at Oswego. More are expected from Buffalo. Another thousand troops are waiting at Sackets Harbor, ready to go on board. "With this force," Chauncey believes, "Fort George and the whole Niagara frontier must fall without great sacrifice of lives."

The Commodore has reason to feel elated. His handling of the fleet during the attack cannot be faulted. Dearborn, old, ill, worn out by his exertions at York, is less certain of an accolade. He himself took no part in an action that cost three hundred casualties—more than twice those of the British. Worse, in the view of the Secretary of War, John Armstrong, Sheaffe has outwitted him by preferring the preservation of his troops to that of his post and "thus carrying off the kernel leaves us only the shell." Armstrong is already planning to replace his ailing general.

For the people of York, the invasion marks a watershed. Nothing can ever be quite the same again. Those who fought the good fight, with weapons or with words, will occupy a special place in the community. The heroes of the day—Allan, for one, and especially Strachan—will become the leaders of the morrow. The lines are drawn; those who aided the Americans, by word as much as by deed, are held to be traitors.

The militia, who saw little action in the battle of York, sustaining no more than ten casualties, are the darlings of the community. The regulars, who bore the brunt of the fighting, are castigated as men who care only about saving their own skins. This is wholly unfair, as is the memorandum that Strachan prepares for Sir George Prevost, the Governor General. The document, running to ten pages and signed by seven eminent citizens, berates Sheaffe, whose name "is odious to all ranks of people." Strachan writes that the citizens of York "are indignant rather than dispirited and while they feel the disgrace of their defeat they console themselves with the conviction that it was owing entirely to their commander."

Sheaffe is attacked for taking the very action that his enemy, Dearborn, is criticized for allowing: getting his troops out of town and destroying the ship in the harbour, an act that Strachan claims "incensed the enemy to such a degree as to expose the town to indiscriminate pillage and conflagration."

Strachan's message to Prevost is blunt: Sheaffe must go. "Without a new commander and more troops this Province must soon be overpowered." At least some members of York's minor aristocracy agree. Mrs. Powell, for one, is planning to draw off all her wine and pack the bottles in sawdust in the event of precipitate flight, for "a miracle alone can save us."

Sir George Prevost cannot agree with Strachan's armchair assessment of his general's conduct, especially as neither the chaplain of York nor any of his colleagues can suggest what *they* might have done in the circumstances. But Sir George is a practical politician and diplomat as well as a general of armies. Clearly Sheaffe has outlived his usefulness in Upper Canada. He will not be sent back as administrator; eventually, a phlegmatic Swiss-born major-general, Francis De Rottenburg, will be sent in his stead; but that is two months in the future. In the meantime, without title or stipend, but with all the power he needs, John Strachan reigns supreme.

TWO

Stalemate on the Niagara Peninsula

May 27–August 1, 1813

————

Following the attack on York, American strategy calls for an immedi-
ate amphibious landing at the mouth of the Niagara River to seize
Fort George and Fort Erie, destroy the defending army, and roll up
the peninsula. For this task the Americans have sixteen warships and
seven thousand men. The British have eighteen hundred regulars dis-
persed along the Niagara frontier; most of the militia have returned
to their farms. Ill and indecisive, Major-General Dearborn dallies
for a fortnight before launching the invasion. It comes at last on May
27, 1813.

NEWARK, UPPER CANADA, MAY 27, 1813

Dawn. Brigadier-General John Vincent, commander of the British
Centre Division, stands with his staff near the lighthouse overlooking Lake Ontario at the Niagara's mouth, trying to peer through
the blanket of fog that masks the water. He is almost certain there
are ships out there, but he cannot be sure. He expects invasion, for

a rocket has already flared up from the American side, but he can only guess where it will come. Nor can he know whether there will be one landing or several.

He is, however, painfully aware that he is badly outclassed. The guns from Fort Niagara across the river have already shattered his imperfect defences, and his own troops, spread out thinly all along the frontier from Newark to the falls, are exhausted from night watches. Vincent himself has had no sleep.

Young William Hamilton Merritt of the Provincial Dragoons, standing beside him, spyglass to eye, points suddenly out into the lake. The curtain of fog lifts, as in a theatre, and there is now revealed to Vincent and his staff a spectacle they will never forget—sixteen ships standing out from the lakeshore, sweeping toward them in a two-mile arc. Behind, on towlines, 134 open boats, scows, and bateaux, crowded with men and artillery, move steadily toward the Canadian side.

Even as Vincent and the others put spurs to their horses and gallop upriver toward Fort George, the cannon begin to thunder—fifty-one guns in action on the lake, another twenty from Fort Niagara, pouring a hail of iron and exploding shells across the fields and roads. The barrage is so powerful that Ely Playter, forty miles away at York, distinctly hears the rumble of the guns. A cannonball tears through the wall of the Carrol house in Newark. Mrs. Carrol, whose husband is a British gunner, hastily wraps her two small boys in bedding and rushes into a neighbouring wheatfield. Another ball ploughs into the ground beside the terrified trio. They leap up and join the throng of refugees heading for Four Mile Creek.

The enemy ships are manoeuvring to catch the British batteries in a crossfire. The effect is shattering. The battery at the lighthouse manages to fire off a single shot before it is destroyed. Another at Two Mile Creek has to be abandoned. As the fleet continues its majestic movement forward, three schooners move close to shore to cover the landing at Crookstown, a huddle of farmhouses near the mouth of Two Mile Creek. In a thicket overlooking this potential invasion point Vincent has hidden a guard of fifty Mohawk under their celebrated Scottish chief, John Norton. A hail of missiles fired at point-blank range pierces the covert, killing two Indians and wounding several before the main body flees.

On board the American flagship *Madison*, Major-General Dearborn, too ill to lead the attack himself, watches nervously as the assault boats move toward the shore. He sees a young naval officer, Oliver Hazard Perry, directing the fire of the schooners from an open boat, standing tall in the stern in full uniform, oblivious to enemy musket fire. Perry is rowed from vessel to vessel, telling each where to anchor to achieve the best field of fire. That done, he boards *Madison*, determined to have nothing further to do with an invasion he believes to be badly planned and ineptly mounted.

Gazing at the churning waters below, Perry falls prey to conflicting emotions. He chafes for action, has come all the way from Lake Erie to take charge of the sailors and marines in the assault—rowing for weary hours under the threat of British cannon, then galloping bareback through dense forests in a driving storm—only to find his advice ignored. He has no intention of taking the blame for any disaster that results.

But Perry has a sudden change of heart. The one man he admires, Colonel Winfield Scott, Dearborn's adjutant-general, is in danger. Scott stands in the leading flatboat with Benjamin Forsyth's green-clad riflemen, the same sharpshooters who led the attack on York, but Perry sees that he is being blown off course and is about to miss the landing point. If Scott and the entire advance guard are not ordered immediately to pull to the windward, they will lose the protection of the covering schooners.

Gone, suddenly, are all Perry's scruples. He begs to be allowed to avert the disaster. Dearborn assents, and Perry leaps back into his gig, picks up Scott, and with his help herds the scattered assault craft back on course.

As the advance guard pulls for the bank, Perry rows swiftly over to *Hamilton*, the closest schooner to shore. He is no sooner alongside than a lookout on the mast shouts that the whole British army is advancing on the double to thwart the landing.

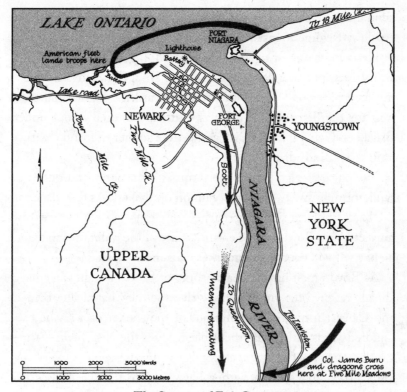

The Capture of Fort George

Most of the American officers do not believe the British will make a stand. This view is reinforced by the presence of a high bank, which conceals the defending troops. But Perry senses danger, sets off to warn Scott, rows hard past *Hamilton*, and slips in and out between the advancing ships. Just as he reaches the lead assault boat, the British appear on the bank and fire a volley, most of which goes over the heads of the riflemen. Confusion follows. Some of the oarsmen stop rowing while the soldiers begin firing wildly in every direction. Perry, fearing that they will shoot each other, yells to them to row to shore.

Scott echoes the order. The big colonel has planned carefully for this moment. Captured at Queenston and exchanged after months as a prisoner in Quebec, he has no intention of letting a less experienced officer bungle the landing. When Dearborn made him adjutant-general, Scott insisted on retaining command of his 2nd Artillery Regiment, insisted also on commanding the assault wave.

He is in charge of twenty boats containing eight hundred men and a three-pounder cannon. His orders are specific: advance three hundred paces only across the beach toward the high bank, then wait for the first wave of infantry—fifteen hundred troops under Brigadier-General John Boyd, a one-time soldier of fortune with a long service in India.

Into the water go Scott's men, through the spray and onto the sand, forming swiftly into line, cannon on the left. As they dash for the bank, the next wave approaches the beach in such a torrent of musketry that Boyd sees the entire surface of the water turn to foam; he himself will count three musket balls in his cloak.

As Boyd's men hit the beach, some of Scott's assault force have already reached the crest of the twelve-foot clay bank. The British and Canadian militia, bursting out of the shelter of a ravine two hundred yards away, hurl them back down the cliff. Scott—a gigantic figure, six feet five inches tall—is unmistakable. One of the Glengarries attacks him with a bayonet. Scott dodges, loses his footing, tumbles back down the bank.

On board *Madison*, Dearborn sees his adjutant-general fall and utters an agonizing cry:

"He is lost! He is killed!"

But Scott has already picked himself up and is leading a second charge up the bank.

The schooners have slackened their covering fire for fear of hitting their own men. Perry, realizing this, pulls over to *Hamilton* and directs its nine guns to pour grape and canister onto the crest. The British retreat to the cover of the ravine, where more troops are forming. Lieutenant-Colonel Christopher Myers, Vincent's acting quartermaster general, now leads a second attack on the men clawing their way up the bank. Once again Scott is forced back.

A scene of singular carnage follows. Two lines of men face each other at a distance of no more than ten yards and for the next fifteen minutes fire away at point-blank range. On the British side, every field officer and most junior officers are casualties. Myers falls early, bleeding from three wounds. The British, fighting against odds of four to one, are forced back, leaving more than one hundred corpses piled on the bank. An American surgeon, James Mann, who lands after the battle is over, counts four hundred dead and wounded men, strewn over a plot no longer than two hundred yards, no broader than fifteen.

Lieutenant-Colonel John Harvey, Vincent's deputy adjutant-general who has arrived with reinforcements, now steps into the wounded Myers's command and leads his shattered force in a stubborn retreat from ravine to ravine back toward the little town of Newark, scarred by shellfire and totally deserted.

Chauncey, meanwhile, has brought his flagship, *Madison*, into the river opposite the British fort. At the same time comes news of another American column massing at Youngstown farther upriver, apparently intent on crossing and cutting off the British retreat. As more troops land on the beach, the Americans form into three columns with the riflemen and light infantry flitting through the woods on the right to get past Harvey's forces and threaten his rear.

Vincent realizes that nothing can save the fort. Tears glisten in his eyes as he dispatches a one-sentence note to Colonel William Claus of the Indian Department, in charge of the garrison, ordering him to blow up the magazine, evacuate the fort, and join the retreating army on the Queenston road.

At the fort, Colonel Claus orders his men to leave, sets several long fuses on the three magazines, tries to chop down the flagpole to retrieve the Union Jack. The axe is blunt, the work only half done when the American advance troops are heard outside the fort. Claus drops his axe, makes a hurried escape.

The American columns move cautiously on the fort, their advance rendered ponderous by the lack of draught animals: the heavy artillery must be manhandled. Winfield Scott, impatient to pursue the British, seizes the riderless horse of the wounded Myers and dashes off at the head of his skirmishers, galloping down the empty streets of Newark and on to the fort, half a mile beyond, in time to capture two British stragglers. From them he learns that the guns are spiked, the magazines about to blow.

Off he gallops, trying to save the ammunition. He is under the wall of the fort when the main magazine goes up, hurling a cloud of debris into the air. A piece of timber falls on Scott, throwing him from his horse, breaking his collarbone. Two officers pull him to his feet and he presses on, forces the gate, stamps out the lighted train leading to the smaller magazines. Then he turns his attention to the flagstaff, partly cut through by Claus. In spite of his injury, he topples it with the blunt axe, claims the flag as a souvenir.

In dashes Moses Porter, the artillery colonel, who has also spotted the British standard flying and wants it for himself.

"Damn you, Scott!" he cries. "Those cursed long legs of yours have got you here ahead of me."

Meanwhile Vincent and his division are retreating swiftly and silently toward the village of St. Davids, the infantry retiring through the woods, the artillery and baggage along the road. Their ultimate goal is Burlington Heights at the head of the lake. The Americans are in danger of winning another hollow victory, and Scott knows it. Painfully, he hoists his big frame back onto his injured horse and gallops off once more in the wake of his own light troops who are already picking up stragglers from the British column.

The original American plan called for Colonel James Burn and his dragoons to cross the river from Youngstown to cut off the British retreat, but this attack has been delayed by the threatening fire of a British battery. Now, with the whole of the Niagara frontier being evacuated, Burn is able at last to land his fresh troops within musket shot of the enemy stragglers.

When he arrives on the Canadian shore, Burn asks Scott to wait fifteen minutes while he forms up his men; then their combined forces can proceed to harry the British retreat.

It is a fatal delay, for neither officer has reckoned on the timidity of the high command. Dearborn, who can scarcely stand and has to be helped about by two men, is incapable of decision; he will claim afterwards that the troops were too exhausted to engage in pursuit, ignoring all evidence that Burn's dragoons are fresh and Scott's skirmishers eager for the fray. Dearborn has turned direct command over to Major-General Morgan Lewis, who finally lands after the battle on the beach is over. Lewis is a politician, not a soldier, a former chief justice and governor of New York State, a brother-in-law of the Secretary of War, and a boyhood friend of the President. He loves playing at commander, revels in pomp and ceremony, and once, in a memorable speech to the New York militia, made a remark that has become a persistent source of ridicule: the drum, General Lewis purports to believe, is "all important in the day of battle."

Lewis is terrified of making a mistake—a bad quality in a commanding officer. He remembers the follies of overconfidence that destroyed Van Rensselaer's army at Queenston and Winchester's at Frenchtown the previous year and decides to play it safe.

He sends two messengers forward to restrain Scott from any further advance. Scott disregards the order.

"Your general does not know that I have the enemy within my power," he tells them. "In seventy minutes I shall bag their whole force, now the dragoons are with me."

But, as Scott waits for the rest of Burn's boats to land, Brigadier-General Boyd himself rides up and gives him a direct order to withdraw to Fort George. Disgusted, Scott abandons his plans. He can see the rearguard of Vincent's army disappearing into the woods. The defeated columns are marching off in perfect order, with much of their equipment intact, a circumstance that lessens the American triumph. Once again the invaders have cracked the shell of the nut but lost the kernel. Trapped all year in the enclave of Fort George, unable to break out for long because of Vincent's raiders lurking on the outskirts, an entire American army will be reduced to illness, idleness, and frustration.

Scott controls his disgust. In spite of a natural impulsiveness, he has learned to curb his tongue in the interests of his career, for he is nothing if not ambitious. But he cannot forgive Boyd, the man who ordered him back to Fort George just as he was about to destroy an army.

In Scott's later assessment, this blustering soldier of fortune is serviceable enough in a subordinate position but "vacillating and imbecile beyond all endurance as a chief under high responsibilities." Notwithstanding this harsh appraisal, Boyd is soon to take charge of all the American forces occupying the Niagara frontier.

Dearborn's immediate inclination is to move his troops to the head of the lake by water and cut off the British retreat. For that venture he needs the enthusiastic co-operation of the fleet and its commodore, Isaac Chauncey. That is not forthcoming. Chauncey, at forty-one, has gone to flesh—a pear-shaped figure with a pear-shaped head, double-chinned and sleepy-eyed. The navy has been his life. He earned his reputation during the attack on Tripoli in 1804 but is better known as a consummate organizer. In command on both lakes, he is really concerned with Ontario, where he is determined to achieve naval superiority. This obsesses him to the exclusion of all else. His task, as he sees it, is to build as many ships as possible, to preserve them from attack, and to destroy the enemy's fleet. But his fear of losing a contest—and thus losing the lake—makes him wary and overcautious. Chauncey will not dare; before he will attack his adversary's flotilla everything must be right: wind, weather, naval superiority. But, since nothing can ever be quite right for Chauncey, this war will be a series of frustrations in which he, and his equally cautious opposite number, Sir James Yeo, flit about the lake avoiding decisive action, fleeing as much from their own irresolution as from the opposing guns, always waiting for the right moment, which never comes.

Now comes word that a British fleet is at the other end of the lake threatening Sackets Harbor. The attack fails, but the Americans panic, briefly setting fire to the partially built warship *General Pike*, thus delaying its launch date. That is enough for Chauncey, who leaves the Niagara frontier, taking all his ships and two thousand troops, a defection that allows Vincent's army to reach the protection of the heights above Burlington Bay. If the Americans are to dislodge them, they must now proceed by land.

To young Billy Green and his brother Levi, the war is a lark. The older settlers may be in a state of panic, believing with some reason that the British are about to desert them, but when the Green brothers hear that the Americans are only a few miles away they cannot restrain their excitement. Nothing will do but that they have a good look at the advancing army.

With the fall of Fort George, the greater part of the Niagara peninsula has been evacuated by the British army. The Americans have taken Fort Erie and are pushing up the peninsula—have already reached Forty Mile Creek, some thirty-one miles from Newark. General Vincent's army has retired to Burlington Heights and dug in, but there is not much hope that his seven hundred regular troops can hold the position against three thousand of the enemy. The militia have been disbanded and sent home—deserted by the British, in the opinion of Captain William Hamilton Merritt, whose volunteer horsemen still continue to harass the forward scouts of the advancing enemy. Like many others, Merritt is convinced that the army will retreat to Kingston, leaving all of the western province in the hands of the invaders.

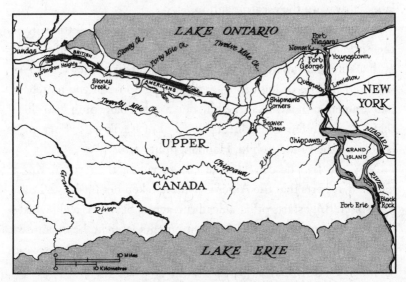

The Niagara Peninsula, 1813

None of this concerns young Billy, a high-spirited youth of nineteen, youngest of Adam Green's seven children. Left motherless almost at birth, shortly after the family moved up from New Jersey, he is known as a loner and a woodsman who can shinny up any tree and swing from branch to branch like a monkey. Now, at six o'clock on a humid spring morning, the two brothers clamber up the Niagara escarpment and make their way south until they reach a point above the American camp at the mouth of Forty Mile Creek.

At noon, hidden from view, they watch the Americans marching by, wait until almost all have passed, then begin to yell like Indians—a sound that sends a chill through the stragglers. "I tell you those simple fellows did run," is the way Billy describes it.

Back along the ridge the brothers scamper, then scramble back down to the road the soldiers have just passed over. Here they run into a lone American, one boot off, tying a rag onto his blistered foot. As he grabs for his musket, Levi Green belabours him with a stick. The resultant yells of pain draw a rattle of musket fire from the rearguard, whereupon the brothers dash back up the slope, whooping Indian-style, until they reach Levi's cabin on a piece of bench land halfway up the escarpment.

The sound of warwhoops and gunfire draws several settlers from their homes, and a small crowd looks down from the brow of the hill at the Americans marching through the village of Stoney Creek—a scattered huddle of log cabins and taverns. Some of the marchers halt long enough to fire at the hill, one musket ball coming so close that it strikes a fence rail directly in front of Levi's wife, Tina, who is holding their oldest child, Hannah, in her arms.

Now the two descend to the village where their sister, Kezia Corman, reports that the Americans have taken her husband, Isaac, a prisoner. Billy starts off at a dead run across Stoney Creek, whistling for his brother-in-law. A few moments later he hears an owl hoot and knows it is Isaac. The missing man has made his escape by pretending to be friendly to the American cause—a plausible enough pretence in this province.

Isaac simply told the major who captured him that he is a Kentuckian and first cousin to William Henry Harrison. It is true; his mother is Harrison's father's sister. The major promptly released him and when Corman explained that he could not get through the American lines, cheerfully gave him the countersign of the day which, appropriately enough, is made up of the first syllables of Harrison's name: *Wil-Hen-Har*.

Billy Green is now in possession of a vital piece of information. He knows what he must do—get a message to the British at Burlington Heights. Back he goes to Levi's farm, borrows his brother's horse, Tip, rides him as far as he can, ties him to a fence, and makes his way to the British lines on foot.

At this very hour, the British are planning to gamble on a night attack against the American camp. Lieutenant-Colonel Harvey has already reconnoitred the enemy position and believes it to be vulnerable. Harvey is by far the most experienced officer in the division. At thirty-four, he is thirteen years younger than his commander, Vincent, but has spent more than half his life on active service in Holland, France, Ceylon, Egypt, India, and the Cape of Good Hope. The illegitimate son of a peer, Lord Paget (so it is whispered), he is married to the daughter of another, Lord Lake.

In an army that has its fair complement of laggards, the hawk-faced Harvey stands out. Landing at Halifax in the dead of the previous winter, he pushed on to Quebec on snowshoes. He has served in enough campaigns to hew to two basic military principles. He is a firm believer first in "the accurate intelligence of the designs and movements of the enemy, to be procured at any price," and second, in "a series of bold, active, offensive operations by which the enemy, however superior in numbers, would himself be thrown upon the defensive."

Harvey now puts these twin precepts into operation. He has not only reconnoitred the enemy himself, but also one of his subalterns, James FitzGibbon of the 49th, an especially bold and enterprising officer, has apparently disguised himself as a butter pedlar and actually entered the American camp and noted the dispositions of troops and guns.

Harvey is able to report to Vincent that the Americans are badly scattered, that their cannon are poorly placed, that their cavalry is too far in the rear to be useful. He urges an immediate surprise attack by night at bayonet point. It is, in fact, their only chance. Ammunition is low; the American fleet may arrive at any moment. If that happens the army must retreat quickly or face annihilation. Vincent agrees and bowing to Harvey's greater experience and knowledge of the ground sensibly puts him in charge of the assault.

Now, thanks to Billy Green, Harvey has the countersign. He asks Billy if he knows the way to the American camp.

"Every inch of it," replies Billy proudly.

Harvey gives him a corporal's sword, which Billy will keep for the rest of his long life, and tells him to take the lead. It is eleven-thirty. The troops, sleeping on the grass, are aroused, and the column sets off on a seven-mile march through the Stygian night. It is so dark the men can scarcely see each other, the moon masked by heavy clouds, the tall pines adding to the gloom, a soft mist blurring the trails. Only the occasional flash of heat lightning alleviates the blackness.

Their footfalls muffled by the mud of the trail, the troops plod forward in silence. Harvey has cautioned all against uttering so much as a whisper and has also taken care to order all flints removed from firelocks to prevent the accidental firing of a musket. Billy Green, loping on ahead, finds he has left the column behind and must retrace his steps to urge more speed; otherwise it will be daylight before the quarry is flushed. Well, someone in the ranks is heard to mutter, that will be soon enough to be killed.

By three, on this sultry Sunday morning, Harvey's force has reached the first American sentry post. After it is over nobody can quite remember the order of events. Someone fires a musket. At least one sentry is quietly bayoneted. ("Run him through," whispers Harvey to Billy Green.) Another demands the countersign and Billy gives it to him, at the same time seizing his gun with one hand and dispatching him with his new sword held in the other. An American advance party of fifty men, quartered in a church, is overpowered and taken prisoner.

The Americans are camped on James Gage's field, a low, grassy meadow through which a branch of Stoney Creek trickles. The main road, down which the British are advancing, runs over the creek and ascends a ridge, the crest marked by a tangle of trees and roots behind which most of the American infantry and guns are located, their position secured by hills on one side, a swamp on the other.

Directly ahead, in a flat meadow below the ridge, the British can see the glow of American campfires. Moving forward to bayonet the sleeping enemy, they discover to their chagrin that the meadow is empty. The Americans have left their cooking fires earlier to take up a stronger position on the ridge.

In the flickering light of the abandoned fires the attackers fix flints; but by now all hope of surprise has been lost, for the attackers are easily spotted in the campfire glow. As they dash forward, whooping like Indians to terrify the enemy (who believe, and will continue to believe, that they have been attacked by tribesmen), they are met by a sheet of flame. In an instant all is confusion, the musket smoke adding to the thickness of the night, the howls of the British mingling with the sinister *click-click-click* of muskets being reloaded. All sense of formation is lost as some retire, others advance, and friend has difficulty distinguishing foe in the darkness.

The enterprising FitzGibbon, seeing men retreating on the left, runs along the line to restore order. The left holds, and five hundred Americans are put to flight; but the British on the right are being pushed back by more than two thousand. The guns on the ridge above are doing heavy damage. Yet, as Harvey has surmised, the American centre is weak, for the guns do not have close infantry support.

Major Charles Plenderleath of the 49th, a veteran of the battle of Queenston Heights, realizes that his men have no chance unless the guns are captured. He calls for volunteers. Alexander Fraser, a huge sergeant, only nineteen, gathers twenty men and with Plenderleath sprints up the road to rush the guns. Two volleys roar over their heads, but before the gunners can reload they are bayoneted. Plenderleath and Fraser cut right through, driving all before

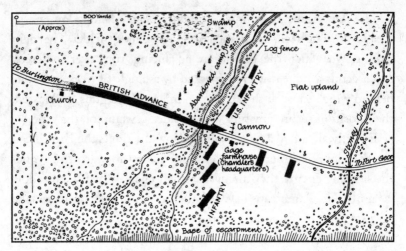

The Battle of Stoney Creek

them, stabbing horses and men with crazy abandon. Fraser alone stabs seven, his younger brother four. The American line is cut, four of the six guns captured, one hundred prisoners seized.

The American commander, Brigadier-General John Chandler, a former blacksmith, tavernkeeper and congressman, owes his appointment to political influence rather than military experience, of which he has none. He will spend the rest of his life defending his actions this night. As an associate remarks, "the march from the anvil and the dram shop in the wane of life to the dearest actions of the tented field is not to be achieved in a single campaign."

The General is up at the first musket shot, galloping about on his horse, shouting orders, trying to rally his badly dispersed troops. He can see the British outlined against the cooking fires but not much more. On the crest of the hill, pocked by unexpected depressions and interspersed with stumps, brushwood, fence rails and slash, his horse stumbles, throws him to the ground, knocking him senseless. When he recovers, all is confusion. Badly crippled, he hobbles about in the darkness crying, "Where is the line? Where is the line?" until he sees a group of men by the guns, which to his dismay do not seem to be firing. He rushes forward, mistaking the men of the British 49th for his own 23rd, realizes his error too late, tries to hide under a gun carriage, and is ignominiously hauled out by Sergeant Fraser, who takes his sword and makes him prisoner.

Chandler's second-in-command, Brigadier-General William Winder—a former Baltimore lawyer and another political appointee—is also lost. He too finds himself among the enemy, pulls a pistol from its holster, and is about to fire when Fraser appears.

"If you stir, Sir, you die," says the sergeant.

Winder takes his word for it, throws down his pistol and sword, and surrenders.

The American command now falls to the cavalry officer, Colonel James Burn, whose troops have been placed too far in the rear to be effective during the attack. Burn and his horsemen roar down on the British, cut through the lines, and open fire, only to find that they are shooting at their comrades in the 16th Infantry, who, with their commander lost, are wandering about firing at one another. Friend and foe are now intertangled, both sides taking prisoners, neither knowing how the battle is going. General Vincent himself, knocked from his horse and separated from the British staff, is lost somewhere in the woods, stumbling about in the wrong direction.

Each force leaves the field believing the other victorious. Heavily outnumbered from the start, with a quarter of his force killed, wounded, or captured, Harvey decides to withdraw without Vincent, before the Americans can recover from their confusion. He takes with him three captured cannon, a brass howitzer, two American generals, and more than one hundred prisoners.

The Americans are also preparing to flee, as William Hamilton Merritt, the leader of the volunteer dragoons, discovers when he rides back to the field shortly after dawn, seeking the missing Vincent. An armed sentry at the Gage farmhouse orders him to halt, but the resourceful horseman decides on a bluff, raps out a query.

"Who placed you there?" Merritt barks.

The sentry, seeing the blue coat of a dragoon, takes him for one of his own officers. Before he can catch his breath, Merritt makes him a prisoner, then, using the same subterfuge, captures a second sentry.

He cannot find Vincent, but he is able to report that the Americans are in a panic, destroying everything that cannot be removed—provisions, carriages, arms, blankets. In their haste, they do not even stop to bury their dead but are gone before noon, littering the road with a stream of discarded baggage and the occasional corpse.

The British return to the Stoney Creek battlefield that afternoon to find guns, stores, and baggage still scattered about the field among the litter of the dead. Some of the American tents are still standing. Vincent turns up at last, exhausted, half-famished, his sword, hat, and horse all missing. Lost in the woods, convinced that his army had been annihilated, he has blundered about for seven miles, expecting at any moment to be captured. This embarrassing footnote to the action has no part in the report that Harvey makes to Sir George Prevost. Nor does the signal contribution of Billy Green, who will for the remainder of his eighty-four years be known locally as Billy Green, the Scout.

The American retreat continues. From Fort George, Dearborn orders Major-General Morgan Lewis, his deputy commander, to make haste to Stoney Creek to attack the British. Lewis, who allowed the British to slip out of his grasp during the capture of Fort George, postpones the advance for half a day—because of a rainstorm! The old politician is not held in great esteem by his fellows. Peter B. Porter, Congressman, War Hawk, and Quartermaster General of New York, comments that Lewis "could not go sixteen miles to fight the enemy, not because his force was too small, but because he had not waggons to carry tents and camp kettles for his army." Porter claims that Lewis's own baggage moves "in two stately wagons—one drawn by two, the other by four horses, carrying the various furniture of a Secretary of State's office, a lady's dressing chamber, an alderman's dining room and the contents of a grocer's shop."

All this ponderous accoutrement is now threatened as the British fleet under Sir James Yeo appears outside the mouth of the Niagara, apparently threatening Fort George. Dearborn, whose physical condition is aggravated by mental stress, nervously dispatches a series of notes urging Lewis to send back all his dragoons and eight hundred foot-soldiers to defend the fort.

Yeo moves his vessels up to Forty Mile Creek, where the Americans are camped. Lewis, who has just arrived on the scene, resolves to retire at once, abandoning his supplies in such haste that the occupying British seize 600 tents, 200 camp kettles, 140 barrels of flour, 150 stands of arms, and a baggage train of twenty boats for which the Americans have neglected to supply an escort.

Within three days of the Battle of Stoney Creek, the situation along the Niagara frontier has been reversed. The Americans had been in full possession of the peninsula, outnumbering the British defenders at least three to one. The command at Montreal was prepared to evacuate most of the province, to sacrifice the militia and pull back the regulars to Kingston. But as the result of a single unequal contest, hastily planned at the last minute and fought in absolute darkness by confused and disorganized men, the invaders have lost control. On June 9, they burn Fort Erie and evacuate all the defence posts along the Niagara River, retiring in a body behind the log palisades of Fort George. Except for a few brief forays, it will be their prison until winter forces them across the river to American soil.

NEAR BEAVER DAMS, UPPER CANADA, JUNE 21, 1813

Lieutenant James FitzGibbon and his Bloody Boys are hot in pursuit of Dr. Cyrenius Chapin, an American surgeon from Buffalo whose band of mounted volunteers has been plundering the homes of Canadian settlers along the Niagara River. Leaving his men hidden near Lundy's Lane, FitzGibbon moves up the road seeking information about Chapin's movements. Ahead he spots a fluttering handkerchief: Mrs. James Kerby, wife of a local militia captain, is trying to get his attention. She runs to him, urges him to flee: Chapin has just passed through at the head of two hundred men.

But FitzGibbon does not retire. Up ahead he has spotted an enemy dragoon's horse hitched to a post in front of Deffield's Inn. He rides up, dismounts, bursts into the inn. An American rifleman covers him, but FitzGibbon, who is wearing a grey-green fustian overall covering his uniform as a disguise, clasps him by the hand, claims an old acquaintance, and having thus thrown the enemy off guard, seizes his rifle barrel and orders him to surrender. The man refuses, clings to his weapon, tries to fire it while his comrade levels his own piece at FitzGibbon. FitzGibbon turns about and, keeping the first rifle clamped in his right hand, catches the other's with his left and forces it down until it points at his comrade. Now FitzGibbon exercises his great strength to drag both men out of the tavern, all three swearing and calling on one another to surrender.

Up runs Mrs. Kerby, begging and threatening. Up scampers a small boy who throws rocks at the Americans. The trio continues to struggle until one of the dragoons manages to pull FitzGibbon's sword from its sheath with his left hand. He is about to thrust it into his opponent's chest when Mrs. Deffield, the tavernkeeper's wife, who has been standing in the doorway all this time, a small child in her arms, kicks the weapon out of his hand. As he stoops to recover it, she drops the infant, wrenches the sword away from the American, and runs off.

FitzGibbon throws one of his assailants against the steps and disarms him. The other is attacked by Deffield, the tavernkeeper, who knocks the flint out of his weapon, rendering it useless. FitzGibbon mounts his horse and, driving his two prisoners before him, makes his escape two minutes before Chapin's main force arrives.

The incident adds to FitzGibbon's reputation as a bold and enterprising guerrilla leader. The Niagara peninsula at this moment is a no man's land, the populace split between those loyal to the British cause and others who flock to the American side. It is not always possible to distinguish between friend and foe in this heterogeneous society of old soldiers, English and Scots immigrants, fervent Loyalists, and rootless new arrivals from America. Old feuds and personal grudges play their own role in the growing schism that sets family against family and alarms the high command.

The two most notorious defectors are Joseph Willcocks, a disgruntled newspaper editor and member of the House of Assembly, and his colleague, Benajah Mallory. The pair are in the act of forming a body of mounted "Canadian Volunteers" to aid the Americans and terrify the Loyalists. Willcocks has some grudges to settle.

For much of the populace the best policy is to lie low and try to keep out of trouble. There are some, however, who are prepared to risk their lives to harass the Americans. It is FitzGibbon's task to aid these partisans—to keep the enemy off balance and penned up in Fort George by a series of ambuscades and skirmishes. With Harvey's blessing he has organized some fifty volunteers from the 49th, provided them with grey-green coveralls as disguises, and trained them in guerrilla warfare. They gallop about the frontier, never sleeping in the same place twice, signalling each other by means of cow bells, which excite no suspicion in this pastoral lowland. They call themselves the Bloody Boys.

FitzGibbon—the man who entered the American camp at Stoney Creek disguised as a butter pedlar—is the perfect leader for such a force. He is a popular officer, unconventional, immensely strong and lithe. The semi-literate son of an Irish cottager, he entered the service too poor to advance himself by the successive purchase of rank. But he was fortunate that Isaac Brock was his commanding officer, for he was Brock's kind of soldier. Fiercely ambitious, almost entirely self-educated, an omnivorous reader in spite of his meagre schooling, FitzGibbon soon came to Brock's attention. Under Brock, he learned grammar, spelling, manners. His patron lent him books, corrected his pronunciation. FitzGibbon can never forget the day when, as adjutant taking dictation from his commander, he mispronounced the word "ascertain" and felt so ashamed that he immediately purchased a spelling book, a dictionary, and a grammar. The three volumes made him so amazed at his own ignorance that he determined to better himself. The orderly room, he has remarked more than once, was his high school, the mess room his university.

He learned also, under Brock, how to handle men. He treats them "as a lady would her piano—that is put them in tune (good humour) before I played upon them." As a result, his men have such faith in him that, as one of them puts it, "if he had told any one of them to jump into the river, he would have obeyed."

On June 22 FitzGibbon, having narrowly escaped Cyrenius Chapin's marauders, takes his men to the two-storey stone house owned by a militia captain, John De Cew, not far from Beaver Dams on Twelve Mile Creek, about seventeen miles from Fort George.

The De Cew house, which FitzGibbon has appropriated as headquarters, forms the apex of a triangle of defence that the British have thrown out to contain Fort George. At the left base of the triangle, seven miles away at the mouth of Twelve Mile Creek, Major Peter De Haren is stationed with three companies of regulars. At the right base, farther up the lake on the heights above Twenty Mile Creek, Lieutenant-Colonel Cecil Bisshopp is posted with a small brigade of light infantry. William Hamilton Merritt's Provincial Dragoons, FitzGibbon's Bloody Boys, John Norton's Mohawks, and Captain Dominique Ducharme's band of Caughnawaga Indians patrol the intervening countryside, forcing back the American pickets and harassing the enemy's own marauders.

It is all very romantic—men on horseback, often in disguise, riding through the night, cutting and thrusting, taking prisoners, making hairbreadth escapes. For those whose homes are plundered and whose menfolk are wounded or killed it is also tragic, but by European standards it is not war. At the very moment when FitzGibbon is struggling with Chapin's dragoons, the Duke of Wellington is hurling 87,000 men against Napoleon's brother Joseph, King of Naples, on the Spanish plain of Vitoria. Wellington's victory costs him five thousand casualties; the French lose eight thousand and are driven back across the Pyrenees. Napoleon's cause is clearly doomed, though not finished, and a wild bacchanalia ensues that makes the looting and burning on the Niagara peninsula seem like very small potatoes indeed.

The following evening, just after sunset, while Wellington's army is recovering from its victory orgy in far-off Spain, a slight and delicate little Loyalist woman in a gingham dress stained with mud makes her appearance at the De Cew house to announce that she has an important message for FitzGibbon. She is Mrs. James Secord, aged thirty-eight, mother of five, wife of a militiaman badly wounded at Queenston Heights. She tells FitzGibbon that she has heard from Americans in Queenston that an attack is being planned on the De Cew headquarters the following day. To carry her warning, she has made her way on foot through the dreaded Black Swamp that lies between Queenston and De Cew's, staying clear of the main roads in order to avoid capture. She is exhausted but game, triumphant after her long journey, which has apparently taken her, at some risk, through the camp of the Caughnawagas.

Laura Secord's adventure, which is destined to become an imperishable Canadian legend, causes FitzGibbon to alert Norton's Mohawks and to keep men posted all night to warn of impending attack. None comes. Is her story, then, a fabrication? Scarcely. She is the daughter of a Loyalist family; her husband is still crippled from wounds inflicted by American soldiers. She has not struggled nineteen miles in the boiling sun from Queenston, through St. Davids and across a treacherous morass on a whim.

In all her long life, Laura Secord will tell her story many times, embellishing it here and there, muddying it more than a little. The Prince of Wales himself will hear of it. Others will add to it: a cow will become part of the legend.

Laura's story will be used to underline the growing myth that the War of 1812 was won by true-blue Canadians—in this case a brave Loyalist housewife who single-handedly saved the British Army from defeat. It dovetails neatly with John Strachan's own conviction that the Canadian militia, and not the British regulars or the Indians, were the real heroes.

But one mystery remains: Laura will never make clear exactly how she heard the rumour of an impending attack on the afternoon or evening of June 21. On this detail she is vague and contradictory, telling FitzGibbon that her husband learned of it from an American officer; telling her granddaughter, years later, that she herself overheard it from enemy soldiers who forced her to give them dinner in Queenston.

Her exhausting odyssey is even more baffling because it is undertaken on the most tenuous of evidence—an unsubstantiated rumour, flimsy as gossamer, nothing more. On June 21 the Americans have made no firm plans to attack De Cew's. Even Lieutenant-Colonel Charles Boerstler, the man chosen to lead the eventual assault, does not know of it until the afternoon of June 23.

Who are these Americans in Queenston on June 21? They must be Chapin's guerrillas, for the regular troops have been called back to Fort George for fear of being cut off. Yet Chapin, by his own statement, knows nothing of any attack on De Cew's—will not hear of it until orders are issued on June 23.

Yet *something* is in the wind. Has someone whispered a warning in Mrs. Secord's ear? Who? It is not in her interest to give her source. News travels on wings here on the Niagara frontier. Who knows what damage might be done if Laura revealed what she knew? Her invalid husband and children could easily be the subject of revenge in this peninsula of tangled loyalties.

Like everybody else who has lived along the border, the Secords have friends on both sides of the line. Before the war people moved freely between the two countries, buying and selling, owning land, operating businesses without regard to national affiliations. Chapin himself was a surgeon in Fort Erie before he helped to found the town of Buffalo. His men are virtual neighbours; the Secords would know most of them. It may be that in later years, when the past becomes fuzzy, Mrs. Secord simply cannot remember the details of her source, though she seems to remember everything else. It is equally possible that she refuses to identify her informant to save him and his descendants from the harsh whispers and bitter scandal of treason.

FORT GEORGE, UPPER CANADA, JUNE 23, 1813

Henry Dearborn is in a bad way. Cooped up in Fort George by a numerically weaker adversary and, in his own words, "so reduced in strength as to be incapable of any command," he has been humiliated by the continuing assaults on the outskirts of his position. Dominique Ducharme's Caughnawagas have just attacked a barque on the Niagara within sight of the fort, killing four American soldiers, wounding seven more, and escaping into the maze of trails that veins the forests along the frontier. It is too much. He has tried to excuse the reverse at Stoney Creek as a "strange fatality," a pomposity which so exasperates the Secretary of War that he hurls the remark back at him in an acid letter that deplores *the two escapes of a beaten enemy.* Armstrong rubs Dearborn's nose in it by underlining the words.

The ailing general knows he must do something to restore his shattered reputation. Why not a massive excursion to wipe out the Bloody Boys? He has only just learned that FitzGibbon has made his headquarters at the De Cew house. Five hundred men and two guns guided by Chapin and his marauders ought to do the job.

The details are handled by his new second-in-command, Brigadier-General John Boyd, who has replaced the ponderous politician Morgan Lewis but is no more popular than his predecessor. Winfield Scott has little use for this former soldier of fortune, while Lewis, who is not unbiased, believes him to be a bully and a posturer. Lewis has cautioned against just the sort of attack that Boyd and Dearborn now contemplate.

The command at Fort George is, in fact, rife with petty jealousies. There is little love lost between Dr. Chapin, who will guide the expedition, and the officer chosen to lead it, Lieutenant-Colonel Charles Boerstler, a thirty-five-year-old regular from Maryland who clearly despises the self-appointed civilian guerrilla. Yet of the two, the surgeon appears to be the more warlike. The sallow-faced Boerstler is uncommonly sensitive to imagined slights. Chapin, a lithe six-footer with a great beak of a nose, piercing blue eyes, and a long face bronzed by the sun, was once bitterly opposed to war with Britain—he still belongs to the Federalist opposition—but has since become an enthusiastic and unorthodox belligerent, known for his boldness as well as his ego. He cannot stand Boerstler, calls him "a broken down Methodist preacher." Boerstler, on his part, has no use for Chapin, thinks him "a vain and boasting liar."

Chapin is so put off by Boerstler's appointment that he tries to get the high command to replace him, but Dearborn and Boyd decide to go with Boerstler, who has been embarrassingly touchy at being passed over on previous occasions and who has for days been pleading for a chance to lead an attack against the British.

Boerstler does not like Boyd and he does not like Winfield Scott, both of whom have been involved in what he considers slights to his abilities. Originally detailed by Lewis to lead the attack on Fort George, he was passed over at the last moment in favour of Scott. Just four days ago, Boyd replaced him on another assignment, again at the last moment—a decision that produced a heated scene between the two commanders. Chapin's remonstrances are in vain. Neither Boyd nor Dearborn is prepared to slight the sensitive Boerstler a third time.

The expedition is hastily and imperfectly planned. No attempt is made to divert the posts at the other two corners of the defensive triangle while De Cew's is being attacked. Nor is there any reserve on which Boerstler can fall back in case of disaster. The problem is a lack of men: half the army is too sick to fight. The shortage is so serious that officers are forced to turn out on night patrol, shouldering muskets like privates. Boerstler has been promised a body of riflemen—essential in the kind of bush fighting that is certain to take place—but these sharpshooters, having been placed on guard, cannot be relieved. He marches off without them.

Captain Isaac Roach, so sick he can scarcely draw his sword, volunteers to go on the expedition with his company in place of an exhausted friend, but he has grave doubts about the mission. He hands his pocketbook to an old comrade, Major Jacob Hindman.

"I have no doubt we shall get broken heads before my return," says Roach, "and if so send my trunk and pocketbook to my family."

His closest cronies, all members of Winfield Scott's family of artillery officers, see him off. None has confidence in Boerstler. He is, in Roach's opinion, "totally unfit to command."

The column reaches Queenston an hour before midnight in absolute silence. Boerstler dispatches patrols to prevent any citizen escaping with news of the troops' advance. (Laura Secord has now been at FitzGibbon's headquarters for more than twenty-four hours.) Lighted candles are prohibited, the men ordered to sleep on their arms. At daybreak the detachment moves on to St. Davids, where it surprises two of Dominique Ducharme's Caughnawaga skirmishers. One is shot; the other escapes to warn Ducharme and his superior, Major De Haren, of the American advance.

Meanwhile the Americans are moving in column up the side of the Niagara escarpment, which the local settlers insist on calling a mountain. They halt at the top, move on for about a mile past an open field and into a defile bordered on both sides by thick woods. It is here that the Battle of Beaver Dams begins.

Each of the leading actors in the tangled drama that follows sees it in retrospect through the distorted lens of his own ego. Some three hours later, when it is all over and men lie dead, wounded, or captive, none can have a clear idea of exactly what happened. Yet each persuades himself that he alone is possessed of the truth.

François Dominique Ducharme sees it as a straightforward victory. He is forty-eight, a veteran of twenty-five years' service in the western

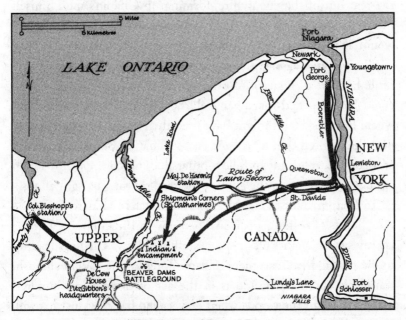

The Battle of Beaver Dams

fur country—a small, agile, incredibly tough skirmisher who now finds himself detailed to Upper Canada in charge of a band of Caughnawagas from the lower province. In his view, the decisions, the tactics, the victory are totally his—and those of his Indians. It is he, Ducharme, who persuades Major De Haren to allow him to move out of his original position in order to ambush the Americans in the woods. It is his Indians who kill every single one of Chapin's advance guard at the outset of the battle. His allies, the Mohawks, who are on the far side of the road, flee at the first musket volley while Ducharme and his followers drive the Americans back to a coulee, surround them, and force a surrender. Or so Ducharme will remember and believe.

To Charles Boerstler, the architect of the American defeat is Dr. Cyrenius Chapin. Boerstler believes that Chapin has led him into a trap, that he knows nothing about the country, has never been within miles of De Cew's, and may well be a traitor since he *is a* former Federalist. Boerstler sees himself as a beleaguered commander, struggling against bad fortune, ordering his wagons and horses to the rear out of the enemy fire, forming up Chapin's men himself in the unaccountable absence of their commander, concealing the wound in his thigh to avoid lowering the troops' morale, and leading a gallant charge against the Indians in the woods—a charge made futile because of his lack of experienced sharpshooters. If only he could have reached that open field beyond the copse of beeches, where his musketeers might have used their parade-ground drill to oust the painted enemy! *If only!* As for Chapin, Boerstler sees him as a coward, reluctant to follow orders, taking cover with his men among the wagons in the gully at the rear, refusing to fight at all.

To Chapin, Boerstler is a blunderer who leans on him for information, boasts of seeking a personal battle with FitzGibbon ("Let me lay my sword against his"), and gratefully follows Chapin's lead up to the pass in the escarpment. Chapin foresees the Indian ambush, warns his commander, and is in the act of driving five hundred natives through the woods when he is called back, against his will, by the timid and hesitant Boerstler who finally orders him to the rear to select gun positions, with clear instructions not to pursue the enemy. Chapin must stand with his men at the guns and take fearful punishment while Boerstler and his troops move farther to the rear. Or so Chapin will come to believe.

One thing is clear: by noon the troops are exhausted. Boerstler, feeling hemmed in by the woods and the hidden Indians, has made the mistake of leading his men forward and keeping them too long exposed to heavy fire. The fault is not entirely his; the detachment was too small, the plans imperfect and hurried. The troops have been up since dawn, have marched eleven miles without refreshment, have fought for three hours under a blazing sun, have exhausted their ammunition. What is to be done?

Time will blur the memories of all the participants, but it does not matter, for at this moment James FitzGibbon appears on the scene carrying a white flag and demanding an American surrender.

FitzGibbon has actually been in the area for some time, having been alerted earlier in the morning by Ducharme's scouts to the presence of an enemy column advancing toward his post. He has reconnoitred the battlefield and sent for his men, but the chances of capturing the Americans do not look good. He cannot depend on the Indians, who are coming and going on whim, some running off, others returning to the struggle; none is capable of forcing a surrender, and their leader, Ducharme, cannot speak English. At best, he thinks, the Americans will manage to untangle themselves and retire to Fort George. At worst, he and his small detachment of forty-four Bloody Boys may themselves be made prisoners. Finally, FitzGibbon decides upon a bluff, strides forward, white flag in hand.

Boerstler sends his artillery captain, McDowell, to meet him. The two parley. FitzGibbon resorts to the tried and true threat: he has been dispatched by Major De Haren to inform the Americans that they are surrounded by a superior force of British, that they cannot escape, and that the Indians, having met with severe losses, are infuriated to the point of massacre—a tragedy that can only be averted if Boerstler surrenders. Boerstler refuses. He is not accustomed, he says, to surrender to an army he has not seen.

FitzGibbon's bluff has been called. There is no unseen army—only Ducharme and his Caughnawagas. Nonetheless, FitzGibbon boldly proposes that the Americans send an officer to examine De Haren's force: that will convince them that the odds against them are overwhelming. Boerstler agrees but declares there will be no surrender unless he finds he is badly outnumbered. FitzGibbon then retires on the pretence that he must consult with De Haren who is, of course, nowhere near the scene. Instead, FitzGibbon runs into Captain John Hall, who has just ridden up with a dozen Provincial Dragoons. Hall agrees, if necessary, to impersonate the absent major.

Back goes FitzGibbon to report that De Haren will receive one of the American officers. Boerstler sends a subaltern who encounters Hall, believing him to be De Haren. Hall, thinking quickly, declares that it would be humiliating to display his force but insists it is quite large enough to compel surrender.

Boerstler, weak from loss of blood, asks for time to decide. FitzGibbon gives him five minutes, explaining that he cannot control the Indians much longer.

"For God's sake," cries Boerstler, "keep the Indians from us!" and, with the spectre of the River Raisin never far from his mind, agrees to surrender.

FitzGibbon faces a problem. How can his tiny force disarm five hundred of the enemy without his subterfuge being discovered—especially when the real Major De Haren is nowhere to be found? Fortunately, a more senior officer, Lieutenant-Colonel John Clark, arrives, followed shortly after by De Haren himself with a body of troops.

FitzGibbon has a further problem: he must explain his deception to De Haren before the Major unwittingly reveals it to the enemy. Moreover, he wants credit for the surrender and fears that De Haren will rob him of it. To his discomfiture, De Haren brushes him aside. Clearly, he is about to offer surrender conditions of his own to Boerstler.

FitzGibbon is not Brock's disciple for nothing. Impulsive action is called for. He steps up quickly, lays his hand on the neck of the Major's horse, speaks in a low, firm voice:

"Not another word, sir; these are my prisoners."

Steps back and cries loudly:

"Shall I proceed to disarm the American troops?"

De Haren cannot but agree.

FitzGibbon is still afraid that the Major will, by some remark, ruin everything. The Americans can easily overwhelm them if the deception is revealed. He quickly orders the troops into file, and as soon as some are formed raps out an order to the men to march, thus driving Boerstler and De Haren forward to prevent further conversation between them.

The marching Americans, still armed, are rapidly approaching FitzGibbon's small force of Bloody Boys. He suggests to De Haren that the captives ground arms at once.

"No," says De Haren harshly, "let them march through between our men and ground their arms on the other side."

What folly! thinks FitzGibbon. *When they see our handful will they really ground their weapons?*

Turns to De Haren: "Do you think it prudent to march them through with arms in their hands in the presence of the Indians?"

At the mention of the dreaded word *Indians*, Boerstler throws up a hand:

"For God's sake, sir, do what this officer bids you."

De Haren agrees, and as the prisoners drop their weapons, the tribesmen appear from behind trees and bushes and rush toward them. Some of Boerstler's men, terrified, seize their weapons once more, whereupon FitzGibbon, springing up on a stump, shouts that no one will be hurt. The Indians are allowed to plunder muskets, knives, swords, and other equipment, but the chiefs, having promised they will not injure their captives, hold their men in check. Ducharme and his Caughnawagas are displeased; they are not allowed to scalp the dead, and much of the plunder goes to the Mohawks, who did little fighting. As Norton, the Mohawk chief, puts it in a long-to-be-remembered aside: "The Caughnawaga Indians fought the battle, the Mohawks got the plunder and FitzGibbon got the credit."

The Battle of Beaver Dams confirms the inability of the invaders to break out of their enclave at Fort George. Boerstler has lost more than five hundred men, including Chapin and twenty-one of his mounted corps. The big doctor is not a prisoner for long. About three weeks later, while being conveyed to Kingston by boat, he succeeds in overpowering his captors and escaping with two boatloads of prisoners. For the United States it is the only bright spot in an otherwise sorry picture.

Dearborn is stunned by the disaster. He describes the Battle of Beaver Dams as "an unfortunate and unaccountable event." But generals must be accountable, and when the news reaches Washington there is an immediate demand for the sick old soldier's removal. Congress is in session when this "climax of continual mismanagement and misfortune" (to quote Congressman Charles Ingersoll) reaches the capital. By this time Dearborn is too sick to care. His officers—those who have not been killed, wounded, captured, or driven to their beds by the fever raging within the fort—urge him to move the army back to American soil at once. A council of war finally agrees to hold fast. Dearborn is removed at last, as much to his own relief as to that of his officers. Only when his replacement is named are eyebrows raised. The new commander, James Wilkinson—Pike's hero—is perhaps the most despised general officer in the army. Before the year is over and Fort George finally returns to British hands, many will long for Dearborn's return.

NEAR FORT ERIE, UPPER CANADA, JULY 10, 1813

James FitzGibbon, concealed behind the willows that fringe the Niagara's high bank, peers through his glass at the American community of Black Rock, directly across the gorge. Here, for the taking, are vast quantities of stores as well as extensive military and naval barracks. FitzGibbon, whose Bloody Boys are hidden in nearby barns, is convinced that a lightning attack against the settlement, if managed with complete surprise, can deal the enemy a serious blow and also serve to stretch the dwindling supplies of the British.

The troops are in a bad way. The commissariat is out of salt, the necessary item to preserve meat. The Green Tigers, as the 49th are dubbed, are in the words of one officer "literally naked." The 41st on the Detroit frontier is in rags and without shoes. A stream of urgent, almost frantic pleas from Major-General Henry Procter at Amherstburg makes it clear that the Right Division is in a bad way.

FitzGibbon lowers his glass to discover that two lieutenant-colonels, Cecil Bisshopp, a regular officer, and Thomas Clark of the 2nd Lincoln militia, have happened upon his hiding place. Both are in uniform, the former resplendent in scarlet and gold braid, and both are walking about in full view of the enemy. FitzGibbon is aghast. The success of his plan depends on keeping the Americans ignorant of the British return to the frontier.

Bisshopp tells FitzGibbon that he has already proposed an attack on Black Rock and has asked the new commander, De Rottenburg (Sheaffe's replacement), for three hundred men to do the job. De Rottenburg has allowed him two hundred. Does FitzGibbon think the barracks can be taken and the stores destroyed or captured with such a small force?

FitzGibbon can barely resist a smile. He has been planning to attack Black Rock with his forty-four Bloody Boys! When Bisshopp hears this, he laughs: "Oh, then! I need ask you no more questions but go and bring the two hundred men."

He orders the impetuous FitzGibbon to wait until the following morning when he and his boys will lead the advance across the river and, if necessary, cover the retreat.

The boats, brought up from their hiding place at Chippawa Creek, push off at two the following morning in a thick mist. A strong current forces FitzGibbon's party well below the landing place. The main party is drifting even farther downriver and FitzGibbon realizes that they will land half an hour later than planned. Nonetheless, he follows orders—to advance immediately upon landing—and leads his men on a concealed march through the woods toward the marine barracks and blockhouse half a mile downriver from Black Rock.

So complete is the surprise that an eight-man picket, all raw militia, is captured before it can give any alarm. FitzGibbon fires the blockhouse and barracks, then, moving rapidly through the town, reaches the army camp at Fort Gibson, guarded by 150 militia.

Peter B. Porter, Quartermaster General for the state of New York, in charge of the militia at Black Rock, has been on watch for most of the night and has just managed to get to sleep in his big stone house on the main street when FitzGibbon's advance guard dashes by. Porter leaps up and, clad only in a linen nightshirt, climbs out of a window at the back, finds a horse, mounts it with some difficulty, and dashes off toward Buffalo to rouse the militia. Five minutes later, Bisshopp's advancing troops seize his house.

In Hawley's Tavern on the river bank a small drama is being enacted. James Sloan, an itinerant pedlar of goods and groceries, is asleep when the sound of FitzGibbon's bugle causes him to jump out of bed. To his astonishment, the tavern is empty; all have fled at the sight of Bisshopp's approaching troops. A luckless baker named Wright, who also tried to escape into the woods, lies dead in the street below.

Sloan decides that bed is the safest place for him and climbs back under the covers. A few moments later he sees a strange Irish face peering at him through the window.

"Sergeant Kelly!" says the face. "Here is a man in bed."

The door bursts open as two Green Tigers enter the room and order Sloan out of bed.

Can't get out of bed, says Sloan, cowering under the covers. *I'm sick.*

The remark enrages the two Irishmen, who swear they'll skivver him where he lies.

At that Sloan jumps up and pulls on his clothes. Sergeant Kelly in a more kindly tone asks if he has any liquor. The pedlar produces a demijohn of cherry bounce, the two soldiers fill their canteens, and all three take several hearty pulls on the jug.

The trio are soon on the best of terms. Sloan's new friends suggest that he return to bed: it is the safest place to be in Black Rock at the moment. Sloan agrees, leaps back under the covers, and the two tipsy Irishmen depart.

But Sloan's curiosity gets the better of him. What is happening out there? Emboldened by cherry bounce, he climbs out of bed, peers through the window at the drama in the street. He can see the naval and military barracks and the fifty-ton schooner *Zephyr* all in flames. British troops are stripping Porter's warehouse and an adjoining store of army property. An officer in a red coat rides up and down the street.

It dawns on the pedlar that he can be an instant hero: he can slip unobserved through the front door of the tavern and capture that officer! His fears vanish as glory beckons. But first he will need a gun; surely, somewhere in this tavern there must be a weapon! He rummages about vainly until he is halted by a cry from the river. Unhappily for him, the boats that brought the British across the Niagara are being poled up to the rendezvous point and are at this very moment passing the tavern. Somebody spots him through a window on the river side and shouts a warning. A cordon of troops surrounds the house and batters at the hall door. Sloan opens it, and two officers, who look more like peasants to him, announce that he is their prisoner. Sloan falls back on an old excuse, says he is too sick to move. It does not work.

They take him to Bisshopp, the officer on the horse whom Sloan thought to capture.

"Young man," says Bisshopp, breaking in on his protestations, "you must go to Canada."

Well, that is all right with James Sloan. The idea, in fact, rather appeals to him. He will see something of a new country and of the famous British Army. When his curiosity is satisfied he will simply nail two or three rails together with strips of bark and, being a strong swimmer, propel himself back across the Niagara.

Sloan cannot help liking Lieutenant-Colonel Bisshopp. He considers him a mild and humane-looking man and guesses his age at about thirty-six. Actually Bisshopp is barely thirty, but his years of service in the guards, as military attaché in St. Petersburg, as aide to Wellington in Portugal, as an infantry officer in Holland, have matured him. The oldest surviving son of a baronet, a one-time

Member of Parliament, he is heir to an ancient title and a considerable fortune. Duty and duty alone keeps him in Canada. Service in this coarse colonial backwater is "complete banishment," and "were it not for the extensive command I have and the quantity of business I have to do, I should hang myself." His men adore him; he thinks more of their welfare than he does of his own. To FitzGibbon, he is "a man of most gentle and generous nature," more beloved by the militia than anyone else.

But FitzGibbon also believes that Bisshopp is lacking in judgement. The events that follow underline the accuracy of that assessment. Having dealt Black Rock a heavy blow, the leader of the Bloody Boys wants to be off before the Americans can rush reinforcements from Buffalo. The British have not lost a man. The boats, brought up from the landing place, are ready to take off the troops. But Bisshopp insists on waiting until eighty or ninety barrels of salt, so precious to the army, are brought out of Porter's warehouse and rolled to the water's edge. That is his undoing.

The owner of the salt, Peter B. Porter, is at this moment galloping about in the woods between Buffalo and Black Rock in his nightshirt, seeking to rally the militia. This war is partially of his making; as chairman of the House Foreign Relations Committee and a key member of Henry Clay's determined little group of War Hawks, he pushed for declaration in the spring of 1812. The war has brought him a measure of wealth, for he is a provisioner to the militia as well as quartermaster, ordering from himself and selling to himself the contents of the warehouse being looted by the British. Now in the Two Mile Woods he encounters a troop of dragoons en route to Black Rock from Buffalo. He orders them to fall back and wait in a field while he proceeds to collect the scattered citizen soldiers.

By seven o'clock, Porter has 250 men formed up in some sort of order, to whose ranks are added thirty Indians, mainly Senecas, under two chiefs, Farmer's Brother and Young King. This is the first time in the war that the Americans have employed Indians as combatants—the first time, in fact, that any large group of natives has wanted to fight on the side of the Long Knives. But these tribesmen feel that their own territory is under attack and so attach themselves to Porter's advancing forces.

Half of Bisshopp's force has already been sent back across the river. The remainder is engaged in loading the boats with salt and other stores when the attack comes. The American militia and the Indians burst from the woods on either flank, catching Bisshopp off guard.

Bisshopp is shaken. As he will ruefully remark, a body of Cossacks could not have surprised him more. He orders the main body of his men to make for the boats, then with FitzGibbon at his side leads a small detachment up a hill to meet the attackers and cover the withdrawal. As he rushes forward, a bullet from an Indian rifle shatters his left thigh. Some of his men turn back and rush to the prostrate figure of their commander.

"Oh, my lads," cries Bisshopp, "dead or alive don't leave me here."

Several assure him that they will lose their own lives rather than see him taken. They carry him down to the boats on the dead run, but before they reach them, he is hit by a second ball in the right wrist. Other members of the rescue party drop around him as he is hoisted into a boat overloaded with escaping soldiers. As the oarsmen pull away, the Americans pour a deadly fire into the little flotilla. Twenty-seven British are killed or wounded, among them Sloan's drinking companion, Sergeant Kelly, who will not recover. And Bisshopp is struck for a third time, high up in the right arm.

His physical wounds are not serious; his mental sufferings are. He cannot forgive himself for the loss of his men, cannot accept the idea that a single soldier should be shot while trying to rescue him. The surgeon who attends him has no fears for his recovery, yet Bisshopp daily grows worse, even when his commanding general, Francis De Rottenburg, pays him a visit and tries to ease his conscience. All he can talk about as his condition worsens is the loss of his men, until one evening, still blaming himself for the tragedy, he expires "without a struggle, nay, without a groan."

Panic! Square sails on the lake . . . white jibs . . . red stripes and blue stars flying from the sterns. With the half-charred *General Pike* finally launched at Sackets Harbor, the naval balance on Lake Ontario has changed again. The Americans are back in force on this humid midsummer morning—at least a dozen vessels standing for the harbour.

By the time the leading vessels anchor off the garrison, the town is all but emptied of men. William Allan, merchant and militia major, leads the exodus, the memory of his earlier imprisonment still seared into his mind. It is true that he and the others have given their parole, but they do not trust the Americans. Along the Niagara frontier other paroled militia officers have been bundled up and taken across the border to captivity on foreign soil. Allan is taking no chances.

He reaches the Playter farmhouse on north Yonge Street. With the help of the two Playter brothers, Allan conceals a boatload of five thousand cartridges and another crammed with baggage in a marsh near the Don River. He himself moves north and hides out in the woods.

Through the silent streets of the empty town, two men make their way to the garrison. Grant Powell has elected to stay and so, of course, has the Reverend Dr. Strachan. (Who would dare imprison *him*?) They reach the garrison about two o'clock and wait developments.

They watch the largest vessels come to anchor at three. The wind is so light that the schooners, trailing behind, must use their sweeps. At four, they see the boats put off. Two hundred and fifty men land without opposition. All available British troops have retired to defend Burlington Heights.

White flag in hand, Strachan tackles the first officer to reach the shore and demands to be taken to the Commodore. Chauncey, with Winfield Scott at his elbow, is cordial enough. Indeed, he expresses regret at the theft of books from the library the previous April, says he has made a search of the fleet for the books, has found several and will return them. Strachan demands to know his intentions, points out that the present inhabitants are only women and children. Does he mean to destroy the community? If so, will he allow the removal of these non-combatants?

Chauncey reassures him: no looting is contemplated, only the seizure of the public stores and the burning of all fortifications. The major purpose of the expedition is retaliation for British attacks on the far side of the lake, especially a recent hit-and-run assault on the little community of Sodus. He does not say it, but the real reason for the expedition, surely, is the need to do *something*. Cooped up in Sackets Harbor and Fort George, denied a naval confrontation by the elusive James Yeo, stalemated in their attempts to seize the Niagara peninsula, the Americans need to simulate action.

Chauncey asks where the public stores are located. Strachan and Powell will not tell him. It does not matter, because Chauncey already knows or soon finds out—knows the state of York's defences, knows the position of the army on Burlington Heights, knows every single transaction that has taken place in York. As he remarks later to Strachan, he "never heard of any place that contained half the Number of persons, Publickly known & avowadly to be Enemys to the Government & Country to be allowed to remain at rest. . . ."

Chauncey knows that some of the public stores are secreted in William Allan's store and that Allan himself, a militia officer under parole, has been collecting and sending information to the British army and aiding in the forwarding of troops. Winfield Scott offers a five-hundred-dollar reward for Allan's capture and sends his men to break into the store. They seize everything, break open several officers' trunks, give away the contents, and burn a large quantity of hemp. Others open the jail and release all the prisoners. When Strachan attempts to protest to Winfield Scott, the American colonel brushes him off, declares he'll seize all the provisions he can find.

In this he has the aid and comfort of a group of disaffected Canadians. John Lyon, one of the ringleaders, brings his wagon down Yonge Street to help the Americans move the captured flour to the boats. His crony Calvin Wood, jailed for sedition, is one of those released from the York jail. Wood and several others go aboard the American ships to give the enemy information; in gratitude, his newfound friends present him with seven barrels of flour.

From these informants Chauncey learns that boatloads of arms, baggage, and ammunition have been hauled up the Don River. It is late in the evening; a half-hearted attempt to storm Burlington Heights has been called off; the fleet is about to leave. Now, however, the Commodore postpones his departure. The following morning the troops disembark, and three armed boats move up the Don seeking the hidden supplies. But Ely Playter and his brother have already squirreled most of them away, and the searchers return disappointed.

The troops evacuate the town, burn the barracks, blockhouses, and all other buildings at Gibraltar Point, and return to the ships, which weigh anchor the following dawn and set sail for Sackets Harbor. Again, unaccountably, the Americans have declined to occupy the capital and cut the line between Kingston and the British forces on the Niagara.

The town breathes more freely. Though the inhabitants do not know it, this is the last time a hostile flotilla will anchor in Toronto Bay. The new centre of action is on Lake Erie, more than two hundred miles to the southwest. Even as Chauncey's fleet sails out of the harbour, a mixed force of British regulars, Canadian militia, and Indians is launching a bloody attack on Fort Stephenson, the American outpost on Sandusky Bay. Farther along the shoreline to the east, Oliver Hazard Perry is about to give his adversary the slip, manoeuvre his brand new fleet out of its prison at Presque Isle, and challenge British naval authority on the lake.

The war has passed York by, but its effects will linger on, long after hostilities end. John Lyon, Calvin Wood, and a clutch of other dissidents will soon find themselves in jail. Charges of sedition, taunts of treason, will be thrown at any who, by deed, word, or even gesture, appeared to espouse the American cause. It will no longer be prudent to praise the American way of life, as Timothy Wheeler, among others, has done in the hearing of his neighbours, or even to attack "the old Tories," as Edward Phillips has done.

A "committee of information" is about to come into being to take depositions from all loyal subjects who wish to inform on their neighbours. Its members are men of impeccable loyalty and substance: the core of the future Family Compact—Strachan, Allan, Thomas Ridout, and the acting attorney general's brother, Captain Peter Robinson, whose name will one day be immortalized by the town of Peterborough. The acting attorney general, John Beverley Robinson, cannot participate in person since the committee's actions, strictly speaking, are illegal. But he is with them in spirit, for "the country must not be lost by a too scrupulous attention to forms." In Upper Canada, during an emergency, individual civil liberties are not a matter of pressing concern. Individualism, after all, is an American concept, "liberty" a Yankee word.

THREE

The Northwest Campaign: 1

The Siege of Fort Meigs

April 12–May 8, 1813

———

While the British Centre Division prepares to defend the Niagara peninsula, the Right Division, with Indian help, plans to attack the American base at Fort Meigs on the Maumee River, near the west end of Lake Erie. The time is propitious. The British, who have captured most of Michigan Territory, control the lake. Most of the American defenders are leaving the garrison, their term of service at an end. If Fort Meigs falls, the American left wing will collapse and the land north of the Ohio is likely to revert to the Indians who fight on the British side under the Shawnee war chief, Tecumseh.

FORT MEIGS, OHIO, APRIL 12, 1813

Major-General William Henry Harrison, commander of the American Army of the Northwest, returning to his headquarters here on the swirling Maumee, looks up at his fortified camp and senses that something is not quite right.

The eight-acre stockade, one hundred feet above the river, is encircled by a fence of fifteen-foot pickets driven deep into the ground for permanence. Permanence? What are those gaps in the fence line? Why are the eight blockhouses unfinished? The British are only a few miles away at Amherstburg across the Detroit River. Hostile Indians are already lurking among the oaks and beeches. Has nothing been done in his absence?

Very little, it seems. Harrison, drumming up reinforcements in the wilderness, left the strengthening of the fort in charge of a brigadier-general of the Virginia militia—Joel B. Leftwich. But Leftwich is not to be found, has in fact taken off with all his men, their six months' tour of duty having ended the previous week. This "phlegmatic, stupid old granny," as a captain of the engineers calls him, stopped all work on the defences, announcing that he could not make the militia do anything—and therefore they might as well stay in their tents out of the mud and the water. Instead of improving the works, they have been permitted to burn the timber intended for the blockhouses and to pull up the pickets for fuel.

The quality of the militiamen assigned to Harrison does not inspire much confidence. Some of the senior officers cannot read or write; many more cannot spell. The reports of the general officers often read like the contents of a six-year-old's exercise book. Harrison, the scholar who reads Latin and Greek, is dismayed to discover that one field officer who has been given a day to fill out a form is unable to manage the task. Few know anything about military customs, drill or discipline. Two Ohio captains after two months in the service still labour under the belief that sergeants of the regular army outrank them; while serving as officers of the guard they meekly ask the NCO's permission to go to dinner!

All this must gall Harrison, the one-time governor of Indiana whose passion is military history. But his brooding features do not betray it. His is an ascetic's face, aquiline, stretched long like pull-toffee. The hollow cheeks, the thin nose, the sombre eyes give him a mediaeval look that masks his feelings.

At the moment he is frustrated over the orders of the new Secretary of War, John Armstrong, who has forbidden him to go on the attack until the ships that the naval commander, Oliver Hazard Perry, is building can control Lake Erie. Harrison is used to having his own way, has enjoyed carte blanche until this month. Now he is being hedged in, ordered to economize. Governor Isaac Shelby of Kentucky is itching to raise fifteen thousand troops to help Harrison avenge last January's massacre at Frenchtown, but Armstrong demurs. The government, he declares, can afford to spend only $1,400,000 a month on this war. Harrison is allotted twenty thousand.

Economy or not, Harrison has been forced to bribe some of the six-month men to hang on at Fort Meigs until reinforcements arrive. He has about twelve hundred troops in camp but only 850 are fit for duty—half of them untrained—against an estimated three thousand British, Canadians, and Indians.

Dismayed by the lack of public spirit among the militia, he has overstepped his authority and urged Governor Shelby to send him an additional fifteen hundred Kentuckians. Shelby, invoking a new Kentucky law, complies at once, and even now these men are on the march down the Maumee Valley. But will they arrive in time? Harrison has offered a bonus of seven dollars a month to any man who will offer to remain on duty until the new recruits appear. Two

The Northwest Frontier

hundred Pennsylvanians agree to stay for fifteen days. The Kentucky troops in camp are hawkish: if the General will lead them against the men who massacred their fellow soldiers at Frenchtown they will follow him without any bribe.

Upon Harrison's return to the fort, the troops are plunged into a whirlwind of activity. The chief engineer has booked sick, but his replacement, Captain Eleazer D. Wood, throws himself into the task of reinforcing the stockade. Harrison, who seems to be everywhere at once, orders his officers to conduct daily drills of the raw recruits to prepare them for the coming siege. It is not easy. Most of the officers need drilling as badly as their men.

They are much better at felling trees, digging trenches, splitting logs and raising bulwarks—an activity that proceeds under Eleazer Wood's direction. Work parties haul in fuel for the garrison and timber to fill breeches in the walls. Others dig wells in preparation for a lengthy siege.

Harrison has known since early April that the British, aware of his reduced state, are preparing an attack and expect a swift and easy contest. His old adversary, Tecumseh, has fifteen hundred tribesmen under his command at Fort Amherstburg on the Canadian side of the Detroit River. Fortunately for Harrison, the British commander, Major-General Henry Procter, has moved tardily, allowing the Americans a breathing space. But now the British have landed in full force at the mouth of the Maumee and are moving up the left bank. One of Harrison's scouting parties discovers them on the twenty-eighth, camped on the site of the old British Fort Miami, and estimates their strength at between fifteen hundred and two thousand. Tecumseh's Indians have already crossed the river and surrounded the American camp, picking off those soldiers foolhardy enough to leave the stockade for water. Fort Meigs is all but cut off, its garrison outnumbered two to one. Harrison's only hope lies in the reinforcements from Kentucky, somewhere on the Upper Maumee, nobody yet knows exactly where.

Métoss, head chief of the Sauks, lies belly down in a thicket close by the walls of the fort, waiting for any thirsty American soldier who attempts to steal down to the river. Like his fellow chief, Black Hawk, he has become a bitter enemy of the Americans—and with reason, for they have managed to squeeze fifty million acres of good Mississippi Valley land out of his people. He has come here to fight the Long Knives at the behest of Robert Dickson the fur trader, now an official of the British Indian Department, whom the Sioux call *Mascotopah*, the Red-Haired Man. Each night Métoss crosses the river from his tepee near the British camp to pick off one of the enemy or take a prisoner. The woods are alive with his fellow tribesmen, creeping behind the stumps and logs that litter the clearing around the fort or clambering into the elms to fire down upon the men within the walls.

He is an imposing figure, Métoss—six feet tall, with classic Roman features, his torso, arms, and thighs daubed with war paint, a circlet of feathers ornamenting his head. To the Americans behind the tall pickets, the encroaching Indians are only shadows, featureless and unreal. To the frontiersmen of Ohio and Kentucky they are no better than animals, without human feelings, to be shot on sight, war or no war. No American jury will convict a white man for murdering an Indian any more than it will censure him for slaughtering buffalo.

Métoss's thirteen-year-old son crouches beside his father, peering into the darkness, playing at being a man. He is his father's favourite. Métoss can deny him nothing, even this moment of danger. He has urged him not to come; but the boy is here.

They are very close to the fort, their temerity fuelled by the Americans' inability to locate them in the gloom. Does Métoss catch the glint of a telescope, flickering in the moonlight, behind the palisade? For once the enemy has him spotted. A moment later comes a flash, a coarse roar, and the whistle of grape-shot—scores of heavy balls released from their skin of canvas, whirling in the air, ripping the bark from the trees, shredding the new leaves of spring, tearing into the bowels of the child beside him, who dies, writhing, in his arms.

Revenge! Back at his tepee, securely pinioned, is Métoss's captive, a young American soldier taken the night before. Wild with grief, the father picks up the small mangled body, carries it to his canoe, slips across the river. All of his terrible despair is funnelled into an implacable purpose: he will purge his sorrow with a stroke of the tomahawk.

The red-headed Dickson, who seems to know everything that transpires in his camp, is there ahead of him. *Do not do this thing*, says Dickson. *Do not destroy this man. Surrender him instead to me—otherwise your father, the King, will look on you with sorrow.*

No other white man and few other native chiefs have Dickson's power over the western tribes. He is the master of the fur country, the protector of his people, their unquestioned champion, spokesman, general. To save them from starvation he has been prepared to beggar himself, and he has never betrayed their trust. Métoss cannot refuse him.

The chief tears off his headdress, struggles with his emotions, goes at last to his tepee. There he pulls a knife from his belt, severs his captive's thongs, takes him by the hand, leads him to Dickson, speaks in a mournful voice:

"You tell me that my Great Father wishes it—take him!"

Then, no longer able to control his emotions, he weeps like a baby.

The boy is buried next day with full military honours. The body is laid out first in Métoss's tent, a small rifle beside it with a quantity of ammunition and provisions for the journey that must follow. A dozen warriors painted black perform a solemn ritual dance. Suddenly, the chief rushes into the midst of the group, frantic with sorrow, his grief violent, ungovernable. They lead him, at last, from the body of his son, and the funeral procession moves off toward the newly dug grave on the river bank under the command of Lieutenant Richard Bullock of the 41st.

The red-coated firing party discharges the customary three rounds. The black-painted warriors follow with volley after volley. And still Métoss cannot control his grief. In the months that follow he becomes attached to Bullock, the officer who headed the firing party, makes him a chief of the Sauks, asks him to exchange names, treats him as a blood relative as if to replace his missing son. But he cannot staunch his tears, and it is the better part of a year before anybody sees him smile.

FORT MEIGS, OHIO, APRIL 28, 1813

Rain drenches the besieged American camp. The flash of lightning competes with the blaze of cannon; the crack of thunder with the roar of musketry. Indian warwhoops add to the cacophony.

Into this hellish night—into the mud, into the unseen tangle of stumps and broken logs, into hidden thickets and lurking shadows— goes a young captain, William Oliver, protected briefly by an escort of dragoons and by the thickness of the night itself. He carries a two-sentence message from Harrison to Brigadier-General Green Clay, in command of the Kentucky reinforcements somewhere on the upper reaches of the Maumee:

> Dear Sir: I send Mr. Oliver to you, to give you an account of what is passing here. You may rely implicitly on him.

The note reveals nothing, for Oliver's chances of getting through are minimal. The real message will be oral. Harrison can only wait and hope while he strengthens his defences. Meanwhile, to raise morale, he composes one of those eloquent general orders for which he is famous:

> Can the citizens of a free country who have taken arms to defend its rights, think of submitting to an army composed of mercenary soldiers, reluctant Canadians goaded to the field by the bayonet, and of wretched, naked savages? Can the breast of an American soldier, when he casts his eye on the opposite shore, the scene of his country's triumphs over the same foe, be influenced by any other feelings than the hope of glory? Is not this army composed

of the same materials with that which fought and conquered under the immortal Wayne? Yes, fellow soldiers, your General sees your countenances beam with the same fire which he witnessed on that glorious occasion; and although it would be the height of presumption to compare himself with that hero, he boasts of being that hero's pupil. To your posts, then, fellow citizens, and remember that the eyes of your country are upon you.

Harrison's order contains all the proper ingredients. It reinforces the American attitude that this war is a fight for freedom, that the British regulars are really mercenaries without a cause, that the Canadians are enslaved and must be goaded to fight. It conjures up the savagery of a so-called civilized nation that fights its colonial wars with unrestrained natives. Finally, it recalls past glories; directly across from Fort Meigs is the site of the Battle of Fallen Timbers, where General "Mad Anthony" Wayne humbled the combined Indian armies.

Harrison's order is also a statement of America's military philosophy. It reminds the young recruits from Ohio and Kentucky that they are citizens first and soldiers second (a truth with which the regulars would wryly agree) and that their commander is a citizen, too, and an equal. This approach, which springs out of the Revolution, is at odds with that of the British, who believe in disciplined professional soldiers following orders without question within the perimeters of a rigid caste system. No British general would ever refer to his men as "fellow citizens"—nor would a Canadian, for that matter.

But Harrison must inspire his artillery with more than words. The British are building gun emplacements on a ridge directly across from the fort, on the north side of the Maumee, concealing their own gunners in a hollow at the rear. A second battery has been moved across the river and is about to bear down on his position. The General sees at once that his own entrenchments will be ineffective against these massed cannon. He must drastically alter his own defensive plan. With Eleazer Wood's engineering help he will criss-cross the camp with a series of traverses—great embankments of earth, buttressed against cannon fire, with caves scooped out at the base in which the half-buried troops can eat and sleep.

The largest of these embankments is planned to run the entire length of the fort. Because it must be constructed in secrecy, Harrison has his second line of tents taken down to leave an open avenue but keeps the first line standing to mask the work of construction. Now the entire camp is employed throwing up this vast wall of earth, three hundred yards long, fifteen feet high, twenty feet thick at the base. The troops work in three-hour shifts, urged on by Wood who is heartened and astonished by their energy and courage.

This is work the raw recruits understand, for they have toiled with pick and shovel on frontier farms for most of their lives. Driven to almost superhuman exertions by the British activity across the river and by the musket balls of the Indians raining down into the camp, they are remarkably cheerful, singing as they work:

Freemen, no longer bear such slaughter,
Avenge your country's cruel woe!
Arouse, and save your wives and daughters,
Arouse, and expel the faithless foe.

The heavy rains turn the camp into a swamp, filling the trenches with water and slowing the work, which must be finished before the British get their cannon into position. But the British, too, are hampered by weather. Their gun emplacements are completed on April 29. Now they must secretly move up their two big twenty-four-pounders. At nine that evening, under cover of darkness, two hundred men straining on drag ropes with several teams of oxen start to haul the heavy ordnance along the river road through mud that reaches to the wagons' axles. It takes six hours to move the guns one mile; the first streaks of dawn are lighting the sky before they are finally in place.

All this ponderous preparation weighs on Tecumseh. It is Harrison he wants—Harrison, the former governor of Indiana who has stolen the Indians' land; Harrison, whose troops have wantonly burned the villages of the Miami, Kickapoo, Potawatomi, and Ottawa;

Harrison, who has sworn to destroy the Indian confederacy, which the Shawnee war chief and his mystic brother, the Prophet, forged on the banks of the Tippecanoe.

Now Harrison is hiding from him, his men burrowing into the earth like frightened animals. Why cannot the so-called victor of Tippecanoe come out into the open and fight like a man? Tecumseh dispatches a blunt challenge to his old enemy:

"I have with me 800 braves. You have an equal number in your hiding place. Come out with them and give me battle. You talked like a brave man when we met at Vincennes and I respected you, but now you hide behind logs and earth like a ground hog. Give me your answer."

There is no reply. The former governor must see once again in the mirror of his memory that swarthy, hazel-eyed figure in un-adorned deerskin who upset so many of his plans, frustrated his at-tempts to buy native territory for a pittance, dared to face him down on his own estate at Vincennes; who has through the magic of his personality, the eloquence of his oratory, and the quickness of his intelligence managed to rally the tribes of the American northwest and bring them over to the British side. It is Tecumseh who is at the root of America's disgrace; his presence at Detroit tipped the scales to give the British a bloodless victory and control of most of Michigan Territory. His example has brought others swarming to the British cause—Sioux, Sauk, Chippewa, and Menominee from the far reaches of the Upper Mississippi; Mohawk from the Grand Valley of Upper Canada; Caughnawaga from the St. Lawrence; and a horde of American Indians from the Old Northwest.

A rumour has spread through the American lines that Major-General Procter has promised Tecumseh all of Michigan Territory and Harrison's head as well, should the British be victorious at Fort Meigs. More than any other enemy leader, Tecumseh is both feared and admired by the Americans. Harrison has no intention of re-sponding to his taunt.

He will not sleep this long night until he has made a full tour of the camp to make certain every man is at his post. His adjutant of the day, who will accompany him, is one Ohio militiaman he can trust—a wiry, twenty-six-year-old draftee named Alexander Bourne. Bourne does not need to be here, one hundred miles from civilization, drenched by the chill rain, living in a muddy cave, preyed on by hostile Indians. The law allows substitutes, and Bourne could easily have afforded to pay a neighbour ninety dollars to serve six months in his place. But, in spite of the pleading of his friends, Bourne refused. Not all of his fellow militiamen were as steadfast. In the first draft of three men from his unit, Bourne's name was seventeenth on the roll. He was taken anyway because the first fourteen ran off to the woods and were hidden by cronies. Now he is an instant officer, promoted of necessity from private to lieutenant because the company sergeant is so drunk he cannot call the roll.

Bourne's first task this night is to inform Major Alexander that he is duty field officer. He finds him drinking brandy in an officers' marquee, protesting he is unfit for duty. Bourne takes him by the arm, and the two stumble through the lines, the Major lamenting his situation, the adjutant doing his best to cheer him up. The General, it develops, is far too occupied to notice the Major's state. Off they all go on their rounds, General and staff, the drunk and the sober, tumbling into ditches, sometimes two or three on top of one another as the British round shot hurtles harmlessly into the river bank below. It is the first time that Bourne, or indeed Harrison himself, has been exposed to the British artillery fire, but Bourne is not dismayed. He and his comrades are determined now to defend the fort to the last, for they are convinced that surrender will mean massacre at the Indians' hands.

As for Harrison, he can only hope that Brigadier-General Green Clay's reinforcements are within striking distance of his besieged garrison.

FORT MEIGS, OHIO, MAY 1, 1813

The artillery barrage, which the British believe will shatter Harrison's strong point, begins at 11 A.M., but before the red flag goes up signalling the first shot, Major-General Procter and his gunners are faced with a frustrating spectacle. Suddenly, as if pulled by an invisible cord, the masking line of tents goes down revealing an immense shield of earth that screens every tent, horse, and man. Behind it, the men lie in trenches and caves hollowed out in the earthen bulwark, awaiting the inevitable.

The first ball has no sooner sped across the river and buried itself in the mud than Harrison turns to his acting quartermaster, a twenty-two-year-old named William Christie.

"Sir," says the General, "go and nail a banner on every battery, where they shall wave as long as the enemy is in view." Christie hurries off to obey.

The British seem to have unlimited ammunition—huge twenty-four-pound balls of solid pig iron, smaller shot weighing twelve pounds, and bombs—heavy iron shells full of black powder, fused to explode directly above the heads of the defenders, spewing jagged bits of shrapnel in all directions.

They are crack shots, these British gunners. John Richardson, a gentleman volunteer with the British 41st, and, at the age of sixteen, a veteran of two previous battles, notes that the big cannon are aimed as accurately as rifles. As a member of the covering party protecting one battery, he asks the bombardier's permission to charge and point one of the pieces and experiences a sense of delight and power to see the ball land exactly where it is aimed.

But although the British send more than 250 missiles crashing into the fort, these do little damage, most burying themselves in the clay of the traverse, now rendered mushy by the incessant rain. Only a handful of men are wounded and only one killed.

Because Harrison is short of ammunition, his own gunners cannot afford the British extravagance. They have 360 shot only for their eighteen-pound cannon, about the same number for their twelves. As the British are also firing twelve-pound balls into the camp, the Major-General sees no reason why these cannot be returned. He offers a gill of whiskey to every man who delivers an enemy ball to the magazine keeper. Before the siege is over, more than one thousand gills have gone down the throats of the resourceful soldiers. To them, it is a happy substitute for water, which is difficult to come by. The well being dug behind the traverse is not finished, and the men are reduced to scooping up the muddy contents of rainwater pools.

The cannonade lasts until eleven at night, commences with re-doubled fury the following dawn. In the next two days the British pour close to one thousand shot into the fort. One militia man, acting on his own, stands on the embankment, warning his comrades of every shot, becoming so skilful that he can predict exactly where each will fall. As he watches the smoke erupt from a British muzzle he calls out "bomb" or "shot," adding a phrase to indicate its destination—a blockhouse, the main battery, the commissary. His friends urge him to take cover, but he refuses until one shot defies his calculations. The smoke from the cannon has moved neither to right nor to left; he cannot gauge the target. He stands motionless, perplexed, silent, until the great ball strikes him full in the chest, tearing him apart.

Now the British gunners concentrate their fire on the magazine. It has been moved out of the traverse for fear that an exploding bomb may fire it and is now within a small blockhouse, which must be covered with earth for full protection.

"Boys," says an officer, "who will volunteer to cover the magazine?"

Nobody moves. The British are hurling red-hot cannonballs, which hiss sickeningly as they sink into the mud, sending up clouds of acrid smoke; one would be enough to blow up the building. Finally a few men hesitantly step forward. The gunners have not yet got the range. Perhaps if they move quickly they can get the job done.

They no sooner reach the blockhouse than a cannonball slices off one man's head. Like men possessed the survivors fling earth on top of the building. Then, to their horror, a bomb falls on the roof, lodges on a brace, spins about like a top. All but one throw them-selves face down into the mud, expecting to be blown to pieces. The holdout reasons that since death is inevitable if the bomb bursts, he might as well take a chance. He seizes a boat hook, pulls the sput-tering missile to the ground, and jerks the fuse from its socket. His comrades rise and complete their job.

Not far away, Lieutenant Alexander Bourne and a fatigue party of Ohio militia men are struggling to complete an entrenchment. Red-hot cannonballs, aimed at the magazine, whiz past the work party, boiling up the mud until the soldiers can stand it no longer. Bourne reports to Eleazer Wood that he cannot keep his men at this dangerous work. The engineer gives him an unlimited order on the commissary for whiskey, telling him to issue it every half-hour and make the men drink it until they become insensible to fear—but not so drunk, he warns, that they cannot complete the job. Thus fortified, the men reel about, drunkenly curse the British, and ply their shovels until the task is finished.

Bourne, the patriot, is a man fascinated by human nature, and here, during the heat of the barrage, he has an opportunity to examine it under stress. As the cannon thunder and the ground shakes and the rain pelts down he notes examples of indifference, courage, foolhardiness, and cowardice—the four human characteristics that are intensified by war.

One man, he observes, a saddler from Philadelphia named Isaac Burkelon, seems totally insensible to fear. He is that oddity found in every army, the man who volunteers for everything—having for a price replaced a wealthy Chillicothe citizen in the draft. Bourne comes out of his blockhouse one morning to find a huge bombshell hurtling toward him. He calls to Burkelon to lie down, but the saddler refuses to muddy his clothes. When the bomb bursts four feet away, hurling him to the ground and covering him with filth, he rises, shakes himself, and laughs as if he had just indulged in a bit of spirited horseplay.

Another in Bourne's company, a sixty-year-old German named Bolenstein, watches another bomb fall outside the blockhouse. It strikes a stump, bounces off it, skips across the ground. Nothing will do but that Bolenstein should go after it, like a youth chasing a football. In vain Bourne calls him to come back; he is already outside the enclosure, and the sentinels, who are under orders to shoot any man who leaves without permission, are cocking their guns and shouting warnings. Bolenstein tells them to fire away—he means to retrieve the bomb and pull out the fuse. Fortunately it fizzles out, and he returns, laughing, with his prize.

By contrast, Bourne's quartermaster, Sutton, is a coward, so afraid of death that he can neither eat nor sleep. He crouches behind a pile of flour barrels, and while his comrades stand laughing at him, a twenty-four-pound ball crashes through the floor above his head, throwing staves and hoops in every direction and covering him with flour. He jumps up, hurls himself into a wet ditch, screaming "Oh Lord! Oh Lord!" to emerge plastered with paste.

To protect themselves from the bombshells, the men dig holes behind the traverse, covering each with a plank on top of which they shovel a protective mantle of earth. At the warning cry "Bomb!" each runs for his mole hole; but as the rain continues and the hollows fill with water they are forced back into the tents to emerge, half-awake, at each warning cry until, exhausted and indifferent to danger, they ignore the alarms, determined not to be disturbed, as one puts it, "if ten thousand bombs burst around them."

By May 3, four British batteries are hammering the fort. Frustrated by Captain Wood's earthen wall, Procter that night sends a force across the river to establish another. These cannon and mortars, hidden in a thicket only 250 yards from the fort, catch the defenders in a brief crossfire. But Wood has already anticipated the move and a new traverse, hastily thrown up at right angles to the old one, renders the fire ineffective.

The following day—the fourth of the siege—the British fire slackens as if the heart had gone out of the gunners. The defenders, in spite of their exhaustion, are in the habit of waving their hats and giving three cheers whenever the guns are silent, receiving each time an echoing yell from Tecumseh's followers in the woods. Now, as the cheering dies, a white flag is seen. Captain Peter Latouche Chambers of the 41st arrives under its protection to ask for a parley with Harrison on behalf of his commander.

Says Chambers: "General Procter has directed me to demand the surrender of this post. He wishes to spare the effusion of blood."

To which Harrison responds with some warmth: "The demand

under the present circumstances, is an extraordinary one. As General Procter did not send me a summons to surrender on his first arrival, I had supposed that he believed me determined to do my duty. His present message indicates an opinion of me that I am at a loss to account for."

Generals, in this war, may fire cannon at one another, but insults are odious. Captain Chambers hastens to correct any impression of incivility:

"General Procter could never think of saying anything to wound your feelings, sir. The character of General Harrison, as an officer, is well known. General Procter's force is very respectable, and there is with him a larger body of Indians than has ever before been embodied."

There it is: the veiled threat that if the fort is taken, the Indians cannot be prevented from massacring the survivors. The threat worked at Michilimackinac early in the war and it worked again at Detroit, when Isaac Brock and Tecumseh terrified William Hull into surrendering not only an army but also most of Michigan. It does not work with Harrison.

"Assure the General," Harrison responds in his stilted fashion, "that he will never have this post surrendered to him upon any terms. Should it fall into his hands, it will be in a manner calculated to do him more honor, and to give him larger claims upon the gratitude of his government, than any capitulation could possibly do."

In short, Harrison is prepared to fight to the last man. He does not like Procter and in this chilly exchange makes little attempt to hide his disdain for the man who every American believes (and with truth) abandoned defenceless and wounded Kentucky troops to the hatchets of the Potawatomi after the battle of the River Raisin in January.

Nonetheless he knows his situation is critical. The fort cannot hold out forever. Once its ammunition is gone, Harrison's men will be at the mercy of an immeasurably stronger and better-trained army of seasoned British regulars and enraged natives.

Midnight comes. The bombardment ceases. Men sleep exhausted in their muddy shelters. And then, out of the blackness comes Captain

William Oliver, Harrison's emissary. He has slipped through the Indian lines, guarded by fifteen dragoons, all virtually invisible on this foggy, moonless night.

Captain Oliver brings heartening news: General Clay and his reinforcements are only two hours away. Harrison realizes he must act at once. He knows that the bulk of the British force is two miles downriver at the old British Fort Miami, that most of Tecumseh's Indians are on the right bank, investing his position. This means that the big guns across the river, harassing his stockade, are lightly manned.

He forms his plan swiftly: he will strike simultaneous blows on both sides of the river. Part of Clay's advancing force will spike the guns on the opposite shore. The remainder will attack the Indians on the near bank. Once the battle is joined, the Americans will burst out of the fort, attack the British battery in their rear, and defeat the British and Indians on the American-held side of the river.

The plan depends on surprise, discipline, and perfect timing. Harrison is only too well aware that Clay's Kentuckians are green, having seen no more than thirty days' service. Nonetheless, it is a gamble he must take. He dispatches his aide, Captain Hamilton, and a subaltern under cover of the black night to carry his orders to General Clay.

BELOW THE MAUMEE RAPIDS, OHIO, MAY 5, 1813

Lieutenant Joseph Underwood lies shivering in the stern of the leading American flatboat in General Clay's flotilla as it sweeps down the Maumee in the wan light of daybreak. Underwood is recovering from a severe attack of measles; his single blanket, wrapped tightly around him, is not enough to protect him from the raw drizzle that beats across the valley. Behind him, swirling in the curves of the river, are seventeen similar craft, each carrying one hundred Kentuckians protected from the arrows of marauding Indians by heavy shields of timber nailed to the bulwarks.

Underwood can hear the rumble of the big guns downriver. As

the little fleet courses on, the rumble grows louder, becomes a deafening roar. The sound seems to well up from the bottom of the flatboat until the atmosphere dances with it and the world vibrates with every volley.

It is Underwood's first experience of cannon fire. He will never forget it. He is only twenty, an ardent Kentucky volunteer, recruited as a private but elected lieutenant in the democratic fashion of the American militia, which will have no truck with the military authoritarianism of Europe. The words of his general still ring in his ears:

"Kentuckians stand high in the estimation of our common country. Our brothers in arms who have gone before us to the scene of action have acquired a fame which should never be forgotten by you—a fame worthy of your emulation—Should we encounter the enemy, *remember the fate of your butchered brothers at the River Raisin—that British treachery produced their slaughter!*"

The devil Procter is up ahead: the moment for revenge has arrived at last.

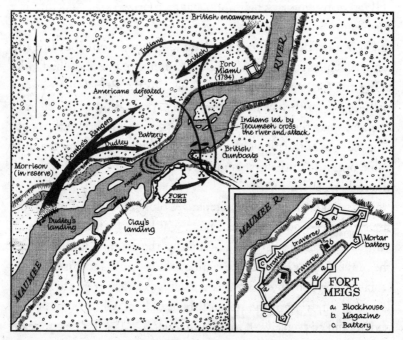

The Battle of Fort Meigs

On the right bank of the river, Underwood spots two men waving at the flotilla. Lieutenant-Colonel William Dudley, in command of the lead boat, dispatches a canoe to pick them up. These are Harrison's emissaries: they have a message for General Clay. Dudley sends them back to Boat Number Thirteen. Underwood watches them go, wondering what their message is. Alas, he and his comrades will never be told the details.

Like most American militia commanders, Green Clay is more politician than soldier. His roots go back to America's beginnings: his great-grandfather first came to Virginia with Sir Walter Raleigh. The Speaker of the House is a cousin; Clay himself has served as a member of both houses of the Kentucky legislature. At fifty-five he is wealthy from land speculation. He is also something of a classical scholar, has named his son (a future ambassador) Cassius Marcellus Clay, a name that will be adopted by succeeding generations of blacks on his tobacco plantation, one of whose descendants will become heavyweight boxing champion of the world.

Harrison's emissary, Hamilton, has memorized a succinct message for Clay:

"You must detach about eight hundred men from your brigade, who will land at a point I will show, about one or one and a half miles above the fort, and I will conduct them to the British batteries on the left side of the river. They must take possession of the enemy's cannon, spike them, cut down the carriages, and return to the boats. The balance of the men under your command will land on the right bank, opposite to the first landing, and will fight their way through the Indians to the fort."

Clay makes his plans: Lieutenant-Colonel William Dudley, the senior officer, now in the lead boat, will land the first twelve craft on the left bank to carry the assault on the cannon. Clay will lead the remaining six boats to the right bank to harass Tecumseh's force.

Hamilton goes off downstream to convey Clay's orders to Dudley. Underwood, lying in the stern of the lead boat, watches him climb aboard and converse with his commander. Dudley is a heavy, fleshy man, "weak and obstinate but brave" in Harrison's assessment, "ignorant and rash" in the later, rueful opinion of Eleazer Wood, the engineer. Like Underwood, Dudley has never heard a hostile gun until this morning. In common with so many other citizen commanders he also suffers from a fatal flaw: he does not bother to explain to his subordinates the full purpose of Harrison's plan—to spike the cannon and get out fast. Lieutenant Underwood, who is second-in-command of Captain John Morrison's company, is told only that the troops will land on the left bank and storm the enemy batteries. And then? Nobody tells him.

Suddenly—gunfire! On the right bank muskets flash as a group of Indians appear. One of the captains is wounded in the head. The troops fire back and the Indians flee, no doubt to warn the British.

It comes home to Underwood that he is about to fight and perhaps to die, and with that realization everything takes on a different hue. The morning may be grey, the wind raw, the rain chill, the brooding woods oppressive, yet the world has never looked brighter or more attractive. He gazes about him at ordinary objects and realizes that for him they may soon disappear forever. His thoughts go back to home, to old friends, and in his mind he bids them farewell. He finds that he is neither frightened nor alarmed but strangely calm with the calmness of melancholy.

His daydream is interrupted as the boats nose into the bank and the troops leap off and form up in three columns, one hundred yards apart. The left column is to swing around on the flank and get behind the British guns while Dudley on the extreme right attacks the batteries from the river side. The centre column, led by Underwood's captain, Morrison, will come up in reserve. Captain Leslie Combs will lead his company of thirty riflemen as an advance party to protect the flank.

Silently, the Kentuckians creep forward. Suddenly Combs's rangers flush a small party of Indians, who after a brief skirmish flee toward the British encampment. At this the troops break their silence and with a tremendous yell fall upon the enemy batteries. The British gunners flee in disorder, and Dudley's men, without bothering to wait for the spikes that are being sent by Harrison to hammer into the powder holes, use ramrods from their muskets to render the cannon powerless.

At this point, everything that Harrison had hoped for has been achieved. The guns have been silenced before Procter's reinforcements can be brought forward or the Indians on the opposite bank can cross the river. It is time to retire, but Dudley's men do not know this. They loiter around the useless guns, confused and disorganized, cheering themselves hoarse. In vain, Harrison, watching from the fort, signals them to return. The troops believe the General is cheering them on and so cheer back.

As the minutes tick by, more Indians appear at the fringe of the woods bordering the open plain on which the British guns are placed. *Indians!* Caution cannot compete with ancestral memories, folk tales, gaudy stories handed down by uncles and grandfathers who have, since the days of Daniel Boone, battled the redskins on the old frontier. Flushed with victory, oblivious to the entreaties of Dudley, who flails about him with a half-pike, the Kentuckians tear after the painted enemy. The slowly retreating tribesmen draw their quarry farther and farther away from the protection of the plain, where the fort's cannon can give them cover, and deeper into a wooded labyrinth, creased by ravines and encumbered by stumps and logs.

Harrison is in anguish.

"They are lost! They are lost!" he cries from his vantage point across the river. "Can I never get men to obey my orders?"

He offers one thousand dollars to any volunteer who will cross over and warn Dudley. A young lieutenant instantly accepts, rushes to the bank, struggles to launch a pirogue, finally gets it into midstream only to realize he is too late. British reinforcements have arrived. The smell of defeat is in the air.

OLD FORT MIAMI, OHIO, MAY 5, 1813

John Richardson, the teenaged gentleman volunteer with the British 41st, is just sitting down to breakfast in a wet shelter made of evergreen boughs when a rabble of gunners dashes into camp crying out that the Americans have seized the batteries.

Richardson looks ruefully at the scanty meal he will never eat—a tough steak of half-cooked beef, a piece of dry bread, a mug of tea made from sassafras root, sweetened with sap from the sugar maple. It is not much of a meal, but here in this sodden camp it is a banquet. Richardson, who has not yet attained his full growth, is perennially ravenous, a condition aggravated by the fact that, being a junior, he is the last to reach the cooking pot. On the forced march that follows, the future novelist thinks more of the uneaten meal and what will happen to it than he does of the approaching conflict.

The sound of musket fire on the left snaps him out of his reverie. The Americans are in possession of the guns: Richardson can see them milling about the batteries. The Scotch mist of dawn has turned to driving rain, rendering the mud knee deep. In this soft pudding the men flounder forward in an attempt to retrieve their losses. One of the 41st falls dead. Captain Peter Chambers—the same officer who dealt with Harrison the day before—seizes the dead man's musket, throws away his own sword, and shouts:

"Who will follow me and retake that battery?"

"I will!" cries little John Richardson. Two other officers and a dozen men push forward with him against the American right flank.

Richardson, who believes this tiny attacking force will be wiped out, is astonished when the Americans give way. He does not yet know that Tecumseh and his Indians have swum the river and sucked the American left flank into the maze of the forest. As the Kentuckians stumble forward, mauled by the elusive native sharp-shooters withdrawing behind logs and stumps, Tecumseh circles around behind them. Caught in an ambush, the green troops are driven back toward the advancing British, trapped between two fires.

Captain Morrison's reserve column has hastened to the rescue of his fellow Americans—too late. Joseph Underwood gets a brief glimpse of Lieutenant-Colonel Dudley, who rails at him for not keeping his men in better line; but the ground is so uneven, the bush so thick that any sort of parade-ground manoeuvre is impossible, especially for raw troops. It is the last time Underwood will see Dudley alive.

Morrison falls, shot through the temple, his optic nerve severed by a musket ball. Underwood does what he can for his sightless captain, then takes command of the company, already falling back under Tecumseh's ambush.

The retreat becomes a rout. The Kentuckians rush back through the woods toward the batteries, where Underwood confidently expects they can re-form and repel the Indians. Men are dropping all around him as he runs. Suddenly he feels something slam into his back—a stunning, deadening blow that pitches him forward onto his hands and knees. He pulls himself to his feet, throws open his waistcoat to see if the ball has passed through his body. There is no sign of it. He stumbles on, emerging at last from the woods onto the open ground where the batteries stand. Somebody seizes his sword: a British soldier.

"Sir," cries his captor, "you are my prisoner!"

Underwood is astonished, looks about, sees the ground littered with discarded muskets.

Says his captor: "Your army has surrendered."

He has difficulty understanding this, stumbles forward to a line of captives, recognizes one of his men, Daniel Smith.

"Good Lord, Lieutenant," says Smith, his eyes brimming with tears, "what does all this mean?"

Underwood tells him what he has himself only just discovered: they have been defeated. Of Dudley's force of 800, fewer than 150 have escaped. The rest are either captured or dead, including the Colonel himself, whose corpse, already scalped, lies somewhere in the forest.

The prisoners are marched downriver toward the old British fort, now not much more than a crumbling ruin. As they are driven forward, the Indians loot them of clothes and possessions. Underwood loses all his outer clothing but manages to hide his watch. Because he has read somewhere that the Indians treat best those who show no fear, he stares sternly at his native captors until one strikes him full in the face with a stick. Underwood decides that humility is a better policy.

On reaching the fort, the prisoners face a hideous ordeal. On their left, some twenty paces back from the river bank, stands a line of armed Indians reaching to the gate of the enclosure. Each man must run this gauntlet, already slippery with blood and flanked by a hedgerow of naked, scalped corpses. Some of the British escorts attempt to prevent the Indians from belabouring the column with tomahawks, war clubs, and rifles, but when one British regular from the 41st is shot through the heart, these attempts cease.

Underwood notices that the men nearest the river bank, and thus farthest from the line of warriors, suffer the most as they try to reach the fort. He determines to run as close as possible to the Indians, who will not be able to shoot him in the curve of the laneway without killing their own people. He dashes forward, feeling the blows of ramrods on his back. The man ahead drops dead. Underwood stumbles across his corpse, but others fall on it, blocking the passageway. In the end he reaches the safety of the fort, badly bruised and bleeding from the wound in his back but still alive.

Within the ruined walls of the old fort, hundreds of Kentucky prisoners mill about. Underwood, exhausted, rests on the ground, his head in the lap of a fellow soldier. But the terror has not ended. A gigantic rawboned brave, face and body painted jet black, climbs on an earthen embankment and harangues the crowd in an angry voice. Some of the British who understand the Potawatomi tongue attempt to reason with him.

"Oh, *Nichee wah!*" they cry, again and again. "Oh, brother, don't do it!"

It is useless. The Indian raises his rifle, shoots a man at the foot of the embankment, reloads, shoots another dead. Panic ripples through the crowd. The big Potawatomi leaps down, draws his tomahawk, sinks it into the head of another victim. Those closest to the attacker scramble to get away, trampling their own comrades including Underwood, who, face down and half smothered by his own gore, can hear the cracking of skulls around him. When he extricates himself, he counts four corpses on the floor, their scalps already dangling from the Potawatomi's belt.

A general massacre seems inevitable. The Indians are already throwing the covers off their rifle locks. Suddenly a tall warrior in fringed deerskin gallops into the fort, makes his way to the heart of the throng, climbs onto the embankment, shouting over the din. The crowd grows quiet, the Indians begin to grunt as the stranger points directly at the murderer and delivers what is clearly a dressing-down. The Potawatomi warrior scowls, shakes his head, turns on his heel, leaves. Only later do the prisoners realize that their deliverer is the celebrated Tecumseh.

Nobody can be sure what the Shawnee war chief has said for none can understand his tongue. It is well known that he abhors torture and the slaying of prisoners—has been opposed to it since his boyhood when he watched a white man slowly roasted at the stake and swore he would never again countenance such savagery. Later the story of his intervention at Fort Miami will take on the trappings of legend, for this is a man who, being larger than life, inspires myth. Some will pretend to recall that he buried his tomahawk in the head of the murderer, but that is fancy. The Shawnee does not need to indulge in violent gestures; his tongue is enough to subdue his followers.

He is Tecumseh and he is unique. After a year of warfare he has managed to hold together the fragile alliance of tribesmen entirely through the iron force of his personality. There are some this day who fancy they see in those dark features omens of despair. Some profess to see tears in the hazel eyes. Others claim that he cries out in passion, "Oh! What will become of my Indians?"—that he seeks out Procter and asks why he has not intervened, that he attacks the British general, sneering, "Begone, you are unfit to command; go and put on petticoats."

It is possible. He has little love for Procter, whom he considers a weak commander. But none can really know what transpires between them, for, apart from Matthew Elliott of the British Indian Department, no one speaks Shawnee—and Elliott is unlikely to tell.

Elliott has seen massacres before, has in fact taken part in several; in that sense he is as savage as the Indians.

The prisoners, secure at last from further attack, are formed up in four lines to be counted. One of the Kentucky men strips off Underwood's mud-streaked bloody garments and offers him his hunting jacket, saved from the looters. As the Indians begin to select prisoners to be taken to the villages for ransom or adoption, the younger men, who are most wanted, try to crowd into the centre of the mob, beyond reach.

Unable to struggle, the wounded Underwood is thrust to the outside. An Indian hands him a piece of meat, and the soldier is certain he intends to carry him off. He decides to act boldly, borrows the Indian's knife, cuts the meat into pieces, offers it to his friends, saving a small bit for himself mostly as a show of politeness, for he has little appetite. When he returns the knife the Indian leaves—he was only being friendly—and Underwood sighs in relief. Shortly he will be paroled to his home in Kentucky. For him the war is over, and he can return to his fledgling law practice. Some day he will be a United States senator, a judge, a presidential elector. And always he will carry in the flesh of his back the leaden musket ball discharged from an Indian gun during the bloody battle of Fort Meigs.

OLD FORT MIAMI, OHIO, MAY 6, 1813

The day after the battle, as dusk descends, John Richardson accompanies Major Adam Muir of the British 41st on a stroll through the Indian encampment, a few hundred yards from the British tents.

A grotesque sight meets his eyes. Here are Chippewa and Menominee warriors decked out in the blue-and-gold uniforms of American officers, strutting about in unaccustomed high leather boots which force them into awkward postures. Here are others— Sioux, Winnebago, Potawatomi—wearing ruffled shirts that contrast with their dusky bodies. Behind them are tepees ornamented with saddles, bridles, rifles, daggers, swords, pistols, many intricately wrought and exquisitely designed. Mingled with these trophies are the scalps of the Americans, half dried, dyed with vermilion, suspended from poles, swinging gently in the night breeze. Interspersed with these grisly trophies are hoops upon which portions of human skin have been stretched—a hand here, a foot there, with the nails still clinging to it—while strewn about the camp are the flayed limbs, half gnawed by packs of wild dogs that roam among the tents.

On the face of it, the plunder suggests a stupendous British victory. Here, for instance, parcelled among the tribesmen, is the personal baggage of Brigadier-General Green Clay, captured after he left his boat in the shadow of the American fort the previous morning. A general officer does not travel light. Clay's camp kit includes a trunk, a portmanteau, flat iron, coffee mill, razor strop and box, inkstand and quills, reams of paper, three halters, shoebrushes, blacking, saddle and bridle, tortoise-shell comb and case, a box of mercurial ointment, silver spoons, mattresses and pillows, three blankets, three sheets, two towels, linen for a cot, two volumes of *M'Kenzie's Travels*, two maps, spyglass, gold watch, brace of silver-mounted pistols, umbrella, sword, two pairs of spurs (one silver), a pair of shoes, bottle-green coat, scarlet waistcoat, blue cashmere and buff cashmere waistcoats, striped jean waistcoat, cotton pantaloons, bottle-green pantaloons, cord pantaloons, short breeches, flannel waistcoat and shirt, five white linen shirts, two check shirts, nine cravats, six chamois, two pairs of thread stockings, three pairs of thread socks, hunting shirt, hat, two pairs of gloves—all in the hands of the Indians.

Yet all this loot is deceptive. While Dudley was attacking the British batteries, Clay himself with six boatloads of Kentucky soldiers was successfully fighting his way into Fort Meigs. And though he lost his personal kit he managed to bring in all the cannonballs and ammunition. Harrison's two sorties, timed to coincide with the attack on the guns, have both been successful. The British battery on the American side of the river has been destroyed, the Indians driven off.

Moreover, under pretence of a prisoner exchange Harrison has been able to take advantage of a brief armistice to bring in the rest of the ammunition the defenders need so badly. A message from Procter, calling on him to surrender, is treated with disdain.

Both sides have reached a stalemate. Harrison is so exhausted from lack of sleep, so miserable from the cold and the driving rain that he has not the strength to compose a detailed account of the affair for the Secretary of War. His men, too, are worn out. The wounded lie untended in the trenches, supported on rails that barely keep their bodies above water. But the fort still stands. Procter has not been able to capture it.

Nor can he. The Indians, loaded with plunder, are drifting back to their villages with their wounded to display their prisoners and their trophies. A deputation of chiefs waits upon the British general to explain that they cannot prevent this exodus; it is the custom after every battle. Only Tecumseh and a handful of followers remain.

The citizen soldiers cannot be relied on either. Another deputation of eight officers from the 1st and 2nd Regiments of the Essex and Kent militia makes it clear that if the men are not allowed to return to their farms to sow their spring wheat and corn, "the consequence must be famine next winter." Indeed, half the militiamen have already taken off; it is beyond the power of any commander to hold on to the rest.

The regulars are in a bad state, suffering from dysentery, ague, and fatigue as a result of wretched weather, poor food, and exhausting fighting. On top of this comes the news that Little York has fallen to the enemy—a piece of intelligence not calculated to lift the army's morale. Procter has no choice but to raise the siege and return to Amherstburg.

Both commanders in their official reports put the best possible face on the battle, overestimating their adversary's strength as well as his losses and minimizing their own.

Procter writes to Sir George Prevost that he believes the enemy's casualties to have been between one thousand and twelve hundred. Harrison assures Armstrong that no more than fifty Kentuckians have been killed and that he has reason to believe that many have escaped up the river to Fort Defiance.

As a result of Procter's report, Prevost's General Order announces "the brilliant result of an action which took place on the banks of the Miami river . . . which terminated in the complete defeat of the Enemy and the capture, dispersion or destruction of 1300 Men by the Gallant division of the Army under the Command of Brig. General Procter. . . ."

Harrison in a similar General Order, issued about the same time, "congratulates the troops upon having completely foiled their foes and put a stop to their career of victory which has hitherto attended their Arms. He cannot find words to express his sence [*sic*] of the good conduct of the Troops of every description and of every corpse [*sic*]."

Only at the end does he temporize:

"It rarely occurs that a General has to complain of the excessive ardor of his men yet such appears always to be the case whenever the Kentucky Militia are engaged. It is indeed the sorce [*sic*] of all their misfortunes. They appear to think that valor alone can accomplish anything. . . . Such temerity although not so disgraceful is scarcely less fatal than Cowardice. . . ."

FOUR

The Northwest Campaign: 2

The Contest for Lake Erie

June–September, 1813

American strategy in the Northwest is to destroy the British-Indian alliance. That will secure their left flank and free thousands of troops for the main struggle farther to the east. But the Americans cannot move their army out of Fort Meigs until they control Lake Erie and the Detroit River, at present British waterways. The spring and summer of 1813 find both sides engaged in a shipbuilding contest for supremacy on the lake—the Americans at Presque Isle, the British at Amherstburg.

ABOARD THE BRIG *CALEDONIA*, EN ROUTE FROM BUFFALO, NEW YORK, TO PRESQUE ISLE, JUNE 13, 1813

Oliver Hazard Perry, the American commodore, returning to Lake Erie after his part in the capture of Fort George, lies tossing in his bunk, a victim of what the doctors call "bilious fever." It is a recurring malady. The invalid looks the picture of health—a tall robust naval commander, his plump cheeks framed by dark, curly sideburns. Those who encounter him are struck by the symmetry of his figure, the grace of his movements. Yet with Perry appearances are deceptive: in moments of stress he falls prey to what is virtually a chronic complaint.

For the past several weeks, the stress has been almost constant: the responsibility of constructing a new fleet from scratch, the long horseback ride along the Niagara followed by the attack on Fort George, and, most recently, a struggle to warp a small flotilla of five vessels out of their haven near Black Rock on the Niagara and on to Presque Isle on Lake Erie, where the major American warships are under construction.

It has not been easy. On Perry's arrival at Black Rock a strong west wind made any movement impossible for a week. Finally, with the help of two hundred soldiers and several teams of oxen, his men managed to haul the boats upstream for three miles in the teeth of the gale. Now at last he is on his way, leading the flotilla in the prize brig *Caledonia*, seized from the British the preceding summer by Lieutenant Jesse Elliott.

Elliott, though junior in rank to Perry, is far better known to the American public, a national hero, awarded a sword by Congress for that daring escapade—the only victory in a string of scandalous defeats. A veteran, also, of the recent attack on York, chosen originally to command on Lake Erie, he finds himself, at thirty-one, superseded by a late arrival four years younger than himself and with less battle experience. In such circumstances only a man devoid of human flaws—and Elliott has his share—could fail to be a little jealous. And Elliott is vain, given to boasting, and not always generous with subordinates, for he likes to retain the credit for any accomplishment.

A bit of a troublemaker (he has already fought one duel, will fight more), he has piqued Perry's right-hand man, Daniel Dobbins, by sneering at his choice of the sheltered harbour of Presque Isle as a shipyard. A shallow sandbar blocks the entrance; Elliott, who has never visited Lake Erie, claims that Perry's big ships cannot get across it. He much prefers his own choice of Black Rock, in spite of the fact that the harbour there is a *cul de sac*, within easy range of British guns at Fort Erie and within striking distance of the British army.

Fortunately, the British have been forced, briefly, to abandon Fort Erie in their scramble up the peninsula. Perry takes advantage of their absence to manoeuvre the five vessels out of their potential trap and, under cover of fog, up the Niagara River into Lake Erie.

The two young naval officers, who as a result of this summer's events will be pitted against each other in bitter controversy, are a study in contrasts. Both are brave men who joined the navy in their teens as midshipmen and fought the Barbary pirates in the Tripolitan wars at the start of the century. There the similarities end. Elliott comes from a long line of black Donegal Irishmen; his kinsman and enemy is that same Matthew Elliott of the British Indian Department who is Tecumseh's friend, Harrison's *bete noire*. Fatherless since the age of nine (the elder Elliott having been slain by Indians), he is hot tempered, brooding, quick to take offence at any imagined slight.

Perry's people are Quakers, his father a retired naval captain. He comes from a family of eight—a brother, Matthew, will one day gain fame by opening Japan to the West. Like Elliott, he has a quick temper but has learned to keep it under control. Most of his colleagues find him quiet, unemotional, sedate, courteous, a little humourless. Dr. Usher Parsons, his surgeon, finds him to be the most remarkable officer he has known for impressing his subordinates with almost reverential awe, inculcating in them a dread of giving their commander offence. He is well read, plays the flute, is a capable fencer, a student of both history and drama, and a fearless and elegant horseman.

He is also a man of considerable moral rectitude. He disdains to indulge in naval profanity and, although it is customary to allow any fleet commander a percentage of construction costs, Perry has refused to take a penny, in sharp contrast to his superior, Chauncey, who is reaping a fortune at Sackets Harbor. "It might influence

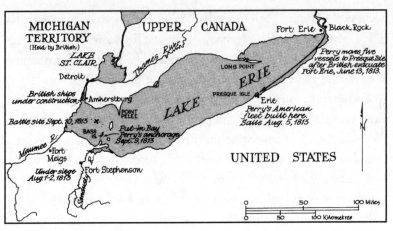

Action on Lake Erie, Summer, 1813

my judgement," says Perry, "and cause people to question my good faith."

Does this paragon have no chinks in his armour? There is one reassuring imperfection. It is said that Perry, who does not give a hang for musket ball or grape-shot, has an almost pathological fear of cows, will trudge through mud to avoid one if he hears so much as a moo. That, and a tendency to succumb to fever after periods of strain, appear to be his only frailties.

The wind, which has bedevilled Perry with its moodiness for the past week, now drops, and the squadron is forced to return to its anchorage at Buffalo. The following morning it sets off again, crawling along the shoreline, sails drooping in a wan breeze. In the first twenty-four hours it moves no more than twenty-five miles.

That night Perry anchors close to shore to escape detection. A man signals from the bank and comes aboard to warn that the British flotilla of five boats, led by the flagship *Queen Charlotte*, has appeared off Presque Isle. Sick or not, Perry is out of his bunk and on deck, ready to do battle. But when, on June 19, he reaches his destination he learns that the British, having finished their reconnaissance, have departed. It is one of the strokes of good fortune that seem to attend Perry's career. The British clearly outgun him, even without their biggest ship, *Detroit*, unfinished at Amherstburg. The fleets will not be equal until Perry completes his two brigs, *Lawrence* and *Niagara*, still under construction here at Presque Isle Bay.

This is the best natural harbour on Lake Erie, a placid sheet of water, three miles long and more than a mile wide, protected from Erie's storms by a six-mile finger of land that curls around the outer edge. A sandbar, six feet below the surface, joins the peninsula to the far shore, effectively barring the harbour from enemy incursion. The advantage is two-edged. Jesse Elliott is not the only one who is convinced that the big brigs under construction will draw too much water to cross the bar, especially with the British fleet lurking just outside.

Now, as the pilots manoeuvre the five light vessels through the narrow channel that splits the sandbar, Perry's men can see the village of Erie crowded along the shoreline—some fifty frame houses, a blacksmith shop, tannery, and court house, the last serving as a sail loft.

The shipbuilders have been here most of the winter, Perry since March. As a result of this season's labours, three of his staff will go into the history books: Noah Brown, his building superintendent, a carpenter since the age of fifteen and the owner of the most flourishing shipyard in New York; Henry Eckford, his architect and designer, a Scottish-born genius, whose own shipyard is next door to Brown's; and the indispensable Daniel Dobbins, organizer and troubleshooter, a seasoned lake captain whose home is here in Erie. Dobbins has seen more of the war than his colleagues, for he was captured by the British in the summer of 1812 and escaped to bring to Washington the early news of Detroit's surrender.

These are young, energetic men—average age, thirty-five. They need to be, for the problems of building sophisticated fighting vessels hundreds of miles from the centre of civilization seem almost insurmountable. Presque Isle's sole resource is timber. Everything else must be hauled in by keel boat and then ox cart, over roads that are no more than tracks wriggling through the forests, punctuated by mudholes, blocked by stumps and deadfalls. Dobbins and Perry have had to travel to Meadville to scrape up steel to make axes. Iron

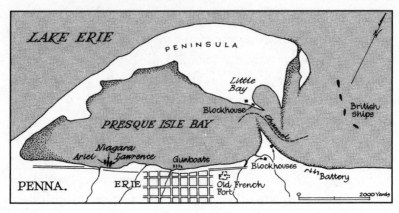

Presque Isle

comes from Bellefonte, spike rods from Buffalo, cables and hawsers
from Pittsburgh, canvas from Philadelphia. Oakum is non-existent;
the gunboats and brigs are caulked with old rope. Dobbins has to
plunder his old schooner *Salina* for scrap iron, rigging, and shot.

Brown's army of axemen, choppers, and sawyers have partially
denuded the surrounding forest, working from dawn to dusk,
hacking down cucumber, oak, poplar, and ash for ribs, white pine
for decks and bulwarks, black oak for planking and frames, red cedar
and walnut for stanchions. It is all handwork; there are no sawmills
within easy reach of the shipyard. So swift has the race been that a
tree on the outskirts of the settlement can be growing one day and
part of a ship the next.

Eckford, who outfitted all five of the vessels brought from Black
Rock, has also designed four of the six being built at Presque Isle, including the two great brigs. Since no conventional craft of those sizes
could get across the sandbar blocking the harbour's mouth, Eckford
has had to design fighting vessels with extremely shallow drafts.

It is trying work. Unavoidable food shortages have caused more
than one strike. Delays have been maddening. Anchors ordered for
May I have not yet arrived. Yet, in spite of it all, the ships are in
the water, nearing completion. Perry confidently expects that his
fleet of eleven vessels will be ready by mid-July. He has, however,
two problems: he does not have enough seamen to man them, and

he still faces the difficult task of getting his biggest ships across the sandbar, beyond which the British are again lurking, ready to tear them to pieces before they can make sail.

SANDWICH, UPPER CANADA, JULY 4, 1813

509

—

FLAMES
ACROSS
THE
BORDER

Major-General Henry Procter, commander of the British Right Division, has never felt so frustrated. On this Independence Day, as his enemies fire rockets into the sky and sound church bells in celebration of their original victory over his countrymen, he vents his spleen in a brace of letters, one to Captain Robert McDouall, General Vincent's aide-de-camp at Burlington Heights, the other— couched in more temperate language—to Sir George Prevost, the Governor General of Canada.

Procter feels abandoned. His naval colleague, the one-armed Captain Robert Heriot Barclay, newly in command on Lake Erie, has returned from his reconnaissance of Presque Isle full of gloom. The new American brigs are already in the water while the British ship *Detroit* is still on the ways at Amherstburg. Procter knows what he should do: he should attack Erie at once and destroy Perry's fleet before it can be fitted; but he has neither men nor supplies for that task.

He is especially piqued at De Rottenburg, Sheaffe's replacement as commander of the forces in Upper Canada. Prevost has promised to dispatch the remainder of the first battalion of the 41st to Fort Amherstburg, but De Rottenburg, faced with the need to invest Fort George, has been dragging his feet. Procter does not believe that the commanding general has any intention of sending him a single man. He is short of gunners, clerks, servants, artificers, as well as fighting men. He is also short of food for his men and of money to pay them. Things are so bad that "we have scarcely the Means of constructing even a Blockhouse."

Captain Barclay is equally desperate for seamen. He has arrived with the merest handful, most of them incompetent, only a few able to speak English. He needs three hundred trained sailors and

marines to man his fleet, but Sir James Lucas Yeo, his superior at
Kingston, will not even send him a shipwright. A super-cautious
commander, Yeo wants to hold on to every man and scrap of material to meet the threat of Chauncey's fleet on Lake Ontario.

It must be obvious to Procter that Prevost, De Rottenburg, and
Yeo consider Lake Erie expendable. Indeed, it has been British
strategy since the start of the war to defend Montreal and Quebec
at any cost, even if it means abandoning Upper Canada. Now, with
the Americans threatening the Niagara peninsula and Chauncey's
fleet menacing the St. Lawrence lifeline, Procter's superiors are more
reluctant than ever to weaken their own thin forces at Kingston
and Burlington Heights. De Rottenburg says as much, bluntly, to
Procter: he "must first secure Command of the lower Lake; after
which there will be no Difficulty in recovering the Command of
the Upper one."

Procter disagrees. On July 11, he ruefully writes to Prevost to point
out that had he received the promised men and supplies, he could
probably have destroyed all of Perry's vessels at Presque Isle, thus
securing command of the lake and making a powerful diversion in
favour of General Vincent's embattled Centre Division.

Across the water, Perry's fleet is rapidly approaching fighting
trim. Barclay's new ship, *Detroit*, along with two gunboats under
construction at Amherstburg, will even the odds on Lake Erie, but
Detroit will not be launched until July 20, let alone rigged. Perry's
shipbuilding problems are minor compared with those of the British.
Canada has no steel or iron mills, no Pittsburghs or Philadelphias,
no manufacturing worthy of the name. Everything but timber-nails,
bolts, pulleys, lead, copper, glass, paint, resin, cordage, sails—must
come from caches in Montreal and Quebec and ultimately from
England. Cannon intended for Barclay's ship have been expropri-
ated by Yeo at Kingston; new ones must be ordered and shipped
across the Atlantic, up the St. Lawrence, across Lake Ontario
(where Chauncey's fleet lies waiting) and, with the Niagara peninsula in flames, by a long land route through the forests of Upper
Canada to Amherstburg.

Now the significance of the American attack on York comes into focus. It was, Chauncey said at the time, a blow from which the British could not recover. Certainly the loss of fifty thousand dollars' worth of stores—guns, ammunition, cables, cordage, canvas, tools, all destined for Barclay's fleet—is making itself felt. Prevost's only solution, which is no solution at all, is to urge Procter to make up his deficiencies by seizing guns and stores from the enemy "whose resources on Lake Erie must become yours." But Procter does not believe his force strong enough to attack Presque Isle with its block-houses and redoubts.

Yet he must do *something*, for the Indians are becoming rest-less. Supplies are so short that they are living mainly on bread; the traditional presents, by which the tribesmen are mollified, have not arrived. They chafe for action; without it even the best efforts of Tecumseh cannot keep them in line. Without a battle to fight, without glory and excitement, without the prospect of loot, scalps, or prisoners to ransom, the Indians will drift away to their villages and Procter's army will be irretrievably weakened.

Procter is made uncomfortably aware that he does not command the Indians. If anything, the Indians command him; they far out-number his own force. To a very large degree his movements are "subject to their Caprices and Prejudices." One group is loyal to Tecumseh and his brother, the Shawnee Prophet, the other—recently arrived from the Far West—to Robert Dickson, the Red-Haired Man. Even Dickson cannot control his followers for long.

Tecumseh and the others insist on mounting a second attack on Fort Meigs. Procter believes, with good reason, that Harrison's stronghold is too tough a nut to crack. Yet he has no choice: if he does not go on the attack he will lose his Indian allies. So Fort Meigs it must be.

Tecumseh has worked out an ingenious plan to take the fort by deception, for he, too, realizes that it cannot be captured without heavy artillery. The trick is to lure the Americans *out* of the fort and fall upon them from an ambush. To that end he proposes to stage a sham battle at some distance from the palisade. Hearing the sounds of conflict, the Americans will believe that reinforcements are on their way to relieve the fort but are being attacked. Tecumseh's hope is that the enemy will burst out of the fort to aid their comrades, whereupon Procter's superior force will cut them up.

Within Fort Meigs, Brigadier-General Green Clay has been preparing for trouble. Spies and deserters have already informed him that the Indians are eager to resume the siege. He himself is bedridden with one of the several fevers that no surgeon can properly diagnose, but he keeps one-third of his force on duty at all times and orders the rest to sleep on their arms. Meanwhile he sends word to Harrison, at Lower Sandusky, that he will presently need reinforcements. If worse comes to worst, he has a suicidal plan: he will fire the magazine and blow up the fort and its occupants rather than face the hatchets and scalping knives of the tribesmen.

Procter's army, five thousand strong, reaches the mouth of the Maumee on July 20. Clay informs Harrison at once. Harrison, who does not yet know the British intentions, responds that he will send reinforcements if needed; meanwhile, Clay is to beware of surprise. Harrison moves his own headquarters nine miles up the Sandusky to Seneca Town. From that point he can co-operate with either Fort Meigs or Fort Stephenson near Sandusky Bay, in case the attack should come at the latter point.

Procter moves up the Maumee, reaches Fort Meigs on the twenty-fifth, places his troops in a ravine on the right bank just below the fort. His cavalry is concealed in a neighbouring thicket. At the same time Tecumseh and his Indians circle around and lurk in the forest close to the road that leads to Lower Sandusky. It is along this road that Harrison's reinforcements must come. If Clay believes they are being attacked he will surely order his men out of the cover of the stockade, expecting to catch the Indians in a trap. At least that is the Shawnee's reasoning.

With his comrades in the 41st back on familiar ground, John Richardson waits impatiently in the concealing skirt of wood, half soaked in the clammy drizzle. Hours pass. Will the sham battle never begin? And when it does begin, will Tecumseh's ruse work?

Finally, from the southeast comes an explosion of musket fire, desultory at first, accompanied by savage yells, then increasing in volume until, approaching the fort, it becomes one incessant roar.

Within the fort, Clay's men hear it too, and are eager to be off to rescue their comrades. The wounded throw away their crutches, the sick abandon their bunks; but Clay restrains them. Harrison's message about reinforcements has arrived only a short time before. Clay simply does not believe that any relief could have come so quickly—especially as Harrison was awaiting word from the fort before committing his men. Clay is convinced that the musket fire is part of a grand deception. But he has difficulty in convincing his officers and restraining his troops, who are indignant at being held back. The fortunate advent of a thunderstorm forestalls what might have been a difficult situation.

Tecumseh has failed, but the Indians are still full of fight. If they cannot take Fort Meigs they are determined to seize Fort Stephenson, the lightly held bastion just upriver from Sandusky Bay. Procter has no choice but to follow where they lead.

SENECA TOWN ON THE SANDUSKY, OHIO, JULY 29, 1813

William Henry Harrison calls a council of his officers, here at his new headquarters, nine miles up the Sandusky. The General has just learned from Clay that Procter has abandoned the attempt on Fort Meigs and may be advancing on Fort Winchester, farther up the Maumee. Harrison does not believe it; the British have nothing to gain there. He assumes, correctly, that Procter will attack Fort Stephenson.

The council of nine is unanimous. The fort, a mile or so upriver from Sandusky Bay, with its weak garrison of 160 soldiers and its huddle of wooden buildings, cannot be held against an army of five thousand. Harrison scribbles an order to the fort's young commander, Major George Croghan:

Immediately on receiving this letter you will abandon Fort Stephenson, set fire to it and repair with your command this night to headquarters. . . .

It is 10 P.M. Harrison's messenger, John Conner, accompanied by
two Indians, sets off in the dark, only to find the swamp and thickets
teeming with Tecumseh's tribesmen, who have come overland from
the Maumee while Procter's force moves by water toward Sandusky
Bay. Conner loses his way and arrives at Fort Stephenson tardily,
just before noon.

Croghan reads Harrison's note and curses roundly. He has already
written to a friend that he will "defend this post to the last extremity." Now he swears that he will fight the British even though he
may be the first man killed in the attack. The lateness of Harrison's
messenger gives him an excuse. He calls a council of his officers and
pens an immediate reply:

> Sir: I have just received yours of yesterday, 10 o'clock P.M., or-
> dering me to destroy this place and make good my retreat, which
> was received too late to be carried into execution. We have deter-
> mined to maintain this place and by heavens we can.

He hands the letter to Moses Wright, a veteran of Tippecanoe
and Fort Meigs and the best rider in the garrison. Tecumseh's men
seem to be lurking behind every tree as Wright gallops through a
hail of bullets. A ball goes through his cap, another clips his heel,
his horse is mortally wounded. When he finally arrives at Harrison's
tent, his clothes are in tatters from forcing his way through the heavy
brush. The General puts down his morning coffee, reads the note in
anger, swears that Croghan ought to be shot immediately for insubordination, and orders him removed from command. Colonel Sam
Wells with an escort of dragoons is sent to relieve him.

Wells and his escort run into an Indian ambush, fight their way
out, and deliver Harrison's blunt note, written by an assistant, to
Croghan:

> Sir: The General has just received your letter of this date informing
> him that you had thought it proper to disobey the order ... deliv-
> ered to you this morning. It appears that the information which

dictated this order was incorrect, and as you did not receive it in the night, as was expected, it might have been proper that you should have reported the circumstance and your situation before you proceeded to its execution. This might have been passed over; but I am directed to say to you that an officer who presumes to aver, that he has made his resolution, and that he will act in direct opposition to the orders of his General, cannot longer be entrusted with a separate command. Colonel Wells is sent to relieve you. You will deliver the command to him and repair with Colonel Ball's squadron to this place.

Young George Croghan is not in the least abashed. He is only twenty-one, handsome and debonair, with a long aristocratic face, high forehead, and Roman nose. He comes from a line of fighting Irish. His family is both affluent and distinguished. His father has an enviable record as a Revolutionary officer. Two of his uncles on his mother's side are famous. One, William Clark, Governor of Missouri Territory, became, with Meriwether Lewis, the first white American to cross the continent to the Pacific. The other, General George Rogers Clark, is known as the Hannibal of the West for his conquest of the country northwest of Vincennes. Croghan himself is a veteran of the Battle of Tippecanoe under Harrison who, in recommending him for a commission in the regulars, wrote that he "possesses all the courage and fire which are so necessary to form a good officer."

Has that courage and fire caused Croghan to overstep the mark? By the time the dragoons escort him to Seneca Town, he has an ingenious explanation for his apparent flouting of orders. He has written the letter, he insists, in such a way as to deceive the enemy should it be captured—for any attempt to withdraw in daylight "would be more hazardous than to remain in the fort under all its disadvantages."

Harrison is mollified and also half convinced by Croghan that the fort can be held. The young major has constructed two new blockhouses and topped the sixteen-foot palisade with heavy logs, calculated to fall on the attackers. He has surrounded the entire stronghold with a ditch eight feet deep and eight feet wide. On the northwest angle of this formidable moat he has placed his only cannon, a six-pounder, and he has evacuated all the women, children, and invalids.

Croghan's enthusiasm is catching. Harrison returns him to his command, warning that if attack seems imminent Croghan is to burn the fort and retire upriver. But Harrison, one suspects, is well aware by now that his young subordinate is reluctant to leave without a fight.

FORT STEPHENSON, OHIO, AUGUST 1, 1813

Major-General Procter's gunboats sweep up Sandusky Bay and enter the river, pushed forward by a spanking breeze. By mid-afternoon they have landed in a cove, about a mile from the fort. Procter has Croghan outgunned. He will storm the palisades with three six-pounders and two 5½ inch howitzers. Croghan has "Old Betsey," an ancient six-pounder left over from the Revolution—nothing more.

Procter has five hundred regulars from the 41st light infantry and some seven hundred Indians—Winnebago, Menominee, Sioux— under the legendary Robert Dickson and Matthew Elliott, the aging superintendent of the British Indian Department. Hidden in the woods between Fort Meigs and Seneca Town are Tecumseh's followers, perhaps two thousand strong. Their presence makes retreat impossible—or so George Croghan will claim.

Harrison does not believe the fort can be held; the British outnumber the defenders seven to one. Procter, on the other hand, does not believe the fort can be taken—or so *he* will claim. Yet he has no choice but to attack. Hundreds of his native allies, disappointed by the failure to seize Fort Meigs, have already deserted him. Tecumseh has trouble holding on to his own people, many of whom are off chasing after cattle. Now Matthew Elliott, Tecumseh's long-time comrade, ailing and so infirm he can hardly sit a horse, issues what amounts to an ultimatum on behalf of the tribesmen: unless the fort is stormed, the British will never be able to bring another Indian into the field of battle.

Procter feels his command slipping away. He does not like the Indians nor their leaders, has never liked them. To him they have become a nuisance and a burden, consuming vast quantities of rations, refusing to take direction from their own chiefs, coming and going as they please. Yet he recognizes their proven value. Without the Indians in 1812, the British could not have held Upper Canada. Procter knows he cannot dispense with them and so agrees to Elliott's plan. If Procter's regulars will storm one face of the fort, Elliott promises, the Indians will storm the other.

But first, Procter decides to use a time-tested tactic: he will attempt to frighten Croghan into surrender by threatening an Indian massacre. Elliott, accompanied by Major Peter Chambers of the 41st approaches the fort under a flag of truce and is met by a young Kentucky subaltern, Edmund Shipp. The British major points out that his commander has a large number of cannon, a sizeable body of troops, and so many Indians that it will be impossible to control them once the fort is captured.

Shipp has already been told what to reply: "My commandant and the garrison are determined to defend the post to the last extremity, and bury themselves in its ruins rather than surrender it to any force whatever."

Elliott intervenes: "You are a fine young man. I pity your situation; for God's sake, surrender and prevent the dreadful slaughter that must follow resistance."

"When the fort shall be taken," Shipp retorts, "there will be none to massacre."

As Shipp turns away, an Indian springs forward, seizes him by the coat, tries to take his sword. Elliott makes a show of aiding Shipp, expressing anxiety for his safety, perhaps to demonstrate that he cannot control his followers.

All this is too much for Croghan, watching from the ramparts.

"What does that mean?" shouts the Major. "Shipp, come in, and we will blow them all to hell."

No sooner is Shipp back inside the palisade than Procter's artillery opens up on the fort. Croghan replies with Old Betsey, but sparingly, to husband his ammunition, moving the six-pounder from place to place to make Procter believe he has more than one piece. Most of the British fire seems to be directed toward the pickets at the northwest angle of the fort. Croghan guesses that the main attack will come at that point. Late that night, he orders his second-in-command to move Old Betsey into a blockhouse where it can rake that portion of the ditch from behind a concealed porthole.

By dawn, Procter has moved his three cannon within 250 yards of the fort. During the day he hurls five hundred balls and shells at the embattled Americans. Now Croghan is certain the attack will come at the northwest angle; anything else will be a feint. He strengthens the pickets with bags of sand and flour, stuffs Old Betsey to the muzzle with half a charge of powder plus grape-shot, double slugs, and even old pieces of pottery, puts his Kentucky sharpshooters in place, and waits for the attack.

Croghan is correct about the British intentions. Procter plans a feint at the south end, sends his second-in-command, Lieutenant-Colonel Augustus Warburton, in a wide circle around the fort to effect the deception. Meanwhile, his main force, led by Lieutenant-Colonel William Shortt and Lieutenant J.G. Gordon, attacks from the north. The assault commences at four, the troops moving forward at the double to the sound of distant thunder, Shortt whistling away, Gordon swearing under his breath, storm clouds gathering on the horizon.

But why this haste? Procter's men are not prepared for a frontal assault on a fortified position. They have no scaling ladders to launch at the sixteen-foot pickets, and their axes are dulled from weeks of misuse. Procter is a flawed commander who tends to panic in circumstances that require steadfastness and resolve. Following his victory at the River Raisin he rushed away, leaving his prisoners to be massacred by the Indians because he feared (wrongly) that Harrison would send reinforcements to attack him. Now the same fear forces him to another hasty decision. He does not know that three days earlier Harrison himself considered withdrawing from Seneca Town and even now half expects Croghan to retire. So Procter, who will later insist that he did not want to attack Fort Stephenson, attacks it half-heartedly and in haste.

The Indians, who had urged the attack in the first place, turn out to be useless. Siege warfare and frontal assaults in the face of cannon fire are not their mode of fighting. They retreat early into a nearby wood and remain as spectators in the battle that follows. As for Warburton's feint against the south wall, it comes too late to be of any use.

Shortt and Gordon lead their men out of the cannon smoke some twenty paces from the ditch that encircles the fort and form them into line for the assault, as the Kentucky sharpshooters open up. The picket fence is higher, the ditch deeper than the attackers had expected. The troops hesitate. Private Shadrach Byfield sees one man about to flee; his neighbour cries that if he doesn't turn around and face the enemy he'll run him through with a bayonet. The two leaders rally the troops with shouts and slogans.

"Cut away at the pickets, my brave boys and give the damn Yankees no quarter," cries Shortt, as he clambers over the bank and leaps into the ditch. He claws his way up the far side to reach the palisade at the northwest corner—the first man to do so—but is thrown back. At this moment, Lieutenant Shipp unmasks Old Betsey, and a dreadful hail of musket balls, grape-shot, and jagged missiles is hurled the full length of the ditch, now filled with struggling men.

Shortt, a slug in his body, twists a handkerchief around his sword and raises it in surrender, but his enemies have already heard his cry for no quarter. A second volley from Shipp's six-pounder cuts him down. Gordon takes over, leaps up at the fence, hacking at the pickets with his sword until a ball strikes him full in the breast, killing him too.

More than fifty men lie dead in the ditch, the victims of Old Betsey's raking fire. Shadrach Byfield is still alive, advancing in the second line. He sees the man directly in front of him fall dead. Then the sergeant on his right drops, and the man on his left receives six balls in his body.

Procter's bugle is sounding the retreat; the attack has failed. The troops fall back under a withering fire to the shelter of a ravine that runs parallel to the ditch. The Americans have lost but one man—a drunkard who climbed to the top of the palisade.

Croghan's men continue to fire at anything that moves in the ditch or the ravine. Byfield, out of ammunition, crawling past his dead and wounded comrades seeking more powder and shot, spots an old friend, bleeding from a wound.

"Bill, how bee'st?" Byfield inquires.

"One of the Americans keeps firing at us, out of one of those loopholes," his comrade replies.

He points to the loophole. Byfield ventures a shot at it, and almost at the same moment his friend falls back.

"Bill, what's the matter?"

"They've shot me again!"

Dark falls. The rising moon casts a wan light in the ditch and ravine where men are groaning and dying, some complaining that Procter has deserted them. The order to retreat has already been passed from company to company in whispers and in Indian language to prevent the enemy hearing.

An American officer cries from the fort that when the British are gone "I will come out and take you in and use you well."

"Why don't you come out now," shouts Byfield, "and we will fight you five to one."

But he knows that he must escape, not fight. As he climbs to the top of the ravine, the flash of a gun catches his eye, and he flings himself forward as a shower of shot falls near him. Then he is up and running toward the British batteries.

As he leaps into a familiar entrenchment he runs into Procter.

"Where are all the rest of the men?" the Major-General asks.

"I don't think there are any more to come," Byfield replies. "They are all killed and wounded."

"Good God," Procter exclaims, with tears in his eyes.

John Richardson, meanwhile, is trying to convince the men in his platoon that they must quit the ravine. It is now half-past nine;

the troops have been lying in the ankle-deep mud for four hours. Richardson's men are separated from the other companies by piles of brushwood. As a result the orders to retire have not reached them. But Richardson can tell from the indistinct sounds beyond that the troops are moving back.

He whispers to his followers that they must move out at once, but the men are fearful they will be spotted in the moonlight. Richardson, piqued, decides to leave them, climbs out of the ravine, and immediately stumbles over a corpse. That sound alerts the garrison, and the entire front of the fort lights up with gunfire. Balls whistle past his head and hiss through the long grass, but in spite of a second volley, the young gentleman volunteer makes his escape—and not a moment too soon, for the troops are already moving to the boats.

In his provision basket Richardson discovers several bottles of port wine, a gift from his family in Amherstburg. Exhausted, starving, and thirsty he proceeds to drain an entire bottle. The effect is instantaneous. Pleasantly inebriated, he settles down in the bottom of one of the boats, enjoying the most delicious moments of repose he has ever experienced. When he awakens, the sun is high in the sky, the lake is glassy, and the men around him are singing and joking, forgetful of the comrades whose dying groans racked their ears only a few hours before.

At the fort, those British still alive are already prisoners. Some have been saved during the night by the defenders, who lowered buckets of water to the wounded, half dead with thirst. Croghan himself, after thirty-six hours of continuous exertion, is too exhausted to send Harrison a detailed report of the battle. No matter. That cautious general is elated by the defeat of the one British officer for whom he has no respect. "It will not be amongst the least of General Procter's mortifications to find he has been baffled by a youth who has just passed his twenty-first year," he writes in a jubilant report to the Secretary of War.

Croghan's victory is the signal for a national celebration and the kind of adulation the American public, desperately short of heroes in this depressing conflict, is prepared to shower on any victor. The young major receives the thanks of Congress and, ultimately, a gold medal, not to mention an elegant sword from the ladies of Chillicothe, Ohio.

The benefits to America of this minor skirmish are more psychological than physical. Procter has lost the respect of his troops, whose resultant low morale will have serious consequences in the days to come. And the Indians are deserting the British. Even Tecumseh, that great optimist, has become disillusioned. He will continue to fight the Long Knives, desperately, hopelessly, but he must know that the long battle for his people and their land is coming to its tragic close.

PRESQUE ISLE BAY, LAKE ERIE, AUGUST 1, 1813

As George Croghan's small force prepares to defend Fort Stephenson, Oliver Hazard Perry rises once more from a sick-bed, inspirited by another stroke of good fortune—"Perry's Luck" it will come to be called. He learns that the British fleet, which has been hovering just outside the bay since July 19, effectively blockading his own flotilla, has unaccountably vanished. His own ships are ready to sail. The moment has come to take them over the sandbar that blocks the entrance.

He shakes off the "bilious" fever that seems to strike him after long periods of stress and fatigue. These have not been easy weeks. He still has not enough experienced seamen or officers to man his ships, and his entreaties to Chauncey, his plump superior on Lake Ontario, have been all but fruitless. Like his opposite number, Yeo, Chauncey wants to keep everything for himself; yet having everything, he does nothing. The two rival commanders, though physical opposites, are psychological counterparts. The slender, rawboned Yeo is ten years younger than his forty-one-year-old adversary, but each fears to tangle decisively with the other. The two fleets continue to slip furtively about the lake, engaging in minor skirmishes, cautiously avoiding all-out action, fleeing when necessary to their respective shelters at Kingston and Sackets Harbor, neither quite sure who has command of the waters, each awaiting the moment when he can outbuild the other, a moment that will never come. Each is convinced, not without reason, that a decisive naval battle on Lake Ontario would cripple one side; and since sailing ships are subject as much to the caprices of wind and weather as to human command, each fears the outcome of such a contest. If Yeo loses the lake, Canada falls; if Chauncey loses, America is humbled. Meanwhile, the two opposing fleets on Erie suffer from a lack of trained seamen.

Perry has no such qualms. He is eager to attack Barclay, even with ships that are only partially manned.

"I long to have at him," he tells Chauncey, and in the same breath pleads, "for God's sake . . . send me men and officers."

He is mortified when Harrison, reporting the second siege of Fort Meigs, asks for naval co-operation, which Perry cannot supply. Chauncey has finally sent him a handful of men, the dregs of his fleet, "a motley set, blacks, soldiers and boys," in Perry's description. A second detachment of sixty is even worse, many worn down by disease, one-fifth suffering from fever and dysentery, one a Russian who speaks no English. The two hundred soldiers who accompanied him from Black Rock have long since been ordered back to Sackets Harbor, and his only defence force is a comic opera regiment of Pennsylvania militia who are too afraid of the dark to stand watch at night. When Perry inquires about these unsoldierly qualms he receives a jarring reply from their commander: "I told the boys to go, Captain, but the boys won't go."

It is clear that Procter, after his failure in May, is wary of attacking any defensive position. But Perry is less concerned about his own defence than he is about his ability to attack. At the moment, his force is clearly superior to Barclay's and will be as long as the British ship *Detroit* remains unfinished.

"What a golden opportunity if we had men," he writes to Chauncey. Yet he is "obliged to bite [his] fingers in vexation" for want of them.

With the enemy out of the way Perry can at last get his new ships into the open lake without fear of molestation. Or is it a ruse? No matter; he must try. Now a new frustration bedevils him. The water has dropped to a depth of only four feet. The two brigs, *Lawrence* and *Niagara*, draw nine. Fortunately, Noah Brown has foreseen just such a calamity and devised a solution—four gargantuan box-like scows, known as camels, which can be floated or sunk at will. By placing a camel on each side of a ship and sinking each of them below the surface, the vessel can be raised by means of ropes and windlasses and set on a series of wooden beams resting on the camels. The scows are then plugged, pumped out, and brought to the surface. With the big ship resting on the supports, the entire ungainly contraption can be floated easily over the bar.

As Perry discovers, the process is more easily described than accomplished. The smaller vessels are lightened and warped over first to act as a protective screen in case Barclay's squadron should reappear. But more armament is needed to meet this threat; *Niagara* is kedged up close to the bar, her port broadside facing the open lake. If the British return, she will act as a floating battery. On shore, batteries support this formidable armament.

Now *Niagara's* twin, *Lawrence*, a fully rigged brig pierced for twenty guns, is hauled forward on her kedge anchors under Dobbins's direction. For three hours, Dobbins's sweating men strip her of armament and ballast. The camels are brought alongside and the brig hoisted two feet; it is not enough. She still draws too much water. The process must be repeated. It is mid-morning, August 4, after "renewed and unparalleled exertions" when she finally floats free.

Officers and men have spent two sleepless nights, but the work is not over. *Lawrence* must be refitted, a task that takes until midnight. Now *Niagara* must be floated over the bar under *Lawrence's* protecting guns. This is an easier operation, for the men have mastered the technique.

But before *Niagara* is free of the bar, trouble appears in the shape of two sails, seen through the haze, on the horizon. Barclay is back.

If there is such a thing as Perry's Luck, there is an antithetical adversity that might be dubbed Barclay's Mischance. The British commodore simply cannot believe Perry can get his big ships over the bar. He had gone off, apparently, to attend a dinner in his honour at Port Dover, where, in reply to a toast, he announced that he expected to return "to find the Yankee brigs hard and fast aground on the bar at Erie . . . in which predicament it would be but a small job to destroy them."

He has returned at a most inopportune moment for the Americans. But Perry's Luck holds as nature conspires to deceive the British. The wind casts such a haze across the mouth of the bay that Barclay is misled into believing that all of Perry's fleet has successfully entered the open lake. Perry dispatches two of his smaller vessels to keep Barclay at bay. A few shots are exchanged, whereupon the British captain, believing himself outgunned, retires. By midnight, August 5, Perry's fleet of eleven, all fully armed, heads out into the lake for a two-day trial run, vainly seeking the elusive British.

Perry's worries are not over. On the evening of August 8, he takes dinner ashore with his only confidant, the purser, Samuel Hambleton, a one-time Maryland merchant, who at thirty-six is closer to Perry than any of the other junior officers, whose average age is less than twenty years.

To Hambleton, Perry unburdens himself. He is at a loss what to do. He has had to pay off a number of volunteers and is left with only those men who signed articles for four months' service. Now he has less than half the crew needed to man the fleet; of these, less than a quarter are regular naval personnel; and his officers have little experience. He knows delay is dangerous yet feels himself ill-prepared to encounter the enemy.

He is still suffering from fever and fatigue. The struggle to get *Lawrence* over the bar has worn him down; for two days he went without food or sleep. And he has just received a caustic letter from Chauncey that has put him in a dark mood. That officer has seized upon his remarks about black reinforcements to read him a lecture on race relations: "I have yet to learn that the colour of the skin, or the cut and trimmings of the coat, can affect a man's qualifications or usefulness."

Chauncey is especially offended because Perry has gone over his head, writing to the Secretary of the Navy directly, on the ground that the distance between Sackets Harbor and Erie is too great to make communication effective. That sounds very much as if Perry were suggesting a separate command on Lake Erie, an idea which, though sensible, annoys and mortifies the senior commander.

Chauncey cannot resist a further taunt:

> As you have assured the secretary that you should conceive yourself equal or superior to the enemy with a force of men so much less than I had deemed necessary, there will be a great deal expected from you by your country, and I trust they will not be disappointed in the high expectation formed of your gallantry and judgement. I will barely make an observation which was impressed on my mind by an old soldier, that is "Never despise your enemy"....

It is too much. In a white heat Perry has just dictated a letter to the Secretary of the Navy requesting that he be removed from his station because he "cannot serve longer under an officer who has been so totally regardless of my feelings."

Does he really mean it? Probably not; the Secretary does not take it seriously, and Chauncey himself will respond at month's end with a mollifying note that will restore relations between the two officers. More important to Perry, the letter has scarcely been dispatched when another arrives. Perry is electrified: Chauncey is sending reinforcements after all! Jesse Elliott is on his way with several officers and eighty-nine seamen. Perry exclaims to his friend Hambleton that this is the happiest moment he has known since his arrival at Erie.

Elliott reaches Presque Isle on August 10. The men he brings are of a better calibre than their predecessors. Perry, whose flagship will be *Lawrence*, gives Elliott command of *Niagara* and allows him to choose his own crew. The ambitious Elliott selects the pick of the crop. *Lawrence*'s sailing master, William Taylor, complains that the vessels of the fleet are unequally manned—the best men are on *Niagara*. But Perry, in his new euphoria, lets Elliott's marked discourtesy pass.

He is more concerned about *Detroit*, nearing completion at Amherstburg and larger than any of his own vessels. He takes care to cruise the lake in battle formation and, since he has only forty seamen who know anything about guns, seizes the opportunity to drill his force. Off Sandusky, he fires a signal shot which on the nineteenth brings General Harrison, his staff, and a crowd of American Indian chiefs on board for a conference. The Indians explore the ship, clamber up the masts, perform a war dance on deck, gawk at the big guns while the two officers settle future strategy. Perry's plan is to force Barclay out of his harbour at Amherstburg. If that fails, he will transport Harrison's army across the lake to attack Procter. His fleet will hold at Put-in Bay, a safe anchorage in the Bass Islands not far from Sandusky Bay.

Here, sickness strikes again. Perry falls dangerously ill once more with fever. His thirteen-year-old brother, Alexander, who has insisted on coming to Erie with him, is also sick. The chief surgeon is too ill to work; his assistant, Usher Parsons, must be carried from ship to ship to minister to the ailing, flat on his back on a cot.

On August 31, with the Commodore still in his bunk, a welcome and unexpected reinforcement of one hundred Kentucky riflemen arrives from General Harrison. Most have never seen a ship before and cannot conceal their astonishment and curiosity. Like the Indians, they scale the masts, plunge into the holds, trot about each vessel from sick bay to captain's cabin, exclaiming over the smallest details. In their linsey-woolsey hunting shirts and pants they are themselves a curiosity to Perry's seamen. He indulges them for a time, then lectures them on ship's etiquette and discipline. They are to act as marines and sharpshooters in the battle to come.

The following day, Perry is well enough to put his squadron into motion toward Amherstburg, hovering outside the harbour as Barclay once blockaded him. *Detroit*, he observes, is now fully rigged. But Barclay declines to come out.

A few days later, three prisoners escape from Fort Amherstburg to warn him that Barclay is preparing for battle. He now has a fairly accurate account of his adversary's strength but overestimates his manpower, which is no greater than his own. In firepower, he outguns Barclay, two to one.

Sickness again strikes him, and he is forced back to his bunk. All his officers are ill with "lake fever." Sick or not, on the evening of September 9 Perry calls a council in the cabin of his flagship. Of his 490 men, almost a quarter are ill; some of the invalids, however, will still be able to fight. All three surgeons are ill, but Usher Parsons manages to stagger in for the meeting.

A long discussion follows. Each commander is given his instructions. Perry, in *Lawrence*, will attack Barclay's flagship, *Detroit*. Elliott, in *Niagara*, will attack the next largest British vessel, *Queen Charlotte*, and so on down the line. Because the British ships are armed chiefly with long guns and the American vessels carry the shorter, more powerful carronades, it is essential for Perry that the fight take place at close quarters. Otherwise his ships will be too far from the British, who with their longer range can batter him to pieces.

Perry leaves nothing to chance. He has already devised a series of signals for the day of action. Now he hands every officer written instructions, each containing one specific admonition: "Engage each designated adversary in close action, at half cable's length." He is wary of those long guns. If he has his way, his powerful short-range carronades will batter Barclay's vessels at point-blank range of one hundred yards.

After an hour's discussion, Perry rises, opens his sea chest, pulls out a strange flag. He has named his flagship *Lawrence* after the newest American naval hero, James Lawrence, who, mortally wounded on the deck of *Chesapeake*, uttered a dying plea: "Don't give up the ship!" Hambleton has had the ladies of Erie sew this slogan in letters of white muslin onto a dark blue flag. Perry exhibits it, tells his officers that when it is hoisted to his masthead it will be the signal for action. It is a curiously negative slogan, especially since Lawrence's men *did* give up the ship. But nobody comments on that.

The officers rise, but Perry is still not satisfied. He calls them back from the deck, goes over his plan once more. He wants to make absolutely sure that they will bring the British fleet into close action. Finally he dismisses them, echoing a phrase of Nelson's: "If you lay the enemy close alongside you cannot be out of your place."

But it is still not enough. As the officers' boats pull away from *Lawrence* to their own ships, Perry stands on deck and repeats Nelson's phrase. He cannot get those long British guns out of his mind. Barclay can easily stand out of range—especially if the wind is right—and reduce his fleet to matchwood before a single American shot strikes him.

It is ten o'clock of a lovely September evening. The moon is full, the lake like black glass, tinselled with silver. From the shore comes the hum of voices around campfires, the *peep-peep* of frogs in Squaw Harbor; from the quarterdecks of the anchored vessels the low murmur of officers, discussing the coming battle; from the fo'c's'les the crackle of laughter—sailors telling jokes, discussing the prospect of prize money.

Perry returns to his cabin; he has letters to write. If battle should come on the morrow and he is victorious, they need not be sent. If he should fall and die, these will be his final messages.

AMHERSTBURG, UPPER CANADA, SEPTEMBER 9, 1813

Ill-prepared as he is, Robert Heriot Barclay knows he must lead his squadron into Lake Erie and fight the Americans. He realizes the odds are against him, that only a miracle can bring him victory. But he has no choice: Amherstburg is on the verge of starvation; his own crews are on half rations; they do not have a barrel of flour left. Procter's fourteen thousand followers, most of them Indians with wives and children, are reduced to a few barrels of pork, some cattle, and a little unground wheat. Barclay has held off until the last moment, hoping for promised reinforcements, guns, and equipment for his new ship, *Detroit*. He can hold out no longer. He must attempt a run to bring provisions from Long Point. But he knows that Perry's fleet awaits him at Put-in Bay, thirty miles to the south-east. He does not intend to shirk the encounter.

Like Perry, he is badly undermanned, in far worse condition than his adversary. The officers do not know their men; the men do not know their ships. He has been pleading for weeks for reinforcements, but the merest handful has arrived, most of them untrained. The troops have not been paid for months and the civilian artificers have refused to do further work on the ships without wages. Procter has warned Prevost that "there are not in the Fleet more than four and twenty *seamen.*" Barclay has echoed these remarks to Yeo: "I am sure, Sir James, if you saw my Canadians, you would condemn every one (with perhaps two or three exceptions) as a poor devil not worth his Salt. . . ."

Prevost has contented himself with penning fatuous letters likely to infuriate both commanders. On reaching the Niagara frontier on August 22, the Governor General ignored all his subordinates' misgivings. Their situation, he agreed, "may be one of some difficulty," but "you cannot fail in honourably surmounting it, notwithstanding the numerical superiority of the enemy's force, which I cannot consider as overbalanced by the excellent description of your troops and seamen: valerous [*sic*] and well disciplined." To which he added (as if mere words could win a battle): "Captain Barclay . . . has only to dare, and the enemy is discomfited."

Procter could not let that pass: "Your Excellency speaks of seamen valorous and well disciplined. Except, I believe, the 25 Captain Barclay brought with him, there are none of that description on this lake. . . ."

Barclay is also short of cannon and equipment because of the spring attack on York. To outfit his new ship, he has been forced to borrow a motley collection of cannon from the ramparts of Fort Amherstburg. The big guns come in half a dozen sizes, each requiring its own ammunition, so that confusion will reign among the untrained gunners in the heat of battle. Nor can they be fired efficiently; the matches and tubes are spoiled or corroded. To set one off, an officer must snap his pistol over the touch-hole, an awkward procedure that slows the rate of fire. Everything on *Detroit* is make-shift: some of the sails, cables, and blocks have been borrowed from *Queen Charlotte* and other vessels, there being no others available in Amherstburg.

Prevost keeps promising that ordnance and men are on their way. On September 1, the reluctant James Yeo landed a dozen twenty-four-pound carronades, destined for Detroit, at Burlington on Lake Ontario, together with two lieutenants, two gunners, and forty-five seamen. The guns have moved no farther, but the seamen have just turned up and are, in Barclay's opinion, "totally inadequate." Sixteen are mere boys.

Prevost assures him that more are on the way; but Barclay cannot wait. At ten o'clock on this calm, moonlit night, as Perry paces his own deck a few leagues away, Barclay's fleet of six warships slips its moorings and moves out of the Detroit River onto the shining waters of the shallow lake.

In Europe, the noose is tightening around Napoleon. Austria has joined the Allied cause. The Prussian marshal, Gebhard Von Blücher, has already dealt the French a stunning setback at Katzbach. In St. Petersburg, three distinguished American diplomats have been cooling their heels since July, attempting, with limited success, to launch peace talks with Britain through the mediation of the Tsar. But none of this can have the slightest effect on the contest being waged here on a silent lake in the heart of a continental wilderness.

What is Barclay thinking as he walks the quarterdeck of his untried ship? Undoubtedly he has examined the odds, which are against him. Perry has ten vessels—three brigs, six schooners, and a sloop (one of which, however, will not get into action). Barclay has six: two ships, a brig, two schooners, and a sloop. Ships and brigs are square rigged, the former with three masts, the latter with two. It is largely on these that the contest will depend.

Barclay's flagship, *Detroit*, is the largest craft on the lake—126 feet in length—at least fifteen feet longer than either of Perry's twin brigs, *Niagara* and *Lawrence*. But firepower counts more than size, and here Perry has the advantage, especially at close quarters. Long guns are most effective at eight hundred yards. At three hundred yards, the stubby carronades can do greater damage. Here, Perry's ships can shatter the British fleet with a combined broadside of 664 pounds. The British, who prefer the longer range, can reply with only 264 pounds of metal. Barclay is also short of trained gunners and seamen. Of his total crew of 440, at least 300 are soldiers, not sailors. But three of every five men in Perry's crews are seamen.

Barclay has one advantage only. Perry's two largest vessels, *Lawrence* and *Niagara*, are inferior to him in long-range firepower. At long range, for instance, the American flagship faces nine times its own firepower. No wonder Perry is desperate to fight at close quarters.

Barclay may not have statistics, but he does have a rough idea of the two fleets' comparative strength. He has carefully taken the measure of the opposing squadron off Amherstburg, climbing to the highest house in the village to examine the vessels through his glass. His strategy is the opposite of Perry's. He must use his long guns to batter the Americans before they can come within range with their stubby carronades. It must be frustrating to realize that so much depends on forces over which he has no control. If he has the "weather gauge"—that is, if the wind is behind him, giving him manoeuvrability—then Perry will be in trouble. But if Perry has the gauge, the wind will drive him directly into the heart of the British fleet.

Tomorrow will tell the tale. For all Barclay knows, it may be his last day on earth. He may emerge a hero, honoured, promoted, decorated. More likely, he will have to shoulder the blame for defeat.

But Barclay is not the kind of man to consider defeat, for he was cast in the mould that has made Britain master of the seas. He is only twenty-eight, but like his contemporaries he has spent more than half his life—sixteen years—in the service of the British navy. Perhaps now his mind harks back to that soft May day in 1798 when at the age of twelve—a small, plump child with rosy cheeks and dark eyes—he took leave of his family and boarded a coach to join a British frigate at Greenock, weeping bitterly because, as he told a sympathetic innkeeper's wife, "I am on my way to sea and will never see father, mother, brothers and sisters again." It is a scene that Barclay cannot put out of his mind. The life of a teenaged midshipman in the British navy is no feather bed. Young Barclay was "ill used," to quote a scribbled remark in an old family register.

It has not been an easy life or a particularly distinguished one. Barclay is a run-of-the-mill officer, no better, certainly no worse, than hundreds of others in the navy that Nelson shaped. "Ill used" fits his career—a wound at Trafalgar, an escape from drowning when a boat capsized, an arm lost in an engagement with the French. He carries with him a combination knife and fork with which to cut and eat his meat, one-handed. His rank is low; he is called a captain because he commands a ship on Lake Erie; officially he is only a commander. Compared with the big three-decked ships of the line, which are the navy's pride, this crude vessel *Detroit*, hammered together from green lumber and awkwardly rigged, must seem pitifully inadequate. Yet it is a command. He is painfully aware that he is second choice: the post was first offered by Yeo to William Howe Mulcaster, who promptly refused it, believing, quite rightly, that there is no honour in a badly equipped, undermanned fleet on a lake that the high command clearly views as a backwater. So the command has devolved on Robert Heriot Barclay, His Majesty's humble, obedient, and sometimes ill-used servant. How will fate, fortune, wind, and circumstance use him in the approaching conflict? Tomorrow will tell.

PUT-IN BAY, LAKE ERIE, SEPTEMBER 10, 1813

Sunrise. High up on the mast of *Lawrence*, Perry's lookout spies a distant silhouette beyond the cluster of islands and cries out, "Sail, ho!"

Perry is out of his bunk in an instant, the cry acting as a tonic to his fever. Up the masthead goes his signal: *Get under way*. Within fifteen minutes his men have hauled in sixty fathoms of cable, hoisted the anchors, raised the sails, and steered the nine vessels for a gap between the islands that shield the harbour.

The wind is against him. He can gain the weather gauge by beating around to the windward of some of the islands; but that will require too much time, and Perry is impatient to fight.

"Run to the lee side," he tells his sailing master, William Taylor.

"Then you will have to engage the enemy to the leeward, sir," Taylor reminds him. That will give the British the advantage of the wind.

"I don't care," says Perry. "To windward or leeward, they shall fight today." Taylor gives the signal to wear ship.

The fleet is abustle. The decks must be cleared for action so that nothing will impede the recoil of the guns. Seamen are hammering in flints, lighting rope matches, placing shot in racks or in circular grummets of rope next to the guns. Besides round shot, to pierce the enemy ships, the gunners will also fire canister and grape—one a formidable cluster of iron balls encased in a cylindrical tin covering, the other a similar collection arranged around a central core in a canvas or quilted bag. Perry's favourite black spaniel is running about the deck in excitement; his master orders him confined in a china closet where he will no longer be underfoot. As the commander collects the ship's papers and signals in a weighted bag for swift disposal in case of surrender, his men are getting out stacks of pikes and cutlasses to repel boarders and sprinkling sand on the decks to prevent slipping when the blood begins to flow.

Usher Parsons is setting up a makeshift hospital in *Lawrence's* wardroom. The brig is so shallow that there is no secure place for the wounded, who must be confined to a ten-foot-square patch of floor, level with the waterline, as much at the mercy of the British cannonballs as are the men on the deck above.

Suddenly, just before ten, the wind shifts to the southeast—Perry's Luck again. The Commodore now has the weather gauge. Slipping past Rattlesnake Island, he bears down on the British fleet, five miles away. Barclay has turned his flotilla into the southwest. The sun bathes his line in a soft morning glow, shining on the spanking new paint, the red ensigns, and the white sails limned against a cloudless sky.

Staring at the fleet through his glass, Perry realizes that Barclay's line of battle is not as he expected. A small schooner, *Chippawa*, armed with a single long eighteen-pounder at the bow, leads the van, followed by a big three-master, which must certainly be *Detroit*. Perry had expected the British lead vessel to be the seventeen-gun *Queen Charlotte*, designated as Elliott's target.

He signals Elliott, up ahead on *Niagara*, to hold up while he draws abreast to question Captain Henry Brevoort, Elliott's acting marine officer, who, being a resident of Detroit, is familiar with the British squadron. Brevoort points out the small brig *Hunter*, standing directly behind *Detroit*, and *Queen Charlotte* behind her, followed by the schooner *Lady Prevost* and a small sloop, *Little Belt*.

Perry changes his battle order at once in order to bring his heaviest vessels against those of the enemy. The ambitious Elliott, who had originally asked to be in the forefront, "believing from the frequent opportunities I had of encouraging the enemy, that I could successfully lead the van," is moved farther back, much to his chagrin; Perry himself intends to take on Barclay. Two American gunboats, *Scorpion* and *Ariel*, will operate off Perry's bow to act as dispatch vessels. *Caledonia*, now in line behind *Lawrence*, will engage the British brig *Hunter*. Elliott in *Niagara* will follow to take on the larger *Queen Charlotte*. The four smaller vessels will bring up the rear.

Perry has all hands piped to quarters. Out come tubs of rations, bread bags, and the standard issue of grog; and out comes the flag that Perry has prepared for this moment.

"My brave lads," he cries, "this flag contains the last words of Captain Lawrence! Shall I hoist it?"

A cheer goes up. Even the sick—those who can walk—come out as Perry, moving from battery to battery, examining each gun, murmurs words of encouragement, exchanges a joke or two with those Kentuckians he knows best, and saves a special greeting for the men from his home state of Rhode Island, who make up a quarter of his fleet:

"Ah, here are the Newport boys! *They* will do their duty, I warrant!"

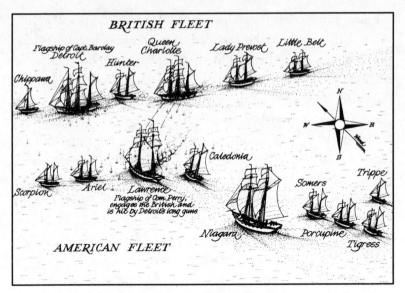

The Battle of Lake Erie: 12:15 p.m.

And to a group of old hands who, with the experience of earlier contests, have removed their cumbersome headgear and tied handkerchiefs around their brows:

"I need not say anything to you: *you* know how to beat those fellows."

A silence has descended on the lake. The British line, closed up tight, waits motionless in the light breeze. The American squadron approaches at an acute angle of fifteen degrees. The hush is deathly. To David Bunnell, a seaman aboard *Lawrence*, it resembles "the awful silence that precedes an earthquake." Bunnell has had a long experience at sea, has served, indeed, in both navies, but now finds his heart beating wildly; all nature seems "wrapped in awful suspense." In the wardroom below, its single hatch closed tight, the lone surgeon, Usher Parsons, sits in the half-light, unable to shake from his mind the horror he knows will shortly be visited upon him. He cannot curb his imagination, which conjures up dreadful scenes mingled with the hope of victory and the prospect of safe return to friends and kin.

At the guns, the men murmur to each other, giving instructions to comrades in case they should fall, relaying messages to wives and sweethearts. In his cabin, Perry rereads his wife's letters, then tears them to shreds, remarking that no enemy shall read them, turns to his friend Hambleton, and declares soberly: "This is the most important day of my life."

Slowly the distance between the two fleets narrows. Minutes drag by; both sides hold their breath. Perry has little control over the speed of his vessels—the gunboats at the rear, being slower, are already lagging badly behind.

One mile now separates the two flagships. Suddenly a British bugle breaks the silence, followed by cheering. A cannon explodes. To Dr. Parsons in the wardroom below, the sound, after the long silence, is electrifying. A twenty-four-pound ball splashes into the water ahead; the British are still out of range.

The American fleet continues to slip forward under the light breeze. Five minutes go by, then—another explosion, and a cannonball tears its way through *Lawrence's* bulwarks. A seaman falls dead, killed by a flying splinter. The British have found the range. "Steady, boys, steady," says Perry.

An odd whimpering and howling echoes up from below. It is Perry's spaniel. The British cannonball has torn its way through the planking of the china closet, knocking down all the dishes and terrifying the animal, who will bark continually during the battle.

Perry calls out to John Yarnell, his first-lieutenant, to hail the little *Scorpion*, off his windward bow, by trumpet. He wants her to open up on the British with her single long thirty-two. He himself orders his gunners to fire *Lawrence's* long twelves, but without effect: the British are still out of range.

Barclay's strategy is now apparent. Ignoring the other vessels in Perry's line, *Hunter*, *Queen Charlotte*, and the other British ships will concentrate their combined fire on *Lawrence*—a total of thirty-four guns. Barclay intends to batter Perry's flagship to pieces before she can get into range, then attack the others piecemeal. The British vessels are in a tight line, no more than half a cable's length (one hundred yards) apart. At this point, Perry's superior numbers have little significance, for, as he pulls abreast of the British, his gunboats are too far in the rear to do any damage. He signals all his vessels to close up and for each to engage her opponent. At 12:15 he finally brings *Lawrence* into carronade range of *Detroit*, so close that the British believe he is about to board.

Now, as the thirty-two-pound canisters spray the decks of his flagship, Robert Barclay suffers a serious stroke of ill fortune. His seasoned second-in-command, Captain Finnis, in charge of *Queen Charlotte*, has been unable to reach his designated opponent, partly because the wind has dropped and partly because Elliott, in *Niagara*, has remained out of range. Finnis, under heavy fire from the American *Caledonia*, determines to move up the British line, ahead of *Hunter*, and punish *Lawrence* at close quarters with a broadside from his carronades. But just as his ship shifts position, he is felled by a cannonball and dies instantly. His first officer dies with him. A few minutes later the ship's second officer is knocked senseless by a shell splinter. It is now 12:30. *Queen Charlotte*, the second most powerful ship in the British squadron, falls under the command of young Robert Irvine, a lieutenant in the Provincial Marine who has already shown daring in two earlier battles. But daring must take a back seat to experience. Irvine is no replacement for the expert Finnis, and all he has to support him is a master's mate of the Royal Navy, two boy midshipmen from his own service, a gunner, and a bo'sun. Barclay has lost his main support.

But *Lawrence* is reeling under the British hammer blows. The tumult aboard the American flagship is appalling. Above the shrieks of the wounded and the dying and the rumblings of the gun carriages come the explosion of cannon and the crash of round shot splintering masts, tearing through bulwarks, ripping guns from carriages. Soon the decks are a rubble of broken spars, tangled rigging, shredded sails, dying men. And over all there hangs a thick pall of smoke, blotting out the sun, turning the bright September noon to gloomy twilight.

Lieutenant John Brooks, head of Perry's marines, the handsomest officer at sea this day, a figure of "manly beauty, polished manners and elegant appearance," turns, smiling, to pass a remark to Perry when a cannonball tears into his hip, rips off a leg, hurls him across the deck. In terrible agony, Brooks screams for a pistol to end his life. Perry orders the marines to take him below. As they bend over him, Brooks's little black servant boy, twelve years old, bringing cartridges to a nearby gun, sees his fallen master and flings himself, sobbing, to the deck. Usher Parsons can do nothing for Brooks, who asks in his pain how long he has to live. A few hours at most, the doctor tells him.

Perry's first-lieutenant, John Yarnell, presents a grotesque appearance. His nose, perforated by a splinter, has swollen to twice its normal size. Blood from a scalp wound threatens to blind him. Parsons binds it with a bandanna, and Yarnell, returning to the deck, walks into a cloud of cattail down, torn from a pile of hammocks by round shot. Wounded a third time, he comes down once more for medical aid, his bloody face covered with down, looking like some gigantic owl. At this bizarre spectacle the wounded men cannot help laughing. "The devil has come for us!" they cry.

Perry seems to bear a charmed life. Men are dropping all around him; he suffers not a scratch. As he stops to give aid to one of his veteran gun captains, the man, drawing himself up, is torn in two by a twenty-four-pound ball. His second-lieutenant, Dulaney Forrest, is standing close to him when a shower of grape strikes him in the chest, knocking him to the deck. It is, fortunately, spent. As Perry asks Forrest if he is badly hurt, the stunned officer regains consciousness and cries, "I am not hurt, sir, but this is my shot!" and pulling out a handful from his waistcoat, pockets it as a souvenir.

The Commodore's little brother, acting as a messenger during the din of battle, is also knocked senseless by a splinter but is otherwise unhurt. Still the Commodore remains untouched. For the next century, American naval men will speak in awe of Perry's Luck. He is not, however, above helping that luck along. Not for Oliver Hazard Perry the glittering full-dress uniform of a Nelson or a Brock. He has no intention of being an easy target and has donned the plain blue jacket of a common sailor.

By 1:30, *Lawrence's* sails are so badly shredded that the brig can no longer be controlled. In spite of the sand, the decks are slippery with blood, which seeps through the seams and drips on the faces of the wounded in the wardroom below. These soon include Perry's closest friend, the purser, Samuel Hambleton, whose shoulder blade has been fractured by a spent cannonball bouncing off a mast. Hambleton lies beside the dying Brooks, who makes a verbal will and asks him to look after his affairs.

The wounded are being taken down the hatch so quickly that Parsons can do little more than secure bleeding arteries and tie a few splints to shattered limbs. There is not time now for the amputations that must follow; only when a leg or arm hangs by a shred does the ailing surgeon stop to sever it.

Nor is there any protection from the battle raging above. At least five cannonballs rip through the walls of Parson's makeshift hospital. The doctor has just finished applying a tourniquet to the mangled arm of a young midshipman, Henry Lamb, when a ball passes through the room, tears the boy out of the surgeon's arms, and throws him against the wall, his body half severed. A seaman brought down with both arms fractured is scarcely in splints before another ball tears off his legs.

On the deck above, the carnage is dreadful as the gun crews are felled by the British grape. Perry calls down through the skylight to Parsons, asking him to send up one of his assistants to man a gun. The call is renewed every few minutes until the doctor has no help left.

Bizarre scenes and unlikely incidents punctuate the action, to remain in the minds of the survivors for years and to form part of the mythology of the battle. Two cannonballs pass through the powder magazine—without igniting it. Another enters the light room, knocks the snuff from a candle into a magazine; a gunner puts it out with his fingers before disaster can strike. One shot punctures a pot of peas boiling on deck and scatters them. David Bunnell, working his gun, notices that a pig has got loose and is greedily eating the peas even though both hind legs have been shot away. Another shot strikes a nearby gun, showering its crew with tiny pieces of gun-metal; one man is riddled from knees to chin with bits of cast iron, some as small as a pinhead, none larger than buckshot. He recovers.

Bunnell is one of the few gunners left who has not been killed or wounded. A shot takes off the head of the man beside him, blowing his brains so thickly into Bunnell's face that he is temporarily blinded. All marines have been ordered down from the masts to replace the gunners, and when the marines are put out of action Perry again calls down the hatch, "Can any of the wounded pull a rope?" Two or three manage to crawl on deck and lend a feeble hand. Wilson May, one of the sick, insists on relieving the men at the pumps so that they can help with the guns. He is not well and must sit down to do the job. At the battle's end he is still sitting there, a bullet through his heart.

The major battle is between *Lawrence* on one side and the two largest British vessels—*Detroit* and *Queen Charlotte*—on the other. Elsewhere, things are going badly for the British. *Hunter*, unable to cope with the American carronades (her own shot is falling short) runs up to the head of the line to assist *Chippawa*. At the rear of the line, the four smaller American craft are battering their two opponents, *Lady Prevost* and *Little Belt*. A ball carries away the former's rudder and she drifts helplessly out of action. Her commander, Lieutenant Edward Buchan, has been driven temporarily insane by a wound in the head. *Little Belt* also loses her commander; she runs to the head of the line and is out of the fight.

But where is Jesse Elliott and the new brig *Niagara*? To the fury of Perry's officers and men, she is standing well off, using her long guns to little effect, too far out of range to bring her carronades into action. Elliott's original orders were to attack *Queen Charlotte*, which is hammering away at Perry's flagship. He has not done so. *Niagara*, twin to *Lawrence*, lurks behind the slower *Caledonia*, every spar in place, her crew scarcely scratched, her bulwarks unscarred.

What has got into Elliott? In the bitter controversy that follows, his supporters will give several explanations and his detractors will make as many charges. Is it a matter of cowardice? Few will believe that. Elliott has shown himself a brave and daring officer and will demonstrate that quality again before the battle is done. Is he merely obeying orders to keep in line behind *Caledonia*? That is scarcely credible (though Elliott will argue it), for Perry's other order—to engage *Queen Charlotte*—was unequivocal. Has the lightness of the wind made it impossible to move closer? If so, how have other ships been able to manoeuvre? And why, if he needs the wind, is his topsail backed and his jib brailed?

None of these alibis make sense. There is, however, one explanation that fits the circumstances. It devolves on Elliott's known character, his ambitions, his mild paranoia. He is nettled at being superseded by a younger man, piqued at being taken out of the van at the last moment, is stubbornly hewing to the letter of Perry's instructions (but only part of them) to stay a cable's length from the vessel ahead. There is, perhaps, more than that. Elliott undoubtedly sees himself as the saviour of the day; when Perry is driven to strike his flag, he, Elliott, will move in.

On *Lawrence*, even the wounded are cursing Elliott.

"Why don't they come and help us?" young Dulaney Forrest asks his superior, the bleeding Yarnell.

"We can expect nothing from that ship," comes the bitter reply.

It is now past two. Perry's flagship is a shambles. Most of her guns are useless, dismounted by the enemy's shot, their breeches torn away, their carriages knocked to pieces. A handful of gunners stick to their posts, firing as quickly as they can. In his haste, David Bunnell sticks a crowbar down the muzzle of his cannon and fires that, too. The gun grows so hot from constant use that it jumps from its carriage. By now five of Bunnell's crew of eight are casualties. He moves to the next gun, finds only one man left, brings up his surviving crew members and tries to get the weapon into action. As he does so he looks down the deck and is shocked by the spectacle—a tangle of bodies, some dead, some dying, the deck a welter of clotted blood, brains, human hair, and fragments of bones sticking to the rigging and planking. Of 137 officers and men aboard *Lawrence*, only 54 have escaped injury or death.

One by one, *Lawrence's* guns fall silent until she lies like a log in the water. Suddenly *Niagara* gets under way. Elliott, apparently believing Perry is dead, takes over and shouts an order to *Caledonia*, directly ahead, to move out of the line and let him pass—ostensibly to go to the aid of the disabled flagship. He does not do so. Instead, he passes *Lawrence* on the windward side, leaving that beleaguered vessel to the mercies of the British.

It is half-past two. Aboard *Detroit*, Barclay has been forced to go below to be treated for a bad wound in the thigh, secure in the belief that he has triumphed. His ship, too, has taken a fearful pummelling, its first officer dead, its spars and yards shattered, many of its guns out of action. The deck is clear of corpses, for the British do not share the American reverence for the dead and throw all bodies, except those of officers, immediately overboard. Here, too, is a bizarre spectacle: a pet bear, roaming the deck unhurt, licking up the blood.

Barclay's optimism is premature. Perry has no intention of giving up. Whatever Elliott's motives may be for staying out of the battle, he has at least left Perry a seaworthy brig, the equal of *Lawrence*, to continue the contest. Perry calls for a boat, takes four men, turns to Yarnell.

"I leave you to surrender the vessel to the enemy," says Perry, and orders his men to pull for *Niagara*. Then he remembers his special flag and calls for it. Hosea Sergeant, the last survivor of Gun Crew Nine, hauls it down, rolls it into a tight wad, tosses it down to the boat.

"If victory is to be gained, I'll gain it," says Perry.

He cannot control his excitement, refuses to sit down until his men, fearful for his life, threaten to ship their oars. On *Detroit*, the British catch glimpses of the craft, half hidden by the gunsmoke. Musket balls whistle past Perry's head, oars are shattered, round shot sends columns of spray into the boat, but Perry's Luck holds. When a twenty-four-pound ball hits the side of the rowboat, Perry tears off his jacket to plug the hole.

On *Lawrence*, some of the wounded are attempting to talk the surviving officers into fighting on.

"Sink the ship!" they cry, and "Let us sink with her!"

But Yarnell has no intention of indulging in further sacrifice. As he reaches *Niagara*, Perry, with "unspeakable pain," sees *Lawrence*'s flag come down. But the British cannot take the prize; all of *Detroit*'s boats have been shattered.

The American commodore is a scarecrow figure as he climbs aboard to greet the astonished Elliott, hatless, his clothes in tatters, blackened from head to foot by gunsmoke, spattered with blood.

"How goes the day?" asks Elliott, a fatuous question considering the state of the flagship.

"Bad enough," says Perry. "We have been cut all to pieces." Then to business: "Why are the gunboats so far behind?"

"I'll bring them up," says Elliott.

"Do so, sir," Perry responds shortly.

Elliott takes the rowboat and in a remarkable display of personal bravery rows off through heavy fire to call the smaller craft forward into battle by speaking-trumpet. He himself takes command of *Somers*, where he indulges in a curious display of temperament. A cannonball whizzes across the deck, causing Elliott to duck. A gun captain laughs. In a fury, Elliott strikes him across the face with his trumpet and then proceeds to arrest the sailing master, whom he believes to be drunk. But he gets the gunboats quickly into action and pours a heavy fire on the British ships.

Perry is also in action. He has hoisted his personal flag on *Niagara* and is intent on cutting directly through the British line—an echo of Nelson's famous feat at Trafalgar.

Barclay, back on deck, his wound dressed, anticipates the tactic. A fresh breeze has sprung up; *Niagara* is bearing down at right angles to his ship. In a few minutes she can rake her from bowsprit to taff-rail, the full length of the vessel, with her broadside of ten guns. It is a manoeuvre that every commander fears.

Barclay knows what he must do. He will have to wear his ship—bring her around before the wind—so that his own broadside of un-damaged guns can be brought to bear upon *Niagara*. Before he can effect the manoeuvre he is struck down again by a charge of grape-shot that tears his shoulder blade to pieces, leaving a gaping wound

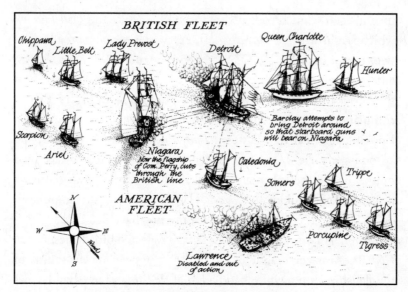

The Battle of Lake Erie: 2:40 p.m.

and rendering his one good arm useless. At the same instant, his second-in-command, John Garland, falls mortally wounded. The ship is now in charge of Lieutenant George Inglis.

As Elliott's gunboats begin to rake the British vessels from the stern, Inglis tries to bring the badly mauled flagship around. But *Queen Charlotte*, which has been supporting Barclay in his battle with *Lawrence*, has moved in too close. She is lying directly astern and in the lee of *Detroit*, which has literally taken the wind out of her sails. Her senior officers are dead, and Robert Irvine has little experience in working a big ship under these conditions. As *Detroit* attempts to come around, the masts and bowsprits of the two ships become hopelessly entangled. They are trapped. *Queen Charlotte* cannot even fire at the enemy without hitting fellow Britons.

Only seven minutes have passed since Perry boarded *Niagara*. Now he is passing directly through the ragged British line, a half pistol-shot from the flagship.

"Take good aim, boys, don't waste your shot!" he shouts.

His cannon are all double-shotted, increasing the carnage. As *Niagara* comes directly abeam of the entangled British ships, Perry fires his starboard broadside, raking both vessels and also *Hunter*, which is a little astern. On the left, Perry fires his port broadside at two smaller British craft, *Chippawa* and the rudderless *Lady Prevost*. The damage is frightful; above the cannon's roar Perry can hear the shrieks of men newly wounded. At this point, every British commander and his second is a casualty, unable to remain on deck. Looking across at the shattered *Lady Prevost*, Perry's gaze rests on an odd spectacle. Her commander, Buchan, shot in the face by a musket ball, is the only man on deck, leaning on the companionway, his gaze fixed blankly on *Niagara*. His wounds have driven him out of his mind; his crew, unable to face the fire, have fled below.

Detroit's masts crumble under Perry's repeated broadsides. *Queen Charlotte*'s mizzen is shot away. An officer appears on the taffrail of the flagship with a white handkerchief tied to a pike—Barclay has nailed his colours to the mast. *Queen Charlotte* surrenders at the same time, followed by *Hunter* and *Lady Prevost*. The two British gunboats, *Chippawa* and *Little Belt*, attempt to make a run for it but are quickly caught. To Perry's joy, his old ship, *Lawrence*, drifting far astern, has once again raised her colours, the British having been unable to board her.

It is three o'clock. Perry's victory is absolute and unprecedented. It is the first time in history that an entire British fleet has been defeated and captured intact by its adversary. The ships built on the banks of the wilderness lake have served their purpose. They will not fight again.

When Elliott boards *Detroit* there is so much blood on deck that he slips, drenching his clothing in gore. The ship's sides are studded with iron—round shot, canister, grape—so much metal that no man can place a hand on its starboard side without coming into contact with it. Elliott sends a man aloft to tear down Barclay's colours, saving the nails as a present for Henry Clay of Kentucky. Says Barclay, ruefully: "I would not have given sixpence for your squadron when I left the deck." He is in bad shape, weak, perhaps near death, from loss of blood and the shock of his mangled shoulder, ill-used once again in the final minutes of this astonishing contest.

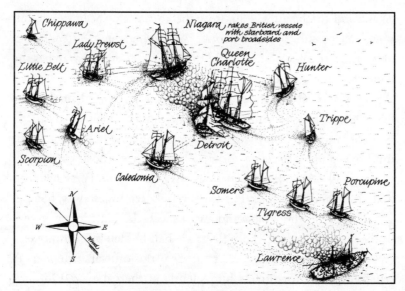

The Battle of Lake Erie: 3:00 p.m.

Perry, meantime, sitting on a dismounted cannon aboard *Niagara*, takes off his round hat and, using it for a desk, scrawls out a brief message to Harrison on the back of an envelope. Its first sentence is destined to become the most famous of the war:

> We have met the enemy and they are ours. Two Ships, two Brigs, one Schooner and one Sloop.
>
>   Yours, with greatest respect and esteem
>
>   O.H. PERRY

To William Jones, Secretary of the Navy, he pens a slightly longer missive to be borne personally to Washington by Dulaney Forrest, who still carries in his pocket the handful of grape-shot plucked from his waistcoat.

> Sir—It has pleased the Almighty to give to the arms of the United States a signal victory over their enemies on this lake. The British squadron ... have this moment surrendered to the force under my command after a sharp conflict. . . .

Around the lake the sounds of the battle have been heard, but none can be sure of the outcome. At Amherstburg, fifteen miles away, Lieutenant-Colonel Warburton, Procter's deputy, watches the contest from a housetop and believes the British to be the victors. At Cleveland, seventy miles away, Levi Johnson, at work on the new court house, hears a sound like distant thunder, realizes the battle is under way. All the villagers assemble on Water Street to wait until the cannonade ceases. Because the last five reports come from heavy guns—American carronades—they conclude Perry has won and give three cheers. At Put-in Bay, only ten miles away, Samuel Brown watches the "grand and awful spectacle" but cannot be sure of the outcome because both fleets are half hidden by gunsmoke.

Perry returns to *Lawrence* to receive the official surrender. A handful of survivors greets him silently at the gangway. On deck lie twenty corpses, including close friends with whom he dined the night before. He looks around for his little brother, Alexander, finds him sound asleep in a hammock, exhausted by the battle. He dons his full-dress uniform and, on the after part of the deck, receives those of the enemy able to walk. They pick their way among the bodies and offer him their swords; he refuses to accept them, instead inquires after Barclay's condition. His concern for his vanquished enemy is real and sincere.

The September shadows are lengthening. Perry's day is over. The fever, which subsided briefly under the adrenalin of battle, still lurks. Oblivious of his surroundings, the Commodore lies down among the corpses, folds his hands over his breast, and, with his sword beside him, sleeps the sleep of the dead.

PUT-IN BAY, LAKE ERIE, SEPTEMBER 11, 1813

The American fleet, its prizes and its prisoners, are back at anchorage by mid-morning. In the wardroom of the battered *Lawrence*, Dr. Usher Parsons has been toiling since dawn, amputating limbs. The seamen and marines are so eager to rid themselves of mutilated members that Parsons has had to establish a roster, accepting his patients for knife and saw in the order in which they were wounded. His task completed by eleven, he turns his attention to the remainder of the disabled; that occupies him until midnight. In all, he ministers to ninety-six men, saves ninety-three.

A special service is held for the officers of both fleets. Barclay, in spite of grievous wounds, insists on attending. Perry supports him, one arm around his shoulder. The effort is too much for the British commander, who is carried back to his berth on *Detroit*. Perry goes with him, sits by his side until the soft hours of the morning when Barclay finally drops off to sleep. The prisoners are struck by the American's courtesy. Now that the heat of battle has passed, he looks on his foes without rancour, makes sure his officers treat them well, urges Washington to grant Barclay an immediate and unconditional parole so that he may recover.

To Barclay, Perry is "a valiant and generous enemy." "Since the battle he has been like a brother to me," he writes to his brother in England. Later, the British commander, who will never again be able to raise his right arm above the shoulder, writes to his fiancée, offering to release her from their engagement. The spirited young woman replies that if there were enough of him left to contain his soul, she would marry him. The inevitable court martial follows, at which Barclay, not surprisingly, is cleared—his mutilated figure drawing tears from the spectators. But the navy, which has used him ill on Lake Erie with help that was too little and too late, puts him on the shelf. Almost eleven years will pass before he is promoted to post rank.

In the meantime, a more acrimonious drama is in the making. Most of Perry's officers are enraged at Elliott's behaviour during the action; but Perry, intoxicated by victory, is in an expansive mood. There is little doubt in his mind that Elliott has acted abominably, but in his elation, as he later tells Hambleton, there is not a man in his fleet whose feelings he would hurt. It is certainly in his power to ruin Elliott's career, but that is not his nature. Nor does he want the decisiveness of his victory marred by any blemish. "It is better to screen a coward than to let the enemy know there is one in the fleet," he remarks, quoting a long-dead British admiral.

In his official report, he cannot ignore his second-in-command; that would be tantamount to condemnation. So he laces his account of the battle with ambiguities:

> At half past two, the wind springing up, Captain Elliott was enabled to bring his vessel, the Niagara, gallantly into close action.

And:

> Of Captain Elliott, already so well known to the government, it would almost be superfluous to speak. In this action he evinced his characteristic bravery and judgement; and since the close of the action, has given me most able and generous assistance.

Perry shows the report to Elliott, who first says he is satisfied but later asks for changes. He does not like the reference to his ship coming into action so late. Perry, fearing he may have gone too far, refuses to revise the document.

Elliott takes to his bed, calls for Dr. Parsons, who can find nothing wrong with him. He calls for Perry, who finds him in "abject condition" and listens sympathetically while Elliott laments that he has missed "the fairest opportunity of distinguishing [himself] that ever a man had." Elliott follows this up with a letter in which he reports that his brother has heard rumours that *Lawrence* "was sacrificed in consequence of a want of exertion on my part individually." He urges Perry to deny this allegation.

The good-natured Perry has already ordered his officers not to write home with their doubts about Elliott's conduct in action and to silence all rumours about any controversy. He can do no less himself. Thus he falls into Elliott's trap and writes a letter (which he will later describe as foolish):

> ... I am indignant that any report should be in circulation prejudicial to your character ... I ... assure you that the conduct of yourself ... was such as to meet my warmest approbation. And

I consider the circumstance of your volunteering and bringing the smaller vessels to close action as contributing largely to our victory. . . .

This letter will be part of the ammunition that Elliott will use in his long and inexplicable battle for vindication. There is more: he is already twisting the arms of his own officers to prepare memoranda in his favour. And after Perry takes his leave of Lake Erie to go to another command, Elliott approaches Daniel Turner of *Caledonia* asking for a certificate praising his conduct in battle. Elliott tells Turner he wants only to calm his wife's fears—she has heard the rumours—and promises on his honour to make no other use of the document. But after Turner complies, Elliott has the certificate published.

And to what end? In the hosannas being sounded across the nation, Elliott shares the laurels equally with his commander. Congress takes the unprecedented step of striking not one but two gold medals—the first time a second-in-command has received one. In this one divines the subtle hand of Elliott's friend and mentor, Mr. Speaker Henry Clay. Elliott's share of the prize money—a staggering $7,140—also equals Perry's. (Chauncey, who begrudged the Erie fleet its seamen, gets one-twentieth of the total, almost thirteen thousand dollars.) As far as the public is concerned, Elliott is a hero. Why does he not keep quiet? But that would be contrary to Elliott's temperament; he is a man with a massive chip on his shoulder and an unbridled hunger for fame. He is also a man with a guilty conscience.

And so, as the news of the great victory spreads, as bonfires flare and triumphant salvos echo across the Union, as public dinners, toasts, orations, songs, and poems trumpet the country's triumph, the seeds of a bitter controversy begin to sprout.

Elliott cannot let the matter die. For the next thirty years the Battle of Lake Erie will be fought again and again, with affidavits, courts of inquiry, books, pamphlets, newspaper articles, even pistols. By 1818, Perry's own good nature evaporates; he calls Elliott "mean and despicable," retracts his letter when Elliott challenges him to a duel. Perry responds by demanding Elliott's court martial (a request that is pigeon-holed by the President). A hasty court of inquiry settles nothing, and even Perry's unfortunate death of yellow fever in 1819 does not still the verbal war. Elliott persists in his unflagging campaign for exoneration. In 1839, when James Fenimore Cooper enters the fray with a book that tends to support Elliott, Perry's friends rush again to his defence, and the literary battle goes on. Nor does it die until the last of the participants have gone to their final rest to join those others who, in the bloom of youth, bloodied the raw new decks of the two fleets that tore at each other on a cloudless September afternoon in 1813.

FIVE

The Northwest Campaign: 3

Retreat on the Thames

September 14–October 5, 1813

―――――――

With Barclay's defeat, Erie becomes an American lake. Because Perry can cruise these waters with impunity, landing troops anywhere, the British cannot hope to hold the territory captured in 1812. Detroit must be evacuated; Amherstburg, on the Canadian side, is threatened. The British have two choices: to meet the coming invasion at the water's edge (always supposing they know where it will come), or retire at once to a defensive position up the valley of the Thames, keeping the army intact and stretching the American lines of supply. The British command favours retreat; the Indians want to stay and fight.

FORT AMHERSTBURG, UPPER CANADA, SEPTEMBER 14, 1813

Tecumseh is in a violent passion. He has just come over from Bois Blanc Island in the Detroit River, where he and his followers are camped, to find that the fort is being dismantled. What is going on?

It looks very much as if Procter is planning to retreat; but Procter has been remarkably evasive with the Indians. On the day after the naval battle he actually pretended that Barclay had won.

"My fleet has whipped the Americans," he told the tribesmen, "but the vessels being much injured have gone into Put-in Bay to refit, and will be here in a few days."

Tecumseh, who is no fool, resents being treated as one. He does not care for Procter. The two have been at loggerheads since Brock's death, a year ago. Brock, in Tecumseh's view, was a *man*; Procter is fit only to wear petticoats. Now the British general fears to face his Shawnee ally with the truth.

Disillusion is gnawing at Tecumseh. Since 1808 he has been the supreme optimist, perfectly convinced that, aided by the compelling new religion of his mystic brother the Prophet, he can somehow weld all the warring and quarrelsome tribes into a mighty confederacy. He is in this war not to help the British but to help his people hold on to their hunting grounds and to their traditional life style. But the war has gone sour, and confederation is not as easy as it once seemed. He cannot convince the southern tribes to join him. And there is more than a suspicion that the young braves who still recognize his leadership are as interested in plunder and ransom money as they are in his grand design.

He is a curious mixture, this muscular Shawnee with the golden skin and hazel eyes who has renounced all pleasures of the flesh to funnel his energies toward a single goal. It is the future that concerns him; but now that future is clouded, and Tecumseh is close to despair. He has already considered withdrawing from the contest, has told his followers, the Shawnee, Wyandot, and Ottawa tribesmen, that the King has broken his promise to them. The British pledged that there would be plenty of white men to fight with the Indians. Where are they?

"The number," says Tecumseh, "is not now greater than at the commencement of the war; and we are treated by them like the dogs of snipe hunters; we are always sent ahead to *start the game;* it is better that we should return to our country and let the Americans come on and fight the British."

Tecumseh's own people agree. Oddly, it has been Robert Dickson's followers, the Sioux, and their one-time enemies the Chippewa, who have persuaded him to remain. But Dickson has gone off on one of his endless and often mysterious peregrinations through the wilderness to the west.

Now, with the fort being dismantled, Tecumseh has further evidence of Procter's distrust. Determined to abandon the British, he goes off in a fury to the home of Matthew Elliott, the Indian Department supervisor at Amherstburg. Ever since the Revolution, Elliott has been friend and crony to the Indians and especially to the Shawnee. At times, indeed, this ageing Irishman seems more Indian than Tecumseh. He fights alongside the Indians, daubed with ochre, has clubbed men to death with a tomahawk and watched others die at the stake—the ritual torture that Tecumseh abhors and prohibits. As events have proved, at both Frenchtown and Fort Meigs, he is less concerned about sparing the lives of prisoners than is Tecumseh. As a result he is, next to Procter, the man whom Harrison's Kentuckians hate most.

Elliott cringes under Tecumseh's fury. The Shawnee warns him that if Procter retreats, his followers will in a public ceremony bring out the great wampum belt, symbolic of British-Indian friendship, and cut it in two as an indication of eternal separation. The Prophet himself has decreed it. Worse, the Indians will fall on Procter's army, which they outnumber three to one, and cut it to pieces. Elliott himself will not escape the tomahawk.

For retreat is not in Tecumseh's make-up; he believes only in attack. The larger concerns of British strategy in this war are beyond him; his one goal is to kill as many of the enemy as possible. He has been fighting white Americans since the age of fifteen, when he battled the Kentucky volunteers. At sixteen, he was ambushing boats on the Ohio, at twenty-two serving as a raider and scout against the U.S. Army. He was one of the first warriors to break through the American lines at the Wabash during one of the most ignominious routs in American history when, in 1791, Major-General Arthur St. Clair lost half his army to a combined Indian attack. The following year Tecumseh answered the call of his elder brother to fight in the Cherokee war, and when his brother was killed became band leader in his stead, going north again to take part in the disastrous Battle of Fallen Timbers on the Maumee, where Major-General Anthony Wayne's three thousand men shattered Blue Jacket's band of fourteen hundred. On that black August day in 1794 Tecumseh, his musket jammed, did his best to rally his followers, waving a useless weapon as they scattered before the American bayonets.

Tecumseh believes in sudden attack: dalliance, even when justified, frustrates him; retreat is unthinkable. When Perry's fleet first appeared outside Amherstburg he could not understand why Barclay did not go out at once to face it.

"Why do you not go out and meet the Americans?" he taunted Procter. "See yonder, they are waiting for you and daring you to meet them; you must and shall send out your fleet and fight them."

Since those bloody days on the Wabash and Maumee, facing St. Clair and Wayne, Tecumseh has used another weapon—his golden voice—to frustrate William Henry Harrison's hunger for Indian lands. Now Harrison, the former governor of Indiana, who did his best to buy up the hunting grounds along the Wabash for a pittance, has Lake Erie to himself. He can land anywhere; and he has a score to settle with Tecumseh, who frustrated his land grab. Tecumseh, too, has a score to settle with Harrison, who destroyed the capital of his confederacy on the Tippecanoe. He cannot wait to get at the General; and he will use the weapon of his oratory to rally his people and blackmail the British into standing fast.

The following morning, he summons his followers from Bois Blanc Island. They squat in their hundreds on the fort's parade ground as Tecumseh strides over to a large stone on the river bank. It is here that announcements of importance are made and here that Tecumseh, the greatest of the native orators—some say the greatest orator of his day—makes the last speech of his life.

It is to Procter, standing nearby with a group of his officers, that Tecumseh, speaking through an interpreter, addresses his words.

First, his suspicions, born of long experience, going back to the peace that followed the Revolution:

"In that war our father was thrown on his back by the Americans. He then took the Americans by the hand without our knowledge, and we are afraid that our father will do so again. . . ."

Then, after a reference to British promises to feed the Indian families while the braves fought, a brief apology for the failure at Fort Meigs: "It is hard to fight people who live like ground hogs."

Then:

"Father, listen. Our fleet has gone out, we know they have fought. We have heard the great guns, but know nothing of what has happened to our father with one arm. Our ships have gone one way and we are much astonished to see our father tying up everything and preparing to run the other, without letting his red children know what his intentions are. You always told us to remain here and take care of our land. . . . You always told us you would never draw your foot off British ground. But now, Father, we see that you are drawing back, and we are sorry to see our father doing so without seeing the enemy. We must compare our father's conduct to a fat animal that carries its tail upon its back. But when affrighted, it drops it between its legs and runs off. . . ."

Tecumseh urges Procter to stay and fight any attempt at invasion. If he is defeated, he himself will remain on the British side and retreat with the troops. If Procter will not fight, then the Indians will:

"Father, you have got the arms and ammunition. . . . If you have any idea of going away, give them to us. . . . Our lives are in the hands of the Great Spirit; we are determined to defend our land; and if it is his will, we wish to leave our bones upon it."

As always, Tecumseh's eloquence has its effect. Some of his people leap up, prepared to attack the British immediately if their leader gives the word. But Tecumseh is placated when Procter promises to hold a council with the tribesmen on September 18.

Procter faces serious problems. The fort is defenceless, having been stripped of its cannon to arm the new ship, *Detroit*. One-third of his troops have been lost to him as a result of Perry's victory. He is out of provisions and must call on Major-General Vincent's Centre Division to send him supplies overland, since the water route is now denied him by the victorious Americans. Harrison not only has a formidable attack force but he also has the means to convey it, unchallenged, to Canada. Procter's own men are battle weary, half famished, and despondent over the loss of the fleet.

He does not have the charisma to rally his followers—none of Brock's easy way with men, or Harrison's. He is in his fiftieth year, a competent enough soldier, unprepossessing in features, and not very imaginative. There is a heaviness about him; his face is fleshy, his body tends to the obese—"one of the meanest looking men I ever saw," in the not unbiased description of an American colonel, William Stanley Hatch. When Brock remarked that the 41st was "badly officered" he undoubtedly meant men like Procter; yet he also must have thought Procter the best of the lot, for he put him in command at Amherstburg and confirmed him as his deputy after the capture of Detroit.

Procter suffers from three deficiencies: he is indecisive, he is secretive, and he tends to panic. When Brock wanted to cross the Detroit River and capture William Hull's stronghold in a single bold, incisive thrust, Procter was against it. When Procter's own army crept up on the sleeping Kentuckians at the River Raisin, Procter hesitated again, preferred to follow the book, wasted precious minutes bringing up his six-pounders instead of charging the palisade at once and taking the enemy by surprise. When he was finally convinced of the fleet's loss on September 13, he held a secret meeting with his engineering officer, his storekeeper, and his chief gunner, ordered the dismantling of the fort and the dispatching of stores and artillery to the mouth of the Thames. But he did not tell his second-in-command, Lieutenant-Colonel Augustus Warburton, who is understandably piqued at being left in the dark. When Warburton protests, Procter curtly tells him he has a perfect right to give secret orders. A right, certainly; but it is an axiom of war that subordinates should be kept informed.

There are good reasons for Procter to withdraw from Fort Amherstburg. Harrison has total mobility. Perry's fleet can now land his troops anywhere along Erie's north shore to outflank the British and take them from the rear. But if Procter moves up the Thames Valley he can stretch Harrison's line of supply and buy time to prepare a strong defensive position. The bulk of the American force is made up of militia men who have signed up for six months. If past experience means anything, Harrison will have difficulty keeping them after their term is up, especially with the Canadian winter coming on.

He must move quickly if he is to move at all; otherwise Harrison will be at his heels, giving him no chance to prepare a defence on ground of his own choosing. And here Procter stumbles. Inexplicably, he has been told by his superiors *not* to retire speedily. "Retrograde movements . . . are never to be hurried or accelerated," Prevost's aide writes from Kingston. And De Rottenburg, at Four Mile Creek on Lake Ontario, believes that the enemy's ships are in no condition to move after the battle—therefore Procter should take time to conciliate the Indians.

Procter, by his secrecy, has already wasted time. Almost a week passes before the promised meeting with the tribesmen. Even if they agree to move with the British, the logistics will be staggering. With women and children, their numbers exceed ten thousand. All must be brought across from Bois Blanc Island and from Detroit (which the British will have to evacuate) and moved up the Thames Valley. The women and children will go ahead of the army along with those white settlers who do not wish to remain under foreign rule. The sick must be removed as well—an awkward business—together with all the military stores. It is a mammoth undertaking, requiring drive, organizational ability, decision, and a sense of urgency. Procter does not display any of these qualities. And when he hears from De Rottenburg, he is given plenty of excuse to drag his feet.

He meets the Indians on September 18. Tecumseh urges that Harrison be allowed to land and march on Amherstburg. He and his Indians will attack on the flank with the British facing the front. If the attack fails, Tecumseh says, he can make a stand at the River aux Canards, which he defended successfully the previous year. When Procter rejects this plan, Tecumseh, in a fury, calls him "a miserable old squaw." At these words, the chiefs leap up, brandishing tomahawks, their yells echoing down from the vaulted roof of the lofty council chamber.

The time for secrecy is past. Procter unrolls a map and explains his position to the Shawnee war chief. If the gunboats come up the Detroit River, he points out, they can cut off the Indians camped on the American side of the river, making it impossible for them to support the British. Harrison can then move on to Lake St. Clair and to the mouth of the Thames, placing his men in the British rear and cutting off all retreat. Tecumseh considers this carefully, asks many questions, makes some shrewd remarks. He has never seen a map like this before. The country is new to him, but he quickly grasps its significance.

Procter offers to make a stand at the community of Chatham, where the Thames forks. He promises he will fortify the position and will "mix our bones with [your] bones." Tecumseh asks for time to confer with his fellow chiefs. It is a mark of his flexibility that he is able to change his mind and of his persuasive powers that after two hours he manages to convince the others to reverse their own stand and follow him up a strange river into a foreign country.

Yet Tecumseh still has doubts. On September 23, after destroying Fort Amherstburg, burning the dockyard and all the public buildings, the army leaves for Sandwich. Tecumseh views the retreat morosely.

"We are going to follow the British," he tells one of his people, "and I feel that I shall never return."

The withdrawal is snail-like. It has taken ten days to remove all the stores and baggage by wagon and scow. The townspeople insist on bringing their personal belongings, and this unnecessary burden ties up the boats, causing a delay in transporting the women, children, and sick. Matthew Elliott, for example, takes nine wagons and thirty horses to carry the most valuable part of his belongings,

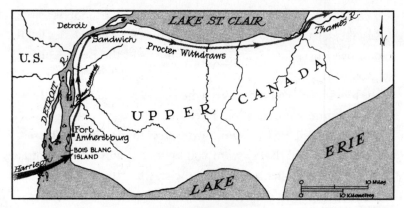

Procter Withdraws

including silver plate worth fifteen hundred pounds. The organization of the military stores is chaotic. Entrenching tools, which ought to be carried with the troops, are shifted to the bottoms of the boats after the craft are unloaded to take them across the bar at the mouth of the Thames. The rest of the cargo is piled on top, making them difficult to reach.

On the twenty-seventh, more than a fortnight after Barclay's defeat, Major Adam Muir destroys the barracks and public buildings at Detroit and moves his rearguard across the river. All of the territory captured by Brock in 1812—most of Michigan—is now back in American hands. At five the same day, Lieutenant-Colonel Warburton marches his troops out of Sandwich.

That same evening, Jacques Baby, a member of a prominent merchant and fur-trading family and a lieutenant-colonel in the militia, gives a dinner for the senior officers of the 41st in his stone mansion in Sandwich. Tecumseh attends wearing deerskin trousers, a calico shirt, and a red cloak. He is in a black mood, eats with his pistols on each side of his plate, his hunting knife in front of it.

Comes a knock on the door—a British sergeant announcing that the enemy fleet has entered the river and is sailing northward near Amherstburg. Tecumseh, whose English is imperfect, fails to catch the import of the message and asks the interpreter to explain. Then he rises, hands on pistols, and turns to General Procter.

"Father, we must go to meet the enemy.... We must not retreat.... If you take us from this post you will lead us far, far away ... tell us Good-bye forever and leave us to the mercy of the Long Knives. I tell you I am sorry I have listened to you thus far, for if we remained at the town ... we could have kept the enemy from landing and have held our hunting grounds for our children.

"Now they tell me you want to withdraw to the river Thames.... I am tired of it all. Every word you say evaporates like the smoke from our pipes. Father, you are like the crawfish that does not know how to walk straight ahead."

There is no reply. The dinner breaks up as the guests join the withdrawing army. Tecumseh has no choice but to follow the British with those warriors still loyal to his cause. By now these number no more than one thousand. The Ottawa and Chippewa bands have already sent three warriors to make peace terms with Harrison. The Wyandot, Miami, and some Delaware are about to follow suit.

In the days that follow, Henry Procter, obsessed by the problems of the Indians, abandons any semblance of decisive command. In 1812 the tribesmen were essential to victory; without them Upper Canada might well have become an American fief. Now they have become an encumbrance. Procter literally fails to burn his bridges behind him—an act that would certainly delay Harrison—because he believes that if he does so the Indians, who follow the troops, will think themselves cut off and abandon the British cause. To Lieutenant-Colonel Warburton's disgust, he purposely holds back the army in order to wait for the Indians. He does not, however, give that reason to his second-in-command but merely says that the troops should rest in their cantonments because of wet weather.

Indeed, he tells Warburton very little. Nor does he stay with the army. Mindful of his pledge to Tecumseh to make a stand at the forks of the Thames, he dashes forward on a personal reconnaissance, leaving Warburton without instructions—an action his officers find extraordinary.

He cannot get the Indians out of his mind. Their presence haunts him; the promises wrung from him at the council obsess him;

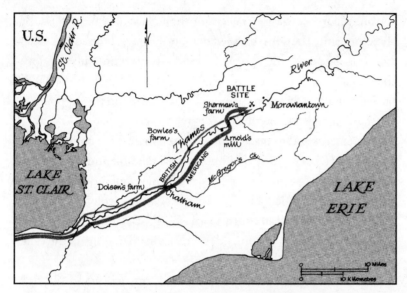

Retreat Up the Thames, September 27–October 5, 1813

Tecumseh's taunts clearly sting. And there is something more: his own superiors have harped again and again on the necessity of placating the tribesmen. De Rottenburg has expressly told him that he must "prove to them the sincerity of the British Government in its intent not to abandon them so long as they are true to their own interests" (which, translated, means as long as the Indians are prepared to fight for the British). Prevost has ordered him to conciliate the Indians "by any means in your power"—promising them mountains of presents if they will only follow the army. It is clear that the high command, taking its cue from the evidence of 1812, believes the Indians hold the key to victory; it does not occur to any that they may be the impediment that leads to defeat. There is also in the minds of Procter and his superiors another fear: if the Indians defect, may they not fall upon the British, destroy the army, and then swell the ranks of the invaders? Procter is caught in a trap: if he loses his native allies the blame will fall on him, but as long as Tecumseh is his ally, Procter is not his own man.

He sends his engineering officer, Captain Matthew Dixon, upstream to the forks of the Thames at the community of Chatham.

Dixon's report is negative: it is not the best place to make a stand. But something must be done, the General says; he has promised Tecumseh. Dixon is badgered into agreeing that the tiny community of Dover, three miles downstream from Chatham, is a slightly better position, but he cannot really recommend it. Procter seizes on this, appoints an assistant engineer, Crowther, to fortify the spot, ordering him to dig entrenchments and to place light guns at two or three points.

His heart is not in it. He and Dixon take off immediately for Moraviantown, twenty-six miles upstream, a much better position already recommended by the eccentric militia colonel and land developer, Thomas Talbot. In his haste, Procter does not think to inform his second-in-command, Warburton, marching up the valley with the army.

The General's intentions are clear: the army will stand and fight at Moraviantown, not at the forks. But Henry Procter will always be able to say he kept his promise to Tecumseh.

FRENCHTOWN, RIVER RAISIN,
MICHIGAN TERRITORY, SEPTEMBER 27, 1813

As the British fire the public buildings in Detroit and move back into Canada, twelve hundred mounted Kentucky riflemen, led by the fiery congressman, Colonel Richard Johnson, gallop along the Detroit road to reinforce Harrison's invasion army. Here they pause at the site of their state's most humiliating defeat to find the bones of their countrymen still unburied and strewn for three miles over the golden wheatfields and among the apple orchards.

The grisly spectacle rekindles the volunteers' thirst for revenge. Here, on a bitterly cold day the previous January, Procter's Indians struck down the flower of Kentucky, massacring them without quarter, butchering the wounded, burning some alive after putting the torch to buildings, holding others for ransom. *Remember the Raisin!* is the only recruiting cry needed in the old frontier commonwealth. Kentucky now has more men under arms than any state in the Union.

The regiment halts to bury the dead. Captain Robert McAfee writes in his diary that "the bones . . . cry aloud for revenge. . . . The chimneys of the houses where the Indians burnt our wounded prisoners . . . yet lie open to the call of vindictive Justice. . . ." The scene is rendered more macabre that night by a tremendous lightning storm "as if the Prince of the Power of the air . . . was invited at our approach to scenes of Bloodshed. . . ."

Its task completed, the regiment rides on toward Detroit, where William Henry Harrison awaits them. Most have been in the saddle since mid-May, after Harrison had asked for reinforcements to relieve Fort Meigs. Richard Johnson was only too eager to answer the call. Without waiting for War Department approval, he issued a proclamation:

> Fort Meigs is attacked—the North Western army is Surrounded . . . nobly defending the Sacred Cause of the Country. . . . The frontiers may be deluged with blood; the Mounted Regiment will present a Shield to the defenseless. . . .
>
> Every arrangement shall be made—there shall be no delay. The soldier's wealth is HONOR—connected with his Country's cause, is its Liberty, independence and glory, without exertions Rezin's [*sic*] bloody scene may be acted over again and to permit [this] would stain the national character. . . .

Such purple sentiments spring easily from Richard Mentor Johnson's pen. At thirty-two a handsome, stocky figure with a shock of auburn hair, he has made a name for himself as an eloquent, if florid, politician. The first native-born Kentuckian to be elected to both the state legislature and the federal congress, he is a crony of Henry Clay and a leading member of the group of War Hawks who goaded the country into war. Like so many of his colleagues, he is a frontiersman by temperament, reared on tales of Indian depredations. His family were Indian fighters by inclination as well as of necessity. He has heard from his mother the story of one siege, when, as she was running from the blockhouse for water, a lighted arrow fell on her son's cradle. Fortunately for Richard Johnson it was snuffed out.

Unlike the aloof New Englanders or the hesitant Pennsylvanians, Kentuckians regard the invasion of Canada as a holy war, "a second revolution as important as the first," in Johnson's belief. It is also seen as a war of conquest: Johnson makes no bones about that. England must be driven from the New World: "I shall never die contented until I see . . . her territories incorporated with the United States."

The "men of talents, property and public spirit" who flock to Johnson's banner in unprecedented numbers—old Revolutionary soldiers, ex-Indian fighters, younger bloods raised on tales of derring-do—agree. All have made their wills, have resolved never to return to their state unless they come back as conquerors "over the butcherly murderers of their countrymen." Robert McAfee, first captain of the first battalion, is typical. On reaching the shores of Lake Erie he foresees in his imagination huge cities and an immense trade—the richest and most important section of the Union. "It is necessary that Canada should be ours," he writes in his journal.

Johnson and his brother, James, have fifteen hundred six-month volunteers under their command, each decked out in a blue hunting shirt with a red belt and blue pantaloons, also fringed with red. They are armed with pistols, swords, hunting knives, tomahawks, muskets, and Kentucky squirrel rifles. Their peregrinations since mid-May have been both exhausting and frustrating, for they have been herded this way and that through the wilderness for more than twelve hundred miles without once firing a shot at the enemy.

At last the action they crave seems imminent. Johnson can hardly wait to get at the "monster," Procter. His men are no less eager as they ride toward Detroit, swimming their horses across the tributary streams, on the lookout for hostile Indians, elated by news of the British withdrawal. On the afternoon of the thirtieth they reach their objective. The entire population turns out to greet them, headed by the Governor of Kentucky himself, old Isaac Shelby, who at Harrison's request has brought some two thousand eager militia-men to swell the ranks of the invading army.

The tide is turning for the Americans. Johnson learns that Harrison has already occupied Amherstburg, surprised that Procter abandoned it without offering resistance. Harrison now has a force of five thousand men, including two thousand regulars. He does not expect to catch Procter because the British have commandeered every horse in the country. It is all he can do to find a broken-down pony to carry the ageing Shelby.

Harrison has one hope: that Procter will make a stand some-where on the Thames. His "greatest apprehensions," as he tells the Secretary of War, "arise from the belief that he will make no halt." In that case, perhaps he ought to move his army up the north shore of Lake Erie aboard the fleet, and attack the British rear.

At dawn on the morning of September 30 he and Shelby meet in a small private room in his headquarters at Amherstburg to discuss tactics. The Governor is here at Harrison's personal request, tech-nically in command of all Kentucky militia.

"Why not, my dear sir, come in person?" Harrison asked him in a flattering letter. "You would not object to a command that would be nominal only. I have such confidence in your wisdom that you in fact should be 'the guiding head and I the hand.'"

Harrison—a scholarly contrast to the ragtag crew of near illiter-ates who officer the militia—cannot resist a classical allusion:

"The situation you would be placed in is not without its parallel. Scipio, the conqueror of Carthage, did not disdain to act as a lieu-tenant of his younger and less experienced brother, Lucius."

It is a shrewd move. Shelby, an old frontiersman and Revolutionary warrior, cannot resist Harrison's honeyed pleas. He is sixty-three, paunchy and double-chinned, with close-cropped white hair. But he commands the respect of Kentuckians, who call him "Old King's Mountain" after his memorable victory at that place in 1780 and flock to his command in double the numbers required.

Harrison wants the Governor's opinion: the army can pursue Procter by land up the Thames Valley or it can be carried by water to Long Point, along the lake, and march inland by the Long Point road to intercept the British.

Shelby replies that he believes Procter can be overtaken by land. With that the General calls a council of war to confirm the strategy. It opts for a land pursuit.

Harrison decides to take thirty-five hundred men with him, leaving seven hundred to garrison Detroit. Johnson's mounted volunteers, brought over early next morning, will lead the van. The remainder of the force, whose knapsacks and blankets have been left on an island in the river, will follow.

The General has the greatest difficulty persuading any Kentuckian to stay on the American side of the Detroit River. All consider it an insult to be left behind; in the end, Harrison has to resort to a draft to keep them in Detroit. The Pennsylvania militia, on the other hand, stand on their constitutional right not to fight outside the territorial limits of the United States.

"I believe the boys are not willing to go, General," one of their captains tells him.

"The boys, eh?" Harrison remarks sardonically. "I believe some of the officers, *too*, are not willing to go. Thank God I have Kentuckians enough to go without you."

Speed is of the essence. As Shelby keeps saying: "If we desire to overtake the enemy, we must do more than he does, by early and forced marches."

And so, at first light on October 2, as Procter dawdles, the Americans push forward, sometimes at a half run to keep up with the mounted men. Johnson asks Harrison's permission to ride ahead in search of the British rearguard. Harrison agrees but, remembering the disaster before Fort Meigs, adds a word of caution.

"Go, Colonel, but remember discipline. The rashness of your brave Kentuckians has heretofore destroyed themselves. Be cautious, sir, as well as brave and active, as I know you all are."

Johnson rides off with a group of volunteers. Not far from the Thames, they capture six British soldiers and learn that Procter's army is only fifteen miles above the mouth of the Thames. It is now nearly sunset, but when the regiment hears this, it determines to move on to Lake St. Clair. In one day Harrison's army has marched twenty-five miles.

The troops set off again at dawn. Since only the three gunboats with the shallowest draft can ascend the winding Thames, Oliver Hazard Perry, who is eager to see action, signs on as Harrison's aide. Harrison concludes that Procter is unaware of his swift approach, for he has not bothered to destroy any bridges to slow the American advance. Then, at the mouth of the Thames, an eagle is spotted hovering in the sky. Harrison sees it as a victory omen, especially after Perry tells him his seamen had noticed a similar omen the morning of the lake battle. The Indians, it seems, are not the only warriors who believe in signs and portents.

That afternoon, the army captures a British lieutenant and eleven dragoons. From these prisoners Harrison learns that the British have as yet no certain information of his advance.

By evening, the army is camped ten miles up the river, just four miles below Matthew Dolsen's farm at Dover, from which the British have only just departed. It has taken Procter's army five days to make the journey from Sandwich. Harrison has managed to cover the same ground in less than half the time.

DOLSEN'S FARM, DOVER, UPPER CANADA, OCTOBER 3, 1813

Augustus Warburton is a confused and perplexed officer. Procter's second-in-command has no idea what he is to do because his commander has not told him. Word has reached him that the Americans are on the march a few miles downstream. His own men have reached the place where Procter decided to make a stand, but Procter has rushed up the river to Moraviantown, having apparently decided to meet the enemy there.

Now Captain William Crowther comes to Warburton with a problem. Procter has ordered him to fortify Dover; he wants to throw up a temporary battery, cut loopholes in the log buildings, dig trenches. But all the tools have been sent on to Bowles's farm seven miles upriver, and there are neither wagons nor boats to bring them back. Crowther is stymied.

It is too late, anyway, for Tecumseh, on the opposite bank, insists on moving three miles upstream to Chatham, at the forks. It was there that Procter originally promised to make a stand and, if necessary, lay his bones with those of the Indians. Tecumseh has not been told of any change of plans.

Nor has Warburton. His officers agree that the Indians must be conciliated. As a result, the army, which has lingered at Dolsen's for two days, moves three miles to Chatham and halts again. Tecumseh—not Procter, not Warburton—is calling the tune.

Tecumseh is in a fury. There are no fortifications at Chatham; Procter has betrayed him! Half his force leaves, headed by Walk-in-the-Water of the senior tribe of Wyandot. Matthew Elliott's life is threatened.

Elliott crosses the river and, in a panic, urges Warburton to stand and fight at Chatham.

"I will not, by God, sacrifice myself," he cries, in tears.

He is a ruined man, Elliott, in every sense, and knows it. Financially, he is approaching destitution. His handsome home at Amherstburg has been gutted by the Kentuckians—the furniture broken, fences, barns, storehouses destroyed. His personal possessions are in immediate danger of capture. And his power is gone: the Indians no longer trust him. Once he was the indispensable man, his influence over the American tribes so great that the British restored him to duty after a financial scandal that would have destroyed a lesser official. Now all that has ended. The frontier days are over. The Old Northwest, which Elliott and his cronies, Simon Girty and Alexander McKee, knew when they fought beside the braves against Harmar, St. Clair, and Wayne, is no more. Except for Tecumseh's dwindling band, the native warriors have been tamed. The old hunting grounds north of the Ohio are already threatened by the onrush of white civilization. Here on the high banks of the Thames, the faltering Indian confederacy will stand or fall.

Warburton asks Elliott to tell Tecumseh that he will try to comply with Procter's promises and make a stand on any ground of the Indian's choosing. He has already sent two messages to Procter, warning him that the enemy is closing in and explaining that he has moved forward to Chatham. But Procter goes on to Moraviantown regardless and, after sending his wife and family off to safety at Burlington Heights, remains there for the night.

The Indians are angered at Procter's inexplicable absence. Tecumseh's brother, the Prophet, says he would like personally to tear off the General's epaulettes; he is not fit to wear them. The army, too, is disturbed. Mutiny is in the air. There is talk of supplanting Procter with Warburton, but Warburton will have none of it, a decision that causes Major Adam Muir of the rearguard to remark that Procter ought to be hanged for being absent and Warburton hanged with him for refusing responsibility.

Early on the morning of October 4 (the Americans have been camped all night at Dolsen's), Warburton gets two messages. The first, from Procter, announces that he will leave Moraviantown that day to join the troops. The second, from Tecumseh, tells him that the Indians have decided to retire to the Moravian village.

Warburton waits until ten; no Procter. Across the river he can hear shots: the Indians are skirmishing with the enemy. Just as he sets his troops in motion another message arrives from Procter, ordering him to move a few miles upriver to Bowles's farm. The column moves slowly, impeded by the Indian women who force it to halt time after time to let them pass. At Bowles's—the head of navigation on the river—Warburton encounters his general giving orders to destroy all the stores collected there—guns, shells, cord, cable, naval equipment. In short, the long shuttle by boat from Amherstburg, which delayed the withdrawal, has been for nothing. Two gunboats are to be scuttled in the river to hinder the American progress.

At eight that evening the forward troops reach Lemuel Sherman's farm, some four miles from Moraviantown, and halt for the night. Here, ovens have been constructed and orders given for bread to be baked; but there is no bread, the bakers claiming that they must look first to their families and friends. Footsore, exhausted, and half-starved, their morale at the lowest ebb, the men subsist on whatever bread they have saved from the last issue at Dolsen's.

Tecumseh, meanwhile, has fought a rearguard action at the forks of the Thames—two frothing streams that remind him, nostalgic-ally, of his last home, Prophetstown, where the Tippecanoe mingles its waters with those of the Wabash. In this strange northern land, hundreds of miles from his birthplace, he hungers for the familiar. His Indians tear the planks off the bridge at McGregor's Creek and when Harrison's forward scouts, under the veteran frontiers-man William Whitley, try to cross on the sills, open fire from their hiding place in the woods beyond. Whitley, a sixty-three-year-old Indian fighter and Kentucky pioneer, has insisted on marching as a private under Harrison, accompanied by two black servants. Now he topples off the muddy timbers, falls twelve feet into the water, but manages to swim ashore, gripping his silver-mounted rifle. Major Eleazer Wood, the defender of Fort Meigs, sets up two six-pounders to drive the Indians off. The bridge is repaired in less than two hours, and the army pushes on.

That evening, Tecumseh reaches Christopher Arnold's mill, twelve miles upriver from the forks. Arnold, a militia captain and an acquaintance from the siege of Fort Meigs, offers him dinner and a bed. He is concerned about his mill; the Indians have already burned McGregor's. Tecumseh promises it will be spared. He sees no point in useless destruction; with the other mill gone, the white settlers must depend on this one.

In these last hours, fact mingles with myth as Tecumseh prepares for battle. Those whose paths cross his will always remember what was done, what was said, and hand it down to their sons and grandsons.

Young Johnny Toll, playing along the river bank near McGregor's Creek, will never forget the hazel-eyed Shawnee who warned him, "Boy, run away home at once. The soldiers are coming. There is war and you might get hurt."

Sixteen-year-old Abraham Holmes will remember the sight of Tecumseh standing near the Arnold mill on the morning of October 5, his hand at the head of his white pony: a tall figure, dressed in buck-skin from neck to knees, a sash at his waist, his headdress adorned with ostrich plumes—waiting until the last of his men have passed by and the mill is safe. Holmes is so impressed that he will name his first-born Tecumseh.

Years from now Chris Arnold will describe the same scene to his grandson, Thaddeus. Arnold remembers standing by the mill dam, waiting to spot the American vanguard. It is agreed he will signal its arrival by throwing up a shovelful of earth. But Tecumseh's eyes are sharper, and he is on his horse, dashing off at full speed, after the first glimpse of Harrison's scouts. At the farm of Arnold's brother-in-law, Hubble, he stops to perform a small act of charity—tossing a sack of Arnold's flour at the front door to sustain the family, which is out of bread.

Lemuel Sherman's sixteen-year-old son, David, and another friend, driving cows through a swamp, come upon Tecumseh, seated on a log, two pistols in his belt. The Shawnee asks young Sherman whose boy he is and, on hearing his father is a militiaman in Procter's army, tells him: "Don't let the Americans know your father is in the army or they'll burn your house. Go back and stay home, for there will be a fight here soon."

Years later when David Sherman is a wealthy landowner, he will lay out part of his property as a village and name it Tecumseh.

Billy Caldwell, the half-caste son of the Indian Department's Colonel William Caldwell, will remember Tecumseh's fatalistic remarks to some of his chiefs:

"Brother warriors, we are about to enter an engagement from which I shall not return. My body will remain on the field of battle."

Long ago, when he was fifteen, facing his first musket fire against the Kentuckians, and his life stretched before him like a river without end, he feared death and ran from the field. Now he seems to welcome it, perhaps because he has no further reason to live. Word has also reached him that the one real love of his life, Rebecca Galloway, has married. She it was who introduced him to English literature. There have been other women, other wives; he has treated them all with disdain; but this sixteen-year-old daughter of an Ohio frontiersman was different. She was his "Star of the Lake" and would have married him if he had only agreed to live as a white man. But he could not desert his people. Now she is part of a dead past, a dream that could not come true, like his own shattered dream of a united Indian nation.

In some ways, Tecumseh seems more Christian than the Christians, with his hatred of senseless violence and torture. He is considerate of others, chivalrous, moral, and, in his struggle for his people's existence, totally selfless. But he intends to go into battle as a pagan, daubed with paint, swinging his hatchet, screaming his war cry, remembering always the example of his elder brother Cheeseekau, the father figure who brought him up and, in the end, met death gloriously attacking a Kentucky fort, expressing the joy he felt at dying—not like an old woman at home but on the field of conflict where the fowls of the air should pick his bones.

LEMUEL SHERMAN'S FARM,
UPPER THAMES, OCTOBER 5, 1813

Procter's troops, who have had no rations since leaving Dolsen's, are about to enjoy their first meal in more than twenty-four hours when the order comes to pack up and march—the Americans are only a short distance behind. Some cattle have already been butchered, but there is no time to cook the beef and there are no pans in which to roast it. Nor is there bread. Ovens have been constructed but again the baker has run off. Some of the men stuff raw meat into their mouths or munch on whatever crusts they still have from the last issue; the rest go hungry.

There is worse news. The Americans have seized all the British boats, captured the excess ammunition, tools, stores. The only cartridges the troops have are in their pouches. The officers attempt to conceal that disturbing information from their men.

The army marches two and a half miles. Procter appears and brings it to a halt. Here, with the river on his left and a heavy marsh on his right, in a light wood of beech, maple, and oak, he will make his stand.

It is not a bad position. His left flank, resting as it does on the high bank of the river, cannot be turned. His right is protected by the marsh. The General expects the invading army to advance down the road that cuts through the left of his position. He plants his only gun—a six-pounder—at this point to rake the pathway. The regulars will hold the left flank. The militia will form a line on their right. Beyond the militia, separated by a small swamp, will be Tecumseh's Indians.

But why has Procter not chosen to make his stand farther upstream on the heights above Moraviantown, where his position could be protected by a deep ravine and the hundred log huts of the Christian Delaware Indians, who have lived here with their Moravian missionaries since fleeing Ohio in 1792? It is to this village that Procter brought his main ordnance and supplies. Why the sudden change of plan?

Once again the Indians have dictated the battle. They will not fight on an open plain; that is not their style. Procter feels he has no choice but to anticipate their wishes.

His tactics are simple. The British will hold the left while the Indians, moving like a door on a hinge, creep forward through the thicker forest on the right to turn Harrison's flank.

There are problems, however, and the worst of these is morale. The troops are slouching about, sitting on logs and stumps. They have already been faced about once, marched forward and then back again for some sixty paces, grumbling about "doing neither one thing or another." Almost an hour passes before they are brought to their feet and told to form a line. This standard infantry manoeuvre is accomplished with considerable confusion, compounded by the fact that Procter's six hundred men are too few to stand shoulder to shoulder in the accepted fashion. The line develops into a series of clusters as the troops seek to conceal themselves behind trees. Nobody, apparently, thinks to construct any sort of bulwark—entrenchments, earthworks, or a barricade of logs and branches—which might impede the enemy's cavalry. No one appears to notice that on the British side of the line there is scarcely any underbrush. But then, all the shovels, axes, and entrenching tools have been lost to the enemy.

The troops stand in position for two and a half hours, patiently waiting for the Americans to appear. They are weak from hunger, exhausted from the events of the past weeks. They have had no pay for six months, cannot even afford soap. Their clothes are in rags, and they have been perennially short of greatcoats and blankets. They are overworked, dispirited, out of sorts. Some have been on garrison duty, far away from home in England, for a decade. They cannot see through the curtain of trees but have heard rumours that Harrison has ten thousand men advancing to the attack. Many believe Procter is more interested in saving his wife and family than in saving them; many believe they are about to be cut to pieces and sacrificed for nothing. And so they wait—for what seems an eternity.

Tecumseh rides up. The men, he tells Elliott, seem to him to be too thickly posted; they will be thrown away to no advantage. Procter obediently robs his line to form a second, one hundred yards behind, with a corps of dragoons in reserve. Now the Shawnee war chief rides down the ragged line, clasping hands with the officers, murmuring encouragement in his own language. He has a special greeting for John Richardson, whom he has known since childhood. Richardson notes the fringed deerskin ornamented with stained porcupine quills, the ostrich feathers (a gift from the Richardson family), and most of all the dark, animated features, the flashing hazel eyes. Whenever in the future he thinks of Tecumseh—and he will think of him often—that is the picture that will remain: the tall sturdy chief on the white pony, who seems now to be in such high spirits and who genially tells Procter, through Elliott, to desire his men to be stout-hearted and to take care the Long Knives do not seize the big gun.

William Henry Harrison, having destroyed Procter's gunboats and supplies, has crossed the Thames above Arnold's mill in order to reach the right bank along which the British have been retreating. The water at the ford is so deep that the men hesitate until Perry, in his role as Harrison's aide, rides through the crowd, shouts to a foot soldier to climb on behind, and dashes into the stream, calling on Colonel Johnson's mounted volunteers to follow his example. In this way, and with the aid of several abandoned canoes and keel boats, the three thousand foot soldiers are moved across the river in forty-five minutes.

William Whitley, the veteran scout, seeing an Indian on the opposite side, shoots him, swims his horse back across, and scalps the corpse. "This is the thirteenth scalp I have taken," he tells a friend, "and I'll have another by night or lose my own."

As the army forms up on the right bank, a message arrives for Harrison. A spy has reported that the British are not far ahead, aiming for Moraviantown. Harrison rides up to Johnson, tells him that foot soldiers will not be able to overtake Procter until late in the day, asks him to push his mounted regiment forward to stop the British retreat.

"If you cannot compel them to stop without an engagement, why FIGHT them, but do not venture too much," Harrison orders.

Johnson moves his men forward at a trot. Half a mile from the British line his forward scouts capture a French-Canadian soldier. The prisoner insists that Procter has eight hundred men supported by fourteen hundred Indians. When Johnson reveals he has only one thousand followers, his informant bursts into tears, begs him to retire. But Johnson has no intention of retreating. He sends back a message to Harrison that the British have halted and are only a few hundred yards distant. If they venture to attack, his men will charge them.

Procter does not attack, and the two armies remain within view of one another, motionless, waiting.

A quarter of an hour passes. Harrison rides up, sends Eleazer Wood forward to examine the situation through his spyglass. Behind him, the American column—eleven regiments supported by artillery—stretches back for three miles. Harrison holds a council of war on horseback. He sees at once that Procter has a good position and divines the British strategy: they will use the Indians on his left on the edge of the morass to outflank him. That he must frustrate. He will attempt to hold the Indians back with a strong force on his left and attack the British line with a bayonet charge through the woods. At the same time Johnson's mounted men will splash through the shallow swamp that separates the British from the Indians and fall on Tecumseh's tribesmen.

Harrison forms up his troops in an inverted L, its base facing the British regulars. Shelby is posted at the left end of the base (the angle of the L). Harrison takes a position on the right, facing Procter. The honour of leading the bayonet charge goes to Brigadier-General George Trotter, a thirty-four-year-old veteran. It is a signal choice, for a high proportion of Trotter's men come from the same Kentucky counties that bore the brunt of the Frenchtown massacre.

An hour and a half passes while Harrison forms his troops. The British, peering through the oaks, the beeches, and the brilliant sugar maples, can catch only glimpses of the enemy, three hundred yards distant. The Americans, waiting to attack, have a better view of the British in their scarlet jackets.

Meanwhile, Richard Johnson has sent Captain Jacob Stucker to examine the shallow swamp through which his troops must gallop in their attack on the Indians. Stucker returns with disappointing news: the swamp is impassable. Finally, the General speaks:

"You must retire, Colonel, and act as a corps of reserve."

But Johnson has a different idea:

"General Harrison, permit me to charge the enemy and the battle will be won in thirty minutes." He means the British—not the Indians.

Harrison considers. The redcoats are spread out in open formation with gaps between the clusters of men. The woods are thick with trees, but there is little underbrush. He knows that Johnson has trained his men to ride through the forests of Ohio, firing cartridges to accustom the horses to the sound of gunfire. Most have ridden horseback since childhood; all are expert marksmen.

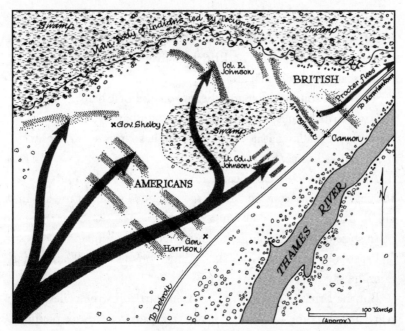

The Battle of the Thames

"Damn them! Charge them!" says Harrison, and changes the order of battle on the spot.

It is a measure, Harrison will later declare, "not sanctioned by anything that I had seen or heard of." But he is convinced that this unorthodox charge will catch the British unprepared.

Now Stucker comes back with welcome news. He has found a way through the intervening swamp. It will not be easy, for the ground is bad. Johnson turns to his brother, James, his second-in-command.

"Brother, take my place at the head of the first battalion. I will cross the swamp and fight the Indians at the head of the second battalion." He explains his reason: "You have a family, I have none."

In the brief lull that follows, one of Harrison's colonels, John Calloway, rides out in front of his regiment and in a stentorian voice, shouts:

"Boys, we must either whip these British and Indians or they will kill and scalp every one of us. We cannot escape if we lose. Let us all die on the field or conquer."

Procter's repeated threat—that he cannot control the Indians—has been turned against him. He has so convinced the Americans that a massacre will follow a British victory that they are prepared, if necessary, for a suicidal attack.

The bugle sounds the charge. Seated on his horse halfway between the two British lines, Procter hears the sound and asks his brigade major, John Hall, what it means. The bugle sounds again, closer.

"It's the advance, Sir," Hall tells him.

An Indian scout, Campeaux, fires his musket. Without orders, the entire British front line discharges a ragged volley at the advancing horsemen.

In spite of their training, the horses recoil in confusion.

Procter looks toward the six-pounder on his left. "Damn that gun," he says. "Why doesn't it fire?"

But the British horses have also been startled by the volley. They rear back, become entangled in the trees, taking the six-pounder with them.

James Johnson rallies his men and charges forward as the second line of British defenders opens fire.

"Charge them, my brave Kentuckians!" Harrison cries in his florid fashion as the volunteers dash forward, yelling and shouting.

"Remember the Raisin!" someone shouts, and the cry ripples across the lines: *Remember the Raisin! Remember the Raisin!*

The volunteers hit the left of the British line. It crumbles. Captain Peter Chambers, one of the heroes of the siege of Fort Meigs, sees his men tumbling in all directions, tries vainly to rally them, finds himself swept back by the force of the onslaught.

"Stop, 41st, stop!" Procter shouts. "Why do you not form? What are you about? For shame. For shame on you!"

The force of the charge has taken Johnson's horsemen right through both British lines. Now they wheel to their left to roll up the British right, which is still holding.

"For God's sake, men, stand and fight!" cries a sergeant of the 41st. Private Shadrach Byfield, in the act of retreating, hears the cry, turns about, gets off a shot from his musket, then flees into the woods.

Not far away stands John Richardson, an old soldier at sixteen, survivor of three bloody skirmishes. A fellow officer points at one of the mounted riflemen taking aim at a British foot soldier. Richardson raises his musket, leans against a tree for support, and before the mounted man can perfect his aim drops him from his horse. Now he notes an astonishing spectacle on his right. He sees one of the Delaware chiefs throw a tomahawk at a wounded Kentuckian with such precision and force that it opens his skull, killing him instantly. The Delaware pulls out the hatchet, cuts an expert circle around the scalp; then, holding the bloody knife in his teeth, he puts his knee on the dead man's back, tears off the scalp, and thrusts it into his bosom, all in a matter of moments. This grisly scene is no sooner over than the firing through the woods on Richardson's left ends suddenly, and the order comes to retreat.

Procter, too, is preparing to make off. The gun crew has fled; the Americans have seized the six-pounder. Hall warns him that unless they move swiftly they will both be shot.

"Clear the road," Hall orders, but the road is clogged with fleeing redcoats. He suggests to the General that they should take to the woods; but Procter, stunned by the suddenness of defeat, does not appear to hear him. No more than five minutes have passed since Harrison's bugle sounded.

"This way, General, this way," says Hall patiently, like a parent leading a child. The General follows obediently. A little later he finds his voice:

"Do you not think we can join the Indians?" For Tecumseh's force on the right of the shattered British line is still fighting furiously.

"Look there, Sir," says Hall, pointing to the advancing Americans. "There are mounted men betwixt you and them." James Johnson's charge has cut Procter's army in two.

They are on the road, riding faster now, for the Americans are in hot pursuit. Procter is desperate to escape the wrath of the Kentucky volunteers, whose reputation is as savage as that of the Potawatomi who slaughtered their countrymen at the River Raisin. For all he knows they may flay him alive before Harrison can stop them.

As Captain Thomas Coleman of the Provincial Dragoons catches up, the General gasps out that he is afraid he will be captured. Coleman reassures him: some of his best men will be detailed to guard him. The General gallops on with the sound of Tecumseh's Indians, still holding, echoing in his ears.

As James Johnson's men drive the British before them, his brother's battalion plunges through the decaying trees and tangled willows of the small swamp that separates the Indians from their white allies. Richard Johnson's plan is brutal. He has called for volunteers for what is, in effect, a suicide squad—a "Forlorn Hope," in the parlance of both the British and the American armies. This screen of twenty bold men will ride ahead of the main body to attract the Indians' fire. Then, while the tribesmen are reloading, the main body will sweep down upon them.

There is no dearth of volunteers. The grizzled Whitley, a fresh scalp still dangling from his belt, will lead the Forlorn Hope. And Johnson will ride with them.

Off they plunge into the water and mud, into a hail of musket balls. Above the shattering dissonance of the battle another sound is heard—clear, authoritative, almost melodic—the golden voice of Tecumseh, urging his followers on to victory. Johnson's tactic is working: the Indians have concentrated all their fire on the Forlorn Hope, and with devastating results—fifteen of the twenty, including William Whitley, are dead or mortally wounded.

But Johnson faces a problem. The mud of the swamp has risen to the saddle girth of the horses. His men cannot charge. Bleeding from four wounds, he orders them to dismount and attack. An Indian behind a tree fires again, the ball striking a knuckle of Johnson's left hand, coming out just above the wrist. He grimaces in pain as his hand swells, becomes useless. The Indian advances, tomahawk raised. Johnson, who has loaded his pistol with one ball and three buckshot, draws his weapon and fires, killing his assailant instantly. Not far away lies the corpse of William Whitley, riddled with musket balls.

Beyond the protecting curtain of gunsmoke, the battle with the Indians rages on as Shelby moves his infantry forward to support the dismounted riflemen. Oliver Hazard Perry, carrying one of Harrison's dispatches to the left wing, performs a remarkable feat of horsemanship as his black steed plunges to its breast in the swamp. The Commodore presses his hands to the saddle, springs over the horse's head to dry land; the horse, freed of its burden, heaves itself out of the swamp with a mighty snort; as it bounds forward, Perry clutches its mane and vaults back into the saddle without checking its speed or touching bridle or stirrup.

Word spreads that Richard Johnson is dead. An old friend, Major W.T. Barry, riding up from the rear echelon to examine the corpse, meets a group of soldiers bearing the Colonel back in a blanket.

"I will not die, Barry," Johnson assures him. "I am mightily cut to pieces, but I think my vitals have escaped." One day he will be vice-president.

Behind him, the cacophony of battle continues to din into his ears as Shelby's force presses forward through the trees. The volume rises in intensity: the advancing Kentuckians shouting their vengeful battle cry; the Indians shrieking and whooping; wounded men groaning and screaming; horses neighing and whinnying; muskets and rifles shattering ear drums; bugles sounding; cannon firing.

The smoke of battle lies thickly over forest and swamp, making ghosts of the dim, painted figures who appear for an instant from the cover of a tree to fire a weapon or hurl a tomahawk, then vanish into the gloom. They are not real, these Indians, for their faces can be seen only in death. Which are the leaders, which the followers? One man, the Kentuckians know, is in charge: they can hear Tecumseh's terrible battle cry piercing the ragged wall of sound. For five years they have heard its echo, ever since the Shawnee first made his presence felt in the Northwest. Yet that presence has always been spectral; no Kentuckian on the field this day—no white American, in fact, save Harrison—has ever seen the Shawnee chief or heard his voice until this moment. He is a figure of legend, his origins clouded in myth, his persona a reflection of other men's perception. Johnson's riders, firing blindly into the curtain of trees, hating their adversary and at the same time admiring him, are tantalized by his invisibility.

Suddenly comes a subtle change in the sound. Private Charles Wickliffe, who has been timing the battle, notices it: something is missing. Wickliffe, groping for an answer, comes to realize that he can no longer discern that one clear cry, which seemed to surmount the dissonance. The voice of Tecumseh, urging on his followers, has been stilled. The Shawnee has fallen.

The absence of that clarion sound is as clear as a bugle call. Suddenly the battle is over as the Indians withdraw through the underbrush, leaving the field to the Kentuckians. As the firing trails off, Wickliffe takes out his watch. Exactly fifty-five minutes have elapsed since Harrison ordered the first charge.

As the late afternoon shadows gather, a pall rises over the bodies of the slain. There are redcoats here, their tunics crimsoned by a darker stain, and Kentuckians in grotesque attitudes that can only be described as inhuman, and Indians, staring blankly at the sky, including several minor chieftains, one dispatched by Johnson, another by Whitley.

But one corpse is missing. Elusive in life, Tecumseh remains invisible in death. No white man has ever been allowed to draw his likeness. No white man will ever display or mutilate his body. No headstone, marker, or monument will identify his resting place. His followers have spirited him away to a spot where no stranger, be he British or American, will ever find him—his earthly clay, like his own forlorn hope, buried forever in a secret grave.

———

John Richardson, fleeing from James Johnson's riders, charges through the woods with his comrades, loses his way, finds himself unexpectedly on the road now clogged with wagons, discarded stores and clothing, women and children. Five hundred yards to his right he sees the main body of his regiment, disarmed and surrounded by the enemy. Instinctively, he and the others turn left, only to run into a body of American cavalry, the men dismounted, walking their horses.

Their leader, a stout elderly officer dressed like his men in a Kentucky hunting jacket, sees them, gallops forward brandishing his sword and shouting in a commanding voice:

"Surrender, surrender! It's no use resisting. All your people are taken and you'd better surrender."

This is Shelby. Richardson, whose attitude towards all Americans is snobbishly British Canadian, thinks him a vulgar man who looks more like one of the army's drovers than the governor of a state— certainly not a bit like the chief magistrate of one of His Majesty's provinces.

He swiftly buries his musket in the deep mud to deny it to the enemy and surrenders. As the troops pass by, one tall Kentuckian glances over at the diminutive teenager and says: "Well, I guess now, you tarnation little Britisher, who'd calculate to see such a bit of a chap as you here?" Richardson never forgets that remark, which illustrates the language gulf between the two English-speaking peoples who share the continent.

Shadrach Byfield at this moment, having fled into the woods at the same time as Richardson, has encountered a party of British Indians who tell him Tecumseh is dead. They want to know whether the enemy has also taken Moraviantown and ask Byfield whether he can hear American or British accents up ahead. At the forest's edge, Byfield hears a distinctive American voice cry, "Come on, boys!" The party retreats at once. Terrified that the Indians will kill him, he gives away what tobacco he has in his haversack and prepares to spend the night in the woods.

Major Eleazer Wood is in full pursuit of Procter, but the General eludes him, stopping only briefly at Moraviantown and pressing on to Ancaster, so fatigued he cannot that evening write a coherent account of the action. Wood has to be content with capturing his carriage containing his sword, hat, trunk, and all his personal papers, including a packet of letters from his wife, written in an exquisite hand.

Moraviantown's single street is clogged with wagons, horses, and half-famished Kentuckians. The missionary's wife, Mrs. Schnall, works all night baking bread for the troops, some of whom pounce on the dough and eat it before it goes into the oven. Others upset all the beehives, scrambling for honey, and ravage the garden for vegetables, which they devour raw.

Richardson and the other prisoners fare better. Squatting around a campfire in the forest, they are fed pieces of meat toasted on skewers by Harrison's aides, who tell the British that they deplore the death of the much-admired Tecumseh.

Now begins the long controversy over the circumstances of the Shawnee's end. Who killed Tecumseh? Some give credit to Whitley, whose body was found near that of an Indian chief; others, including Governor Shelby, believe that a private from Lincoln County, David King, shot him. Another group insists that the Indian killed by Richard Johnson was the Shawnee; that will form the most colourful feature of Johnson's subsequent campaign for the vice-presidency.

But nobody knows or will ever know how Tecumseh fell. Only two men on the American side know what he looks like—Harrison, his old adversary, and the mixed-blood Anthony Shane, the interpreter, who knew him as a boy. Neither is able to say with certainty that any of the bodies on the field resembles the Indian leader.

The morning after the battle, David Sherman, the boy who encountered Tecumseh in the swamp, finds one of his rifled flintlock pistols on the field. That same day, Chris Arnold comes upon a group of Kentuckians flaying the body of an Indian to make souvenir razor strops from the skin.

"That's not Tecumseh," Arnold tells them.

"I guess when we get back to Kentucky they will not know his skin from Tecumseh's," comes the reply.

In death, as in life, the Shawnee inspires myth. There are those who believe he was not killed at all, merely wounded, that he will return to lead his people to victory. It is a wistful hope. "Skeletons" of Tecumseh will turn up in the future. "Authentic" graves will be identified, then rejected. But the facts of his death and his burial are as elusive as those of his birth, almost half a century before.

As the Americans bury their dead and those of their enemy in two parallel trenches, Shadrach Byfield moves through the wilderness with the Indians, still fearful that he will be killed by his new companions. Toward sunset on his second night in the wild, to Byfield's relief and delight the party stumbles upon one of his comrades, also drifting about in the woods. That night they sleep out in the driving rain, existing on a little flour and a few potatoes. The following night they find an Indian village where they are treated kindly and fed pork and corn. At last, after a further twenty-four hours of wandering, their shoes now in shreds, they run into a group of fifty escapees whom Lieutenant Richard Bullock has gathered together. With Bullock in charge, the remnants of the 41st make their way to safety.

John Richardson, meanwhile, is marched back to the Detroit River with six hundred prisoners. Fortunately for him, his grandfather, John Askin of Amherstburg, has a son-in-law, Elijah Brush, who is an American militia colonel at Detroit. Askin writes to his daughter's husband to look after his grandson. As a result, Richardson, instead of being sent up the Maumee with the others, is taken to Put-in Bay by gunboat, where he runs into his own father, Dr. Robert Richardson, an army surgeon captured by Perry and assigned to attend the wounded Captain Barclay.

The double victories on Lake Erie and the Thames tip the scales of war. For all practical purposes the conflict on the Detroit frontier is ended. At Twenty Mile Creek on the Niagara peninsula, Major-General Vincent, expecting Harrison to follow up his victory, falls into a panic, destroys stocks of arms and supplies, trundles his invalid army back to the protection of Burlington Heights. Of eleven hundred men, eight hundred are on sick call, too ill to haul the wagons up the hills or through the rivers of mud that pass for roads.

De Rottenburg is prepared to let all of Upper Canada west of Kingston fall to the Americans, but the Americans cannot maintain their momentum. Harrison's own supply lines are stretched taut; the Thames Valley has been scorched of fodder, grain, and meat; his six-month volunteers are clamouring to go home. Harrison is a captive of America's hand-to-mouth recruiting methods. He cannot pursue the remnants of Procter's army, as military common sense dictates. Instead, he moves back down the Thames, garrisons Fort Amherstburg, and leaves Brigadier-General Duncan McArthur in charge of Detroit.

The British still hold a key outpost in the Far West—the captured island of Michilimackinac, guarding the route to the fur country. It is essential that the Americans seize it; with Perry's superior fleet that should not be difficult. But the Canadian winter frustrates this plan. For that adventure the Americans must wait until spring. Instead, Harrison takes his regulars and moves east to Fort George, from which springboard he hopes to attack Burlington Heights.

Once again victory bonfires light up the sky; songs written for the occasion are chorused in the theatres; Harrison is toasted at every table; Congress strikes the mandatory gold medal. One day, William Henry Harrison will be president. An extraordinary number of those who fought with him will also rise to high office. One will achieve the vice-presidency, three will rise to become governors of Kentucky, three more to lieutenant-governor. Four will go to the Senate, at least a score to the House.

For Henry Procter there will be no accolades. A court martial the following year finds him guilty of negligence, of bungling the retreat, of errors in tactics and judgement. He is publicly reprimanded and suspended from rank and pay for six months.

Had Procter retreated promptly and without encumbrance, he might have joined Vincent's Centre Division and saved his army. But it is the army he blames for all his misfortunes, not himself. In his report of the battle and his subsequent testimony before the court, he throws all responsibility for defeat on the shoulders of the men and officers serving under him. The division's laurels, he says, are tarnished "and its conduct calls loudly for reproach and censure." But in the end it is Procter's reputation that is tarnished and not that of his men. To the Americans he remains a monster, to the Canadians a coward. He is neither—merely a victim of circumstances, a brave officer but weak, capable enough except in moments of stress, a man of modest pretensions, unable to make the quantum leap that distinguishes the outstanding leader from the run-of-the-mill: the quality of being able in moments of adversity to exceed one's own capabilities. The prisoner of events beyond his control, Procter dallied and equivocated until he was crushed. His career is ended.

He leaves the valley of the Thames in a shambles. Moraviantown is a smoking ruin, destroyed on Harrison's orders to prevent its being used as a British base. Bridges are broken, grist mills burned, grain destroyed, sawmills shattered. Indians and soldiers of both armies have plundered homes, slaughtered cattle, stolen private property.

Tecumseh's confederacy is no more. In Detroit, thirty-seven chiefs representing six tribes sign an armistice with Harrison, leaving their wives and children as hostages for their good intentions. The Americans have not the resources to feed them, and so women and children are seen grubbing in the streets for bones and rinds of pork thrown away by the soldiers. Putrefied meat, discarded in the river, is retrieved and devoured. Feet, heads, and entrails of cattle—the offal of the slaughterhouses—are used to fill out the meagre rations. On the Canadian side, two thousand Indian women and children swarm into Burlington Heights pleading for food.

Kentucky has been battling the Indians since the days of Daniel Boone. Now the long struggle for possession of the Northwest is over; that is the real significance of Harrison's victory. The proud tribes have been humbled; the Hero of Tippecanoe has wiped away the stain of Hull's defeat; and (though nobody says it) the Indian lands are ripe for the taking.

The personal struggle between Harrison and Tecumseh, which began at Vincennes, Indiana Territory, in 1810, has all the elements of classical tragedy. And, as in classical tragedy, it is the fallen hero and not the victor to whom history will give its accolade. It is Harrison's fate to be remembered as a one-month president, forever to be confused with a longer-lived President Harrison—his grandson, Benjamin. But in death as in life, there is only one Tecumseh. His last resting place, like so much of his career, is a mystery; but his memory will be for ever green.

SIX

The Assault on Montreal

October 4–November 12, 1813

With Michigan Territory and Detroit back in American hands and the campaign on the Niagara peninsula at a standstill, the United States reverts to its original strategy—to thrust directly at the Canadian heartland, attacking either Montreal or Kingston and cutting the lifeline between the Canadas. Two armies—one at Fort George, a second at Sackets Harbor—will combine for the main attack. A third, at Plattsburgh on Lake Champlain, will act in support, either joining in the massive thrust down the St. Lawrence or creating a diversion if the attack should focus on Kingston.

SACKETS HARBOR, NEW YORK STATE, OCTOBER 4, 1813

Major-General James Wilkinson, Dearborn's replacement as the senior commander of the American forces, returns to his headquarters after a month at Fort George, shivering from fever, so ill that he must be helped ashore. He has been ailing for weeks; as a result, the projected attack on Montreal—or will it be Kingston?—has moved by fits and starts. The combined forces from Sackets Harbor and Fort George should have been at the rendezvous point—Grenadier Island, near the mouth of the St. Lawrence—long before this. Winter is approaching, but they have only just begun to move.

At fifty-six, Wilkinson is an odd choice for commander-in-chief. He is almost universally despised, for his entire career has been a catalogue of blunders, intrigues, investigations, plots, schemes, and deceptions. Outwardly he is blandly accommodating, with a polished, easy manner. Behind those surface pretensions lurks a host of less admirable qualities: sensuality, unreliability, greed for money, boastfulness, dishonesty. No other general officer has pursued such an erratic career. Long before, as brigadier-general, he was forced to resign because of his involvement in a cabal against George Washington. As clothier-general he resigned again because of irregularities in his accounts. As a key figure in the "Spanish Conspiracy," a plan to split off the southwest into a Spanish sphere of influence, he resigned once more. His colleagues are unaware that he has taken an oath of allegiance to the Spanish crown and draws a pension from that government of four thousand dollars a year.

Yet he is nothing if not resilient. After the Spanish scandal he rejoined the army, rose again to brigadier-general, plotted to discredit his commander, Anthony Wayne, then narrowly escaped indictment for his association with Aaron Burr. He faced a court martial for conspiracy, treason, disobedience, neglect of duty, and misuse of

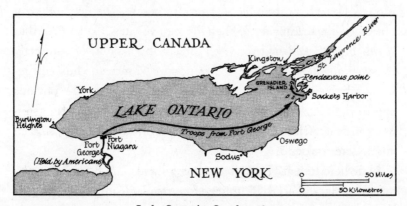

Lake Ontario, October, 1813

public money but, to President Madison's dismay, the court cleared him. Now here he is, the President's deputy, in charge of the most important military post in the United States—a living example of the poverty of military leadership in his country's army.

He has been too long away from his headquarters; indeed, it is questionable whether he should have left, for the Secretary of War, John Armstrong, has quit Washington to be at the centre of the war and has all but taken over in his absence. Sick or not, the shivering general must look in on Armstrong, who shares quarters with Wilkinson's second-in-command, the ineffectual Morgan Lewis, who is Armstrong's brother-in-law.

Armstrong would like to have Wilkinson's job. He fancies himself a shrewd military strategist and is not without experience, having served on the staff in the Revolution and later as a brigade commander in the militia. He likes to be called General and peppers his letters to his army commanders with military axioms and advice. Madison has no confidence in him, and James Monroe, the Secretary of State, is an avowed enemy; but Armstrong, through a politically opportune marriage, has powerful friends in New York who helped him secure his present post.

The Secretary's instincts are often sound but his execution indecisive. It has always been obvious to him that the key to victory in Canada lies in the capture of Kingston, but in his orders to Wilkinson he has covered himself carefully to escape blame for future defeat. Kingston, he declares, "represents the *first* and *great* object of the campaign." Then he equivocates, explaining that it can be attacked in two ways: directly by assault, or indirectly by sweeping down the St. Lawrence to Montreal, thus cutting its supply line. The Secretary is an expert at making the obvious appear significant. Whether Wilkinson chooses to attack Kingston or Montreal, Armstrong can always point out that he suggested an alternative course.

Now here he is at Sackets Harbor, a handsome figure, about to turn fifty-six, with a proud, unlined face, regular features, and hooded eyes, aristocratic by nature, pugnacious by temperament—"eminently pugnacious," in Martin Van Buren's phrase—ambitious, caustic, but like Wilkinson outwardly convivial.

They make a strange pair, the general and the politician who hold the fate of Canada in their hands. Friends once, then enemies, they are friends again, or seem to be. While serving together in 1792 they had such a falling out that Armstrong, charged by Wilkinson with fraud, left the army in disgust. That has been patched up; Wilkinson is the Secretary's choice as commander. But it is an uneasy alliance. To the ailing general, Armstrong's presence is unsettling. He feels his command undermined, his prestige lessened, for the Secretary has been bustling about, making free with advice that, not surprisingly, is accepted as command.

Wilkinson is so sick that he has almost ceased to care. Weakened by a series of paroxysms, he tells Armstrong he is incapable of command and wants to retire. The Secretary insists he is indispensable, assures him that he will soon recover, and remarks to one of his staff, "I would feed the old man with pap sooner than leave him behind." It is indicative of their relationship that the "old man" is scarcely a year older than Armstrong.

Indecision marks their deliberations. Neither can make up his mind whether the main attack should be on Kingston or on Montreal. Whichever objective one favours, the other opposes. Almost at their first encounter, Wilkinson vigorously espouses Montreal. Armstrong differs but covers himself with a cloud of ambiguities. A fortnight later both men trade positions, Armstrong arguing that circumstances have changed. But when Wilkinson asks for a direct order in writing, the Secretary declines, referring him to his earlier letter about "direct" and "indirect" attacks.

It is becoming obvious that neither man expects an attack on Kingston or Montreal to succeed; in this documentary confrontation they are carefully protecting themselves from future charges of failure.

Armstrong, the would-be commander, is the author of a pompous little book entitled *Hints to Young Generals*. "The art of war," he has written, "rests on two [principles]—concentration of force and celerity of movement." It cannot be said that the army is moving with celerity at Sackets Harbor. Nineteen days are spent loading the boats with provisions, a task the contractor's agent believes could be done in five. The boats are encumbered with hospital stores instead of guns and powder, and these stores are scattered throughout the flotilla without any plan.

This is especially significant because the squadron, when it does move, will resemble a floating hospital—a term specifically used by William Ross, the camp surgeon. In September, some seven hundred men and officers lie ill; that number will double within two months.

The chief causes are bad food—which, in Dr. Ross's words, has "destroyed more soldiers than have fallen by the sword of the enemy"—and wretched sanitation. The meat is rotten, the whiskey adulterated, the flour so bad that "it would kill the best horse in Sacket's Harbor." The greatest offender is the bread, which when examined is found to contain bits of soap, lime, and, worst of all, human excrement. The bakers take their water from a stagnant corner of the lake, no more than three feet from the shore. Into the lake pours all the effluent from a cluster of latrines a few yards away. Naked men knead the dough. Nearby is a cemetery housing two hundred corpses, together with the contents of a box of amputated limbs marked "British arms and legs," buried in no more than a foot of sandy soil. But although the troops are weak from dysentery and the leading officers have been warned of the problem, nothing is done. His subordinates are convinced that Wilkinson is too ill to be told and too weak (from the same condition) to act upon the information if he were.

The word from Major-General Wade Hampton, meanwhile, is not such as to inspire confidence. Hampton's army of four thousand regulars and fifteen hundred militia at Lake Champlain has been ordered to support Wilkinson's attack. The difficulty is that Hampton hates Wilkinson so much that he will not take orders from him. Indeed, he has secured the ambiguous agreement of the Secretary of War that his will be a separate command. Unfortunately,

Armstrong has also assured Wilkinson that Hampton really will act under his orders. The result is that although Wilkinson has sent directions to Hampton, two hundred miles away, Hampton has not deigned to answer. In the end all communication between the two generals has to be passed through Armstrong.

Hampton's army has reached Châteauguay Four Corners, just south of the border, after a dismal attempt to follow Armstrong's instructions to create a diversion near the Canadian village of Odelltown. The attack failed on September 21 because of unseasonably hot weather. Horses and men were so desperate with thirst that the entire force had to withdraw and march seventy miles to its present situation.

Now Hampton too seems to be covering himself against failure. He reports that his troops are raw and that illness is increasing daily. "All I can say is it shall have all the capacity I can give it," he writes, lamely.

Armstrong tells him to hold fast at Four Corners "to keep up the enemy's doubts, with regard to the real point of your attack"—a necessary order, since Armstrong himself does not know where the real point of attack will be. Finally, on October 16 he instructs Hampton to move down the Châteauguay River and cross the border, either as a feint to support the thrust against Kingston or to await the main body of Wilkinson's army on its movement down the St. Lawrence to Montreal.

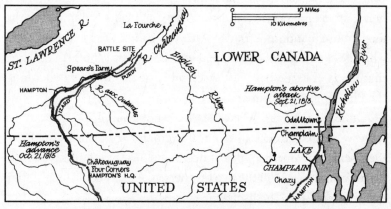

Wade Hampton's Movements, September–October, 1813

At this point, more than half of Wilkinson's combined forces have yet to reach the rendezvous point at Grenadier Island. A winter storm has been raging for a week, lashing the waters of the lake with rain, snow, and hail. Those few boats that do set off are destroyed or forced back to harbour. Do Wilkinson and Armstrong really believe they can seize Canada before winter?

By October 19, when the weather abates and the main body sets off, the ground is thick with snow. And still no one can be sure whether Kingston or Montreal will be the main point of the attack.

CHÂTEAUGUAY FOUR CORNERS,
NEW YORK STATE, OCTOBER 21, 1813

For the past eighteen days, two Canadian farmers, Jacob Manning and his brother, David, have been held captive by the Americans in a log stable on Benjamin Roberts's farm, where Wade Hampton's army is camped. Suddenly word comes that the Major-General himself wishes to speak to them.

The Mannings are spies—part of a small group recruited by the British from the settlers of Hemmingford and Hinchinbrook townships just north of a border that was, until war broke out, little more than an imaginary line. This is smugglers' country. The settlers know one another intimately and, no matter what their allegiance, still continue an illicit trade—the Americans sneaking barrels of potash into Canada for sale in Montreal, the Canadians slipping over the line, pulling hand sleds loaded with ten-gallon kegs of hard-to-get whiskey. So much beef is shipped into Canada for the British Army that herds of cattle have left discernible tracks in the woods along the Hinchinbrook frontier.

For some time the Mannings have been supplying the British with reports of American troop movements. But on the night of October 2, an American patrol descended on their farmhouse near Franklin and surprised the two brothers asleep. Since that night they have been held under suspicion.

They are brought under guard to Hampton's headquarters at

Smith's Tavern, where the Major-General himself receives them. A large and imposing Southerner in his sixtieth year, Hampton is known for his impatience, his hauteur, and his hasty temper. Subordinates and superiors find him difficult to get along with, perhaps because he is a self-made man with all the stubbornness, pride, and ego that this connotes. An uneducated farm boy—orphaned early in life by a Cherokee raid that wiped out most of his family, including his parents—he is well on his way to becoming the wealthiest planter in the United States. He has a hunger for land—greed might be a better word—and has made a fortune in speculation, much of it bordering on the shady. In South Carolina he is the proprietor of vast plantations that support thousands of slaves, some of whom wait upon him here at Four Corners, to the raised eyebrows of the northern settlers. He is both a politician and a soldier, with a good Revolutionary record and a background that includes a stint in Congress and several other public offices. Now, entering his seventh decade, he seems to have lost his drive—the panache that made him one of General Thomas Sumter's most daring officers. He is not popular. Morgan Lewis has flatly refused to serve under him; several other officers at Fort Niagara have sworn they would resign their commissions if Hampton were placed in charge of that frontier.

His orders are to cross the border and march down the Châteauguay to the St. Lawrence. If Wilkinson attacks Kingston, this move will confuse the British. Otherwise, his army will join Wilkinson's on its sweep to Montreal.

Hampton is as much in the dark regarding British and Canadian strength and intentions as the British are of American strength and strategy. That is why he has called for the Manning brothers. He wants David Manning to take his best black charger, gallop to Montreal, and bring him back an estimate of the British defence force there. There will be no danger, the General assures Manning; no one will suspect him, and if he does his job well there will be a handsome reward.

Manning refuses.

"Are you not an American?" Hampton demands.

"Yes," says Manning. "I was born on the American side and I have many relations, but I am true to the British flag."

He is a Loyalist—a Tory who refused to fight against the British during the Revolution and was forced to move north of the border.

Hampton's famous temper flares. He roughly tells the Manning brothers that they are in his power and will be sent to the military prison at Greenbush if they do not toe the line.

The two backwoodsmen are not cowed. They reply, cheekily, that anything will be better than confinement in a filthy stable; perhaps they will be treated like human beings at Greenbush.

Hampton tries a different tack, asks if there is a fort at Montreal. When they tell him that none exists, he refuses to believe it. He takes the two men to the tavern window overlooking the Roberts farm and proudly points out the size of his army.

Spread out before them, the brothers see an imposing spectacle: thousands of men striking their tents, cavalry cantering about, the infantry drilling in platoons. Clearly, Hampton is about to move across the Canadian border.

The General proudly asks how far the Mannings think a force of that size can go. Again, Jacob Manning cannot resist a cheeky answer.

"If it has good luck it may get to Halifax," he says—for Halifax is the depot to which prisoners of war are sent.

Angered, Hampton orders his officer of the guard, a local militiaman named Hollenbeck, to take the brothers back to the stable and keep them there for three days to prevent word of his advance reaching the British.

But Hollenbeck is an old friend and neighbour.

"Do you want anything to eat?" he asks.

"No," says Jacob.

"Well, then, put for home," says Hollenbeck. Off go the brothers with news of Hampton's advance.

Theirs is not the only intelligence to reach the British. Hampton's forward troops under Brigadier-General George Izard are already across the border. At four o'clock they reach Spears's farm at the junction of the Châteauguay and Outarde rivers and rout a small

Canadian picket, which sounds the alarm. For weeks the border country has been in a state of tension, not knowing exactly where the American attack on Lower Canada will come. Now it is clear that Hampton's main force will advance along the cart track that borders the Châteauguay. His object is the St. Lawrence River and, surely, Montreal.

In the coming battle the defence of Canada will fall almost entirely to the French-Canadian militia. More than three hundred are already moving up the river road to a rendezvous point in the hardwood forest not far from the future settlement of Allan's Corners— the Sedentary Militia from Beauharnois in homespun blouses and blue toques, and two flank companies of the 5th Battalion of Select Embodied Militia in green coats with red facings. This is the notorious Devil's Own battalion recruited from the slums of Montreal and Quebec, and so called because of its reputation for thievery and disorder.

The following morning a more reliable force of Canadian Fencibles and Voltigeurs arrives. The latter unit consists not of habitants but of voyageurs, lumbermen, and city-bred youths. They have been drilled all winter like regulars by their leader, a thirty-five-year-old career soldier, Lieutenant-Colonel Charles-Michel d'Irumberry de Salaberry. They wear smart grey uniforms and fur hats and are used to fighting in their bare feet.

De Salaberry, who has been given charge of the Châteauguay frontier by his superior, the Swiss-born Major-General de Watteville, is that unique product of Lower Canada, the French-Canadian aristocrat. But he is no fop. De Rottenburg refers to him as "my dear Marquis of cannon powder." Short in stature, big-chested and muscular, he is a strict disciplinarian—brusque, impetuous, often harsh with his men. Dominique Ducharme, the victor at Beaver Dams, now back in Lower Canada, cannot forgive him for dispatching him to track down six deserters, whom he ordered shot. (Ducharme, had he known what would be their fate, would have let them escape.) De Salaberry's Voltigeurs, however, admire their leader because he is fair minded.

This is our major, [they sing]
The embodiment of the devil
Who gives us death.
There is no wolf or tiger
Who could be so rough;
Under the openness of the sky
There is not his equal.

In the de Salaberry vocabulary, one word takes precedence over all others: honour. He cannot forget his father's remark to Prevost's predecessor, Sir James Craig. The elder de Salaberry openly opposed Craig, who wanted to destroy the rights of French Canadians. When Craig threatened to remove his means of livelihood, Ignace de Salaberry retorted: "You can, Sir James, take away my bread and that of my family, but my honour—never!"

The Voltigeurs no doubt know the story of the scar their colonel carries on his brow. It goes back to his days in a mixed regiment in the West Indies, when a German duellist killed his best friend.

The duellist: "I come just now from dispatching a French Canadian into another world."

De Salaberry: "We are going to finish lunch and then you will have the pleasure of dispatching another."

But it is the German who is dispatched, de Salaberry merely scarred.

He has been a soldier since the age of fourteen; three younger brothers have already died in the service. His father's patron and his own was the Duke of Kent, father of a future queen. The Duke prevented him from making an unfortunate marriage; the bride he later chose is a seigneur's daughter.

For weeks, de Salaberry has been spying on Hampton's pickets at Châteauguay Four Corners. Now he is prepared to meet the full force not far from the confluence of the Châteauguay and the English River.

He has chosen his position with care. Half a dozen ravines cut their way through the sandy soil at right angles to the Châteauguay

River. These will be his lines of defence. The first three are only two hundred yards apart, the fourth half a mile to the rear. At least two more lie some distance downriver near La Fourche, where Major-General de Watteville's reserves and headquarters will be stationed.

By midday on October 22, de Salaberry has his axemen constructing breastworks of felled trees and tangled branches on the forward tip of each ravine. A mile or more in front of the leading ravine—a coulee forty feet deep on Robert Bryson's farm—they build a vast abatis extending in an arc from the river's gorge on the left to a swamp in the forest on their right.

The axemen are still hacking down trees and piling up slash when de Salaberry is reinforced in a dramatic fashion. In Kingston, on October 21, Sir George Prevost had decided to send a battalion of Select Embodied Militia—a mixed bag of French-Canadian and Scottish farmers—to Châteauguay. He called on their commander, Lieutenant-Colonel George Macdonell, to ask how soon the battalion could be under way.

"As soon as my men have done dinner," replied the Colonel, who is known through the county as Red George to distinguish him from a score of other Glengarry Macdonells.

Now Prevost has come post-haste to Châteauguay where, to his astonishment, he encounters Red George. The battalion has made the trip in just sixty hours without a man absent.

That same day, October 24, as Hampton's main body moves up along the road his engineers have hacked through the bush, a spy watches them go by and carefully counts the guns, the wagons, and the troops, immediately sending detailed reports to the British.

More than fourteen hundred of Hampton's militiamen, he writes, have refused to cross the border. The Americans are badly clothed, having so little winter gear that they have had to cast lots for great-coats. The Virginians are not used to the Canadian weather. One regiment of a thousand Southerners has lost half its force to "a kind of distemper." He has also heard a report that Major-General Wilkinson is bringing his army down the St. Lawrence by boat and plans to join Hampton in an assault on Montreal.

Now the British are aware of the full American strategy. Hampton has upwards of four thousand men assembled at Spears's farm. All that stands between him and the St. Lawrence are the sixteen hundred militiamen seven miles downriver. The brunt of the attack will be borne by de Salaberry's three hundred Canadian Voltigeurs and Fencibles manning the forward ravines. They wait behind the tangle of roots and branches, knowing that they are heavily outnumbered and outgunned. The spy has counted nine pieces of field artillery, a howitzer, and a mortar and suspects there is more moving toward the Canadian lines by an alternative route.

Who is this secret agent who seems to know everything that is going on at Spears's farm and Four Corners? He is, of course, David Manning, the Loyalist farmer, whom Wade Hampton believes to be safely behind bars at Greenbush. But Hampton has not reckoned on the uncertain loyalties of the border people. He does not know, will never know, that Hollenbeck, his sergeant of the guard, is not only David Manning's friend and neighbour but also an informant who is perfectly prepared to salute the Stars and Stripes in public while secretly supplying the British with all the information and gossip they require.

SPEARS'S FARM, CHÂTEAUGUAY RIVER, LOWER CANADA, OCTOBER 25, 1813

Major-General Wade Hampton considers the problem of de Salaberry's defence in depth and realizes he cannot storm those fortified ravines without serious loss. He decides instead on a surprise flanking movement that will take the French Canadians in the rear.

He summons Robert Purdy, Colonel of the veteran U.S. 4th Infantry, and gives him his orders. Purdy will take fifteen hundred elite troops, cross the Châteauguay River at a nearby ford, proceed down the right bank under cover of darkness, bypass de Salaberry's defences on the opposite shore, recross the river at dawn by way of a second ford, and attack the enemy from behind their lines. Once Hampton hears the rattle of Purdy's muskets, he will launch a frontal attack on the abatis, thus catching de Salaberry's slender force between the claws of a pincer.

It is an ingenious plan on paper, impossible to carry out in practice. Hampton is proposing that Purdy and his men, accompanied by guides, plunge through sixteen miles of thick wood and hemlock swamp in pitch darkness. That would be difficult in familiar territory; here it becomes a nightmare. The guides prove worthless, have, in fact, warned Hampton that they are not acquainted with the country. But Hampton is bewitched by a fixed idea; nothing will swerve him.

The result is disaster. Hampton accompanies the expedition to the first ford, then returns to camp. The night is cold; rain begins to fall; there is no moon. On the far side of the river Purdy's men flounder into a creek, stumble through a swamp, trip over fallen trees, stagger through thick piles of underbrush. Any semblance of order vanishes.

After two miles the guides themselves are lost. Purdy realizes he cannot continue in the dark. The men spend the night in the rain, shivering in their summer clothing, unable to light a fire for fear of betraying the plan.

At the camp, Hampton receives a rude shock. A letter arrives from the Quartermaster General relaying Armstrong's instructions to build huts for the army's winter quarters at Four Corners—south of the border. *Winter quarters at Four Corners!* Hampton has been expecting to winter at Montreal. The order can have one meaning only: Armstrong doubts that the expedition will reach its objective. The fight goes out of Hampton. Heartsick, he considers recalling Purdy's force but realizes that in the black night it cannot be found.

Dawn arrives, wan and damp, the dead leaves of autumn drooping wetly from the trees. In a tangle of brush and swamp, Purdy shakes his men awake. On the opposite bank, the American camp is all abustle, the forward elements already in motion along the wagon road that leads to the French-Canadian position.

In spite of his intelligence system, de Salaberry is not expecting an attack this morning. A party of his axemen, guarded by forty

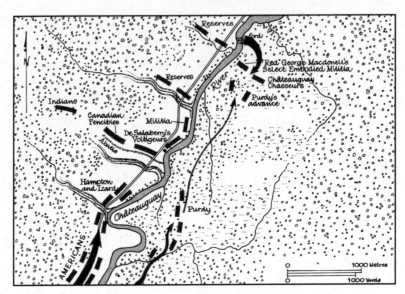

The Battle of Châteauguay: Phase 1

soldiers, is strengthening the abatis a mile in front of the forward
ravine when, at about 10 A.M., the first Americans come bounding
across the clearing, firing their muskets. De Salaberry, well to the
rear, hears the staccato sounds of gunfire, moves up quickly with
reinforcements. The workmen have scattered, and the Americans,
cheering lustily, push forward, only to be halted by musket fire.

De Salaberry—a commanding figure in his grey fur-trimmed
coat—moves forward on the abatis, climbs up on a large hemlock
that has been uprooted by the wind, and, screened from enemy view
by two large trees, watches the blue line of Americans moving down
the river road toward him. The firing has sputtered out; the expected
attack does not come.

Hampton is waiting to hear from Purdy across the river. The
Americans settle down to cook lunch. On the Canadian side of the
abatis a company of Beauharnois militia kneel in prayer and are told
by their captain that having done their duty to their God, he now
expects they will do their duty to their King.

Meanwhile, de Salaberry's scouts have discovered Purdy's presence on the east bank of the river—a few stragglers emerging briefly

from the dense woods along the far bank. Purdy is badly behind schedule; his force of fifteen hundred has got no farther than a point directly across from de Salaberry's forward position. Back goes word to Red George Macdonell, who has been given the task of guarding the ford in the rear. Macdonell sends two companies of his Select Embodied Militia across the river to reinforce a small picket of Châteauguay Chasseurs who, despite their formidable title, are untrained local farmers, co-opted into the Sedentary Militia of Lower Canada.

The Canadians move through the dense pine forest, peering through the labyrinth of naked trunks, seeking the advancing Americans. Purdy's advance guard of about one hundred men is splashing through a cedar swamp when the two forces meet. Both sides open fire. Macdonell's men stand fast, but the Chasseurs turn and flee. The American advance party also turns tail and plunges back through the woods where the main body, mistaking them for Canadians, opens fire, killing their own men.

Purdy, thinking the woods full of enemies, attempts to regroup and sends a messenger to Hampton, asking for reinforcements. The courier heads for Spears's farm, only to discover that Hampton is no longer there, having moved downriver. As a result, Hampton has no idea whether Purdy has achieved his objective. Nor can he tell what is happening on the far bank because of the thickness of the forest.

Finally, at two o'clock Hampton decides to act. He orders Brigadier-General George Izard to attack in line. Izard, another South Carolina aristocrat, is a professional soldier of considerable competence. His well-drilled brigade moves down the road toward the vast tangle of the abatis.

Behind their breastwork, de Salaberry's Voltigeurs watch as a tall American officer rides forward. After the battle is done, some will claim to remember his cry in French, which will become a legend along the Châteauguay:

"Brave Canadians, surrender yourselves; we wish you no harm!"

At which de Salaberry himself fires, the American drops from his horse, and the battle—such as it is—is joined.

De Salaberry shouts to his bugler to sound the call to open fire. The noise of sporadic musketry mingles with the cries of a small body of Caughnawaga Indians stationed in the woods to the right of the Canadian line. The Americans, firing by platoons, as on a parade ground, pour volley after volley into the woods, believing that the main Canadian force is concentrated there. The lead balls whistle harmlessly through the treetops.

Now Red George Macdonell sounds his own bugles as a signal that he is advancing. Other bugles take up the refrain; de Salaberry sends buglers into the woods to trumpet in all directions until the Americans believe they are heavily outnumbered. Izard hesitates—a fatal error, for he loses momentum. Two other ruses reinforce his misconception about the Canadian strength. Some of Macdonell's men appear at the edge of the woods wearing red coats, then disappear, reverse their jackets, which are lined with white flannel, and pop out again, appearing to be another corps. In addition, twenty Indians are sent to dash through the forest to the right of the Canadian line, appearing from time to time brandishing tomahawks. The ruse is similar to the one used by Brock against Hull the previous year: the Americans are led to believe that hundreds of savages are lurking in the depths of the woods.

"Defy, my damned ones!" cries de Salaberry. "Defy! If you do not dare, you are not men!"

The battle continues for the best part of an hour, the Americans firing rolling volleys, platoon by platoon, the half-trained Canadians returning the fire raggedly. There are few casualties on either side. Izard does not attempt to storm the abatis.

Now de Salaberry turns his attention to the action on the far side of the river. The two Canadian companies that drove off Purdy's forward troops have been advancing cautiously toward his position and are now tangling with his main force.

De Salaberry hurries to the river bank, climbs a tree, and begins to shout orders to Captain Charles Daly of the Embodied Militia, speaking in French so the Americans cannot understand him. At the same time he lines up his force of Voltigeurs, Indians, and

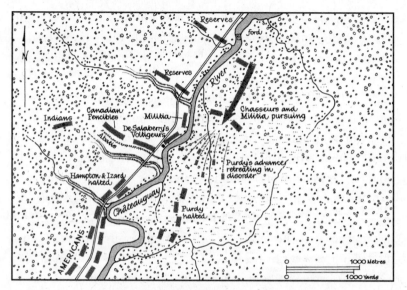

The Battle of Châteauguay: Phase 2

Beauharnois militia along his side of the river to fire on Purdy's men, should they emerge from the woods.

As the two forces face each other in the swampy forest, Daly orders his men to kneel before they fire, a manoeuvre that saves their lives. Purdy's overwhelming body of crack troops responds with a shattering volley, but most of it passes harmlessly over the Canadians' heads.

Now Purdy's force swoops forward on the river flank of the Canadians, determined to take them from the rear. The situation is critical, but as the Americans burst out of the woods and onto the river bank, de Salaberry, watching through his glass, gives the order to fire. The bushes on the far side erupt in a sheet of flame. The Americans, badly mangled, retreat into the forest; exhausted by fourteen hours of struggle, they can fight no more.

A lull comes in the skirmishing. Hampton, sitting his horse on the right of his troops, is in a quandary. A courier has just swum the river with news of Purdy's predicament. The Major-General is rattled, angry at Purdy for not reporting his position sooner, unaware that the original message has gone astray.

He considers his options. Izard has not attempted to storm the abatis; to do so, Hampton is convinced, would cause heavy casualties. He believes there are five to six thousand men opposing him. In fact, there is only a fraction of that number. De Salaberry has perhaps three hundred men in his advanced position. Macdonell has about two hundred in reserve. The remainder (apart from the two companies across the river) are several miles back at La Fourche, where the English River joins the Châteauguay. These do not number more than six hundred, and none have been committed to battle. De Salaberry, either by accident or by design, has failed to inform Major-General de Watteville of the American advance—a delinquency that nettles his senior and might easily provoke a court martial in the event of failure.

De Salaberry is a bold officer. His defensive position is strong. But it is Hampton's failure of nerve more than de Salaberry's brilliance of execution that decides the outcome of the so-called Battle of Châteauguay. In reality, it is no more than a skirmish, with troops on both sides peppering away at each other at extreme range and to little effect. De Salaberry, on his side of the river, has lost three men killed, eight wounded.

Hampton's heart is not in it. Purdy is bogged down, the afternoon is dragging on, rain is in the offing, twilight but a few hours away. A host of emotions boils up inside the hesitant commander: jealousy of Wilkinson, who will gain all the glory if Hampton, by a victory, helps him to seize Montreal; anger at Armstrong, who he rightly believes is resigned to defeat; and, most telling, a lack of confidence in himself. He does not have the will to win. Much of his force has yet to be engaged in battle. His artillery has not been used. Izard's brigade has fallen silent. Suddenly, the Major-General sends an order to Purdy to break off the engagement on the right bank and tells his bugler to sound the withdrawal.

De Salaberry's men watch in astonishment as the brigade retires in perfect order. Oddly, they make no attempt to harass it, waiting instead for a rally that never comes. Their colonel, expecting a renewed attack at any moment, has sent back word to all the houses along the river to prepare for a retreat and to burn all buildings. It is not necessary.

Of this Colonel Purdy, hidden in the forest, is unaware. As the sun sets he starts to move his wounded across the river on rafts and sends a message to his commander asking that a regiment be detached to cover his own landing. He is shocked and angered to discover that Hampton has already retreated three miles, deserting him without support.

The following morning the once.elite detachment straggles into Hampton's camp, many without hats, knapsacks, or weapons, their clothing torn, half starved, sick with fatigue, their morale shattered. Purdy is thoroughly disgusted. Several of his officers have behaved badly in the skirmish, but when Purdy tries to arrest them for desertion or cowardice, Hampton countermands the order. Purdy reports to the General that someone in the commissary is selling the troops' rations, but Hampton brushes away the complaint. The sick, in Purdy's view, are being so badly neglected that many have died from want of medical care. In common with several other officers, Purdy is convinced that Hampton is drinking so heavily that he is no longer able to command.

De Salaberry, meanwhile, feels snubbed by the British high command. Sir George Prevost, who arrived on the field with de Watteville shortly after the victory, is his usual cautious self. The brunt of the struggle has been borne by a handful of French-Canadian militia. One thousand fresh troops, held in reserve, are available to harass the enemy. De Salaberry is eager to do just that, but neither senior commander will allow it. Both are remarkably restrained in their congratulations, perhaps because of de Salaberry's delinquency in not informing them of the American attack. And de Salaberry himself is embittered because, he believes, he has not been given sole credit for repulsing the invaders. "It grieves me to the heart," he declares to the Adjutant-General, "to see that I must share the merit of the action." For Prevost and de Watteville insist on a portion of the glory.

Hampton meanwhile orders his entire force back across the border to Four Corners "for the preservation of the army"—a statement that would astonish the British, who are convinced that the Americans are planning a second attack. On October 28, Indian scouts confirm Hampton's decision.

It has been, as de Salaberry asserts in a letter to his father, "a most extraordinary affair." In this battle in which some 460 troops forced the retirement of four thousand, the victors have lost only five killed and sixteen wounded with four men missing. (The American casualties number about fifty.) It has been a small battle but for Canada profoundly significant. A handful of civilian soldiers, almost all French Canadian, has, with scarcely any help, managed to turn back the gravest invasion threat of the war. Had Hampton managed to reach the St. Lawrence to join with Wilkinson's advancing army, who would give odds on the survival of Montreal? And with Montreal gone and Upper Canada cut off, the British presence in North America would be reduced to a narrow defensive strip in the lower province. On a military sand table, the battle of Châteauguay seems no more than a silly skirmish. Yet without this victory, what price a Canadian nation, stretching from sea to sea?

GRENADIER ISLAND, THOUSAND ISLANDS,
NEW YORK STATE, OCTOBER 28, 1813

"All our hopes," James Wilkinson writes to the Secretary of War, "have been very nearly blasted." Two days have passed since Hampton's defeat at Châteauguay (a calamity unknown to Wilkinson) and the great flotilla designed to conquer Montreal—or will it be Kingston first?—is still stuck at its rendezvous point. The troops are drenched from the incessant rains, boats are smashed, stores scattered, hundreds sick, scores drunk.

Wilkinson puts the best possible face on these disasters, relying on the Deity to solve his problems:

"Thanks to the same Providence which placed us in jeopardy, we are surmounting our difficulties and, God willing, I shall pass Prescott on the night of the 1st or 2nd proximo, if some unforeseen obstacle does not present to forbid me."

Unforeseen obstacles have already presented themselves in quantity. On the journey from Sackets Harbor to Grenadier Island—a mere eighteen miles—the flotilla was scattered by gales so furious that great trees were uprooted on the shores. Some boats have not yet arrived.

A third of all the rations have been lost. It is virtually impossible to disentangle the rest from the other equipment. Shivering in the driving rain, the men have torn the oilcloths off the ration boxes for protection, so that the bread becomes soggy and inedible. Hospital stores have been pilfered—the hogsheads of brandy and port wine, which the doctors believe essential for good health, tapped and consumed. The guard is drunk; the officer in charge finds he cannot keep his men sober. The boats are so badly overloaded that they have become difficult to row or steer. Sickness increases daily. One hundred and ninety-six men are so ill that Wilkinson—himself prostrate with dysentery—orders them returned to Sackets Harbor. In spite of the army's shortage of rations, the American islanders prefer to sell their produce to the British on the north shore. When Jarvis Hanks, a fourteen-year-old drummer boy with the 11th U.S. Infantry, tries to buy some potatoes from a local farmer for fifty cents a bushel, the man refuses, saying he can get a dollar a bushel in Kingston. That night, Hanks and his friends steal the entire crop.

Some of the officers are still half convinced that Wilkinson intends to attack Kingston. Chauncey, in fact, does not learn until October 30 that the Major-General has made up his mind to take the flotilla down the river, joining with Hampton to attack Montreal. The Commodore is, in his own words, "disappointed and mortified." He clearly does not believe that such a plan has much chance of success, for the season is far advanced.

Three brigades finally set out for the next rendezvous point, at French Creek on the American side of the river directly opposite Gananoque. Brigadier-General Jacob Brown manages to get down the river; bad weather forces the other two back. The bulk of the army arrives on November 3, followed by Wilkinson, now so ill that he has to be carried ashore.

Wilkinson Moves on Montreal, October 31–November 11, 1813

The disillusioned Chauncey, who feels that his navy has been relegated to the position of a mere transport service for the army, is supposed to be guarding the entrance to the St. Lawrence to protect Wilkinson's flotilla from pursuit by British gunboats. But while Chauncey's squadron lurks in the south channel, Sir James Yeo's daring second-in-command, Captain William Howe Mulcaster (the same officer who refused the Lake Erie command) nips down the north channel, evades the Americans, moves down to French Creek, skirmishes with Brown's brigade, then whips back to Kingston to report at last that Montreal is the enemy's objective.

The tangle with Mulcaster again delays Wilkinson. The full flotilla does not leave French Creek until November 5.

Providence has at last smiled on the ailing general; the valley of the St. Lawrence is bathed in an Indian summer glow as six thousand men in 350 boats, forming a procession five miles long, slide down the great river, flags flying, brass buttons gleaming, fifes and drums playing, boatmen chorusing. There is one drawback: Mulcaster is not far behind.

On November 6, the flotilla reaches Morristown. Wilkinson is four days later than his most pessimistic promise to Armstrong. Now he must halt, for he fears the British guns at Prescott, a dozen miles downstream. He decides to strip his boats of all armament, march his men along the river bank, hauling the supplies in wagons, and

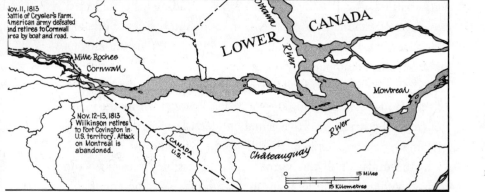

pass Prescott with the lightly manned boats under cover of darkness. That will cost him another day.

While the boats are being unloaded and the troops formed, he issues a proclamation to the British settlers along the river, urging the farmers to remain at home, promising that the persons and property of non-combatants will be protected.

These sentiments might as well be directed to the wind. This is Loyalist country, and the settlers are already priming their muskets to harass the American flotilla. The river shortly becomes a shooting gallery, with gunfire exploding from the bushes at every twist in the channel.

At noon, Colonel William King, Hampton's adjutant-general, arrives with the official news of the debacle at Châteauguay. Morgan Lewis takes King downriver to find Wilkinson, who is reconnoitring Prescott. The three men sit on a log as King describes Hampton's defeat, adding that "our best troops behaved in the most rascally manner."

"Damn such an army!" Wilkinson cries. "A man might as well be in hell as command it."

Still, Hampton's force remains intact—that is some consolation. The two armies number close to eleven thousand men—more than enough, surely, to seize Montreal.

At eight that night the river is shrouded in a heavy fog. Brown, the officer of the day, gives the order to move. Out into the water they go with muffled oars. The fog lifts, and Brown's leading gig is subjected to a fearful cannonade. Fifty twenty-four-pound balls are hurled at her from the Canadian shore but with no effect, for the guns are out of range and set too high to do any damage. Brown halts the flotilla, waiting for the moon to set. Its pale light, gleaming on the bayonets of the troops trudging along the shore, has helped identify the manoeuvre to the British, as have signal lights flashing in the homes of certain Ogdensburg citizens friendly to the British cause.

In the midst of all this uproar the irrepressible Winfield Scott arrives. Wilkinson had left him in charge of a skeleton command at Fort George until relieved by the New York State militia. Now, having left his own brigade with the Secretary of War's permission, he has ridden for thirty hours through the forests of northern New York in a sleet storm. Taken aboard Wilkinson's passage boat, he is stimulated by the bursting of shells and rockets and the hissing of cannonballs. Scott finds it sublime, though he distrusts and despises his general—an "unprincipled imbecile," in Scott's acid view. Years before he was court-martialed for referring publicly to Wilkinson as a liar, a scoundrel, and a traitor. But the ambitious Scott has learned that the road to promotion and power must not be strewn with invective and keeps his feelings to himself. The two men, who have no use for one another, conceal their mutual antipathy behind masks of cordiality.

Wilkinson leaves the passage boat and returns to his gig. Scott, knowing his reputation, is convinced he is drunk, but it is more likely that he is simply intoxicated from repeated draughts of opium, prescribed to ease his dysentery, an ailment that has now spread to most of the older officers, including his second-in-command, Morgan Lewis.

Wilkinson's condition is so serious that he is finally forced to go ashore and relieve himself at Daniel Thorpe's farmhouse on the river bank a mile below Ogdensburg. Benjamin Forsyth of the rifle company meets him and helps him up the bank with the aid of another officer. Wilkinson is muttering to himself, hurling imprecations at the British, threatening to blow the enemy's garrison to dust and lay waste the entire countryside. The two officers sit him down by the hearth, post a guard at the door to keep the spectacle from prying eyes, and try to decide what to do. By this time Wilkinson is singing bawdy songs and telling obscene stories, to the horror of Thorpe, who also believes him to be drunk. Finally, the General begins to nod and, to the relief of all, allows himself to be put to bed.

November 7 dawns clear and bright, a perfect day for sailing. But the British have reinforced every bend with cannon and sharpshooters. Wilkinson detaches an elite corps of twelve hundred soldiers to clear the bank, with Forsyth's riflemen detailed as a rearguard. By nightfall the flotilla has moved only eight miles.

Wilkinson is losing his nerve. In his weakened condition he imagines himself in the grip of forces he cannot control. Providence has been fickle, wrecking all his plans for a speedy descent down the river. He has little faith in his own army, especially the contingent from Sackets Harbor. He knows that he has been held up too long, giving Mulcaster every chance to catch him from the rear: the word is that two armed schooners and seven gunboats have already reached Prescott carrying a thousand—perhaps fifteen hundred—men. In his fevered imagination, the General magnifies the forces opposed to him. The farmers on the Canadian shore have been purposely stuffing their interrogators' heads with wild stories about the dangers ahead—the terrifying rapids, batteries of guns at every narrows, savage Indians prowling the forest, no fodder for the horses. It is said that the army will face five thousand British regulars and twenty thousand Canadian militia—a fantastic overstatement.

On November 8, Wilkinson, who can hardly rise from his bunk, calls a council of war. It agrees, hesitantly, to continue on to Montreal. Still concerned about the forces gathering on the Canadian side, the Major-General orders Jacob Brown to disembark his brigade and take command of the combined forces clearing the north shore.

Ahead lies the dreaded Long Sault, eight miles of white water in which no boats can manoeuvre under enemy fire. Brown's job is to clear the banks so that the flotilla can navigate these rapids without fear of attack. Harassed now from the rear, Wilkinson cannot get under way until Brown reaches the head of the rapids. Wilkinson moves eleven miles and, with Mulcaster nipping at his heels, stops again.

The following day, November 10, Mulcaster's gunboats move in to the attack. At the same time, Brown's force on the shore runs into heavy resistance. By the time Brown has cleared the bank, the pilots refuse to take the boats through the white water. The flotilla moves two miles past John Crysler's farm to Cook's Point, a mile or two above the Long Sault. The troops on shore build fires from the farmers' rail fences and shiver out the night in the rain and sleet. Jarvis Hanks, the drummer boy in the 11th, pulls a leather cap over his head and curls up so close to the fire that by morning both his cap and his shoes are charred. Brown, meanwhile, has gone aboard Wilkinson's passage boat to find out exactly who is in charge. But Wilkinson is too sick to see him. It has taken eight days for the fleet to move eighty miles. A log drifting down the river could make the same distance in two.

JOHN CRYSLER'S FARM, ST. LAWRENCE RIVER,
UPPER CANADA, NOVEMBER 11, 1813

Dawn breaks, bleak and soggy. John Loucks, one of three troopers in the Provincial Dragoons posted with three companies of Canadian Voltigeurs and a few Indians a mile ahead of the main British force, spots a movement through the trees ahead. A party of Americans is advancing from Cook's Point, where Wilkinson's flotilla is anchored. A musket explodes from the woods on his left, where a party of Indians is stationed. The Americans reply with a volley that kicks the sand in front of the troopers' horses. Off goes young Loucks at a gallop, heading for the headquarters of the British commander, Lieutenant-Colonel Joseph Wanton Morrison.

As the three dragoons dash through the ranks of the 49th Regiment, Lieutenant John Sewell is in the act of toasting a piece of breakfast pork on the point of his sword. He needs hot nourishment, for he has slept on the cold ground all night, his firelock between his legs to protect it from the icy rain, laced with sleet. Now it seems, there will be no time for breakfast, as his company commander shouts to him:

"Jack, drop cooking, the enemy is advancing."

The British troops are scrambling into position behind a stout rail fence, but the warning is several hours premature. All that Loucks has encountered is an American reconnaissance party. A regular officer chides him gently for his precipitate gallop: it is perfectly all right to fall back, he explains, but it is bad form to ride so fast in the face of the enemy.

At his headquarters in the Crysler farmhouse, hard by the King's Highway that runs along the river bank, Colonel Morrison assesses his position. He has been chasing Wilkinson in Mulcaster's gunboats for five days, ever since word reached Kingston that the main American attack would be on Montreal. Now he has caught up with him. Will the Americans stand and fight or will the chase continue? With a force of only eight hundred men to challenge Wilkinson's seven thousand, Morrison is not eager for a pitched battle. But if he must have one, it will be on ground of his choosing—a European-style battle here on an open plain where his regulars can manoeuvre, as on a parade ground, standing shoulder to shoulder in two parallel lines, each man occupying twenty-two inches of space, advancing with the bayonet, wheeling effortlessly when ordered, or moving into echelon—a staggered series of platoons, each supporting its neighbour.

This is the kind of warfare for which his two regiments have been trained: Brock's old regiment, the 49th, known as the Green Tigers both from the facings on their lapels and for the fierceness of their attack; and his own regiment, the 89th. The Green Tigers have had their fill of fighting, from Queenston to Stoney Creek, but the 89th are new to North America. Morrison, their commanding officer and senior commander on the field, has just turned fifty. Like his father before him, he has served half his life in the British Army, shifted from continent to continent wherever his country needs him, from Holland, where he was wounded, to the Caribbean, to Canada. He

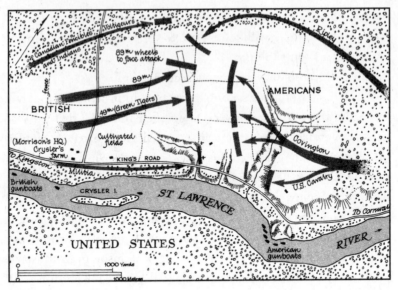

The Battle of Crysler's Farm: Phase 1

has never handled a battalion in battle; but he has been singled out as an attentive and zealous officer, and he has solid support in John Harvey, his second-in-command, and Charles Plenderleath of the 49th, both veterans of Stoney Creek.

He has chosen his position carefully, anchoring his thin line between the river on his right (where Mulcaster's gunboats will give support) and an impenetrable black ash swamp about half a mile to his left. His men are protected by a heavy fence of cedar logs, five feet high. Ahead for a half-mile stretches a muddy field covered with winter wheat, cut with gullies and bisected by a stream that trickles out of the swamp to become a deep ravine running into the St. Lawrence.

Behind the fence, the 49th occupies the right, close to the river and to the King's Highway that runs along the bank. The 89th is on the left, nearer the swamp; its soldiers wear scarlet coats, but the battle-seasoned 49th hide their distinctive tunics with grey overcoats.

Half a mile forward of this main body are lighter troops, including Canadian Fencibles. Another half-mile farther on are the skirmishers—Indians and Voltigeurs, the latter almost invisible in their grey homespun, concealed behind rocks, stumps, and fences.

Though heavily outnumbered, Morrison is counting on the ability of the British regulars to hold fast against the more individualistic Americans. Here the contrast between the two countries, so recently separated and estranged, becomes apparent. Wilkinson's men are experienced bush fighters, brought up with firearms, blooded in frontier Indian wars, used to taking individual action in skirmishes where every man must act on his own if he is to escape with a whole skin. But the British soldier is drilled to stand unflinching with his comrades in the face of exploding cannon, to hold his fire until ordered so that the maximum effect of the spraying muskets can be felt, to move in machine-like unison with hundreds of others, each man an automaton. The British regular follows orders implicitly; the American volunteer is less subservient, sometimes to the point of anarchy. This British emphasis on "order" extends, in Canada, to government. If the Canadians accept a form of benevolent dictatorship, or at least autocracy, it is because they have opted for a lifestyle different from that of their neighbours, a lifestyle based on British attitudes and institutions. Under the impetus of war, that attitude is hardening.

Morrison has one advantage of which he is unaware. The American high command is prostrate. In separate boats anchored at Cook's Point, the chief of the invading army and his second-in-command both lie deathly ill, unable to direct any battle. Lewis, confined to a closet-like cabin and dosing himself on blackberry jelly, is even less capable than his enfeebled superior. Wilkinson, unable to rise from his bunk, awaits word from Jacob Brown on shore that the rapids ahead have been cleared of British troops. At 10:30 a dragoon arrives with the expected reassurance. The Commander-in-Chief is in a quandary. Mulcaster is directly astern. What if the British gunboats should slip past him? He gives a tentative order to the flotilla to get under way and orders Brigadier-General Boyd, on land, to begin marching his men toward Cornwall. Even as he does so he is alerted to the presence of British redcoats on Crysler's field. At the same time Mulcaster begins to lob shot in his direction. Wilkinson decides to destroy the small British force before moving on.

This confusion and delay does not sit well with John Boyd on shore. Since early morning, he has been subjected to a variety of conflicting orders. At noon, a violent storm further reduces the morale of the troops who have now been under arms for nearly forty-eight hours. Boyd rides impatiently to the river bank where he finally receives a pencilled order to put his troops in motion in twenty minutes as soon as the guns can be put ashore. It is the last order he receives from Wilkinson.

Boyd will command the American forces in the battle to follow. A one-time soldier of fortune who for twenty years sold his services to a variety of Indian princes, including the Nizam of Hyderabad and the Peshwa of Poona, he exchanged his turban and lance in 1808 for a colonel's eagle in the U.S. 4th Infantry. Commissioned brigadier-general at the opening of the war, he does not enjoy the esteem of his peers. Brown cannot stand him. Scott considers him imbecilic. Lewis, in a vicious indictment, describes him as "a combination of ignorance, vanity, and petulance, with nothing to recommend him but that species of bravery in the field which is vaporing, boisterous, stifling reflection, blinding observation." Not the best man to put up against British regulars.

Boyd's first move is to send Lieutenant-Colonel Eleazar Ripley's regiment across the muddy fields and over a boggy creek bed to probe Morrison's forward skirmishers in the woods on the British left. Ripley advances half a mile when a line of Voltigeurs suddenly rises from concealment and delivers two volleys at his men who, disregarding the cries of their officers, leap behind stumps and open individual fire until, their ammunition exhausted, they run back out of range. Ripley retires with them but soon returns to the attack with reinforcements and drives the Voltigeurs back.

John Sewell, the British lieutenant whose breakfast was so rudely interrupted, is standing with his fellow Green Tigers in the thin line formed by the two British regiments when he sees the grey-clad Voltigeurs burst from the woods on his left, pursued by the

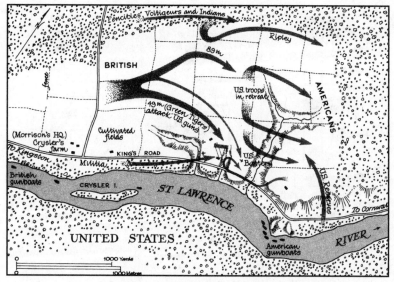

The Battle of Crysler's Farm: Phase 2

Americans. The situation is critical. If Ripley's men can get around the 89th, which holds the left flank, and attack the British from the rear, the battle is as good as lost.

Morrison now executes the first of a series of parade-ground manoeuvres, wheeling the entire 89th Regiment from its position in line, facing east, to face north—*en potence*, to use the military term. Emerging from the woods, the Americans encounter a solid line of scarlet-coated men firing muskets in unison. They break and run. The contrast between the fire of the opposing forces is so distinct that the women and children hiding in Captain John Crysler's cellar can easily tell the American guns from the British: the former make an irregular pop-pop-pop; the latter, at regular intervals, resound "like a tremendous roll of thunder."

Thwarted in his attempt to turn the British left, Boyd now advances his three main brigades across the open wheatfields in an attempt to seize the British right. Leonard Covington, the forty-five-year-old Marylander who commands the 3rd Brigade—a veteran of Anthony Wayne's frontier army—is fooled by the grey coats of the 49th directly in front of him.

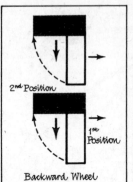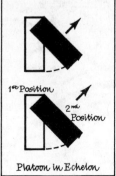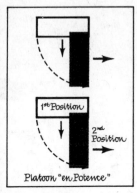

British Infantry Tactics at Crysler's Farm

"Come, lads, let me see how you will deal with these militia men," he shouts.

But the disguised Tigers are already executing another familiar drill—moving into echelon, a line of staggered platoons, which, supported by six-pounders, fire rolling volleys against the advancing Americans.

The action has now become general, a confused mêlée of struggling men, half obscured by dirty grey smoke, weaving forward and backward, floundering in the ankle-deep mud, splashing and dying in the stream beds, tumbling into gullies, clawing their way out of ravines until no one, when it is over, is able to produce a coherent account of exactly what went on.

Certain key moments emerge from the fog of battle. In one of several assaults on the British line, Brigadier-General Covington falls mortally wounded while attempting to seize the British cannon. His second-in-command is also killed. This critical loss, followed by the loss of two more senior officers, causes confusion in the American 3rd Brigade.

At about the same time, the American artillery, hauled from the boats and late getting into position, begins to harass the advancing British. Morrison orders Plenderleath to attack the guns with the heavy troops of the 49th, for unless they can be silenced the grapeshot will cut the outnumbered British to pieces.

Plenderleath's Green Tigers are about 120 yards from the enemy. Off they go through the deeply ploughed field, trampling the grain, kicking up the mud, tearing down two snake fences that bar their path, unable to fire back as they struggle with the heavy logs under a galling hail of shot from the American six-pounders.

John Sewell, advancing with his company into the hail of grape, sees his captain killed, takes over, and suddenly spies a squadron of American dragoons galloping down the King's road on his right. He realizes the danger: if the horsemen get around the flank, they can wheel about and charge the British from the rear. Fortunately, another drill book manoeuvre exists to meet this threat. Captain Ellis on the right wing executes it under Plenderleath's command, wheeling his men backward to the left to face the line of cavalry. Sewell notes that the entire movement, which the Americans believe to be a retreat, is carried out with all the coolness of a review as the commands ring out over the crash of grape and canister: *Halt . . . Front . . . Pivot . . . Cover . . . Left wheel into line . . . Fire by platoons from the centre to the flank.* The effect is shattering as the wounded American horses, snorting and neighing, flounder about, their saddles empty.

At the same time, a light company of the 89th stationed well ahead of the main ravine charges the American artillery, captures a six-pounder, and kills its crew. By now the whole American line is giving way, and the retreat is saved from becoming a rout only by the presence of American reserves.

Wilkinson, who has spent the day in his bunk lamenting his ill fortune at not being with his men, tries to prevent a pell-mell rush to the boats, exclaiming that the British will say that the Americans were running away and claim a victory. He sends a message to Boyd, asking if he can maintain himself on the bank that night to preserve some vestige of American honour. Boyd's answer is a curt *No:* the men are exhausted and famished; they need a complete night of rest.

Boyd now busies himself with the mandatory report of the day's action, which is, as always in defeat, a masterpiece of dissembling. He cannot actually claim victory but comes as close to it as he can, larding his account with a litany of alibis:

. . . though the result of this action were not so brilliant and decisive as I could have wished, and the first stages of it seemed to promise, yet when it is recollected that the troops had been long exposed to hard privations and fatigues, the inclement storms from which they could have no shelter; that the enemy were superior to us in numbers [*sic*], and greatly superior in position, and supported by 7 or 8 heavy gunboats; that the action being unexpected, was necessarily commenced without much concert; that we were, by unavoidable circumstances long deprived of our artillery; and that the action was warmly and obstinately contested for more than three hours, during which there were but a few short cessations of musketry and cannon; when all these circumstances are recollected, perhaps this day may be thought to have added some reputation to the American arms. And if, on this occasion, you shall believe me to have done my duty, and accomplished any of your purposes, I shall be satisfied. . . .

Wilkinson, in his report to the Secretary of War, does not shilly-shally. He inflates the British strength from 800 to 2,170, bumps up the British casualties from 170 to 500, and declares that "although the imperious obligations of duty did not allow me sufficient time to rout the enemy, they were beaten. . . ."

But it is Wilkinson who is beaten. "Emaciated almost to a skeleton, unable to sit my horse, or to move ten paces without assistance," he seeks an excuse to give up the grand campaign and receives it the morning after the battle in the form of a letter from General Hampton.

The two armies were supposed to meet just below the Long Sault, at St. Regis opposite Cornwall. Wilkinson's flotilla makes the passage, but Hampton is not there and never will be. It is impossible, he reports, to transport enough supplies to the St. Lawrence to feed the army; his arrival would only weaken the existing force; the roads are impracticable for wheeled transport; his troops are raw, sick, exhausted, dispirited. He intends to go back to Plattsburgh on Lake Champlain and strain every effort to throw himself on the enemy's flank along the old Champlain-Richelieu invasion route. This is mere posturing. He intends to do nothing.

Now Wilkinson has his scapegoat. Montreal, just three days downriver, is virtually defenceless. Hampton's apparent feint at Châteauguay and his sudden withdrawal has convinced Prevost to withdraw the bulk of the British troops to Kingston. Wilkinson still has some seven thousand soldiers. But neither he nor his generals have the will to continue. A hastily summoned council of war agrees to abandon the enterprise.

Wilkinson goes to some effort to make it clear that the defeat of the grand plan is entirely Hampton's fault. In his General Order on November 13 he announces that he is "compelled to retire by the extraordinary unexampled, and apparently unwarrantable conduct of Major General Hampton."

To Armstrong he writes that, with Hampton's help, he would have taken Montreal in eight or ten days. Now all his hopes are blasted: "I disclaim the shadow of blame because I have done my duty. . . . To General Hampton's outrage of every principle of subordination and discipline may be ascribed the failure of the expedition. . . ."

The army drifts eighteen miles down the St. Lawrence to Salmon Creek and moves up that tributary to the American hamlet of French Mills, soon to be known as Fort Covington in honour of the dead general. Here, in a dreary wilderness of pine and hemlock, with little shelter and hard rations, it passes a dreadful winter. Sickness, desertions, and venality do more damage than any British force. Clothing is hard to come by. Little Jarvis Hanks, the drummer boy, has no pantaloons and is forced to tailor himself a pair out of one of his two precious blankets. Driven to subsist on contaminated bread, the men sicken by the hundreds and die by the score. So many men are mortally stricken that funeral dirges are banned from the camp for reasons of morale. By the end of the year almost eighteen hundred are ill. Food is so scarce the sick must subsist on oatmeal, originally ordered for poultices. All of the efficient officers have gone on furlough or are themselves ill with pneumonia, diarrhea, dysentery, typhoid, or atrophy of the limbs, a kind of dry rot. The remainder, ex-ward politicians mostly, fatten their pocketbooks by selling army rations to British and Americans alike, and drawing dead men's pay.

The defeat on the St. Lawrence wrecks the careers of the men who bungled the grand attack. Wilkinson, convalescing in a comfortable home at Malone, New York, and bitterly blaming everybody but himself for the debacle, must know that his days are numbered. Hampton will shortly resign, to the relief of all. Lewis and Boyd have each taken a leave of absence and will not be heard of again.

Jacob Brown, promoted to major-general, and George Izard, Hampton's efficient second-in-command, represent the new army. When the force at French Mills breaks up the following February, Brown takes two thousand men to Sackets Harbor to continue the struggle for the Niagara frontier while Izard marches the rest to Plattsburgh.

Along the St. Lawrence, the settlers begin to rearrange the fragments of their lives. The north shore has been heavily plundered of cattle, grain, and winter forage. Fences have been ripped apart to build fires—the sky so illuminated it sometimes seemed as if the entire countryside was ablaze. Cellars, barns, and stables have been looted. Stragglers, pretending to search for arms, rummaged through houses, broke open trunks, stole everything from ladies' petticoats to men's pantaloons. Fancy china, silver plate, jewellery, books—all went to the plunderers in spite of Wilkinson's proclamation that private property would be respected.

The American advance has left a legacy of bitterness. Dr. William "Tiger" Dunlop, an assistant surgeon with the 89th, working with the wounded of both armies in the various farmhouses that do duty as makeshift hospitals, discovers that he cannot trust some of the Loyalist farmers near the stricken Americans, so great is their hatred of the enemy.

Fortunately, this brief explosion in their midst marks the last military excursion down the great river. For John Crysler and his neighbours, the war is over. In spite of James Wilkinson's hollow boast that the attack on Montreal is merely suspended and not abandoned, the St. Lawrence Valley will never again shiver to the crash of alien musketry.

SEVEN

The Niagara in Flames

November–December, 1813

With the news of Procter's defeat on the Thames, General Vincent hastily moves his Centre Division back to Burlington Heights, leaving the Niagara peninsula a no man's land. The Americans, hived in Fort George, cannot break out except for brief forays against the surrounding countryside. The regulars have departed to join Wilkinson. William Henry Harrison and his men have come and gone. The new American commander, Brigadier-General George McClure, a New York militia officer, is planning to move up the peninsula with his citizen soldiers in an attempt to dislodge Vincent's army.

SHIPMAN'S CORNERS (ST. CATHARINES),
UPPER CANADA, NOVEMBER 28, 1813

Captain William Hamilton Merritt and two of his Provincial Dragoons, their uniforms concealed by long greatcoats, lurk by a bridge over Twelve Mile Creek, spying out the countryside. Disloyalty is rife; traitors abound. Joseph Willcocks, the Canadian turncoat, is an hour away, riding at the head of an armed troop of former Canadians on one of his nightly attacks against his one-time neighbours. To young Captain Merritt's bitter disappointment, he has just missed tangling with him.

Two dissident Canadians mistake the three dragoons for members of the invading army. From them, Merritt learns that the Americans are marching out of Fort George, heading for Burlington Heights, and that their advance post is already at Shipman's.

Merritt is forty miles from the nearest British post. If the Americans discover his presence he will certainly be captured—and there are enough enemy sympathizers about to spread the news. These are confusing times. Villages change hands, often overnight. Pickets, advance parties, mounted marauders from both sides gallop about seeking each other and often confusing themselves, for it is not always possible to tell friend from foe: men from both sides speak the same language; not everyone wears a uniform, and some who do so, like Merritt and his men, are disguised.

The three dragoons retire slowly through the night until they reach the Runchey farmhouse at Twenty Mile Creek. Here they run directly into two enemy horsemen, and an odd little charade takes place. Merritt, posing as an American, affects a Yankee accent. The Americans, seeing through the deception, pretend to be British. A scuffle follows and shots are fired, just as two more horsemen ride up.

These are also Merritt's men—his sergeant-major and his cornet, Amos McKenney, both hot on the trail of another traitor—but Merritt does not recognize them in the dark, and an incredible mixup ensues. Merritt shoots off McKenney's cap, believing him to be an American. McKenney's horse, startled by the shot, lurches and throws him to the ground. Merritt's own horse is exhausted from the night ride, and so the young captain leaps into the empty saddle and dashes away. Only when he reaches headquarters at Dundas and recognizes the bridle does he realize, with a sinking heart, that he may have shot his best friend and comrade.

McKenney is not dead, only unhorsed and stunned. He lights out for the woods, spends the rest of the night stumbling through

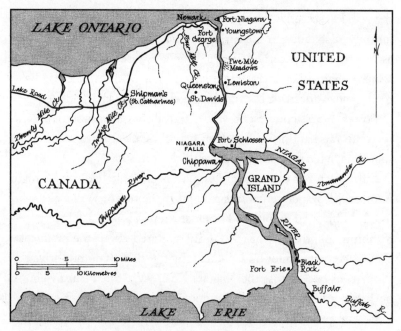

The Niagara Frontier, December, 1813

the undergrowth, trying to keep away from the enemy whom he can hear crashing through the bushes, hot on his trail. When dawn arrives, the "enemy" turns out to be his own sergeant-major, who has also spent the night fleeing from an unseen adversary—who turns out to be McKenney. The embarrassed pair make their way back to Dundas, to the relief of their crestfallen commander.

At twenty, William Hamilton Merritt is that inevitable product of war—a young-old man. He has already had more than a year of almost uninterrupted warfare—a mounted guerrilla veteran of a dozen skirmishes, hair-breadth escapes, shoot-outs, midnight rides, sleepless nights, sudden forays, hurried retreats. He is well educated, having studied the classics under John Burns, the Presbyterian minister at Newark, and mathematics and surveying under Richard Cockrel, the noted Ancaster schoolmaster—learning that will stand him in good stead in the future when he builds the first Welland Canal. At sixteen, Merritt operated a two-hundred acre farm and a general store. At nineteen, his commercial ambitions were interrupted by the war. He served in his father's Niagara Light Dragoons until the unit was disbanded in the spring of 1813. From that point on, as far as Merritt was concerned, it was somebody else's war. But General Vincent had other ideas. Here was a man who knew every back road, lane, and creek bed in the Niagara peninsula and—equally important—was conversant with the loyalties of every settler. Who better to raise and lead a troop of fifty Provincial Dragoons? Since that time, Merritt has been in the thick of it.

Since October, all his energies have been funnelled into a single purpose: he desperately wants to capture the traitor Willcocks, who briefly kidnapped his father. The elder Merritt is now safely returned to Shipman's, the rest of the family scattered about the peninsula. Young Merritt cannot understand why the British do not drive the Americans back across the Niagara River. What is the army about, he keeps asking himself. Why doesn't Vincent go on the attack? Have our great men given up the idea of regaining the country?

He is still puzzling over this lack of initiative at a party on November 29 when a midnight order calls on him to move at once with his dragoons to Forty Mile Creek. He is to join Colonel John Murray, the army's inspecting field officer, who is close on the trail of the treasonous Willcocks. "King Joe," as Merritt sardonically calls him, is reported to be in the vicinity with 250 men, but when Merritt's troop arrives after an all-night ride, they have already slipped away.

By this time Brigadier-General George McClure's main army of sixteen hundred New York militia has reached Shipman's. Willcocks, acting as his advance scout, somehow manages to inflate Murray's light force into an army. He warns McClure that two or three thousand British troops are on their way to meet the American threat.

Does McClure believe this nonsense, or is he merely seeking a way out? His bravado is well known, his bravery held in lower esteem. "Your general will lead you to victory and share the dangers with you," he told his brigade in September. Now, on the strength of a rumour, he is prepared to fold up and retire.

He calls the usual council of war. His officers tell him what he wants to hear: it would be madness to go on. And so it would, for the British, having beaten Wilkinson, are now able to rush regular troops back to Upper Canada and, with a new commanding general, Gordon Drummond, in charge, to go immediately on the offensive.

The morning after the council, McClure counts his men to discover that six hundred—one-third of his army—have not waited for their December 9 discharge but have simply deserted. In a panic, he realizes that he has left Fort George almost defenceless. Seizing some cattle and flour from the settlers, he makes a hasty withdrawal.

Now the eager Murray asks Vincent's permission to move forward but is told he cannot take his main body past Forty Mile Creek or his outposts past Twelve Mile Creek. Vincent, it appears, is no more anxious to tangle with McClure than the American is with him. His health has failed him and he is about to be replaced.

Merritt worries about his father. On December 8 he persuades the commander of Murray's advance picket to let him go on to Shipman's to round up any suspicious characters who may be helping the Americans. His real purpose is to bring his father to safety. That done he returns to Forty Mile Creek where he receives a stiff dressing-down from Colonel Murray for disobeying orders. But a moment later Murray himself disobeys instructions. When Merritt reports a rumour that McClure has threatened to lay waste the countryside if the British dare advance, Murray agrees to move his entire force forward to Twenty Mile Creek, in direct contravention of Vincent's orders. To Merritt, this is not far enough; he fears for the safety of the community at Shipman's.

He returns to Twelve Mile Creek and publicly assembles all the available militia, a ruse that convinces McClure's scouts that the greater part of Vincent's Centre Division has already reached that spot.

Merritt has had little sleep for three nights. At two on the morning of December 10, having just bedded down in a nearby farmhouse, he is dispatched on another errand—to ride immediately to Beaver Dams to prevent a cache of flour from falling into American hands. When he returns to Shipman's, the exhausted dragoon is surprised to discover that Colonel Murray has moved forward. Orders or no orders, the aggressive Murray is determined to march on Fort

George this very night. The town of Newark is in flames, burned by the Americans: every house, every barn, every shop, every public building. It is a bad business; but Merritt cannot help a moment of inward elation, for it means that the Americans are leaving Canada.

NEWARK, UPPER CANADA, DECEMBER 10, 1813

Snow. Snow falling in a curtain of heavy flakes. Snow blowing in the teeth of a bitter east wind off the lake. Snow lying calf deep in the streets, whirling in eddies around log buildings, creeping under doors, piling in drifts at the base of snake fences. Snow clogging the brims of top hats, crusting mufflers, whitening horses' manes, smothering the neat gardens of summer. No day, this, to be out in the storm; better to crouch by hearth or kitchen stove, making peep-holes in the frosted windows from which to view the white world from behind the security of solid walls. But not on this day, for there is no security in Newark. Before darkness falls there will be few walls standing in this doomed village.

On Queen Street, in Joseph McCarthy's store, a violent quarrel is in progress. The American commander, George McClure, is hotly defending his decision to burn the town against the vehement pro-tests of Dr. Cyrenius Chapin, the partisan leader from Buffalo.

McClure is in a near panic. Armstrong has ignored his repeated request for reinforcements. Harrison and his veterans are gone. With the threat to Montreal at an end, the British can again turn their attention and their troops to the Niagara country. Fort George is virtually defenceless, for all of McClure's militia, having reached the end of their period of enlistment, have recrossed the river in a body and are dispersing to their homes. Threats, bribes, entreat-ies have not persuaded them to stay. Indeed, they have been in a state of near mutiny on learning that they will not receive their pay before demobilization. McClure has gone to the extreme of offering an extra two dollars a month to any man who will remain. To his chagrin and disgust, dozens take the money, then desert.

To hold the captured British fort—the only American foothold on the peninsula—McClure has some seventy regulars plus Joseph Willcocks's small corps of about one hundred Canadian Volunteers. Merritt's hoax has convinced the General that the entire British army is on its way from Twelve Mile Creek. Willcocks has just lost five men, one of whom has been handed over to the Indians—an act that strikes terror into the hearts of others. A council of war has speedily concluded that the fort must be abandoned and destroyed before the British arrive.

McClure attempts to justify the decision to burn the town by brandishing a letter from Armstrong, written the previous October:

> Understanding that the defense of the post committed to your charge may render it proper to destroy the town of Newark, you are hereby directed to apprise its inhabitants of this circumstance, and invite them to remove themselves and their effects to some place of greater safety.

This is hardly a *carte blanche* to destroy the village, since McClure has no intention of defending the fort. He argues, however, that the British mean to attack Fort Niagara, the American stronghold across the river. By burning Newark he will deny them comfortable billets.

McClure is not much of a soldier. A Londonderry Irishman, he has been carpenter, miller, contractor, merchant, land speculator, and, above all, a New York State politician. The spoils have included a judgeship and command of the 8th Brigade of state militia, the latter an inconsequential post because there are no militia left to command. Like so many other political appointees to military rank, he is a better boaster than tactician. Chapin, himself a citizen soldier, has little use for him. He censures McClure for countenancing the plundering of buildings and the burning of private homes by the undisciplined militia during an abortive October venture to Twenty Mile Creek; indeed, Chapin suspects that McClure shared in the spoils. On his part, the General hates Chapin, calls him a "damned rascal," and has been heard to wish that the enemy would capture him.

Does McClure really intend to burn Newark for the reasons he advances to Chapin? If he means to deny the British shelter, why does he not destroy the new barrack buildings at Fort George? Why does he not burn the fifteen hundred new tents that lie within its walls? Is there, perhaps, a second, more emotional reason to visit such misery on the women, children, and non-combatants of Newark?

Behind the bumbling militia general there can be discerned a more intriguing figure, another enemy of Chapin's and one of McClure's chief advisers, the turncoat Joseph Willcocks. Now a commissioned lieutenant-colonel in the American army, Willcocks is a former resident of the doomed community. It was from here that he edited his virulent newspaper, the *Upper Canadian Guardian or Freeman's Journal.* That publication was not designed to placate the true-blue Loyalists who make up the town's elite and whom the Americans, with memories of the Revolution, still disparage as "Tories."

Now, as McClure rides through the streets of the Loyalist village at the head of his burning party, torches and lanterns lit, directing his men to various corners of the town to fire houses and public buildings, Willcocks rides beside him, settling old scores and cursing anyone who protests as a Tory.

He is a curious, even baffling specimen, this Willcocks. His motivations are more complex than those of his two chief associates, Benajah Mallory, now his second-in-command, and Abraham Markle. Like so many of their fellow citizens, these two came to Canada from the United States, lured by cheap land and low taxes; in spite of service in the Upper Canadian legislature, their loyalties have never been firm. But Willcocks is not an American. He is the scion of an upper-class British family living in Ireland. He fought for the British at Queenston Heights. Why is he presiding at the destruction of his adopted village?

The answer lies partly in Willcocks's mercurial personality and partly in his continuing search for a patron—a father figure, perhaps—who can advance his interests. He is a handsome man at forty, reasonably well educated and with an aptitude for making friends, though it is noticed that the friends he makes are generally those who can give him a push up the ladder of his ambition.

His first patron in Upper Canada was a distant cousin, Peter Russell, who, as Administrator of the province, was the most powerful man next to the governor. Russell gave him a job and a home but threw him out when Willcocks made advances to the Administrator's half-sister.

His next backer was Chief Justice Allcock, with whom he also lived and whose influence secured him a better post as Sheriff of York. When Allcock was moved to Lower Canada, Willcocks sought a new benefactor and found him in the person of the new Puisne Judge of the Court of King's Bench, Robert Thorpe. That encounter marked a watershed in Joseph Willcocks's life. Under Thorpe's dark influence, the model civil servant became a thorn in the side of the government that employed him. Thorpe was aggrieved at not being appointed Chief Justice and shortly became the backer of those opposition elements in the legislature who gathered about the Irish lawyer and malcontent, William Weekes. If Weekes was Thorpe's tool, so was Willcocks. Having lost his government job and launched his scrappy little newspaper, Willcocks became a member of the lower house. And after Weekes was killed in a duel in 1806, Willcocks became the centre of the opposition forces.

In Willcocks's resistance to the closed circle of elitists at York can be seen the faint stirrings of a movement, interrupted by war, that a quarter of a century later will burst into open revolt. His Irish upbringing, his re-education under Thorpe and Weekes, his breach with Russell—all these have contributed to a vaguely formed political philosophy that makes him a foe of arbitrary power. In his newspaper, Willcocks hinted so broadly at bribery in the legislature that he was thrown in jail. It did not disconcert him. He fought hard, if vainly, for common school education—an American idea shunned by those who believe that schooling should be reserved for the sons of the privileged. He also opposed the strengthening of the militia. At the war's outset he successfully blocked Isaac Brock's call to suspend the laws of *habeas corpus* and to invoke martial law. "I am flattered at being ranked among the enemies of the King's Servants in this colony," he declared. "I glory in the distinction."

Then, suddenly, he reversed himself to become Isaac Brock's humble and obedient servant. It is these sudden right-angle turns in Joseph Willcocks's chequered career that baffle his friends and disconcert his enemies. Brock, who had every reason to hate and despise him, went out of his way to meet him and beg his aid. Among the proud and stiff-necked arbiters of the province's destiny, Brock must have stood out as a man of exquisite charm and affability. Once again Willcocks found himself in the shadow of an older patron, this time the most powerful man in the province, one who made a point of flattering him. Would he undertake a mission of some delicacy in the interests of his country? Willcocks succumbed and was dispatched to secure the loyalty of the Grand River Indians. Later, still under Brock's influence, he fought bravely at Queenston where his patron was killed.

Brock's crusty successor, Roger Sheaffe, no diplomat, had little time for such as Joe Willcocks. But the Americans had. During the second occupation of York, when the Americans seemed to be winning, some of Willcocks's friends went over to the enemy. Willcocks joined them, and here he is in Newark again, the civil servant-turned-radical-turned-soldier-turned-traitor, riding beside his commander, a green band and a white cockade in his hat identifying him proudly as a Canadian Volunteer, shouting threats and imprecations at his former neighbours.

Many have not heeded McClure's warning, given early this morning, believing that the threat to burn the town is an empty gesture. Now, roughly turned out into the blowing snow, they see their homes and all their belongings consumed by fire. The able-bodied citizens are with the militia or in prison at Fort Niagara. Only women, children, and sick old men remain. Two babies are born this night in the light of the leaping flames.

Mrs. Alex McKee, whose husband is a prisoner at Niagara, struggles to save what she can. Her family owns seven buildings, including two houses, a well-stocked store, and a soap and candle factory.

They pack fifteen trunks with their most valuable effects and ship them off to Eight Mile Creek to be buried and covered with brushwood. She saves one article—a large teatray—as a sleigh to protect her little daughter's bare feet from the snow. It is a vain effort; the child's toes are soon frozen.

Eliza Campbell, widow of the fort major, cannot leave her home because she has three small children to care for. She lives in a handsomely furnished storey-and-a-half building, surrounded by two acres of land with fruit trees and a barn. Now, forced from her house without time to gather anything but money, she watches as the soldiers plunder her furniture and fire the two buildings. A moment later, one of Willcocks's men takes all her money.

John Rogers, a boy of nine, watches his mother carry a beautiful mantelpiece out into the street before her house is reduced to ashes. His parents have friends and relatives among the American officers but have been told that if their home were to be spared, they would be tagged as disloyal by their neighbours.

Mrs. William Dickson lies ill in bed in her handsome mansion, the first brick house in Newark. Her husband, a brother of the Robert Dickson whom the Sioux call the Red-Haired Man, is a prisoner in Fort Niagara. Like others who are unable to walk, Mrs. Dickson is carried out of her house, bed and all, and plumped down in the snow while Willcocks's men put the torch to the building, destroying everything—damask curtains, cherry and walnut furniture, a full set of India table china, stores, stoves, clothing, pictures, and, above all, one of the finest libraries in Upper Canada—a thousand books purchased in England at a cost of three thousand dollars. It is surely no coincidence that Dickson has long been an enemy of Joseph Willcocks—ever since the day, seven years before, when he killed Willcocks's political patron, William Weekes, in a duel.

McClure's intelligence, much of it based on Willcocks's exaggerated reports, is faulty. The British as yet have no intention of attacking either Fort George or Fort Niagara. But Colonel Murray, seeing the flames from a distance, decides to ignore his orders, march on the town, and seize the fort. He calls out the militia, instructs Captain

Merritt to commandeer axes and scaling ladders, and puts his column in motion. Refugees are already streaming out of the town seeking shelter. The nearest farmhouse, four miles away, cannot handle them all. Some women and children walk up to ten miles that night through the swirling snow. The spectacle enrages Murray's men, fuelling a desire for revenge that Murray is in no mood to dampen.

At nine in the evening, Murray's advance enters the smouldering village. McClure's troops make a hasty retreat across the ice-choked Niagara River. They have blown up Fort George's main magazine and spiked the guns but left the new barracks intact, together with a quantity of ammunition and all fifteen hundred tents.

By the time William Merritt enters the town, Newark is a heap of coals, the streets clogged with furniture and only one house still standing—that of his brother-in-law. Ninety-eight houses, barns, and stables have been destroyed. Four hundred people are homeless. All public buildings—jail, court house, library—are in ashes. Two churches have been fired. In McEwen's smokehouse, the refugees seek what shelter they can. Others crouch against chimneys or in root houses or cellars, hastily roofed with boards.

In the hearts of the homeless and the soldiers there is one common emotion: a desire for retaliation. The senseless burning of Newark will send an echo down the corridors of history, for it is this act, much more than the accidental firing of the legislature at York, that provokes a succession of incendiary raids that will not end until the city of Washington itself is in flames.

ST. DAVIDS, UPPER CANADA, DECEMBER 18, 1813

It is close to midnight as Colonel John Murray looks over the force that is about to march to the river and embark on the attack against Fort Niagara, the American stronghold on the far side. He turns to Captain Thomas Dawson of the grenadiers of the 100th, who will lead the Forlorn Hope:

"What description of men have you got, Dawson, for the advance? Can you rely on them?"

"I can, Colonel. I know every one of them. They can all be depended on."

"Yes, Dawson, I dare say, but what I mean, are they a desperate set? I want men who have no conscience, for not a soul must live between the landing place and the fort. There must be no alarm."

"They are just that description of men, Colonel."

They are, in fact, the flower of Upper Canada. Young Allan MacNab is here, not yet turned sixteen; one day he will be premier. Lieutenant Richard Bullock, one of the few officers who escaped capture at the Thames, is here, and half a dozen officers from the Lincoln Militia—Loyalists with names like Kerby, Ball, Hamilton, and Servos, local gentry burning for revenge after the destruction of Newark.

The secret attack on the American fort has been a week in the planning, ever since McClure's hasty departure from Fort George. For the past several days, Merritt and his dragoons have been gathering boats for the midnight voyage across the river. Exhausted from lack of sleep and a bout of grippe brought on by fatigue and cold, Merritt finds to his bitter disappointment that he can no longer stand upright and must miss the night's excitement.

Lieutenant-General Gordon Drummond—De Rottenburg's replacement as commander in Upper Canada and as Prevost's second-in-command—has come down from Little York to St. Davids to mastermind Murray's attack. A bolder and more innovative leader than his predecessor, he has left nothing to chance. The force of 562 men is taken from the 100th Regiment, the Royal Scots, and the veteran 41st. The Forlorn Hope will dispose of the American advance guard. One body will storm the main gate of the fort; another will attack the southern salient; a third will scale the eastern bastion. One officer, Daniel Servos, carries a stick of cordwood to jam into the gate if necessary. A party of axemen has been detailed to chop down the pickets and open the way to the fort's rear. Silence is essential. Oars are to be muffled, muskets carried at the shoulder, unloaded, bayonets fixed, to prevent the clash of arms. The troops have all been warned that any sound will bring instant death. The killing is to be silent. "The bayonet is the weapon on which the success of the attack must depend," Drummond declares.

The boats slip across the narrow river in just fifteen minutes, landing two and a half miles above the fort. It is intensely cold, the night moonless, a soft blanket of snow muffling the sound of marching feet.

At Youngstown, Captain Dawson and his enormous sergeant, Andrew Spearman, spot an American soldier posted outside a tavern door. This must be the advance guard. Spearman creeps up on the shivering sentry, chokes him into silence, demands the official countersign, then dispatches him with a single bayonet thrust.

Some of the Forlorn Hope peer through the window. The twenty members of the American picket are inside, protecting themselves from the cold. The officers are playing whist. When it is all over someone will claim that one of the Americans asked, "What's trump?" and one of the Canadians replied, "Bayonets are trump!" Perhaps; it is a night for legend.

The door crashes open; the Forlorn Hope dashes in—young Allan MacNab in the forefront. The advance guard dies under the bayonets of the British and the force moves on. A mile or so later a second picket is also dispatched, silently, ruthlessly, and the company marches on along the frozen river road.

What Murray does not know is that two days before, a deserter has alerted McClure to the possibility of just such an attack. McClure has warned the fort's commander, Captain Nathaniel Leonard, to keep his men on guard and to place grenades at strategic points to resist the enemy.

Fort Niagara is no easy target. Its bastions bristle with twenty-seven pieces of artillery. Three strong towers overlook the palisades. Four hundred and thirty men, of whom some fifty are sick, guard the ramparts. But where are these men? Sound asleep in their tents, in spite of the warning. Where is McClure? In Buffalo, attempting to justify his attack on Newark. And where is Captain Leonard? At home with his family, three miles beyond. The evidence suggests that the captain is more than a little drunk and that his officers, after a night of gaming and tippling, are sleeping it off in the belief that the threatened attack, which has failed to materialize on two previous nights, is merely a figment of the deserter's imagination.

The ice crackles under the tread of the soldiers' boots, but the sound is borne away on the gusts of a northeast wind. Only one man is on horseback: Lieutenant-Colonel Hamilton of the British 100th, who, having lost a leg in Holland, cannot march but refuses to remain behind. Suddenly Hamilton's horse neighs loudly. From a stable near the fort comes an answering neigh. The force halts at once. Surely these sounds must alert the garrison! *Silence.* Relieved, the men shuffle forward.

At three o'clock they reach the main gate to find the drawbridge down. They have arrived at the very moment when the sentries on the river side are being changed. Spearman, the big sergeant, advances alone across the bridge, reaches the sentry box, is challenged, gives the countersign, and in an approximation of a Yankee accent says he has come from Youngstown. As the sentry turns, Spearman strangles him to death.

Shouting and cheering, the storming party dashes across the bridge, awakening the garrison. A cannon booms from the roof of one of the towers. Lieutenant Maurice Nolan of the 100th rushes through the lower door and vanishes into the gloom. His comrades hear the clash of steel on steel, the hoarse roar of musketry. Nolan is dead, his chest pierced by a bayonet, a musket ball, and three buckshot. Three American corpses lie beside him, one killed by a pistol shot, the others with their skulls cleft by sword blows. In a fury, Nolan's men proceed to massacre the survivors until other officers stop them.

Meanwhile, Major Davis Byron Davies of the 100th is attacking a second blockhouse. Random fire has already killed one of his men, wounded two others. Davies seizes an American prisoner, threatening him with instant death unless he guides him to the inner stairs, waits until he hears the Americans reloading their muskets, seizes the interval to force the door, and in the light of flaming torches carried by his men finds his way up the twisting staircase, shouting to his followers to bayonet everybody. The Americans have no stomach for the fight; one man is killed; sixty-four surrender.

Panic-stricken, a group of Americans tries to escape from the sally port, only to be driven back by the grenadiers of the Royal Scots. Colonel Murray saves most of their lives by making them lie down, receiving a painful bayonet wound in the hand for this act of mercy.

It is soon over. The Americans have lost sixty-five dead and sixteen wounded, all by the bayonet, the British six dead, five wounded. Fourteen officers, including the tardy Captain Leonard, who returns at dawn, are captured with 350 others. The considerable booty includes twenty-nine cannon, seven thousand muskets and rifles, seven thousand pairs of shoes, and a vast cache of clothing, much of it originally captured from the British, the whole being valued at one million dollars. To William Hamilton Merritt's delight, Murray allows him and his troops a share of the prize money as a reward for their services. Every private soldier will receive two pounds sterling, the officers much more.

At five that morning a cannon shot from the newly captured fort signals victory to Major-General Phineas Riall, the peppery little Irishman who has replaced the ailing Vincent as officer commanding the Centre Division. Riall has been waiting on the far shore for this signal to invade Lewiston with a thousand men and five hundred Indians.

Drummond has agreed to use the natives only if they can be kept under control—a specious argument, surely. Does Drummond, of all people—the first Canadian-born general officer—actually believe the Indians can be controlled? Or that Matthew Elliott and William Caldwell, the Indian Department officers who will lead them in battle, will be able to control them? They have shown no disposition to do so on previous occasions.

Riall's force lands without opposition at Five Mile Meadows, half way between Lewiston and the lake. There is little to stand in his way as he sets out to make a clean sweep up the river. The handful of militia at Lewiston has deserted. Their commander was told to expect a three-cannon warning from Fort Niagara if invasion came;

he ignored the single cannon shot at three o'clock—the only gun fired by the defenders—believing it a false alarm. Snug in bed, the citizens now find the British and Indians on their doorsteps. They flee from their homes, half-dressed, many without shoes or stockings, the men on horseback, the roads leading to Buffalo a tangle of wagons, farmers' carts, and sleighs, many toppling over, passengers cursing their drivers, in the pell-mell escape.

Mrs. Solomon Gillette, waiting for her husband to return home, hears the sound of the signal cannon, wakes her ten-year-old son, Orville, and sets about milking. The task is nearly complete when blood-curdling yells split the air. Three Indians in war paint and feathers appear, loot the barn, drink the milk, head for the house. Orville dashes off, dodging between the haystacks; but his mother cannot flee, for she has left three younger children in the house. More Indians arrive, seize a demijohn of whiskey, threaten to kill the children. She holds the two youngest in her arms while Jervis, aged seven, clings to her skirts. Through the open door she spies a British officer, resplendent in scarlet, and springs into the street, pleading for rescue. The Indians fire a volley. Little Jervis falls dead at her feet. As the officer dashes up to save the surviving trio, one of the Indians tears the scalp from the dead child's head.

At the same time, on Centre Street, her husband, Solomon, is taken prisoner. As he is led away he sees his eldest boy, Miles, aged nineteen, being brought along the opposite side by a party of tribesmen. Miles, a veteran of the Battle of Queenston Heights, struggles with his native captors, shoots one, tries to break away, and is shot and scalped in front of his father. Mrs. Gillette and her two babies make their way through the snow for 270 miles, finally reaching her father's farm in Columbia County. It is June before she learns that ten-year-old Orville is safe and Christmas before she knows that her husband is alive and a prisoner in Canada. The shattered family is not reunited until the spring of 1815.

Joseph Willcocks's second-in-command, Benajah Mallory, arrives post-haste with sixty turncoat Canadian Volunteers to fight a delaying action that will allow the settlers time to escape. But soon every building in the vicinity is reduced to ashes. Within a day, the Niagara frontier from the fort to Tonawanda Creek, including the Tuscarora village, Lewiston, Youngstown, and Manchester (the future Niagara Falls), have been depopulated and reduced to smoking ruins.

For this devastation Brigadier-General McClure is blamed. In Buffalo he is the subject of universal excoriation for what one American (in the *Pittsburgh Gazette*) calls the "wanton and abominable act" of firing Newark. As he marches at the head of his men down the main street, his ears ring with cries and taunts: "Shoot him down! Shoot him!" Cyrenius Chapin's followers lead the pack, some even firing their muskets at the embattled general. Chapin is briefly jailed for mutiny but almost immediately released by the citizens themselves.

McClure cannot stay in Buffalo. He is a pariah. Brigadier-General Timothy Hopkins finds that the militia will not serve under him. His own soldiers have lost confidence in him. His officers are convinced that he is unfit to command. Universally detested, he slinks off to Batavia and turns his militia command over to Major-General Amos Hall.

The British, meanwhile, are advancing on Fort Schlosser. Marching with the advance is the indestructible Private Shadrach Byfield of the 41st light company, back in service again after his escape on the Thames and fresh from the attack on Fort Niagara. A mile and a half from its objective, the group seizes a forward guardhouse, manages to take eight prisoners before the rest escape. Byfield and a handful of men are ordered to guard the prisoners while the main force moves on to Schlosser.

The night is dark, the countryside unknown, the trails through the woods labyrinthine. Byfield's party takes the wrong fork and almost immediately runs into trouble. Footsteps can be heard behind them. Friend or enemy? No one wants to find out, but at last Byfield volunteers to go back alone, runs into a shadowy figure—an American—threatens to blow his brains out, and makes him a prisoner. It is the officer of the guard who made his escape during the confusion of the attack.

An affecting little scene follows. The American complains that someone has stolen his boots. Byfield rummages in his pack and generously offers him a pair of his own as well as a tot of rum to warm him, whereupon the prisoner breaks into sobs, exclaiming he had not expected to be treated so well.

There are more tears to come. As Byfield brings his prisoner to Fort Schlosser, now in British hands, he spots the body of an American officer sprawled on the floor. His captive spots it too and begins to weep bitterly, for this battered and bleeding corpse was once his dearest friend.

Byfield and the others burn the fort, destroy all the buildings, throw the provisions into the river. Then, on December 22, all of the army save for a small garrison force at Fort Niagara returns to the Canadian side, and the people of Buffalo and Black Rock, who have been expecting an imminent attack, breathe more easily. Their relief is premature. A week later, the attack is launched.

BUFFALO, NEW YORK, DECEMBER 30, 1813

Margaret St. John—the widow St. John, as she is now known—has no sense of danger, even though she can hear the booming of cannon downriver at Black Rock. She has seen General Amos Hall's troops move out, two thousand strong, with men like Chapin and Mallory in the van, and is convinced the militia can thwart any British attempt at landing.

She is not easily rattled, for she is a child of the frontier: her father was a long-time missionary to the Indians. She has lived all her life in log communities, in the shadow of dark forests, always on the rim of civilization. She has raised eleven children under the most primitive conditions, often without a doctor's help. Now, at forty-five, she is self-reliant, domineering, a little irritable at times, but always in total control.

She has no way of knowing that the American defence of Black Rock is a total disaster, that almost half of General Hall's volunteers have fled at the first alarm, that the British, having launched a successful two-pronged attack, are even now marching on Buffalo, fourteen hundred strong, with the Indians in the vanguard, their passage only slightly impeded by a few bold defenders.

Like a clap of thunder the alarm gun booms, and panic grips the village. The first of the retreating militia come dashing through town, followed by a column of refugees. The terrible word *Indians!* passes, in a scream, from house to house.

The flight from Buffalo begins at once as horses, oxen, and sleighs are commandeered; as babies are thrown into open carts along with furs, jewellery, bread, silverware, provisions. Those who cannot find transport set out on a dead run through the light snow over half-frozen ruts.

Into the St. John cottage at the corner of Main and Mohawk comes an old friend, Dr. Josiah Trowbridge. He begs the widow to leave at once, warns that the Indians will kill her if she stays, offers her his horse, promises to take care of the children.

"I can't do it," says Margaret St. John. "Here is all I have in the world, and I will stay and defend it."

All she has in the world are two buildings: the big family house which, since the accidental drowning of her husband and one son the previous summer, has been leased as a hotel, and the little unfinished storey-and-a-half cottage into which she and eight of her children have been forced to squeeze.

Across Main Street, her son-in-law, Asaph Bemis, is hastily packing a wagon. He offers to take the six youngest St. John children, three boys and three girls, along with his own wife and baby to safety. He packs them in with the bedding and household goods, whips his horses and is off.

The Indians are advancing down Guideboard Road, the militia fleeing ahead. One of Mrs. St. John's neighbours, Job Hoysington, stops; he wants one more shot at the redskins, he says. The others dash on, leaving him behind. His scalped corpse and rifle will not be found until the snow melts in the spring.

Next door to the St. Johns lives Sally Lovejoy, a tall, spirited woman of thirty-five. She, too, has no intention of leaving unless she can take her big trunk, containing her most precious belongings, with her. When no wagon can be found to handle the trunk, she determines to stay. Her husband, Henry, is fighting with the militia. Young Henry, her thirteen-year-old son, wants to fight, too; during Bisshopp's raid on Black Rock he carried a musket bigger than himself. Now his mother tells him to run away:

"Henry, you've fought against the British: you must run. They'll take you prisoner. I am a woman; they'll not harm me."

The town is in a state of anarchy. People are fleeing in every direction, some heading up Seneca Street toward the Indian reservation, others galloping up Main toward Williamsville or Batavia, more moving up the beach toward Pratt's Ferry at the river and on to Hamburg.

An ox team lurches by, pulling a sled crammed with wounded soldiers; another, loaded with household goods, carries a settler's family and three exhausted women who have begged a ride; a ragged party of militia straggles through town, still carrying the muskets they have never fired. Friendly Seneca Indians clip-clop past on ponies, their women up behind, babes in arms. Children are lost and found again. One woman, holding her baby, tumbles off her horse into a bed of quicksand and is hauled out at the last moment. A farmer from Hamburg arrives with a load of cheese, grasps what is happening, dumps his wagon and loads it with refugees.

Families are separated. Job Hoysington's wife, unable to wait any longer for her husband (already dead), sets out on foot with her six children, turns two of them over to a passing rider, and does not locate them for weeks; they are found in two separate counties, miles apart. Few save anything of value, and those who try are often thwarted. One silversmith throws his stock into a pillowcase; he hands it to a stranger who offers to save it but is never seen again.

Some stay to fight. One group, led by one of Oliver Hazard Perry's naval gunners, rushes to the river where the *Chippawa*, late of Perry's fleet, is wintering. They seize an old twelve-pound cannon and trundle it up Main Street to the corner of Niagara. There they see the British advancing—a long line of brilliantly uniformed men, bayonets gleaming in the morning sunlight.

The cannon speaks, without much effect. It is so badly overloaded by the eager civilians that on the third shot it bounds off the carriage.

Dr. Cyrenius Chapin is convinced that further resistance is useless. He determines to surrender the town to the British.

"Don't fire that gun," says Chapin.

Robert Kane, a mason by trade, doesn't want to give up.

"I *will* fire it," says Kane. "I will cleave any man who touches it."

Seth Grosvenor runs up to the St. John cottage looking for help to hoist the heavy gun back on its carriage. But every able man has gone.

Grosvenor is in tears.

"If I had help," he says, "I could drive the British back."

At this moment, Mrs. St. John sees a group of men on horseback coming from Court Street. She runs out into the road as the leading rider draws rein.

"For mercy sake's do turn back and help Mr. Grosvenor manage that cannon and defend the town," she cries, "and let General Hall go; he must be an awful coward."

The rider raises his hat but trots on with the others. Somebody tells Mrs. St. John that she has been talking to the General himself. Well, she retorts, if she had known that she would have had more to say.

Suddenly the Bemis wagon, with the St. John children hanging on for dear life, flies past. At North Street they found the way blocked by oncoming Indians—friendly Senecas pursued by British tribesmen. With bullets whizzing around his head, Asaph Bemis managed to turn the cart around and now, as he rattles down Main Street, calls to his mother-in-law that he must take the lakeshore road but will be back for the rest of the family as quickly as possible.

As the wagon passes the head of Niagara Street, young Martha St. John looks out and catches a confused glimpse of the British army drawn up on Niagara Square and a man on horseback facing them holding a white flag over one shoulder. It is 10 A.M. The man is Cyrenius Chapin, who has tied the flag to his cane. The British accept his surrender but later repudiate it because Chapin has no official standing in the community. He is made prisoner once more, being placed under heavy guard because of his previous escape. He has already sent his two daughters, aged eleven and nine, out of town on foot to try to reach his farm at Hamburg, ten miles away. He has no idea where they are now.

Down the street at Pomeroy's Bakery some famished militiamen are gobbling up Pomeroy's bread when the cry comes, "Run, boys, run!" Looking north, they see a long line of Indians trotting down Washington Street in single file. Gripping the bread in one hand and their muskets in the other, they flee the village.

Several Indians and their women are in the St. John house, looking for plunder. Next door, Mrs. St. John sees an Indian pulling down the curtains from Mrs. Lovejoy's windows. Her spirited neighbour grapples with the invader.

"Don't risk your life for property," cries Mrs. St. John.

But Mrs. Lovejoy replies, "When my property goes, my life shall go with it."

Each witness to the grisly scene that follows will remember it from a slightly different focus. Mrs. Lovejoy struggles with the Indian over—what? A silk shawl? The blankets? The curtains? One thing is clear to Mrs. St. John, watching in dismay through her window: she sees her neighbour strike at the Indian with a carving knife; she sees him raise his hatchet; she sees the hatchet fall. But she does not dare enter the house to determine Sally Lovejoy's fate.

A British colonel rides up.

"Why are you not away?" he asks, crossly.

She replies that she has nowhere to go but the snow, asks protection for her house. He sends her to Major-General Riall, who gives her his own interpreter as a guard.

Now, from the corner of Main and Seneca comes a crackle of flames, a whiff of wood smoke. An officer and a squad of men are moving from house to house, torches in hand. Soon the Lovejoy home is fired. Mrs. St. John and her two remaining daughters, Maria and Sarah, with the help of Pettigrew, the hired man, go into the house, take out the body of Mrs. Lovejoy, and lay it on a pile of boards beside a fence. Then they manage to extinguish the fire. At night, with the help of old Judge Walden, the women carry the corpse back into the house and place it on the cords of the bedstead. Later, some of the villagers return to visit the home and are moved to tears by the spectacle of Sally Lovejoy, clad in her black silk dress, her long, ebony hair reaching through the cords to the floor.

Meanwhile, the Bemis family and the six younger St. John children have reached Pratt's Ferry to find a long queue waiting to cross the river. Men, women, children, soldiers, oxen, horses, wagons of every description from great timber haulers to tiny go-carts scarcely big enough for a baby mill about at the water's edge.

Suddenly, Martha St. John hears a loud groan from the multitude and, turning, sees tall pillars of brown smoke billowing above the treetops. As the refugees realize that their homes are being destroyed, a sound of wailing and sobbing, mingled with women's shrieks, ripples across the crowd.

The Bemises are among the last to get across the river; after nineteen trips, James Johnson, the ferryman, gives up and follows the others in their flight. The family's destination is a tavern at the little community of Willink. Three miles before they can reach it, the wagon breaks down. The three St. John sisters, Margaret, Parnell, and Martha, decide to trudge on through the deep snow, leaving the Bemis couple and the four younger children to spend the night in the cart. As they pick their way along the strange road their nerves are shaken by a weird spectacle: wads of burning matter from Buffalo, born on the wind, hurtle over their heads like meteors.

It is past dawn when, numb with cold, they finally reach the tavern. In a large room in front of a log fire they recognize their neighbours. Here are the two Chapin girls, who have walked ten miles from Buffalo through the snow. And here is the family of Samuel Pratt, whose wife, Sophia, seeing Martha blue with cold, takes the girl in her arms by the fire and rubs her frostbitten fingers. There is breakfast for all, for the resourceful Mrs. Pratt was in the act of baking bread when the alarm sounded; she stuffed the dough into a pillowcase and brought it with her.

Shortly afterwards the rest of the St. John family arrives, carried by the two horses, having spent a ghastly night in the cold.

In the days that follow, the widow St. John struggles to save her cottage. The British are determined to burn every house in Buffalo as well as all public buildings, army stores, and—this is the official reason for the attack—four schooners from Perry's fleet, which are stranded for the winter at the river's mouth.

The morning after the attack, the St. John barn goes up in flames.

"They say I must burn your barn," cries old Pettigrew, the hired man, wiping his eyes.

"Oh well," says Mrs. St. John, "it cannot be helped." He takes a burning brand from the hearth and sets it on fire.

They cannot save the big house, which is her livelihood. When the British first fire it, she and her daughters struggle to extinguish the flames with pails of water from the well. But the respite is brief.

In vain Mrs. St. John exclaims that the British, by burning the hotel, are destroying her income.

"We have left you one roof, and that is more than the Americans left for our widows when they came over," she is reminded. The St. John hotel goes up in flames, as does the Lovejoy home next door, corpse and all; thus are the Canadians avenged for the burning of Newark.

The flames of Buffalo die down, but this is not the end. Fire breeds fire, revenge seeds more revenge. Before this war is ended, more homes will be put to the torch on both sides of the border, from the humblest cottage to the executive mansion of the President himself.

The British depart, keeping a garrison in Fort Niagara. The people of Buffalo trickle home to the blackened ruins of their village. The St. John children are shocked at the spectacle before them: all that is left of their big house are the cellar walls, two chimneys, and the front step. The frontier from Buffalo through Black Rock to Eighteen Mile Creek is a blackened smear. The British have destroyed 333 buildings. In Buffalo only three are still stand-ing—the jail and the blacksmith shop, which would not burn, and the little cottage on Main Street, just twenty-two feet square, that the widow St. John, through the force of her will, managed, against all odds, to preserve.

EIGHT

Marking Time

January to June, 1814

With the burning of Buffalo, the campaign of 1813 ends. It is again too cold to fight. Since the war began, only a few square miles of territory have changed hands: the British hold Michilimackinac Island; the Americans occupy Amherstburg. Both sides change their high commands and prepare for another invasion, neither knowing where it will come. On Lake Ontario and Lake Champlain the rival navies engage in a new shipbuilding contest, constructing the world's largest lake vessels. And in St. Petersburg, Russia, three American diplomats try vainly to negotiate for peace with the British, with the Tsar as mediator.

ST. PETERSBURG, RUSSIA, JANUARY 6, 1814

The Russian Christmas. It is bitterly cold; the Fahrenheit thermometer shows twenty-five below. A skin of ice glitters on the colossal bronze statue of Peter the Great; a crust of snow sheaths the cornice of the church of St. Catherine; a frieze of icicles droops from the carved façades of the Hermitage and the Winter Palace. On the gravelled promenades, the snow squeaks beneath the runners of the one-horse sleighs that dart along the frigid banks of the Neva.

It is eleven o'clock. Above the great colonnade of the new church of Our Lady of Kazan—perhaps the most magnificent building in the city—the bells are ringing for a *Te Deum* to mark the recent successes of the Allies over Napoleon. Just one year ago, all Europe was opposed to Russia; now all Europe is with her in the holy crusade against the French. Wellington is through the Pyrenees and into France—and the Iberian peninsula is lost to Bonaparte. Blücher and Bernadotte have stopped him at Leipzig. The Continental system is smashed, the Empire crumbling.

Within the great church, dwarfed by the lofty domes, the gigantic columns, the gargantuan icons, a thin congregation listens to a proclamation from the Tsar, read by a chamberlain. The Russian Emperor is absent at army headquarters in Frankfurt, but the Empress is here, of course, and several grand dukes and at least one grand duchess. The diplomatic corps, however, is poorly represented. Thus the three Americans present, in their blue and gold uniforms (newly designed for such occasions), are more than usually conspicuous and more than usually uncomfortable. The church doors are continually opening and shutting, and after two hours of hymns, prayers, and chanting, they are thoroughly chilled.

The trio's discomfort is more than physical. Two are fed up with Russia, and each is fed up with the others' company. They are supposed to be treating for peace through the good offices of the Emperor Alexander, but now, with Napoleon approaching final defeat, peace with England seems nearly as distant as the Emperor himself. For almost six months they have waited for some official word: will the British agree to accept Alexander as a mediator in the dispute with their former colony? They are fairly certain that the answer is No, but it has not come officially; so they remain, diplomatic prisoners, shackled to a chill environment by the constraints of protocol.

All three are distinguished public servants, but none more distinguished than the leader of the delegation, John Quincy Adams, an old Russia hand who has been Minister Plenipotentiary here in

St. Petersburg since 1809. Son of the second president of his country, a former senator, he has only recently turned down a confirmed appointment to the Supreme Court.

See him now, standing rigidly beneath the vaulted dome (for, as one of his colleagues has ruefully observed, no one sits down in a Russian church)—a short, stout figure of forty-six, the humourless face as chilly as the Russian winter, the high, bald pate gleaming like polished marble. If he is impatient with the interminable ceremony he gives no sign; yet for Adams this is time pirated from intellectual inquiry. He begrudges every wasted moment, does his best to stay out of society's grasp, rises before six, beds down early, feels a sense of overpowering guilt if he cannot spend at least five hours daily in reading and study. He gobbles up everything: science, philosophy, the classics, the Bible. No night passes in which he does not set out the minutiae of the day in a voluminous journal. In this exhaustive work every official gesture is recorded along with his own reading and observations—everything save his deepest, most intimate emotions. Gazing at the sky one frosty November night in 1813, he observes a constellation that he cannot identify, marks down the position on a slip of paper, leafs through Lalande's *Astronomy*, discovers to his discomfiture that it is the constellation Orion—one familiar to every schoolboy. *Mortification!* To be ignorant of something he should have known thirty years before! He must, of course, record his own humiliation in his journal: "I am ashamed at my age," he writes, "to be thus to seek for the very first elements of practical astronomy."

To James Ashton Bayard, standing next to him, Adams is the coldest of fish: "He has little talent for society and does [not] appear to enjoy it. His address is singularly cold and repulsive. His manners are harsh and you seldom perceive the least effort to please anyone." These first impressions, expressed a few days after his initial encounter with Adams, have hardened during the ensuing months, exacerbated no doubt by Bayard's own ill health (a concomitant of the wretched Russian weather) and his increasing homesickness.

As senators, Bayard and Adams were political opponents and, in a sense, still are. Bayard, a Federalist, was originally opposed to the war but, unlike some of his colleagues, supported the government once the declaration was made. He knows that the war—"a hopeless project"—has been tearing his country apart and feels it his solemn duty "not to refuse to the government any means in my power which could aid in extricating the Country from its embarrassments." Of the three envoys he is the least sophisticated—a tall, greying senator from Delaware, ill at ease in court circles, unable to make small talk in diplomatic French, unaccustomed to the finger-bowl etiquette of multi-course banquets.

The third member of the trio, Albert Gallatin, is Bayard's direct opposite, an alert and cultured Genevan who has served his adopted country as Secretary of the Treasury for almost thirteen years. He is fluent in French, witty, and has no trouble fitting into the Russian social routine, which, beginning as it does at two in the afternoon and ending at two or three the following morning, encourages the kind of late rising that is anathema to Bayard and Adams. Yet Gallatin is no lie-abed. Of the three, his mind is the sharpest, his diplomatic talents the most polished. He is about to turn fifty-three, a swarthy, compact figure with a flat, forthright face and a prominent nose. Nor has his career reached its peak: more than three decades of public service lie before him.

Gallatin and Bayard share apartments in the same building—the best rooms in the city—but each man keeps to himself, the two scarcely speaking except on official business, each going his own way in a separate carriage. On this Christmas night, with the *Te Deum* finally at an end, Bayard makes his way to Adams's quarters to pour out his resentment at his fellow lodger, who he imagines has adopted a superior air toward him. Gallatin, at the moment, is in a curious position. He has only recently learned that the Senate has refused to ratify his appointment as envoy. Though the Russians continue to treat him as a diplomat, he is, in fact, only a private citizen. Bayard does not trust him. He is convinced that Gallatin, on his return to Washington, will blame the failure of the peace negotiations on the Senate's rejection.

Adams does not yet know it, but Bayard has been making equally unkind remarks about him, Adams, in private. After six months in the Russian capital, Bayard is at the end of his tether. At first it was all very novel, very entrancing. The orphan boy from Philadelphia, sought out with his colleagues for special treatment by his Russian hosts ("a rare act of civility not heretofore experienced by any Foreigner"), was subjected to a glittering circuit of architectural wonders—palace after palace, church after church, museum after museum. There were country weekends in dazzling châteaux, theatre parties, operas, recitals, and, above all, banquets where under glistening chandeliers he rubbed shoulders with dukes and duchesses, counts and countesses, princes and princesses, never at ease with the gold and silver plate, never certain of which arm to offer to what lady. He quickly tired of all this magnificence: "There is nothing so homely in my own Country, the sight of which would not please me better. . . ."

As Bayard's exile lengthened, the social circus palled the more. The waters of the Neva brought on attacks of diarrhea. The Russian women began to look unattractive. Their dress he found tasteless, their dinners laborious; the weather was "gloomy and detestable" and the people "as cold as their climate in its most frosty season."

For Gallatin, who moves easily among the nobility—staying for supper at the homes of his hosts, playing endless games of Boston, strolling through the gardens with the ladies, joking in his exquisite French—the long wait is just as frustrating. He has not come here to socialize but to try to end a war that neither side wants to continue.

Yet it does continue, for there is the matter of national honour. The Americans have no intention of asking the British to discuss peace terms; they must never be seen to come on bended knee! On the contrary, they hope to get a good deal more out of the peace agreement than they originally expected. James Monroe, the American Secretary of State, believes that the United States can annex all or most of Canada as it has recently acquired Louisiana. It would be, he argues, in Great Britain's best interests because she would no longer have to bear the expense of supporting her North American colonies. The Americans, in fact, are prepared to offer advantages in trade as part of the bargain.

But all this depends on the British accepting the mediation that Alexander I, Emperor of Russia, has happily extended. There is the rub. It has long been obvious to the three envoys that the British have no intention of accepting the offer—have, indeed, officially rejected it. From the British point of view, the war in North America is a family quarrel to be settled directly between the belligerents without the interference of a foreign potentate. The Americans have already been made aware of this, but until they hear *officially*—from the Tsar himself—it would be a breach of protocol to leave the country, a rebuff to a friendly nation. And so the war goes on; men die in the mud of Crysler's Farm and the swamps of Châteauguay; women and children shiver, homeless, in the snows of Newark and Buffalo; farm boys cough out their lives in the tattered tents of French Mills.

The situation is complicated by the war in Europe, the difficulty and slowness of communication, the byzantine manoeuvrings of the Russian court, and the Emperor's own vain, wistful fancy that, in the end, the British may come round. The envoys have never met Alexander; he is hundreds of miles away, his days fully occupied with the problem of Napoleon. Their only contact with the Russian Emperor is through his foreign minister, the courtly Count Romanzoff, who is, unfortunately, so out of favour with his royal master that he is not always aware of what is going on.

The envoys have been trapped in the sunless Russian capital since July. Now it is January and still no word from the Tsar of all the Russias—a sign of poor Romanzoff's fall from grace. The delay is maddening. A letter takes two months to reach Washington; that means a four-month hiatus before any report can be acknowledged. News of the war is obtained tardily from the English newspapers. In the American view, these are dreadfully biased, although it has not been possible to disguise the magnitude of Barclay's defeat on Lake Erie. But the Americans have yet to learn of Wilkinson's disastrous attempt on Montreal or of the attacks along the Niagara frontier.

Gallatin, who now considers himself a private citizen no longer bound by official etiquette, is determined to leave as soon as possible. Bayard wants to leave with him—an intention that offends

Adams's sense of protocol. Adams is also irked to learn that the pair are planning to visit the Emperor Alexander at Frankfurt and then proceed to London, apparently to sound out the British on the subject of direct peace talks. The fact that the two have concocted the plan behind his back annoys him almost as much as the plan itself. For Adams is convinced that neither man can do any good by going to England "unless our Government has totally changed its principles."

The rock on which any peace negotiations must founder, in Adams's view, is the matter of impressment. The forcible seizure of British deserters from American ships on the high seas is the only remaining reason for this savage border war. Madison has explicitly told his envoys that the question of impressment cannot be set aside. But the British have flatly announced that they will refuse to discuss it. After their weary internment in the Russian capital, both Gallatin and Bayard have softened on the matter. Their inclination now is to yield; it seems the only way peace can be obtained.

Meanwhile, Adams helps Bayard prepare a note to Count Romanzoff that will allow him to leave the country without creating an international incident. He is determined to depart on the twenty-first—six months to the day after his arrival. Delicate negotiations follow; more "notes"—the mortar of diplomacy—are exchanged. On the eighteenth a note arrives from the Count indicating that if Bayard sends another note asking for an audience of leave, he can immediately quit Russia. "No words can express my joy," he scribbles in his diary. Off goes the note on the twentieth. Back comes another on the twenty-first: the Empress Mother will receive him on the twenty-third.

On that day, a Sunday, the dowager receives him. They discuss the war, agree on the hope that it will not last long. *We know you are against the war*, the Empress murmurs . . . *and that you should be glad of.* He presses his lips to her wrinkled paw, bows his way out, moves on to the apartments of the Grand Dukes Nicholas and Michael and the Grand Duchess Ann, nibbles at their outstretched knuckles. Finally, he is free.

The following day, a little procession takes off for the west—
Bayard in a four-horse calèche, Gallatin in a four-horse carriage,
six servants bringing up the rear in a six-horse landau. Somehow
Gallatin's carriage becomes separated on leaving the city, runs into
a snowbank, and is stalled for several hours. Bayard trots on. It will
be May, and the start of a new campaign along the embattled border,
before the two reach London.

John Quincy Adams is relieved to see the last of them. In his view,
three heads are not better than one. The endless, niggling arguments
over the precise phrasing of diplomatic notes is such that one took
an entire week to compose; Adams is convinced that he could have
done it alone in two hours. "In the multitude of counsellors there is
safety," he has noted, "but there is not despatch." It is a portent of
things to come.

In the frustrating months of waiting, Adams, the clear thinker,
the scientific dabbler, the cool logician, has come perilously close to
paranoia, half-convinced that his two colleagues, who make a habit
of going directly to Count Romanzoff, are conspiring behind his
back, trying to manoeuvre him out of the peace negotiations—a suspicion reinforced by their joint trip to London. Now a few days after
their departure, the consul, Levitt Harris, comes to him to report
what Bayard has been saying behind his back. The alleged remarks
are scarcely damaging, but they fuel Adams's own suspicions that
Bayard has also been turning Gallatin against him. He tells Harris
that he hopes "never again to be placed in relations which would
make it necessary to associate with Mr. Bayard." It is a vain fancy.
When peace negotiations finally begin the two men will find themselves colleagues once more. But many months will pass and much
blood be spilled before that becomes a reality.

YORK, UPPER CANADA, FEBRUARY 15, 1814

In the charred capital, His Honour, the President of the Legislative
Council and Administrator of the Province, is pleased to open the
session of both houses with what the official proceedings will describe

(as always) as "a most gracious speech." The setting is new—Jordan's Hotel and Tavern must do duty as a public edifice now that the Parliament Buildings lie in ashes—and so is the President himself, who has come down from Kingston for the occasion.

He is Lieutenant-General Gordon Drummond, an unknown quantity to the handful of legislators assembled to hear him (their number depleted by capture and disaffection). They know, of course, that he is a Canadian, the first native-born general officer to take command of both the army and the civil government. He is forty-two, a New Brunswicker who has been a soldier since the age of seventeen. He must have military talent: he rose from lieutenant to colonel in just three years. His regiment, the famous 8th or King's, saw bloody action in Holland and continued to distinguish itself under its Canadian leader in the West Indies, the Mediterranean, and Egypt.

Since 1811, Drummond has been Sir George Prevost's second-in-command in Canada. Clearly he is made of sterner stuff than the despised Sheaffe or the easy-going De Rottenburg. But is he another Brock? He is certainly as handsome as Brock—with his angular, chiselled face, his thin aristocratic nose, and his dark, tight curls. (Does he use a curling iron in the fashion of the time?) John Strachan, the armchair general, who is not a member of the legislature but whose long shadow hangs over it, has reservations. Drummond, Strachan finds, is an excellent man "and a very superior private character," but somehow he lacks Brock's panache. "He seems to be destitute of that military fire and vigour of decision which the principal commander of this country must possess in order to preserve it. . . ."

Nonetheless, in his speech to the legislature Drummond is forthright. He knows what he wants. He wants one-third of each militia regiment embodied for up to twelve months' military service. He wants the wretched provincial roads improved. He wants to continue the practice of banning all distillation of grain, for the province is teetering on the edge of starvation and every kernel of wheat, oats, and rye is needed for food. Most of all he is concerned about disaffection. The jail at York is bursting with prisoners accused of treason and sedition. The population is heavily American—at best apathetic, at worst disloyal.

So Drummond demands stern measures: a denial of the right of *habeas corpus* in certain cases; the right to confiscate the property of convicted traitors; the right to enforce martial law when necessary. The legislature allows him the first two. When it denies him the third Drummond makes it very clear who is in charge. His executive council, which he dominates (it has been reduced to three members), hastily gives him the power he seeks. He expects the lower house to censure him for it, as it censured De Rottenburg, but without it he cannot impress provisions for his troops from the reluctant settlers. Democracy, such as it is in Upper Canada, goes out the window as Drummond shows his iron fist.

He feels shackled by lack of money. At Long Point and Port Dover, debts incurred by Brock eighteen months before have yet to be paid. In consequence, the settlers will not sell their produce to the army. Small debts cannot be discharged because neither coinage nor army bills are available in denominations under twenty-five pounds. If a merchant is owed twenty pounds, he collects nothing; if he is owed forty pounds, he loses fifteen. What money does come in is scarcely enough to pay off old debts. As a result, Drummond is forced to accept loans from York merchants to cover the spending.

There are further complications: Canadians, prejudiced against paper money, want gold because the Americans are flooding the country with forged bills. There is also the problem of compensation. Everybody from John Crysler on the St. Lawrence to Isaac Dolsen on the Thames is demanding relief for war damages. Early in March, with the legislature still in session, Drummond pays a flying visit to the Thames Valley and returns to report that the entire region has been drained of its resources. There is no house that does not have a claim for reparations. The mills have been burned, the houses looted, the livestock killed or dispersed. Drummond estimates that at least thirty thousand pounds will be needed just to pay existing obligations.

The troops are in a state of discontent over the lack of pay. Some have received nothing for six months. At Fort Niagara, the captured stronghold on the American side of the river, Colonel Robert Young reports an increasing number of desertions among soldiers who are usually steady and well behaved. Pay is not the only problem. The men of Drummond's old regiment, the King's, are suffering so badly from ague and dysentery that the regiment's medical officer recommends its immediate removal. By mid-March, Major-General Riall, Vincent's replacement, reports that desertions have been increasing to an alarming degree from "that cursed Fort," as he calls it.

Riall wants to reduce the garrison and decrease the area of the fort. But Drummond has no intention of abandoning his toehold on the American bank of the Niagara. When the invasion comes, the five or six hundred men hived in the fort can stand off at least ten times their number. The best Drummond can do is to replace the King's with another regiment. Meanwhile, Riall must hold his thin line along the river, as Brock did before him, and be prepared to deploy at the moment the enemy's invasion point is known.

As soon as the river and the lakes are open the British 103rd will reinforce Riall's Centre Division (now called the Right). Drummond does not relay to Riall Prevost's assessment of that regiment: ". . . men who [have] long lost sight of everything that is honest and honourable. Convicts taken from the hulks to be made soldiers— but who answer to no other purpose than that of bringing the profession into discredit and disrepute. . . ." Of all the corps last sent to Canada, Prevost believes the 103rd to be the worst. On a recent foray to destroy American stores and river craft, fifty-one of its members deserted to the enemy.

Drummond has no idea where the Americans will strike. Their movements, are, to say the least, confusing. The best part of an American division has moved from French Mills (Wilkinson's winter quarters) to Sackets Harbor and then on toward the Niagara frontier, only to turn about and march back again. Drummond cannot know it, but this is the result of an ambiguous order sent by the Secretary of War and misinterpreted by Jacob Brown. Drummond determines to sit tight, maintain his main force at Burlington Heights, and when the American intentions are known, march at the head of his army to reinforce Major-General Riall's slender defence along the Niagara.

At the moment, the weather is his enemy. An unexpected mild spell in February has frustrated a daring and unconventional attack that Drummond planned against the American fleet, wintering at Put-in Bay. The plan called for seventeen hundred men to hack a road through the forest, seize Amherstburg, cross the Detroit River, and push on to attack the ships with bill hooks, hatchets, and muskets. But the ice is too soft and the expedition must be aborted. At the same time the weather along the Niagara is so bad, the snow so deep, that no progress can be made to strengthen "that cursed Fort."

In mid-March, Drummond prorogues the legislature and returns to his headquarters at Kingston. One further problem continues to occupy him: he is convinced that some exemplary trials are needed "to overawe the spirit of disaffection in the province." John Beverley Robinson, the youthful acting attorney general, is preparing abstracts against some thirty persons for high treason. Most have left the country, but there are eight or nine who he believes can be convicted. An additional twenty remain to be indicted. These will be civil trials. As Robinson points out, "Executions of traitors by military power would have comparatively little influence. The majority of people would consider them arbitrary acts of punishment."

The accused traitors are Canadian civilians who joined groups of armed American raiders under Joseph Willcocks's second-in-command, Mallory, during the guerrilla activity the previous November. Captured by the Oxford and Norfolk militia during two encounters at Port Dover and Chatham, they have been languishing in the York jail, waiting to be tried by a special commission.

Robinson is convinced that the trial must take place as close to the homes of the accused as possible—in the London district. He well knows that the settlers in that region are generally indifferent to the interests of the autocratic government at York (in which they have little real say) and, if not indifferent, are often actively pro-American. But now the war has come to their doorstep. Willcocks, Mallory, Markle have all conducted raids on their settlements, robbing them of cattle and household goods, burning barns and homes, making prisoners of those neighbours who have joined the militia. The accused are known to them as men who actively supported the raiding parties. Some of the prospective jurors, in Robinson's words, "voluntarily resorted to arms to subdue them." Therefore it is fair to suppose that "men who risqued their lives in the apprehension of these traitors will be well satisfied to have them punished as they deserve."

To all this Drummond assents. He is anxious to have the trials take place as swiftly and as publicly as possible. For the future security of the province, a number of unfortunate farmers are shortly to be brought before a jury of their peers at the Union Hotel in Ancaster (for the London district is held to be too close to the border) and, in accordance with the ancient law still on the statute books, to be hanged, drawn, and quartered if found guilty. Nothing else, the authorities are convinced, will serve to stiffen the spines of a wavering population.

GOTHENBURG, SWEDEN, APRIL 14, 1814

Henry Clay, Speaker of the House of Representatives, and his colleague, Jonathan Russell, the two newest members of what is now a five-man American peace commission, step off the gangplank of the U.S. corvette *John Adams*, which has brought them here from New York. Since the bay is choked with ice and the river frozen, they must travel twelve miles by sleigh to reach their lodgings in the heart of the town, where they confidently expect to meet the three other plenipotentiaries, now charged with dealing directly with the British—but on neutral ground.

But where *are* the others? Where are Adams, Bayard, and Gallatin, the original threesome who are to form part of the expanded commission? And where are the British negotiators? Nobody knows. Clay and Russell dispatch notes to Amsterdam and St. Petersburg informing the missing trio of their new appointment. A week passes before they learn that Bayard and Gallatin are in London. As for

Adams, he has not yet left the Russian capital, but long before the letter can reach him he will be off to Reval on the Gulf of Finland, waiting for the ice to shift in the Baltic. Men of goodwill on both sides have been murmuring about peace in North America for the best part of a year, but the possibility of any face-to-face negotiation seems as remote as ever.

The five wanderers have been chosen partly for their public stature, partly for their negotiating ability, partly for what they represent. Adams and Bayard are both known to be, in James Monroe's words, "friendly to peace"—especially Bayard, a confirmed Federalist, whose party has always opposed the war. Russell and Clay are in the other camp, notably the silver-tongued Clay who, as leader of the War Hawks, helped goad the country into war in 1812. Monroe, the Secretary of State, has regional considerations also in mind. Thus Adams represents the Eastern states, Bayard the Middle, Clay the South and West, and Russell the commercial interests. As for Gallatin, as a former member of the Cabinet he stands as a buffer, the great conciliator between hawks and doves, eastern and western interests. For the negotiators must negotiate with each other as well as with the enemy.

Clay comes to Gothenburg reluctantly. He would much rather remain in Washington as Speaker, but he cannot in conscience resist this call to public service. America needs tough-minded men who will stand up to the nefarious British, and Clay is nothing if not tough-minded. It is possible to believe that without his persistence in the winter of 1811–12, the United States might not have gone to war.

His instructions and those of his colleagues are clear. The most important item on the future agenda is that of impressment. "This degrading practice must cease; our flag must protect the crew; or the United States cannot consider themselves an independent Nation." The words are Monroe's, but they might easily have sprung from Clay's own lips in the months before war was declared. Impressment is what this brutal, frustrating, inconclusive war is all about—that and the British Orders in Council establishing a blockade on the high seas. Those Orders were repealed, not at the eleventh hour, alas, but at the thirteenth, a tardiness on Britain's part that frustrated any hope of peace. Now, however, Monroe and his president, James Madison, are insisting that the whole matter of blockades—their legality and illegality—be settled by formal treaty.

Third, but not least, is the question of Canada. Here the American government's view has hardened. Canada—or at least part of it—must be ceded to the Union. Joint use of the Great Lakes will surely mean another war; it was in those common waters that the British gained control of the Indians with the resultant massacres: "The cupidity of the British Traders will admit of no control. The inevitable consequences of another war, and even of the present, if persevered in by the British Government, must be to sever those provinces by force from Great Britain. Their inhabitants themselves, will soon feel their strength, and assert their independence."

Nothing can be settled, however, until the British appoint negotiators, and this has not been done. Clay is eager to get started, but events seem to be moving at the speed of treacle. He wants Gallatin and Bayard to get to Gothenburg as quickly as possible. What are they doing in the enemy capital, anyway? Yet neither man shows any sign of moving, while Russell, the former American chargé d'affaires in London, must go off to Stockholm to present his credentials as American ambassador to Sweden. Like Adams, he will hold two jobs at the same time.

So Clay frets, all alone, in Gothenburg. He is not used to sitting still, has none of John Quincy Adams's cool patience. (That earnest diplomat is bettering himself in Reval waiting for the ice to break by working his way through the Duc de Sully's interminable memoirs of life under Henry IV of France.) Clay, the hot-tempered Kentuckian, is used to getting his way, whether in a duel, a poker game, or on the floor of the House. Now, as he paces impatiently about his new lodgings—a lank, nervous figure, his long, bony face reflecting his frustration—he must know that events have overtaken him, "wonderful events . . . astonishing events," to be sure, but events, nevertheless, that may have an adverse effect on the peace talks.

He is scarcely in Gothenburg a week before the news filters through that the Allies have seized Paris (on March 31), that Napoleon has abdicated, and that a new Bourbon king, Louis XVIII, is about to ascend the throne. Clay is bowled over by this dramatic and unexpected news. Napoleon, the master of Europe for more than a decade, humbled and shipped off to an obscure Mediterranean isle! Clay has anticipated peace, but *this*—this is like a revolution! No human sagacity could have foreseen it, he tells the American ambassador in Paris.

Bayard and Gallatin, who arrived in London in the midst of its delirium over Bonaparte's downfall, report to Clay some of the new facts of life. As the bells peal and the rockets explode and the people cheer the end of twenty years of war, Gallatin explains that "the complete success obtained by this country in their European contest has excited the greatest popular exultation, and this has been attended with a strong expression of resentment against the United States."

The popular feeling is entirely in favour of continuing the war. People talk of taking over the Great Lakes, pushing back the American border, dividing the Union by seducing New England back into the Imperial fold. The British now have a seasoned army sitting idle, which they cannot demobilize too quickly, as well as a superabundant naval force. The people are demanding "the chastisement of America," and even though their political leaders are less eager to continue the war, "they will not, certainly, be disposed to make concessions, nor probably displeased at a failure of negotiations." Impressment will never be repealed.

In spite of Clay's earnest hope that he will shortly leave London for Gothenburg, Gallatin is determined to stay, hoping to open direct negotiations with the British leaders, especially Lord Castlereagh, the foreign secretary.

Indeed, it has become clear that the Swedish city is the wrong place for negotiations. The British much prefer a neutral town— in Holland, say—as close as possible to London, for it is obvious that the real negotiations will be in the hands of Lord Liverpool, the Prime Minister, Lord Bathurst, the colonial secretary, and Castlereagh. Whoever are chosen as plenipotentiaries will be little more than messenger boys for the trio of peers at Whitehall. Both Gallatin and Bayard are agreed on the need for a change of location.

Meanwhile Clay receives disturbing news from Crawford, the American ambassador in Paris, who tells him that unless America either excludes the whole question of impressment from the agenda, or at least agrees to postpone it, there is no chance for any peace negotiation. The matter, he points out delicately, has become largely academic: the European war is over; Britain has too many sailors, does not need to impress anyone.

There is more. The news of Wilkinson's disgrace the previous November on the St. Lawrence has placed "all the continental powers under the direct influence of our enemy." The posturing general has turned America's potential friends against her.

The British are taking their own time naming envoys to the peace talks, which, it is finally decided, will be held at Ghent in Belgium. At last, on May 15, Christopher Hughes, secretary to the American mission, who has begged to go to London, learns unofficially who they are to be: Admiral Gambier, "a Mr. Golsby (or Goldburn)," and a Mr. Adams. They are, in short, nonentities, unknown to the Americans, equally unknown to the British public.

Admiral James Gambier, aged fifty-eight, is a blundering and sedentary flag officer with remarkably little sea experience (less than six years), known as much for his failures as for his successes, as well as for his piety and his narrow morality, which some call hypocrisy.

Henry Goulburn is so little known that Hughes, among others, gets his name wrong. He is an under-secretary for war and the colonies, a run-of-the-mill diplomat at thirty but more forceful than his two colleagues.

William Adams is an obscure Admiralty lawyer, placed on the commission because of his expertise in maritime law, on which much of the future negotiation is expected to hinge.

The choice of this threesome suggests two British attitudes. First, they hold the Americans in contempt. The United States has sent a first-class team of plenipotentiaries to Europe; the British have responded with second-class negotiators. Second, as suspected, the real decisions will be made by Great Britain in Whitehall, not at Ghent. But the British, in their hauteur, have placed themselves at a disadvantage. Their choices are no match for five tough, high-powered Americans.

In Gothenburg, winter gives way to spring, but Henry Clay is in no mood to bask in the zephyrs of late May. With Russell still in Stockholm he is all alone, his sense of isolation aggravated by a lack of knowledge of the outside world. Two weeks have passed without news from England, and the last letter could scarcely have improved his temper—a burbling report from Hughes, the commission secretary, exclaiming over the beauty of the English lawns and gardens, the extraordinary size of the capital, and "the perfect state of cultivation" of the countryside. Clay does not need this kind of report from enemy territory; it is bad enough to be cooped up here in a foreign town whose very Englishness has given it the sobriquet of "Little London."

Clay is eager now for peace, as he once was for war, but events are moving at a crawl. The boredom is driving him to distraction. He has no one to talk to, having dispatched his secretary to Amsterdam to intercept the latest news from Washington. Adams is somewhere in mid-Baltic among the ice floes, a fortnight overdue. Hughes remains in London, against Clay's wishes, goggling over the estates of the aristocrats. Gallatin is there too, still trying to see the Tsar of Russia, who has thus far eluded him—still hoping to get the negotiations moving. Bayard has set out for Ghent but has got no farther than Paris. "Perhaps never was a joint mission so disjointed & scattered," Russell remarks in a moody letter from Stockholm.

Clay will not soon find an outlet for his frustration. Two more months will slip by before the British and Americans finally meet face to face at the Hôtel d'Alcantara in Ghent. Meanwhile, the same spring that brings a bloom to the pasque flower in Sweden heralds a renewal of the war in Canada. Men are dying from musket fire and round shot, and the bloodiest battles still lie ahead.

Lieutenant-General Gordon Drummond has come down from Kingston to board Commodore James Yeo's spanking new flagship, *Prince Regent*. His purpose: to reconnoitre the Americans' chief naval base and centre of operations. Yeo and his opposite number, the sleepy-eyed Chauncey—those two "heroes of defeat," in Winfield Scott's sardonic phrase—have both declined to fight a decisive battle. Theirs has been a war, instead, of carpenters and shipwrights. All winter long at Kingston and Sackets Harbor, hundreds of men have been hammering at vessels that will never fight, each one bigger and better armed than the last. Now Drummond intends to discover how far the American shipbuilding program has progressed and, if possible, to frustrate it.

He would dearly love to mount an all-out attack on Sackets Harbor, wreck the garrison, and destroy Chauncey's partly built fleet. That would give the British undisputed control of Lake Ontario, where the fortunes of war have see-sawed over the past eighteen months. But the base is well fortified. Drummond needs at least eight hundred reinforcements to make the attempt. These the cautious governor general Sir George Prevost has denied him, fearing that it would denude Lower Canada of regular troops, leaving Montreal open to American capture.

Drummond arrives aboard *Prince Regent* to find Yeo lying in his cabin, prostrated by illness (as who is not in this war of invalids?). The following morning, May 25, the General sets off in a canoe to look over the harbour. He approaches within a mile and a half, peers through his glass, observes that Chauncey's new vessels have their topgallants across and are ready to take to the lake except for the largest ship, *Superior*, which is not yet rigged.

Once this sixty-four-gun double-decker is launched, the two fleets will again be almost equal in firepower. All winter long the rival commanders have struggled to outbuild each other. When Chauncey learns that Yeo is constructing the largest ship ever to ply an inland

671
—
FLAMES
ACROSS
THE
BORDER

lake—almost as large as Nelson's *Victory*—he orders that his own flagship be increased in size. When Yeo, in reply, undertakes to build the largest ship in the world—*St. Lawrence*, a gigantic three-decker, mounting 120 guns—Chauncey makes plans to go him one better.

The road from Albany to Sackets is jammed with wagon trains hauling supplies for the new fleet. On Canada's Atlantic coast, four sloops of war are laid up in order to supply seamen for the vessels being built at Kingston. Every skilled carpenter in Montreal has been rounded up to work on the British fleet. At Sackets Harbor, four hundred shipwrights are toiling in shifts. The cost on both sides is horrendous. The British have secretly hired two hundred ox teams from Vermont and New Hampshire to haul guns and cable to Kingston. It costs two thousand pounds to bring six thirty-two-pounders into the naval yard, a thousand pounds to haul in a single large cable from Sorel. Small wonder that the government's bills in Upper Canada go unpaid.

Shortly after Drummond returns to *Prince Regent*, one of his spies confirms his assessment. *Superior* is still short of heavy guns, rigging, and cable, all held up at Oswego Falls because of the British blockade. As long as the fleet lurks outside the harbour, these essentials, which can be moved only by water, are denied to Chauncey: his biggest ship lies helpless and unarmed.

The American commander, however, has a plan to run the blockade using nineteen bateaux, which move at night, hide in small inlets by day. Drummond discovers the scheme, sends off a detachment of gunboats to capture the blockade runners. The Americans flee up a winding creek, the Big Sandy, and ambush their pursuers, killing, wounding, or capturing the entire British force. From this point the Americans haul their cannon, cable, and supplies sixteen miles overland to the shipyard. With the naval balance about to change again on the lake, Drummond and Yeo call off the blockade.

Will the enemy now attack Yeo before his great ship, still building at Kingston, is ready? Drummond does not believe they will—not until *their* great ship is ready. Even then, he suggests, they are unlikely to seek an encounter. He advises Yeo to stay on the defensive until the mighty *St. Lawrence* is ready to sail. Then, perhaps, the British can venture out of Kingston harbour and destroy the American fleet. Drummond does not consider a more likely possibility—that Chauncey, discovering Yeo's superiority, will commence construction of another ship to equal the odds, that Yeo will then follow suit, and that long after the war is over four more great vessels, all unfinished, never to be launched, will be on the ways at Kingston and Sackets Harbor, preparing to fight a battle that can never take place.

BUFFALO, NEW YORK, JUNE 4, 1814

Winfield Scott, newly promoted to brigadier-general, has been drilling his raw recruits unmercifully since March 24, preparing for an expected invasion of Canada. Now he draws up his brigade in a hollow square on the training ground to witness the execution of five men sentenced to be shot for desertion. The prisoners stand before them, dressed grotesquely in white robes—their winding sheets— with white caps on their heads and red targets over their hearts.

Five graves stand open before them. Beside each grave lies a coffin. Each of the condemned men is made to kneel between coffin and grave as the firing party approaches. For every prisoner there are twelve riflemen.

Officers load the weapons, return them to the firing party. The chaplain murmurs a short prayer. The white caps are pulled down over the eyes of the victims. As soon as the order is given, the guns explode and five men drop as one, some toppling into the open graves, others sprawling across their coffins. One struggles feebly. A sergeant approaches, aims the muzzle of his piece a yard from the victim's head, blows him into eternity.

Suddenly a murmur ripples across the ranks as one of the corpses slowly rises to his knees and is helped to his feet.

"By God," he says, "I thought I was dead!"

He has been judged too young to die. This is Brigadier-General Scott's blunt method of telling him he has been reprieved by having his men fire blank cartridges.

The gesture is typical of Scott, a harsh disciplinarian and self-taught tactician who has, at last, been given the command he has sought for so long. Brevetted a brigadier-general in March, he is now, at twenty-eight, the youngest general officer in the American army and the symbol of a new attitude. The tired veterans of another war—Hampton, Wilkinson, Dearborn, and others—are out of the army. John Armstrong has all but scrapped the stale tradition of seniority. George Izard, aged thirty-eight, has been promoted; so has Eleazar Ripley, aged thirty-two. And Jacob Brown, at thirty-nine, is now major-general in command of the Northern Army. Amos Hall no longer leads the New York militia. His replacement is Henry Clay's congressional crony and War Hawk, the ebullient Peter B. Porter.

In this new pantheon one name is unaccountably missing, that of William Henry Harrison, surely an able commander and, some believe, the best-qualified man to lead the new invasion. But Harrison has resigned. He cannot—*will* not—work under Armstrong, cannot abide the Secretary's repeated interference in his command. Armstrong, on his part, has accepted Harrison's resignation without demur. For the Secretary of War, William Henry Harrison is too independent.

The new head of the Northern Army, Jacob Brown, is an aggressive and imaginative commander but with little regular experience, and certainly no tactician. He remains at his headquarters at Sackets Harbor and leaves the training of the army to Winfield Scott at Buffalo. Scott is in his element. No more ambitious officer exists in the United States. For two years he has actively sought promotion, frustrated to the point of fury by the imbecilities—a typical Scott word—of the past two years. Compromised at Queenston Heights by a well-meaning but green commander, deserted by a craven militia, captured, and imprisoned by the British in the winter of 1812–13, held back during the attack on Fort George by the incompetence of Boyd, maddened by Wilkinson's posturing on the St. Lawrence, he is finally on his own, able at last to put into practice those military theories that he has soaked up from his voluminous reading.

He may not know everything about war, but he acts as if he does. His fellow officers shrink from arguments on tactics or strategy, for Scott is able at a moment's notice to clinch the debate by quoting an incontrovertible authority. His baggage wagon carries Scott's considerable library—a variety of military works, biographies of the great soldiers of history, and the latest texts on drill and strategy imported from Europe. In future years, when Scott is the nation's leading soldier, this will come to be known as "the Scott tradition."

In Scott, the army has found a remarkable commander. He is a little pompous and more than a little vain but has reason to be both. He has studied Greek, Latin, and French, rhetoric, metaphysics, mathematics, political economy, philosophy, and law. He is an omnivorous reader: Plutarch, Shakespeare, Milton, Adam Smith, John Locke. He rides well, holds his liquor, plays chess, knows how to keep a conversation going. He is also a gourmet who believes that a knowledge of good food and its preparation is one of the accomplishments of a gentleman and a soldier—a view not lost on the army cooks.

He is also pugnacious. As a boy of thirteen he defended his Quaker schoolteacher from a drunken brawler, knocking the man down with a single blow. A furrowed skull is evidence of a successful duel. In his full-dress uniform, the long-legged Scott—a towering six-foot-five—cuts a handsome figure and knows it. When he received his first uniform—a sartorial symphony of blue and gold, scarlet and white—he strutted for two hours before two full-length mirrors, admiring himself.

He is a man of colossal ego, superbly confident of his own abilities, which, happily for him, are considerable. Here at Buffalo his military library comes into its own. Since the government has not provided him with a text on infantry tactics, Scott has dug into his baggage to discover a dog-eared copy of the French regulations issued by Napoleon and has made it his military Bible. Since March he has been acting as a drill sergeant, beginning with the officers, teaching them to march in column and line, to wheel and deploy, to load and fire their muskets with some degree of efficiency, to charge with fixed bayonets.

For three months, ten hours a day, Scott drills his men, allowing nothing to interrupt him except darkness or rain. Once the officers are schooled, the lower ranks are put to work. In the morning, the corporals drill their squads. At eleven, the captains take over. At one the entire brigade, complete with officers and musicians, turns out for four more hours. To Jarvis Hanks the drummer boy, who has come overland from French Mills with his comrades, Winfield Scott is "the most thorough disciplinarian I ever saw."

There has been some grumbling and a flurry of desertions. But now with four corpses lying on the drill ground and a fifth prisoner fainting dead away from the shock of his resurrection, there will be no more. Indeed, officers and men alike are gaining a new respect for themselves, as well as for their commander, who now finds them "healthy, sober, cheerful and docile." Scott has left nothing to chance. A stickler for cleanliness, he has borne down so hard on sanitary conditions that the army has lost only two men from illness.

The camp is secure. Scott has organized night patrols, guards, sentinels, outposts. He insists on civility, etiquette, and courtesy and lays down rules to enforce "these indispensable outworks of subordination." Woe to the soldier who forgets to salute a junior lieutenant! Woe to the officer who fails to return the salute.

He also has at his command an intelligence arm—a small force of spies, which he personally directs. They are mainly Americans with friends living north of the border, or disaffected Canadians who can come and go fairly freely. Scott's practice is to throw them out to the rear of the British right flank as far as Burlington Heights and even to York. The spies hide in the homes of sympathizers who visit the British posts to find out for them what Scott wants to know.

Scott has at least one captive traitor in the British midst, an anonymous captain in one of the regular regiments who has volunteered to pass along military secrets. "I hold him," Scott tells Armstrong in his florid fashion, "by one of the strongest cords that bind the human heart—a sentiment of steady and determined revenge. I know his private history."

Thus, the new brigadier is able to inform the War Department in Washington of the exact British strength at York, Lake Simcoe, Burlington Heights, Fort George, Fort Niagara, Queenston, Chippawa, and Fort Erie. He has details of new fortifications, emplacements, blockhouses, supply depots. He knows the topography of the Niagara peninsula, the distance between communities, the state of the roads, the best places to effect a landing. In short, he is preparing for the next invasion of Canada, carefully and methodically. His men, in his own words, "sigh for orders to beat up the enemy's quarters."

Some, however, have carried the beating up too far in the smash-and-grab raids launched by the Americans along the shoreline of Lake Erie. Abraham Markle, the man who directs Scott's spies to the homes of dissident Canadians, is not above settling old scores—and therein lies danger. Markle is a crony of Joseph Willcocks, an officer in the Canadian Volunteers, a former member of the Upper Canadian legislature who defected about the same time as his fellow turncoat. He is responsible for urging that the homes of old Revolutionary Tories in the Long Point area be destroyed. On May 16, he guided a raiding party across the lake, ostensibly to destroy public property. Instead, it burned every house, barn, and private building between Port Dover and Turkey Point—an act of revenge, for their owners were among those who burned Buffalo the previous December.

That is too much for Scott. The last thing he wants is a continuation of the tit-for-tat incendiary war that flared up the previous winter. He calls a court of inquiry which disavows the act, but it is too late. Sir George Prevost is outraged; he has already indicated that as far as the British are concerned, vengeance for the destruction of Newark ended with the burning of Buffalo. Now he asks the navy, patrolling the eastern seaboard, to act to deter further American raids. Vice-Admiral Alexander Cochrane is happy to cooperate. He issues an order to "destroy and lay waste such towns and districts as you may find assailable. . . ." The firing of private property becomes official British policy. It will not be tempered until Washington itself is in flames.

It is late evening. From the open window of the dining room in Weisinger's Tavern on the outskirts of town comes the sound of revelry and hoarse voices raised in song. What is this? "Rule Britannia"? "God Save the King"? It is too much for the crowd of Southerners gathered below the open windows. They surge forward, maddened by the foreign voices, and try to rush the stairs, only to be halted by Dan Weisinger himself, a man of substance and authority who has been selling claret to the revellers at thirty dollars a case and has no intention of losing their custom.

The celebrants are prisoners of war. The captured officers from Barclay's fleet are here as are those of the 41st taken at the Battle of the Thames. The group includes the young gentleman volunteer from Amherstburg, John Richardson, now a tall seventeen-year-old.

After eight months in captivity, things have eased. No longer fettered in stifling prisons, Richardson and his comrades are on parole, dressed in the grey cotton blouses affected by Kentucky riflemen. A Frankfort banker has guaranteed their bills so that they are able this night to celebrate the birthday of the mad old king, George III, in a style to which, as officers of His Majesty, they have become accustomed.

For John Richardson it has been a remarkable experience, thanks largely to the American connections of his maternal grandfather, the Canadian fur trader John Askin, Sr., who is the father-in-law of Elijah Brush, the American commander of the militia at Detroit. For many a family living along the international border this is a civil war in more than one sense, for the Brush family has been remarkably civil to their enemy kinsman.

In Chillicothe, another member of the family, Henry Brush, took Richardson under his wing, supplied him with a private apartment, regular meals, and a horse. As Richardson put it, "no individual in the character of a prisoner of war had less reason to inveigh against his destiny."

Now he is in Frankfort with the others. The news of Napoleon's defeat has put a new complexion on the war. Lodged in the town's principal hotel, they are paid the regulation three shillings a day—more than sufficient for their board, which includes three hearty meals and all the whiskey they can drink.

In the garden, taking their daily constitutional, the British have been objects of an intense if hostile interest by the long-limbed Kentuckians who come to stare and gibe, surprised to discover that their enemies are white and not like the Indians, as they have been taught to believe. When the prisoners reply to the Kentuckians' jeers in kind, young Richardson records the odd comments, delivered "in their usual nasal drawling tone."

Tarnation if these Britishers don't treat us as if we were their prisoners than they ours.

Roar me up a sapling if they aren't mighty saucy.
By Christ, I've the swiftest horse, the truest rifle, and the prettiest sister in the whole state of Kentucky, but I'd give 'em all to have one long shot.

This zoo-like atmosphere is soon dissipated as the government puts the prisoners on parole and tells them they can leave for Canada if they can pay their way. The field officers depart; the others remain, enjoying the run of the town.

Most Kentuckians cannot forget that some of these men were present at the River Raisin and again at Fort Meigs, when the Indians had their way with wounded prisoners. Yet there are others, perhaps with stronger reasons to be bitter, who have long since forgiven and forgotten. One of these is George Madison, the American major who surrendered to Procter at the Raisin. Another is Madison's friend Betsey Hickman, daughter of the disgraced General Hull and widow of Captain Paschal Hickman who, after his capture at Frenchtown, was tomahawked by the Potawatomi and allowed to choke to death in his own blood.

Major Madison cannot forget that the British in Lower Canada treated him well. He determines to return the compliment and helps arrange parole for the officers. As for Betsey Hickman, she has known Richardson since he was a small boy, for the Hulls of Detroit and the Askins of Amherstburg were old friends and neighbours before the war. As far as she is concerned, such friendships cannot be shattered by politics, and so John Richardson becomes a regular guest in her home.

He is more than a little in love with the buxom Betsey, even though she has three teenaged daughters not much younger than himself. In spite of the tragedies of the previous eighteen months—her father sentenced to be shot, her husband cruelly slaughtered—she retains her beauty and her good humour. She is both rich and desirable. When a tall, husky Kentuckian named James starts to pay her court, Richardson seethes. In the younger man's mind, James is "a man of vulgar bearing and appearance ... evidently little used to the decorum necessary to be preserved in the society of females." When James goes so far as to smoke a cigar in the presence of ladies, Richardson cannot resist a comment on his bad manners. James glares at him, leaves the room, and from then on appears to avoid the youth.

Meanwhile, word has arrived of a prisoner exchange. Richardson hurries to the Hickman home to murmur his goodbyes, then, late at night, heads back to his quarters only to find the malevolent James barring his path.

"You have escaped me once," says James (or so the future novelist and playwright will recall it), "but I'll take good care you don't again."

A stiletto flashes. A hand grips Richardson by the collar. He wriggles free, dashes off, hears a shrill whistle from behind as a group of James's friends leap from their hiding place in pursuit. Fear spurs him on—up a slope, over a garden wall, down a pathway, through a stubborn gate, home to the tavern.

Next day Richardson loses no time in recounting the story to the Hickman family, whereupon, to his immense satisfaction, the spirited Betsey announces that James will never again darken her door. It is as well Richardson is leaving, for James is armed, but a paroled prisoner is allowed neither weapons nor a lock on his door.

Off goes Richardson next morning with his fellow officers, each attired in a light Kentucky frock fastened by a red Morocco belt with a silver buckle. They mount their horses and follow their escort through the streets, heading north toward Canada with the blessings of George Madison and a knot of friends ringing in their ears and the scowls of the rest of the populace engraved on their memories. Richardson half expects another ambush or perhaps a single shot from a long Kentucky rifle; as the company trots along he examines every tree lest it hide an enemy. There is nothing.

John Richardson's war is over, but his life is just beginning. The events of these crowded teenage years will become grist for the literary mill he is constructing; and the people he has encountered—Tecumseh, Betsey, George Madison's daughter Agatha, even the ill-humoured James—will, in thin fictional disguises, achieve an immortality of sorts in the literary works that flow from his pen.

ANCASTER, UPPER CANADA, JUNE 18, 1814

John Beverley Robinson, acting attorney general for the province, veteran of Queenston Heights, leading member of the ruling aristocracy, ward and disciple of the Reverend Dr. John Strachan, is penning a careful letter in his slanting copperplate to General Drummond, via his aide, Captain Robert Loring.

He weighs his words carefully, for, as a result of what he writes, some men will die gruesomely while others will live. At the Union Hotel on the main street of this little village, the trials for high treason, soon to be known (a little unfairly) as the Bloody Assizes, are coming to an end. It is Robinson's task to sum up the evidence for Drummond and to indicate which of the guilty men should be executed and which, if any, should be reprieved.

A handsome, personable young man with delicate, almost feminine features, at the age of twenty-three he carries the burden of justice in Upper Canada on his shoulders. (The solicitor general, D'Arcy Boulton, captured en route to England, now languishes in a French jail.) He is not without experience of the world. He has seen men die, including his predecessor, John Macdonell, Brock's stricken aide, who was also the senior partner in the law firm to which Robinson was articled. He owes his present position to John Strachan and to Mr. Justice William Dummer Powell, one of the three senior jurists who have been taking the treason cases here in rotation.

Strachan, who has an ability to spot talent, took Robinson under his wing as a small boy, paid his tuition at his famous Cornwall school, invited him into his household, counselled him, and ever since has bombarded his protege with letters of advice, reproof, praise, caution. For most of his life, young Robinson has struggled to achieve the standards his foster father set for him. It has not been easy.

Like many others this sickly spring, he has been so ill that it has required an enormous effort to come from York to Ancaster to preside at the prosecution of the twenty-one men charged with high treason. Yet come he must, "for I shall enjoy very little rest or comfort until these prosecutions are ended."

Strachan cannot resist telling him how to run the trial:

"Do not indulge yourself in asperity of expression against the Prisoners—a dignified statement of the magnitude of their crime will have more weight. . . . In addressing the jury appeal to their reason rather than their passion. . . . Much depends upon the success of the first trial, bring forward the greatest offender.

"In regard to your opposing Barristers. Be cool—neither harsh nor supercilious. Boldly demand authorities for random objections. This will frequently confound the objector. . . .

"Be not surprised at unexpected objections. . . . On such occasions you may assume a bolder tone—remind the court that the public have rights as well as their Prisoners, that if frivolous objections are allowed to defeat substantial justice Society cannot exist. . . ."

Whether or not Robinson has taken Strachan's advice, he has been remarkably successful. Of seventeen persons tried, thirteen have been convicted. Four trials remain, but two will have to be held over until the fall, for the evidence arrived too late. The others proceed on the morrow.

Robinson has handled the cases without any Crown officers to assist him, with no one to share the responsibility of public prosecutor, with the enemy in possession of part of the district in which the court sits. He has been meticulously correct, resisting all pressure for summary justice, some of which comes from the Administrator himself, for Drummond keeps importuning him to speed things up and to offer the wavering public some spine-stiffening examples of treason unmasked before the summer campaign gets under way.

Now Robinson, mulling over the records of the accused, decides that eight have no claim to mercy. The remainder, he suggests, might escape with something less than the maximum penalty, but "an unconditional free pardon should in no case be granted." There are some extenuating circumstances, however.

There is, for instance, the confused case of Samuel and Stephen Hartwell, former Americans who returned to their native country immediately war was declared and were captured at Detroit as bona fide prisoners of war. Upper Canada is full of people not unlike the Hartwells—recent arrivals from the United States who do not yet think of themselves as British or Canadian, who have little interest (and even less say) in the government of the province, whose loyalties are tenuous if not non-existent, who have no desire to fight their former countrymen, and who may, indeed, feel that they are traitors if they do. Unlike the Hartwells, who made their personal loyalties clear at the outset and crossed back over the border, most of these rootless farmers sit tight, suppress their feelings, try to stay out of trouble. Technically the Hartwells are traitors, but Robinson is well aware of the problem and realizes that "from the former relations between the two countries many cases of such nice discrimination may arise." That being the case, "perhaps from political motives even, it is best not to strain the law to its utmost rigor. . . ."

There is also the murky case of Jacob Overholzer, "an ignorant man from Fort Erie of considerable property and a good farmer . . . not a man of influence or enterprise [who] it is thought acted as he did from motives of personal enmity to the persons thus taken away who are not of themselves men of good character." Ninety-six of Overholzer's neighbours have signed a petition asking a pardon for this "unfortunate but honest old man," whom they describe as "peaceable, sober and industrious . . . and a good neighbour." No other prisoner has received such an accolade.

Overholzer is a victim of circumstance, a model farmer and also a newly arrived American, a target for private grudges and public revenge by reason of the depredations of the enemy along the Niagara. After the burning of Newark some of his neighbours threatened to seize his land and burn his buildings. Three of his enemies stole his horses, harnesses, and household goods. When Overholzer complained to the authorities, the thieves turned on Overholzer, branding him as a traitor for his part in a recent American raid. This confused series of charges and countercharges might well have blown over had it not been for the temper of the times. The magistrate who heard the case originally dismissed the charges as nothing more than an example of unneighbourly spite. Now they have been dredged up again, and Overholzer's defence is rejected.

Robinson leaves the matter of clemency to Drummond, but urges that one or two sentences be carried out as swiftly as possible, to awe the populace. The following Monday—June 20—the last two accused are found guilty. On Tuesday, the convicted men are brought from the temporary jail in the Union Mill, a building owned, ironically, by Abraham Markle, another traitor tried *in absentia*. Standing in the dock, with the public looking on, the fifteen farmers listen to the sentence in the form presented for centuries by the Common Law:

"That each of you are to be taken to the place from whence you came and from thence you are to be drawn on hurdles to the place of execution, whence you are to be hanged by the neck, but not until you are dead, for you must be cut down while alive and your entrails taken out and burned before your faces, your head then to be cut off and your bodies divided into four quarters and your heads and quarters to be at the King's disposal. And may God have mercy on your souls."

Thomas Scott, the Chief Justice, hastens to assure Drummond that "in point of fact this sentence is never exactly executed; the executioner invariably taking care not to cut the body down until the criminal is dead, but the sentence of the law is always pronounced." He adds that "the impressions which those convictions have made on the public mind will be, so far as I can judge, striking and lasting. . . ."

It is Scott's view, and Robinson's, that only the worst of the traitors need be executed, perhaps one for each of the London and Niagara districts, "since example is the chief end of punishment and . . . the punishment of a few would have an equal, and I even think a more salutary effect in this province, than the punishment of many."

Scott adds that "the very novelty and horror of the punishment of that crime will have a most powerful effect. . . ."

Upper Canada has always been a docile and law-abiding province. Scott, speaking for the ruling clique, wants to keep it that way. For beneath the placid surface can be discerned the ferment of American-style democracy and republicanism, the political philosophies of the enemy, fuelled by American victories on Lake Erie and the Thames. That must be stamped out ruthlessly.

Drummond mulls over Robinson's and Scott's advice, decides that the eight listed in Robinson's letter shall die. At Burlington Heights, on July 20, the sentences are carried out after a fashion. A rude gallows with eight nooses awaits the victims, who are driven in two wagons to the scene. Once the nooses are adjusted, the wagons are driven off, leaving the prisoners to strangle. Their contortions are such that a heavy brace comes loose and falls, striking one of the dying men on the head and mercifully putting an end to his struggles. Later all eight heads are chopped off and publicly exhibited.

Of the remainder of the accused, one manages to escape. Three are eventually banished from Canada for life. But Garrett Neill, "an ignorant and inconsiderable man," Isaac Pettit, who joined the rebels because he could not stand to be called a coward, and Jacob Overholzer, the victim of his neighbours' rancour in this incendiary conflict, surrender to a different fate. Confined in the crowded and stinking military prison at Kingston, they contract a virulent form of typhus and succumb, one by one, to the disease three months after the war is over.

NINE

The Struggle for the Fur Country

May–September, 1814

The watershed of the Upper Mississippi, though technically American, is an economic no man's land, where British traders operate easily. Guarding the entrance to this domain is Michilimackinac Island, ceded to the United States after the Revolution and captured by the British in July, 1812. For economic reasons as well as military, the Americans must recapture it. The lateness of the season prevented such an expedition following Harrison's victory on the Thames in October, 1813. But there is no doubt that, when spring comes, the Americans will try again.

MICHILIMACKINAC ISLAND, LAKE HURON, MAY 18, 1814

To the infinite relief of the half-starved British garrison, a long line of bateaux, laden with stores, provisions, weapons, and soldiers, arrives at this captured American fort after more than three weeks of battling the shrieking gales and grinding ice floes of the great inland sea. The new commander, Lieutenant-Colonel Robert McDouall of the Glengarry Fencibles, a Scot with eighteen years' regular service, steps ashore and takes command from Captain Richard Bullock of the 41st.*

The British are determined to hold this great lump of Precambrian schist, for if they lose it they lose control of the western fur trade. Every craft moving southwest toward Green Bay, or to the Wisconsin-Fox portage, or to the headwaters of the Mississippi-Missouri system must come within reach of its guns. Sir George Prevost, the Governor General, is well aware of its significance. As he explains in a letter to Lord Bathurst: "Its geographical position is admirable. Its influence extends and is felt amongst the Indian tribes at New Orleans and the Pacific Ocean; vast tracts of country look to it for protection and supplies, and it gives security to the great establishments of the Northwest and Hudson's Bay Companies by supporting the Indians on the Mississippi."

Prevost is convinced that Mackinac is the only barrier preventing American expansion westward to the Red River. If it falls, the enemy will monopolize the fur trade of the Northwest.

Washington's first blunder of the war—some say the greatest—was the failure to alert the American commander at Michilimackinac that war had been declared. The subsequent British occupation inspired the northwestern tribes to join the British and led directly to the loss of Detroit. Now, with Detroit again in American hands and control of Lake Erie wrested from the British, this mini-Gibraltar is in peril.

All winter long, Captain Bullock has been doing his best to strengthen the fort. The garrison has survived only through careful rationing. The troops have been without meat since March, existing on local corn and fish. Now, on this bright May day, soldiers and civilians crowd to the shoreline to help unload the barrels and sacks of provisions.

Until this moment, the beleaguered Bullock had no idea whether the first boats to arrive after the spring breakup would fly the Stars

---

* Not to be confused with Lieutenant Richard Bullock, also of the 41st, a coincidence of nomenclature that has misled many historians.

and Stripes or the Union Jack. But while the Americans dallied, McDouall dared. By crossing the lake at the moment of the breakup, he has beaten the enemy to the island and shortened the odds against its capture.

He is a courageous and resourceful officer, a former aide to Procter and a veteran of the midnight battle at Stoney Creek. He brings with him ninety members of the Royal Newfoundland Regiment, together with a party of shipwrights, twenty-one seamen, eleven gunners in charge of four field pieces, and twenty-nine large bateaux. The journey has been made from York through the snows along the old overland route to Nottawasaga Bay and then across the lake, the boats dodging between the grinding floes, the men half frozen on the oars. Yet McDouall has lost only one boat and managed to save its cargo and its crew.

A few days later a second reinforcement arrives—two hundred picked Indian warriors, mainly Sioux and Winnebago, led by the Red-Haired Man, the legendary Robert Dickson. McDouall has certainly heard of Dickson—who has not?—the most celebrated Indian leader in the Northwest, the most admired and the most mysterious. Like McDouall, he is a Scot, gigantic of frame and full of face, with a shock of flaming hair that has given him the Sioux cognomen of *Mascotopah*. No other white man commands the respect of the tribes as Dickson does; the contrast between him and some other leading members of the Indian Department is startling. Unlike Matthew Elliott (dead now of exhaustion and old age), he is highly literate. Unlike Thomas McKee, a hopeless drunkard, he is temperate. Unlike John Norton, who is jealous of his superiors and suspected by some of his followers, he commands the absolute loyalty, even love, of his people. Most of the others forsook their Indian women for white brides; not Dickson. He remains faithful to his Sioux wife. One cannot imagine Dickson standing by, as Elliott and the others did at Fort Miami, while the tribesmen attacked defenceless prisoners; he will not allow his people to kill or torture captives. No one in the department matches his reputation for humanity, courage, integrity, zeal.

That is Sir George Prevost's assessment. Dickson and his Indian followers were the key to the capture of Michilimackinac by the British in 1812. The following January, the Governor General persuaded the Red-Haired Man to give up the fur trade and become a government employee—agent to the Indians of the Northwest. When Elliott and his colleagues at Amherstburg tried to put obstacles in Dickson's way, Prevost promoted him to a separate command, naming him Assistant Superintendent of Indian Affairs in Michigan Territory and all captured lands, reporting directly to Procter.

Thus Dickson is both diplomat and military leader. His task is to unite all the diverse and squabbling tribesmen against the Long Knives. In this cause, his peregrinations are extraordinary. He vanishes into the wilderness for months at a time, turns up unexpectedly, vanishes again. Though no one can ever be sure where Dickson is, one thing is certain: he covers astonishing distances in remarkably short periods of time. Leaving Montreal in mid-January, 1813, he set off on a fifteen-hundred-mile journey that few, if any, have equalled, travelling to Fort George, Amherstburg, Detroit, the Wabash, Chicago, Green Bay, and eventually arriving at Prairie du Chien on the Upper Mississippi in mid-April. He went on to Mackinac, took part with his Indians in the siege of Fort Meigs and the attack on Fort Stephenson, pushed on to Kingston to pick up presents for the Indians, moved overland from York by way of Lake Simcoe and the Nottawasaga River, crossed Lake Huron to Mackinac again, then set off for Garlic Island on Lake Winnebago, where he spent the winter.

He has lived a life of hardship without complaint while his brothers, Thomas and William, occupy fine homes at Queenston and Newark. On Lake Winnebago, while the Americans were burning William's brick mansion in Newark, the Red-Haired Man was close to starvation. By February, he and his Indians had only eight handfuls of wild rice, ten pounds of black flour, two shanks of deer, three frozen cabbages, and a few potatoes left on which to exist.

By March, his situation was desperate. "I am heartily sick of this place," he wrote. "There is no situation more miserable than to see objects around you dying of hunger and [to be] unable to give them but little assistance. I have done what I could for them and in consequence will starve myself."

He loves his people. He could easily leave them, but that is not his way. He hangs on until the snow melts in April, then goes off to Prairie du Chien to recruit more followers to the British cause. That accomplished, he sets off with his tribal army to defend Michilimackinac.

With Dickson's arrival, McDouall seizes the opportunity to deliver to the assembled chiefs the kind of flowery speech required of army commanders. He chooses the King's birthday—the same day on which John Richardson and his fellow prisoners decide to toast their sovereign in the hostile Kentucky capital.

The Americans, McDouall asserts in his Scots burr, are intent on destroying the Indians and seizing their lands:

"My children, you possess the Warlike spirit of your fathers. You can only avoid this horrible fate by joining hand in hand with my warriors in first driving the Big Knives from this Island and again opening the great road to your country. . . ."

The speech is popular and so is the speaker. The Indians like the way McDouall treats them. Dickson finds "the greatest satisfaction in conducting the Indian business in conjunction with him."

The British are ready, and indeed eager, to defend the island; but the Americans do not come. The Indians grow restless. Some want to head down the lake and fight the enemy on the water—a dangerous proposal in the light of the Americans' known naval strength.

Then, on June 21, two voyageurs beach a small bark canoe under the brow of the frowning cliffs and inform McDouall that an American raiding party, three hundred strong, has seized Prairie du Chien on the Upper Mississippi. Its leader is General William Clark, Governor of Missouri Territory. The following day, the Tête du Chien, one of the leading chiefs of the Winnebago, arrives with a grisly tale. Clark, on capturing the settlement, seized eight Winnebago, cajoled them at first with kindness, set food before them, and then as they were eating had them murdered in cold blood. Only one escaped. Worse was to follow. Clark shut up four others in a log building and then shot them. One was the Tête du Chien's brother, and another the wife of Wabasha, first chief of the Sioux.

The Indians are screaming for revenge, and McDouall is faced with a difficult decision. His task is to hold the fort: dare he chance an expedition down the Mississippi to recapture the outpost and to exact revenge for Clark's depredations? To do so is to weaken his own position and to leave Michilimackinac wide open to enemy attack from across the lake.

He has little choice. If he does not accede to the Indians' wishes he loses the support of the tribes. If that happens the Americans will win the Upper Mississippi—the gateway to the Canadian Northwest: "The total subjugation of the Indians on the Mississippi would either lead to their extermination . . . or they would be spared on the express condition of assisting them to expel us from Upper Canada."

The chiefs of the Winnebago and the Sioux ask two favours of McDouall. They want a white man from the Indian Department to command the expedition, and they want an artillery piece. McDouall cannot spare more than eighteen of his regulars, but he assigns Sergeant James Keating of the Royal Artillery to accompany a force of civilian volunteers with a brass three-pounder. William McKay, an officer of the North West Company, is appointed temporary lieutenant-colonel in charge of the force. Two members of the Indian Department, Thomas G. Anderson and Joseph Rolette, decked out in red coats and epaulettes, with red feathers in their hats, are detailed to raise two companies of local volunteers while Dickson detaches part of his Indian force—two hundred Sioux, three hundred Winnebago.

On June 28, this hastily assembled strike force sets off down Lake Michigan to be joined by seventy-five Menominee, twenty-five Chippewa, and a company of Green Bay Fencibles, while McDouall, in his fort above the cliffs of Mackinac, awaits the inevitable attack upon his island.

Daybreak. From the island's highest promontory, McDouall's sentinels see the blurred outlines of half a dozen sailing ships emerging from the fog—part of Perry's former fleet on Lake Erie. The long-expected invasion of the island is about to begin.

McDouall cannot understand why the Americans have waited so long. The breathing space of several weeks has given him time to strengthen his defences. If the Americans had come even a week or so earlier, he would not have had at his disposal those Indians who have just returned from the expedition down the Mississippi. He would like to have the remainder of the Mississippi force, but at least he has the consolation of knowing that the Union Jack flies over Prairie du Chien. The upper river is a British waterway and will remain so if McDouall can hold Michilimackinac.

Why the delay? The answer is to be found in American procrastination, hesitancy, bad planning, wrong decisions. The expedition was projected as long ago as April, then cancelled (in the mistaken belief that the British were not eager to command the upper lakes), and revived again. The fleet did not sail until July, when it set out for a British supply base reported at Macadesh Bay on the southeastern extremity of Lake Huron. Nobody, as it turned out, knew how to get there. Nobody had thought to bring a pilot who could lead the fleet through the maze of fog-shrouded islands and sunken rocks behind which the bay was concealed.

At that point, the fleet's commander, Captain Arthur Sinclair, in an incredible decision, overruled the army commander, Lieutenant-Colonel George Croghan, defender of Fort Stephenson. Croghan wanted to make sail for Mackinac without delay; Sinclair insisted on first attacking and burning the deserted British fort on St. Joseph's Island, forty miles to the north.

Now, at last, the Americans are standing off Mackinac—the big brigs *Lawrence* and *Niagara*, the smaller schooners *Scorpion* and *Tigress*, and two gunboats. With one thousand soldiers, Croghan outnumbers the defenders two to one. On the island, the older settlers gaze upon the fleet with mixed feelings, some anxious for an American victory so that they may renew acquaintances and cement old loyalties, others fearful that should the invasion succeed, they may be hanged as traitors. Allegiances on this rock-bound island are fragile. In two decades it has changed hands three times.

From his vantage point in the fort, 120 feet above the village, McDouall is uneasy. His defences are in good shape, but he has only 140 soldiers. The Indians are an unknown quantity, "as fickle as the wind." Worse, he is desperately short of supplies. Dickson's followers have so badly depleted his stores that he has had to refuse rations to their wives and children and to reduce those of his white garrison. The enemy can beat him merely by sitting still, blockading the island, starving him into submission.

But the Americans plan an assault. The big guns are already booming, but the range is too far; and when the fort's cannon return the fire, the fleet moves into the lee of Bois Blanc Island. Here McDouall's sentries spot an American work party on shore, clearing an area for artillery. Three hundred Indians in bark canoes swiftly put a stop to that, seizing one luckless American who has tarried too long to pick raspberries. The British save him from death and from him learn something of the enemy strength and plans.

It is Croghan's idea to land on a beach on the southwest side of the island where an open field and sparse woods, almost devoid of undergrowth, will allow him to fight a set-piece battle, which the Indians abhor. He intends to "annoy the enemy by gradual and slow approaches." Incredibly, nobody on the American side has paid any attention to the island's natural defences. When Sinclair attempts to batter the fort with his guns, he discovers he cannot elevate them enough to do any damage. The shells fall harmlessly in the gardens of the villagers, who have sought safety within the bastion. Sinclair now realizes that the island is "a perfect Gibraltar." One hundred and twenty feet above the fort the British have a second gun, which Sinclair's naval cannon cannot reach. Faced with the loss of artillery support, Croghan decides to launch his assault from the only other beach on the island, at its far northwest corner—a fatal mistake.

This is ideal Indian country. A labyrinth of trees and tangled undergrowth extends almost to the water's edge, cut by narrow footpaths and thin cart tracks, unsuitable for the massing of troops or guns. Equally serious is the distance of this landing place from the army's objective. The fort lies at the other end of the island, three miles away, at the crest of a steep slope. McDouall's men are already blocking all the paths but one (which they will use) to slow the assault.

Fog shrouds the lake. A week passes before the ships can move. Then, on August 4, in clear weather, the fleet moves up to within three hundred yards of the beach and one thousand men push off in rowboats, supported by a sheet of fire from the American carronades.

In one of these craft stands Croghan's young deputy, Major Andrew Hunter Holmes, resplendent in blue and gold. Croghan's guide, Ambrose Davenport, a Mackinac resident exiled to the United States after the British victory in 1812, has urged Holmes to wear nothing more distinct than a common hunting suit, lest the Indians make him a target. But the stubborn major declares that the uniform was meant to be worn, and he intends to wear it. If it should be his day to fall, he says, then he is willing to die.

The troops land in a hail of musket balls. The thickets are alive with Indians, gorgeously plumed, hideously painted. Croghan halts his men at the edge of a small clearing. In the woods, at the far end he can see the British line, two artillery pieces at its centre, the riflemen forming an arc on either side.

McDouall has stripped his fort of defenders, leaving only twenty-five untrained militia behind, taking the field with 140 soldiers and some 350 tribesmen. The regulars lurk behind a ridge, protected by a hastily built abatis of roots and tangled branches. The Indians hold the flanks.

McDouall's two guns, a six-pounder and a three-pounder, open fire but without effect. The Americans return it. Now McDouall's defensive strategy is thrown into disarray by a false rumour. Sinclair's two brigs, it is said, are landing men farther down the island. To prevent entrapment, he pulls back. Most of the Indians follow.

A small group of Menominee—Dickson's followers—hold fast on the left flank under their celebrated chief, Tomah, concealed behind rocks, boulders, and trees that they have hacked down to form a breastwork. One of the younger braves, Yellow Dog, wants to follow McDouall and turns to his uncle, L'Espagnol, a huge, raw-boned Menominee, said to be part Spanish.

"Let us go with the others," says Yellow Dog.

"No," says L'Espagnol. "I shall remain; if you wish to go you can, but you ought to show proper respect for your uncle by standing by him."

At this juncture, Croghan determines to outflank the retiring British by circling around their left on the lake side. He orders Major Holmes to lead his men in a charge through the woods.

Yellow Dog spots the gaudily dressed officer, his silver braid glinting in the sunlight. As a reward for his fidelity, L'Espagnol gives the young man the honour of shooting the American leader. On come the enemy, the officers casually swinging their swords. The Indians, uttering their war cry, open fire. Yellow Dog's gun misses fire, but Holmes falls dead with five bullets in his body, one of them from L'Espagnol's gun. The warrior runs forward, seizes Holmes's cap and sword, and vanishes into the forest.

The charge peters out as quickly as it began—and at fearful cost. Holmes's second-in-command falls, seriously wounded. Two of the senior officers are mortally stricken. McDouall, hearing the Indian cries, returns only to be forced back by Croghan's regulars advancing in ragged line. But the Indians on the flanks—the same Indians McDouall despised as "fickle as the wind"—are too much for the Americans. At last Croghan realizes what he should have known at the outset—that he cannot possibly move his men three miles through this snarled jungle, especially with the guns on the heights above him.

He has lost twenty dead, forty-four wounded. The Indians scalp the corpses, loot their belongings, and are prevented from killing the wounded only by McDouall's stern discipline.

Holmes's body, stripped, is found by his black servant who hides it under a covering of bark until a truce party recovers it the following day. It is taken aboard *Lawrence* which, with the gunboats, is returning to Detroit loaded with one hundred sick and wounded and a portion of the soldiers. But Sinclair and Croghan remain on Lake Huron with *Niagara, Tigress*, and *Scorpion*, determined to blockade the lake. If the Americans cannot take the British stronghold by force, they intend to starve it into surrender.

NOTTAWASAGA BAY, GEORGIAN BAY,
LAKE HURON, AUGUST 13, 1814

Sinclair's reduced fleet anchors in the small harbour, debouching men and guns to attack the British supply base a mile or so up the Nottawasaga. In this way he hopes to strangle the supply line to Mackinac Island. A prisoner from a British gunboat, captured during the excursion to St. Joseph's Island, has described this secret route, which runs from Little York to Lake Simcoe, across a short portage into the Nottawasaga River, and thence down to Georgian Bay. Sinclair has also learned that the British sloop *Nancy* is expected to take on supplies for Mackinac deposited earlier at the river's mouth. What he does not know is that Lieutenant Miller Worsley of the Royal Navy has been alerted to their presence.

When McDouall saw the American fleet hovering off his shore, he realized that he must get word to Nottawasaga to hold back *Nancy* for fear of capture. To carry this message by fast canoe across three hundred miles of treacherous water to the British post up the river he chose a remarkable man, Robert Livingston. An Indian Department courier, Livingston knows every foot of the fur country. He has logged nine thousand miles by canoe in the service of his department. In this War he has been taken prisoner twice, escaped twice, suffered five wounds, two of which have not yet healed. A tomahawk cost him the sight of his right eye, a musket ball is lodged in his thigh, spear wounds have scarred his shoulder and forehead. No matter; he has managed to beat the American navy to the river's mouth to find the sloop loaded with six months' provisions, ready to sail. Warned by Livingston of the American presence on the lake, Worsley and his twenty-one seamen haul the little craft three miles up the narrow, winding river, impeded by overhanging boughs and rocks jutting from the shallow water. They conceal the vessel behind a bald ridge, protected by a hastily built blockhouse and a twenty-four-pound cannon, then await developments.

Their attempt at concealment fails. Sinclair and Croghan can see the vessel's masts above the ridge. Worsley and Livingston with twenty-one sailors, nine voyageurs, and twenty-three Indians are badly outnumbered by Croghan's three hundred assault troops. The next day, the Americans hammer at the blockhouse with a four-pounder, to no effect. At noon they unload two howitzers, move them forward under cover, and lob shells into the British position. There is a shattering explosion: a shell has hit the magazine. Worsley leads his men into the forest as a train of powder, previously laid, sputters its way to *Nancy*, blowing up the ship and everything aboard—shoes, leather, candles, flour, pork—all destined for the starving fort.

Sinclair spots a packet flung from the exploding blockhouse—correspondence between McDouall and Montreal. Now for the first time he has an inkling of the island's desperate condition. He can safely return to Lake Erie with Croghan leaving *Tigress* and *Scorpion* behind, one to hover at the mouth of the Nottawasaga, the other to guard the entrance to the French River, the terminal point on the Ottawa River portage route. If the two schooners do their job, nothing will get through to Michilimackinac. If necessary, he tells *Tigress*'s commander, he may also cruise around St. Joseph's Island to intercept the great fur canoes of the North West Company. Thus, with total command of the huge lake, the Americans can squeeze the British dry and seize the fur country.

But Sinclair has reckoned without young Miller Worsley who, with his men, has retreated fifteen miles up the Nottawasaga. Here, unknown to the Americans, is another cache of supplies: one hundred barrels of flour, two big bateaux, and the canoe that Livingston brought from Mackinac. On August 18, Worsley and Livingston load

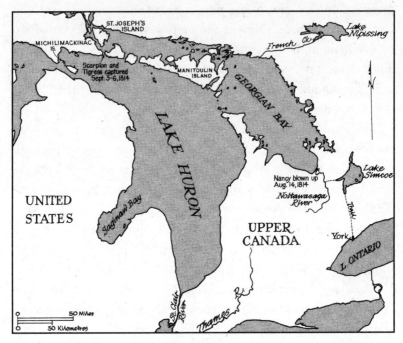

Lake Huron, Summer, 1814

men and provisions into the three craft and set off to row and paddle for 360 miles along the north shore to the British garrison.

Six days later, within eight miles of St. Joseph's Island, they are greeted by an unexpected sight: the two American schooners, *Tigress* and *Scorpion*, cruising in tandem down the Detour channel, seeking the North West Company's fur canoes. At once Worsley hauls up his boats, conceals the supplies, crams all the men into Livingston's big canoe, and as dusk falls slips past the enemy at a distance of no more than one hundred yards.

When he reaches Michilimackinac on August 31, he finds the garrison on half rations, eating their horses and paying ballooning prices to the settlers—a dollar and a half for a loaf of bread. McDouall is more than willing to fall in with Worsley's bold offer to lead an attack on both American vessels to clear the lake of the enemy.

The next day, Worsley's force sets off in four bateaux. The naval commander and his seamen are in one boat. Fifty members of the Newfoundland Fencibles, experienced boatmen and fishermen, occupy the other three. Robert Dickson follows with two hundred Indians in nineteen canoes.

At sunset on September 2, this formidable flotilla reaches the Detour channel. The following day Worsley and Livingston paddle off by canoe to seek the American schooners. They come upon one, *Tigress*, anchored in the channel only six miles away. That night the four bateaux set out, the men rowing with muffled oars. At nine, they see the dark outline of the schooner against the night sky. Two bateaux slip around to the port side, two to the starboard. Worsley is within ten yards of the vessel before he is hailed. He makes no reply. A burst of musket fire and the roar of a cannon follow, but by this time his men have clambered aboard and are fighting hand to hand with officers and crew. It is a short, fierce struggle; every American officer is wounded including the sailing master, Stephen Champlin, Perry's friend and kinsman, whose thigh bone is shattered, rendering him a cripple for life.

Somebody tries to burn *Tigress's* signal book, but one of the British seizes it. Now Worsley has the flag code. He sends Livingston off in a canoe to find *Scorpion*. Livingston returns in two hours to report the schooner fifteen miles down channel but beating up toward *Tigress*.

Worsley plans a bold deception. He will keep the American pennant flying, hide his soldiers, dress the officers in American uniforms. The charade is in readiness when *Scorpion*, unsuspecting, comes up and anchors two miles away on the night of September 5.

At dawn, Worsley slips his cable and bears down on the other ship, using his jib and foresail only. His men lie on deck, hidden under their greatcoats. The signal flags deceive the Americans; no officer walks *Scorpion's* deck. A gun crew, busy scrubbing the planking, pays no attention to *Tigress* until it is within ten yards.

By then it is too late. The grappling-irons are out, the muskets are exploding, men are pouring over the side, seizing the bewildered Americans. It is over in five minutes, to Sinclair's subsequent mortification.

Thus ends the war on the northern lakes. Mackinac Island is relieved. Lake Huron is again an English sea. The fur country, almost as far south as St. Louis, is under British control and will remain so until the horse trading at Ghent restores the status quo.

TEN

The Last Invasion

July–November, 1814

Unable to seize either Kingston or Montreal, the Americans decide to make another drive at the Niagara peninsula. Jacob Brown, newly promoted to major-general, plans to seize Fort Erie, march down the Niagara and, with the help of the navy, capture Fort George, then move on to Burlington Heights. With the European war ended, Britain is planning to ship massive reinforcements to Canada, but these have not yet arrived. When Lieutenant-General Gordon Drummond asks Sir George Prevost for more men, he is told there are none to spare. His five thousand troops, scattered from York to Fort Erie, are not enough to contain the enemy attack.

BEFORE FORT ERIE, UPPER CANADA, JULY 3, 1814

It is two o'clock on a black, rainy morning when Winfield Scott in the lead boat of the American invasion force, thirty-five hundred strong, leans over the bulwark to check the depth of the water with his sword. It is less than knee deep. As musket balls whiz above his head, Scott leaps over the side and is about to shout "Follow me!" when the boat swerves in the current and he steps into a hole.

"Too deep!" gurgles Scott, as he disappears below the surface.

The warning cry prevents 150 men from drowning. The boat backs water as her crew struggles to haul the big brigadier-general, heavily encumbered by cloak, high boots, sword, and pistols, aboard. No one laughs; Scott is sensitive about his dignity. A moment later, in the shallows of a small cove near Fort Erie, he goes over the side again. His men follow. The British pickets gallop away.

Thus begins the third major invasion of the Niagara frontier, proposed less than a month before—and in the most casual fashion—by John Armstrong, the American Secretary of War.

"To give . . . immediate occupation to your troops, and to prevent their blood from stagnating, why not take Fort Erie?" the Secretary suggested to Major-General Jacob Brown, almost as though he were planning a weekend outing. Scott, with his sense of history, would have liked to wait a day and seize his objective on the anniversary of his country's independence, but the impatient Brown is not to be delayed. After capturing Fort Erie, he plans to seize the strategically important bridge over the Chippawa and march downriver to Fort George, where he fully expects Commodore Chauncey to be waiting, ready to give him heavy support from his reinforced fleet.

One officer opposes Brown's plan. Scott's fellow brigadier-general, Eleazar Wheelock Ripley, believes the force is too small to make an impression upon the peninsula and that if the British dominate Lake Ontario the Americans are likely to be cut off and captured. When Brown attempts to reason with him, Ripley sullenly offers his resignation. Brown curtly tells him to follow orders, and Ripley does so—but tardily. Ripley goes down in Brown's mental notebook as a hesitant, untrustworthy officer.

The British garrison at Fort Erie is heavily outnumbered by Ripley's and Scott's regulars and by more than one thousand militia volunteers and Indians under Amos Hall's replacement, Congressman Peter B. Porter. At five it surrenders. For the Americans it has been a long, weary day; after more than twenty-four hours of constant movement, young Jarvis Hanks, the drummer boy, cannot stay awake and finds himself dropping off to sleep on the march.

But the following day—July 4—is as glorious as its name: the rain dispersed, the sky cloudless, a haze of heat already shimmering over the grain fields and fruit orchards that border the Niagara. Through this smiling countryside, for twelve hours Winfield Scott and his brigade drive back the forward elements of Major-General Phineas Riall's thinly extended Niagara army, the soldiers on both sides choking in the dust and sweating in the blazing sunlight.

At dusk, the British withdraw across the Chippawa bridge to the safety of their entrenched camp. Scott prudently moves back a mile behind Street's Creek.

Riall has been on the gallop since eight in the morning, gathering his troops and dispatching appeals to York for reinforcements. At the British camp on the north side of the Chippawa, all is fever and bustle as troops and refugees pour in. Riall's defensive position is well chosen, for the sluggish creek is unfordable, and there is no other bridge for miles upstream. The Chippawa cuts the peninsula in two: no invading force can roll up the frontier without seizing and holding this bridge.

To frustrate such an attempt, Riall has his army dug in on the north side of the creek and an artillery battery on the south side amid a cluster of houses and warehouses that forms the community of Chippawa. The settlement marks the southern terminus of the portage route around Niagara Falls, where schooners and wagon trains switch cargoes to circumvent the great cataract. Tomorrow it will be a battlefield. The residents have already fled to the protection of the British camp, and a long line of refugees snakes along behind.

For more than twelve months these victims of a baffling and mysterious war—old men, women, small children—have been harassed and plundered by raiding parties from across the river. Their horses are spavined, for the best animals have all been stolen or eaten. The remaining wagons are broken down. Everything of value has long since been taken—livestock, flour, bacon, household goods, silverware, cutlery. Half starved through the winter, their able-bodied men seconded to the militia, their fields sometimes unsown, oftener ravaged, they cross the bridge and seek a camping place in the open fields beyond the British lines.

As dusk falls, Winfield Scott's advance brigade is reinforced by Ripley. A force of Pennsylvania militia under Peter B. Porter is also on the way. By noon the following day, Jacob Brown will have five thousand fighting men and Seneca Indians to contest the bridge at the Chippawa. Riall will have two thousand. As midnight approaches and more reinforcements straggle into camp and bed down, the two armies, more than a mile apart, slumber and await the approach of a bloody tomorrow.

CHIPPAWA, UPPER CANADA, JULY 5, 1814

It is seven o'clock of a bright midsummer morning. Captain Joseph Treat of the U.S. 21st Infantry has been up all night on picket duty. He is lame, worn down by fatigue and burdened by extra responsibility, for the second-in-command of his company is not only ill but also under arrest. As well, a fall from a horse a few days earlier has rendered him unfit for duty. But he has refused to report sick and has marched with his regiment to Street's Creek.

As the lemon sun begins to warm the meadows along the Niagara, an order reaches him to march his forty men back to camp. Comes a rattle of musketry from the British picket lines. Treat's men throw themselves to the ground, hidden in the waist-high grass. He orders them to their feet, but when the enemy fires again his new recruits break and run toward the rear, directly into the muzzles of their own cannon.

Treat, running after his men, calls on them to halt, form up, return and face the enemy. At this moment, Major-General Jacob Brown arrives on the scene.

The new commander of the Army of the North is a big, handsome figure, with a smooth oval face and clear searching eyes. He comes from a long line of Pennsylvania Quaker farmers but has also been schoolmaster, surveyor, land speculator, and—more significantly—a smuggler. Smuggling is an honourable calling in Sackets Harbor, Brown's home; most of the male populace engages in it. Brown, however, is no minor smuggler. A road is named for him, Brown's Smuggler's Road, and his nickname, "Potash Brown," comes directly from the illicit potash trade across the border. His smuggler's resourcefulness—aggressive action, swift decisions—has already stood him in good stead as an army commander; he is several cuts above the posturing and indecisive leaders he has replaced. Quick to act, he is also quick to anger—too quick, sometimes. His worst fault is a refusal ever to admit he is wrong. Now he is enraged at what he sees: an officer running away with his men in the face of enemy fire. As Treat tries vainly to explain, his sergeant runs up to report that one of the men hiding in the grass has not risen. Brown is aghast: a wounded man deserted by his cowardly officer! Captain Treat again tries to explain, but Brown brusquely sends him off to bring back the wounded man, then strips him of command, charges him with cowardice, and rides away. Treat is outraged; it will take ten months and all his persistence to clear his name.

All that morning, to Brown's annoyance, the skirmishing continues. The Americans are camped on the south side of Street's Creek, the British on the north side of the Chippawa. Between these two streams lies an empty plain, three-quarters of a mile wide, bordered on the east by the river, on the west by a forest. At noon, Brown determines to clear the forest of British pickets—Indians and militia—who are exposing his whole camp to a troublesome fire.

He decides to employ Peter B. Porter's mixed brigade of Indians and Pennsylvania militia who, having crossed the river at midnight, are marching toward the camp. He rides out to meet them and explains his plan.

Porter is touchy where the militia are concerned and jealous of the regulars who, he believes, get better treatment than his civilian army. Brown flatters him, explaining that it is necessary to drive the British out of the forest and that the militia and Indians are better equipped for bush fighting than the regulars.

Porter suspects he is about to become a sacrificial goat. He can see no prospect of glory in this kind of skirmish, which can end only in retreat. And Porter desperately needs a moment of glory after the humiliations visited on him at Black Rock. (Can he ever forget being forced from his home in his nightshirt?) He is a pugnacious man with a pugnacious face—bulldog nose, snapping black eyes—pugnacious in politics (Henry Clay's leading War Hawk) and pugnacious in war. He does not lack zeal: he has scoured the countryside for volunteers, not always with success. Almost half of his Pennsylvanians have refused to cross into Canada—another setback to add to his litany of mortifications. But he has, by dint of oratory and persuasion, managed to attract four hundred Senecas to the American cause.

Brown hastens to assure the belligerent militia general that there is not a single British regular on the south side of the Chippawa-only militia. At the moment this is true. Further, he promises that Winfield Scott's brigade will cover Porter's right in case the British should attack.

Porter agrees. The Pennsylvanians are less than enthusiastic. Their rations have been left behind. At two o'clock the troops are given two biscuits per man, the first food they have eaten that day. Captain Samuel White, who expects to enjoy a good supper later on, gives one of his biscuits away, only to learn, belatedly, of the projected attack. When Porter calls for volunteers, White and two other officers, with some 150 others, volunteer as privates.

White watches in fascination as the Indians tie up their heads with yards of white muslin, then paint their faces, making red streaks above the eyes and forehead, rubbing their hands on burnt stumps to streak charcoal down their cheeks. That accomplished, Porter leads his force of several hundred in single file through the woods on the left.

He does not know, of course, that Phineas Riall, the British commander, has decided to mount an all-out attack on the American position. Riall has sent a screen of militia and Mohawks under John Norton to cover his right flank in the same woods through which

Porter's men are advancing. At the same time he is forming up his regulars to cross the Chippawa bridge and advance against Jacob Brown's army.

Riall is a Tipperary Irishman, short, stout, near-sighted, gutsy, but without much fighting experience. He is impetuous to the point of rashness. He has badly underestimated the size of the enemy force and believes, wrongly, that the enemy plans a two-pronged attack, with Chauncey's fleet bombarding the lakeshore above Newark. Consequently, he has weakened his force by sending a regiment back to Queenston. Yet he does not order out the militia from the neighbouring countryside or call on the 103rd Regiment, eight hundred strong, at Burlington Heights, which could be rushed to the scene within two days. When the three hundred members of the exhausted and badly mauled King's Regiment arrives from York early in the morning, Riall decides he has an army strong enough to attack.

Besides the King's, he has two regular regiments: the Royal Scots under Lieutenant-Colonel John Gordon and the 100th under the remarkable Marquis of Tweeddale, a physical giant, famous as a swordsman, horseman, gambler, and fox hunter, thrice wounded under Wellington, limping from a game leg. A recent arrival, Lord Tweeddale comes to Canada with a towering reputation for chivalry, dash, and eccentricity. Stories about him are rife in the camp: how, on one memorable long march with Irish recruits, he appointed a rearguard with shillelaghs to hurry on the laggards; how he knocks his men down when they get drunk, bails them out when they are in trouble, thinks nothing of leaping from his horse and shouldering a private soldier's knapsack to march as an example to his troops; how he once risked his life under fire to swim a river and rescue the wife of a German hussar, forgotten during a retreat. His baggage on the Peninsula included cases of champagne and claret, which he often served in his own mess to captured officers. At his waist he carries two pistols presented by Wellington himself following a cavalry action.

Lord Tweeddale is in bed, suffering from a violent case of ague—a vague term that could mean anything from influenza to malaria—when he receives Riall's order. He replies that he is "in the cold fit of the disease" but expects the hot fit shortly. Riall agrees to postpone the attack for an hour when, presumably, the Marquis will be hot enough for action. By four o'clock the troops are drawn up on a plain between the two creeks, hidden from the Americans by a screen of bushes along the Chippawa.

At this moment, Peter B. Porter is moving his men in file through the woods, blissfully unaware of his predicament. Just ahead, masked by trees and underbrush, a strong enemy column is advancing toward him. A few yards to his right, on the plain beyond the forest's rim, Riall's scarlet-coated regulars are drawn up in battle order, bayonets gleaming. When he realizes that he is caught between the two forces, Porter shouts the traditional cry: *"Sauve qui peut."* In an instant his column is in full retreat, the Indians bounding ahead, many carrying their small sons, whom they have brought into battle, on their shoulders. Porter himself is scarcely able to keep ahead of the pursuing British until he reaches the safety of Street's Creek. Once again, the bellicose congressman has been frustrated in his search for glory.

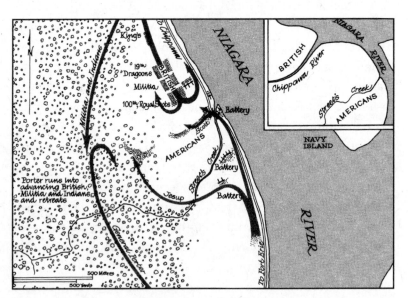

The Battle of Chippawa

Not all of his men outrun the enemy. Captain Samuel White, who volunteered to fight as a private under Porter, is surrounded by enemy Indians with two fellow officers from the Pennsylvania militia, Lieutenant-Colonel John Bull and a Major Galloway. An Indian seizes his coat, another his vest, a third his neck-cloth. Soon he is stripped to his shirt and pantaloons. Everything including his watch is taken.

Galloway has lost his boots and must walk barefoot. A more ghastly fate awaits the Colonel. The party has proceeded less than half a mile to the rear when one of the guard whoops, raises his rifle, and shoots him through the body. Bull falls, reaches out to Galloway for help, and is dealt a tomahawk blow through the skull. His captors scalp him and leave the corpse where it fell. As they hurry their two remaining prisoners through the woods, White expects a similar fate at any moment. A vagrant thought courses through his mind: why hadn't he eaten the second biscuit in his rations while he had the chance? If he lives, he is unlikely to have supper.

———

Major-General Jacob Brown sees the clouds of dust and hears the firing in the forest. He rightly concludes that the British are moving to the attack. It is five o'clock. Winfield Scott, in full uniform, has decided, in the cool of the afternoon, to drill his brigade in grand evolutions on Dan Street's meadow. But now his commander dashes up on horseback.

"You will have a battle!" cries Brown, and quickly outlines the situation. Scott is sceptical. He will march and drill his brigade, he says, but he does not believe he will encounter five hundred of the enemy.

Nonetheless, he moves his men at a smart double across the Street's Creek bridge. To his discomfiture, he discovers that the British have placed nine field guns on the far side. Fortunately, the grape and cannonballs pass harmlessly over the heads of the jogging soldiers. The drummer, Jarvis Hanks, watches them skip across the surface of the creek. Nathan Towson, perhaps the best artillery officer in the American army, has already brought his own guns down and is replying to the British volleys.

From his position in front of Chippawa Creek, Riall, the British commander, sees Scott's brigade advancing and is deceived by their uniforms. Unable to obtain regulation U.S. Army blue cloth, Scott has had to outfit his men in grey.

"Why," exclaims Riall, "it is nothing but a body of Buffalo militia!" (warm memories of the rout at Black Rock the previous December).

Scott forms his troops into line and, because he believes a commander should appear a little arrogant before a battle, roars out a rallying cry to his troops. Independence Day is over but:

"Let us make a new anniversary for ourselves!"

As the Americans, dressing smartly by the right, begin a steady advance under British artillery fire, Riall revises his opinion.

"Why, those are regulars!" the little Irishman exclaims, with an oath.

The months of parade-ground toil are paying off. Scott's men move inexorably forward, halting, loading, firing in unison. Young Hanks stands by the side of Sergeant Elias Bond, drum slung over one shoulder, holding the sergeant's ramrod in his other hand, saving so much time that the sergeant manages to get off sixteen rounds before advancing.

Scott's line comes on in perfect order, Towson's battery of twelve-pounders covering his right. On his left flank, Major Thomas Jesup with the 25th Regiment, pushing through the woods only just vacated by Porter's fleeing militia, manages to outflank the British. Noting this, Scott decides upon a difficult manoeuvre, holding back his centre and advancing his wings so that they extend beyond the British flanks, half surrounding the columns. Cannonballs tear into the advancing line, but the Americans close up the ranks with the steadiness of veterans.

Brown now orders Eleazar Ripley's brigade forward to support Scott. In the 21st Battalion a brand-new private marches in the ranks, musket on shoulder. He is Captain Joseph Treat, victim of the morning's encounter with Brown, still smarting from the unfairness of his dismissal.

Scott has no idea where Ripley's brigade is—or Porter's. He continues to move back and forth around his U-shaped formation, encouraging his men. Towson's accurate fire has all but silenced the British cannon. A shot strikes the British magazine, reducing the British stock of ammunition, throwing the gunners into confusion. Towson now begins to belabour the British columns with canister.

The British, only two hundred yards from the American line, attempt a charge through the deep furrows and three-foot grass of the meadow. They are beaten back. Gordon, the colonel of the Royals, falls, shot in the mouth, unable to speak. The Eighth Marquis of Tweeddale, riding at the head of his regiment, is forced to dismount. The fire from Towson's canister is now so heavy—the big iron balls spraying in every direction—that both British regiments come to a standstill. Lord Tweeddale calls to the captain of his grenadier company to resume the advance, but even as the order is given, the officer is killed. He calls to a lieutenant, who at that moment is grievously wounded. He calls to his next in line, a young subaltern; he, too, is killed. A ball ploughs into Tweeddale's game leg, cutting his Achilles tendon; he cannot move. His men hoist him onto his horse and begin to take down a fence to let him through to the rear. Up rides a squadron of American cavalry, their commander demanding Tweeddale's surrender. The imperturbable peer retorts that he will order his men to shoot the officer and fire on his squadron if he does not retire on the instant. As the Americans turn back, Tweeddale turns over his command to the only officer remaining on his feet, and rides away.

The British line is breaking. Winfield Scott, preparing for a bayonet charge, rides out in front of the 11th Infantry and cries:

"The enemy says the Americans are good at long shot but cannot stand the cold iron. I call upon you instantly to give the lie to the slander. *Charge!*"

It is all but over. Riall, who has exposed himself fearlessly, riding out in front of his troops during the entire encounter almost as if he were courting death, realizes he must withdraw. He calls upon the King's Regiment, held in reserve, to cover the retreating troops as they move across the Chippawa bridge, ripping up the planking as they go. Miraculously he is unscratched, though his cloak is riddled with bullet holes. He leaves behind mounds of dead, among them some of his bravest officers. In little more than two hours he has lost almost one-third of his effective force.

The Americans do not pursue. Riall is too well entrenched, his guns too well positioned. A light rain sweeps across the battlefield as Scott's men trudge back through the mud. As dusk falls the two armies occupy the identical positions they did the previous evening, with one difference: more than eight hundred men are dead, wounded, or missing.

———

Captain Samuel White, herded as a prisoner through the woods and fields, continues to ask himself why he and his fellow Pennsylvanian, Major Galloway, are still alive. His captor slips in a furrow, falls, but never relaxes his grip. For an instant the American contemplates escape, but realizes that that would mean instant death. Ahead, he can see the last of the British retreating across the Chippawa bridge. The Indians push White forward with such violence that he almost falls. They gain the bridge with the last of the rearguard, the American cannonballs rolling after them, one shot falling within yards of White himself. A moment later, the bridge is destroyed.

Now, thinks White, I'm safe. The British will protect me.

To his indignation, they do nothing of the sort but urge the Indians to run the prisoners still farther:

Who have we got there—a damn Yankee? Well, damn him, run him well, he's not half run yet.

White is almost at the end of his tether. It's impossible, he thinks; I cannot run twenty rods farther. But run he must; mouth agape, breath coming in hoarse gasps—and not for twenty rods but for more than a mile to the Indian encampment, poked in the back whenever he slackens pace.

At last, at the rear of the camp, he is halted and allowed to collapse. It is some time before he can find his voice to ask for water.

Eventually, a group of Canadian officers arrive. The Indians disperse, and White is taken to the British camp, where he is reunited with Major Galloway. The two are taken to Riall's headquarters, where the testy general peppers them with questions, few of which seem relevant.

Riall asks the size of Brown's army, but when White replies that it numbers five thousand, Riall refuses to believe him.

"That is not true, sir, you know it is not, you have more than double that number."

Commanders do not like to be beaten except by an overwhelming force, and Riall, the wishful thinker, is no exception.

The prisoners sleep that night on bare ground. Soaked with sweat after his exertions, Captain White shivers with cold until the sergeant in charge lends him his coat and a kerchief to cover his head. Equally welcome is a tot of rum. The sergeant himself has been a prisoner, knows what it is like, remembers that he was well treated by his American captors. But he is not allowed to draw rations for his charges and so must feed them from his own supply.

On the afternoon of the third day White sees a British horseman racing down the banks of the Chippawa at full speed to report that the Americans are bridging the creek upstream and are about to outflank the British position.

The camp comes alive. Horses are hitched to gun tumbrels; baggage wagons are heaped with supplies; cannons roar on both sides as the British artillery covers Riall's retirement. Soon the army is in full retreat along the road toward Queenston as Winfield Scott, swimming the Chippawa at the head of his brigade, occupies the abandoned camp.

White and three fellow prisoners march at the rear of the retiring army, watching with amusement as camp kettles tumble out of the escaping wagons, rattling at high speed along the river road. Riall, who realizes at last that he is outnumbered, decides to retreat to Fort George. There he will try to hold on until his superior, Gordon Drummond, can arrive with reinforcements. Drummond, at Kingston, makes plans to leave immediately for the head of the lake, pushing on the 89th Regiment (victors at Crysler's Farm) and the

Glengarry Light Infantry. But it will be some time before these can reach the Niagara frontier. Meanwhile, Riall's situation is critical. The Americans occupy Queenston Heights. Fort George cannot hold out long against enemy bombardment. If Chauncey's fleet arrives from Sackets Harbor it can blast these crumbling defences into rubble with its naval guns. Once again, the peninsula is in peril.

All this is of no consequence to Captain Samuel White and his fellow prisoners. Before reaching Fort George they are marched to a large brick house surrounded by British troops. From the windows, White can see wounded officers being carried toward Newark, each in a blanket held by four men. The prisoners have no rations—the entire garrison is close to starvation from lack of supplies. When at last they are given beef, they eat it raw, being too ravenous to wait to cook it.

A few days later they are herded aboard a schooner bound for York, so crowded with wounded men that they are forced to remain on deck for the entire journey. Luckily, one of the officers gives them a bottle of rum. It is the last liquor White will see until the following March when, with the war over and after many hardships, he finds himself safely home in Adams County, Pennsylvania.

QUEENSTON, UPPER CANADA, JULY 10, 1814

Second-Lieutenant David Bates Douglass has just arrived on the Niagara frontier, fresh from West Point, with a company of young engineers. Here, on the heights above the town, almost at the very spot where Brock fell, he looks down on the American camp and feels a surge of emotion.

On the horizon, five miles distant, he can see the silvery surface of Lake Ontario. Three hundred feet below, cutting through a jungle of foliage, the Niagara plunges out of the turmoil of the rapids and wriggles toward open water. He gazes down with pounding heart on the village of Queenston, surrounded by an open plain, white with American tents. He can see long lines of troops under arms, columns in motion, cavalry galloping about, gunners drilling—no fancy plumage, no glitter, only hundreds of men in close-buttoned grey tunics and plain white belts, wielding Brown Bess muskets. (These distinctive uniforms, Winfield Scott's makeshifts, will soon be adopted permanently for the cadets at West Point in recognition of the victory at Chippawa.) In the distance, near the river's mouth, Douglass spots a flash of colour—the Union Jack waving over the two forts, Niagara and George—and, here and there, as the sun's rays catch it, the glitter of an enemy bayonet.

His company descends the heights and enters the vast semicircle of tents. The troops are in good spirits, some splashing about in the river. Jarvis Hanks disports himself by leaping from the third storey of a dockside warehouse, thirty feet above the swirling Niagara, thinking of the mill pond back home in the green mountains of Vermont.

Jacob Brown has no time for such frivolity. A dozen problems occupy the American commander's mind. He has lost confidence in one of his brigade commanders, Eleazar Ripley, who has disapproved of the campaign from the start. Can this force of fewer than five thousand actually hope to conquer the Niagara peninsula and hold Upper Canada? Ripley thinks not; such an action can only lead to a senseless effusion of blood. To the impetuous Brown, Ripley is far too cautious. Brown prefers Scott's panache. The big brigadier's tactics may occasionally be questionable—he took a long chance at Chippawa, advancing so swiftly that his flanks were unprotected—but his very audacity makes up for it.

Brown has reason for his impatience. He has rushed his army to Queenston because he believes he has a rendezvous this day with Commodore Chauncey and the fleet. With Chauncey's ships transporting men and guns from Sackets Harbor, Brown is confident he can take Fort George and then move up the peninsula, seizing Burlington Heights, York, and finally Kingston, effectively ending the war.

But there is no sign of Chauncey. For three days, Brown waits and frets. On July 13, he dispatches a letter by express:

I have looked for your fleet with the greatest anxiety since the 10th. . . . For God's sake let me see you . . . at all events have the politeness to let me know what aid I am to expect from the fleet of Lake Ontario.

But there is no unified command among the U.S. forces, no chief of combined operations. The navy is a law unto itself, jealous of its prerogatives. What Brown does not know is that Chauncey lies so ill with fever that he can scarcely make a decision. One thing, however, is clear: the ailing commodore has no intention of turning his spanking new vessels over to a second-in-command; nor does he intend to use them as mere transports for the army. These are *fighting* ships, not barges! In his myopia, Chauncey conceives that his only duty is to do battle with the British fleet—in his own time. And there is nothing anybody can do about that—not Brown, not Armstrong, not even the President.

Brown is aware that as each day passes the British forces grow stronger. The frontier is in a ferment. Guerrilla warfare rages on both sides. The militia in the London district is called out. Civilians harry the troops. Farmers leave their fields and flock into Burlington Heights and to Twenty Mile Creek, where Major-General Riall has his headquarters.

The Canadian population is so hostile to the invaders that, in an act of revenge, the troops of Colonel Isaac Stone descend upon the Loyalist village of St. Davids and burn it to the ground. Brown, in one of his furies—and with bitter memories of the retaliation that followed McClure's ravaging of Newark—dismisses Stone. The Colonel pleads that he, personally, was three miles away at the time, but Brown is not in a mood to accept excuses. The accountability for the outrage, he says, must rest with the senior officer. It is a harsh principle, indicative of Brown's frustration.

He cannot even blockade Fort George from his position at Queenston. Parties continue to slip in and out of that thinly held garrison. On July 20, Brown—still expecting the fleet—moves his army up before the fort, a move urged by the aggressive Winfield Scott against the advice of most senior officers.

But Scott can do no wrong in Brown's eyes. Hanks, the drummer boy, watches wide-eyed as the tall brigadier rides forward within range of the British cannon, telescope in hand, to reconnoitre the fort. A shell buzzes toward him. Scott raises his sword, sights it at the bomb, sees that it will fall directly upon him, spurs his horse, wheels about and escapes. A moment later, the missile drops on the exact spot he has vacated.

Without siege guns, Brown realizes he can do nothing against the fort. Those guns are at Sackets Harbor and can be transported to the scene only by Chauncey's fleet—and there is no sign of Chauncey. Chagrined, Brown moves his army back to Queenston, having lost two days in a pointless exercise. At last, on July 23, he learns the hard truth: a letter from Sackets Harbor makes it clear he will get no help from the navy.

The odds have changed dramatically. Brown's army has been reduced to twenty-six hundred effective soldiers. But the British have somewhere between three and four thousand. Lieutenant-General Drummond is on his way from York to take personal command. Morrison's 89th has arrived to reinforce Riall. The British have sent troops across the Niagara to the American side, apparently planning to march up the river and threaten Brown's flank and rear. All of Brown's reserve supplies are at Fort Schlosser, in the direct path of this movement. Brown loses no time. On July 24, he moves back to Chippawa. There he will attempt to refit and reinforce his army and, leaving both forts in British hands, bypass them and move up the peninsula to seize Burlington Heights.

The zealous Winfield Scott does not want to wait. So eager is he for the contest that he wants to move on Burlington that very night. Brown restrains him. Sometimes Scott is *too* eager, a failing that will be brought home to both men in less than twenty-four hours at the junction of Portage Road and Lundy's Lane.

CHIPPAWA, UPPER CANADA, JULY 25, 1814

It is five o'clock of a sultry day, the Americans at rest or drill, bathing, washing clothes, checking arms. David Douglass watches curiously as Winfield Scott's brigade heads out in column across the creek in the direction of the Falls.

His friend and superior, Colonel Eleazer Wood, explains what is happening. The British are believed to be crossing the Niagara at Queenston to seize Lewiston, dash upriver, overwhelm the American depot at Fort Schlosser opposite the American camp, and threaten Brown's army. More troops are thought to be moving toward the American camp on the Canadian side. Scott has been ordered to march on Queenston—an action designed to force the enemy back to the Canadian side of the river—and report on the British dispositions.

Douglass, eager to be part of the action, gets permission to ride with Wood in the vanguard of Scott's brigade.

Actually, the Americans are misinformed. Brown has been operating on rumour. He is convinced that the main British attack will come on his supply depot at Schlosser, directly across the river, but Gordon Drummond, now on the scene, has cancelled that movement. In fact, his deputy, Riall, is massing British troops three miles away at Lundy's Lane, the main route between the Falls and the head of Lake Ontario. Riall has established a strong defensive force on this road to keep watch on the American camp at Chippawa. Drummond, meanwhile, having landed at the mouth of the Niagara, is marching to Riall's aid with eight hundred men.

Brown's weakness is his stubbornness and inflexibility. He finds it difficult to change his mind once it becomes fixed—a trait that has been impressed on the unfortunate Captain Treat and also on the cautious brigadier, Ripley. Earlier in the day, Colonel Henry Leavenworth, officer of the day, reported seeing two companies of British infantry and a troop of dragoons at Wilson's Tavern near the Falls. Leavenworth tries to warn Brown that these must be the advance guard of the British army; he cannot believe that Drummond would trust such a force so close to the enemy without sizeable support. But Brown cannot be budged. Off goes Scott toward Queenston with Nathan Towson's artillery, dragoons and volunteers—upwards of twelve hundred men. But Riall has three times that number, with more on the way.

The widow Wilson's tavern, one of the few buildings not burned by American partisans, overlooks the famous Table Rock, just above the Falls. As Scott's column comes into view, David Douglass sees eight or ten British officers hastily mount their horses. Some ride off briskly, but three or four face about and coolly examine the advancing Americans through glasses. They wait until the column is within musket shot, whereupon their leader, an officer "of dignified and commanding mien," waves a military salute, wheels and rides away. In the distance, through the woods beyond, Douglass can hear a series of bugle signals.

Wood and Douglass are the first men to enter the tavern.

"Oh, sirs!" cries Mrs. Wilson, "if you had only come a little sooner you would have caught them all."

"Where are they and how many?"

"It is General Riall," says the widow, "with eight hundred regulars, three hundred militia and Indians, and two pieces of artillery."

At this moment Winfield Scott enters, questions the tavern-keeper closely, then sends Douglass back to camp with word that Scott is about to engage the British army at Lundy's Lane.

It does not occur to the eager brigadier-general to wait for reinforcements from Brown or even to sound out the enemy's strength. It is an axiom of warfare that one does not engage an entrenched enemy piecemeal. But the aggressive Scott moves forward blindly until, suddenly, he realizes that he is heavily outnumbered by the forces directly ahead of him. The widow Wilson's information, perhaps by design, was deceptive.

Scott is now within cannon shot of the red frame Presbyterian church, which occupies a high knoll one hundred yards to the left of the river road. To the right of the church is a small graveyard, and below it an orchard. The British hold the knoll and the ground around it, their line in the shape of a crescent with seven big field guns at the centre. Scott is caught in the curve of this crescent. Behind the ridge, Lieutenant-General Gordon Drummond's advancing reinforcements, including the veteran 89th, are already forming up.

What is Scott to do? Fall back? He does not know that Riall is preparing to do just that, believing, in his own blindness, that Brown's entire army is before him. Only Drummond's timely arrival countermands Riall's order to withdraw.

Scott ponders. He is in a tight spot. If he advances he may be torn to shreds. If he turns back, he may panic the main army. There is another consideration, undoubtedly the paramount one for a man like Scott. He and his brigade have a reputation to uphold. His name is magic; his men can do no wrong. Can he suffer the ignominy of a retreat? A more cautious, less egotistical officer— Ripley, for one—might accept that. Scott cannot. He decides to push ahead against overwhelming odds, not waiting for Brown's army, to glory, honour, and acclaim, even if it means the sacrifice of his brigade.

On his right, between road and river, is a thick wood. Scott orders Major Thomas Jesup to creep through this covering with his battalion, work around the British flank, and seize the Queenston road in the rear. With the support of Towson's artillery, he himself will lead a frontal assault on the hill.

Jesup finds a narrow trail through the woods, moves slowly forward, and, as darkness begins to fall, hits the British in the flank, driving back a detachment of militia and two troops of dragoons. He is about to cross the Queenston road to attack the batteries at the rear of the knoll when he realizes that more British reinforcements are on their way from Queenston. If he crosses the road, he will be caught between two bodies of the enemy. He switches plans, determines instead to harass the new arrivals.

It is now so dark that it is impossible to distinguish friend from foe. On Jesup's flank, one of his captains is surprised by a party of men emerging from the gloom.

"Make way there, men, for the General," a British voice barks out.

"Aye, aye, Sir!" comes the quick-thinking reply.

As his aide rides past, the Americans surround the British general and his staff.

"What does all this mean?" asks the astonished Riall.

The Battle of Lundy's Lane: Phase 1

"You are prisoners, Sir," comes the answer.

"But I am General Riall!"

"There is no doubt on that point; and I, Sir, am Captain Ketcham of the United States Army."

Riall, bleeding from a wound that will cause him to lose his arm, mutters, half to himself:

"Captain Ketcham! *Ketcham!* Well, you *have* caught us, sure enough."

Jesup's prisoners, who include Drummond's aide, Captain Robert Loring, are sent back to Scott, eliciting a cheer from his hard-pressed brigade. For Scott is in trouble, his three battalions torn to pieces by the cannon fire of the British. The 22nd, its colonel badly wounded, breaks and runs into the 11th in the act of wheeling. That battalion breaks too, its platoons scattering, all its captains killed or wounded, its ammunition expended. The brigade has been reduced to a single battalion, the badly mauled 9th, reinforced by a few remnants of the beaten regiments. The attack is a failure.

British reinforcements are pouring in—Drummond's detachment from Queenston, another twelve hundred from Twelve Mile Creek. Winfield Scott can only hope that his message has got through to Brown and aid is on its way.

———

David Bates Douglass, his horse lathered, crosses the Chippawa bridge, the distant sound of cannon fire assaulting his ears, and reports directly to Major-General Brown, who immediately orders out Ripley's brigade to reinforce the embattled Scott. He does not, however, immediately send off Porter's Pennsylvania militia; clearly the stubborn commander is not yet convinced that the entire British force on the Niagara frontier is engaged at Lundy's Lane. And so the American army goes into battle piecemeal.

Douglass's commander, Colonel William McRee, sends him back to the scene of the action. It is dark when he arrives at Wilson's Tavern, brilliantly lit and ready to receive the wounded. He rides on, soon sees the dim outlines of a hill surmounted by flashing cannon. Wounded soldiers limp past as he gallops on, the balls whizzing over his head, knocking the limbs off trees.

As Douglass reaches Scott's lines, Colonel McRee overtakes him.

"Come," says McRee, "let's see what these fellows are doing."

The two ride down to the left of the action, guided in the pitch dark by the flash of musketry. McRee spurs his horse directly toward the British lines, draws up at the foot of the knoll, examines the action, turns to his junior.

"That hill is the key to the position and must be taken," he says.

Brown gallops up. Ripley's force is not far behind, the men advancing on the run to keep up with their mounted leader. It is Brown's intention to withdraw Scott's shattered brigade and to move Ripley's fresh troops into line. A wan moon, half obscured by the smoke of battle, occasionally reveals the carnage on the hill above—heaps of corpses, grey uniforms intermingled with scarlet.

McRee advises Brown that victory lies in the seizure of the British cannon on the brow of the hill, just below the church. As Ripley's troops move into line, Brown turns to Colonel James Miller, a veteran of Tippecanoe and the siege of Detroit:

"Colonel Miller, will you please to form up your regiment and storm that height."

"I'll try, sir," replies Miller, and this modest reply becomes in the years that follow an American rallying cry on the order of *Don't give up the ship* and, as well, the motto of Miller's regiment, the 21st.

Miller does more than try. Brown has dispatched Robert Nicholas's raw 1st Regiment, newly arrived from garrison duty on the Mississippi frontier, to act as a diversion to "amuse the infantry," as he quaintly puts it. Nicholas's troops give way in disorder, but Miller, on their left, leads his three hundred men forward under cover of the shrubbery to the shelter of a rail fence, directly below the guns. He can see the slow matches of the British gunners glowing in the dark, only a few yards away. He whispers to his men to lean on the fence, gain their breath, aim carefully, and fire. A single volley routs the gunners and Miller's regiment has possession of seven brass cannon. But the British line rallies, surges forward with fixed bayonets, and a hand-to-hand battle follows, the blaze of the opposing muskets crossing one another—the Americans, as is their custom, loading their muskets with one-ounce iron balls and three buckshot to add to the carnage. The guns remain in their hands.

It is ten o'clock. The moon is down. In the blackness of a hot night the armies struggle for two hours for possession of the guns with what one of Miller's officers calls "a desperation bordering on madness." Seldom more than twenty yards apart, the opposing lines occasionally glimpse the faces of their enemies and the buttons on their coats in the flash of the exploding muskets. Drummond, cold as ice, refuses to give an inch. Ripley's men, moving to support Miller, can hear the British commander's rallying cry: "Stick to them, my fine fellows!" Ripley orders his men to hold their fire until their bayonets touch those of their opponents, so that they can use the musket flashes to take aim.

Later, the surviving participants will try to bring order out of chaos in the reports they submit, writing learnedly of disciplined flank attacks, battalions wheeling in line, withdrawals, charges, the British left, the American right, making the Battle of Lundy's Lane sound like a parade-ground exercise. But in truth the actual contest, swirling around the shattered church on the little knoll, is pure anarchy—a confused mêlée in which friend and foe are inextricably intermingled, struggling in the darkness, clubbing one another to death with the butts of muskets, mistaking comrades for foes, stabbing at each other with bayonets, officers tumbling from horses, whole regiments shattered, troops wandering aimlessly, seeking orders.

In the blackness, a British non-commissioned officer approaches David Douglass and salutes, mistaking him for one of his own officers:

"Lieutenant-Colonel Gordon begs to have the three hundred men, who are stationed in the lane below, sent to him, as quick as possible, for he is very much pressed."

Douglass draws him closer, pretending not to hear distinctly, and when he approaches, seizes his musket and draws it over the neck of his horse. The man is mystified:

"And what have I done, Sir? I'm no deserter. God save the King and dom the Yankees!"

In the darkness, the light company of the British 41st is almost shattered by an American ruse. Shadrach Byfield, his stomach warmed by a noggin of rum after a seven-mile dogtrot from Queenston, hears someone in a loud voice call upon his captain to form up on the left. Who is calling? From what regiment? It is too dark to tell, but the regiment's guide insists the voice belongs to an enemy. The bugle sounds for the company to drop. A moment later it is hit by a musket volley; two corporals and a sergeant are wounded. Byfield and his fellows leap up, fire back, and charge forward, driving the Americans away.

Jacob Brown, having sent Miller up the hill to seize the British guns, moves along the Queenston road with his aides to the rear of

Lundy's Lane and is almost captured in the dark. Only the cry of a British officer—"*There are the Yankees!*"—saves him. Now he comes upon Major Jesup, fighting his way back to rejoin Scott's shattered brigade. Wounded and in pain, Jesup asks for orders and is told to form on the right of the American 2nd Brigade.

Confusion! The British reinforcements, hurried into the line in the dark, mistake friends for enemies. The Royal Scots pour a destructive fire into the Glengarry Fencibles stationed in the woods to the west of the church. The British 103rd blunders by error into the American centre and is extricated only with difficulty and heavy casualties.

Jacob Brown vaguely discerns a long line of soldiers in the dark, tries to discover who they are, rides out in front. The line appears to be advancing. An aide spurs his horse, rides forward, and in a firm voice cries out: "What regiment is that?"

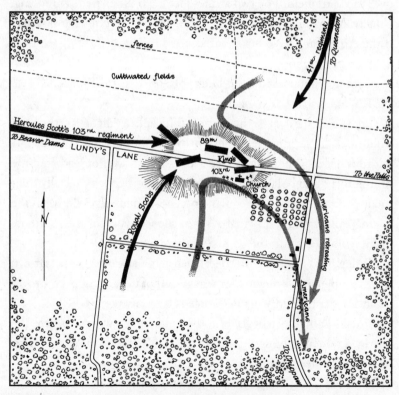

The Battle of Lundy's Lane: Phase 2

"The Royal Scots, Sir," comes the unexpected reply.

Brown and his suite throw themselves behind their own troops to await the attack.

Porter's Pennsylvanians have arrived at last and are placed on the left flank of the American regulars in time to face a British charge.

"Show yourselves, men, and assist your brethren!" cries Porter.

Alexander McMullen, one of the Pennsylvania volunteers, hears a shower of musket balls pass over his head like a sweeping hail storm. Fortunately for him, the British on the knoll above are having difficulty depressing their weapons.

The battle seesaws. A pause follows each rally while each side distributes cartridges and flints or searches the bodies of the dead for ammunition. Now, as Porter's corps ascends the hill, a stillness falls over the battlefield. The two armies face each other, neither moving. Finally, McMullen hears a British officer's voice inquiring hoarsely if the Americans have surrendered.

No reply. Nobody moves.

A young lieutenant named Dick at last breaks the silence: *We will NEVER surrender!*

On the American right some of Joseph Willcocks's turncoat Volunteers falter and fall back, firing their muskets sporadically without orders. The British respond with a shower of lead, and the militia turns and bolts. As the Pennsylvania officers try to rally their men, Colonel Nicholas's regulars interpose themselves between the fleeing militia and the British. Again silence, save for the murmurs of the volunteers and the groans of the dying.

Ripley, hard pressed with the British again advancing, asks Brown to order up Scott's brigade—or what is left of it—for support. Brown hesitates. Scott's badly mauled force is the only reserve he has. If he commits it now he will have nothing left with which to deal the enemy a finishing blow should the tide of battle turn. Nonetheless, he grants Ripley's request.

Winfield Scott forms up his skeleton brigade in a second line behind the American right wing. He has decided upon another bold stroke—a dash past the captured guns, piercing the British line and rolling around to take it from the rear.

"Are these troops prepared for the charge?" he asks Henry Leavenworth.

The loyal Leavenworth, the only surviving battalion commander, is given no chance to reply.

"Yes, I know, they are prepared for anything!" Scott cries and orders them into close column, shouting out an order that has almost become a cliché: "Forward and charge, my brave fellows!"

The tired troops follow their commander into the jaws of disaster. Gordon Drummond has anticipated the move and protected his flanks with the battle-seasoned 89th Regiment, whose commander, Morrison, has already left the field, grievously wounded. Kneeling in the cover of a grain field, the British regulars hold their fire, await Drummond's order, and, at twenty paces, let loose a volley that routs Scott's troops. The British pursue the fleeing Americans at bayonet point.

In the darkness and smoke, all is confusion. Forced down the hill and to the left of the line, Scott—who has had two horses shot from under him—again tries to lead a charge. The 89th, in hot pursuit, mistakes his force for their fellow battalion, the Royal Scots, and lets him escape.

Now Scott finds himself with the remainder of his assault party directly in front of two British regiments, the 103rd and the 104th. Fortunately for him, *they* mistake him for the British 89th.

"The 89th!" warns a British officer, just as his men are about to decimate Scott's ranks.

"The 89th!" call out the Americans, realizing the British mistake.

Scott leads his detachment back toward his own lines, only to blunder into two more British regiments, the real Royal Scots and the 41st, who are too far forward of their own line. A bitter hand-to-hand struggle ensues, the opposing troops standing toe to toe, slashing and hacking at each other. Up come the Glengarries to support the British regulars, but they too are confused in the darkness, mistaking the Royals and 41st for American regiments. As the two British forces grapple with one another, Scott's men are able at long last to retire.

Scott moves to Jesup's detached battalion on the extreme right of the American line and asks after his wound. A moment later he is prostrated by a one-ounce ball that shatters his left shoulder joint. Scott is in a bad way, for he is a mass of bruises from two falls from horseback and from the rebound of a spent cannonball that ploughed into his right side. Two men move him to the rear and place him against a tree where, on reviving, he finds he cannot raise his head from pain and loss of blood.

Brown, meanwhile, is on the far side of the field with Porter's volunteers. A musket ball passes through his right thigh, but he remains on his horse. His aide falls mortally wounded. Now the American commander suffers a violent blow from a spent cannonball. Badly winded and bleeding, he determines to turn his command over to Scott. On learning that Scott is wounded, he passes it to Ripley.

It is past eleven o'clock and the battlefield is silent. As if by agreement, both sides cease fighting. Henry Leavenworth, in command of Scott's brigade, counts his men, finds he has fewer than two hundred, confers with Jesup, agrees that the troops ought to return to camp. The British have quit the hill and may at any moment cut off the American withdrawal. Almost every battalion commander has been disabled; the men are exhausted and suffering from a raging thirst, for there is no water. Some have left the field. There are no reserves; Brown has committed every man.

For Alexander McMullen of the Pennsylvania militia, these will be, in retrospect, the most trying moments of his life. Sweating heavily during the attack up the hill, he had opened his vest and shirt. Now he shivers in the night air, and not only from the midnight chill; the prospect of imminent death disturbs him more. He hopes against hope that he will not have to struggle one more time up that terrible slope, now strewn with corpses.

It is clear to all, including Brown, that the army must retire. Major Hindman of the artillery encounters the wounded general, who orders him to collect the guns and march to camp.

But how are the captured guns to be removed? Most of the horses are dead, the caissons blown up, the guns unlimbered, the men exhausted, the drag ropes non-existent. Hindman decides to try to bring away one of the brass twenty-four-pounders, assigns a junior officer, Lieutenant Fontaine, to get it ready, then goes in search of horses. But Drummond, bleeding from a wound in the neck, is already forming his battle-weary British for a final assault. Once more his battered battalions press up the slope and retrieve the guns just as Hindman returns with horses and wagons. Fontaine dashes through the ranks on horseback; the rest of his party is captured.

The British are too exhausted to harass the retreating Americans. Most of the men have marched eighteen miles on this hot July day, some twenty-one. They throw themselves down among the corpses and in their sleep are scarcely distinguishable from the dead. Ripley's troops straggle back to the camp at Chippawa, plunge into the river to slake their thirst, then fall into their tents.

It has been the bloodiest battle of the war, the casualties almost equal on both sides. The British count some 880 officers and men killed, wounded, or captured, the Americans almost as many (although some will charge that Brown has purposely underestimated his returns). William Hamilton Merritt, leader of the Provincial Dragoons and now an American captive, is one who will not fight again.

Both sides claim victory. Drummond reports that the day has "been crowned with complete success by the defeat of the enemy and his retreat to the position of Chippawa. . . ."

Brown declares that "the enemy . . . were driven from every position they attempted to hold . . . notwithstanding his immense superiority both in numbers and position, he was completely defeated. . . ."

Nothing will ever shake Winfield Scott's conviction that the Americans won a brilliant victory, for which he was largely responsible. Certainly his men bore the brunt of the fighting. Of a total of 860 American casualties, Scott's brigade suffered 516. Scott is contemptuous of Brown; he considers him a flawed commander and is stung by Brown's report of the action, which, he feels, does not give him sufficient praise. It is "lame and imperfect, unjust and incomplete."

A few doubts are raised about Scott's wisdom in immediately attacking Riall's position. Was such rashness necessary? Would it not have been better to wait for the rest of the army? Did not Scott, in his search for glory, needlessly sacrifice hundreds of men? After all, what advantage did the Battle of Lundy's Lane give to Brown's army, apart from raising American morale?

These hard questions are drowned in the chorus of jubilation that follows the battle. Scott, in dreadful pain, his life at times despaired of, achieves during his convalescence a triumph that might have brought a blush to the cheek of a Roman conqueror. Medals, swords, banquets, addresses, honours of every kind—including a promotion to major-general—are heaped upon him. A national hero, he can do no wrong. He will continue to serve his country for another half century, every ambition achieved—General-in-Chief, Old Fuss and Feathers, the Nestor of the Republic—all because of a bloody and indecisive battle fought on a Stygian night at the margin of Lundy's Lane.

CHIPPAWA, UPPER CANADA, JULY 26, 1814

In his tent at 1 A.M., the wounded Jacob Brown sends for Brigadier-General Ripley, orders him to reorganize the troops, feed them, and then with every available man march back to the battlefield at dawn to meet the British.

It is a foolish order. Ripley's effective force does not exceed fifteen hundred. It is scarcely conceivable that they can retake the hill after only a few hour's sleep. Nonetheless, Ripley sets off the following morning at daybreak.

Samuel Tappan, a company commander in the 21st Regiment, marches with him. Tappan's situation suggests Ripley's problem. The previous day he took forty-five men into battle of whom seventeen were casualties. But such is the state of confusion and morale in Brown's battered army that Tappan has been able to muster only nine men on this march back down the Queenston road.

Ripley sends Tappan and another officer forward through the woods on the left to reconnoitre. As the two emerge from the thickets a mile from the battlefield, they see Drummond's army posted on the heights above, the guns on a knoll near the road, the flanks protected by the river on one side and a thick forest on the other. Tappan realizes that the Americans are outnumbered.

Neither side has any stomach for a fight. Ripley withdraws to Chippawa and prepares to move the entire army farther back. Brown is furious. He has lost all confidence in Ripley, who he is convinced "dreaded responsibility more than danger." On his shoulders he places all the blame for the loss of the British guns and, by implication (though he can never say it), for the defeat at Lundy's Lane—forgetting his own harsh retort to the disgraced Colonel Stone, after the burning of St. Davids, that accountability must rest with the senior officer.

Ripley demands a court of inquiry—he has many supporters, including Miller and Jesup—but the President intervenes before the first witness is finished. Congress has already decided that Ripley and everybody else involved in the battle is a hero. Nobody in Washington wants to sully the legend of victory at Lundy's Lane with adverse testimony.

Brown is borne across the Niagara with the other wounded, but the recriminations do not end. His report of the battle, dictated to an aide, does not satisfy some of the chief participants. Three of Scott's commanders—Leavenworth, Jesup, and Colonel Hugh Brady of the 22nd—are bitter, feeling that they have been denied the kind of glowing praise that will bring them glory and promotion. Porter, too, is bitter: his militiamen have not received proper credit for their part in the Battle of Chippawa; they have been treated as "the tools and drudges of the regular troops." He himself has not been given the command he expects. He frets, in a letter to the Governor of New York, that because his casualties are so low "it will seem that we were cowardly and did not do our duty."

It is well that his men are not privy to that callous statement. As Ripley prepares to withdraw to Fort Erie, one of Porter's men, the Pennsylvanian Alexander McMullen, passes down his own line and views "a scene of distress . . . which I hope I may never witness again." Porter may bemoan his few casualties, but it seems to McMullen that every tent contains at least one wounded man, each still wearing his blood-soaked uniform. John McClay, the company quartermaster, struck in the forehead by a musket ball, his skull cracked open, lies groaning on his back, his face covered with gore, a wild look in his eyes. In a nearby house, his cousin, Thomas Poe, lies mortally wounded. McMullen helps carry him across to the waiting boats. Poe shakes his hand weakly.

"Alexander," he says, "you will never see me again in this world." A few minutes later he expires.

McMullen notes that of one hundred men who came with him from Franklin County, only twenty-five are whole. He counts forty wagons moving toward the river, loaded with wounded men. Knocked about in the lumbering carts, they suffer horribly.

McMullen begins to feel giddy. Attacked by a high fever and a violent headache, he scrambles into one of the wagons, where the jolting all but deranges him. He climbs out, attempts to walk, falls, is finally helped along by one of the regulars.

In a meadow near Fort Erie, the army halts. The men drop where they stand. David Douglass, the engineer who brought Scott's message to Brown the previous day, is so tired he stretches out on the first available wagon and slumbers without complaint on a heap of crowbars, pickaxes, and spades. Alexander McMullen flops down in the meadow under a single blanket as the rain pours down in torrents.

The British do not have the strength to follow. In a crumbling log shack near Lundy's Lane, the assistant surgeon of the 89th, Dr. Dunlop, struggles to save the wounded. The chief surgeon is so ill he has been shipped home. The chief assistant, also ill, has exhausted his strength helping bring down the wounded. Tiger Dunlop works alone.

The casualties lie in tiered berths from which they must be moved in order to have their wounds dressed—an excruciating operation. As more men are herded into the makeshift hospital, they are laid on straw on the floor. By noon, Dunlop has 220 men to attend.

There is no time for niceties. Limbs that might be saved are amputated to forestall gangrene. The heat is stifling, the flies thick. Maggots breed in open wounds, causing dreadful irritation. For two days and nights, Dunlop seldom sits down, pausing only to eat and change his clothes. On the third day he collapses, and for five hours nothing can wake him. Refreshed, he plunges in again.

An American militiaman is brought in—a big, powerful farmer from New York State, about sixty years old. He is suffering grievously. A ball has shattered his thigh bone, another has passed through his body, wounding him mortally. His ageing wife arrives from across the river under a flag of truce to find her husband writhing in agony on a bed of straw. Stunned at what she sees about her, she takes her husband's head in her lap, the tears running down her face, and sits in a stupor until awakened by a groan from the dying man. She clasps her hands together, looks about her wildly, and cries out:

"O that the King and the President were both here this moment to see the injury their quarrels lead to—they surely would never go to war without a cause that they could give as a reason to God at the last day, for thus destroying the creatures that He hath made in his own image."

Half an hour later, her man is dead.

BLACK ROCK, NEW YORK STATE, AUGUST 13, 1814

Well before dawn, eleven hundred British soldiers under the command of Lieutenant-Colonel J.G.P. Tucker slip across the Niagara River to the American side in nine boats on a mission, which, if successful, could force the enemy out of Canada.

The Americans have retreated to the protection of Fort Erie and are constructing a vast fortified camp, with the original fort forming a bastion at one corner. They are supplied and reinforced by rowboats from Buffalo and protected by batteries set up along the American side of the river. Tucker's task is to destroy the supply depots, disperse the troops at Black Rock, and wreck the batteries, leaving the American flank exposed. If he succeeds, the Americans will not be able to hold Fort Erie, and Gordon Drummond will not have to mount a long and costly siege.

These are seasoned troops. Half come from the veteran 41st Regiment, which has fought in Upper Canada since the start of the war. Only a hard core of originals remain, however. Private Shadrach Byfield of Wiltshire is one. Of the 110 men in his company who marched into Detroit with Isaac Brock in the summer of 1812, fewer than fifteen are left. Most, including Byfield himself, have been wounded at least once.

At twenty-five, Shadrach Byfield is a survivor. He missed death by inches at the River Raisin, survived the bloody siege of Fort Meigs, escaped from the ditch after the failed attack on Fort Stephenson, was one of the few who slipped through Harrison's fingers after the debacle on the Thames, took part in the capture of Fort Niagara, emerged unscratched after storming up the hill at Lundy's Lane. Now, as dawn breaks, he prepares once more to face hostile guns.

Tucker is counting on surprise. He expects to land before dawn, seize the bridge over Sacjaquady Creek, and move to his objective. But the Americans are waiting for him behind a breastwork of logs. The far side of the bridge, obscured from the attackers, has also been rendered impassable.

As Tucker's force lands and moves up the narrow path in the dark, three hundred sharpshooters, protected by the logs, begin to pick them off.

A strange thing happens: the veterans are seized by an unaccountable panic. They crouch, duck, flatten themselves in the face of the deadly fire. It is more than possible that they have seen enough fighting for a time, that they are used up by the bloody events of the previous week. Nevertheless, their officers rally them, and the column moves on, dashing across the bridge at the double quick only to discover that the planking at the far end has been torn up. The column recoils, but its momentum is such that many of the men are thrown into the water. An attempt is made to rebuild the floor of the bridge, but the American riflemen keep up such a steady fire that the task must be abandoned.

Shadrach Byfield, staring across the creek, sees one of the Americans climb above the breastwork only to fall back, struck by a British ball. At almost the same moment a bullet strikes Byfield's right arm, just below the elbow. One of his comrades cuts his uniform away, and Byfield staggers to the rear, finds a doctor, and asks him to amputate the arm. The surgeon refuses, believes the limb can be saved, orders Byfield into one of the boats.

To General Drummond's disgust, the remains of Tucker's entire force returns to Canada, its mission a failure.

"The indignation excited in the mind of the Lieut.-General . . . will not permit him to expiate on a subject so unmilitary and disgraceful," his General Order declares. ". . . it is . . . the duty of all officers to punish with death on the spot any man under their command who may be found guilty of misbehaviour in front of the enemy. . . . Crouching, ducking, or laying down when advancing under fire are bad habits and must be corrected."

With the Americans daily reinforcing their camp at Fort Erie, Drummond has been cheated of an easy victory. It will now require a vigorous and undoubtedly a bloody effort to dislodge them.

To Shadrach Byfield, all this is of minor importance. The doctors have done their best to save his arm, but mortification has set in. It must come off. That is a heavy blow, for he is a weaver by trade.

He seeks out a fellow soldier whose own arm has recently been amputated.

"Bill, how is it to have the arm taken off?"

"Thee woo't know, when it's done," Bill reassures him.

Several orderlies are detailed to blindfold and hold him down before the surgeon goes to work with knife and saw, but Byfield waves them away. There'll be no need of that, he says, stolidly. The operation seems to take forever and is very painful, but he bears it well. Then, his stump dressed, he goes off to bed, mercifully groggy from a draught of mulled wine.

Later, he asks for his severed arm. An orderly replies casually that it has been thrown onto a dung heap. Enraged, Byfield leaps out of bed, tries to strike the man with his one good hand. Then, nothing will do but that he search through the heap, find the missing appendage, look about for lumber, somehow manage to nail a coffin together, and give his arm a decent burial.

Byfield's fighting days are over. He returns to England where he and his family must make do on a pension of nine pence a day, later raised to fifteen through his own importuning. One night he dreams that he is working at his old trade, wakes his wife, tells her he is certain that, arm or no arm, he can weave cloth.

"Go to sleep," says she. "There was never such a thing known as a person having but one arm to weave."

But in his sleep Byfield works out his destiny. The following day he visits a blacksmith, draws the design of an instrument similar to one in his dream and, thus equipped, finds work at his former trade with a clothier at Staverton Woods, not far from his home in Wiltshire. There, from time to time, he looks back on his youthful adventures. Those memories begin to blur until he cannot quite remember which battle came first or what the places were called or what his companions looked like. Certain incidents stand out sharply—the spectacle of an Indian throwing a wounded man into the fire after Lundy's Lane, for instance—but it is all a little unreal, rather like one of his dreams. Only his missing forearm testifies to the reality of his experience on the embattled border of a strange, cold colony, an ocean and more away.

THE BRITISH CAMP BEFORE FORT ERIE,

UPPER CANADA, AUGUST 14, 1814

After a week of bombarding the American fortifications, Lieutenant-General Gordon Drummond is convinced that the time has come to attack. A shell has just landed on the American magazine chest. Drummond is certain that it has caused heavy casualties. With the Americans off balance he will this very night assault the fort from three sides.

Drummond and his opposite number, Brigadier-General Edmund Pendleton Gaines (Ripley's replacement) are like blind men, groping to test each other's strength. Both have miscalculated. Because the British entrenchments are hidden behind a screen of trees, Gaines can only guess at Drummond's force, which he estimates at five thousand. Actually, Drummond has fewer than three thousand men. Drummond is misled by his spies and informers into believing the Americans have fifteen hundred troops. In fact, Gaines has almost twice that number. Drummond has made another error: the explosion of the magazine has produced few casualties. And Gaines, shrewdly reading his opponent's mind, is now expecting an immediate attack.

Drummond plans a simultaneous assault on each of the three major gun batteries that protect the corners of the fifteen-acre encampment. The camp is surrounded on three sides by embankments, ditches, and palisades. Directly ahead, at the near corner, not more than five hundred yards from the forward British lines, the Lieutenant-General can see the outlines of the old fort, now bristling with cannon. One hundred and fifty yards to the left, on the edge of the lake, is a second artillery battery commanded by David Douglass. The two are connected by a vast wall of earth, seven feet high, eighteen feet thick. Half a mile up the lake, and also connected to the fort by an enclosed rampart, is Nathan Towson's battery of five guns, perched on a conical mound of sand, thirty feet high, known as Snake Hill and joined to the lake by a double ditch and abatis. If Drummond's plan succeeds, his assault forces will strike all three batteries at the same time and seize the encampment.

At 4 P.M. his main force sets off. Its task is to attack Towson's battery on Snake Hill. Drummond orders it to march down the Garrison Road, screened from view by the forest, to rendezvous on the far side of the American encampment, and to attack at two the following morning. The General orders the troops to remove the flints from their firelocks and to depend entirely upon the bayonet, identifying the enemy in the dark by their white pantaloons. Loud talking is prohibited and the roll is to be called every hour to frustrate desertions.

This last is a curious instruction. Does Gordon Drummond actually expect a body of his men to steal away in the dark of the night?

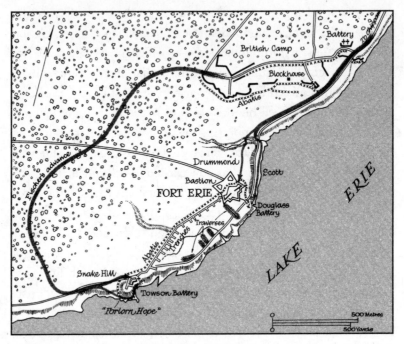

The Siege of Fort Erie

Clearly he does. The bulk of the thousand-man force attacking the Towson battery is made up of soldiers from the de Watteville regiment, a foreign corps recruited twenty years before in Switzerland but shattered during the Peninsular campaign and now heavily interlaced with prisoners of war and deserters from Napoleon's armies—French, German, Dutch, Italian, Polish, and Portuguese. Their commander, Lieutenant-Colonel Victor Fischer, is an able officer; he has under his command a smattering of British regulars from the King's and the 89th. They may stiffen the backs of the less-disciplined de Wattevilles, but the motley foreign corps forms the majority.

Drummond considers the attack on Snake Hill to be the key to success. If Fischer and his men can capture that end of the encampment, victory is certain. But why has he committed his poorest troops to this critical night attack? In his eagerness to rid the peninsula of the invading army, Drummond is acting precipitately. He has not bothered to reconnoitre the defences at Snake Hill, where a vast abatis of tangled roots and branches can inhibit any assault force. Nor does he plan to soften those defences with cannon fire— he has purposely refrained from bombarding the position in order to conceal his real purpose from Gaines. Secure in his overconfident conviction that the Americans are outnumbered and demoralized, he plunges ahead in the belief that he can conquer by surprise alone.

He has divided his force. While Fischer assaults the far end of the camp, two smaller detachments will attack the near end. The General's nephew, Lieutenant-Colonel William Drummond of Keltie, will lead 360 men against the ramparts of the original fort. Lieutenant-Colonel Hercules Scott will lead another seven hundred against the Douglass battery on the lakeshore and against the embankment that connects it to the old fort. Scott's regiment is the notorious 103rd, originally the New South Wales Fencibles, known in that colony as "the rum regiment," brought up to strength before sailing for Canada by the recruitment of released convicts. Two of its companies are composed of boys below fighting age.

Two more antithetic characters than Hercules Scott and William Drummond could scarcely be found in a single army corps. Scott is a bitter man who despises his commanding officer. He does not believe that the assault on the American encampment has any hope of success. But he is a courageous officer and can be expected to do his duty. He sleeps that night in the drenching rain under a piece of canvas suspended from a tree and jauntily tells his surgeon, "We shall breakfast in the fort in the morning." Privately he is less optimistic; he has already written out a brief will and mailed it to his brother, for he is half convinced that he will not return from the attack.

Only in this respect does he resemble the General's nephew. Every army knows at least one field officer like William Drummond— colourful, dashing, eccentric, ruthless—the sort of leader that men will follow into the mouths of cannon. Such men rarely rise above field rank, for they are either killed in action or barred from promotion by their own quirkiness. There does not seem to be a nerve in Drummond's body. Perhaps he lacks the imagination to be afraid.

He is a fatalist who spends the day in high spirits, spinning yarns with a wide circle of cronies, then as the bugles sound turns solemnly to his friends, and remarks:

"Now, boys! We never will all meet together here again; at least I will never again meet you, I feel it and am certain of it."

A thick rain is falling; soon it becomes a torrent. The General's nephew leaves the leaky hut in which the others are smoking and talking, finds a rocket case, stows himself away in it, and is soon fast asleep as if this were not his last day on earth.

Beyond the American camp, the same downpour soaks Fischer's mixed bag of British regulars and foreign mercenaries as they move through the forest.

It is two in the morning. In a clump of dripping oaks, three hundred yards in front of Snake Hill, a picket of one hundred Americans hears the steady *swish-swish* of the approaching column and sounds the alarm. Surprise, the essence of Drummond's plan, has not been achieved.

Towson's artillery is already in action. The British attackers are illuminated in a sheet of flame, a pyrotechnical display so bright that Snake Hill will shortly be dubbed Towson's Lighthouse.

Now Fischer comes up against the formidable abatis that the Americans have constructed between Snake Hill and the lake— thousands of tree trunks, four to six inches in diameter, their branches cut off three feet above the base, pointing in all directions and forming an impassable tangle. Unable to breach this labyrinth and the embankment behind it, Fischer's Forlorn Hope dashes around the end on the American left and into the lake in the hope of taking the defenders from the rear. The current is swift, the channel a maze of slippery rocks. The men struggle in waist-deep water. Part of the Forlorn Hope does reach the rear of the battery to fight hand to hand with the defenders, but two companies of Eleazer Wood's 21st, especially detailed for such an emergency, pour a galling fire on those who follow.

Panic seizes the men of the de Watteville regiment struggling in the water. Some, dead or badly wounded, are being borne into the Niagara River by the stiff current. Shouting wildly, they break in confusion, turn tail, and plunge directly into the King's, carrying those veterans with them like a torrent. Only the seasoned 89th holds fast. The hundred men of the Forlorn Hope who have managed to penetrate the American defences are killed or captured.

Fischer, meanwhile, is attempting to storm the Towson battery with the rest of his force, only to find that his scaling ladders are too short to reach the parapet. Worse, he cannot reply to the heavy fire being poured down on him because, to ensure secrecy, his men have been ordered to remove the flints from their muskets. He charges the parapet five times before giving up. His losses are heavy. Many of the de Watteville regiment have deserted and are hiding in the woods. The King's, too, have been badly mauled during the panic. Only the 89th, which maintained its order, is intact.

Drummond's principal attack has failed. Success now depends entirely on the forces of his flamboyant nephew and those of the embittered Hercules Scott.

———

At the other end of the American camp, David Bates Douglass has kept his men on the *qui vive*, warned by his commander, Brigadier-General Gaines, that a British attack is certain. Midnight passes without incident; then two o'clock. Nothing. Stretched out on his camp bed, Douglass begins to doubt that the assault will come. Slowly, the tension that has been keeping sleep away subsides and he slips into slumber.

Still asleep, he hears—what? A musket shot? Or is it part of his dream? Another volley follows. His body responds before his brain; he is on his feet before he is awake. In the distance, on the far left, comes another volley. This is no dream!

The cry "To arms! To arms!" ripples along his line of tents. The reserve is aroused and formed in the space of sixty seconds. On Douglass's left, the American 9th battalion, bayonets fixed, has already formed a double line. His own corps is wide awake and standing to their guns, the primers holding their hands over the priming to protect it from dampness, the firemen opening their dark lanterns, lighting their slow matches.

Up the river, at Snake Hill, the sky is brilliantly lit with rocket flares, bomb bursts, and musket fire. The sound of small arms and artillery, blended together, becomes a continuous roar like a stupendous drum roll.

Douglass has seen the signal rockets rise from the woods in front of him in answer to those from Fischer's column, but there is yet no hint of an attack on his battery. As the minutes tick by, tension starts to build.

"Why don't the lazy rascals make haste?" someone whispers.

It is another axiom of war that the more complex the plan the more unlikely it is of success. Drummond's three attacks were supposed to take place simultaneously—difficult enough in broad daylight, let alone pitch darkness. Hercules Scott's men should have assaulted Douglass's position the instant Fischer's rockets went up, but his battalion is still moving along the lakeshore, just below the embankment, as yet unseen but certainly heard. The tramp of seven hundred pairs of feet on the soft sand and the low whispers of the officers keeping their men together carries clearly through the night air:

"Close up . . . Steady! . . . Steady men, steady . . . Steel . . . Captain Steel's company."

The sound of plodding feet grows louder. Then, as if on a signal, a sheet of fire blazes, and the batteries along the entrenchment from the water to the fort open up in reply.

It is three o'clock. Douglass is firing his cannon at point-blank range, cramming each to the muzzle with round shot, canister, and bags of musket balls—stuffing each barrel so full that he can touch the last piece of wadding with his hand.

From the direction of the old fort comes a sudden cry:

"Cease firing! You are firing on your own men!"

As Douglass considers, the fire slackens momentarily. But the voice was stiffly British; this, he guesses is a *ruse de guerre*. A second voice calls out in an American twang:

"Go to hell. Fire away, there, why don't you?" and the cannonade continues.

Hercules Scott's column surges forward with scaling ladders, seeking to surmount the breastwork. Again and again the British are repulsed. Of twenty officers, only four escape without wounds. More than half the regiment are casualties. By dawn it is clear that the attempt has failed.

On Scott's right, Drummond of Keltie is more successful. He forms up his men in a deep ravine, unbuckles his sword, and asks his friend Dunlop, the surgeon, to keep it for him; he prefers a boarding pike and pistol. Then he leads his 350 men in a dash across the open plain to the fort.

Twice his men attempt to scale the walls with ladders and are beaten back. Finally, hidden under the smoke of the big guns, they creep along the outer ditch, scale the north bastion of the old fort, and leap into the upper storey.

"Give the damn Yankees no quarter!" shouts William Drummond.

The gunners desert their cannon as British and Americans struggle hand to hand with pikes, bayonets, spears. One of the American defenders, Lieutenant John McDonough, badly wounded by a bayonet, asks for quarter, but Drummond, in a rage, shoots him with his pistol. It is his final act. A moment later, the General's brash nephew falls dead, shot through the heart and bayoneted.

The British manage to take possession of one side of the fort but are subject to heavy fire from the blockhouse above. The battle seesaws, neither side giving way, until suddenly beneath their feet comes a trembling followed by a roar and an appalling explosion. The magazine in the north bastion has blown up, either by accident or by design.

Douglass, over a hundred yards away, feels the ground shake under him, then sees a jet of flame shoot up from the fort for more than a hundred feet into the night sky, followed by a shower of stone, earth, chunks of timber, bits of human bodies. One of his own men falls dead, struck by the debris.

The carnage is ghastly. The Americans, protected by the walls of the barracks, are spared, but the British attackers are torn, crushed, mangled. Some, flung from the parapet, die on the bayonets of their comrades in the ditch below. Nothing can stem the panic that follows. Believing the entire fort to be mined, the men break and flee across the plain to the safety of the British trenches.

Only a few escape the blast. Captain John Le Couteur, who made the snowshoe trip from New Brunswick in 1813, is blown off the parapet, falling twenty feet into the ditch, winded but unharmed. As he dashes toward the British camp, he sees an officer on a stretcher and asks who it is.

"Colonel Scott, sir, shot through the head."

Le Couteur can see the bullet wound in Hercules Scott's forehead. The commander of the British 103rd can no longer speak, and only the slight pressure of his hand reveals that he is conscious. He has only moments to live.

At this spectacle, Captain Le Couteur flings down his sabre and cries out: "This is a disgraceful day for Old England!"

"For shame, Mr. Le Couteur," someone calls. "The men are sufficiently discouraged by defeat."

"Don't blame him," says another. "It's the high feeling of a young soldier."

Another officer turns about—General Drummond.

"Where is Colonel Scott?" the General asks.

"Oh, Sir! He is killed, just being brought in by his men."

"Where is Colonel Drummond?"

"Alas, Sir! He is killed, too. Bayoneted."

At the memory of his commander's death and that of three-quarters of his own men, Le Couteur bursts into tears.

The General is heartsick, and not just over the death of his nephew. Clearly he has underestimated the size of the American force and the strength of its defences and overestimated the effect of his artillery barrage. He has no time for recriminations. If the American commander knows what he is about, he will counterattack at once while the British are off balance and in disarray and before Fischer's broken column can return. Drummond has fewer than one thousand effective troops to put into the line. They wait in their trenches for the counterblow. It does not come. Brigadier-General Gaines has not grasped his opponent's weakness.

The British losses are appalling. More than nine hundred men—one-third of the army—are dead, wounded, or missing. Six battalions are so badly shattered they are no longer fit for field duty. The drummer Jarvis Hanks, visiting the ditch outside the fort in the morning, counts 190 bodies, the faces burned black, many horribly mutilated, one or two still alive but dying, a confusion of torn arms and legs heaped about, one human trunk bereft of head or limbs, "too sickening to look upon." Men move about in the ditch picking the pockets of the dead and dying. William Drummond's body lies under a cart, naked except for his shirt. American soldiers have looted it of epaulettes, money, and a gold watch.

Gordon Drummond blames both the "misconduct of this foreign corps," the de Watteville regiment, and the happenstance of the explosion for his misfortune. It is the failure of the mission more than the deaths of good men that appalls him. "The agony of mind I suffer from the present disgraceful, and unfortunate conduct, of Troops committed to my superintendence wounds me to the Soul," he writes to Sir George Prevost. He does not consider that his own hasty planning and faulty intelligence may have contributed to the debacle. But then, no commander on either side during this maladroit war has yet written—will ever write—"I blame myself."

Prevost knows better. He chides Drummond gently in two letters, which the Americans intercept and Drummond never receives. It has been, the Governor General remarks, "a costly experiment," but no doubt the Lieutenant-General will profit from the experience. He can say no more; Drummond is the best he has. He can scarcely replace him.

Gaines is jubilant, but his elation is short lived. Gordon Drummond has no intention of abandoning the investment of Fort Erie. The cannonade increases in fury. One aiming point is the chimney above Gaines's headquarters. On August 29, a shell strikes it, drops through the roof, smashes the General's writing desk, and wounds him so badly that he is evacuated to Buffalo, his part in the war at an end.

Within the encampment, as the rain pelts down and the bombardment goes on and autumn approaches, elation gives way to dismay. Was Ripley right, after all? Is it possible for the invasion force to seize the peninsula and march on to conquer York and Kingston? The Americans have won a significant victory on paper, but nothing has changed. They hold exactly fifteen acres—no more, and Drummond's army blocks any further advance.

THE BRITISH CAMP BEFORE FORT ERIE,
SEPTEMBER 17, 1814

Tiger Dunlop, the British army surgeon, is at dinner, well behind the lines, when the sound of gunfire interrupts his meal. Two American columns have left the safety of the fort and are attacking the British batteries two miles in front of the main camp. Jacob Brown, back on the Canadian side, is making one last attempt to break Gordon Drummond's siege of the American encampment.

Dunlop rushes out without waiting for orders. By the time he reaches the forward trenches with the other officers, the skirmish is all but over. He sees the Indians bounding forward, yelling and flinging their tomahawks. He comes upon American corpses, their skulls cleft to the eyes by the throwing hatchets. He searches the battlefield for wounded men and comes upon one of his bandsmen carrying in a blanket a mortally wounded American officer, gulping water from a canteen. Dunlop proposes to dress his wounds, but the officer refuses.

"Doctor," he gasps, "it's all in vain, my wound is mortal and no human skill can help me—leave me here with a canteen of water and save yourself. . . ."

Dunlop takes him back to a hut; when he returns from his medical duties, the American is dead. Dunlop asks his identity and is told he is Jacob Brown's confidant and David Bates Douglass's friend, Colonel Eleazer Wood, the engineer.

Dusk is falling as the Americans regain the shelter of their fort and the British return to their camp. Two British batteries have been damaged, at appalling loss. Brown counts 511 casualties, Drummond

565. Both sides claim victory, each exaggerating the other's strengths and losses. Neither will admit it, but the war on the Niagara frontier has again reached a stalemate. Drummond is low on ammunition and food, his troops miserable and diseased, desertions on the increase, his camp a heaving swamp. He is reinforced the next day but still has no more than two thousand effectives. On September 21, in a driving torrent of rain, he abandons the siege and moves quietly back to the original British position on Chippawa Creek. Brown, his own strength diminished by British cannon fire and the disastrous sortie, is too weak to follow. The two forces resemble equally matched prizefighters, staggering about the ring in the last round, scarcely able to raise their arms in combat.

Both commanders are hungry for fresh troops. On September 28, George Izard arrives at Batavia, New York, having marched all the way from Lake Champlain with four thousand seasoned American troops. He is determined to drive the British out of Fort Niagara, but Brown wants instead to repeat the Battle of Chippawa. On October 10, Izard moves his army across the river and three days later is skirmishing with the British outposts at Street's Creek. In all this there is a weary sense of *déjà vu*.

Drummond suffers an agony of frustration. His force is not strong enough to go on the attack, but he is convinced that with two more regiments he could drive the Americans back across the river and finish the war in Upper Canada. He pleads with Prevost for supplies and men. Commodore Yeo is sitting at Kingston with the fleet. The new ship, *St. Lawrence*, is almost ready. Why can't the navy supply him?

Drummond's frustrations are nothing compared to Izard's. In his projected sweep across the Chippawa and up the peninsula to seize Burlington Heights and York, the Major-General has counted on Chauncey. Now he discovers to his chagrin that the American commodore, having learned of Yeo's superiority on the lake, has fled to the shelter of Sackets Harbor and will not come out. Izard cannot conceal his bitterness; Chauncey's timidity has destroyed all hope of any forward movement.

Drummond, meanwhile, is feverishly awaiting the arrival of the 9th Regiment from Kingston. Yeo reluctantly agrees to carry some troops and provisions across the lake but is so fearful of overloading his great new ship, *St. Lawrence*, that he carries only a small number of men; the rest are forced to struggle on by land over roads little better than rivers of mud. Drummond is as bitter at Yeo's caution as Izard is at Chauncey's. To both naval commanders their ships are too precious to be risked in battle and too grand to be used as transports.

Both opposing generals are dispirited and both are ill. Drummond is so sick that he asks to be sent home. Izard is so sick he cannot write to the Secretary of War. The troops on both sides are weak from dysentery. The weather grows worse each day.

The fight has gone out of the men on the Niagara frontier. The American militia, without pay for three months, are mutinous. Izard can see no practical reason to remain on the Canadian side of the river and so, after several days' wait for clement weather, embarks his troops. By November 1 all are back on their own soil. Nobody has the temerity to recall the gloomy prophecies of the perverse and discredited brigadier-general Eleazar Ripley.

And what of Fort Erie, over which so much blood has been spilled? In Izard's view, it is worthless: "It commands nothing, not even the entrance of the strait." It is "a weak, ill-planned . . . hastily repaired redoubt."

On November 5, Gordon Drummond, guided by a sixth sense, dispatches James FitzGibbon, one-time leader of the Bloody Boys and now a captain with the Glengarry Light Infantry, to travel upriver to see what is happening at the fort. FitzGibbon finds it deserted. The Americans have blown up the works, dismantled everything of value, and vanished across the Niagara.

FitzGibbon rides through the rubble of the deserted encampment. Except for a dozen cases of damaged cartridges, the enemy has left nothing. Five months have passed since Winfield Scott first leaped ashore in its shadow. Yet no territory has been captured; none given up. The invasion has ended just as the last one did the previous December. Thousands are dead, more are crippled, hundreds are in prison. In the glowing reports of the opposing commanders, scores of officers have achieved immortality of a sort, their deeds of heroism, zeal, steadfastness, loyalty, leadership, and resolve recorded for all time. But where in this crumbling, rain-swept redoubt—its walls spattered with old blood, its ramparts scarred by cannon fire—is the glory? Where the victory? Here, as at Chippawa and Lundy's Lane, the dead lie mouldering in common graves. To what purpose have they fought? For whose honour have they bled? For what noble principle have they fallen? Even the suave diplomats, charged with treading the delicate pathway toward peace in the ancient Flemish city of Ghent, can no longer be certain.

ELEVEN

The Burning of Washington

August, 1814

Heeding Sir George Prevost's request to create diversions along the eastern seaboard of the United States in support of the struggle in Canada and also as a reprisal against American raids on Canadian private property—especially the vengeful burning of Port Dover in the spring—British ships have for months been harassing settlements on Chesapeake Bay. Now, with the war in Europe ended and reinforcements available, the British plan to attack the gunboats guarding Washington and, at the same time, mount a land raid on the capital.

BENEDICT, CHESAPEAKE BAY, MARYLAND, AUGUST 19, 1814

Lieutenant George Gleig, an eighteen-year-old subaltern in the British 85th, clambers off a landing launch, loaded down with equipment, sweltering in his thick wool uniform, feeling the effects of ten weeks on shipboard. Since leaving France at the end of May he has been almost constantly cooped up in a tiny stateroom with forty fellow officers, without exercise, subject to seasickness, threatened with typhoid—not the best preparation for a long march in the August heat with the prospect of a battle at the end.

The villagers have deserted Benedict, but now the empty streets come alive as forty-five hundred British soldiers—Wellington's Invincibles—pile out of the boats and sort themselves into three brigades. Some begin to forage for extra food. Gleig finds three ducks, and the following morning he and his friend Lieutenant Codd manage to buy a pig, a goose, and a couple of chickens from a solitary farm wife. But before they can enjoy their feast, the bugle sounds assembly.

As the three brigades march off toward Washington, their commander, Major-General Robert Ross, a blue-eyed Irishman of forty-seven, one of Wellington's best officers, rides past to the cheers of his men. Ross has some doubts about this venture. His troops, languishing aboard ship, are badly out of shape. He has no cavalry and only three small field guns. The terrain ahead, cut by streams and bordered by forests, can be easily defended. He has been persuaded, however, by his naval colleague, Rear-Admiral George Cockburn, that a two-pronged attack up Chesapeake Bay is practical—with the fleet seizing the American flotilla of gunboats and the army marching on the capital by a parallel route.

Ross is new to North America, but Cockburn has been skirmishing off the coast for more than a year and knows every inlet in the long, narrow bay. At forty-two he is a seasoned commander, famous for his lightning thrusts at American seaboard settlements. In an earlier decade he might have been a buccaneer. The plan to seize and burn Washington is his.

Ross's column manages only six miles. The march is a horror, the men groaning under their heavy baggage, choking with dust, half dead from heat and fatigue. Scores fall exhausted by the wayside. George Gleig has never felt so tired, though he remembers that during the Peninsular campaign he often marched thrice this distance without difficulty.

Surprisingly, the British advance is unimpeded. No one has blocked the road or burned any bridges. Except for a few shots fired from the woods there is no harassment on the flanks, no attempt at ambush. The real enemy is the weather. In August, Maryland is a furnace.

Still, General Ross has misgivings. Admiral Cockburn, having chased the Americans into a cul-de-sac and forced them to blow up their gunboats, arrives on horseback to stiffen his colleague's resolve. The high command is also nervous. At two in the morning of August 24, both commanders are awakened by a courier from their commander-in-chief, Vice-Admiral Sir Alexander Cochrane, who orders them to return at once.

A whispered argument follows between Ross and Cockburn as Ross's aides strain to listen. Clearly Cockburn wants to go on, in spite of orders. They hear the phrase "stain upon our arms." They hear him pledge success. They see Ross waver and finally, as dawn breaks, see him strike his head and say: "Well, be it so, we will proceed."

George Gleig has spent a sleepless night on picket duty, two miles ahead of the main British force, with only sixteen men, fearing imminent capture. He has no time to rest, for when he returns to camp at five, the army is ready to march. He can hardly drag one foot ahead of the other, but he knows that Washington is only a few miles ahead, across the Potomac. Just past the community of Long Old Fields the road forks, one route leading directly to the capital, the other circling around to the right, a longer distance through the village of Bladensburg. Ross leads his weary men onto the direct fork, then suddenly reverses his column and opts for the Bladensburg road. His plan is to throw the Americans off guard; they will not have been expecting this. Nor have his men. By the time they reach the village in the scorching sun, they have marched fourteen miles and some are lying dead from exhaustion by the wayside.

It is noon as the troops trudge into the village. They have already seen huge clouds of dust in the distance and realize that the Americans are marching to meet them. But Bladensburg is empty of the enemy; the Americans have not fortified it, an error that causes relief. Few have the stomach for street fighting.

On the heights above the village, directly ahead and beyond the single bridge that crosses the Potomac's shallow eastern branch—

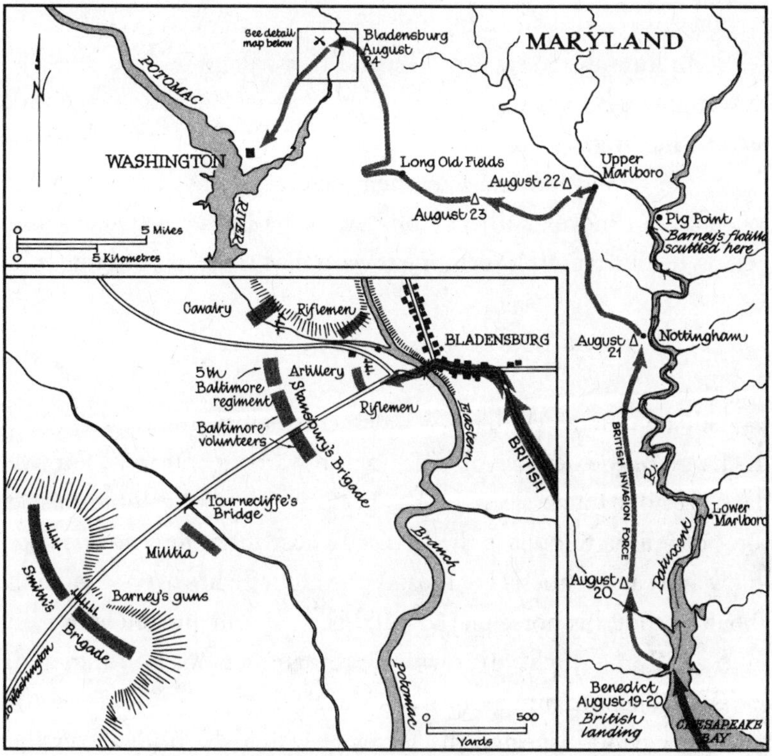
MARYLAND
WASHINGTON
POTOMAC
RIVER
See detail map below
Bladensburg August 24
Long Old Fields
August 22
August 23
Upper Marlboro
Pig Point
Barney's flotilla scuttled here
Nottingham
August 21
BRITISH INVASION FORCE
Lower Marlboro
August 20
Patuxent
Benedict August 19-20
British landing
CHESAPEAKE BAY
5 Miles
5 Kilometres
Cavalry
Riflemen
BLADENSBURG
5th Baltimore regiment
Artillery
Stansbury's Brigade
Riflemen
Baltimore volunteers
Eastern
BRITISH
Tournecliffe's Bridge
Militia
Branch
Smith's Brigade
Barney's guns
to Washington
Potomac
500
Yards

The British March on Washington, August 19–24, 1814

surprisingly still intact—George Gleig in the light brigade can see the enemy drawn up in line. Few are in uniform, some in blue, some in black, many in hunting jackets or frock coats. To Gleig they look like "country people," in stark contrast to the disciplined British regulars.

Gleig's brigade commander, Colonel William Thornton, thinks so, too. He does not want to wait for the rest of the army: the American militia, he insists, cannot stand a determined bayonet charge, supported by rocket fire. When Harry Smith, the General's aide, urges caution, Thornton becomes furious, and when Ross supports him, Smith is flabbergasted.

"General," he says, "neither of the other brigades will be up in time to support this mad attack and if the enemy fight, Thornton's brigade must be repulsed."

But Ross has made up his mind.

"If it rain militia," says the General, "we will go on."

Off goes Thornton on his grey horse, sword flashing in the sun, leading his brigade through the streets. As he reaches the river, the American guns open up. A moment before, George Gleig had felt he could not move another step; now, as the Battle of Bladensburg begins, he finds himself sprinting toward the bridge like a young colt.

WASHINGTON, D.C., AUGUST 24, 1814

Brigadier-General William Winder, the Baltimore lawyer placed in charge of the defence of Washington, worries and frets. For five days, without much sleep, he has been trying frantically to raise a force of militia to oppose the British, whose intentions he does not know and cannot guess. For most of the night he has been stumbling about on foot, his horse played out, his right arm and ankle in pain from a fall in a ditch. His own subordinates cannot find him and, for a time, believe him a captive of the British.

Now, having inspected the forces guarding the bridge over the east branch of the Potomac—the entrance to the city—he snatches an hour's sleep on a camp cot. If the British do intend to attack Washington, he reasons, they will probably come this way by the direct route from Long Old Fields. On the other hand, they may have another objective—Annapolis, perhaps, or Fort Warburton. He cannot tell. It is also possible they may take a more roundabout route to the capital, through Bladensburg. What to do? If he goes to Bladensburg, he leaves the other route wide open.

Few believe the British intend to attack Washington. The Secretary of War is one doubter. "They certainly will not come here," John Armstrong has declared. "What the devil will they do here? No! No! Baltimore is the place . . . that is of so much more consequence." This incredulity helps explain why so few have answered the call to arms.

Winder's military career has not been glorious. Captured by the British as he blundered about in the dark at Stoney Creek and exchanged a year later, he holds his present post partly because he is available and partly because he is a nephew of Maryland's governor, whose state has not been the most enthusiastic supporter of the war. That blood relationship, however, has not paid off. Of six thousand Marylanders called out by federal draft on July 4, only 250 were under Winder's command the day the British landed. The Pennsylvania record is even worse. That state was supposed to supply five thousand men but has sent none because its militia law has expired, and no one has yet got around to renewing it.

Winder should have fifteen thousand men—the number called for by the government. Two days before he could count only three thousand. Now, with the redcoats only eight miles away, more troops are trickling in. None are trained because the government would not call on them until the danger was "imminent." And some will not see action because of a maddening bureaucracy. As Winder fidgets and waits for word of the British line of march, seven hundred frustrated arrivals from Virginia are vainly attempting to get arms from the War Department. The clerk in charge arrives at last and begins doling out flints, one at a time, counting each carefully. When an officer tries to speed things up, he starts the count over again. These men will not see action today.

Because he cannot be sure of the British intentions, Winder has had to divide his forces. Two thousand Marylanders under Brigadier-General Tobias Stansbury occupy Bladensburg. Some arrived only the previous night and have hardly had time to settle in. Another six hundred are on their way from Annapolis; Winder does not know where they are. At the Potomac bridge on the eastern outskirts of Washington, ready to march in either of two directions, he has fifteen hundred District of Columbia militia under Brigadier-General Walter Smith. In addition, there are a handful of regulars, a couple of hundred dragoons, and four hundred naval men, anxious to get into action now that the flotilla has been destroyed.

The sun is scarcely up before Winder receives mortifying news from General Stansbury at Bladensburg. Fearing the British may take another route and cut him off, he has moved his exhausted Marylanders out of the village and back toward Washington. Winder orders him forward again. Stansbury's troops, who have been up most of the night, return as far as the heights above Bladensburg, commanding the bridge across the river, but do not occupy the village.

At ten, Winder's scouts gallop in and the General finally learns the British intentions: they have taken the longer route through Bladensburg. That is where he must oppose them. He moves to combine his forces, orders General Smith to march his brigade off immediately to join Stansbury. An hour later he follows as does most of the Cabinet, including the President. James Monroe, the Secretary of State, a onetime colonel in the Revolutionary army, dashes on ahead. It has always been his ambition to be commander-in-chief of the American forces in this war; now he has a chance to display his military acumen.

On the heights above the village, John Pendleton Kennedy of the crack United Company of the 5th Baltimore Light Dragoons—the "Baltimore 5th," as they are known—can hardly keep himself awake. He has actually had the novel experience of sleeping while on the march. What began as a glittering adventure—banners flying, bands playing, the populace huzzahing at every corner—has taken a darker turn. His comrades belong to the elite of Baltimore—barristers, professionals, wealthy merchants; he and his five friends have even brought along a black servant, Lige, to wait on them. But now the picnic is over. Routed out in the dark only hours after arriving, their kits in disarray, marched and countermarched in the night, they are used up. Kennedy has lost his boots in the midnight scramble to retire and is wearing dancing pumps on his swollen feet.

The British are only three miles away, but now another mix-up bedevils the Baltimore 5th. Having taken their position on the left of the forward line, supporting the riflemen and artillery, they are suddenly ordered back a quarter of a mile to an exposed position which leaves the forward guns and rifles without support. This is the work of Monroe, the Secretary of State, who has butted in, uninvited and without the knowledge of General Stansbury. By the time Winder arrives to inspect the lines, it is too late to make any change.

Stansbury's force is deployed in two ragged lines: the sharpshooters (most of whom have only muskets, not rifles) and cannons well forward, the three Maryland regiments some distance behind with the crack 5th on the left, its field of fire impeded by an orchard. These will bear the brunt of the British attack. A mile to the rear, another line is hastily forming as the troops arrive—Smith's brigade from Washington and several hundred footsore militia from Annapolis, who have already marched sixteen miles. None, save a few regulars and the naval detachment, have had any recent training because, as the Secretary of War has told Winder, the best way to use the militia is on the spur of the occasion—to bring them to fight as soon as called out.

The Secretary of War is the last of the Cabinet to arrive on the heights above Bladensburg. The President is already here, a small, frail figure in black, two borrowed duelling pistols at his waist. He stands behind Stansbury's lines with the Attorney General and the Secretaries of State, War, and Treasury. This is a motley crew, their personal relations fraught with jealousies, hatreds, ambitions. Armstrong has no use for Winder, who was not his choice for commander-in-chief; he has pointedly ignored the General's letters pleading for reinforcements. Monroe and Madison have little liking for Armstrong, whom they see as a possible political rival. Armstrong for once has nothing to say; having made no effort to defend the capital, he must realize that his days in office are numbered.

Up rides William Simmons, another Armstrong-hater, recently fired from his job with the War Department. Now, however, he has buried his bitterness in the common cause. Spotting Monroe, he offers to ride into the village and scout out the enemy. He gets to Lownde's Hill, on the far side of town, and sees, in the near distance, a great cloud of dust. Back he gallops to discover that the presidential party is in front of its own lines, moving down toward the Bladensburg bridge. Simmons warns the President that the British advance has already reached the village.

"The enemy in Bladensburg!" Madison exclaims in surprise. His party wheels about as Simmons vainly calls after them:

"Mr. Madison, if you stop, I will show them to you. . . ."

Only Richard Rush, the Attorney General, checks his horse. Simmons points out the redcoats entering the town, whereupon Rush too wheels about and gallops off, with Simmons riding after him, shouting that he has left his hat behind.

By 12:30, the battle is joined. Henry Fulford in the Baltimore 5th watches in amazement as the American cannons and sharpshooters pour a hail of fire onto the bridge. The British redcoats, dashing across, seem to take no notice; they move like clockwork: the instant a platoon is cut down it is filled up by men from the rear without the least confusion. George Gleig, on the bridge, has a different view: an entire company ahead of him is cut to pieces, and he has the grisly experience of trampling on his dead and dying comrades.

Without pausing for the rest of the British to come up, Colonel Thornton leads his men against the forward American skirmishers. Flinging aside their heavy packs, Gleig and the others drive the riflemen back into the woods, only to be faced with the main body of Marylanders. The Baltimore 5th surges forward, forcing the redcoats back to the river's edge. The carnage is dreadful. Almost every British officer is hit. Gleig's friend, Lieutenant Codd, falls dead beside him—the pair will never again forage for chickens. Not far away, crouching in the willows, Captain John Knox realizes he had never seen such fire. So many officers are down that he can expect promotion—if he lives. "By the time the action's over, the devil is in it if I am not a walking Major or a dead Captain," he tells himself. Harry Smith has been right; Thornton was too impetuous; he should have waited for the rest of the army.

Now, however, Major-General Ross has his Congreve rockets in position. Long tubes filled with powder, they operate on the same principle as a Fourth of July firework. They are hopelessly inaccurate but make a terrifying scream as they whoosh over the heads of the raw American troops, who have never before encountered anything like them. The Baltimore 5th, on the left of the line, stands fast, but the two regiments on the right break in panic. With its flanks exposed, the 5th also falls back. Officers dash about, vainly attempting to rally their fleeing men, but the retreat has become a rout.

John Kennedy, still in his dancing pumps, flings away his musket and joins the mob, carrying a wounded comrade to safety. Henry Fulford has only one idea in mind: to head for the woods, lie down, and sleep; instead, the musket balls and grape shot drive him into a swamp from which he later makes his way to a friendly farmhouse.

The rear line of Americans has only just formed when the fleeing Marylanders come dashing through. (Madison and his Cabinet have long since galloped off.) It stands briefly, then breaks. Only the naval veterans under Commodore Joshua Barney hold fast at their guns until out of ammunition. Barney, badly wounded in the thigh, cannot understand the rout.

"Damn them," he growls to his British captors, "there were enough of them to have eaten every one of you!"

The road to Washington and the city beyond is filled with fleeing militia. Winder, who has made no plans to gather his troops at a rallying point in case of retreat, decides to abandon the capital, an order that causes anguish among General Smith's brigade of Washington militia. Many vanish to their homes to look after their families. Those who can be collected are marched eighteen miles beyond the city to Montgomery Court House.

For the moment, the British are too exhausted to follow. George Gleig pursues the fleeing troops for a mile before he collapses and slakes his thirst in a muddy pool. He is lucky to be alive: a musket ball has torn the arm of his jacket, another has seared his thigh. He gathers what men he can and returns to join his battered regiment. It is dark before the scattered remains of his company can be collected. Then, tired or not, the light brigade marches triumphantly off toward the abandoned capital, the sky ahead bright with the glow of leaping flames.

———

Dolley Madison waits in the President's house, listening to the rumble of cannon and seeing, in the distant sky, the flash of rockets. She has no intention of leaving until she hears from her husband.

Two pencilled messages have arrived, warning her to be ready to depart at a moment's notice. In the driveway stands her carriage loaded with trunks containing all the Cabinet papers. A wagon, recently procured, contains some silver plate and personal belongings.

Four artillerymen, posted at two cannons guarding the mansion, have deserted their posts. French John Siousa, her personal servant, offers to spike the guns and lay a trail of powder to the door, to destroy the house if necessary. Mrs. Madison will have none of it. At three, two messengers, grimy with dust, gallop up with orders from the President to leave immediately. She will not do so until she can rescue Gilbert Stuart's full-length portrait of George Washington. She and French John attack the frame with carving knife and axe. With the canvas rolled and placed in friendly hands, the First Lady of the United States climbs into her carriage and rolls through the streets of the capital, crowded with soldiers, senators, women and children, with carriages, horses, wagons and carts loaded with household furniture, all fleeing toward the wooden bridge on the west side of town.

Half an hour later, the President arrives with his party, exhausted and humiliated. All his theoretical ideas about the value of democratic volunteers have been shattered.

"I could never have believed that so great a difference existed between regular troops and a militia force if I had not witnessed the scenes of this day," he remarks. At dusk, he too leaves the city.

From his handsome four-storey house at the corner of First and A streets, Washington's leading physician, Dr. James Ewell, has been gloomily watching the retreat. He sees the Secretary of War in full flight, followed by crowds of riders, some of whom bawl out: "Fly, fly! The ruffians are at hand! . . . send off your wives and children!" In the distance a cloud of dust envelops the retreating army. Shaken with horror, the doctor turns to find his wife in convulsions, crying repeatedly, "Oh, what shall we do? What shall we do?" while his two daughters scream at her side. He decides to quit his own home and move his family to a neighbouring house. The owner, a Mrs. Orr, is so sick that Ewell is sure nobody will harm her or those she shelters.

General Ross and Rear-Admiral Cockburn enter the city at the head of the 3rd Brigade, which has escaped most of the fighting. From a large brick house on their right comes the crackle of musket fire, killing the General's horse and hitting four soldiers, one mortally. At once the Admiral's aide, James Scott, leads a party to the building and smashes down the door. The house, only recently occupied by Albert Gallatin, now treating for peace at Ghent, is empty. Up come the light companies of the 21st and demolish the building with Congreve rockets. At almost the same time, the retreating Americans blow up the navy yard. For the next forty-eight hours, Washington will be aglow.

The victors push into Capitol Square. Ahead lies the seat of government, a Greek temple, inviting destruction. It is not easy to fire the Capitol. In the lower storey only the frames, sashes, shutters, and doors will burn. The troops chop away with axes, tear open some rockets as tinder, and spread a trail of fire from room to room. In the House of Representatives there is better fodder for the incendiaries—galleries and stages of yellow pine, mahogany desks, tables, chairs. Piled in the centre of the great domed chamber, they make a gargantuan bonfire, the heat so intense that glass melts, stone cracks, columns are peeled of their skin, marble is burned to lime. So bright is this pyre that George Gleig, bivouacked outside the city, can see the faces of his men reflected in the glow. He recalls the burning of San Sebastian; except for that, he realizes, he has never in his life witnessed a scene more strikingly sublime. But to the people of Washington, so certain of victory that thousands made no preparation to flee, the spectacle is pure horror.

The Treasury building is next, then the President's Mansion. Here an advance party finds a table set for forty, apparently in anticipation of a victory dinner. Instead, the real victors toast the Prince Regent while Cockburn sardonically raises his glass to "Jemmy," as he calls the President. Looting precedes the flames. Everyone takes a souvenir. The Admiral urges a local bookseller to help himself—but not to anything expensive; the most luxurious items, he says, must feed the blaze. Ross helps pile furniture in the

Oval Room while some of the seamen procure fire from a nearby beer house.

That done, the Admiral and the General enjoy dinner at Barbara Suter's boarding house. Cockburn blows out the candles, preferring, he says, the light cast by the burning buildings. An officer enters to ask if the War Department should be fired. Tomorrow, says the General; the men are exhausted.

Ross prepares to bed down in Dr. Ewell's empty house, then apologizes when its owner arrives, offers to go elsewhere. When Ewell insists, the General reassures him that his family is quite safe.

"I am myself a married man, have several sweet children and venerate the sanctities of conjugal and domestic relations," Ross declares—at least, that is the way the much-relieved physician remembers it.

Later Ross tells Ewell he regrets burning the Capitol library and says he would not have fired the President's Mansion had the First Lady remained. "I make war neither against letters nor ladies," he explains.

But the burning goes on the following day—private homes as well as public buildings to a value of more than a million dollars go up in smoke. Cockburn, riding a white mare with a black foal following, makes his way to the office of the violently anti-British newspaper, the *National Intelligencer*. Bowing to the entreaties of several women who fear the flames will spread to their homes, he spares the building but orders his men to destroy the contents. Out into the street go books, papers, type as the axes do their work.

"Be sure that all the C's are destroyed," says Cockburn, "so that the rascals can have no further means of abusing my name. . . ."

Dolley Madison, meanwhile, arriving at a small tavern sixteen miles from town, finds herself excoriated by a group of women fugitives who blame the administration for all their troubles. Her escort forces open the door against their protests just as a violent storm breaks. It is the worst in living memory.

In Washington, the sky goes black, a torrent of rain sweeps through the blazing buildings, damping the flames, while a hurricane tears the roofs off houses, whirling them into the air like sheets of paper. George Gleig, camping on Capitol Hill with his company and used to the soft rains of the English countryside, has never experienced anything so terrifying. Only the jagged flashes of lightning relieve the darkness. His company is dispersed, the men fleeing for shelter or throwing themselves flat to the ground to prevent the tempest carrying them off. Several houses topple, burying thirty soldiers in the debris. The wind is so strong that two cannon are lifted from their mounts and hurled several yards.

For two hours the storm rages. When it is over, Ross decides it is time to move out. The withdrawal takes place at night and in secret, the populace ordered to remain indoors under pain of death. Fuel is added to the burning buildings and a handful of men detailed to leap about in the light of the flames to fool the enemy. The army moves out in silence. Four days later, unmolested, it is back at Benedict, embarking on the ships.

For the first time, the war has been carried to the heart of the United States. When Madison commenced hostilities two summers before, expecting an easy victory and, possibly, a new state in the Union, he could hardly have foreseen that he would one day be cowering in a hovel outside the capital, fearing imminent capture. Now, as the people of Washington return to their gutted city and Ross and Cockburn plan a new attack on Baltimore, another army of British regulars—the largest yet assembled—is preparing to cross the border and march on New York. What began as the invasion of Canada has now become the invasion of America, and in spite of the peace talks in Ghent, it is not yet over.

TWELVE

The Battle of Lake Champlain

September, 1814

With thousands of Wellington's veterans shipped across the Atlantic to reinforce his thin army, Sir George Prevost can at last go on the offensive. He intends to march his troops—eleven thousand strong— down the Richelieu-Champlain corridor and take the war into New York State. To succeed he must seize Plattsburgh on Lake Champlain and destroy the newly built American fleet anchored in Plattsburgh Bay. All year, the two opposing navies on the lake have been engaged in a shipbuilding contest. As the British flotilla nears completion and Prevost's army marches south, the American commodore, Thomas Macdonough, awaits the coming attack.

ABOARD U.S. *SARATOGA*, PLATTSBURGH BAY,
NEW YORK, SEPTEMBER 4, 1814

Sunday dinner aboard the flagship of Commodore Thomas Macdonough, commander of the American fleet on Lake Champlain. The Commodore's gig arrives bringing a guest, a Yale student, John

H. Dulles of Philadelphia. As the sun approaches the meridian, a pre-dinner service is held on deck, and young Dulles notes that the three hundred members of the naval congregation are more than usually devout. He remarks on this to the Commodore, who replies, drily, "You must not be deceived by an inference that it is from pious feelings altogether." He smiles and adds, "There are other considerations controlling their conduct." There are indeed. Thomas Macdonough is totally in control of his fleet. Dulles, chatting with some junior officers, is "struck with the palpable evidence of the one pervading spirit of a master mind."

In spite of the stalemate on the Niagara peninsula, the war is far from over. On this Sunday afternoon, as Gordon Drummond continues to lob cannonballs at Fort Erie and the five Americans at Ghent begin, at last, to fence with their British counterparts, Sir George Prevost's vast army is marching down the western shore of Lake Champlain, virtually unopposed. A few miles to the north,

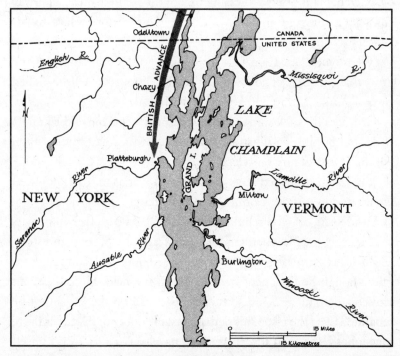

Lake Champlain, 1814

a new British fleet is nearing completion. But here on Thomas Macdonough's flagship, all is calm.

In his cabin, Macdonough quietly discusses the possibilities of the coming action. If the British destroy his fleet, he explains, Sir George Prevost can march his army, unobstructed, to the capital at Albany—even on to New York City, there to dictate an ignominious peace. The next few days will be decisive.

Dulles is impressed by Macdonough, who speaks "with the singular simplicity and with the dignity of a Christian gentleman." The Commodore looks younger than his thirty-one years. He has a light, agile frame and a bony face—all nose and jaw. His faith in a living God is unbounded. To Dulles he quotes from the epistle of St. James with its naval illustrations:

"He that wavereth is like a wave of the sea driven with the wind," and "Behold the ships, though so great, are turned about with a very small helm."

The chaplain offers a blessing before the midday meal. Halfway through a message arrives, which the Commodore relays to his officers:

"Gentlemen . . . I am just informed by the commander of the army that the signs of advance by the British forces will be signalled by two guns, and you will act accordingly."

He leaves the table and the conversation livens. One of the juniors makes so bold as to illustrate a remark with an oath, whereupon another turns to him and declares:

"Sir, I am astonished at your using such language. You know you would not do it if the Commodore was present."

Dead silence as the rebuke sinks in. What a curious company is this! Hardly the blasphemous and salty fraternity of song and story.

But then, no one would describe Thomas Macdonough as salty, though he has spent half his life in the navy. He is a devout Episcopalian, his religion so much a part of him that it cannot be separated from the rest of his personality. He does not flaunt his faith, for he has learned in fifteen years of naval service to keep himself under tight control, to curb a tendency toward impetuosity—even rashness. He is known as an amiable, even placid officer, not one to betray emotion.

And he is a survivor. One of Stephen Decatur's favourite midshipmen, he saw active service in the Mediterranean. He is brave and he is tough. Once, in hand-to-hand fighting on a Tripolitan gunboat when his cutlass broke, Macdonough wrested a pistol from his nearest assailant and shot him dead. Later he survived an epidemic of yellow fever that killed all but three of his shipmates. Two years of service on Lake Champlain, however, have worn him down, leaving him prey to the tuberculosis that will eventually kill him.

As on Erie and Ontario, the British and Americans on Lake Champlain have been engaged in a shipbuilding race. It has not been easy for Macdonough, who has had to compete with Chauncey for men and supplies. Yet, with the help of Noah Brown, the New York shipbuilding genius who worked on Perry's fleet, he has outdone Perry. In the spring, Brown launched the twenty-six-gun *Saratoga*, larger than any of Erie's vessels. Then, when Macdonough discovered that the British were building an even larger vessel, *Confiance*, he undertook to construct a second, the twenty-gun *Eagle*, launched in a record seventeen days after the keel was laid. Now he has outstripped the British, for *Eagle* has joined his squadron while the British flagship has yet to be rigged.

The creation of Macdonough's fleet has been a masterpiece of organization and ingenuity. One vessel, the seventeen-gun *Ticonderoga*, is a former steamer, transformed by Brown into a schooner. Guns, cannon, shot, cables, and cordage have been hauled hundreds of miles to the shipyards at Otter Creek. Here, in the saw pits, green timber has been turned into planking while local blacksmiths have hammered out nails, bolts, fastenings, wire. Besides his two large vessels and *Ticonderoga*, Macdonough has three smaller sloops, six two-gun galleys, each manned by forty oarsmen, and four smaller galleys—sixteen vessels in all.

Now, with Prevost's army sweeping everything before it, Macdonough waits for the British fleet. He knows he cannot beat it in the open water, where the British long guns can savage his vessels at a comfortable distance. He must force them to come to him—to do battle within the confines of Plattsburgh Bay, where his powerful short-range carronades may hammer them to matchwood.

Will Downie, the British commander, hold his fleet outside the bay? Macdonough thinks not: at this season the possibility of a destructive gale is too great. But once they enter the bay, Macdonough can fight at a site of his own choosing.

The long narrow lake runs north and south, with the prevailing winds blowing from the north. Macdonough expects the British fleet will sweep up the lake toward its objective with the north wind behind it. Once the ships round Cumberland Head, however, they must turn into the wind in order to manoeuvre into the bay. They may, of course, drive directly across the mouth of the bay, but that is unlikely, for it would place them within range of the shore batteries on the far side.

With this in mind, Macdonough carefully places his fleet in a chain across the bay, stretching from the shallows near Crab Island on his right to Cumberland Head on his left. The chain runs almost north and south; that will force the British to attack bows on, a position that will allow Macdonough to rake their vessels from bow to stern. Nor can the British stand off out of range and batter the Americans with their long guns. Macdonough has so chosen his position in the cramped bay that there is not enough room.

He intends to fight at anchor, forcing the British to come to him, his vessels little more than floating batteries. It can be dangerous. He must be aware that Nelson destroyed two fleets at anchor—the French on the Nile, the Danes at Copenhagen. But Nelson had the wind behind him. By hitting the enemy line on the windward he was able to bear down on the opposing fleet and roll it up, ship by ship. Downie, the British commodore, cannot duplicate Nelson's feat from the leeward; the geography of Plattsburgh Bay makes that impossible. It is hard enough with lake vessels of shallow drafts and flat bottoms to beat up, close-hauled, against the wind.

Macdonough plans one further precaution. He must be able to manoeuvre quickly at anchor, without putting on sail. To do that, he equips his flagship, *Saratoga*, with a series of anchors and cables

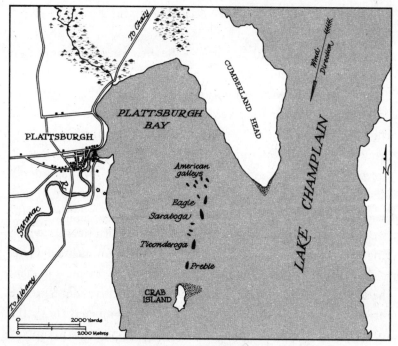

Macdonough at Anchor, Plattsburgh Bay, September, 1814

that will allow him to twist it about in any direction—through an arc of 180 degrees if necessary—in order to bring his guns to bear on targets of opportunity.

He cannot know what the British will do. He can only make an educated guess, based on his knowledge of the winds, the geography of the lake, his own capabilities, and the enemy's objectives.

The British are determined to seize Plattsburgh and destroy its defenders. To accomplish that and to continue on through the state, they must have naval support. That they cannot have without a naval victory. For once, the approaching winter is to the Americans' advantage. With the season far advanced, Macdonough is betting that Prevost will not hazard a blockade but will opt immediately for a combined attack by Downie's squadron and his formidable army. If he does, and if the God in whom the Commodore so devoutly believes gives him favourable winds, Macdonough is calmly confident of victory.

Sir George Prevost's mighty army—the greatest yet assembled on the border—pours into Plattsburgh's outskirts in two dense columns, brushing aside the weak American defenders like ineffectual insects.

These are Wellington's veterans. With Napoleon confined to Elba and the conflict in Europe at an end, sixteen thousand were brought across the Atlantic to finish the war in North America. Prevost has at least eleven thousand on this march through upper New York State. The logistics are awesome. To maintain its new army in Canada, Britain must ship daily supplies weighing forty-five tons across the ocean—a drain upon the British treasury which English property owners, facing new taxes, are beginning to deplore.

At eight in the morning, Major John E. Wool attempts to stem the scarlet tide. He has no chance. The heavy British column presses forward at a steady 108 paces to the minute, completely filling the roadway and routing the militia. An artillery captain tries to support Wool. His cannonballs tear heavy lanes through the British ranks, but the disciplined veterans march inexorably on, filling the gaps as they go. They disdain to deploy into line. Instead, as the bugles sound, the flanking companies toss aside their knapsacks, rush forward at a smart double, and disperse the fleeing Americans at bayonet point even as the main body marches on.

Prevost's brigades are under the direct control of Major-General De Rottenburg, who commands three battle-wise major-generals from Wellington's army—Manley Power, Thomas Makdougall Brisbane, and Frederick Philipse Robinson. They have been hand picked by the Iron Duke himself; he considers them the best he has. Not surprisingly, all three are sceptical of the colonial high command. Neither Prevost, De Rottenburg, nor the Adjutant-General, Colonel Baynes, now promoted to major-general, have much battle experience.

As the troops march into Plattsburgh against light resistance, Robinson has further cause to question Prevost's capabilities. He has already realized that the army is moving on its objective without any carefully thought-out plan. Now, as he approaches the Saranac River, the major obstacle between the American redoubts and the advancing British, his doubts are confirmed.

Prevost proposes an immediate attack. Is Robinson prepared to launch his demi-brigade in an assault on the heights across the river?

Robinson is always ready, but he has some questions:

Is the river fordable and, if so, where? What is the ground like on the other side? How far will the men have to march to reach the American redoubts? Are experienced guides available?

To his dismay, he is told that no one has the answers to any of these queries.

Robinson's men have been on the march since five in the morning. It is now three o'clock. He suggests to Prevost that the staff do its best to get all possible information and if it cannot be procured before dark, to defer the attack until daybreak. Guides, he says, are essential; they must be obtained at any price.

Undoubtedly his mind goes back to Wellington's crossing of the Bidassoa between Spain and France. There the Duke employed men disguised as fishermen to sound out the fords and the ground and to guide the attacking columns. But Prevost is no Wellington. It seems to Robinson that the high command is convinced that it is impossible to get reliable information and that it is simply wasting good money to try. Prevost is a penny-pincher; he has a secret service fund but withholds it from his generals.

It is clear now that no attempt will be made on the American redoubts until the following day. As Prevost camps his army on a ridge north of Plattsburgh, Robinson, the old campaigner, makes a personal reconnaissance of the village below: the scattered houses, perhaps eighty in number, four hotels, a few shops and public buildings; the river, spanned by two bridges, the planking of each removed by the retreating Americans; on the heights on the south side, three redoubts, two blockhouses, and, near the lake, a battery of big guns. He notes that the redoubts are not yet finished and that the guns are *en barbette*—not mounted. They can, he believes, easily be silenced during an assault.

He is an old hand at this, for he has been a soldier since the age of thirteen in Virginia, when he was commissioned an ensign at the outbreak of the American Revolution. At fifteen, he took a company into action at Horseneck. Since then his has been a life of action. Wounded three times—once fighting in America, twice in the Peninsular campaign—he is known as an officer of high and daring spirit, chosen to lead the advance in the successful assault on San Sebastian, mentioned several times in dispatches, noted for taking a village against a heavy artillery barrage without firing a shot. His lineage is distinguished, his family tree studded with clerics, jurists, and generals. John Beverley Robinson is his first cousin.

Robinson has urged that his assault force be called out and in position by first light, but dawn comes and no orders reach him. Sir George Prevost is having second thoughts.

Prevost is not Robinson's kind of general. The qualities that have made him a good administrator in the defence of Canada—prudence, conciliation, sober second thoughts, a tendency to delay—now work against him. He is essentially a diplomat; circumspection is his hallmark. He prefers to slide around a problem rather than meet it head on. He cannot bring himself even to write a harsh letter. His reproofs to subordinates are so delicately phrased that they seem almost like praise.

At forty-seven, he is in the prime of his career, his body supple, his face not unhandsome, though his official portrait cannot disguise the worried, hesitant cast of his eyes. These have not been easy years for George Prevost. His conciliation of the French Canadians, however admirable, has made him unpopular with the Anglophone elite in Quebec, who feel he is coddling a defeated race. His strategy, dictated by Great Britain, has been to remain strictly on the defensive, husbanding his inadequate forces. For more than two years his instincts have been to hold fast, to let the enemy come to him, to seek delay by armistice, to avoid costly mistakes. In this he has been spectacularly successful. Except for two small enclaves at Amherstburg and Fort Erie (the latter soon to be abandoned) and some foraging parties trampling their way up and down the Thames

Valley, the Americans have failed to gain a foothold in Canada. The conquest of British North America is no closer to reality than it was in the summer of 1812. For this, Prevost can take much credit.

Now, however, events have taken an about-turn. For the first time, the Americans are outnumbered—and by the best troops in the world. An entire British division has penetrated deep into enemy territory. If Prevost is to succeed he must accommodate himself to a changed set of circumstances, put aside old habits, abandon the strategy of the previous twenty-seven months.

He cannot do it, cannot bring himself to launch an assault even against the weakly held entrenchments before him. The best American troops, four thousand in number, have already left to support Jacob Brown on the Niagara frontier—an incomprehensible decision by John Armstrong that galled their leader, Major-General Izard—but Prevost still hesitates. He remembers the three previous assaults on entrenched positions at Fort Meigs, Fort Stephenson, and Fort Erie, all abortive. The Americans, it seems, fight like demons behind their ditches and their abatis.

He cannot make up his mind. Robinson, fretting in his head-quarters, receives an order to attend a meeting at six o'clock on the morning of the seventh. Before he can attend, it is countermanded. At eight, Sir George sends for him alone. He has decided that he cannot move on the Plattsburgh redoubts without the support of the fleet. It is just as well, for Robinson discovers, to his dismay, that in the midst of all this soul searching no one has thought to mount the British artillery to support the proposed assault.

At this point, a change comes over Sir George Prevost. In his impatience to bring the fleet down the lake at once, the sedulous diplomat becomes alarmingly shrill. Testy letters urging Captain Downie to get moving travel north by express rider. Prevost, who has been irritated by Sir James Yeo's vacillations, no doubt believes that the navy on Lake Champlain is dawdling. But Downie cannot move until his biggest ship, *Confiance*, is fitted; nor can he be blamed, since he has been in command for only three days. Yet Prevost knows he must attack soon. The fall season is far advanced. The maples that arch over the narrow roads are beginning to turn. Frost is in the air. The weather, which has halted every American advance into Canada, will soon be his enemy.

The notes to Downie grow more petulant, nettling the naval commander, forcing him to move before he is ready, goading him to fight on the enemy's terms and on the enemy's site, with a ship scarcely fitted and a crew yet untried.

MILTON, VERMONT, SEPTEMBER 7, 1814

In spite of his governor's opposition to the war, Jonathan Blaisdell, a Milton house builder, has decided to answer the call of his country and cross the lake to Plattsburgh to help repulse the invading British. Vermonters are undergoing a change of heart now that the war has been carried to their doorstep. Farmers who once sat out the war in opposition to the Hawks in Washington are abandoning their fields, heading for the lake by the hundreds, climbing aboard any vessel that will transport them quickly to Plattsburgh.

Jonathan Blaisdell is so eager to get at the British that he and two companions decide to ride their horses across a low sandbar to the island of South Hero in the lake. From there they plan to catch a boat to Plattsburgh. They are almost drowned in the attempt and end up, soaking wet, at Fox's Tavern on the Vermont shore.

More Vermonters crowd in, also intent on crossing. Two hours pass; the moon rises, encouraging another attempt. One hundred volunteers, strung out in a long line across the shallows, finally reach the island. The following day a sloop carries them to the scene of the action.

Until this week, Vermonters have cared so little about the war that they have not hesitated to continue the border smuggling that has been their livelihood—not just the usual livestock, cheese, fish, grain, tobacco, and potash but also the actual materials of war. Only the vigilance of Macdonough's fleet has prevented the British from equipping *Confiance* with spars, masts, naval stores, and caulking towed up the lake as recently as July by resourceful Vermont entrepreneurs.

Prevost's incursion has done what George Izard's troops could not accomplish: it has turned the Vermonters into patriots and war hawks. Within three days, twenty-five hundred volunteers flock to the colours to be greeted personally by the new commander at Plattsburgh, Brigadier-General Alexander Macomb. In an inspired gesture, he pins an evergreen bough in the hat of their leader, Samuel Strong—a symbol of the zeal of his Green Mountain Boys.

Macomb has need of these citizen soldiers. Since the unexpected departure of Major-General Izard and his four thousand regulars, the safety of the fort has depended on fewer than three thousand troops of whom about half are effective soldiers, the remainder either sick or untrained. On a man-to-man basis, the British outnumber the Americans more than three to one, but even that ratio is deceptive. Prevost has the cream of Wellington's army; Macomb's best soldier is no better than Prevost's worst.

The leading citizens of Plattsburgh have little faith in Macomb's ragtag army. They want him to retire gracefully to spare a wanton sacrifice of lives. Macomb has no such intention. If worst comes to worst, he intends to blow up the town. Most of the inhabitants have already fled.

Prevost's decision to wait for the fleet gives Macomb a week in which to strengthen his defences, gather reinforcements, and raise the morale of his small, largely untrained army. His three major redoubts are positioned in a triangle on the heights of a small peninsula that stretches like a fat thumb between the lake and the Saranac River. Each is protected by ditches, palisades, abatis.

Like Scott, Brown, and Izard, Macomb belongs to a younger generation of general officers, the new team thrown up by the war that will reshape the American army in the years to come. He is a chubby thirty-two, big chested, plump cheeked, blue eyed, bursting with health and good nature—the kind of man who will always seem younger than his years. The son of a Detroit fur merchant, raised in the shadow of an army camp, dandled on the knees of officers during his childhood, he is all soldier. Now he labours under extraordinary difficulties.

But Macomb intends to do his duty, and to that duty he brings an imaginative mind and a sensitive understanding of leadership. He is a strong believer in the military virtues of deception, intelligence, and morale. He may be short on manpower but he is long on acumen.

He makes it a point to issue arms and ammunition personally to the young volunteers crowding into the village, to address them in groups, thanking them for their *esprit*, and to advise them to act in small bands as partisans.

He goes out of his way to deceive Prevost. He never mounts a guard without parading all of his troops to give an impression of great numbers. He burns the buildings in front of the forts to clear the ground and reveal any potential assault force. In the glow of these fires, he marches platoons of reserves as if they were reinforcements. In spite of the rain he keeps a third of his regular force on the parapets each night.

Macomb is aware that spies are operating among his troops, passing as militia volunteers. He spreads the word that George Izard's army is within hailing distance and that he now has ten thousand militia under his command with an additional ten thousand on the way, then watches with satisfaction as the bogus soldiers steal across the Saranac bridge at night, carrying the news to Prevost.

He intends to get the most out of his small force. Even the sick are put to work manning two six-pounders at the makeshift hospital on Crab Island. Meanwhile, Macomb gives instructions to mask the roads leading to the river by planting pine trees on them and covering the bare areas with leaves, at the same time opening the entrances to old, unused roads. By these methods, he hopes the advancing British may lose their way.

The British, however, are confident of victory. On the tenth, Prevost again calls Major-General Robinson to his quarters to advise him that the fleet will be up with the first fair wind and that he must keep his brigade at the ready to ford the river and attack the three American redoubts. Robinson has only one request: he *must* be at the fords by daybreak, not a second later. To this the Governor General agrees.

At Putnam Lawrence's occupied house near the lake, a group of British officers are celebrating the morrow's victory. Soldiers roll up casks and barrels, stand them on end, lay boards across to make a table. The casks are brimming with wine and Jamaica rum. The table is laid with linen, china, glass, silver. The British toast the capture of Plattsburgh and victory over the American fleet.

Plattsburgh, someone is heard to say, will make quite a nice breakfast in the morning.

CHAZY, LAKE CHAMPLAIN, NEW YORK,
SEPTEMBER 10, 1814

Captain George Downie, commander of the British squadron, is irritated beyond measure by the persistent entreaties of Sir George Prevost. Since the British army reached Plattsburgh, the Governor General has been bombarding him with letters, each touchier than the last, urging him to move the fleet up the lake so that he can launch his assault on the American bastions.

"I need not dwell with you upon the Evils resulting to both services from delay," Prevost wrote on September 9, adding that he has directed an officer of the Provincial Cavalry to remain at Downie's headquarters until the fleet moves. Even though the fleet was not ready, Downie tried that very day to get under way, only to be forced back by adverse winds.

Now he holds a more insulting letter from Prevost. It seems to hint that Downie has been deceiving him about the weather:

I ascribe the disappointment I have experienced to the unfortunate change of wind, & shall rejoice to learn that my reasonable expectations have been frustrated by no other cause.

Reasonable expectations! Prevost's phrase stings Downie. All expectations have been unreasonable. He has been in charge of the fleet for no more than a week, does not know the lake, does not know the men, is unfamiliar with the strategic situation. His flagship, the frigate *Confiance*, is scarcely in fighting trim. Twenty-five carpenters are still on board fitting her with belaying pins, cleats, breaching blocks. There has been no time to scrape the green planks of her decks free of oozing tar. The firing mechanisms for her long cannon have not arrived; her gunners will have to make do with carronade locks. She is still taking on newly arrived marines and soldiers: there has been no time for the officers to be able to recognize, much less know, the men who will serve under them.

This last-minute scramble means that there will be no time for a shakedown cruise. The big frigate will go into action with a strange crew who have scarcely had a chance to fire her guns or hoist her sails. Yet it could all have been avoided if Sir James Yeo—or Prevost—had not been obsessed with the shipbuilding war on Lake Ontario. Not until Macdonough's *Saratoga* appeared on the lake in late May did the British commanders wake up to their peril. Now they are paying for their inattention.

Downie shares his disgust over Prevost's letter with his second-in-command, Captain Daniel Pring, whom he has just replaced as senior commander on the lake.

"I will not write any more letters," he declares to Pring. "This letter does not deserve an answer but I will convince him that the naval force will not be backward in their share of the attack."

In short, goaded by Prevost, he will not wait for the enemy to emerge from the safe harbour at Plattsburgh to meet him on the open lake. He will chance a direct bows-on attack against Macdonough's anchored fleet.

Downie is prepared to attempt this dangerous action only because Prevost has told him that he will launch his land assault at the same time. Once the shore batteries have been stormed and taken, Downie believes, Macdonough will be in peril. With the captured guns turned on him he will have to quit his anchorage and, during the confusion, the British will have the advantage.

At midnight, the wind switches to the northeast. Downie weighs anchor, and the fleet slips southward toward Plattsburgh Bay carrying one thousand men, including the riggers and outfitters still straining to complete their work.

At five, the fleet reaches Cumberland Head. Here Downie scales his guns—clears out the bores, which have never been fired, with blank cartridges. This is the signal, pre-arranged with Prevost, to announce his arrival and to co-ordinate a simultaneous attack by the land forces.

In the hazy dawn, Downie boards his gig, nudges it around the point, and examines the American fleet through his glass.

Macdonough's four large vessels are strung out in line across the bay, with the gunboats in support—the twenty-gun brig *Eagle* at the northernmost end, followed by the larger *Saratoga*, twenty-six guns, the schooner *Ticonderoga*, seven guns, and the sloop *Preble*, seven guns, at the rear. With twenty-seven long cannon and ten heavy carronades, Downie's *Confiance* is more than a match for Macdonough's flagship. On the other hand, the combined batteries of *Saratoga* and *Eagle* can hurl a heavier weight of metal than can Downie's two largest vessels, *Confiance* and *Linnet*, the latter a brig of sixteen guns under Captain Pring.

With this in mind, Downie plans his attack. *Confiance* will take on the American flagship *Saratoga*, first passing *Eagle* and delivering a broadside, then turning hard a-port to anchor directly across the bows of Macdonough's ship. *Linnet*, supported by the sloop *Chubb*, will engage *Eagle*. In this way the two largest American vessels will be under fire from three of the British. The fourth and smallest British vessel, the sloop *Finch*, and eleven gunboats will hit the American rear, boarding the former steamer *Ticonderoga* and at the same time attacking the little *Preble*.

Back on his flagship, Downie calls his officers to a conference, outlines his strategy, and speaks a few words of encouragement to the ship's company:

"Now, my lads, there are the American ships and batteries. At the same moment we attack the ships our army are to storm the batteries. And, mind, don't let us be behind."

They answer with a cheer.

At almost the same time, Macdonough's men kneel on the deck of *Saratoga* as their commander reads a short prayer:

"Thou givest not always the battle to the strong, but canst save by many or by few—hear us, Thy poor servants, imploring Thy help that Thou wouldst be a defence unto us against the face of the enemy. Make it clear that Thou art our Saviour and Mighty Deliverer, through Jesus Christ, our Lord."

From the mast of the flagship, Macdonough's signal reminds his men why they are fighting:

Impressed seamen call on every man to do his duty.

In that message there is unconscious irony. It is well that Macdonough is not a party to the peace talks at Ghent where both the British and American negotiators have already decided to toss the whole bitter matter of impressment into the dustbin.

As the British fleet turns into line abreast, a silence falls over the bay. It is not broken until the ships come within range. *Eagle* hurls the first shot at Downie's *Confiance*, which has moved into the van. The ball splashes well short of its objective. *Linnet*, passing the American flagship en route to its target, fires a broadside that does little damage except to shatter a crate containing a fighting game-cock. The rooster flies into the rigging, crowing wildly, a touch of bravado that raises a cheer from *Saratoga*'s crew.

Downie, gazing anxiously at the headland, wonders to James Robertson, his First Officer, why Prevost has not commenced his attack. On *Saratoga*, Macdonough personally sights a long twenty-four and fires the first shot at his opponent's flagship. The heavy ball strikes the tall frigate near the hawse hole and tears its way the full length of the deck, killing and wounding several of Downie's crew and demolishing the wheel.

Now the action becomes general. Grey smoke pours from the guns, cannonballs ricochet across the glassy waters of the bay, chain-shot tears through the rigging. Through this maelstrom, *Confiance* sails toward her objective, sheets tattered, hawsers shredded, two anchors shot away. But the wind is erratic, and Downie realizes he cannot cross the head of the American line as he had hoped. He is forced to anchor more than three hundred yards from Macdonough's *Saratoga*—a manoeuvre he executes with great coolness under the other's hammering fire—but in doing so he loses two port anchors and fouls the kedge anchors at his stern. That will cost *Confiance* dear.

Downie's guns have not yet fired. His long twenty-fours have been carefully wedged with quoins for point-blank fire and double-shotted for maximum effect. Now, at a signal, a sheet of flame erupts from the British flagship, and more than seven hundred pounds of cast iron strike *Saratoga*. The effect is terrible. The American frigate shivers from round top to hull, as if from a violent attack of ague. Macdonough sees half his crew hurled flat on the deck. Forty are killed or wounded; the scuppers are running with blood. The Commodore's right-hand man, Lieutenant Peter Gamble, is among the dead, killed instantly while on his knees, sighting the bow gun.

Saratoga replies to *Confiance*, broadside for broadside. As George Downie stands behind one of his long twenty-fours, commanding the action, an enemy ball strikes the muzzle, knocking the gun off its carriage and thrusting it back into the commander's midriff. Downie falls dead, his watch flattened, his skin unbroken. For the British, it is a critical loss.

Linnet and *Chubb* have moved up to support *Confiance* in her battle with the two big American vessels. But a series of withering broadsides from *Eagle* so badly cripples *Chubb* that with half her crew casualties, her sails in tatters, her boom shaft and halyards wrecked, her hammock netting ablaze, her commander wounded, and only six men left on deck, she drifts helplessly and finally strikes her colours.

At the end of the line, *Finch* and the British gunboats are attacking the schooner *Ticonderoga* and the little sloop *Preble*. The latter wilts under the onslaught, cuts her cable, and drifts out of action. But only four of the British gunboats remain to do battle. The rest flee the action, their militia crews cowering in the bottoms under a shower of grape and musket fire, while the commander of the flotilla bolts to the hospital tender, remaining there until the

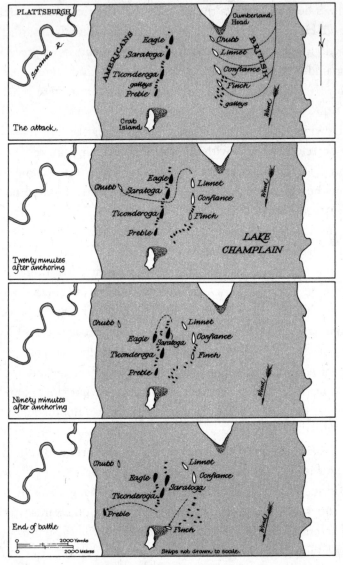

The Battle of Lake Champlain

end of the battle, eventually evading court martial only by escaping while en route to trial.

Ticonderoga wards off *Finch*, which is raking her from the stern, but is herself in trouble, taking water, her pumps struggling to keep up with the inflow. *Finch*'s commander, Lieutenant William Hicks, brandishing a cutlass to bring the terrified pilot into line, tries to wear the British sloop in the light erratic wind and finds himself stuck fast on a reef near Crab Island, where he fights a brief engagement with the invalids manning their six-pounders. He, too, is out of action.

The four remaining British gunboats, sweeps thrashing the water, come within a boathook of *Ticonderoga*. Her commander, Lieutenant Stephen Cassin, a commodore's son, coolly walks the taffrail amid a shower of shot, directing his men to ward off the boarders. His second-in-command is cut in two by a cannonball and hurled into the lake. A sixteen-year-old midshipman, Hiram Paulding—a future rear-admiral—mans the guns, finds the slow match useless, and repeats Barclay's action on Erie by discharging his pistol into the powder holes. In between the cannon blasts he continues to fire the pistol at the British, still vainly trying to scramble aboard.

But the main battle is at the head of the line between the American *Saratoga* and *Eagle* and the British *Confiance* and *Linnet*. *Eagle*, with most of her starboard guns rendered useless, cuts her cable and changes position to bring her port broadside into action. In doing so she positions herself to threaten *Confiance* but leaves Macdonough's flagship exposed to *Linnet*'s raking broadsides.

Linnet's cannons batter *Saratoga*'s long guns into silence. All but one of Macdonough's carronades have been dismounted in the action or wrecked by overzealous crews who overload in the absence of experienced officers. Hardly a man on either flagship has escaped injury. Macdonough is lucky. As he bends over a gun to sight it, a spanker boom, sliced in two by cannon fire, knocks him briefly insensible. A little later he suffers a grislier mishap: the head of his gun captain, torn off by British round-shot, comes hurtling across the deck, strikes him in the midriff, knocking him into the scuppers. He is winded but unharmed.

Now the naval bolt on *Saratoga*'s last carronade breaks, throwing the heavy gun off its carriage and hurling it down the hatch. Macdonough is in trouble. He has no guns left on the starboard side and only one officer. In most situations this would be enough to force him to strike his colours, but Macdonough has prepared for such an emergency. He turns to the complicated series of spring cables, hawsers, and kedge anchors that will allow him to wind his ship: to swing it end for end so that he can bring the seventeen guns on his port side—none of which has been fired—to bear upon his opponent.

It is a difficult and awkward manoeuvre, requiring careful timing and skill—a knowledge of when to raise one anchor, when to drop another. Now it must be done under the hazard of enemy fire.

Fortunately that fire has slackened, for the British ships too are in a bad way, and the guns of *Confiance* are firing too high. The seamen, new to the frigate, to each other, and to their officers, have had no gun drill. The cannon have been set for point-blank range, but at each blast they leap up on their carriages. The quoins, which are supposed to wedge them in place, are loosened, causing the muzzles to edge up. As a result, more damage is done to hammocks, halyards, spars, and pine trees on the shore than to the opposing vessels.

Macdonough manages to wind his ship half-way round until she is at right angles to her former position. There she sticks, stern facing *Linnet*'s broadside. The British brig rakes the battered American flagship and the line of sweating seamen straining at the hawser. A splinter strikes the Commodore's sailing master, Peter Brum, as he runs forward to oversee the manoeuvre. It slices through his uniform, barely touching the skin but stripping him of his clothing. Naked, he continues his task.

Slowly, Brum and Macdonough get the ship turning again until the first of her portside carronades comes into play against *Confiance*. The gun crews go to work as the frigate continues her half circle and, one by one, the heavy guns open fire.

On *Confiance*, Downie's young successor, James Robertson, is attempting the same manoeuvre but with less success. His frigate is in terrible shape, her masts like bunches of matches, her sails like bundles of rags, her rigging, spars, and hull shattered. Almost half her crew are out of action. The wife of the flagship's steward, in the act of binding a wounded seaman's leg, is struck by a ball that tears through the side of the ship, carries away her breasts, and flings her corpse across the vessel. One of Nelson's veterans aboard *Confiance* is heard to remark that compared to this action, Trafalgar was a mere fleabite. The ship's carpenter has already plugged sixteen holes below the waterline, but a great seven-foot gash in her hull, where a plank has been torn away, cannot be mended. To keep her from sinking it has been necessary to run in all the guns on the port side—most are useless anyway—and double shot those on the starboard to keep the holes above the water.

Because her anchors have been torn away it is almost impossible for Robertson to duplicate Macdonough's manoeuvre, but he is trying, swinging the frigate by putting a new spring on the bow cable—a daring feat under fire. Half-way round, she sticks fast at right angles to her enemy, *Saratoga*, whose newly freed guns can rake her from bowsprit to taffrail. At this point, Robertson's crewmen refuse to do more. Why should they? they ask. Most of the British gunboats have not entered the battle. And where is the promised army support? Not a musket, not a cannon has been heard on the land side. Reluctantly, Robertson hauls down his colours.

Linnet, under Daniel Pring, fights on for fifteen minutes more—the water rising so quickly in her lower deck that the wounded must be lifted onto chests and tables—then she, too, surrenders. Hicks, aboard *Finch*, stuck on a shoal, sees the flags go down and follows suit. Only the gunboats escape. The battle, which has lasted for two hours and twenty minutes, is over.

The senior British officers join Robertson and proceed to *Saratoga* to surrender their swords. As they step aboard, Macdonough meets them, bows. Holding their caps in their left hands and their swords by the blades, they advance, bowing, and present their weapons. Macdonough bows once more.

"Gentlemen, return your swords into your scabbards and wear them," he says. "You are worthy of them." He takes Robertson by the arm and walks the deck with his prisoners.

A twenty-one-year old Vermont farmboy, Samuel Shether Phelps, seeing the engagement has ended, takes a rowboat, pulls for *Saratoga*, climbs onto the deck, almost slips in the blood, picks his way between the wounded and dead. Years later, when he is a state senator, he will be able to tell his children that the man he saw walking the deck, cap pulled low over his eyes, face and hands black with powder and smoke, was Commodore Thomas Macdonough, the legendary hero of the Battle of Plattsburgh Bay.

PLATTSBURGH, LAKE CHAMPLAIN,
NEW YORK, SEPTEMBER 11, 1814

Major-General Frederick Philipse Robinson has been up since before dawn, fidgeting over the tardiness of his commander-in-chief. His task is to lead two brigades across the Saranac and then to assault the heights with artillery support. His men should have been at the ford by daybreak; Prevost has promised him that. But the order has not come and now it is almost eight. Why the delay?

Prevost heard from Downie as early as 3:30 A.M. that the fleet was on its way, but the men are not yet in motion; instead, they have been told to cook breakfast. Something else troubles Robinson: the heaviest artillery has not yet arrived, nor are there batteries in place to receive the big guns. They cannot possibly be put in action before late morning.

From Cumberland Head Robinson hears the distant boom of cannon: Downie is scaling his guns, the signal that he is about to attack. An order comes from Prevost to attend at headquarters. The meeting takes an hour as Prevost reviews his plans. As Robinson turns to leave, the Governor General looks at his watch.

"It is now nine o'clock," he says. "March off at ten."

Clearly, Prevost expects the sea battle to go on all day. But as the two brigades move off in full view of the contest, *Preble, Finch*, and *Chubb* are already out of action. On Robinson's left, Major-General Brisbane leads his brigade against the lower bridge, his flank protected by the water. Robinson's force heads for Pike's ford.

After a mile and a half, the troops are faced by a bewildering pattern of cart tracks leading into a thick wood. The army halts as

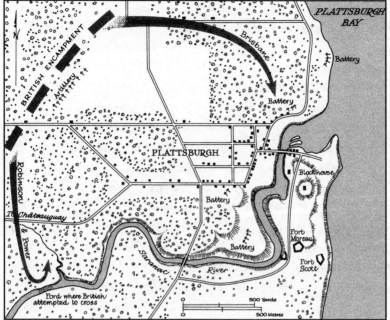

Plattsburgh, September 11, 1814

the guides argue over the route. Finally the force retraces its steps and after an hour's delay arrives at the river. Macomb's deception has paid dividends.

From the bay comes the sound of cheering. A victory? By whom? Robinson dispatches an aide to find out. Meanwhile, he orders his men to rush the Saranac. They race down the bank and splash across the shallow ford in the face of heavy fire from four hundred American riflemen concealed on the far shore. The defenders scatter as the brigades form on the far side in perfect order. As Robinson rides forward to give orders for the attack, his aide returns with a message from Baynes, the adjutant-general:

> I am directed to inform you that the "Confiance" and the brig having struck their colours in consequence of the frigate having grounded, it will no longer be prudent to persevere in the service committed to your charge, and it is therefore the orders of the

Commander of the Forces that you will immediately return with the troops under your command.

Robinson and his fellow general Manley Power are thunderstruck and chagrined, but they give the order to retire.

Major-General Brisbane tells Prevost that he will carry the forts in twenty minutes if given permission, but Prevost will not grant it. He knows that even if he does seize the redoubts he cannot hold the ground while the lake remains under American control. With the American militia rushing to the colours and reinforcements on the way, the enemy can sail down Champlain and cut off his rear. The roads are in dreadful condition, winter is approaching, his lines of supply and communication are stretched thin.

Prevost has also intercepted a letter from a Vermont colonel to Macomb announcing that the recalcitrant governor of that state, Martin Chittenden, is marching from St. Alban's with ten thousand volunteers, that five thousand more are on their way from St. Lawrence County, New York, and four thousand from Washington County. Almost twenty thousand men! Prevost sees himself surrounded by a guerrilla army of aroused civilians lurking in the woods, blocking the roads, stealing into his camp under cover of night, demoralizing his men, scorching the earth, murdering stragglers. What he does not know is that the letter is a fake. Macomb has outwitted him by an old ruse. Has Prevost forgotten that Brock used an identical forgery to convince Hull, at Detroit, that he was surrounded by thousands of Indians?

The Governor General moves his army back so swiftly that it reaches Chazy before Macomb realizes his adversaries have departed. He cannot know it, but even at this moment the British are facing another setback at Baltimore. Here, in a vain attack, Ross meets his death and a poetic young lawyer named Francis Scott Key, watching the rockets' red glare over the embattled Fort McHenry, is moved to compose a national anthem for his country to celebrate the sight of the Stars and Stripes flying bravely in the dawn's early light to signal British defeat.

Robinson is sick at heart over Prevost's "precipitate and disgraceful" move back to Canada. "Everything I see and hear is discouraging," he writes to a friend. "This is no field for a military man above the rank of a colonel of riflemen. . . . This country can never again afford such an opportunity, nothing but a defensive war can or ought to be attempted here, and you will find that the expectations of His Majesty's ministers and the people of England will be utterly destroyed in this quarter."

And, he might add, across the channel in the Belgian city of Ghent, where the news from Lake Champlain will have its own effect on the long-drawn-out negotiations for peace.

THIRTEEN

Ghent

August–December, 1814

Down the cobbled streets of the ancient Flemish town this Sunday morning, past greasy canals and spiky guild houses, comes a minor diplomat with a very English name—Anthony St. John Baker, secretary to the British peace mission. He crosses the Place d'Armes, enters the Hôtel des Pays-Bas, asks for the American commission, is met by James Bayard's secretary, George Milligan, who points him in the direction of the Hôtel d'Alcantara, a three-storey building, cracked and weatherbeaten, on the Rue des Champs. It is said to be haunted—so spooky that servants are hard to hire—but if so, the ghosts have fled the arrival of the five American plenipotentiaries who have leased it for the peace talks and who have given it the wry title of "Bachelor's Hall."

Bayard, the handsome Federalist senator from Delaware, is alone when Baker calls to invite the Americans to meet the following day with the British at his temporary lodgings in the Hôtel du Lion d'Or. Why not meet here? Bayard asks innocently: an excellent room is available. But the Englishman will have none of it, refuses with exquisite politeness even to look at the room. The American, with equal civility, tells him that an answer will be forthcoming later in the day.

Thus are fired the opening shots in the long, weary diplomatic war that will be waged here in this ancient clothmakers' town, to parallel the real war being fought four thousand miles away on the Canadian border. On this very Sunday morning, as the two diplomats spar over the choice of a meeting place, Gordon Drummond unmasks his cannon before Fort Erie and begins his futile week-long bombardment.

The four American negotiators (Jonathan Russell is out of town) meet at noon to discuss what John Quincy Adams calls "an offensive pretension to superiority" on the part of the British. By every rule of diplomatic etiquette, the British should come to *them*! Adams hauls out a heavy tome by Georg Friedrich von Martens, the German expert on international law, to prove this point. Bayard finds a case in Ward's *History of the Law of Nations* where the British themselves had resisted a similar overture. Henry Clay urges that this assumption of superiority be resisted, but Albert Gallatin is not so sure; the Swiss-born ex-cabinet minister is not inclined to slow the negotiations with questions of ceremony.

The discussion drags on for two hours until dinner. Adams proposes that they agree to meet the British "at any place other than their own lodgings." Gallatin suggests softening the phrase to "any place that may mutually be agreed upon." It is the first of many occasions when the former secretary of the treasury will curb his colleagues' irritability.

Thus the stage is set for five months of frustrating bargaining and much hair-splitting. The Americans have already spent a month in Ghent attending functions in their honour, bartering for lodgings, traipsing up and down the narrow streets sightseeing, gazing at the canals and the oils of the Van Eycks, lingering over wine and cigars (to Adams's great displeasure), and, in the absence of the British, sounding each other out on the peace terms. Surprisingly, the disharmony that existed in the last days in St. Petersburg has vanished. Adams, who once hoped never to deal with Bayard again, now finds him the best of companions.

The following day, at one, the Americans take the measure of the three British negotiators. Vice-Admiral Lord Gambier, the titular chairman, is pompous but genial, the epitome of the desk admiral who has seldom been to sea, a big man with an enormous glistening bald head surrounded by a frizzle of greying hair. He is vice-president of the British Bible Society, a fact that sits well with John Quincy Adams.

Dr. William Adams (no kin to John Quincy) is an Admiralty lawyer and, though he prides himself on his wit and humour, is a garrulous bore, his mind stuffed with legalisms, his tongue more cutting than witty. He is such a nonentity that it is said that Lord Liverpool, when questioned about him, could not remember his name.

Henry Goulburn, the youngest of the trio, is of different mettle. A confirmed Yankee-phobe who can scarcely conceal his dislike of everything American, he will struggle in the days ahead to curb his natural irritability in the interests of diplomacy. This thirty-year-old public servant is the real chairman of the British mission and the closest of the three to the British government.

After the usual professions of a sincere and ardent desire for peace (which neither side believes of the other), the meeting gets down to business. Goulburn, for the British, suggests four topics for discussion:

First, the question of impressment, the only stated reason for the war.

Second, the absolute necessity of pacifying the Indians by drawing a boundary line for their territory.

Third, a revision of the border between Canada and the United States.

Fourth, no renewal of a former agreement allowing the Americans certain fishing privileges on Canadian waters and shores "without an equivalent."

From this and from the two days of discussion that follow, two things become clear:

First, neither side is much interested in discussing impressment. The issue, which has inflamed American public opinion since the *Chesapeake* crisis of 1807, which perhaps more than anything else brought on the war and on which both sides have refused to budge an inch, is now dead. The need has passed; the war in Europe is over. In the bitter exchanges that follow, nobody will bother to mention the forcible seizure of British deserters from American ships. Yet thousands have died or been maimed or rendered homeless because of the emotion it engendered.

Second, the British are determined to stick on the question of Indian rights. It is, they insist, a *sine qua non*—an indispensable condition. Without it there can be no peace. Behind their determined stand lie years of promises to the native peoples on both sides of the border: the cultivation of Tecumseh and his federation, the pledges of Brock, Elliott, Dickson, and others that the Great White Father will never forsake his tribal allies.

At this first meeting, the British intentions toward the Indians are so vague that in the days that follow the Americans press for more details. The request seems to irritate Goulburn and his colleagues, but finally they blurt it out: Great Britain wants an Indian buffer state separating the United States from Canada, an area in which neither Canadians nor Americans can purchase land. Though the British decline to go into more detail—they have said too much already—the Americans wake up to the fact that they are being asked to cede a great chunk of their country to people who have been massacring and scalping their soldiers. To this they cannot agree. And, since the British trio in Ghent are mere messenger-boys for a more formidable trio of peers in London—Liverpool, Castlereagh, and Bathurst—negotiations cease until London is heard from.

Nine days pass. During the hiatus, Lord Gambier and Dr. Adams attend a cosy little dinner party given by the Americans; Goulburn stays away, pleading laryngitis. It is August 13, the eve of Drummond's costly attack on Fort Erie, but there is no talk of war. Innocuous pleasantries are batted about the table like shuttlecocks. Gambier tells of meeting Adams's distinguished father and discusses the British Bible Society. Dr. Adams and his namesake discuss their common heritage and conclude they are not cousins.

An entire week from the eleventh to the eighteenth is taken up preparing a report of the negotiations for the American Secretary of State, James Monroe, each of the five taking it upon himself to revise and amend the phraseology of the others. The following day the British announce that they have heard at last from their government. At a meeting that afternoon, they spell out their new demands:

First, the Indian buffer state must extend to the line settled upon at the Treaty of Greenville in 1795. That means that most of Ohio and the future states of Indiana, Illinois, Wisconsin, and Michigan will become Indian territory. Unless the Americans immediately sign a provisional article, subject to ratification by their government, the conference will be suspended.

Second, since the United States has clearly intended to conquer Canada and since Canada is the weaker of the two nations, the British—but not the Americans—must be allowed to keep naval vessels on the Great Lakes and to build forts along their shores for their security.

Third, in order to link her Atlantic colonies with Canada, Britain requires a corner of the state of Maine for a connecting road.

In addition, she wants to perpetuate her right to navigate the Mississippi, as agreed upon in an earlier treaty. This, it develops, is in exchange for American fishing rights in Canadian territory.

The Americans are stunned. Gallatin, in his courteous way, asks what is to be done with the hundred thousand white settlers who now occupy the proposed Indian buffer state. Why, replies the Admiralty lawyer Dr. Adams, they must shift for themselves.

In John Quincy Adams's opinion, the tone of the British is peremptory, their language even more overbearing than before. A confirmed pessimist, he is convinced that the talks are at an end, an opinion shared by the others except Clay. They ask that the British proposals be put in writing and, on August 21, sit down to respond. That takes four days. Adams's first draft is considered too offensive by Gallatin, too flowery by Clay, too ungrammatical by Russell. At eleven o'clock on the evening of the twenty-fourth—two hours past Adams's bedtime—they are still at it, altering, erasing, patching, until no more than a fifth of Adams's original document remains. Finally, on the twenty-fifth—the night of the burning of Washington—the note to the British is signed. Simply put, it rejects the idea of an Indian state and of British military sovereignty over the Great Lakes.

Each side now expects the other to break off negotiations and go home, yet neither wants to be blamed for shattering the hopes of peace. The Americans are convinced that the British tactics are to delay negotiations in the hope of strengthening their hand with victories on the other side of the Atlantic. But they cannot believe the British will back down in the face of this latest rejection.

The days drag by with no official word from the British, although there is a good deal of unofficial socializing, much of it tight-lipped, in which each side tries to sound out the other. On September 1, John Quincy Adams drops in on Henry Goulburn and is convinced from the conversation that the British are holding up an answer to the American note only "to give a greater appearance of deliberation and solemnity to the rupture." It appears to Adams that Goulburn is inflexible, that behind the bland mask of diplomacy there smoulders an abiding hatred of everything American.

Goulburn talks continually of the need to secure Canada from the threat of American annexation. This is the real reason for the Indian buffer state.

"The Indians are but a secondary object," he declares, in a moment of callous candour. "As the Allies of Great Britain she must include them in the peace. . . . But when the boundary is once defined it is immaterial whether the Indians are upon it or not. Let it be a desert. But we shall know that you cannot come upon us to attack us without crossing it."

So much, then, for the moral commitment to Britain's native supporters. The security of Canada has been substituted. But the great and real object, Adams is convinced, is "a profound and rankling jealousy at the rapid increase of population and of settlements in the United States, an impotent longing to thwart their progress and to stunt their growth."

Goulburn is equally convinced that the United States does not want peace and is negotiating only to find some means of reconciling the American public to a continuation of the war. He believes they will find that excuse in the Indian boundary question. He is certain that negotiations are at an end, and that does not entirely displease him. Like so many of his class he still regards the Americans as colonial upstarts—vulgar republicans who must be taught a lesson.

On September 5, the British negotiators bounce the ball back to the Americans. With only a slight modification (a suggestion to discuss any counter-proposal or modification to the Indian question), the note, though longer, does not depart from the original British stand. It is up to the Americans, the British say, to decide whether to continue the peace talks, to refer to Washington for instructions, or to "take upon themselves the responsibility of breaking off the negotiation altogether."

Four of the American commissioners—all but Henry Clay—are convinced that this is the end, and Clay is half convinced. But Clay is a consummate card player and knows the value of a poker face. He has a gut feeling that if the Americans stand firm, the British may back off. He is partial to a game called Brag, in which both sides attempt to out-bluff one another. On September 5, Clay decides to out-Brag the British. He writes to Henry Goulburn, asks him to arrange for his passport: he plans, he says, to return home immediately. Goulburn himself may not be averse to this, but there are others more senior in Whitehall who, faced with the mounting war costs and the growing war weariness, may take a different view.

WALMER CASTLE, KENT, ENGLAND, SEPTEMBER 11, 1814

In the murky confines of Henry VIII's grotesque, turreted fortress—as sombre and heavy as its occupant—the second Earl of Liverpool is harbouring some gloomy second thoughts about the depth of his country's moral commitment to her Indian allies.

The question of the Indians, the Prime Minister tells his colonial secretary, Lord Bathurst, is "one of growing embarrassment." Of course, they must be included in the peace treaty. *But . . .* (one can almost see the cold eyes narrow, the heavy jaw grow firmer), is it really necessary to insist on the *sine qua non* of an Indian buffer state, a kind of sylvan Utopia between the Ohio and the Great Lakes where the natives can gambol, knocking off deer and wild turkey, and cultivating their fields of maize? The Prime Minister hardly thinks so, in fact has never really believed the *sine qua non* would stick. Of course, if a *specific* promise has been made, then honour requires it be kept. But has it been made? Clearly, Lord Liverpool believes that nothing specific has ever been promised the Indians beyond the vague pledge that their Father across the water would never desert them. Now their Father proposes to desert them by watering down British demands, once declared irrevocable, to a simple stipulation that the Indians shall be restored to all the rights and privileges they enjoyed before the war—a promise subject to many interpretations.

Liverpool wants to set the Indian question aside in order to get on to more important matters. He is perfectly prepared to yield on the exclusive military occupation of the Great Lakes. What he really wants is to hold what the British have gained by conquest, specifically, Michilimackinac and Fort Niagara. If he can get these, and Sackets Harbor into the bargain, then he will waive all claims to a chunk of Maine. If the Americans stick on Sackets Harbor because the British do not occupy it, he proposes to delay negotiations in the hope that Sir George Prevost will seize it, as well as Plattsburgh, or some other piece of American territory. The American suspicions are well founded: it has long been British strategy to stretch out negotiations until further military successes in North America strengthen their hand. Wellington's troops have been pouring into Canada since July. If only Prevost would move! Gazing over the misty headland toward the Strait of Dover, Liverpool, the titular

Lord Warden of the Cinque Ports, cannot know that Prevost *is* moving—but backwards, toward Chazy and the border.

Henry Clay is right. The last thing the British prime minister wants is a sudden break at Ghent. He blames his commissioners for taking "a very erroneous view of our policy," and has taken steps to make sure that Goulburn, now quite baffled by the twists and turns of British manoeuvring, understands it. If the peace talks founder on the absurd question of an Indian state and British control of the lakes, Liverpool is certain that the war will become very popular in America.

The British press is howling for revenge, crying that the Americans must be chastised for daring to make war on the world's most powerful nation. But the Prime Minister is a realist. The ten-year struggle with Napoleon has imposed a crushing financial burden on his country. The powerful English landowners are aroused over the increase in the property tax, which must be continued if the war in North America goes on. The commercial and maritime interests want to return to business as usual. Liverpool must rid himself of this nuisance war as soon as practicable—but on the best possible terms.

In Ghent, Goulburn has reported, a little gleefully, that the American government does not want peace, but Lord Liverpool believes otherwise. He is well aware that the United States is teetering on the edge of bankruptcy; that it is having difficulty obtaining further loans to finance the war; and that if the war does continue for another year, financial disaster will certainly result. He also recognizes that there is danger in this, for "the war would then be rendered a war of despair, in which all private rights and interests would be sacrificed to the public cause."

Goulburn must be made to understand this. Next morning, Lord Bathurst undertakes to do just that. Four days later, the chagrined young diplomat receives Bathurst's instructions and, in his dismay, pens a sarcastic answer:

> I . . . cannot sufficiently thank you for so clearly explaining what are the views and objects of the government with respect to

negotiations with America. Before I received it, I confess that I was impressed with the idea that the government did not wish negotiation to be protracted unless there was a prospect of a successful issue. . . .

"I do not deem it possible to conclude a *good peace* now," Goulburn adds, a little bitterly, "as I cannot consider that a good peace which would leave the Indians to a dependence on the *liberal policy* of the United States."

Goulburn is not seduced by the proposed new clause in the treaty. High-flown phrases about restoring the natives to their pre-war privileges cannot obscure the fact that the Great White Father *is* abandoning his children to an uncertain future. The whole history of the United States has been one of merciless exploitation of the Indians. Can the tribes south of the border expect anything different from the established policy of grabbing their lands and moving them farther and farther beyond the frontier? Later in the month, Goulburn raises a second, more practical objection to the new British policy. Will not post-war America attempt to exclude the British from "that trade which we carried on previous to the war with those Indians as independent nations?" The Americans have already made that clear.

But the British prime minister has all but put the Indians out of his mind in the interests of ending the conflict:

"Goulburn and our other commissioners evidently do not feel the inconvenience of the continuance of the war. I feel it strongly, but I feel it as nothing now compared with what it may be a twelve-month hence, and I am particularly anxious, therefore, that we should avoid anything, as far as may be in our power, which may increase our difficulties in concluding it."

In the international game of Brag, it seems, Henry Clay, the loose-limbed Kentucky gambler, holds all the cards.

Henry Clay, after three days of sightseeing among the Gothic spires and cobbled squares of the Flemish capital, is surprised on this autumn Monday to receive from Henry Goulburn a graceful, if uncharacteristic, little note accompanying a packet of newspapers from the United States.

"If you find Brussels as little interesting as I have done," Goulburn writes sweetly, "you will not be sorry to have the occupation of reading the latest Newspapers which I have received, I therefore inclose them to you and shall be glad to have them back by tomorrow evening. I take this opportunity of mentioning that I do not propose leaving this late [*sic*] Tuesday morning in case you should be desirous of extending your excursion. . . ."

But Clay's excursion as well as his disposition is ruined as soon as he opens the papers, which Goulburn, on specific instructions from Lord Bathurst, has so charitably sent him. *Washington in flames!* In the days that follow, Clay's normal optimism gives way to despair. He trembles whenever he picks up a late newspaper. Everything seems to be going wrong: Chauncey's refusal to co-operate with Jacob Brown at Fort George; Drummond (whom he believed captured) threatening Gaines's army and consequently Chauncey's fleet; and now this!

It is not the destruction of public property that wounds him "to the very soul"; it is his country's disgrace—"that a set of pirates and incendiaries should have been permitted to pollute our soil, conflagrate our Capital, and return unpunished to their ships."

Adams is equally downcast. "We must drink the cup of bitterness to the dregs," he writes to his wife, Louisa. Bayard is wrought up to such a pitch of fury that, he declares to Adams, the desecration of Washington should "make every American take his children to the altar and swear them to eternal hatred of England."

In this heated atmosphere the negotiations continue at Ghent, never face to face, always by diplomatic note, both sides giving a little, the British still "arrogant, overbearing and offensive," in Adams's view, and the Americans never as bold or spirited as he thinks they ought to be. The British send off their draft notes to be re-drafted by the real negotiators in England; the Americans spend days arguing over grammar, phraseology, style, tone, length, punctuation. When Adams tries to moralize, peppering each missive with references to God, Providence, and Heaven, Clay cries "Cant!" and Russell, who is in Clay's shadow, laughs openly. Gallatin, the conciliator, ends up writing most of the final drafts.

Not being faced with such wrangles, the English messenger-boys find time heavy on their hands. They have taken up headquarters in the former convent of Chartreux on the outskirts of the town, and here, in John Quincy Adams's observation, they live "as secluded as if they were monks." Lord Gambier, whom Adams quite likes (he appears "an excellent and well meaning man") asks if the Americans have made many acquaintances. Indeed they have, attending a continual round of theatres and dinner parties. The old admiral, who is not much of a mixer, has made only one—the Intendant and his family. Goulburn, who has brought over his wife and small son (the latter recovering from "infantile fever") spends his time with his family. Both he and Dr. Adams are, to the Americans, typical snobbish Britishers who dislike everything that is not English and make no secret of their tastes. The latter, whom Bayard considers "a man of no breeding," boasts that he has not been to the theatre in ten years and reveals that his real enthusiasm is for Indian jugglers. The Americans greet this with a slight sneer; they, too, are not immune to snobbishness.

By late October, the exchange of paper and the instructions from London and Washington serve to clarify and pare down the real issues between the two countries. The backing and filling is accompanied, as always, by long ideological arguments, legalese, appeals to morality, and charges, both imagined and real, of perfidy, greed, lack of principle. But all that is for the public record. The real differences between the antagonists can be described by two Latin phrases: *status quo ante bellum* and *uti possidetis*. The Americans are prepared now to settle for the same conditions that existed before the war—to act, in short, as if the war had never taken place. The British, flushed with success and expecting momentary news of the fall of Sackets Harbor and Plattsburgh, want to keep what they have conquered by right of possession.

The news of Prevost's defeat and the failure of the British attack on Baltimore's Fort McHenry, coming at the end of October, puts a new complexion on the negotiations. Liverpool is furious over Prevost's incompetence. The war in North America has cost ten million pounds, and now this! Stalemate! Is there no end to it? Liverpool grasps at a straw: why not send the Duke of Wellington to Canada to take charge of the army? Such a gesture might easily speed up negotiations; the Duke is known to be anxious for peace with America if the terms are honourable. "Honour" has become a key word. *Peace with honour.* Both sides are more interested in saving face than they are in clinging to bits of real estate or keeping promises to obscure native chieftains. If honour can be satisfied, blood will cease to flow on the morrow. Financially, the Americans are more desperate than the British. Gallatin has just informed Monroe that not a dollar can be obtained in Europe to finance the war. Nonetheless, among the spires of Ghent the rival commissions must continue their diplomatic ritual dance. It has seven more weeks to go.

Three months have passed since the two teams first faced each other. Since that date, Mackinac Island has been relieved, *Tigress* and *Scorpion* captured, Fort Erie attacked, defended, and abandoned, Washington burned with all of Jefferson's papers, Baltimore and Plattsburgh besieged. Francis Scott Key has written "The Star Spangled Banner," John Armstrong has been fired as Secretary of War, and Duncan McArthur's mounted Kentuckians have laid waste the valley of the Thames. Thousands have been killed including William Drummond, Hercules Scott, George Downie, Joseph Willcocks, Robert Ross, and an innocent old Loyalist farmer, William Francis, murdered for no good reason in his bed at Long Point by American partisans.

Along the thousand miles of embattled border, from Montreal to the western margins of Lake Huron, everything is as it was when the year began. The Americans hold Amherstburg. The British occupy Michilimackinac and Fort Niagara. In Ghent there is progress of a sort. The American mission, with British agreement, is actually composing the outline of a peace treaty.

Shortly after five on these raw November mornings, John Quincy Adams pulls himself out of bed, lights a tallow candle, stokes the fire in the grate, warms his numbed fingers, and starts to work on a draft of the document, knowing from bitter experience that his colleagues are waiting to tear it to pieces.

Almost immediately he runs into a confrontation with Henry Clay. Since the Peace of 1783, New Englanders have enjoyed the right to catch and dry their fish in British territory in return for free access, by the British, to the Mississippi. Adams, the New Englander, wants to retain that right; Clay, the Southerner, is opposed.

It would be difficult to find two statesmen more unlike in temperament, habit, or conviction than John Quincy Adams and Henry Clay. By an ironic coincidence, their rooms adjoin one another so that as Adams rises at daybreak, he can often hear Clay preparing to go to bed. Clay loves to linger over dinner, drawing on strong cigars and fortifying himself with table wine before his customary late night card game. Adams bitterly begrudges these wasted moments; at one point he even decided to take dinner by himself, only to be dissuaded by a surprisingly persuasive Clay. Adams is a sour pessimist devoid of humour; Clay has a gambler's optimism. Adams's features are so arranged that he seems to be perpetually scowling. Clay's high cheek bones, long face, and winsome mouth make him appear forever good humoured.

Adams finds it difficult to curb his anger when Clay dismisses the fisheries question as trifling. The Kentuckian will on no account permit the Mississippi to be turned into a British waterway. If that means giving up New England's fishing rights, so be it. In the end, however, Clay proposes an ingenious way out of the impasse: the matter of the fisheries, he says, is linked irretrievably to the recognition of American independence; it does not require negotiation. Adams does not demur.

As usual, John Quincy discovers, to his chagrin, that three-quarters of his draft is struck out by the others. One paragraph, however, he is determined to include. Monroe has instructed the commission that peace can be concluded if both sides will agree to return to the prewar situation—*status quo ante bellum*—leaving the sticky points about boundaries and commerce to future negotiation. Adams believes that the time has come to face the British with this proposal.

It is now November 10. What Henry Clay and his colleagues do not know is that only the previous day the Duke of Wellington put a damper on Lord Liverpool's hopes. What is the point of his going to Canada, he asks Castlereagh, until the British control the lakes? There is worse: the Duke does not believe that Britain has a right to demand any cession of territory from the United States. The war has been successful: the Americans have not succeeded in their plan to seize Canada. But neither have the British been able to carry the war to the enemy's territory.

"Why stipulate for the *uti possidetis?*" Wellington asks. "You can get no territory; indeed, the state of your military operations, however creditable, does not entitle you to demand any: and you only afford the Americans a popular and creditable ground, which I believe their Government are looking for, not to break off the negotiations, but to avoid to make peace."

That does it. Goulburn, blissfully unaware of this turn of affairs, is prepared to break off negotiations in Ghent because of the American insistence on a return to pre-war status. As far as he is concerned it is only a matter of tactics. But Liverpool knows the game is up. France is in a turmoil; the preparations over the coming Congress of Vienna are unsatisfactory from a British point of view; the revolt in England against continuing the property tax is becoming alarming; rents are depressed. Great Britain has larger concerns—the balance of power in Europe being one—than the border war in North America. It is "desirable to bring the American war if possible to a conclusion," Liverpool tells Castlereagh. Parliament would violently oppose its continuance "upon what is called a new principle."

On November 26, the British commissioners inform the Americans in a series of marginal notes to the draft treaty that *uti possidetis* has been abandoned and that the "new principle," *status quo ante bellum*, is accepted. The original questions—impressment, blockade—are tossed aside, although the British still want access to the Mississippi and assurance that the Indians will be restored to their pre-war privileges.

It is a difficult document for Henry Goulburn to swallow. He does not like giving way to the Americans and is especially reluctant to do so now since almost everything he originally demanded on behalf of his government has been abandoned. But orders are orders. His conscience pricks him on the matter of the Indians: "I had till I came here no idea of the fixed determination which prevails in the breast of every American to extirpate the Indians and appropriate their territory," he tells Bathurst, "but I am now sure that there is nothing which the people of America would so reluctantly abandon as what they are pleased to call their natural right to do so."

It is all over but the wrangling. "We have everything but peace in our hands," Adams reports to his wife. The remaining obstacles are so trifling that neither nation would tolerate a war over them. Yet these obstacles, which Adams calls insignificant, occupy another month.

On December 1, the two commissions meet officially face to face for the first time since August 18, talk for three hours, settle little. The talks go on, the notes fly back and forth, hairs are split, words stricken, phrases expunged, concessions made, until by December 10 only two points of contention remain: the whole matter of the Mississippi River and the American fisheries, together with British insistence on hanging on to Moose Island, an obscure pinpoint in Passamaquoddy Bay.

The real argument is not with the British. It is, again, between Clay and Adams. Adams is convinced that the British are sticking in order to cause a split in the Union. If New England loses its fishing rights in Newfoundland, Massachusetts will be at loggerheads with Kentucky.

But Clay stalks back and forth across the room shouting over and over again:

"I will never sign a treaty upon the *status quo ante bellum* with the Indian article, so help me God!"

This acrimony spills over the next morning at the old Chartreux convent, when Adams, on behalf of his colleagues, rejects any British right to Moose Island. At that Goulburn loses control, and for two hours the verbal battle seesaws to no solution. Yet both sides are fully aware that neither country will continue the war over these minor debating points.

It is this awareness and the sheer weariness induced by the long bitter arguments that, in the end, produce a peace treaty. Like the exhausted troops stalemated along the Niagara frontier, the negotiating teams are worn out, dispirited, ready to agree to almost anything. In the end, all five agree to say nothing at all about the fisheries or the Mississippi or anything else; all these disputed points can be settled by others after peace is proclaimed. The British agree to everything, with some minor reservations, but even that does not satisfy Clay, who suggests breaking off negotiations then and there. At that, Albert Gallatin, whose clear mind, good humour, and calm mien have guided the five-man ship through some rough shoals, becomes uncharacteristically impatient. He has no objection, he says, to Mr. Clay amusing himself as long as he thinks proper, but as soon as he chooses to be serious he will propose a conference with the British tomorrow.

Adams has come to admire Gallatin, in whose character he sees "one of the most extraordinary combinations of stubbornness and flexibility that I ever met within man."

Indeed, Adams has come to respect the members of the commission with whom he has been closeted since July. He admires the once-despised Bayard for "the most perfect control of his temper . . . real self command" and has a good word for Russell, who has taken a lesser part in the negotiations. And Clay? Well, he understands Clay, in spite of their differences of belief and inclination. Both suffer from fits of temper, and Adams is nothing if not ruthlessly honest with himself. In Clay he sees his emotional mirror image. "There is the same dogmatical, overbearing manner, the same harshness of look and expression, and the same forgetfulness of the courtesies of society in both." But "nothing of this weakness has been shown in our conferences with the British plenipotentiaries. From two of them, and particularly from Mr. Goulburn, we have endured much; but I do not recollect that one expression has escaped the lips of any one of us that we would wish to be recalled."

It is all but over. Ghent, which has been their home for six months, will soon recede into memory. Adams's long solitary walks by the canal, Clay's all night card parties, the brittle social repartee with their antagonists, the long, lazy dinners, the manoeuvring, the wrangling, the casuistry, Goulburn's frustrations, Gambier's pontifications, Gallatin's mediation—all this is part of history.

On the morning of December 24, most of the plenipotentiaries on both sides are occupied by scribbling—they must prepare fair copies of the new treaty, six in all. The ceremony of signing is set for three o'clock, but the Americans are not ready and cannot meet for another hour. At four, their carriage draws up before the big, grey convent of Chartreux and, with their secretary, Hughes, the five men in long dark coats embroidered in gold enter the long dark room for their final duties.

A few small errors remain to be altered. Then with pen and ink, sand and sealing wax, the documents are rendered official, subject to ratification in Washington and London. Lord Gambier hands the three British copies to John Quincy Adams, whereupon the future president of the United States turns his over to the Admiral, remarking, as he does so, that he hopes this will be the last treaty of peace between Great Britain and the United States. It is half-past six on Christmas Eve—an appropriate anniversary for a peace treaty.

And what does the treaty say? In eleven articles and more than three thousand words it says very little. Nothing about impressment or blockade, those bitter bones of contention that caused tempers to flare, swords to be unbuckled, and war to explode. Nothing about fishing rights, captured territory, boundaries, control of the lakes, or any of the other fractious issues over which the representatives of two countries have broiled and bickered. And so little about the Indians that this question too amounts to nothing.

It is as if no war had been fought or, to put it more bluntly, as if the war that was fought was fought for no good reason. For nothing has changed; everything is as it was in the beginning save for the graves of those who, it now appears, have fought for a trifle:

Porter Hanks, late of Michilimackinac, torn in two by a British cannonball; Isaac Brock, dead with a rifle bullet in his heart on the slippery slopes of Queenston; Henry Clay's brother-in-law, vainly pleading for his life at the River Raisin, slaughtered and scalped; Zebulon Pike, pillowed on a British standard, gasping out his last moments; young Cecil Bisshopp, expiring from gangrene after the debacle at Black Rock; Robert Barclay's shoulder mangled, Shadrach Byfield's arm sliced off, John McClay's skull cracked open—all for eleven pages of paper that change nothing.

And more: a seven-year-old child, Jervis Gillette, slain on the streets of Lewiston in December, 1813; a bewildered immigrant, Jacob Overholzer, rotting in a Kingston jail; Métoss's small son shot dead before Fort Meigs; Sally Lovejoy, killed in her front parlour at Buffalo; and a nameless, sixty-year-old farmer dying in his wife's arms in a makeshift tent near Lundy's Lane—for what?

History will ignore all but a handful of these victims. In the official statements, and the unofficial ones, too, the war will be described as if it were a football game, with much emphasis on strategy and tactics, on valour and "honour," but much less on cowardice, shame, horror, and confusion. Lake Erie and Fort McHenry will go into the American history books, Queenston Heights and Crysler's Farm into the Canadian, but without the gore, the stench, the disease, the terror, the conniving, and the imbecilities that march with every army.

Men will write that the War of 1812 was the making of the United States: for the first time she was taken seriously in Europe; that it was also the making of Canada: her people were taught pride through a common resistance to the invaders; that bloody and insane though it may have been, Lundy's Lane and Stoney Creek produced the famous undefended border between the two nations.

True. But in terms of human misery and human waste—the tall ships shattered by cannonball and grape; the barns and mills gutted by fire; villages put to the torch, grain fields ravaged, homes looted, breadwinners shackled and imprisoned; and thousands dead from cannon shot and musket fire, gangrene, typhus, ague, fever, or simple exposure, can anyone truly say on this crisp Christmas Eve that the game was ever worth the candle?

The Legacy

LIKE A RUNAWAY MACHINE, the war, which ended officially at the close of 1814, continued on its own momentum into the new year. It is entirely characteristic of this bloody and senseless conflict that its bloodiest and most senseless battle should have been fought a fortnight after the peace treaty was signed. The secretary of the commission, Christopher Hughes, was still on the high seas on January 8, the document in his dispatch case, when Wellington's brother-in-law, Sir Edward Pakenham, led eight thousand troops in an ill-timed and badly planned frontal attack against Andrew Jackson's army near New Orleans. In half an hour, Jackson's collection of American regulars, Kentucky sharpshooters, and bayou pirates, secure behind their bulwarks of cotton bales, smashed the assault, killing or wounding some two thousand British soldiers. Pakenham himself was slain.

The foray against New Orleans had been ordered by the British government weeks before, even as the commissioners bickered in Ghent. Its purpose was to hasten the peace negotiations and, with a victory, to force better terms from the Americans. Ironically, the final document was signed almost at the moment when the doomed Pakenham took up his new command.

But no one on the swampy shores of the shallow Pontchartrain knew that the war was over; nor would they know for another month. The Battle of New Orleans, renowned in song and story, had no military significance, was fought to no purpose. In Andrew Jackson, however, the Union had a future president and in the victory a cause for rejoicing after the shame of Washington.

The news of the battle reached the capital early on February 4. Six days later, Christopher Hughes arrived with the treaty. The American commissioners had been nervous about its reception, but now, with the bells pealing and the bonfires blazing, there was no cause for worry. The country entered into a paroxysm of joy. Nobody cared about the details; few ever inquired. The words on everybody's lips were VICTORY and PEACE.

Having won the last battle, the Americans were convinced that they won the War of 1812. Having stemmed the tide of invasion and kept the Americans out of their country, Canadians believed that *they* won the war. Having ceded nothing they considered important, the British were serene in the conviction that *they* won it. But war is not a cricket match. The three nations that celebrated peace were beggared by the conflict, their people bereaved, their treasuries emptied, their graveyards crowded. In North America, the charred houses, the untended farms, the ravaged fields along the border left a legacy of bitterness and distrust.

But the real losers were the Indians. When Black Hawk of the Sauks heard the details of the Peace of Ghent, he wept like a child. A few weeks before he had delivered a prophetic speech: "I have fought the Big Knives and will continue to fight them, until they retire from our lands." And fight them he did. In 1832, the Black Hawk War rekindled Tecumseh's dream of an Indian confederacy. It was a war doomed, as all Indian revolts were doomed, to failure.

The news of the peace did not reach Mackinac Island until May. Lieutenant-Colonel McDouall, still in command, was "prostrated with grief." For three years the British had held the key to the Northwest; now they were giving it up. Clearly the British negotiators, "egregiously duped," in McDouall's bitter phrase, had no comprehension of Mackinac's significance. The Peace of Ghent meant the end of British influence and British fur trade in the Upper Mississippi.

The Indians knew betrayal when they saw it. *"Father!"* Sausamauee of the Winnebago cried out to McDouall in his anguish, "you promised us repeatedly that this place would not be given up . . . it would be better that you had killed at once, rather than expose us to a lingering death. . . . The peace made between you and the Big Knives *may* be a lasting one; but it cannot be for us, for we hate them; they have so often deceived us that we cannot put any faith in them."

The tribes realized that the British had deceived them, too. Three summers before, Brock and Tecumseh had ridden proudly together into the defeated fort at Detroit, symbols of mutual respect between the British and the natives. What price now the pledges of the Great White Father to his children? What meaning the long years of sacrifice by Robert Dickson, starving with his adopted people in the land of the Sioux and Winnebago? Like the Indians, Dickson was ruined by the war. Unable to return to the Upper Mississippi, he moved west to the Red River settlement and ended his days in obscurity.

For the Indians, the conflict was waged for real goals, not empty phrases. Political and military leaders constantly used the clichés of warfare to justify bloodshed and rampage. Words like *honour . . . liberty . . . independence . . . freedom* were dragged out to rally the troops, most of whom, struggling to save their skins, knew them to be empty. But for Tecumseh, Roundhead, Métoss, Black Hawk, and all the native statesmen for whom this war meant tribal survival, these words were real. Honour stood for personal bravery, not a carefully ambiguous document announcing peace. Liberty meant freedom to roam the plains and forests, not the right to be independent of Great Britain. Of the thousands who fell in battle—reluctant Canadian farmers, drafted American militia, career British regulars, foreign mercenaries—few fought for an ideal. But the Indians did.

It is true that the young braves, like so many of their white counterparts, were also in the war for loot and drink, for adventure and glory, for escape from routine. But when the war ended, the white soldiers knew that if they lived they could go home. Where was home for the Indians?

All three English-speaking nations could be sure that when peace was declared, business would continue as before. But not the Indians. The British gave back Mackinac and Fort Niagara; the Americans returned Amherstburg to Canada. Boundary disputes were resolved by commission; a treaty ended the shipbuilding war on the Lakes; the Undefended Border was proclaimed with pride. But the Indians did not get back their hunting grounds.

In the summer of 1815, the United States signed fifteen treaties with the tribes, guaranteeing their status as of 1811. But it did not return an acre of land. The dream of an Indian state never came true. Did the British ever believe it would? The war that bolstered national feeling on both sides of the border crippled the pride of the native peoples. As civilization marched westward, the Indians retreated. Tecumseh's tribe, the Shawnee, found themselves drifting from reservation to reservation in Kansas and Oklahoma. The Winnebago of Green Bay, ravaged by war and disease, moved to Iowa, then Minnesota, and finally Nebraska. The Miami ended on reservations in Kansas, the Potawatomi in Oklahoma.

By that time, the War of 1812 was remembered only in terms of catchphrases: *Don't give up the ship . . . We have met the enemy and they are ours . . . Push on, brave York Volunteers.* History gave the conflict short shrift; and yet, for all its bunglings and idiocies, it helped determine the shape and nature of Canada. Like the Battle of Waterloo, it was, to use Wellington's phrase, "a near run thing." The balance might have been tipped another way had the leadership on either side been more incisive, the weather less capricious, or the Gods of War less perverse. A change of wind on Lake Champlain could have led to the capture of upper New York State. The sniper's bullet that killed Isaac Brock undoubtedly helped prolong the struggle.

Events, not individuals, it is said, control the course of history. The War of 1812 suggests the opposite. Canada's destiny, for better or for worse, was in the hands of human beings, subject to human caprices, strengths, and emotions. If the ambitious Winfield Scott had waited for the army at Lundy's Lane, if the haughty Commodore Chauncey had deigned to support Jacob Brown at Fort George, could Upper Canada have held out? Tecumseh was unique. If he had not been born, would another have risen in his place?

Human failings frustrated American strategy. If Kingston or Montreal had fallen, Ontario would be an American state today. But Dearborn and Wilkinson were flawed commanders. An American Brock might have pierced the heartland of the nation and cut the jugular between the two provinces. But the invaders were reduced to hacking vainly at the country's extremities.

The war helped set the two countries on different courses. National characteristics were evolving: American ebullience, Canadian reserve. The Americans went wild over minor triumphs, the Canadians remained phlegmatic over major ones. Brock was knighted for Detroit, but there were no gold medals struck, no ceremonial swords, banquets, or fireworks to mark Châteauguay, Crysler's Farm, Stoney Creek, or Beaver Dams. By contrast, Croghan's defence of Fort Stephenson was the signal for a paroxysm of rejoicing that made him an overnight hero in the United States.

American hero worship filled the Congress, the Senate, and the state legislatures with dozens of war veterans. Three soldiers— Harrison, Jackson, and Zachary Taylor—became president. But there were no Canadian Jacksons because there was no high political office to which a Canadian could aspire. The major victories were won by men from another land who did their job and went home. Brock and de Salaberry were Canada's only heroes, Laura Secord her sole heroine. And Brock was not a Canadian.

The quality of boundless enthusiasm, which convinces every American school child that the United States won the war, is not a Canadian trait. We do not venerate winners. Who remembers Billy Green, John Norton, Robert Dickson, or even William Hamilton Merritt? The quintessential Canadian hero was a clergyman, not a soldier, a transplanted Scot, a supporter of entrenched values, a Tory of Tories. Dour, earnest, implacable, John Strachan acquired a reputation for courage and leadership that made him a power in Upper Canada and helped freeze its political pattern.

Strachan's thrust was elitist. He believed implicitly in everything the Americans had rejected: an established church, a limited franchise, a ruling oligarchy. He despised Americans, loathed Americanisms. "Democracy" and "republicanism" were hateful words. The York elite, linked by intermarriage and soon to be dubbed the Family Compact, wanted no truck with elected judges or policemen, let alone universal male suffrage.

The war helped entrench certain words in the national lexicon and certain attitudes in the national consciousness. Three words— *loyalty, security,* and *order*—took on a Canadian connotation. *Freedom,* tossed about like a cricket ball by all sides, had a special meaning, too: it meant freedom from the United States. *Liberty* was exclusively American, never used north of the border, perhaps because it was too close to *libertine* for the pious Canadians. Radicalism was the opposite of loyalty, democracy the opposite of order.

Loyalty meant loyalty to Britain and to British values. Long after Confederation, John A. Macdonald could bring an audience to its feet by crying: "A British subject I was born; a British subject I will die"—meaning that he would never die an American. On this curiously negative principle, uttered by the first prime minister of an emerging nation, did the seeds of nationalism sprout.

At the start of the war, Upper Canada was largely American, though its leaders were not. But by 1815, the Americans had become The Enemy. They had ravaged the Thames Valley, burned every house along the Niagara, and laid waste the St. Lawrence. It was no longer prudent to espouse American ideas: in 1813 farmers had been jailed in York for that crime. The example of Willcocks, Markle, and Mallory, the three turncoats, could not go unremarked. Before the war, as elected members of the lower house, they had opposed the established order. Now they stood convicted, *in absentia*, of high treason.

British colonial rule meant orderly government, not the democracy of the uneducated mob. The war enshrined national stereotypes: the British redcoats were seen as a regimented force, the Kentucky militia as an unmannerly horde. The pejorative was "Yankee." In the Canadian vernacular, Yankees were everything the York and Montreal elite were not: vulgar, tobacco-chewing upstarts in loud suits, who had no breeding and spoke with an offensive twang. Tiger Dunlop, the British surgeon, captured this attitude when he described how a servant told Red George Macdonell that a Yankee officer was waiting to sell him some smuggled beef. He knew he was a Yankee, he said, "for he wore his hat in the parlour and spit on the carpet." The stereotype persisted into the next century as the political cartoons of the post-war years demonstrate.

The Invasion of Canada did not initiate that snobbery: it had been part of the English attitude toward the upstart colony since the days of the Revolution. But the bitterness of war made it acceptable, even desirable, in Canada.

Angered by the strident boastings of American generals that this was "a war of extermination" (Hull) or "a war of conquest" (Smythe); hardened in the crucible of fire that destroyed old loyalties and encouraged new hatreds; goaded by those who had a vested interest in maintaining the *status quo;* and inspired by a new nationalism springing from the embers of conflict, few Canadians found it possible to consider, at least openly, the American way as a political choice for the future.

The alternative was already in place—the British colonial way: comfortable, orderly, secure, paternalistic. From that, for better or worse, we have never entirely detached ourselves. The flames of war have long since died; the agony has been forgotten, the justification long obscured. But the legacy of that bitter, inconclusive, half-forgotten conflict still remains.

Aftermath

John Quincy Adams became Secretary of State in 1817 under President James Monroe and, with Henry Clay's help, defeated Andrew Jackson for the presidency in 1824. He did not serve a second term but was a congressional representative from 1831 to 1848, the year of his death.

William Allan became a member of the Legislative Council of Upper Canada in 1825 and served on the Executive Council from 1836 to 1840. A pillar of the Family Compact, he died in 1840.

John Armstrong's political career ended with the burning of Washington. Failing in an attempt to be elected to the Senate, he spent his remaining days in farming and writing. In his *Notices of the War of 1812* he attempted to vindicate his record. He died in 1843.

Robert Barclay waited eleven years after the Battle of Lake Erie before he achieved post rank. He was made a captain in 1824, fathered eight children, died in 1837.

James Bayard died in June, 1815, six months after the conclusion of the peace talks at Ghent.

Alexander Bourne helped found a town on the Maumee, named it Perrysburg, became canal commissioner for Ohio, and laid down most of the waterways in that state. He died in 1848.

John Boyd was discharged from the army in 1815. Toward the end of his life he was naval officer for the Port of Boston. He died in 1830.

Jacob Brown became commander of the U.S. Army in 1821, continuing until his death in 1828.

Cyrenius Chapin continued his medical practice in Buffalo until his death in 1838.

Isaac Chauncey continued his naval career, helped negotiate a treaty with Algiers, and ended his years as president of the Board of Navy Commissioners, charged with the administration of the service. He died in 1840.

Henry Clay again became Speaker of the House of Representatives, entered the Senate in 1831, ran unsuccessfully against Andrew Jackson for the presidency in 1832. He remained in public life until his death in 1852.

George Croghan married a member of the powerful Livingston family of New York, served as postmaster in New Orleans in 1824 and inspector general of the regular army, and fought in the Mexican War. Drink clouded his last years. He died of cholera in New Orleans in 1849.

Henry Dearborn left the army in 1815 after being turned down for the post of Secretary of War. In 1822 he was made Minister to Portugal. He died in 1829.

Robert Dickson helped Lord Selkirk establish his colony on the Red River. He died in 1823.

David Bates Douglass returned to West Point as an instructor and later taught civil engineering and architecture at New York University. From 1834 to 1836 he was engineer in charge of New York City's water supply.

Gordon Drummond succeeded Sir George Prevost as Governor General. He returned to England in 1816, was promoted to full general. He died in London in 1854.

Dominique Ducharme was appointed Indian agent at Lake of Two Mountains, Quebec, a post he held until his death in 1853.

William "Tiger" Dunlop became a journalist in England, returned to Canada with John Galt, in the service of the latter's Canada Company, and represented Huron Riding in the Legislative Assembly from 1841 to 1846. He died in 1848.

Jesse Elliott remained in the navy, becoming commander-in-chief of the Mediterranean Fleet in 1835. Disgruntled officers preferred thirteen charges against him, and he was suspended from the navy for four years. A new administration in Washington remitted part of the suspension and he was given, in 1844, command of the Philadelphia Navy Yard. He died in 1845.

James FitzGibbon rose to become a full colonel and acting adjutant-general. He was leader of the loyalist forces at Montgomery's Tavern who helped suppress William Lyon Mackenzie's rebellion in 1837. He returned to England in 1846, was appointed military knight of Windsor, and died in 1860.

Edmund Gaines took part in several Indian wars, quarrelled openly with Winfield Scott, successfully defended himself at a court martial for insubordination during the Mexican War, and was a constant thorn in the War Department's side. He died, unrepentant, in 1849.

Albert Gallatin became U.S. Minister to France and later to Great Britain. In 1831 he became president of the National Bank in New York. He died in 1849.

George Gleig fought at Waterloo then studied at Oxford, took orders, was named chaplain general of the British forces in 1844. A prolific writer, he produced biographies of Wellington and Clive. He died in 1888.

Henry Goulburn became a member of the Privy Council in 1821 and chief secretary to the Lord-Lieutenant of Ireland. For most of his parliamentary career after 1828 he held cabinet posts, notably that of Chancellor of the Exchequer. He died in 1856.

Billy Green lived all his life in Saltfleet township. He ran a sawmill on the original Green land and died in his eighty-fourth year in 1877.

Wade Hampton was reputed to be the wealthiest planter in the United States at the time of his death in 1835.

Jarvis Hanks had a long career as a teacher, signpainter, silhouette artist, and portraitist; he studied medicine, exhibited with the National Academy of Design in New York, fathered ten children, and died in Cleveland in 1853.

William Henry Harrison entered Congress in 1816 and became a Senator in 1825. In 1840 he nudged out Henry Clay as Whig presidential candidate. His military record and his slogan "Tippecanoe and Tyler, too" won him a landslide victory. One month after his inauguration, he died of pneumonia.

John Harvey became successively Lieutenant-Governor of New Brunswick, Governor of Newfoundland, and Lieutenant-Governor of Nova Scotia. He was knighted in 1834 and at the time of his death, in 1852, was a lieutenant-general.

Thomas Jesup rose to be Quartermaster General of the American army. His distinguished forty-two-year service in that post has never been equalled. He died in 1860.

Richard Johnson ran for vice-president in 1837 using the slogan "Rumpsey, Dumpsey, Colonel Johnson killed Tecumseh." His four years in office were undistinguished. He died in 1850.

Morgan Lewis became president of the New York Historical Society and a founder of New York University. He lived to be ninety, dying in 1844.

Thomas Macdonough was promoted to captain immediately after the naval battle on Lake Champlain. He died at sea of tuberculosis in 1825 at the age of forty-two.

Alexander Macomb rose to become commanding general of the U.S. Army, a post he held from 1828 until his death in 1841.

Benajah Mallory was outlawed and his Canadian property forfeited. He lived in Rochester after the war, but his subsequent career is not known.

Abraham Markle also forfeited his lands. After the war he moved to the Wabash and died in obscurity. His family remained at Newark.

William Hamilton Merritt became an enthusiastic promoter of the first Welland canal and one of the great figures in canal transportation in Canada. He entered politics in 1832, served as president of the Executive Council of the Province of Canada from 1848 to 1851, was Chief Commissioner of Public Works, and later a member of the Legislative Council of Canada. He died in 1862.

Joseph Morrison served in Ireland, India, and Burma, was promoted to brigadier-general, and died at sea in 1826.

Usher Parsons enjoyed a distinguished academic and medical career after leaving the navy. He helped organize the American Medical Association and published fifty-six books and articles. He died in 1868.

Oliver Hazard Perry died in Venezuela of yellow fever while descending the Orinoco River six years after his great victory.

Peter B. Porter ran unsuccessfully for Governor of New York in 1817, served on the boundary commission that followed the Treaty of Ghent, and was briefly Secretary of War in 1828–29. He died at Niagara Falls in 1844.

Sir George Prevost, recalled to face a court martial in connection with his defeat at Plattsburgh, died in 1816, one week before the hearing.

Henry Procter, suspended as a result of his defeat on the Thames, died in 1822.

The Prophet, Tecumseh's mystic brother, was given a small pension by the British government and died in Kansas in the mid-1830s.

Phineas Riall was named governor of Grenada in 1816, was knighted in 1833, and died in Paris, a full general, in 1850.

John Richardson's works include his long poem *Tecumseh, Warrior of the West*, his novel *Wacousta*, his personal history of the war, and a number of further novels, the best-known being *The Canadian Brothers*. His military career included three years of service with the British Auxiliary Legion in Spain from 1834 to 1837. In the early 1840s he edited two periodicals from Brockville. He moved to Montreal and later to New York, where he died in poverty at the age of sixty.

Eleazar Ripley demanded a court martial to vindicate his character after Jacob Brown blamed him for losing the guns at Lundy's Lane. But President Madison held that Congress's gold medal was vindication enough. Ripley left the army in 1820 and became a politician. He died in 1839.

Frederick Philipse Robinson was briefly Lieutenant-Governor of Upper Canada in the summer of 1815. He died, a full general and a Knight Commander of the Bath, in 1852, in his eighty-eighth year.

John Beverley Robinson rose to become Chief Justice of Upper Canada, Speaker of the Legislative Council, and president of the Executive Council. He was one of the guiding spirits of the Family Compact, was created a baronet in 1854, and died in 1863.

Jonathan Russell continued as U.S. Minister to Sweden and Stockholm until 1819. In 1822 he became embroiled in a bitter controversy with his former colleague, John Quincy Adams, arising from a dispute between Clay and Adams at the time of the Ghent negotiations. Adams successfully accused Russell of treachery and the resultant controversy is said to have caused Russell's retirement from public life. He died in 1832.

Charles-Michel de Salaberry, created a Commander of the Bath in 1817 for his victory at Châteauguay, was appointed to the Legislative Council of Lower Canada the following year. He died in 1829.

Winfield Scott became general-in-chief of the U.S. Army in 1841. Victorious in the war with Mexico in 1847, he ran for the presidency in 1852 but was badly beaten by Franklin Pierce. He retired in 1861 on the eve of the Civil War and died five years later at the age of eighty.

Sir Roger Hale Sheaffe rose to become a full general. He died at Edinburgh at the age of eighty-two.

John Strachan, one of the pillars of the Family Compact, was a member of the Executive Council of Upper Canada from 1818 to 1836. In 1839 he became Bishop of Toronto. He was the first president of King's College—the future University of Toronto—and also the founder of Trinity College. He died in 1867, in his ninetieth year.

John Vincent achieved the rank of full general. He died in London in 1848 at the age of eighty-three.

James Wilkinson talked himself into an acquittal before a court martial of his juniors—much to President Madison's disgust—and spent his declining years justifying his career in three carefully edited

volumes of documents, *Memoirs of My Own Times*. He died in
Mexico in 1825.

Sir James Yeo died on a voyage home from Africa in 1818, aged
thirty-five.

Author's Note and Acknowledgements

This book is the second of two dealing with the War of 1812 as it affected Canada and Canadians. Except for a short account of the burning of Washington, I have confined the narrative to the border struggle. Other events, such as the siege of Baltimore, the Battle of New Orleans, and the naval encounters along the Atlantic seaboard have already been dealt with capably by British and American writers.

My own work, which looks at the war from a Canadian point of view, is not intended primarily as a military or political history. These exist. Thus, I have not thought it necessary to list every military unit that fought along the border between 1812 and 1815. Nor have I attempted to go into minuscule detail on minor tactical points. Some lesser skirmishes—Prevost's attack on Sackets Harbor in 1813, Wilkinson's abortive attempt against the Lacolle Mill in 1814, to name two—have been omitted.

This is, rather, a *social* history of the war, the first to be written by a Canadian. I have tried to tell not only what happened but also *what it was like;* to look at the struggle not as a witness gazing down from a mountaintop but as a combatant struggling in the mud of the battlefield; to picture the war from the viewpoints of private soldiers and civilians as well as from those of generals and politicians; to see it through the eyes of ordinary people on both sides—farmer and housewife, traitor and spy, drummer boy and Indian brave, volunteer, regular, and conscript.

For this reason, both books have been based largely on primary sources—letters, military dispatches, documents, reports, diaries, journals and memoirs. I have invented nothing. Dialogue is reproduced exactly as reported by those who were present. If I have on occasion entered the minds of the participants it is because they themselves reported their own thoughts and feelings. This raw material, scattered over two continents, was gathered by my assistant, the indispensable Barbara Sears. I find it difficult to express properly my admiration for her industry and tenacity.

She and I would like to thank the various people and institutions who helped search out the documents which form the underpinnings of these books:

From the Metropolitan Toronto Central Library, Edith Firth and the staff of the Canadian History Department; Michael Pearson and the staff of the History Department; and Norma Dainard, Keith Alcock, and the staff of the newspaper section. From the Public Archives of Canada, Patricia Kennedy, Gordon Dodds, Bruce Wilson, Brian Driscoll, Glenn T. Wright, and Grace Campbell. From the *Dictionary of Canadian Biography*, Robert Fraser. From Parks Canada, Robert Allen of Ottawa and the staffs at Fort George and Fort Malden. And these individuals: Peter Burroughs, Esther Summers, Bob Green, Paul Roney, and Patrick Brode.

Also: the Public Archives of Ontario; the Library of Congress, Manuscript Division, Washington; the U.S. National Archives; the Public Record Office, London; the Filson Club, Louisville, Kentucky; the National Library of Scotland; the William L. Clements Library, University of Michigan; the Indiana State Library; and the historical societies of Vermont, New York, Rhode Island, Buffalo and Erie County, Delaware, Maryland, Kentucky, and Pennsylvania; and the Lundy's Lane and the Niagara Falls Historical Societies.

I am again grateful to those friends and professionals who read the manuscript in draft form and made so many useful suggestions, especially to Janice Tyrwhitt, Charles Templeton, Jack McClelland, Maggie Dowling, and Elsa Franklin. My wife, Janet, the best proofreader I know, again prevented me from grammatical embarrassment, and my editor, Janet Craig, rescued me once more from inconsistency. Research notes were organized under the supervision of my secretary, Ennis Armstrong, who also typed much of the manuscript in its various stages. To all these I say thank you. There will be errors; I hope they are minor; they are all mine.

Kleinburg, Ontario
March, 1981

Notes

Abbreviations used:

ASPFR	American State Papers, Foreign Relations
ASPMA	American State Papers, Military Affairs
ASPNA	American State Papers, Naval Affairs
BHS	Buffalo Historical Society
DAB	*Dictionary of American Biography*
DNB	*Dictionary of National Biography*
LC	Library of Congress
OBA	Ontario Bureau of Archives
PAC	Public Archives of Canada
PAO	Public Archives of Ontario
PRO	Public Record Office
RIHS	Rhode Island Historical Society
SBD	*Select British Documents*
SN	Secretary of the Navy
SW	Secretary of War
UCS	Upper Canada Sundries
USNA	United States National Archives

PRELUDE: NEW BRUNSWICK GOES TO WAR

p.391 l.33   Le Couteur, pp. 490–500, *passim;* Squires, pp. 118–36, *passim.*

OVERVIEW

p.399 l.2   Cruikshank, *Documentary History,* V: 151, regulations; Sheaffe, "Letterbook," p. 346, Sheaffe to Prevost, 13 March 1813.
p.399 l.16   Dunlop, p. 40.
p.399 l.20   Scott, p. 31.

p.399 l.26 Ibid., p. 35.

p.399 l.29 Jackson, *Black Hawk*, p. 71.

p.400 l.13 Ibid.

p.403 l.17 Cruikshank, *Documentary History*, V: 87, Dearborn to SW, 3 March 1813.

THE CAPTURE OF LITTLE YORK

p.406 l.3   PAO, Strachan Papers, Strachan to Brown, 26 April 1813.

p.406 l.12 Ibid.

p.406 l.23 Ibid.

p.406 l.33 Strachan, *Letterbook*, p. 18, Strachan to McGillivray, n.d.

p.407 l.7   Ibid.

p.407 l.22 PAO, Strachan Papers, Strachan to Brown, 20 Oct. 1807.

p.407 l.23 Ibid., Strachan to Brown, 21 Oct. 1809.

p.407 l.32 Ibid., Strachan to Brown, 13 July 1806.

p.408 l.17 Strachan, *Sermon*.

p.408 l.35 *Niles Register*, 28 Oct. 1815.

p.409 l.7   Hollon, pp. 205–6.

p.409 l.11 Quoted in Lossing, p. 586.

p.409 l.12 Ibid.

p.409 l.16 Terrell, pp. 130–31.

p.409 l.25 Ibid., pp. 27–28.

p.410 l.2   Quoted in Hollon, p. 202.

p.410 l.25 Cruikshank, *Documentary History*, V: 162–63, Brigade orders, 25 April 1813.

p.410 l.34 Cumberland, pp. 14–15.

p.411 l.6   Ibid.

p.411 l.7   Humphries, p. 7.

p.411 l.13 Cruikshank, *Documentary History*, V: 147, Sheaffe to Bathurst, 5 April 1813; W. Wood, SBD, II: 89, Sheaffe to Prevost, 5 May 1813.

p.411 l.15 W. Wood, SBD, II: 92, Sheaffe to Prevost, 5 May 1813.

p.411 l.22 Firth, p. 279, Ely Playter Diary, 26 April 1813.

p.411 l.24 Magill, *passim*.

p.411 l.30 PAC, UCS, RG 5, A1, vol. 17, no. 116, McGill to Sheaffe, 17 May 1813.

p.412 l.5   PAC, UCS, State Books, vol. F, report on Mrs. Derenzy's application; Derenzy to De Rottenburg, 5 July 1813; deposition signed by Leah Allan, S. Heward, W. Loe, 23 July 1813.

p.412 l.18 Firth, p. 292, Wilson to Wilson, 5 Dec. 1813.

p.412 l.23 Ibid., p. 279, Ely Playter Diary, 26 April 1813.

p.412 l.29 *The Yankee* (Boston), 2 July 1813.

p.412 l.34 Firth, p. 279, Ely Playter Diary, 26 April 1813.

p.413 l.3   Ibid., p. 294, Strachan to Brown, 26–27 April 1813.

p.413 l.13   PAO, Strachan Papers, Strachan to Brown, 9 Oct. 1808.

p.413 l.27   Ibid.

p.413 l.33   Firth, p. 294, Strachan to Brown, 26 and 27 April 1813.

p.414 l.14   Ibid., pp. 279–80, Ely Playter Diary, 27 April 1813.

p.414 l.28   PAC, RG 8, vol. 923, pp. 12–16, Brock to Lt.-Col. Green, 8 Feb. 1804.

p.415 l.3   C. Elliott, *Scott*, p. 73.

p.415 l.10   W. Wood, SBD, II: 89–91, Sheaffe to Prevost, 5 May 1813.

p.415 l.12   Ibid., p. 89.

p.415 l.31   Ibid., pp. 89–90.

p.415 l.33   Cruikshank, *Documentary History*, V: 193, Chewett, Strachan, et al. to ?, 8 May 1813.

p.416 l.6   W. Wood, SBD, II: 89–90, Sheaffe to Prevost, 5 May 1813.

p.416 l.12   Firth, pp. 304–5, Pearce account.

p.416 l.14   Cumberland, p. 17.

p.417 l.6   Cruikshank, *Documentary History*, V: 179–80, Fraser to ?, May 1813.

p.417 l.13   Firth, p. 304, Pearce account.

p.418 l.6   Cruikshank, *Documentary History*, V: 180–81, Fraser to ?, May 1813; ibid., p. 207, Finan journal; W. Wood, SBD, II: 90, Sheaffe to Prevost, 5 May 1813; Loyal and Patriotic Society, p. 229.

p.418 l.19   *Anglo-American Magazine*, December 1853, p. 565.

p.418 l.26   Firth, p. 304, Pearce account.

p.418 l.30   Cruikshank, *Documentary History*, V: 181, Fraser to ?, May 1813; Lossing, p. 588.

p.418 l.33   Firth, p. 280, Ely Playter Diary, 27 April 1813.

p.419 l.7   W. Wood, SBD, II: 90–91, Sheaffe to Prevost, 5 May 1813; Firth, p. 280, Ely Playter Diary, 27 April 1813; Cruikshank, *Documentary History*, V: 193–94, Chewett, Strachan, et al. to ?, 8 May 1813; Cruikshank, "Contest for . . . Lake Ontario in 1812 and 1813," p. 176.

p.419 l.9   Cruikshank, *Documentary History*, V: 181, Fraser to ?, May 1813.

p.419 l.16   Cruikshank, "Contest for . . . Lake Ontario in 1812 and 1813," p. 176; *Documentary History*, V: 194, Chewett, Strachan, et al. to ?, 8 May 1813.

p.419 l.24   Cruikshank, *Documentary History*, V: 208, Finan journal.

p.419 l.32   Firth, p. 294, Strachan to Brown, 26 and 27 April 1813.

p.420 l.2   W. Wood, SBD, II: 91, Sheaffe to Prevost, 5 May 1813.

p.420 l.6   Firth, pp. 304–5, Pearce account.

p.420 l.15   Ibid., p. 280, Ely Playter Diary, 27 April 1813.

p.420 l.24   Ibid.; W. Wood, SBD, II: 86, Sheaffe to Prevost, 30 April 1813; ibid., p. 91, Sheaffe to Prevost, 5 May 1813.

p.420 l.32   Firth, p. 280, Ely Playter Diary, 27 April 1813; PAC, RG 5, A1, vol. 19, no. 49, Saunders petition.

p.421 l.1   Cruikshank, *Documentary History*, V: 182, Fraser to ?, May 1813.

p.421 l.14   Ibid.

p.421 l.22   Ibid., p. 183, statement of killed and wounded.

p.421 l.31   Firth, p. 280, Ely Playter Diary, 27 April 1813; PAC, RG 5, A1, vol. 26, petition, Gugins to Gore.

p.421 l.33   Cumberland, p. 27; Cruikshank, *Documentary History*, V: 183, statement of killed and wounded.

p.422 l.2   Cruikshank, *Documentary History*, V: 182, Fraser to ?, May 1813.

p.422 l.7   *Niles Register*, 5 June 1813.

p.422 l.11   Cruikshank, *Documentary History*, V: 182, Fraser to ?, May 1813.

p.422 l.16   Ibid., p. 170, Chauncey to SN, 28 April 1813.

p.422 l.20   *Niles Register*, 5 June 1813.

p.422 l.29   Firth, pp. 294–95, Strachan to Brown, 26–27 April 1813.

p.423 l.15   Cruikshank, *Documentary History*, V: 210–11, Finan journal.

p.423 l.23   Firth, p. 295, Strachan to Brown, 26–27 April 1813.

p.423 l.32   Ibid., p. 280, Ely Playter Diary, 27 April 1813.

p.424 l.9   Ibid., pp. 280–81.

p.424 l.17   Ibid., p. 295, Strachan to Brown, 26–27 April 1813.

p.424 l.19   Cruikshank, *Documentary History*, V: 196, Chewett, Strachan, et al. to ?, 8 May 1813.

p.424 l.29   Ibid.; Firth, p. 295, Strachan to Brown, 26–27 April 1813.

p.425 l.7   Cruikshank, *Documentary History*, V: 196, Chewett, Strachan, et al. to ?, 8 May 1813.

p.425 l.10   Firth, p. 295, Strachan to Brown, 26–27 April 1813.

p.425 l.19   Cruikshank, *Documentary History*, V: 196, Chewett, Strachan, et al. to ?, 8 May 1813.

p.425 l.22   OBA, 9th Report, p. 143.

p.425 l.29   Firth, pp. 301–2, statement of Major Givins's losses; p. 296, Strachan to Brown, 26–30 April 1813.

p.426 l.10   Kerr, p. 14.

p.426 l.29   Firth, p. 307, Beaumont Diary, 27 April 1813.

p.426 l.32   Ibid., p. 295, Strachan to Brown, 26–28 April 1813.

p.428 l.7   Ibid.

p.428 l.9   Cruikshank, *Documentary History*, V: 224, memo, Thomas Ridout, 5 May 1813.

p.428 l.17   Selby, pp. 20–21.

p.428 l.30   Firth, p. 281, Ely Playter Diary, 28–30 April 1813.

p.428 l.33   Ibid., p. 282.

p.429 l.8   T. Palmer, *Historical Register*, Chauncey to Jones, 4 June 1813.

p.429 l.10   Firth, p. 308, Beaumont Diary, 1 May 1813.

p.429 l.23   Cruikshank, *Documentary History*, V: 172, *New York Statesman*, 29 May 1813.

p.429 l.32   PAC, RG 5, A1, vol. 16, Cutter information against John Lyon et al., 16 Aug. 1813; Cutter information against James Mulat et al., 16 Aug. 1813.

p.430 l.3   PAC, RG 5, A1, vol. 16, Palmer information against Elijah Bentley, 23 Aug. 1813.

p.430 l.15   PAC, RG 5, A1, vol. 16, Mulholland information against Finch, 24 Aug. 1813.

p.430 l.20   Firth, p. 293, Wilson to Wilson, 5 Dec. 1813.

p.430 l.22   *Niles Register*, 4 Nov. 1815, p. 160.

p.430 l.32   PAC, MG 24, F13, Chauncey to SN, 7 May 1813.

p.431 l.8   Cruikshank, *Documentary History*, V: 199–200, Chewett, Strachan, et al. to ?, 8 May 1813; *The Yankee* (Boston), 2 July 1813.

p.431 l.12   Cruikshank, *Documentary History*, V: 199–200, Chewett, Strachan, et al. to ?, 8 May 1813.

p.431 l.16   Kerr, p. 19.

p.431 l.22   PAC, MG 24, F13, Chauncey to SN, 7 May 1813.

p.431 l.28   Ibid., Chauncey to SN, 11 May 1813.

p.432 l.1   Armstrong, *Notices*, I: 227.

p.432 l.17   Cruikshank, *Documentary History*, V: 201, Chewett, Strachan, et al. to ?, 8 May 1813.

p.432 l.20   Ibid.

p.432 l.25   Ibid.

p.432 l.27   Ibid., p. 200.

p.432 l.31   Firth, p. 312, Powell to Powell, I 6 June 1813.

STALEMATE ON THE NIAGARA PENINSULA

p.435 l.3   W. Wood, SBD, III, pt. 2: 574, Merritt narrative; Cruikshank, *Documentary History*, V: 250, Vincent to Prevost, 28 May 1813.

p.435 l.8   Cruikshank, *Documentary History*, V: 250, Vincent to Prevost, 28 May 1813.

p.435 l.16   Cruikshank, "Battle of Fort George," p. 23.

p.435 l.21   Ibid., p. 24.

p.435 l.22   PAO, Ely Playter Diary, 27 May 1813.

p.435 l.27   "Reminiscences of American Occupation," p. 25.

p.435 l.30   Cruikshank, "Battle of Fort George," p. 24.

p.435 l.31   Ibid.

p.436 l.3   Ibid.

p.436 l.10   Mackenzie, *Perry*, pp. 107–9.

p.436 l.27   Ibid., p. 108.

p.438 l.2   Ibid., p. 109.

p.438 l.8   Cruikshank, "Battle of Fort George," p. 25.

p.438 l.13   Boyd, p. 16, Miller to a general, n.d.

p.438 l.25   C. Elliott, *Scott*, p. 97.

p.438 l.23   Lossing, p. 599.

p.438 l.28   Mackenzie, *Perry*, p. 109.

p.438 l.32   Scott, p. 88.

p.438 l.35   Boyd, pp. 4–5.

p.439 l.4   W. Wood, SBD, II: 103–7, Vincent to Prevost, 28 May 1813; Boyd, p. 5; Cruikshank, "Battle of Fort George," p. 26.

p.439 l.7   Cruikshank, "Battle of Fort George," p. 29.

p.439 l.12   W. Wood, SBD, II: 103–7, Vincent to Prevost, 28 May 1813.

p.439 l.19   Cruikshank, "Battle of Fort George," p. 26.

p.439 l.24   W. Wood, SBD, II: 106, Vincent to Prevost, 28 May 1813; Cruikshank, *Documentary History*, VI: 180, Hamilton to Henderson, 4 July 1813; ibid., V: 246, Clegg to Claus, 27 May 1813.

p.439 l.29   Cruikshank, *Documentary History*, V: 304, diary of Col. Claus.

p.440 l.10   Scott, pp. 89–90.

p.440 l.14   C. Elliott, *Scott*, p. 99.

p.440 l.17   Cruikshank, "Battle of Fort George," p. 27.

p.440 l.22   Scott, p. 90.

p.440 l.31   Ibid., pp. 90–91; C. Elliott, *Scott*, p. 100.

p.441 l.10   Cruikshank, "Battle of Fort George," p. 27.

p.441 l.19   C. Elliott, *Scott*, p. 100.

p.441 l.22   Scott, p. 91.

p.442 l.4   Quoted in H. Adams, VII: 188.

p.443 l.6   M. Thompson, "Billy Green," p. 175.

p.443 l.18   W. Wood, SBD, III, pt. 2: 576, Merritt narrative.

p.444 l.13   M. Thompson, "Billy Green," p. 175.

p.445 l.12   Ibid., pp. 175–76.

p.445 l.27   Morgan, p. 219.

p.445 l.29   Ibid.

p.445 l.35   FitzGibbon, p. 69.

p.446 l.4   W. Wood, SBD, II: 142–45, Vincent to Prevost, 6 June 1813; ibid., pp. 139–41, Harvey to Baynes, 6 June 1813.

p.446 l.13   M. Thompson, "Billy Green," p. 176.

p.446 l.22   Ibid., p. 177.

p.446 l.26   Ibid., p. 176.

p.446 l.33   Ibid.

p.446 l.35   Biggar, p. 387.

p.447 l.11   Cruikshank, *Documentary History*, VI: 33–34, *Niles Register*, 19 Oct. 1816, Chandler narrative.

p.447 l.14   Ibid., p. 13, FitzGibbon to Somerville, 7 June 1813; W. Wood, SBD, II: 139–41, Harvey to Baynes, 6 June 1813.

p.447 l.16   Biggar, p. 387.

p.447 l.23   Cruikshank, *Documentary History*, VI: 13–14, FitzGibbon to Somerville, 7 June 1813.

p.448 l.3   Ibid., pp. 16–17, FitzGibbon memo, 1 Jan. 1854.

p.448 l.10   Quoted in Cruikshank, "Stoney Creek," p. 10.

p.448 *l.16*   Cruikshank, *Documentary History*, VI: 27, Chandler to Dearborn, 18 June 1813.

p.448 *l.18*   Ibid., p. 50, letter from a U.S. officer, 22 June 1813.

p.449 *l.2*   Ibid., p. 27, Chandler to Dearborn, 18 June 1813; Cruikshank, "Stoney Creek," p. 11.

p.449 *l.9*   Cruikshank, *Documentary History*, VI: 14, FitzGibbon to Somerville, 7 June 1813; ibid., p. 17, FitzGibbon memo, 1 Jan. 1854.

p.449 *l.15*   Cruikshank, "Stoney Creek," p. 16.

p.449 *l.19*   W. Wood, SBD, III, pt. 2: 580, Merritt narrative.

p.449 *l.25*   Ibid., II: 140–41, Harvey to Baynes, 6 June 1813.

p.449 *l.35*   Ibid., III, pt. 2: 580, Merritt narrative.

p.450 *l.5*   Ibid., II: 139–41, Harvey to Baynes, 6 June 1813; Lossing, p. 604.

p.450 *l.8*   Cruikshank, *Documentary History*, VI: 56, Evans to Vincent, 8 June 1813.

p.450 *l.12*   Ibid., pp. 116–19, *Niles Register*, 19 Oct. 1816, Chandler narrative; Cruikshank, "Battle of Fort George," p. 16.

p.450 *l.16*   W. Wood, SBD, II: 139–41, Harvey to Baynes, 6 June 1813.

p.450 *l.19*   Cruikshank, "Battle of Fort George," p. 16.

p.450 *l.27*   Ibid., pp. 16–17.

p.450 *l.31*   Ibid., p. 17.

p.450 *l.34*   Cruikshank, *Documentary History*, VI: 62, Evans to Harvey, 10 June 1813.

p.451 *l.2*   Ibid., pp. 77–78, no. 7, Dearborn to Lewis.

p.451 *l.8*   Ibid., p. 63, return, 10 June 1813.

p.452 *l.24*   FitzGibbon, pp. 76–77; Cruikshank, *Documentary History*, VI: 116–17, *Montreal Gazette*, 6 July 1813; ibid., pp. 202–4, Askin to Askin, 8 July 1813.

p.453 *l.30*   Morgan, p. 194.

p.453 *l.32*   FitzGibbon, p. 56.

p.453 *l.35*   Morgan, p. 194.

p.454 *l.2*   FitzGibbon, p. 64.

p.454 *l.18*   Cruikshank, *Documentary History*, VI: 150–51, report of court of inquiry; W. Wood, SBD, III, pt. 2: 584–85, Merritt narrative.

p.455 *l.10*   Cruikshank, *Documentary History*, VI: 127–28, Laura Secord narrative.

p.455 *l.14*   Moir, pp. 107–8, certificate of James FitzGibbon, 11 May 1827.

p.455 *l.35*   Ibid.; PAO, Misc. coll., Story of Laura Ingersoll Secord as related by Laura Secord Clark, 1933.

p.456 *l.6*   Cruikshank, *Documentary History*, VI: 130–31, Boerstler narrative.

p.456 *l.11*   Chapin, p. 10.

p.456 *l.32*   Cruikshank, *Documentary History*, VI: 95–96, Dearborn to Armstrong, 20 June 1813.

p.457 *l.5*   Cruikshank, *Documentary History*, VI: 126, Ducharme to ?, 5 June 1826.

p.457 l.8   Ibid., p. 95, SW to Dearborn, 19 June 1813; ibid., p. 6, Dearborn to SW, 6 June 1813.

p.457 l.14   Chapin, p. 10.

p.457 l.34   Ibid., p. 40, Chapin to Armstrong, 26 April 1838.

p.457 l.35   Cruikshank, *Documentary History*, VI: 132, Boerstler narrative.

p.458 l.12   Ibid., p. 136; Chapin, p. 10.

p.458 l.13   Chapin, p. 10.

p.458 l.17   Cruikshank, *Documentary History*, VI: 151, report of court of inquiry, 17 Feb. 1815.

p.458 l.20   Ibid., p. 146, Roach journal.

p.458 l.23   Ibid., p. 131, Boerstler narrative.

p.458 l.29   Ibid., p. 148, Roach journal.

p.458 l.32   Ibid.

p.458 l.35   Ibid., p. 131, Boerstler narrative.

p.459 l.6   Ibid., p. 126, Ducharme to ?, 5 June 1826.

p.460 l.12   Ibid., pp. 126–27.

p.460 l.28   Ibid., pp. 130–37, Boerstler narrative.

p.460 l.12   Chapin, pp. 9–15.

p.461 l.15   Cruikshank, *Documentary History*, VI: 133–34, Boerstler narrative; FitzGibbon, p. 87.

p.461 l.35   FitzGibbon, p. 87.

p.462 l.10   Ibid.

p.462 l.20   Chapin, p. 14.

p.463 l.27   FitzGibbon, pp. 89–91.

p.463 l.35   Cruikshank, *Documentary History*, VI: 151, Roach journal; ibid., pp. 120–21, FitzGibbon to Kerr, 30 March 1818; ibid., p. 127, Ducharme to ?, 5 June 1826; W. Wood, SBD, III, pt. 2: 585, Merritt narrative.

p.464 l.4   Cruikshank, *Documentary History*, VI: 141, Boerstler to Dearborn, 25 June 1813; ibid., p. 114, return of prisoners, 24 June 1813.

p.464 l.7   Ibid., pp. 142–44, *Buffalo Gazette*, 29 July 1813.

p.464 l.14   Quoted in Cruikshank, "Fight in the Beechwoods," p. 22.

p.464 l.18   Ibid., p. 21.

p.464 l.20   Cruikshank, *Documentary History*, VI: 187, SW to Dearborn, 6 July 1813.

p.464 l.32   Ibid., p. 228, statement by FitzGibbon.

p.465 l.3   PAC, MG 24, F4, Bisshopp Papers, Hackett to Bisshopp, 20 July 1813; PAC, RG 8, vol. 679, pp. 108–9, Fulton to Prevost, 18 June 1813.

p.465 l.13   Cruikshank, *Documentary History*, VI: 228, statement by FitzGibbon.

p.465 l.26   Ibid., p. 228.

p.465 l.35   Ibid.

p.466 l.4   Ibid.

p.466 l.12   Cruikshank, *Documentary History*, VI: 223–24, Porter to Dearborn, 13 July 1813; "Burning of Buffalo," p. 263; "Village of Buffalo," pp. 92, 193.

p.467 l.29   Cruikshank, *Documentary History*, VI: 228–30, Sloan recollection.

p.468 l.3   PAC, MG 24, F4, Bisshopp Papers, Bisshopp to sister, 21 March 1813.

p.468 l.5   Ibid.

p.468 l.7   FitzGibbon, p. 110.

p.468 l.10   Ibid.

p.468 l.17   PAC, MG 24, F4, Bisshopp Papers, Hackett to Bisshopp, 20 July 1813.

p.468 l.30   Cruikshank, *Documentary History*, VI: 224, Porter to Dearborn, 13 July 1813.

p.468 l.33   Ibid., pp. 224–25.

p.469 l.10   PAC, MG 24, F4, Bisshopp Papers, Hackett to Bisshopp, 20 July 1813.

p.469 l.16   Ibid.

p.469 l.21   Ibid.

p.469 l.25   Cruikshank, *Documentary History*, VI: 230, Sloan recollection; FitzGibbon, p. 110.

p.469 l.26   PAC, MG 24, F4, Bisshopp Papers, Hackett to Bisshopp, 20 July 1813.

p.469 l.35   Ibid.

p.470 l.4   Firth, p. 316, *Kingston Gazette*, 10 Aug. 1813.

p.470 l.17   Ibid., p. 319, Allan to Baynes, 3 Aug. 1813.

p.470 l.23   Cruikshank, *Documentary History*, VI: 302, Powell and Strachan to Freer, 2 Aug. 1813.

p.471 l.9   Ibid., pp. 302–3.

p.471 l.15   Ibid., p. 303.

p.471 l.21   Firth, p. 319, Allan to Baynes, 3 Aug. 1813.

p.471 l.31   Ibid.; Cruikshank, *Documentary History*, VI: 303, Powell and Strachan to Freer, 2 Aug. 1813.

p.471 l.35   PAC, RG 5, A1, vol. 16, information of George Cullen, 16 Aug. 1813.

p.472 l.3   Ibid.; also Wm. Huff information, 7 Sept. 1813.

p.472 l.11   Firth, pp. 282–83, Ely Playter Diary.

p.472 l.15   Cruikshank, *Documentary History*, VI: 308–9, Chauncey to SN, 4 Aug. 1813.

p.472 l.35   PAC, RG 5, A1, vol. 16, Wm. Forrest information, 16 Aug. 1813; Jacob Anderson information, 18 Aug. 1813.

p.473 l.10   Ibid., Robinson to De Rottenburg, 16 Aug. 1813.

THE SIEGE OF FORT MEIGS

p.475 l.9   Harrison, II: 417, Harrison to SW, 15 April [?] 1813; E. Wood, "Journal," p. 371.

p.475 l.21   E. Wood, "Journal," pp. 378–79.

p.475 l.28 Harrison, II: 427, Harrison to SW, 21 April 1813.

p.475 l.32 Bourne, p. 41.

p.476 l.13 USNA, M221/57/S126, Shelby to SW, 20 March 1813; Harrison, II: 428, SW to Harrison, 27 April 1813.

p.476 l.16 Lossing, p. 475.

p.476 l.18 E. Wood, "Journal," p. 383; Harrison, II: 430.

p.477 l.4 Harrison, II: 416, Harrison to Shelby, 9 April 1813; E. Wood, "Journal," p. 377; USNA, M221/57/S126, Shelby to SW, 20 March 1813.

p.477 l.16 E. Wood, "Journal," p. 384.

p.477 l.19 Harrison, II: 416, Harrison to SW, 9 April 1813.

p.477 l.28 E. Wood, "Journal," p. 385.

p.477 l.30 Harrison, II: 430, Harrison to SW, 28 April 1813.

p.480 l.5 Richardson, *Richardson's War*, pp. 155–58.

p.480 l.17 Lossing, p. 478.

p.481 l.7 Ibid., p. 482.

p.481 l.30 Ibid.

p.481 l.31 Averill, p. 23.

p.482 l.10 E. Wood, "Journal," pp. 387–90.

p.482 l.19 Winter, pp. 122–23.

p.482 l.29 Richardson, *Eight Years*, p. 135.

p.483 l.12 Randall, p. 486.

p.484 l.13 Bourne, pp. 139–40, 148–49.

p.484 l.27 Ibid., pp. 148–49.

p.485 l.6 E. Wood, "Journal," pp. 389–90.

p.485 l.12 Lossing, p. 483.

p.485 l.24 Richardson, *Eight Years*, p. 136.

p.485 l.28 "Siege of Fort Meigs," p. 59.

p.485 l.31 McAfee, *History*, p. 262.

p.486 l.4 Howe, p. 865.

p.486 l.16 Ibid., p. 868, Lorraine's narrative.

p.486 l.26 Ibid., p. 869, Lorraine's narrative.

p.486 l.35 Ibid.

p.488 l.9 Bourne, pp. 151–53.

p.488 l.17 Howe, p. 869.

p.488 l.24 Harrison, II: 431, Harrison to SW, 5 May 1813; "Siege of Fort Meigs," p. 60; E. Wood, "Journal," p. 392.

p.488 l.29 E. Wood, "Journal," p. 393.

p.489 l.23 Howe, p. 865.

p.490 l.3 E. Wood, "Journal," p. 394; Harrison, II: 432, Harrison to SW, 5 May 1813; Lossing, p. 485.

p.490 l.22 Harrison, II: 432, Harrison to SW, 5 May 1813; McAfee, *History*, p. 265.

p.491 l.9	Howe, p. 869, Underwood narrative; Draper MSS, Tecumseh Papers, 6YY23, Underwood narrative.
p.491 l.15	Lossing, p. 480.
p.492 l.7	Draper MSS, Tecumseh Papers, 6YY23, Underwood narrative.
p.492 l.27	Brannan, pp. 158–59, Clay to Harrison, 13 May 1813.
p.492 l.31	Ibid.
p.492 l.32	Ibid.
p.492 l.35	Harrison, II: 443, Harrison to SW, 13 May 1813.
p.493 l.1	E. Wood, "Journal," p. 394.
p.493 l.9	Draper MSS, Tecumseh Papers, 6YY23, Underwood narrative.
p.493 l.24	Howe, p. 870, Underwood narrative.
p.493 l.29	Lossing, p. 485.
p.494 l.2	Richardson, *Eight Years*, p. 138.
p.494 l.10	Howe, p. 870; "General Orders,"p. 11, General Order, 6 May 1813.
p.494 l.22	Bourne, p. 39.
p.495 l.30	Richardson, *Eight Years*, pp. 137–38; *Richardson's War*, pp. 150–51.
p.496 l.6	Howe, p. 870, Underwood narrative.
p.496 l.26	Ibid.
p.497 l.2	Draper MSS, Tecumseh Papers, 6YY22, Combs to Laughlin; Howe, p. 871, Underwood narrative.
p.497 l.7	Draper MSS, Tecumseh Papers, 6YY22, Combs to Laughlin.
p.497 l.10	*New Monthly Magazine*, December 1826.
p.497 l.19	Howe, p. 871, Underwood narrative.
p.498 l.2	Draper MSS, Tecumseh Papers, 6YY23, Underwood narrative.
p.498 l.10	Ibid., 6YY22, Combs to Laughlin.
p.499 l.16	Howe, p. 873, Underwood narrative.
p.499 l.24	Richardson, "Canadian Campaign," p. 169; *Richardson's War*, pp. 158–59.
p.500 l.6	Ibid.
p.500 l.25	Lossing, p. 480.
p.501 l.2	Ibid., pp. 487–88; Richardson, *Richardson's War*, pp. 152–53; Brannan, pp. 152–54, Harrison to Armstrong, 9 May 1813; E. Wood, "Journal," p. 401.
p.501 l.9	W. Wood, SBD, II: 35, Procter to Prevost, 14 May 1813.
p.501 l.19	Ibid.; Richardson, *Richardson's War*, p. 160.
p.501 l.24	Richardson, *Richardson's War*, pp. 160–61.
p.501 l.32	W. Wood, SBD, II: 35, Procter to Prevost, 14 May 1813.
p.501 l.35	Brannan, p. 156, Harrison to SW, 13 May 1813.
p.502 l.6	W. Wood, SBD, II: 39, General Order, 21 May 1813.
p.502 l.12	"General Orders," p. 13, General Order, 9 May 1813.
p.502 l.19	Ibid., pp. 15–16.

p.505 l.4   Metcalf, p. 95, Elliott to Chauncey, 11 Oct. 1812.

p.505 l.8   Rosenberg, pp. 55–56.

p.505 l.28   Parsons, *Battle*, p. 33.

p.506 l.2   Dutton, p. 209.

p.506 l.7   Snow, p. 13.

p.506 l.13   RIHS, Parsons Diary, 13–15 June 1813.

p.506 l.17   W. Dobbins, *History*, p. 322.

p.506 l.20   Ibid.; W. Wood, SBD, II: 246, Barclay to Vincent, 17 June 1813.

p.507 l.35   Rosenberg, p. 38.

p.508 l.3   Ibid., pp. 38–41.

p.508 l.4   Ibid., pp. 39–40.

p.508 l.17   Ibid., p. 24.

p.509 l.11   PAC, RG 8, vol. 679, p. 177, Procter to McDouall, 4 July 1813; ibid., pp. 181–86, Procter to Prevost, 4 July 1813.

p.509 l.16   W. Wood, SBD, II: 245–46, Barclay to Vincent, 17 June 1813.

p.509 l.29   PAC, RG 8, vol. 679, p. 177, Procter to McDouall, 4 July 1813; ibid., p. 181, Procter to Prevost, 4 July 1813.

p.510 l.2   W. Wood, SBD, II: 248–49, Barclay to Procter, 29 June 1813; ibid., p. 259, Barclay to Prevost, 16 July 1813.

p.510 l.6   Ibid., p. 253, Procter to Prevost, 11 July 1813.

p.510 l.15   Ibid.

p.510 l.20   Ibid.

p.511 l.5   Cruikshank, *Documentary History*, VI: 256, Prevost to Bathurst, 20 July 1813; PAC, MG 24, F13, Chauncey Papers, Chauncey to SN, 7 May 1813.

p.511 l.8   W. Wood, SBD, II: 251, Prevost to Procter, 11 July 1813.

p.511 l.10   PAC, RG 8, vol. 679, p. 177, Procter to McDouall, 4 July 1813.

p.511 l.14   W. Wood, SBD, II: 255, Prevost to Procter, 12 July 1813.

p.511 l.22   Ibid., p. 44, Procter to Prevost, 9 Aug. 1813.

p.511 l.30   Ibid.

p.512 l.4   Richardson, *Eight Years*, p. 140.

p.512 l.14   Harrison, II: 474, Clay to Harrison, 20 June 1813; "General Orders," pp. 21–22, General Order, 21 July 1813; Howe, p. 878.

p.512 l.22   Harrison, II: 494, Harrison to SW, 23 July 1813.

p.512 l.31   Richardson, *Eight Years*, pp. 140–41; Averill, p. 31.

p.513 l.3   Richardson, *Eight Years*, pp. 140–41; *Richardson's War*, p. 178.

p.513 l.13   Howe, p. 878; Harrison, II: 499, Clay to Harrison, 26 July 1813.

p.513 l.17   W. Wood, SBD, II: 44–45, Procter to Prevost, 9 Aug. 1813; Richardson, *Richardson's War*, pp. 178–79.

p.513 l.23   McAfee, *History*, p. 322.

p.513 l.27   Ibid.

p.513 l.31   Harrison, II: 502, Harrison to Croghan, 29 July 1813.
p.514 l.6   McAfee, *History*, pp. 322–23.
p.514 l.9   Charles Williams, "George Croghan," p. 388.
p.514 l.16   Harrison, II: 503, Croghan to Harrison, 30 July 1813.
p.514 l.25   Filson Club, Scrapbook MSS B1/F489, Wright to Duncan, 7 May
             1869.
p.515 l.10   McAfee, *History*, pp. 323–24.
p.515 l.24   LC, Eustis Papers, Harrison to Eustis, 6 Jan. 1812.
p.515 l.31   Harrison, II: 528, Croghan to editor of *Liberty Hall*, 27 Aug. 1813.
p.516 l.8   Ibid., p. 528; Charles Williams, "George Croghan," p. 387.
p.516 l.15   Harrison, II: 510, Harrison to SW, 4 Aug. 1813.
p.516 l.16   McAfee, *History*, p. 324.
p.516 l.22   Harrison, II: 512, Harrison to SW, 4 Aug. 1813.
p.516 l.23   Ibid., p. 514, Croghan to Harrison, 5 Aug. 1813; ibid., p. 528, Croghan
             to editor of *Liberty Hall*, 27 Aug. 1813.
p.516 l.26   W. Wood, SBD, II: 45, Procter to Prevost, 9 Aug. 1813.
p.517 l.2   Ibid.
p.517 l.11   Ibid.
p.517 l.19   Harrison, II: 512–13, Harrison to SW, 4 Aug. 1813.
p.517 l.23   Lossing, p. 501.
p.517 l.26   Harrison, II: 513, Harrison to SW, 4 Aug. 1813.
p.517 l.28   Lossing, p. 501.
p.517 l.35   *Niles Register*, 4 Sept. 1813.
p.518 l.9   McAfee, *History*, pp. 325–26.
p.518 l.17   Harrison, II: 515, Croghan to Harrison, 5 Aug. 1813; Filson Club,
             Scrapbook MSS B1/F489, Wright to Duncan, 7 May 1869.
p.518 l.26   *Niles Register*, 4 Sept. 1813.
p.518 l.30   Richardson, *Richardson's War*, pp. 179–80.
p.519 l.12   *Niles Register*, 4 Sept. 1813.
p.519 l.16   Byfield, p. 365.
p.519 l.24   Lossing, p. 503.
p.519 l.27   Ibid.
p.519 l.30   Richardson, *Richardson's War*, p. 180.
p.519 l.35   Byfield, p. 365.
p.520 l.3   *Niles Register*, 4 Sept. 1813.
p.520 l.4   Filson Club, Scrapbook MSS B1/F489, Wright to Duncan, 7 May
             1869.
p.520 l.33   Byfield, pp. 365–66.
p.521 l.23   Beasley, pp. 23–24.
p.521 l.26   *Niles Register*, 4 Sept. 1813.
p.521 l.33   Harrison, II: 512, Harrison to SW, 4 Aug. 1813.
p.523 l.14   Quoted in Mackenzie, *Perry*, p. 122.
p.523 l.16   Ibid., pp. 125–26.

p.523 l.18   Ibid., p. 126.

p.523 l.21   Ibid., pp. 126–27; Dodge, p. 18; Brown, p. 93.

p.523 l.27   Dutton, p. 100.

p.523 l.34   Quoted in Snow, p. 19.

p.524 l.4   W. Dobbins, *History*, p. 390, Champlin narrative.

p.524 l.13   Rosenberg, pp. 50–51.

p.524 l.19   W. Dobbins, *History*, p. 329.

p.524 l.28   Rosenberg, p. 51.

p.524 l.35   Ibid., pp. 51–52; W. Dobbins, *History*, p. 390, Champlin narrative.

p.525 l.8   Lossing, p. 515.

p.525 l.14   W. Dobbins, *History*, p. 331.

p.525 l.22   Parsons, "Brief Sketches," p. 176.

p.525 l.29   Mackenzie, *Perry*, pp. 139–40.

p.526 l.2   Quoted in Mackenzie, *Perry*, p. 142.

p.526 l.16   Ibid., pp. 142–43.

p.526 l.21   Ibid., p. 146.

p.526 l.29   Ibid., pp. 139–40.

p.527 l.3   *Documents in Relation to the Differences*, p. 33, Wm. Taylor's affidavit.

p.527 l.8   Dutton, p. 115.

p.527 l.16   Harrison, II: 525, Harrison to SW, 22 Aug. 1813; Dutton, p. 119.

p.527 l.21   Dutton, p. 123; Parsons, *Battle*, pp. 7–8.

p.527 l.30   Mackenzie, *Perry*, pp. 155–56.

p.527 l.35   Ibid., pp. 157–58.

p.528 l.2   W. Dobbins, *History*, pp. 340–41.

p.528 l.11   Dutton, p. 140.

p.528 l.15   Ibid., p. 142; W. Dobbins, *History*, p. 342.

p.528 l.23   Dutton, p. 142.

p.529 l.5   Mackenzie, *Perry*, p. 169; W. Dobbins, *History*, p. 342.

p.529 l.18   W. Dobbins, *History*, p. 342.

p.529 l.21   Dutton, p. 143.

p.529 l.27   W. Wood, SBD, II: 274, Barclay to Yeo, 12 Sept. 1813.

p.529 l.29   Ibid., pp. 303–4, Barclay narrative.

p.530 l.2   Ibid., p. 274, Barclay to Yeo, 12 Sept. 1813.

p.530 l.8   Cruikshank, *Documentary History*, VII: 95–96, Procter to Freer, 3 Sept. 1813.

p.530 l.10   W. Wood, SBD, II: 266, Procter to Prevost, 29 Aug. 1813.

p.530 l.13   Ibid., pp. 268–69, Barclay to Yeo, 1 Sept. 1813.

p.530 l.23   Cruikshank, *Documentary History*, VII: 49, Prevost to Procter, 22 Aug. 1813.

p.530 l.27   W. Wood, SBD, II: 264, Procter to Prevost, 26 Aug. 1813.

p.530 l.31   Ibid., p. 265.

p.531 l.4   Cruikshank, "Contest for . . . Lake Erie," p. 377.

p.531 l.10   Ibid.

p.532 l.7   Dodge, pp. 15–19.

p.532 l.11   Ibid., p. 17.

p.532 l.17   Ibid., p. 8.

p.533 l.2   A.B. Burt, "Barclay," p. 170.

p.533 l.5   Ibid.

p.533 l.21   W. Wood, SBD, II: 298, Barclay narrative.

p.533 l.27   W. Dobbins, *History*, p. 343.

p.534 l.9   Maclay, I: 504.

p.534 l.19   Parsons, *Battle*, p. 13.

p.534 l.28   Burges, pp. 121–22, Parsons to Perry.

p.534 l.32   Dodge, p. 20.

p.535 l.6   Cooper, *History of the Navy*, II: 453–54; Lossing, pp. 521–22; *Documents in Relation to the Differences*, pp. 31–32, Wm. Taylor's affidavit.

p.535 l.12   J. Elliott, *Speech*, p. 6.

p.535 l.23   Ibid.; Mackenzie, *Perry*, pp. 173–74.

p.535 l.28   Lossing, p. 520.

p.536 l.4   Mackenzie, *Perry*, p. 175.

p.536 l.12   Bunnell, p. 133.

p.536 l.17   Burges, p. 122, Parsons to Perry.

p.537 l.4   Mackenzie, *Perry*, p. 176.

p.537 l.13   Ibid.; Burges, p. 122, Parsons to Perry.

p.537 l.16   Mackenzie, *Perry*, p. 177.

p.537 l.17   Lossing, p. 522.

p.537 l.18   Parsons, *Battle*, p. 13.

p.537 l.27   Paullin, p. 180, Yarnell testimony.

p.538 l.4   W. Wood, SBD, II: 275, Barclay to Yeo, 12 Sept. 1813; *Documents in Relation to the Differences*, pp. 31–32, Wm. Taylor's affidavit; Mackenzie, *Perry*, p. 178.

p.538 l.23   W. Wood, SBD, II: 275, Barclay to Yeo, 12 Sept. 1813.

p.539 l.7   Mackenzie, *Perry*, pp. 185–86; Parsons, "Brief Sketches," pp. 173–74; Parsons, *Battle*, p. 12.

p.539 l.16   Parsons, *Battle*, p. 13.

p.539 l.25   Lossing, pp. 524–25.

p.539 l.28   Ibid.

p.540 l.6   Parsons, "Brief Sketches," pp. 173–74, 176.

p.540 l.11   Parsons, "Surgical Account," p. 314.

p.540 l.19   Ibid.

p.540 l.24   Ibid.

p.541 l.1   Bunnell, p. 117.

p.541 l.5   Ibid.

p.541 l.8   Parsons, *Battle*, p. 12.

p.541 l.12   Dutton, pp. 154–55.

p.541 l.23   Maclay, p. 516; Cruikshank, "Contest for . . . Lake Erie," p. 383.

p.541 l.30   Paullin, pp. 180–81, Yarnell testimony; *Documents in Relation to the Differences*, p. 17, Lt. Turner's affidavit; ibid., p. 18, Parsons's affidavit; ibid., p. 25, Lt. Stevens's affidavit.

p.542 l.19   Dutton, p. 156.

p.542 l.32   Bunnell, pp. 114–15; Brown, p. 90.

p.542 l.33   Paullin, pp. 84–85, list of killed and wounded; Emerson, pp. 233–35, muster roll of fleet.

p.543 l.5   *Documents in Relation to the Differences*, p. 27, Lt. Champlin's affidavit.

p.543 l.14   Dutton, p. 169; W. Wood, SBD, II: 318, George Young testimony.

p.543 l.32   Paullin, p. 181, Yarnell testimony; Cleveland City Council, *Inauguration*, p. 84, Chapman narrative; *Documents in Relation to the Differences*, p. 26, Forrest to ?, 29 Jan. 1821; BHS, A.C. Goodyear Collection, box 1, Fairchild to Lossing, 12 Oct. 1853.

p.543 l.35   Parsons, "Surgical Account," p. 314.

p.544 l.3   Paullin, p. 80, Perry to Jones, 13 Sept. 1813.

p.544 l.13   Dutton, pp. 160–61.

p.544 l.22   Dutton, p. 161; *Documents in Relation to the Differences*, p. 26, Lt. Stevens's affidavit; ibid., p. 28, Lt. Champlin's affidavit.

p.545 l.3   W. Wood, SBD, II: 276, Barclay to Yeo, 12 Sept. 1813; Mackenzie, *Perry*, p. 195.

p.545 l.13   Mackenzie, *Perry*, pp. 192–93; J. Elliott, *Speech*, p. 8; W. Wood, SBD, II: 276, Barclay to Yeo, 12 Sept. 1813.

p.545 l.17   Bunnell, p. 115.

p.546 l.6   W. Wood, SBD, II: 276, Barclay to Yeo, 12 Sept. 1813.

p.546 l.11   Lossing, p. 528.

p.546 l.18   J. Elliott, *Speech*, p. 8.

p.546 l.20   Parsons, *Battle*, p. 13.

p.546 l.31   J. Elliott, *Speech*, p. 8.

p.546 l.33   Cooper, *History of the Navy*, II: 467n.

p.547 l.8   Paullin, p. 43, Perry to Harrison, 10 Sept. 1813.

p.547 l.16   Ibid., p. 49, Perry to Jones, 10 Sept. 1813.

p.548 l.4   W. Wood, SBD, II: 272, Procter to de Rottenberg, 12 Sept. 1813.

p.548 l.10   Lossing, p. 533.

p.548 l.12   Brown, p. 88.

p.548 l.22   Parsons, *Battle*, p. 14; W. Dobbins, *History*, p. 352.

p.549 l.4   Parsons, *Battle*, p. 14; Parsons, "Surgical Account," p. 315.

p.549 l.10   Dutton, p. 177.

p.549 l.15   Mackenzie, *Perry*, p. 280.

p.549 l.21   A.B. Burt, "Barclay," p. 177.

p.549 l.23   Ibid.

p.549 l.31   Mackenzie, *Perry*, p. 220.

p.549 l.35   Parsons, *Battle*, p. 18.

p.550 l.5   Paullin, pp. 80–82, Perry to Jones, 13 Sept. 1813.

p.550 l.14   *Documents in Relation to the Differences*, p. 10, charges against Perry.

p.550 l.16   Parsons, *Battle*, p. 17.

p.550 l.19   *Documents in Relation to the Differences*, p. 22, Perry to Elliott, 18 June 1818.

p.550 l.22   Mackenzie, *Perry*, p. 218, Elliott to Perry, 19 Sept. 1813.

p.551 l.3   Ibid., pp. 218–19, Perry to Elliott, 19 Sept. 1813.

p.551 l.12   *Documents in Relation to the Differences*, pp. 17–18, Lt. Turner's affidavit.

p.551 l.22   ASPNA, I: 566, 570, 572.

RETREAT ON THE THAMES

p.553 l.12   PRO, WO71/243, Procter court martial, Warburton testimony.

p.554 l.6   Drake, p. 187.

p.554 l.35   Ibid., p. 186.

p.555 l.23   PRO, WO71/243, Procter court martial, Wm. Jones testimony.

p.555 l.25   Ibid.; ibid., Hall testimony.

p.556 l.16   Drake, p. 187.

p.557 l.5   PRO, WO71/243, Procter court martial, appendix 7, Tecumseh's speech, 15 Sept. 1813.

p.557 l.8   Ibid.

p.557 l.21   Ibid.

p.557 l.29   Ibid.

p.557 l.33   Ibid., Hall testimony.

p.558 l.15   Hatch, p. 116.

p.558 l.34   PRO, WO71/243, Procter court martial, Warburton testimony.

p.559 l.16   Ibid., App. 26, Baynes to Procter, 18 Sept. 1813.

p.559 l.19   W. Wood, SBD, II: 282, Harvey to Procter, 17 Sept. 1813.

p.560 l.6   Richardson, "Canadian Campaign," p. 252.

p.560 l.16   PRO, WO71/243, Procter court martial, Hall testimony.

p.560 l.19   Ibid., Warburton testimony.

p.560 l.23   Ibid., Hall testimony.

p.560 l.27   Ibid., Warburton testimony.

p.560 l.29   Drake, p. 191.

p.560 l.34   PRO, WO71/243, Procter court martial, Evans testimony.

p.561 l.1   Horsman, *Matthew Elliott*, p. 212.

p.561 l.6   PRO, WO71/243, Procter court martial, Dixon testimony.

p.561 l.12   Ibid., Warburton testimony, Evans testimony.

p.561 l.18   Quaife, *War on the Detroit*, p. 141.

p.562 l.10   Ibid., pp. 141–42.

p.562 l.16   Harrison, II: 555, Harrison to SW, 30 Sept. 1813.

p.562 l.24   PRO, WO71/243, Procter court martial, Chambers testimony, Hall testimony.

p.562 l.28   Ibid., Warburton testimony.

p.562 l.33   Ibid.

p.563 l.6   W. Wood, SBD, II: 283, Harvey to Procter, 17 Sept. 1813.

p.563 l.9   Ibid., p. 285, Prevost to Procter, 6 Oct. 1813.

p.564 l.7   PRO, WO71/243, Procter court martial, Dixon testimony.

p.564 l.11   Ibid.

p.565 l.7   McAfee, "Papers," 27 and 28 Sept. 1813.

p.565 l.22   Ibid., 19 May 1813.

p.566 l.5   Meyer, p. 81.

p.566 l.9   Ibid.

p.566 l.10   USNA, M221/54/J148, Johnson to SW, 16 April 1813.

p.566 l.15   "Visit," p. 202.

p.566 l.19   McAfee, "Papers," 26 July 1813.

p.566 l.28   Ibid., *passim*.

p.566 l.30   "Visit," p. 202.

p.567 l.2   McAfee, "Papers," 30 Sept. 1813; Sholes, pp. 523–24.

p.567 l.9   Harrison, II: 550–51, Harrison to SW, 27 Sept. 1813; ibid., p. 550, Harrison to Meigs, 27 Sept. 1813.

p.567 l.12   Ibid., p. 555, Harrison to SW, 30 Sept. 1813.

p.567 l.22   Ibid., p. 493, Harrison to Shelby, 20 July 1813.

p.567 l.27   Ibid.

p.568 l.5   McAfee, *History*, pp. 380–81.

p.568 l.10   Harrison, II: 558, Harrison to SW, 9 Oct. 1813.

p.568 l.14   McAfee, *History*, p. 364.

p.568 l.21   Ibid., p. 382.

p.568 l.32   "Visit," p. 203.

p.569 l.3   McAfee, "Papers," 2 Oct. 1813.

p.569 l.12   McAfee, *History*, p. 383; Harrison, II: 558, Harrison to SW, 9 Oct. 1813.

p.569 l.16   Harrison, II: 558, Harrison to SW, 9 Oct. 1813.

p.569 l.19   Ibid.

p.570 l.2   PRO, WO71/243, Procter court martial, Crowther testimony.

p.570 l.10   Ibid., Warburton testimony.

p.570 l.18   Ibid.; ibid., Caldwell and Chambers testimony.

p.571 l.3   Ibid., Chambers testimony.

p.571 l.5   Ibid., Warburton testimony.

p.571 l.7   Tucker, *Tecumseh*, p. 307.

p.571 l.15   Richardson, *Richardson's War*, p. 226.

p.571 l.20   PRO, WO71/243, Procter court martial, Warburton testimony.

p.571 l.31   Ibid.; ibid., Evans, Chambers, Crowther testimony; Appendix 6, Procter defence.

p.572 l.3   Ibid., Evans testimony.

p.572 l.26   Holmes, p. 8.

p.572 l.33   Lauriston, p. 89.

p.573 l.5   Holmes, p. 8.

p.573 l.14   Arnold, p. 3.

p.573 l.21   Lossing, p. 560.

p.573 l.28   Tucker, *Tecumseh*, p. 309.

p.574 l.25   Richardson, *Richardson's War*, p. 232, Bullock to friend, 6 Dec. 1813; PRO, WO71/243, Procter court martial, Gilmore and Crowther testimony.

p.574 l.29   Ibid., Evans and Hall testimony; Richardson, *Richardson's War*, p. 230, Bullock to friend, 6 Dec. 1813; W. Wood, SBD, II: 323–27, Procter to De Rottenburg, 23 Oct. 1813.

p.575 l.2   PRO, WO71/243, Procter court martial, Warburton testimony.

p.575 l.10   W. Wood, SBD, II: 323–27, Procter to De Rottenberg, 23 Oct. 1813.

p.575 l.28   Richardson, *Richardson's War*, p. 232.

p.575 l.33   Ibid., pp. 232–33.

p.576 l.4   PRO, WO71/243, Procter court martial, Evans testimony.

p.576 l.18   Ibid., Hall testimony.

p.576 l.32   Ibid.; Richardson, *Richardson's War* p. 212.

p.577 l.9   Mackenzie, *Perry*, pp. 236–37.

p.577 l.13   Wickliffe, p. 46, Wickliffe to editor of *Bardstown Gazette*, 25 Nov. 1859.

p.577 l.21   *Kentucky Gazette*, 28 Nov. 1835, p. 2.

p.577 l.29   Ibid.

p.577 l.34   McAfee, "Papers," 5 Oct. 1813.

p.578 l.16   Ibid.; Harrison, II: 561–62, Harrison to SW, 9 Oct. 1813; Young, pp. 71, 72.

p.578 l.29   *Kentucky Gazette*, 28 Nov. 1835, p. 2.

p.579 l.1   Ibid.

p.579 l.4   Harrison, II: 562, Harrison to SW, 9 Oct. 1813.

p.579 l.11   *Kentucky Gazette*, 28 Nov. 1835, p. 2.

p.579 l.17   Young, p. 74.

p.580 l.11   PRO, WO71/243, Procter court martial, Hall testimony.

p.580 l.12   McAfee, "Papers," 5 Oct. 1813.

p.580 l.14   PRO, WO71/243, Procter court martial, Hall testimony.

p.580 l.17   Ibid., Chambers and Muir testimony.

p.580 l.21   McAfee, "Papers," 5 Oct. 1813.

p.580 l.23   Young, p. 79.

p.580 l.27   PRO, WO71/243, Procter court martial, Chambers testimony.

p.580 l.29   Ibid., Lefevre and Hall testimony.

p.580 l.35   Byfield, p. 368.

p.581 l.14   Richardson, *Richardson's War*, pp. 223, 210.

p.581 l.29 PRO, WO71/243, Procter court martial, Hall testimony.

p.582 l.4 Ibid., Coleman testimony.

p.582 l.24 Young, pp. 81–85; "Visit," pp. 204–5.

p.582 l.32 "Visit," p. 205.

p.583 l.8 Mackenzie, *Perry*, pp. 241–42.

p.583 l.13 Meyer, p. 134.

p.584 l.6 Wickliffe, p. 47.

p.584 l.11 Ibid., p. 46.

p.585 l.17 Richardson, *Richardson's War*, pp. 210–11.

p.585 l.26 Byfield, pp. 369–70.

p.585 l.33 Cruikshank, *Documentary History*, VII: 195–96, Hall to Harvey, 5 Oct. 1813; McAfee, *History*, p. 393; Sholes, p. 525.

p.586 l.4 Watson, p. 130.

p.586 l.8 Richardson, *Richardson's War*, p. 213.

p.586 l.29 Arnold, p. 4.

p.587 l.13 Byfield, pp. 369–71.

p.587 l.30 Cruikshank, *Documentary History*, IV: 187, Vincent to De Rottenberg, 15 Nov. 1813.

p.588 l.24 Ibid., General Order, 9 Sept. 1815.

p.588 l.30 W. Wood, SBD, II: 323–27, Procter to De Rottenberg, 23 Oct. 1813; PRO, WO71/243, Procter court martial, Procter's defence, *passim*.

p.588 l.31 Richardson, *Richardson's War*, p. 216, General Order, 24 Nov. 1813.

p.589 l.13 Harrison, II: 577, armistice with Indians, 4 Oct. 1813.

THE ASSAULT ON MONTREAL

p.590 l.13 Wilkinson, III: 209, Bull testimony; ibid., p. 351, Wilkinson defence.

p.592 l.22 ASPMA, I: 464, Armstrong to Wilkinson, 8 Aug. 1813.

p.593 l.2 Skeen, "Mr. Madison's Secretary," p. 338.

p.593 l.18 Wilkinson, III: 354, Wilkinson's defence.

p.593 l.28 ASPMA, I: 470, extract from journal, 4 Oct. 1813; Armstrong, *Notices*, II: 206, 207–8, Armstrong to Wilkinson, 19 Oct. 1813; ibid., p. 209, Wilkinson to SW, 19 Oct. 1813; Wilkinson, III: 298.

p.594 l.1 Armstrong, *Hints*, p. 10.

p.594 l.4 Wilkinson, III: 98–99, Thorne testimony.

p.594 l.6 Wilkinson, III: 290–91, Brooks testimony; ibid., p. 109, Ross testimony.

p.594 l.9 Ibid., Ross testimony.

p.594 l.11 Ibid., App. 9, Ross's observations.

p.594 l.14 Ibid.

p.594 l.16 Ibid.

p.594 l.21 Ibid.

p.594 l.23 Ibid.

p.595 *l.5*   Brannan, p. 188, Wilkinson to Armstrong, 6 Aug. 1813; ibid., p. 190, Armstrong to Wilkinson, 9 Aug. 1813; ibid., p. 199, Armstrong to Wilkinson, 6 Sept. 1813.

p.595 *l.11*   ASPMA, I: 459, Hampton to Armstrong, 22 Sept. 1813.

p.595 *l.15*   Ibid.

p.595 *l.19*   Ibid., p. 460, Armstrong to Hampton, 28 Sept. 1813.

p.595 *l.23*   Ibid., p. 461, Armstrong to Hampton, 16 Oct. 1813.

p.596 *l.6*   Wilkinson, III, Totten testimony.

p.596 *l.14*   Sellar, *Histories*, pp. 89–90.

p.596 *l.25*   Ibid., pp. 76–77.

p.596 *l.30*   Ibid., p. 89.

p.597 *l.25*   ASPMA, I: 461, Armstrong to Hampton, 16 Oct. 1813.

p.598 *l.31*   Sellar, *Histories*, p. 90.

p.599 *l.1*   Ibid., pp. 92–93.

p.599 *l.16*   Dunlop, p. 10; Sellar, *Histories*, p. 88; W. Wood, SBD, II: 423, 428, *Gleaner* article.

p.599 *l.23*   W. Wood, SBD, II: 428, *Gleaner* article; Lighthall, p. 24.

p.599 *l.28*   David, p. 6.

p.600 *l.7*   Ibid., p. 7.

p.600 *l.14*   Ibid., p. 10.

p.600 *l.23*   Sellar, *Histories*, pp. 86–87.

p.601 *l.10*   W. Wood, SBD, II: 402–3, *Quebec Mercury*, 9 Nov. 1813.

p.601 *l.20*   Sellar, *Histories*, pp. 95–96.

p.601 *l.22*   Lighthall, p. 15.

p.601 *l.27*   PAC, RG 8, vol. 680, p. 316, Manning to Robertson, 24 Oct. 1813.

p.601 *l.35*   Ibid.

p.602 *l.20*   Sellar, *Histories*, p. 121, Milne to de Salaberry, 26 Nov. 1813.

p.603 *l.2*   Brannan, pp. 249–52, Hampton to Armstrong, 1 Nov. 1813.

p.603 *l.9*   Ibid., p. 276, Purdy report.

p.603 *l.20*   Ibid.; ibid., pp. 249–52, Hampton to Armstrong, 1 Nov. 1813; Sellar, *Histories*, p. 99; Sellar, *U.S. Campaign*, pp. 8–9.

p.603 *l.21*   Brannan, pp. 249–52, Hampton to Armstrong, 1 Nov. 1813.

p.604 *l.5*   W. Wood, SBD, II: 404, *Quebec Mercury*, 9 Nov. 1813; ibid., p. 392, Prevost to Bathurst, 30 Oct. 1813.

p.604 *l.8*   Ibid., p. 428, Morrison statement.

p.604 *l.17*   Ibid., p. 411, *Quebec Mercury*, 9 Nov. 1813.

p.605 *l.9*   Ibid., p. 426, *Gleaner* article.

p.605 *l.14*   Ibid., p. 427, Morrison statement.

p.605 *l.17*   Suite, p. 23.

p.605 *l.23*   Brannan, pp. 249–52, Hampton to Armstrong, 1 Nov. 1813; ibid., p. 276, Purdy report.

p.605 *l.25*   Ibid., pp. 249–52, Hampton to Armstrong, 1 Nov. 1813.

p.606 *l.7*   Sellar, *Histories*, p. 105.

p.606 l.16 Suite, p. 51.

p.606 l.23 Ibid.

p.607 l.2 W. Wood, SBD, II: 407, *Quebec Mercury*, 9 Nov. 1813.

p.607 l.7 Lighthall, p. 20.

p.607 l.12 Ibid., p. 21; W. Wood, SBD, II: 407, *Quebec Mercury*, 9 Nov. 1813.

p.607 l.19 Sellar, *U.S. Campaign*, p. 10.

p.608 l.20 W. Wood, SBD, II: 390, General Order, 27 Oct. 1813.

p.608 l.31 Brannan, p. 251, Hampton to Armstrong, 1 Nov. 1813.

p.609 l.1 W. Wood, SBD, II: 427, Morrison statement.

p.609 l.8 Brannan, p. 276, Purdy report.

p.609 l.14 USNA, M221/57/T233, S. Thayer.

p.609 l.16 Brannan, p. 278, Purdy report.

p.609 l.20 Ibid.

p.609 l.29 W. Wood, SBD, II: 388–90, General Order, 27 Oct. 1813; ibid., pp. 392–93, Prevost to Bathurst, 30 Oct. 1813.

p.609 l.32 Ibid., p. 397, de Salaberry to Baynes, 1 Nov. 1813.

p.610 l.5 Ibid., p. 391, de Salaberry to his father, 29 Oct. 1813.

p.610 l.7 Ibid., p. 395, 26 Oct. 1813, return of killed, wounded and missing.

p.610 l.20 ASPMA, I: 473, Wilkinson to Armstrong, 28 Oct. 1813.

p.610 l.31 Ibid.

p.611 l.16 Wilkinson, III, Thorn, Ross, and Eustis testimony; ASPMA, I: 474, Wilkinson to Armstrong, 1 Nov. 1813.

p.611 l.22 BHS, Hanks Memoir, p. 12.

p.611 l.27 Cruikshank, *Documentary History*, IV: 104, Chauncey to SN, 30 Oct. 1813.

p.611 l.35 ASPMA, I: 477, Wilkinson journal.

p.612 l.4 Cruikshank, *Documentary History*, IV: 105, Chauncey to SN, 30 Oct. 1813.

p.612 l.10 Ibid., p. 123, Mulcaster to Yeo, 2 Nov. 1813.

p.612 l.12 Ibid., p. 155, Chauncey to SN, 11 Nov. 1813.

p.613 l.1 ASPMA, I: 477, Wilkinson journal, 6 Nov. 1813.

p.613 l.6 W. Wood, SBD, II:441, Wilkinson proclamation, 6 Nov. 1813.

p.613 l.18 Wilkinson, III: 129, Lewis testimony.

p.614 l.8 ASPMA, I: 477, Wilkinson journal, 6 Nov. 1813; Lossing, p. 550.

p.614 l.16 Scott, p. 107.

p.614 l.29 Swift, *Memoirs*, 6 Nov. 1813; Wilkinson, III, Pinkney testimony.

p.615 l.6 Wilkinson, III: 211–12, App. 13; Swift, *Memoirs*, 6 Nov. 1813.

p.615 l.11 ASPMA, I: 477, Wilkinson journal, 7 Nov. 1813.

p.615 l.26 Ibid., 8 Nov. 1813; Sellar, *U.S. Campaign*, p. 17; Wilkinson, III, App. 24, council of war, 8 Nov. 1813.

p.615 l.31 Wilkinson, III, App. 24, council of war, 8 Nov. 1813.

p.616 l.3 ASPMA, I: 477–78, Wilkinson journal, 8–9 Nov. 1813; ibid., General Order, 10 Nov. 1813.

p.616 l.17   ASPMA, I: 475, Wilkinson to SW, 16 Nov. 1813; ibid., p. 478, Wilkinson Journal, 10 Nov. 1813; Wilkinson, III, Lee testimony; BHS, Hanks Memoir, p. 13.

p.616 l.27   Way, p. 203.

p.617 l.4   Smart, Sewell narrative, 11 Nov. 1860.

p.619 l.29   USNA, M221/54/L162, Lewis to SW, 14 Nov. 1813; Wilkinson, III, Bull and Pinkney testimony; Delafield, p. 99.

p.620 l.2   ASPMA, I: 475, Wilkinson to SW, 16 Nov. 1813.

p.620 l.10   Wilkinson, III, Boyd testimony.

p.620 l.21   DAB.

p.620 l.31   Salisbury, n.p.

p.621 l.1   Smart, Sewell narrative, 11 Nov. 1860.

p.621 l.13   Way, p. 213.

p.622 l.2   Cruikshank, *Documentary History*, IV: 166, memo on Plenderleath, 1 Jan. 1854.

p.622 l.6   Ibid.

p.622 l.18   Sellar, *US. Campaign*, p. 23.

p.622 l.23   W. Wood, SBD, II: 442, Morrison to De Rottenburg, 12 Nov. 1813.

p.623 l.19   Smart, Sewell narrative, 11 Nov. 1860.

p.623 l.24   Sellar, *U.S. Campaign*, p. 24.

p.623 l.31   Wilkinson, III, Pinkney testimony.

p.624 l.16   Brannan, p. 268, Boyd to Wilkinson, 12 Nov. 1813.

p.624 l.21   Cruikshank, *Documentary History*, IV: 194, Wilkinson to SW, 18 Nov. 1813.

p.624 l.26   ASPMA, I: 475–76, Wilkinson to SW, 16 Nov. 1813.

p.625 l.1   Ibid., p. 462, Hampton to Wilkinson, 8 Nov. 1813.

p.625 l.9   Ibid., p. 476, Wilkinson to SW, 16 Nov. 1813.

p.625 l.14   Ibid., p. 479, General Order, 13 Nov. 1813.

p.625 l.19   Ibid., p. 478, Wilkinson to SW, 17 Nov. 1813; Wilkinson, III, Wilkinson to SW, 24 Nov. 1813.

p.625 l.25   Wilkinson, III, App. 9, Ross to Inspector General.

p.625 l.28   BHS, Hanks Memoir, p. 14.

p.625 l.31   Wilkinson, III, App. 9, note by Ross.

p.625 l.33   Ibid.

p.625 l.35   Brannan, p. 286, Izard to Wilkinson, 6 Dec. 1813.

p.626 l.2   Sellar, *US. Campaign*, p. 28.

p.626 l.23   PAC, RG 19 E5A, claims Numbers 380, 390, 396, 397, 400, 409, 430, 437, 459.

p.626 l.29   Dunlop, p. 23.

p.628 l.4   Unless otherwise noted, source for this section is W. Wood, SBD, III, pt. 2, Merritt narrative.

p.630 l.28   McClure, p. 16.

p.630 l.32   Cruikshank, "Drummond's Campaign," p. 10.

p.631 l.7   McClure, p. 16.

p.632 l.19   Kirby, p. 4.

p.632 l.31   Cruikshank, *Documentary History*, IV: 264, McClure to Tompkins, 10 Dec. 1813; ibid., IX: 49, McClure to public.

p.633 l.2   Ibid., IV: 264, McClure to Tompkins, 10 Dec. 1813.

p.633 l.6   Ibid.

p.633 l.8   McClure, pp. 17, 18.

p.633 l.15   ASPMA, I: 484, Armstrong to McClure, 4 Oct. 1813.

p.633 l.33   Chapin, pp. 22–23; Cruikshank, *Documentary History*, IX: 122, Chapin to public.

p.636 l.32   "Reminiscences of American Occupation," p. 20.

p.637 l.12   Ibid., pp. 21–22.

p.637 l.17   Ibid., p. 21.

p.637 l.27   Ibid., p. 20; PAC, RG 19 E5A, vol. 3740, Dickson claim.

p.637 l.35   W. Wood, SBD, III, pt. 3: 607–8, Merritt narrative.

p.638 l.2   Ibid., p. 607.

p.638 l.11   Cruikshank, *Documentary History*, IV: 270, Murray to Vincent, 12 Dec. 1813, ibid., p. 275, Murray to Vincent, 13 Dec. 1813.

p.638 l.19   W. Wood, SBD, III, pt. 2: 607, Merritt narrative; "Reminiscences of American Occupation," pp. 21, 24.

p.639 l.6   Kirby, p. 6.

p.639 l.13   Mather, p. 272.

p.639 l.20   W. Wood, SBD, III, pt. 2: 608–9, Merritt narrative.

p.640 l.2   Cruikshank, *Documentary History*, IX: 3, Harvey to Murray, 17 Dec. 1813; Kirby, p. 7.

p.640 l.11   Mather, p. 272.

p.640 l.16   Cruikshank, *Documentary History*, IX: 19, Driscoll narrative.

p.640 l.27   Ibid., VI: 270–71, General Order, 12 Dec. 1813.

p.641 l.3   Ibid., IX: 45, McClure to SW, 25 Dec. 1813.

p.641 l.18   Ibid., pp. 19–20, Driscoll narrative.

p.641 l.28   Ibid., p. 20.

p.642 l.2   Cruikshank, *Documentary History 1814*, pp. 298–99, Murray to Baynes, 17 April 1814.

p.642 l.6   Cruikshank, *Documentary History*, IX: 20, Driscoll narrative.

p.642 l.14   Ibid., p. 13, return of enemy's losses, 19 Dec. 1813; ibid., p. 14, General Order, 19 Dec. 1813.

p.642 l.17   W. Wood, SBD, II: 499, General Order, 24 Sept. 1814.

p.642 l.23   Ibid., p. 492, Drummond to Prevost, 20 Dec. 1813.

p.643 l.3   Cruikshank, *Documentary History*, IX: 14, Riall to Drummond, 19 Dec. 1813; "Military Service of 1813/14," pp. 102–3.

p.643 l.32   Clara Williams, pp. 315–22.

p.644 l.8   Cruikshank, *Documentary History*, IX: 31, *New York Evening Post*, 11 Jan. 1814.

p.644 l.10   Ibid., p. 46, McClure to Granger, 25 Dec. 1813.

p.644 l.13   Ibid., pp. 45–46, McClure to SW, 25 Dec. 1813; ibid., pp. 52–53, Spencer to Tompkins, 26 Dec. 1813.

p.644 l.19   Ibid., p. 53, Spencer to Tompkins, 26 Dec. 1813; ibid., p. 61, McClure to Granger, 28 Dec. 1813.

p.645 l.12   Byfield, pp. 373–74.

p.646 l.17   Lossing, p. 637.

p.647 l.8   "Village of Buffalo," p. 198; "Burning of Buffalo," p. 342.

p.647 l.23   "Burning of Buffalo," p. 338; Ketchum, p. 303; Johnson, p. 260.

p.647 l.31   Johnson, p. 251.

p.648 l.2   Wilner, I: 248.

p.648 l.14   "Burning of Buffalo," p. 335; "Village of Buffalo," p. 197.

p.648 l.23   "Burning of Buffalo," pp. 341–42.

p.648 l.35   Ibid., p. 338.

p.649 l.4   Johnson, p. 254.

p.649 l.7   Ibid., p. 251.

p.649 l.12   Ibid., p. 254.

p.649 l.19   "Burning of Buffalo," p. 342.

p.650 l.8   Ibid.

p.650 l.13   Ibid., pp. 342–44.

p.650 l.21   Ibid., p. 338.

p.650 l.28   Ibid., p. 339.

p.651 l.4   Ibid., pp. 339–40.

p.651 l.23   Ibid., p. 345.

MARKING TIME

p.655 l.13   J.Q. Adams, *Memoirs*, II: 552, 30 Dec. 1813.

p.655 l.26   Ibid., pp. 547–48, 18 Nov. 1813.

p.655 l.29   Bayard, "Papers," p. 427, diary, 3 Aug. 1813.

p.656 l.5   Ibid., p. 211, Bayard to Bayard, 23 April 1813.

p.656 l.34   J.Q. Adams, *Memoirs*, II: 556–57, 30 Dec. 1813.

p.657 l.5   Bayard, "Papers," p. 451, diary, 8 Sept. 1813.

p.657 l.14   Ibid., pp. 242–43, Bayard to Bayard, 27 Aug. 1813.

p.657 l.18   Ibid., p. 488, diary, 22–26 Dec. 1813.

p.657 l.19   Ibid., p. 483, diary, 11 Nov. 1813.

p.657 l.35   Ibid., pp. 226–29, Monroe to Gallatin and Bayard, 23 June 1813.

p.659 l.8   J.Q. Adams, *Memoirs*, II: 555–57, 11 Jan. 1814.

p.659 l.28   Bayard, "Papers," p. 496, diary, 19–21 Jan. 1814.

p.659 l.35   Ibid., pp. 496–97, diary, 23 Jan. 1814.

p.660 l.13   J.Q. Adams, *Memoirs*, II: 497, 30 July 1813.

p.660 l.26   Ibid., p. 574, 1 Feb. 1814.

p.661 l.27   Henderson, p. 50, Strachan to Gore, 1 Jan. 1814.

p.661 l.35   OBA, *Report*, no. 7, pp. 433–35, Drummond speech, 15 Feb. 1814.

p.662 l.9   PAC, CO42/355/49–51, Drummond to Bathurst, 5 April 1814.

p.662 l.17   PAC, RG 8, vol. 682, pp. 163–69, Drummond to Prevost, 5 March 1814.

p.662 l.20   Ibid., p. 59, Drummond to Prevost, 27 Jan. 1814.

p.662 l.25   PAC, CO42/156/133, Prevost to Bathurst, 10 March 1814.

p.662 l.33   PAC, RG 8, vol. 682, pp. 163–69, Drummond to Prevost, 5 March 1814.

p.662 l.35   Ibid., p. 59, Drummond to Prevost, 27 Jan. 1814.

p.663 l.3   W. Wood, SBD, III, pt. 1, Young to Riall, 14 March 1814.

p.663 l.8   Ibid., p. 97, Riall to Drummond, 15 March 1814.

p.663 l.16   Ibid., p. 99, Harvey to Riall, 23 March 1814.

p.663 l.26   PAC, CO42/156/133, Prevost to Bathurst, 10 March 1814.

p.664 l.15   PAC, RG 5, A1, vol. 16, Robinson to Loring, 4 April 1814.

p.664 l.22   Ibid.

p.665 l.8   Ibid.

p.665 l.26   Clay, I: 881, Clay and Russell to Monroe, 20 April 1814.

p.666 l.13   Monroe, V: 281, views.

p.666 l.19   Ibid., p. 277.

p.666 l.23   Clay, I: 856, Clay to ?, 27 Jan. 1814.

p.666 l.30   Ibid., pp. 857–58, Monroe to American Commissioners, 28 Jan. 1814.

p.667 l.14   Ibid., p. 859.

p.667 l.28   J.Q. Adams, *Memoirs*, II: pp. 584–89.

p.667 l.35   Clay, I: 885, Clay to Monroe, 23 April 1814; ibid., p. 896, Clay to Wm. Crawford, 10 May 1814.

p.668 l.9   Ibid., p. 896, Clay to Crawford, 10 May 1814.

p.668 l.17   Gallatin, I: 612, Gallatin and Bayard to Monroe, 6 May 1814.

p.668 l.24   Ibid.

p.668 l.27   Ibid., p. 607, Gallatin to Clay, 22 April 1814.

p.668 l.31   Ibid.

p.669 l.4   Ibid., p. 606.

p.669 l.11   Clay, I: 907–8, Crawford to American Commissioners, 13 May 1814.

p.669 l.15   Ibid., p. 910, Crawford to Clay, 15 May 1814.

p.669 l.21   Ibid., p. 914, Hughes to Clay, 16 May 1814.

p.670 l.15   Ibid., p. 925, Clay to Russell, 27 May 1814; ibid., p. 913, Hughes to Clay, 16 May 1814.

p.670 l.29   Ibid., p. 921, Russell to Clay, 22 May 1814.

p.671 l.28   Cruikshank, "Contest for . . . Lake Ontario in 1814," p. 125.

p.673 l.3   Ibid., *passim*.

p.673 l.35   Hanks, p. 55.

p.676 l.8   Ibid.

p.676 l.14   C. Elliott, *Scott*, p. 108.

p.676 l.16   Ibid., p. 147.

p.676 l.20   Scott, p. 19.

p.676 l.35   USNA, M221/57/S489, Scott to SW, 17 May 1814.

p.677 l.19   Cruikshank, "John Beverley Robinson," pp. 211–12.

p.677 l.23   Cruikshank, *Documentary History 1814*, pp. 330–31, return of property destroyed; ibid., p. 331, Talbot to Loyal and Patriotic Society.

p.677 l.33   Ibid., pp. 414–15, Cochrane to Croker, 18 July 1814.

p.678 l.9   Richardson, "Canadian Campaign," pp. 538–51, *passim*.

p.681 l.20   PAC, RG 5, A1, vol. 16, p. 6845, Robinson to Loring, 18 June 1814.

p.682 l.28   PAO, Robinson Papers, Strachan to Robinson, 2 June 1814.

p.682 l.33   PAC, RG 5, A1, vol. 16, p. 6846, Robinson to Loring, 18 June 1814.

p.683 l.2   Robinson, *Life*, p. 56, J.B. Robinson narrative.

p.683 l.10   PAC, RG 5, A1, vol. 16, p. 6852, Robinson to Loring, 18 June 1814.

p.683 l.28   Ibid., p. 6851.

p.683 l.33   Ibid., p. 6847.

p.684 l.31   PAC, RG 5, A1, vol. 16, pp. 6872–73, Warren to Loring, 20 June 1814.

p.684 l.32   PAO, RG 22/05/12a, Criminal Assize Minute Book B, 21 June 1814.

p.685 l.2   PAC, RG 5, A1, vol. 16, Scott to Drummond, 14 July 1814.

p.685 l.4   Riddell, "Ancaster 'Bloody Assize,'" p. 214, Scott to Drummond, 28 June 1814.

p.685 l.9   PAC, RG 5, A1, vol. 16, Scott to Drummond, 5 July 1814.

p.685 l.11   Ibid., Scott to Drummond, 8 July 1814.

THE STRUGGLE FOR THE FUR COUNTRY

p.687 l.2   "Copies of Papers," pp. 575–76, 583–85.

p.687 l.14   PAC, CO42/157/7–10, Prevost to Bathurst, 10 July 1814.

p.687 l.28   W. Wood, SBD, III, pt. 1: 269, Bullock to Loring, 26 Feb. 1814.

p.688 l.14   Cruikshank, "Nancy," p. 79.

p.688 l.17   Tohill, p. 110.

p.689 l.9   PAC, RG 8, vol. 257, p. 45, Prevost to Bathurst, 26 Jan. 1814.

p.690 l.2   Tohill, p. 108.

p.690 l.18   PAC, CO42/157/7–10, Prevost to Bathurst, encl. McDouall speech to Indians.

p.690 l.21   PAC, RG 8, vol. 257, p. 287, Dickson to Freer, 18 June 1814.

p.691 l.15   W. Wood, SBD, III, pt. 1: 254, McDouall to Drummond, 16 July 1814.

p.691 l.28   Ibid., p. 255.

p.691 l.33   Grignon, p. 272.

p.692 l.20   *Niles Register*, 10 Sept. 1814, Croghan to SW, 9 Aug. 1814.

p.692 l.23   Ibid.

p.692 l.29   Van Fleet, pp. 108–9.

p.692 l.33   W. Wood, SBD, III, pt. 1: 278, McDouall to Prevost, 14 Aug. 1814.

p.693 l.8   Ibid.

p.693 l.9   Ibid., p. 275.

p.693 l.12   Cruikshank, "Nancy," p. 96, McDouall to Drummond, 17 July 1814.

p.693 l.21   May, p. 34; Van Fleet, p. 112.

p.693 l.26   *Niles Register*, 10 Sept. 1814, Croghan to SW, 9 Aug. 1814.

p.693 l.33   Ibid.

p.694 l.8   Van Fleet, p. 221.

p.694 l.12   *Niles Register*, 10 Sept. 1814, Croghan to SW, 9 Aug. 1814.

p.694 l.35   W. Wood, SBD, III, pt. 1: 274–75, McDouall to Prevost, 14 Aug. 1814.

p.695 l.10   May, pp. 36–37.

p.695 l.21   Ibid.

p.695 l.30   *Niles Register*, 10 Sept. 1814, Croghan to SW, 9 Aug. 1814.

p.695 l.31   Cruikshank, "Nancy," p. 105, return of killed and wounded, 11 Aug. 1814.

p.696 l.3   Ibid., pp. 101–3, Sinclair to SN, 9 Aug. 1814; Van Fleet, p. 58; May, p. 38.

p.696 l.6   Cruikshank, "Nancy," pp. 101–3, Sinclair to SN, 9 Aug. 1814.

p.696 l.16   Ibid.

p.696 l.29   Cruikshank, "Battle of Fort George," p. 60.

p.697 l.6   Cruikshank, "Nancy," p. 84.

p.697 l.18   *Niles Register*, 24 Sept. 1814, Croghan to McArthur, 23 Aug. 1814.

p.697 l.28   Ibid., 12 Nov. 1814, Sinclair to SN, 15 Aug. 1815.

p.698 l.9   Cruikshank, "Nancy," pp. 120–21, Worsley to Yeo, 15 Sept. 1814.

p.698 l.15   Ibid.; May, p. 39.

p.699 l.4   W. Wood, SBD, III, pt. 1: 277–78, McDouall to Drummond, 9 Sept. 1814.

p.699 l.35   Cruikshank, "Nancy," pp. 120–23, Worsley to Yeo, 15 Sept. 1814; W. Wood, SBD, III, pt. 1: 279, Bulger to McDouall, 7 Sept. 1814.

THE LAST INVASION

p.702 l.6   Scott, pp. 122–23.

p.702 l.14   Cruikshank, *Documentary History 1814*, p. 403, SW to Brown, 10 June 1814.

p.702 l.19   Scott, pp. 121–22.

p.702 l.22   Cruikshank, *Documents Relating to the Invasion . . . 1814*, p. 78, Brown memo, 9 July 1814.

p.702 l.29   Ibid., pp. 72, 77; Elliott, *Scott*, p. 56.

p.702 l.34   Cruikshank, *Documentary History 1814*, p. 26, Porter to Tompkins, 3 July 1814; Scott, p. 123.

p.703 l.2   BHS, Hanks Memoir, p. 40.

p.703 l.12   Scott, pp. 125–26.

p.704 l.8   Cruikshank, *Documentary History 1814*, p. 408, monthly return, Gen. Brown's division, 1 July 1814.

p.704 l.18   Treat, p. 45, Everett testimony.

p.704 l.28   Ibid., pp. 10, 19, 20.

p.705 l.14   Ibid., p. 20.

p.705 l.18   Ibid., p. 20 and *passim.*, Cruikshank, *Documentary History 1814*, p. 39, Brown to SW, 7 July 1814.

p.705 l.35   J.L. Babcock, "Campaign of 1814," p. 126, Porter to Stone, 26 May 1840.

p.706 l.3   Ibid.

p.706 l.13   Cruikshank, *Documentary History 1814*, p. 473, Jesup narrative; ibid., p. 372, McMullen narrative.

p.706 l.18   J.L. Babcock, "Campaign of 1814," p. 126, Porter to Stone, 26 May 1840.

p.706 l.31   White, pp. 14, 15.

p.707 l.3   W. Wood, SBD, III, pt. 1: 115–16, Riall to Drummond, 6 July 1814.

p.707 l.8   Ibid., III, pt. 2: 613, Merritt narrative.

p.707 l.15   Ibid., III, pt. 1: 115, Riall to Drummond, 6 July 1814; ibid., part 2, p. 615, Merritt narrative.

p.707 l.29   Hay, p. 70.

p.708 l.4   Ibid., pp. 72–73.

p.708 l.13   J.L. Babcock, "Campaign of 1814," p. 127, Porter to Stone, 26 May 1840.

p.708 l.17   Ibid., p. 129.

p.709 l.17   White, pp. 17, 18.

p.709 l.26   Scott, pp. 127–28; Cruikshank, *Documents Relating to the Invasion . . . 1814*, p. 75, Brown memo.

p.709 l.29   Ibid., p. 128.

p.709 l.32   Hanks, p. 56.

p.710 l.8   Scott, pp. 128–29.

p.710 l.12   Ibid.

p.710 l.15   Ibid., p. 127.

p.710 l.21   Hanks, p. 56.

p.710 l.25   C. Elliott, *Scott*, p. 161.

p.710 l.30   Ibid., pp. 161–62.

p.710 l.35   Cruikshank, *Documents Relating to the Invasion . . . 1814*, p. 75, Brown memo; Treat, p. 13.

p.711 l.6   Cruikshank, *Documentary History 1814*, p. 45, Scott to Adj. Gen., 15 July 1814.

p.711 l.25	Hay, pp. 73, 74.
p.711 l.30	Scott, p. 134.
p.712 l.4	W. Wood, SBD, III, pt. 1, Riall to Drummond, 6 July 1814; ibid., p. 119, return of killed and wounded, 5 July 1814; Cruikshank, "Lundy's Lane," p. 19.
p.712 l.10	W. Wood, SBD, III, pt. 1: 119, return of killed and wounded, 5 July 1814; Cruikshank, *Documentary History 1814*, p. 43, return of killed and wounded.
p.713 l.9	White, pp. 20–23.
p.713 l.30	Ibid., pp. 23–27.
p.713 l.33	W. Wood, SBD, III, pt. 1: 126, Riall to Drummond, 9 July 1814; ibid., p. 128, Drummond to Prevost, 13 July 1814.
p.714 l.4	Ibid., pp. 127–28.
p.714 l.20	White, pp. 27–28.
p.715 l.8	Douglass, pp. 1, 5.
p.715 l.13	Hanks, p. 56.
p.715 l.24	Cruikshank, *Documents Relating to the Invasion . . . 1814*, p. 77, Brown memo; *Documentary History 1814*, p. 475, Jesup narrative.
p.716 l.2	Cruikshank, *Documentary History 1814*, p. 64, Brown to Chauncey, 13 July 1814.
p.716 l.10	Cruikshank, *Documents Relating to the Invasion . . . 1814*, Brown to Armstrong, 25 July 1814; "Lundy's Lane," p. 22; *Documentary History 1814*, p. 126, Chauncey to SN, 10 Aug. 1814.
p.716 l.28	Cruikshank, *Documents Relating to the Invasion . . . 1814*, pp. 72–73, memorial of David Secord; ibid., p. 74, Stone to Tompkins, 25 July 1814.
p.716 l.33	Davis, p. 143.
p.717 l.6	Hanks, p. 57.
p.717 l.13	Cruikshank, *Documentary History 1814*, p. 87, Brown to SW, 25 July 1814.
p.717 l.15	Cruikshank, "Lundy's Lane," p. 29.
p.717 l.20	W. Wood, SBD, III, pt. 1: 144–45, Drummond to Prevost, 27 July 1814.
p.717 l.28	Cruikshank, *Documentary History 1814*, p. 466, Brown diary.
p.718 l.12	Douglass, p. 13.
p.718 l.15	Cruikshank, *Documentary History 1814*, p. 477, Jesup narrative.
p.718 l.22	W. Wood, SBD, III, pt. 1: 145, Drummond to Prevost, 27 July 1814.
p.718 l.35	Cruikshank, *Documentary History 1814*, p. 477, Jesup narrative.
p.719 l.19	Douglass, pp. 13–15.
p.720 l.4	W. Wood, SBD, III, pt. 1: 145–46, Drummond to Prevost, 27 July 1814.
p.720 l.14	Scott, pp. 140–41.
p.720 l.19	Ibid., p. 140.
p.720 l.27	Cruikshank, *Documentary History 1814*, p. 478, Jesup narrative.

p.721 l.8	Douglass, p. 21.
p.721 l.11	Cruikshank, *Documentary History 1814*, p. 478, Jesup narrative.
p.722 l.1	Ibid., p. 356, evidence at trial of Lt. Blake.
p.722 l.3	Ibid., pp. 335–37, Leavenworth to ?, 15 Jan. 1815.
p.722 l.5	W. Wood, SBD, III, pt. 1: 144, Drummond to Prevost, 27 July 1814.
p.722 l.28	Douglass, pp. 15–16.
p.722 l.32	Cruikshank, *Documentary History 1814*, p. 468, Brown diary.
p.723 l.9	Douglass, p. 16.
p.723 l.15	Cruikshank, *Documentary History 1814*, p. 98, Brown to SW, 7 Aug. 1814.
p.723 l.26	Ibid., p. 105, Miller to ?, 28 July 1814.
p.723 l.30	Ibid., p. 106, Allen to brother, 26 July 1814.
p.723 l.32	Ibid., p. 347, evidence of Capt. MacDonald.
p.723 l.35	Cruikshank, "Lundy's Lane," p. 38.
p.724 l.2	Cruikshank, *Documentary History 1814*, p. 347, evidence of Capt. MacDonald.
p.724 l.23	Douglass, p. 21.
p.724 l.33	Byfield, p. 378.
p.725 l.5	Cruikshank, *Documentary History 1814*, pp. 469–70, Brown diary.
p.725 l.10	James, *Military Occurrences*.
p.726 l.6	Cruikshank, *Documentary History 1814*, p. 470, Brown diary.
p.726 l.11	Ibid., p. 375, McMullen narrative.
p.726 l.20	Ibid.
p.726 l.27	Ibid.
p.726 l.33	Cruikshank, *Documents Relating to the Invasion . . . 1814*, p. 60, Brown to SW, 7 Aug. 1814.
p.727 l.9	Cruikshank, *Documentary History 1814*, p. 339, Leavenworth to ?, 15 Jan. 1815.
p.728 l.2	Cruikshank, "Lundy's Lane," p. 39.
p.728 l.10	Scott, p. 145.
p.728 l.16	Cruikshank, *Documentary History 1814*, p. 471, Brown diary.
p.728 l.25	Ibid., p. 340, Leavenworth to ?, 15 Jan. 1815.
p.728 l.32	Ibid., p. 376, McMullen narrative.
p.728 l.35	Ibid., p. 352, Col. Hindman statement.
p.729 l.3	Ibid., pp. 348–49, evidence of Capt. MacDonald.
p.729 l.6	Ibid., p. 352, Col. Hindman statement.
p.729 l.10	Ibid.
p.729 l.20	W. Wood, SBD, III, pt. 1: 157, District General Order, 26 July 1814; Cruikshank, *Documentary History 1814*, pp. 420–21, report of killed and wounded.
p.729 l.25	W. Wood, SBD, III, pt. 1: 152, District General Order, 26 July 1814.
p.729 l.28	Cruikshank, *Documentary History 1814*, Austin to SW, 29 July 1814.
p.729 l.32	Ibid., pp. 420–21, report of killed and wounded.

p.729 l.35 LC, Jesup MSS, Scott to Jesup, 5 Sept. 1814.

p.730 l.20 Cruikshank, *Documents Relating to the Invasion . . . 1814*, p. 61, Brown to SW, 7 Aug. 1814.

p.730 l.24 Cruikshank, *Documentary History 1814*, p. 472, Brown diary.

p.730 l.30 Ibid., p. 353, Lt. Tappan statement.

p.731 l.4 Ibid., pp. 353–54.

p.731 l.25 LC, Jesup MSS, Scott to Jesup, 5 Sept. 1814.

p.731 l.31 Cruikshank, *Documentary History 1814*, pp. 102–3, Porter to Tompkins, 29 July 1814.

p.732 l.18 Ibid., pp. 376–77, McMullen narrative.

p.732 l.23 Douglass, p. 23.

p.733 l.3 Cruikshank, *Documentary History 1814*, p. 378, McMullen narrative.

p.733 l.21 Dunlop, pp. 33–35.

p.733 l.32 Cruikshank, *Documentary History 1814*, pp. 118–19, Harvey to Conran, 2 Aug. 1814.

p.734 l.16 Byfield, pp. 378–79.

p.734 l.35 Ketchum, pp. 201–2; Cruikshank, *Documentary History 1814*, p. 120, Tucker to Conran, 4 Aug. 1814.

p.735 l.7 Byfield, p. 379.

p.735 l.16 Cruikshank, *Documentary History 1814*, p. 427, District General Order, 5 Aug. 1814.

p.736 l.23 Byfield, pp. 379–83.

p.736 l.27 Douglass, p. 26; W. Wood, SBD, III, pt. 1: 178, Drummond to Prevost, 15 Aug. 1814.

p.737 l.9 Douglass, pp. 26, 27; Cruikshank, *Documentary History 1814*, p. 157, Ripley to Gaines, 17 Aug. 1814.

p.737 l.24 W. Wood, SBD, III, pt. 1: 178–82, Drummond to Prevost, 15 Aug. 1814; Douglass, pp. 24–27.

p.737 l.33 Cruikshank, *Documentary History 1814*, pp. 139–40, General Order, 14 Aug. 1814.

p.738 l.11 Yaple, pp. 24–25; Cruikshank, *Documentary History 1814*, p. 138, General Order, 14 Aug. 1814; *Journal of the Society for Army Historical Research*, vol. 22 (1943–44), pp. 318–19.

p.739 l.3 Douglass, p. 26.

p.739 l.14 Cruikshank, *Documentary History 1814*, pp. 138–39, General Order, 14 Aug. 1814.

p.739 l.18 Cruikshank, "Siege," p. 13.

p.739 l.28 Cruikshank, *Documentary History 1814*, pp. 169–70, Young to Scott, 20 Dec. 1814.

p.740 l.5 Dunlop, p. 51.

p.740 l.9 Ibid., p. 52.

p.740 l.20 Cruikshank, *Documentary History 1814*, pp. 156–57, Ripley to Gaines, 17 Aug. 1814; Douglass, p. 27.

p.740 l.33   Cruikshank, *Documentary History 1814*, p. 153, Gaines to SW, 23 Aug. 1814; ibid., pp. 144–45, Fischer to Harvey, 15 Aug. 1814; ibid., pp. 156–57, Ripley to Gaines, 17 Aug. 1814.

p.741 l.5   W. Wood, SBD, III, pt. 1: 188–89, Fischer to Harvey, 15 Aug. 1814; ibid., pp. 189–94, Drummond to Prevost, 16 Aug. 1814; Cruikshank, *Documentary History 1814*, pp. 156–57, Ripley to Gaines, 17 Aug. 1814.

p.741 l.14   Cruikshank, "Siege," p. 20.

p.742 l.12   Douglass, p. 27.

p.743 l.1   Ibid., pp. 27–28.

p.743 l.7   Cruikshank, "Siege," p. 22.

p.743 l.12   Dunlop, p. 52.

p.743 l.17   Cruikshank, *Documentary History 1814*, pp. 153–54, Gaines to SW, 23 Aug. 1814.

p.743 l.23   Ibid., p. 154.

p.743 l.33   Douglass, p. 29.

p.744 l.4   W. Wood, SBD, III, pt. 1: 179–80, Drummond to Prevost, 15 Aug. 1814.

p.744 l.27   Cruikshank, *Documentary History 1814*, pp. 168–69, Couteur to Couteur, 29 July 1814.

p.745 l.5   W. Wood, SBD, III, pt. 1: 192–93, return of killed and wounded, 15 Aug. 1814.

p.745 l.13   BHS, Hanks Memoir, pp. 27–28.

p.745 l.20   Wood, SBD, III, pt. 1: 189, Drummond to Prevost, 16 Aug. 1814.

p.745 l.27   Cruikshank, *Documentary History 1814*, pp. 174–76, Prevost to Drummond, 26 Aug. 1814.

p.745 l.35   Douglass, p. 33.

p.746 l.28   Dunlop, pp. 48–49.

p.746 l.31   Cruikshank, *Documentary History 1814*, p. 214, report of killed and wounded; W. Wood, SBD, III, pt. 1: 197–99, return of killed and wounded, 17 Sept. 1814.

p.747 l.8   Cruikshank, *Documentary History 1814*, p. 225, Drummond to Prevost, 21 Sept. 1814.

p.747 l.17   Ibid., p. 233, Izard to SW, 28 Sept. 1814.

p.747 l.19   W. Wood, SBD, III, pt. 1: 211, Drummond to Prevost, 11 Oct. 1814; ibid., p. 217, Drummond to Prevost, 15 Oct. 1814.

p.747 l.25   Ibid., pp. 217–18, Drummond to Prevost, 15 Oct. 1814.

p.747 l.35   Cruikshank, *Documentary History 1814*, p. 256, Izard to SW, 16 Oct. 1814.

p.748 l.6   Ibid., p. 243, Prevost to Drummond, 11 Oct. 1814; W. Wood, SBD, III, pt. 1: 223, Drummond to Prevost, 20 Oct. 1814.

p.748 l.10   W. Wood, SBD, III, pt. 1: 231, Drummond to Prevost, 23 Oct. 1814.

p.748 l.11   Cruikshank, *Documentary History 1814*, p. 284, Izard to SW, 2 Nov. 1814.

p.748 l.17   Ibid., p. 286.

p.748 l.23   Ibid.

p.748 l.32   W. Wood, SBD, III, pt. 1: 243, Drummond to Prevost, 5 Nov. 1814.

THE BURNING OF WASHINGTON

p.751 l.3   Barrett, pp. 117–32.

p.751 l.10   Ibid., pp. 131–33.

p.751 l.33   Ibid., p. 134.

p.752 l.14   Lord, p. 98.

p.752 l.28   Barrett, p. 138.

p.753 l.5   Ibid., p. 138; Lord, p. 119.

p.753 l.14   Sir H. Smith, pp. 158–59.

p.754 l.2   C. Ingersoll, p. 175.

p.754 l.7   Barrett, p. 138.

p.754 l.15   ASPMA, I: 556–57, Winder narrative.

p.754 l.24   Ibid.

p.754 l.28   Ibid., p. 581, Gen. Van Ness statement, 23 Nov. 1814.

p.755 l.8   Ibid., p. 539, Armstrong to Johnson, 17 Oct. 1814; ibid., p. 554, Winder narrative, 26 Sept. 1814.

p.755 l.20   Ibid., p. 569, Col. George Minor statement.

p.755 l.31   Ibid., pp. 553–54, Winder narrative.

p.756 l.1   Ibid., p. 557.

p.756 l.3   Ibid.

p.756 l.9   Ibid.

p.756 l.26   Marine, pp. 105–11.

p.756 l.34   ASPMA, I: 536, Monroe to ?, 13 Nov. 1814; ibid., p. 573, Wm. Pinkney statement, 16 Nov. 1814; C. Ingersoll, p. 174.

p.757 l.7   ASPMA, I: 560–62, Gen. Stansbury report, 15 Nov. 1814; ibid., pp. 563–65, Smith statement, 6 Oct. 1814; ibid., p. 563, Lt.-Col. Sterrett statement, 22 Nov. 1814.

p.757 l.11   Ibid., p. 552, Winder narrative, 26 Sept. 1814.

p.758 l.4   Ibid., p. 596, Wm. Simmon letter, 28 Nov. 1814.

p.758 l.10   Marine, pp. 113–14.

p.758 l.12   Barrett, p. 140.

p.758 l.20   Ibid., p. 138.

p.758 l.24   Ibid., p. 153.

p.759 l.2   Marine, pp. 112–13.

p.759 l.5   Ibid., p. 114.

p.759 l.13   "Old Sub," p. 456.

p.759 l.20   ASPMA, I: 530, Johnson report; ibid., p. 565, Smith statement, 6 Oct. 1814.

p.759 l.29   Barrett, p. 139.

p.760 l.4 D. Madison, *Memoirs*, pp. 108–9, Dolley Madison to Anna.

p.760 l.8 Ibid., p. 109.

p.760 l.18 Ibid., pp. 110–11; C. Ingersoll, p. 206; Barrett, pp. 146–47.

p.760 l.24 Lord, p. 151.

p.760 l.35 Ewell, p. 7.

p.761 l.11 Barrett, p. 143.

p.761 l.21 Padover, p. 473, Latrobe to Jefferson, n.d.

p.761 l.25 Barrett, p. 145.

p.761 l.32 Smith, p. 111, Smith to Kirk-patrick; DNB, Ross entry.

p.762 l.2 Lord, p. 169; D. Madison, *Memoirs*, p. 112.

p.762 l.7 C. Ingersoll, p. 186.

p.762 l.14 Ewell, p. 13.

p.762 l.18 Ibid., p. 16.

p.762 l.28 C. Ingersoll, p. 189; Sir H. Smith, p. 112, Smith to Kirkpatrick.

p.762 l.33 C. Ingersoll, p. 208.

p.763 l.9 Barrett, p. 148.

p.763 l.15 Ibid., pp. 148–50.

THE BATTLE OF LAKE CHAMPLAIN

p.765 l.10 Hill, pp. 180–81.

p.766 l.16 Ibid., p. 181.

p.766 l.22 Ibid.

p.766 l.27 Ibid.

p.767 l.17 Macdonough, p. 138.

p.767 l.20 Folsom, p. 247.

p.767 l.25 Ibid.

p.769 l.3 Macdonough, p. 172.

p.770 l.8 Robinson, "Expedition to Plattsburgh," p. 505.

p.770 l.13 W. Wood, SBD, III, pt. 1: 357, Macomb to SW, 15 Sept. 1814.

p.770 l.21 Ibid., p. 358; Lossing, p. 862.

p.771 l.16 Robinson, "Expedition to Plattsburgh," p. 509.

p.771 l.24 Ibid., p. 512.

p.771 l.35 Ibid., p. 510.

p.772 l.14 Ibid.

p.773 l.26 Ibid., p. 510.

p.773 l.34 W. Wood, SBD, III, pt. 1: 379–81, Downie to Prevost, 7 Sept. 1814; ibid., Prevost to Downie, 8 Sept. 1814.

p.774 l.7 Ibid.; ibid., p. 377, Yeo to Croker and enclosures, 29 Sept. 1814.

p.774 l.20 Hill, p. 182.

p.774 l.32 Macdonough, p. 150.

p.775 l.7 Richards, p. 91.

p.775 l.12 W. Wood, SBD, III, pt. 1: 356, Macomb to SW, 15 Sept. 1814.

p.776 l.9   Richards, p. 90.

p.776 l.16   Ibid., p. 87.

p.776 l.23   Ibid., p. 92.

p.776 l.30   Ibid., pp. 93–94.

p.777 l.1   Bathurst, p. 291, Robinson to Merry, 22 Sept. 1814.

p.777 l.10   C. Muller, *Proudest Day*, p. 348, n. 2.

p.777 l.20   W. Wood, SBD, III, pt. 1: 381, Prevost to Downie, 9 Sept. 1814.

p.777 l.27   Ibid., p. 383, Prevost to Downie, 10 Sept. 1814.

p.778 l.3   Ibid., p. 461, Pring statement.

p.778 l.5   Ibid., p. 421, Cox testimony.

p.778 l.10   Ibid., pp. 411–12, Brydon testimony.

p.778 l.24   Ibid., p. 442, Pring testimony.

p.778 l.34   Ibid., p. 437.

p.779 l.8   Ibid., p. 414, Brydon testimony.

p.779 l.29   Mahan, II: 377.

p.779 l.35   W. Wood, SBD, III, pt. 1: 471, Robertson statement; ibid., p. 414, Brydon testimony.

p.780 l.8   Folsom, p. 253.

p.780 l.11   Macdonough, p. 176.

p.780 l.23   Lossing, p. 867.

p.780 l.30   Ibid., pp. 866–67.

p.781 l.6   Macdonough, p. 178; Folsom, p. 253.

p.781 l.16   Macdonough, pp. 179–80; Roosevelt, p. 392.

p.781 l.21   Roosevelt, p. 393.

p.781 l.28   W. Wood, SBD, III, pt. 1: 422–23, Bodell testimony.

p.783 l.5   Macdonough, p. 180; W. Wood, SBD, III, pt. 1: 430, Lt. Bell testimony; ibid., pp. 484, 490, Hicks testimony.

p.783 l.15   Macdonough, p. 181.

p.783 l.21   *Niles Register*, supplement, vol. 7, p. 135, Henley to SN, 12 Sept. 1814.

p.783 l.31   Folsom, p. 254; P. Palmer, *Lake Champlain*, p. 204.

p.784 l.6   Clark, p. 83, Macdonough to SN, 11 Sept. 1814.

p.784 l.25   Lossing, pp. 871–72.

p.785 l.9   W. Wood, SBD, III, pt. 1: 383–84, Robertson to Pring, 15 Sept. 1814; ibid., pp. 418–19, Brydon testimony; P. Palmer, *Lake Champlain*, p. 205.

p.785 l.19   W. Wood, SBD, III, pt. 1: 373–77, Robertson to Pring, 12 Sept. 1814.

p.785 l.24   Ibid., pp. 490–91, Hicks testimony.

p.785 l.33   Macdonough, p. 185.

p.786 l.6   Ibid., p. 188.

p.786 l.24   Robinson, "Expedition to Plattsburgh," p. 510.

p.788 l.2   Ibid., pp. 511–12.

p.788 l.6   Lossing, p. 874.

p.788 l.18   Ibid., p. 875.

p.788 l.28   W. Wood, SBD, III, pt. 1: 360, Macomb to SW, 15 Sept. 1814.

p.789 l.8   Bathurst, pp. 292–93, Robinson to Merry, 22 Sept. 1814.

GHENT

p.791 l.5   J.Q. Adams, *Memoirs*, III: 3–4, 7 Aug. 1814.

p.791 l.23   Ibid.; Clay, I: 963, Clay to Monroe, 18 Aug. 1814.

p.791 l.27   Ibid.

p.792 l.35   J.Q. Adams, *Memoirs*, III: 5–6.

p.793 l.24   Ibid., p. 9.

p.794 l.4   Ibid., p. 15.

p.794 l.26   Ibid., pp. 17–19; Clay, I: 968–70, journal, 19 Aug. 1814.

p.794 l.30   J.Q. Adams, *Memoirs*, III: 19.

p.794 l.34   Ibid., p. 20.

p.795 l.7   Ibid., pp. 20–23.

p.795 l.9   ASPFR, III: 711–13, U.S. to British Commissioners, 24 Aug. 1814.

p.795 l.24   J.Q. Adams, *Memoirs*, III: 25; *Writings*, V: 112, Adams to Monroe, 5 Sept. 1814.

p.795 l.33   J.Q. Adams, *Writings*, V: 112, Adams to Monroe, 5 Sept. 1814.

p.796 l.4   Ibid., p. 119.

p.796 l.10   Wellington, IX: 221, Goulburn to Bathurst, 5 Sept. 1814.

p.796 l.19   Ibid., p. 249, draft note, 1 Sept. 1814.

p.796 l.21   Clay, I: 972, Clay to Crawford, 22 Aug. 1814.

p.796 l.28   Clay, I: 973, Clay to Goulburn, 5 Sept. 1814.

p.797 l.20   Bathurst, pp. 286–87, Liverpool to Bathurst, 14 Sept. 1814; Wellington, IX: 240, Liverpool to Bathurst, 11 Sept. 1814.

p.797 l.30   Bathurst, p. 287, Liverpool to Bathurst, 14 Sept. 1814.

p.798 l.10   Wellington, IX: 214, Liverpool to Castlereagh, 2 Sept. 1814.

p.798 l.28   Ibid., p. 240, Liverpool to Bathurst, 11 Sept. 1814.

p.799 l.4   Ibid., p. 265, Goulburn to Bathurst, 16 Sept. 1814.

p.799 l.8   Ibid., p. 266.

p.799 l.21   Ibid., p. 287, Goulburn to Bathurst, 26 Sept. 1814.

p.799 l.29   Bathurst, p. 289, Liverpool to Bathurst, 15 Sept. 1814.

p.800 l.12   Clay, I: 982, Goulburn to Clay, 3 Oct. [?] 1814.

p.800 l.25   Ibid., pp. 988–89, Clay to Crawford, 17 Oct. 1814.

p.800 l.27   J.Q. Adams, *Writings*, V: 161, Adams to Louisa Adams, 18 Oct. 1814.

p.800 l.30   Ibid.

p.801 l.2   J.Q. Adams, *Memoirs*, III: 51.

p.801 l.13   J.Q. Adams, *Writings*, V: 174, Adams to Louisa Adams, 28 Oct. 1814.

p.801 l.22   Ibid., p. 175.

p.801 l.24   Ibid., p. 108, Adams to Louisa Adams, 30 Aug. 1814; ibid., p. 205, Adams to Louisa Adams, 22 Nov. 1814.

p.802 l.8   Wellington, IX: 367, Liverpool to Castlereagh, 21 Oct. 1814.

p.802 l.9 Ibid., p. 383, Liverpool to Castlereagh, 28 Oct. 1814.

p.802 l.11 Ibid., p. 405, Liverpool to Castlereagh, 4 Nov. 1814.

p.802 l.19 Gallatin, I: 642, Gallatin to Monroe, 26 Oct. 1814.

p.804 l.8 J.Q. Adams, *Memoirs*, III: 60–66.

p.804 l.23 Castlereagh, pp. 186–89, Wellington to Liverpool, 9 Nov. 1814.

p.804 l.27 Wellington, IX: 432, Goulburn to Bathurst, 14 Nov. 1814.

p.804 l.34 Ibid., p. 438, Liverpool to Castlereagh, 18 Nov. 1814.

p.804 l.35 Ibid.

p.805 l.7 Clay, I: 1001, British to U.S. Commissioners, 26 Nov. 1814.

p.805 l.18 Wellington, IX: 452–54, Goulburn to Bathurst, 25 Nov. 1814.

p.805 l.21 J.Q. Adams, *Writings*, V: 219, Adams to Louisa Adams, 29 Nov. 1814.

p.806 l.4 J.Q. Adams, *Memoirs*, III: 101–3.

p.806 l.8 Ibid., p. 108.

p.806 l.25 Ibid., p. 120.

p.806 l.28 J.Q. Adams, *Writings*, V: 238, Adams to Louisa Adams, 16 Dec. 1814.

p.807 l.8 Ibid., pp. 237–39.

p.807 l.30 J.Q. Adams, *Memoirs*, III: 126.

AFTERVIEW

p.811 l.28 Bulger, p. 132, Bulger Report, 18 April 1815.

p.811 l.35 Ibid., p. 143, McDouall to Bulger, 2 May 1815.

p.816 l.9 Dunlop, p. 22.

Select Bibliography

UNPUBLISHED MANUSCRIPT MATERIAL

Public Archives of Canada:
RG 8, "C" series *passim*, British Military Records
CO 42, vols. 143–163 (Lower Canada); vols. 351–355 (Upper Canada). Colonial Office, original correspondence, Secretary of State.
RG 19 E5(a), Department of Finance, War of 1812 Losses, vols. 3728–3768 *passim*
Upper Canada Sundries RG 5 A1, vols. 16, 19, 26
Upper Canada Sundries, state books, vol. F
MG 24 F4 Bisshopp Papers
MG 24 F13 Chauncey Papers

Public Archives of Ontario:
Ely Playter Diary
Strachan Papers
Robinson Papers

U.S. National Archives:
RG 107 Records of the office of the Secretary of War
M6, reels 5–7, Letters sent by the Secretary of War
M221, reels 42–67, Letters received by the Secretary of War
Library of Congress:
William Eustis Papers
Thomas Jesup Papers

Wisconsin Historical Society:
Draper MSS, Tecumseh Papers

Rhode Island Historical Society:
Usher Parsons Diary

Buffalo Historical Society:
A.C. Goodyear Collection
Jarvis Hanks Memoir

Public Record Office, London:
WO 71/243, Court martial of Henry Procter

Filson Club:
Scrapbook MSS B1/F489

PUBLISHED PRIMARY SOURCES

[Adams, John Quincy.] *Memoirs of John Quincy Adams, Comprising Portions of His Diary from 1795 to 1848*, vols. III and IV, edited by Charles Francis Adams. Philadelphia: J.B. Lippincott, 1874.

—— *The Writings of John Quincy Adams*, vol. IV, *1811–1813*, edited by Worthington Chauncey Ford. New York: Macmillan, 1914.

Armstrong, John. *Hints to Young Generals. By an Old Soldier.* Kingston, N.Y.: 1812.

—— *Notices of the War of 1812*, 2 vols., vol. I, George Dearborn, 1836; vol. II, Wiley & Putnam, 1840.

Babcock, James L. (ed.). "The Campaign of 1814 on the Niagara Frontier," *Niagara Frontier*, vol. 10 (1963).

Barrett, Charles Raymond Booth. *The 85th King's Light Infantry.* London: Spottiswoode, 1913.

[Bathurst, Henry.] *Report on the Manuscripts of Earl Bathurst Preserved at Cirencester Park*, prepared by Francis Bickley. London: Historical Manuscripts Commission, vol. 76, 1923.

Bayard, James. "Letters of James Asheton Bayard," *Delaware Historical Society Papers*, vol. 31 (1901).

—— "Papers of James Bayard," edited by Elizabeth Donnan, in *Annual Report of the American Historical Association for the year 1913*, vol. II. Washington: 1915.

Booth, Mordecai. "The Capture of Washington in 1814 As Described by Mordecai Booth," *Americana*, vol. 28 (1934).

Bourne, Alexander. "The Siege of Fort Meigs, year 1813. An eyewitness account," *Northwest Ohio Quarterly*, vols. 17 and 18 (1945 and 1946).

Boyd, John P. *Documents and Facts Relative to the Military Events during the Late War.* Boston, 1816.

Brannan, John (ed.). *Official Letters of the Military and Naval Officers of the United States, during the War with Great Britain in the Years 1812, 13, 14 & 15.* Washington: Way & Gideon, 1823.

[Brenton, E.B.] *Some Account of the Public Life of the Late Lieutenant-General Sir George Prevost, Bart., Particularly of His Services in the Canadas. . . .* London: Cadell, 1823.

Brown, Samuel. *Views of the Campaigns of the Northwest Army & c. . . .* Burlington, Vt., 1814.

Bulger, Alfred (ed.). "The Bulger Papers," *State Historical Society of Wisconsin Collections*, vol. 13 (1895).

Bunnell, David C. *The Travels and Adventures of David C. Bunnell. . . .* Palmyra, N.Y.: J.H. Bortles, 1831.

"The Burning of Buffalo," *Buffalo Historical Society Publications*, vol. 9 (1906).

Byfield, Shadrach. "Narrative," *Magazine of History*, extra no. 11, 1910.

[Castlereagh, Viscount.] *Correspondence, Despatches and Other Papers of Viscount Castlereagh*, edited by C.W. Vane, vol. IX. London, 1848–53.

[Chandler, John.] "General John Chandler of Monmouth, Maine, with Extracts from His Autobiography," edited by George Foster Talbot, *Maine Historical Collections*, vol. 9 (1887).

Chapin, Cyrenius. *Chapin's Review of Armstrong's Notices of the War of 1812.* Black Rock, N.Y.: D.P. Adams, 1836.

Clark, Byron N. "Accounts of the Battle of Plattsburgh from Contemporaneous Sources," *Vermont Antiquarian*, vol. 1 (1903).

[Clay, Henry.] *The Papers of Henry Clay*, vols. I and II, edited by James Hopkins. Lexington, Ky.: University of Kentucky Press, 1959 and 1961.

"Copies of Papers on File in the Dominion Archives at Ottawa, Canada, Pertaining to Michigan As Found in the Colonial Office Records," *Michigan Pioneer and Historical Collections*, vol. 25 (1896).

Combs, Leslie. "Account of Fort Meigs," *American Historical Record*, vol. I, 1872.

"Correspondence between Hon. William Dickson Prisoner of War and Gen. Dearborn, 1813," *Niagara Historical Society Papers*, no. 28.

Cruikshank, E.A. (ed.). *The Documentary History of the Campaign upon the Niagara Frontier 1812–1814.* 9 vols. Welland: Lundy's Lane Historical Society, 1896–1908.

——(ed.). *Documents Relating to the Invasion of the Niagara Peninsula by the United States Army Commanded by General Jacob Brown in July and August 1814.* Niagara-on-the-Lake: Niagara Historical Society Publications, no. 33, 1920.

Delafield, Julia. *Biographies of Francis Lewis and Morgan Lewis.* New York: A.D.F. Randolph, 1877.

Dobbins, Daniel and Dobbins, William. "The Dobbins Papers," *Buffalo Historical Society Publications*, vol. 8 (1905).

Documents in Relation to the Differences Which Subsisted between the Late Commodore O.H. Perry and Captain J.D. Elliott. Boston, 1834.

Douglas, John. *Medical Topography of Upper Canada.* London: Burgess and Hill, 1819.

[Douglass, David Bates.] "An Original Narrative of the Niagara Campaign of 1814," edited by John T. Horton, *Niagara Frontier*, vol. 11 (1964).

Dunlop, William. *Tiger Dunlop's Upper Canada....* Toronto: McClelland and Stewart, 1967.

Edgar, Matilda. *Ten Years of Upper Canada in Peace and War, 1805–1815; Being the Ridout Letters....* Toronto: W. Briggs, 1890.

Elliott, Jesse D. *Speech ... delivered in Hagerstown, Md., on 14th Nov. 1843.* Philadelphia: G.B. Zeiber & Co., 1844.

Ewell, James. "Unwelcome Visitors to Early Washington," *Records of the Columbia Historical Society*, vol. 1 (1897).

Finan, Patrick. *Journal of a Voyage to Quebec in the Year 1825.* Newry, Ireland: Alexander Peacock, 1828.

Firth, Edith (ed.). *The Town of York, 1793–1815.* Toronto: Champlain Society for the Government of Ontario, University of Toronto Press, 1962.

[Gallatin, Albert.] *The Writings of Albert Gallatin*, vol. I, edited by Henry Adams. Philadelphia: J.B. Lippincott, 1879.

"General Orders. Fort Meigs to Put-in Bay April–September 1813," *Register of the Kentucky Historical Society*, vol. 60 (1962).

Grignon, Augustin. "Seventy-two Years' Recollections of Wisconsin," *State Historical Society of Wisconsin Collections*, vol. 3 (1856).

[Hanks, Jarvis.] "A Drummer Boy in the War of 1812: The Memoir of Jarvis Frary Hanks," edited by Lester Smith, *Niagara Frontier*, vol. 7 (1960).

[Harrison, William Henry.] *Messages and Letters*, 2 vols., edited by Logan Esarey. Indiana Historical Collections, vols. 8 and 9. Indianapolis: Indiana Historical Commission, 1922.

Hatch, William S. *A Chapter in the History of the War of 1812 in the Northwest. . . .* Cincinnati: Miami Printing & Publishing, 1872.

Hay, George. "Recollections of the War of 1812," *American Historical Review*, vol. 32 (1926).

Howe, Henry. *Historical Collections of Ohio*, vol. II. Cincinnati, 1902.

Izard, George. *Official Correspondence. . . .* Philadelphia, 1816.

Jackson, Donald (ed.). *Black Hawk, an Autobiography*. Urbana, Ill.: University of Illinois Press, 1964 [reprint].

Kentucky Gazette.

Klinck, Carl F. (ed.). *Tecumseh: Fact and Fiction in Early Records*. Englewood Cliffs, N.J.: Prentice-Hall, 1961.

Lajeunesse, Ernest J. (ed.). *The Windsor Border Region*. Toronto: University of Toronto Press, 1960.

"Lawe and Grignon Papers," *Reports and Collections of the State Historical Society of Wisconsin*, vol. 10 (1883).

[Le Couteur, John.] "The March of the 104th Foot from Fredericton to Quebec, 1813," edited by Maj. M.A. Pope, *Canadian Defence Quarterly*, vol. 7 (1930).

"List of Losses Claimed on Houses Burned in Niagara Dec. 13th, 1813," *Niagara Historical Society Publications*, no. 27 (n.d.).

Loyal and Patriotic Society of Upper Canada. *The Report of the . . . Society . . . with an Appendix, and a List of Subscribers and Benefactors*. Montreal: W. Gray, 1817.

McAfee, Robert. "The McAfee Papers," *Register of the Kentucky Historical Society*, vol. 26 (1928).

McClure, George. *Causes of the Destruction of the American Towns on the Niagara Frontier and Failure of the Campaign of the Fall of 1813*. Bath, N.Y., 1817.

Macdonough, Rodney. *The Life of Commodore Thomas Macdonough, U.S. Navy*. Boston: Fort Hill Press, 1909.

McKenney, Thomas L. *Memoirs. . . .* New York: Paine & Burgess, 1846.

[Madison, Dolley.] *Memoirs and Letters of Dolly Madison*, edited by her grand-niece. Port Washington, N.Y.: Kennikat Press, 1971 [reprint].

[Madison, James.] *The Writings of James Madison*, vol. VIII, *1808–1819*, edited by Gaillard Hunt. New York, London: G.P. Putnam's Sons, 1908.

Mann, James. *Medical Sketches of the Campaigns of 1812, 13, 14*. Dedham, Mass., 1816.

Manning, William R. (ed.). *Diplomatic Correspondence of the United States: Canadian Relations, 1784–1860*, vol. I. Washington: Carnegie Endowment, 1940.

"Military Service of 1813/14 As Shown by the Correspondence of Major General Amos Hall," *Buffalo Historical Society Publications*, vol. 5 (1902).

[Monroe, James.] *The Writings of James Monroe*, vol. V, *1807–1816*, edited by Stanislaus Murray Hamilton. New York, London: G.P. Putnam's Sons, 1901.

New Monthly Magazine, 1826.

Niles Weekly Register, 1812–15.

[Norton, Jacob Porter.] "Jacob Porter Norton, a Yankee on the Niagara frontier in 1814," edited by Daniel R. Porter, *Niagara Frontier*, vol. 12 (1965).

"Old Sub," *United Service Journal*, 1840, part I.

Ontario, Bureau of Archives. *Report of the Bureau of Archives for the Province of Ontario, 1st–15th, 1903–1918/19*, no. 7 (1910) and no. 9 (1912). Toronto: King's Printer, 1904–20.

Padover, Saul (ed.). *Thomas Jefferson and the National Capital. . . .* Washington: U.S. Government Printing Office, 1946.

Palmer, T.H. (ed.). *The Historical Register of the United States*, 4 vols. Philadelphia, 1814–16.

Parsons, Usher. *The Battle of Lake Erie*. Providence, R.I.: Rhode Island Historical Society, 1854.

—— "Brief Sketches of the Officers Who Were in the Battle of Lake Erie," *Inland Seas*, vol. 19 (1963).

—— "A Surgical Account of the Battle of Lake Erie," *New England Journal of Surgery and Medicine*, October, 1818.

Paullin, Charles O. (ed.). *The Battle of Lake Erie: A Collection of Documents, Chiefly by Commodore Perry. . . .* Cleveland: Rowfant Club, 1918.

[Pike, Zebulon Montgomery.] *The Journals of Zebulon Montgomery Pike*, edited by Donald Jackson. Norman, Okla.: University of Oklahoma Press, 1966.

Quaife, Milo M. (ed.). *War on the Detroit: The Chronicles of Thomas Verchères de Boucherville, and The Capitulation by an Ohio Volunteer*. Chicago: Lakeside Press, 1940.

"Reminiscences of American Occupation of Niagara from 27th May to 10th Dec. 1813," *Niagara Historical Society Publications*, no. 11 (n.d.).

Richardson, John. "A Canadian Campaign," *New Monthly Magazine*, London, 1827.

—— *Eight Years in Canada*. Montreal: H.H. Cunningham, 1847.

[Richardson, John.] *The Letters of Veritas. . . .* Montreal: W. Gray, 1815.

[Richardson, John.] *Richardson's War of 1812 . . .* , edited by Alexander C. Casselman. Toronto: Historical Publishing, 1902.

Roach, Isaac. "Journal of Major Isaac Roach, 1812–1824," *Pennsylvania Magazine of History and Biography*, vol. 17 (1893).

Robinson, C.W. "The Expedition to Plattsburgh upon Lake Champlain, Canada 1814," *Journal of the Royal United Service Institute*, vol. 61 (1916).

Scott, Winfield. *Memoirs of Lieut.-General Scott, Written by Himself*, 2 vols., vol. I. New York: Sheldon, 1864.

[Sheaffe, Roger Hale.] "Documents Relating to the War of 1812: the Letterbook of Gen. Sir Roger Hale Sheaffe," *Buffalo Historical Society Publications*, vol. 17 (1913).

[Sholes, Stanton.] "A Narrative of the Northwestern Campaign of 1813," edited by Milo M. Quaife. *Mississippi Valley Historical Review*, vol. 15 (1929).

"The Siege of Fort Meigs," *Register of the Kentucky Historical Society*, vol. 19 (1921).

Slater, D. "An Old Diary," *Journal and Transactions of the Wentworth Historical Society*, vol. 5 (1908).

Smart, James. "The St. Lawrence Project. . . ." Unpublished paper in Queen's University Library, Kingston, Ont.

Smith, Sir Harry. *The Autobiography of Lt. General Sir Harry Smith . . .* , vol. I. London: John Murray, 1901.

[Smith, Margaret Bayard.] *Forty Years of Washington Society . . .* , edited by Gaillard Hunt. London: T. Fisher Unwin, 1906.

[Strachan, John.] *John Strachan: Documents and Opinions*, edited by J.L.H. Henderson. Toronto: McClelland and Stewart, 1969.

[Strachan, John.] *The John Strachan Letterbook, 1812–1834*, edited by George Spragge. Toronto: Ontario Historical Society, 1946.

Strachan, John. *A Sermon Preached at York . . . August 2nd, 1812*. York, 1812.

Swift, Joseph Gardner. *Memoirs of General Joseph Gardner Swift*. Worcester, Mass., 1890.

Treat, Joseph. *The Vindication of Captain Joseph Treat. . . .* Philadelphia, 1815.

United States Congress, *American State Papers: Foreign Relations*, vol. III. Washington: Gales & Seaton, 1832.

—— *American State Papers: Indian Affairs*, vol. I. Washington: Gales & Seaton, 1832.

—— *American State Papers: Military Affairs*, vol. I. Washington: Gales & Seaton, 1832.

—— *American State Papers: Naval Affairs*, vol. I. Washington: Gales & Seaton, 1832.

"The Village of Buffalo in the War of 1812," *Buffalo Historical Society Publications*, vol. 1 (1897).

"Visit of Col. R.M. Johnson to Springfield 18–20 May 1843. Report from State Register 26 May 1843," *Journal of the Illinois State Historical Society*, vol. 13 (1921).

Wellington, Duke of. *Supplementary Despatches: Correspondence and Memoranda of Field Marshal Arthur Duke of Wellington*, vol. IX. London, 1862.

White, Samuel. *History of the American Troops during the Late War.* . . . Baltimore, 1829.

Wilkinson, James. *Memoirs of My Own Times*, 3 vols. Philadelphia, 1816.

Wood, Eleazer. "Eleazer D. Wood's Journal of the Northwestern Campaign," in George Cullum, ed., *Campaigns of the War of 1812–15.* . . . New York: J. Miller, 1879.

Wood, William C.H. (ed.). *Select British Documents of the Canadian War of 1812*, Champlain Society, vols. 13–15, 17. Toronto: The Society, 1920–28.

York [Upper Canada] *Gazette:* 1812–13.

SECONDARY SOURCES

Adams, Henry. *A History of the United States of America during the Administrations of Thomas Jefferson and James Madison.* New York: Charles Scribner's Sons, 1889–91.

Allen, Robert S. "The British Indian Department and the Frontier in North America, 1755–1830," *Canadian Historic Sites: Occasional Papers in Archeology and History*, no. 14 (1975).

Anderson, David. "The Battle of Fort Stephenson," *Northwest Ohio Quarterly*, vol. 33 (1961).

Anglo American Magazine, December, 1853.

Arnold, Thaddeus. "The Battle of the Thames and Death of Tecumseh," unpublished manuscript, Chatham and Kent Historical Society.

Averill, James P. *Fort Meigs: A Condensed History.* . . . Toledo, O., 1886.

Babcock, Louis L. "The Siege of Fort Erie," *New York State Historical Association Proceedings*, vol. 8 (1909).

—— *The War of 1812 on the Niagara Frontier.* Buffalo: Buffalo Historical Society, 1927.

Bailey, John R. *Mackinac, Formerly Michilimackinac.* Lansing, Mich.: 1895.

Bannister, J.A. "The Burning of Dover," *Western Ontario Historical Notes*, vol. 21 (1965).

Bayles, G.H. "Tecumseh and the Bayles Family Tradition," *Register of the Kentucky Historical Society*, vol. 46 (1948).

Baylies, Nicholas. *Eleazer Wheelock Ripley of the War of 1812*. Des Moines, Ia.: Brewster, 1890.

Beasley, David R. *The Canadian Don Quixote: The Life and Works of Major John Richardson, Canada's First Novelist*. Erin, Ont.: Porcupine's Quill, 1977.

Beirne, Francis F. *The War of 1812*. New York: Dutton, 1949.

Berger, Carl. *The Sense of Power: Studies in the Ideas of Canadian Imperialism, 1867–1914*. Toronto: University of Toronto Press, 1970.

Bethune, Alexander N. *Memoir of the Right Reverend John Strachan D.D., LL.D., First Bishop of Toronto*. Toronto: Henry Rowsell, 1870.

Biggar, E.B. "The Battle of Stony Creek," *Canadian Magazine*, vol. 1 (1893).

Blanco, Richard L. "The Development of British Military Medicine, 1793–1814," *Military Affairs*, February, 1974.

Boissonnault, Charles-Marie. *Histoire politico-militaire des Canadiens-Français*. Trois Rivières: Editions du Bien Public, 1967.

Brett-James, Anthony. *Life in Wellington's Army*. London: Allen and Unwin, 1972.

Buell, W.S. "Military Movements in Eastern Ontario during the War of 1812," *Ontario Historical Society Papers and Records*, vol. 10 (1913).

Burges, Tristam. *The Battle of Lake Erie*. Philadelphia: William Marshall, 1839.

Burns, R.J. "God's Chosen People: The Origins of Toronto Society, 1793–1818," *Canadian Historical Association, Historical Papers*, Toronto, 1973.

Burt, Alfred L. *The United States, Great Britain and British North America from the Revolution to the Establishment of Peace after the War of 1812*. New Haven: Yale University Press, 1940.

Burt, A. Blanche. "Captain Robert Heriot Barclay, R.N.," *Ontario Historical Society Papers and Records*, vol. 14 (1916).

Butler, Mann. *A History of the Commonwealth of Kentucky*. . . . Cincinnati: J.A. James, 1836.

Caffrey, Kate *The Twilight's Last Gleaming: The British Against America, 1812–1815*. New York: Stein and Day, 1977.

Chalou, George C. "The Red Pawns Go to War: British-American Indian Relations, 1810–1815." Ph.D. dissertation, University of Indiana, 1971.

Cleaves, Freeman. *Old Tippecanoe: William Henry Harrison and his Time*. New York: Charles Scribner's Sons, 1939; reprinted, New York: Kennikat Press, 1969.

Cleveland City Council. *Inauguration of the Perry Statue at Cleveland*. Cleveland: Cleveland, Fairbanks, Benedict, 1861.

Coffin, William F. *1812: The War and Its Moral: A Canadian Chronicle.* Montreal: J. Lovell, 1864.

Coles, Harry L. *The War of 1812.* Chicago: University of Chicago Press, 1965.

Colquhoun, A.H.U. "The Career of Joseph Willcocks," *Canadian Historical Review*, vol. 7 (1926).

Cook, Samuel F. *Mackinaw in History.* Lansing, Mich.: R. Smith, 1895.

Cooper, James Fenimore. *The Battle of Lake Erie. . . .* Cooperstown, N.Y.: H. & E. Phinney, 1843.

—— *The History of the Navy of the United States of America*, vol. II. London, 1839.

—— "Oliver Hazard Perry," *Graham's Magazine*, vol. 22 (1843).

Coutts, Katharine B. "Thamesville and the Battle of the Thames," *Ontario Historical Society Papers and Records*, vol. 9 (1908).

Craig, G.M. *Upper Canada: The Formative Years, 1784–1841.* Toronto: McClelland and Stewart, 1963.

Cramer, C.H. "Duncan McArthur: The Military Phase," *Ohio State Archaeological and Historical Quarterly*, vol. 46 (1937).

Cruickshank, David A. "The Plattsburgh Campaign, September 1814." M.A. thesis, Queen's University, 1971.

Cruikshank, E.A. "The Battle of Fort George," *Niagara Historical Society Publications*, no. 1 (1896).

—— "The Battle of Lundy's Lane," *Lundy's Lane Historical Society Publications*, vol. 1, part 7 (1893).

—— "The Battle of Stoney Creek and the Blockade of Fort George," *Niagara Historical Society Publications*, no. 3.

—— "The Contest for the Command of Lake Erie in 1812–13," *Royal Canadian Institute Transactions*, vol. 6 (1899).

—— "The Contest for the Command of Lake Ontario in 1812 and 1813," *Royal Society of Canada Transactions*, ser. 3, sect. 2, vol. 10 (1916).

—— "The Contest for the Command of Lake Ontario in 1814," *Ontario Historical Society Papers and Records*, vol. 21 (1924).

—— "The County of Norfolk in the War of 1812," *Ontario Historical Society Papers and Records*, vol. 20 (1923).

"Drummond's Winter Campaign," *Lundy's Lane Historical Society Publications*, vol. 1, part 3 (n.d.).

—— "An Episode of the War of 1812: The Story of the Schooner 'Nancy,'" *Ontario Historical Society Papers and Records* vol. 9 (1910).

—— "The Fight in the Beechwoods," *Lundy's Lane Historical Society Publications*, vol. 1, part 6 (1895).

—— "From Isle aux Noix to Chateauguay," *Royal Society of Canada*

Transactions, ser. 3, sect. 2, vol. 7 (1913).

—— "Harrison and Procter," *Royal Society of Canada Proceedings*, ser. 3, sect. 2, vol. 4 (1910).

—— "John Beverley Robinson and the Trials for Treason," *Ontario Historical Society Papers and Records*, vol. 25 (1929).

—— "Laura Secord's Walk to Warn Fitzgibbon," *Niagara Historical Society Publications*, no. 36 (1924).

—— "Robert Dickson, the Indian Trader," *State Historical Society of Wisconsin Collections*, vol. 12 (1892).

—— "The Siege of Fort Erie," *Lundy's Lane Historical Society Publications*, vol. 1, part 14 (1905).

—— "A Study of Disaffection in Upper Canada," *Royal Society of Canada Transactions*, ser. 3, sect. 2, vol. 6 (1912).

Cumberland, Barlow. *The Battle of York*. Toronto: Wm. Briggs, 1913.

—— "The Navies on Lake Ontario in the War of 1812," *Ontario Historical Society Papers and Records*, vol. 8 (1907).

Currie, Emma. *The Story of Laura Secord and Canadian Reminiscences*. St. Catharines, 1913.

Curzon, S.A. "The Story of Laura Secord," *Lundy's Lane Historical Society Publications*, vol. 1, part 9 (1891).

Dale, Allan. "Chateauguay," *Canadian Geographical Journal*, vol. 11 (1935).

Dangerfield, George. "Lord Liverpool and the United States," *American Heritage*, vol. 6 (1955).

David, Laurent Oliver. *Le Héros de Chateauguay*. Montreal: Cadieux et Jerome, 1883.

Davis, P.M. "The Four Principal Battles of the Late War," *Magazine of History*, extra no. 55 (1917).

Dawson, Moses. *A Historical Narrative of the Civil and Military Services of Major-General William H. Harrison. . . .* Cincinnati, 1824.

Dictionary of American Biography, 22 vols. New York: Charles Scribner's Sons, 1928–58.

Dictionary of Canadian Biography, vol. IX: *1861–1870*. Toronto: University of Toronto Press, 1976.

Dictionary of National Biography, 22 vols. Oxford: Oxford University Press, 1885–1900.

Dobbins, William. *History of the Battle of Lake Erie*. Erie, Pa.: Ashby Printing Co., 1913.

Dodge, Robert. *The Battle of Lake Erie*. Fostoria, O.: 1967.

Douglas, R. Alan. "Weapons of the War of 1812," *Michigan History*, vol. 47 (1963).

Drake, Benjamin. *Life of Tecumseh, and of His Brother the Prophet, with a Historical Sketch of the Shawanoe Indians.* Cincinnati: E. Morgan, 1841.

Dutton, Charles Judson. *Oliver Hazard Perry.* New York: Longmans, Green, 1935.

Eaton, Clement. *Henry Clay and the Art of American Politics.* Boston: Little, Brown, 1957.

Elliott, Charles W. *Winfield Scott: The Soldier and the Man.* New York: Macmillan, 1937.

Emerson, George D. *The Perry's Victory Centenary. Report of the Perry's Victory Centennial Commission, State of New York.* Albany: J.B. Lyon, 1916.

Engelman, Fred L. *The Peace of Christmas Eve.* New York: Harcourt, Brace and World, 1962.

Ermatinger, C.O. "The Retreat of Procter and Tecumseh," *Ontario Historical Society Papers and Records,* vol. 17 (1919).

Erney, Richard A. "The Public Life of Henry Dearborn." Ph.D. dissertation, Columbia University, 1957.

Everest, Allan S. "Alexander Macomb at Plattsburg, 1814," *New York History,* vol. 44 (1963).

FitzGibbon, Mary Agnes. *A Veteran of 1812: The Life of James FitzGibbon.* Toronto: W. Briggs, 1894.

Folsom, William R. "The Battle of Plattsburg," *Vermont Quarterly,* vol. 20 (1950).

Forester, C.S. *The Age of Fighting Sail: The Story of the Naval War of 1812.* Garden City, N.Y.: Doubleday, 1956.

—— "Victory at New Orleans," *American Heritage,* vol. 8 (1957).

—— "Victory on Lake Champlain," *American Heritage,* vol. 15 (1963).

Fortescue, Sir John. *A History of the British Army,* 13 vols., vols. VIII and IX. London: Macmillan, 1917.

Fraser, John. *Canadian Pen and Ink Sketches.* Montreal, 1890.

Gilpin, Alec. *The War of 1812 in the Old Northwest.* Toronto: Ryerson Press; East Lansing, Mich.: Michigan State University Press, 1958.

Goltz, Charles H. "Tecumseh and the Northwest Indian Confederacy." Ph.D. dissertation, University of Western Ontario, 1973.

Gosling, D.C.L. "The Battle at Lacolle Mill, 1814," *Journal of the Society for Army Historical Research,* vol. 47 (1969).

Graves, Donald E. "The Canadian Volunteers, 1813–1815," *Military Collector and Historian,* vol. 31 (1979).

Green, Ernest. *Lincoln at Bay: A Sketch of 1814.* Welland, 1923.

—— "New Light on the Battle of Chippewa," *Welland County Historical Society Papers and Records*, vol. 3 (1927).

Gurd, Norman S. *The Story of Tecumseh*. Toronto: W. Briggs, 1912.

Hamil, Fred Coyne. *The Valley of the Lower Thames, 1640–1850*. Toronto: University of Toronto Press, 1951.

Hamilton, Edward P. "The Battle of Plattsburgh," *Vermont History*, vol. 31 (1963).

Hammack, James W., Jr. *Kentucky and the Second American Revolution: The War of 1812*. Lexington, Ky.: University of Kentucky Press, 1976.

Hare, John S. "Military Punishments in the War of 1812," *Journal of the American Military Institute*, vol. 4 (1940).

Havighurst, Walter. *Three Flags at the Straits: The Forts of Mackinac*. Englewood Cliffs, N.J.: Prentice-Hall, 1966.

Henderson, J.L.H. *John Strachan*. Toronto: University of Toronto Press, 1969.

Hill, Ralph Nading. *Lake Champlain, Key to Liberty*. Taftsville, Vt.: Countryman Press, 1977.

Hitsman, J. Mackay. *The Incredible War of 1812: A Military History*. Toronto: University of Toronto Press, 1965.

—— "Sir George Prevost's Conduct of the Canadian War of 1812," *Canadian Historical Association Report*, 1962.

Hodge, Frederick, W. (ed.). *Handbook of American Indians North of Mexico*, 2 vols. Washington: Smithsonian Institution, Bureau of American Ethnology, Bulletin no. 30, 1906; reprinted, New York: Pageant Books, 1959.

Hollon, William E. *The Lost Pathfinder: Zebulon Montgomery Pike*. Norman, Okla.: University of Oklahoma Press, 1949.

Holmes, T.K. "Pioneer Life in Kent County," *Kent Historical Society Papers and Addresses*, vol. 1 (1914).

Horsman, Reginald. *Matthew Elliott, British Indian Agent*. Detroit: Wayne State University Press, 1964.

—— *The War of 1812*. New York: Knopf, 1969.

Hough, Franklin B. *A History of St. Lawrence and Franklin Counties, New York.* . . . Albany: Little & Co., 1853.

Humphries, Charles. "The Capture of York," *Ontario History*, vol. 51 (1959).

Hurd, Duane H. *History of Clinton and Franklin Counties, New York*. Philadelphia: J.W. Lewis, 1880.

Ingersoll, Charles J. *Historical Sketch of the Second War between the United States of America and Great Britain.* . . . Philadelphia: Lea and Blanchard, 1845–49.

Ingersoll, James H. "The Ancestry of Laura Secord," *Ontario Historical Society Papers and Records*, vol. 23 (1926).

Ingraham, Edward. *A Sketch of the Events Which Preceded the Capture of Washington by the British*. Philadelphia, 1849.

Ingram, George. "The Story of Laura Secord Revisited," *Ontario History*, vol. 57 (1965).

Irving, L. Homfray. *Officers of the British Forces in Canada during the War of 1812–15*. Welland: Tribune Print. for Canadian Military Institute, 1908.

Jackson, Donald. "How Lost Was Zebulon Pike?" *American Heritage*, vol. 16 (1965).

Jacobs, James R. *Tarnished Warrior: Major-General James Wilkinson*. New York: Macmillan, 1938.

James, William. *A Full and Correct Account of the Military Occurrences of the Late War between Great Britain and the United States of America*, 2 vols. London, 1818.

Jarvis, Russell. *A Biographical Notice of Commodore Jesse D. Elliott.* . . . Philadelphia, 1835.

Johnson, Crisfield. *A Centennial History of Erie County, New York.* . . . Buffalo: Matthew and Warren, 1876.

Kelton, Dwight H. *Annals of Fort Mackinac*. Detroit: Detroit Free Press, 1888.

Kerr, W.B. "The Occupation of York," *Canadian Historical Review*, vol. 5 (1924).

Ketchum, William. *An Authentic and Comprehensive History of Buffalo . . . ,* vol. II. Buffalo: Rockwell, Baker & Hill, 1864–65.

Kirby, William. *Annals of Niagara*. Welland: Lundy's Lane Historical Society, 1896.

Koke, Richard J. "The Britons Who Fought on the Canadian Frontier: Uniforms of the War of 1812," *New York Historical Society Quarterly*, vol. 45 (1961).

Land, J.H. "The Battle of Stoney Creek," *Journal and Transactions of the Wentworth Historical Society*, vol. 1 (1892).

Lauriston, Victor. *Romantic Kent, the Story of a County*. Chatham: Shepherd Printing, 1952.

Lighthall, William Douw. *An Account of the Battle of Chateauguay.* . . . Montreal: W. Drysdale, 1889.

Lord, Walter. *The Dawn's Early Light*. New York: W.W. Norton, 1972.

Lossing, Benson J. *The Pictorial Field-book of the War of 1812.* . . . New York: Harper and Brothers, 1868.

Lower, Arthur R.M. *Canadians in the Making: A Social History of Canada.* Toronto: Longmans, Green, 1958.

Lyman, Olin. *Commodore Oliver Hazard Perry and the War on the Lakes.* New York: New Amsterdam Book Co., 1905.

McAfee, Robert. *History of the Late War in the Western Country.* . . . Lexington, Ky.: Worsley and Smith, 1816.

Mackenzie, Alexander S. *Commodore Oliver Hazard Perry . . . His Life and Achievements.* Akron, O.: J.K. Richardson, 1910 [first published 1840].

McKenzie, Ruth. *Laura Secord: The Legend and the Lady.* Toronto: McClelland and Stewart, 1971.

Maclay, Edgar Stanton. *A History of the United States Navy from 1775 to 1901.* New York: D. Appleton, 1901.

Macmillan Dictionary of Canadian Biography, 4th ed., edited by W. Stewart Wallace and W.A. McKay. Toronto: Macmillan, 1978.

Magill, M.L. "William Allan and the War of 1812," *Ontario History,* vol. 64 (1972).

Mahan, Alfred T. *Sea Power in Its Relations to the War of 1812,* 2 vols. Boston: Little, Brown, 1905.

Mahon, John K. *The War of 1812.* Gainesville: University of Florida Press, 1972.

Marine, William M. *The British Invasion of Maryland, 1812–15.* Baltimore, 1913.

Mason, Philip P. (ed.). *After Tippecanoe: Some Aspects of the War of 1812.* Toronto: Ryerson Press; East Lansing, Mich.: Michigan State University Press, 1963.

Mather, J.D. "The Capture of Fort Niagara, 19th December 1813," *Canadian Defence Quarterly,* vol. 3 (1926).

May, George S. *War, 1812* [Lansing?]: Mackinac Island State Park Commission, 1962.

Mayo, Bernard. *Henry Clay, Spokesman of the New West.* Boston: Houghton Mifflin, 1937.

—— "The Man Who Killed Tecumseh," *American Mercury,* 1930.

Metcalf, Clarence S. "Daniel Dobbins, Sailing Master, U.S.N. . . ." *Inland Seas,* vol. 14 (1958).

Meyer, Leland Winfield. *The Life and Times of Colonel Richard M. Johnson of Kentucky.* New York: Columbia University Press, 1932.

Moir, John S. "An Early Record of Laura Secord's Walk," *Ontario History,* vol. 51 (1959)

Morgan, Henry J. *Sketches of Celebrated Canadians.* . . . Quebec: Hunter, Rose, 1862.

Muir, R.C. "Burford's First Settler, Politician and Military Man—Benajah Mallory," *Ontario Historical Society Papers and Records*, vol. 26 (1930).

Mullaly, Frank B. "The Battle of Baltimore," *Maryland Historical Magazine*, vol. 54 (1959).

Muller, Charles G. *The Proudest Day: Macdonough on Lake Champlain*. New York: John Day, 1960.

—— "Commodore & Mrs. Thomas Macdonough, Some Light on Their Family," *Delaware History*, vol. 9 (1960).

Muller, H.N. "A 'Traitorous and Diabolic Traffic': The Commerce of the Champlain-Richelieu Corridor during the War of 1812," *Vermont History*, vol. 44 (1976).

—— "Smuggling into Canada: How the Champlain Valley Defied Jefferson's Embargo," *Vermont History*, vol. 38 (1970).

Oman, Sir Charles. *Wellington's Army, 1809–1814*. London: Arnold, 1913.

Palmer, Peter. *History of Lake Champlain, from . . . 1609 . . . to . . . 1814*, 3rd ed. New York: Frank F. Lovell, 1885[?].

Perkins, Bradford. *Castlereagh and Adams: England and the United States, 1812–1823*. Berkeley: University of California Press, 1964.

Quaife, Milo M. "Governor Shelby's Army in the River Thames Campaign," *Filson Club History Quarterly*, vol. 10 (1936).

—— *The Yankees Capture York*. Detroit: Wayne University Press, 1955.

Quisenberry, A.C. "Colonel George Croghan," *Register of the Kentucky Historical Society*, vol. 10 (1912).

—— "Kentuckians in the Battle of Lake Erie," *Register of the Kentucky Historical Society*, vol. 9 (1911).

Randall, E.O. "Tecumseh, the Shawnee Chief," *Ohio Archaeological and Historical Society Publications*, vol. 15 (1906).

Raudzens, George. " 'Red George' Macdonell, Military Saviour of Upper Canada?" *Ontario History*, vol. 62 (1970).

Richards, George H. *Memoir of Alexander Macomb, the Major-General Commanding the Army of the United States. . . .* New York: McElrath, Bangs, 1833.

Riddell, William R. "Benajah Mallory, Traitor," *Ontario Historical Society Papers and Records*, vol. 26 (1930).

—— "An Echo of the War of 1812," *Ontario Historical Society Papers and Records*, vol. 23 (1926).

—— "The Ancaster 'Bloody Assize' of 1814," *Ontario Historical Society Papers and Records*, vol. 20 (1923).

—— "The First Canadian War-time Prohibition Measure," *Canadian Historical Review*, vol. 1 (1920).

—— "Joseph Willcocks, Sheriff, Member of Parliament, Traitor," *Ontario Historical Society Papers and Records*, vol. 24 (1927).

Robinson, Sir Charles W. *Life of Sir John Beverley Robinson, Bart., C.B., D.C.L.* . . . Toronto: Morang, 1904.

Roosevelt, Theodore. *The Naval War of 1812.* . . . New York: G.P. Putnam's Sons, 1883.

Rosenberg, Max. *The Building of Perry's Fleet on Lake Erie, 1812–13.* [Harrisburg?!: Pennsylvania Historical and Museums Commission, 1968.

Roske, Ralph J. and Donely, Richard W. "The Perry-Elliott Controversy: A Bitter Footnote to the Battle of Lake Erie," *Northwest Ohio Quarterly*, vol. 34 (1962).

Ryerson, Adolphus Egerton. *The Loyalists of America and Their Times, from 1620 to 1816*, 2 vols, 2nd ed. Toronto: W. Briggs, 1880.

Salisbury, George. *Battle of Crysler's Farm* [pamphlet], n.d.

Selby, Charlotte, "Memoirs," unpublished, courtesy Joyce Douglas.

Sellar, Robert. *The Histories of the County of Huntingdon and of the Seigniories of Chateaugay and Beauharnois.* . . . Huntingdon, Que.: Canadian Gleaner, 1888.

—— *The U.S. Campaign of 1813 to Capture Montreal.* . . . Huntingdon, Que., 1914.

Skeen, C. Edward. "Mr. Madison's Secretary of War," *Pennsylvania Magazine of History and Biography*, vol. 100 (1976).

—— "Monroe and Armstrong, a Study in Political Rivalry," *New-York Historical Society Quarterly*, vol. 57 (1973).

Smelser, Marshall. "Tecumseh, Harrison and the War of 1812," *Indiana Magazine of History*, vol. 65 (1969).

Smith, Alison. "John Strachan and Early Upper Canada, 1799–1814," *Ontario History*, vol. 52 (1960).

Smith, J.H. "The Battle of Stoney Creek," *Journal and Proceedings of the Hamilton Association*, 1896–97.

—— "Historical Sketch of the County of Wentworth," *Wentworth Historical Society Papers and Records*, vol. 10 (1922) [first published 1897].

Snow, Richard. "The Battle of Lake Erie," *American Heritage*, vol. 27 (1976).

Squires, William Austin. *The 104th Regiment of Foot (the New Brunswick Regiment), 1803–1817*. Fredericton: Brunswick Press, c. 1962.

Stacey, C.P. "Another Look at the Battle of Lake Erie," *Canadian Historical Review*, vol. 39 (1958).

—— *The Battle of Little York*. Toronto: Toronto Historical Board, 1963.

—— "The Ships of the British Squadron on Lake Ontario, 1812–14," *Canadian Historical Review*, vol. 34 (1953).

Stanley, George F.G. "British Operations in the American Northwest, 1812–15," *Journal of the Society for Army Historical Research*, vol. 22 (1943–44).

—— "The Indians in the War of 1812," *Canadian Historical Review*, vol. 31 (1950).

—— "The New Brunswick Fencibles," *Canadian Defence Quarterly*, vol. 16 (1938).

Stone, William. *The Life and Times of Sa-Go-Ye-Wat-Ha or Red Jacket*, 2nd rev. ed. Albany, 1866.

Suite, Benjamin. *La Bataille de Châteauguay*. Quebec: R. Renault, 1899.

Suthren, Victor. "The Battle of Châteauguay," *Canadian Historic Sites: Occasional Papers in Archeology and History*, no. 11 (1974).

Terrell, John Upton. *Zebulon Pike: The Life and Times of an Adventurer*. New York: Weybright and Talley, 1968.

Thompson, E.J. "Laura Ingersoll Secord," *Niagara Historical Society Publications*, no. 25 (1913).

Thompson, Mabel W. "Billy Green, the Scout," *Ontario History*, vol. 44 (1952).

Tohill, Louis A. "Robert Dickson, Fur Trader on the Upper Mississippi," *North Dakota Historical Quarterly*, vol. 3 (1928).

Tucker, Glenn. *Poltroons and Patriots: A Popular Account of the War of 1812*, 2 vols. Indianapolis: Bobbs-Merrill, 1954.

—— *Tecumseh: Vision of Glory*. Indianapolis: Bobbs-Merrill, 1956.

Upton, Emory. *The Military Policy of the United States*. Washington: Government Printing Office, 1907.

Van de Water, Frederic F. *Lake Champlain and Lake George*. Indianapolis: Bobbs-Merrill, 1946.

Van Fleet, James A. *Old and New Mackinac. . . .* Ann Arbor, 1870.

Wallace, W.S. *The Story of Laura Secord: A Study in Historical Evidence*. Toronto: Macmillan, 1932.

Warner, Mabel V. "Memorials at Lundy's Lane," *Ontario Historical Society Papers and Records*, vol. 51 (1959).

Watson, O.K. "Moraviantown," *Ontario Historical Society Papers and Records*, vol. 28 (1932).

Way, Ronald. "The Day of Crysler's Farm," *Canadian Geographical Journal*, vol. 62 (1961).

Wickliffe, Charles A. "Tecumseh and the Battle of the Thames," *Register of the Kentucky Historical Society*, vol. 60 (1962).

Wilkinson-Latham, Robert. *British Artillery on Land and Sea, 1790–1820*. Newton Abbot: David and Charles, 1973.

Williams, Charles. "George Croghan," *Ohio Archaeological and Historical Society Publications*, vol. 12 (1903).

Williams, Clara S. "An Experience of 1813," *Buffalo Historical Society Publications*, vol. 26 (1922).

Williams, John S. *History of the Invasion and Capture of Washington and of the Events Which Preceded and Followed*. New York: Harper & Brothers, 1857.

Wilner, Merton. *Niagara Frontier: A Narrative and Documentary History*, 4 vols. Chicago: S.J. Clarke, 1931.

Winter, Nevin O. *A History of Northwest Ohio*. . . . Chicago: Lewis Publishing, 1917.

Wise, S.F. and Brown, R. Craig. *Canada Views the United States: Nineteenth-Century Political Attitudes*. Toronto: Macmillan, 1967.

Yaple, R.L. "The Auxiliaries: Foreign and Miscellaneous Regiments in the British Army, 1802–1817," *Journal of the Society for Army Historical Research*, vol. 50 (1972).

Young, Bennett H. "The Battle of the Thames," *Filson Club Publication* no. 18 (1903).

Zaslow, Morris and Turner, Wesley B. (eds.). *The Defended Border: Upper Canada and the War of 1812*. Toronto: Macmillan, 1964.

Index - Invasion of Canada

Adams, 192, 233; *see also* Detroit
Adams, John Quincy, quoted, 30
Alexander I, 323
Alexander, John, 206, 210
Allen, Jane, 298, 324
Allen, Lt.-Col. John, 278, 298,300,
301, 310, 319
Amherstburg, 34, 113–14, 119, 125,
168, 322
Ammerman, Albert, 315–16
Armistice, Prevost-Dearborn,
158–59, 192, 212–16, 218
Armstrong, John, 320
Army of the Centre, 205
Army of the Northwest, 87, 89, 112,
118, 133, 230, 276, 281, 283–84; as
prisoners, 226–27
Askin, Charles, 178, 180, 185, 187,
244
Askin, Capt. James, 305
Askin, John Jr., 105, 108, 174
Askin, John Sr., 23–24, 105, 161, 238,
325
Astor, John Jacob, 105–7, 111, 324
Atherton, William, 291, 304, 313–17,
328–31

Atlantic provinces, 21

Bâby, Lt.-Col. François, 125, 135,
188–89
Bâby, James, 125
Bâby, Lt.-Col. Jean-Baptiste, 162,
305
Ball, Lt. John, 244
Barbados, 130
Barron, Capt. James, 29
Barron, James, 48–49, 51, 66
Barton, Capt. Robert, 71
Baynes, Lt.-Col. Edward, 153,
158–59, 221; and armistice, 158
Beall, Melinda, 139–40
Beall, William K., 115–18, 128,
139–40
Beamer, John, 142
Beaver Dams, Battle of, 329
Beniteau, Jean-Baptiste, 134
Berkeley, Vice-Adm. George, 29
Bermuda, 321
Berthe, Jean-Baptiste, 164
Big Canoe, 108
Bisshopp, Lt.-Col. Cecil, 271
Black Bird, 200, 295

Black Partridge, 200, 201
Black Rock, N.Y., 213, 233, 270
Black Snake, *see* Wells, Billy
Black Swamp, 94, 291
Bloom, Lt.-Col., 254
Bloomfield, Gen., 274
Blue Jacket, 149
Blythe, Ebenezer, 319
Bois Blanc Island, 168
Boismier, Jean-Baptiste, 135
Bordeau, Joseph, 304
Borodino, battle of, 225
Bourbon Blues, 283
Bower, Gustavus, 317
Boyle's Inn, 118
Brant, John, 254, 257, 260
Brant, Joseph, 222, 257
Brice, Pvt. John J., 313
Brigham, Pvt. William, 71, 75
British Army (regulars) 19, 24, 99,
    136–38
British Indian Dept., 33–34, 42–43,
    187, 324
Brock, Irving, 219
Brock, Isaac, 24, 32–33, 64, 105, 106,
    107, 115, 122, 132, 140, 168, 173,
    178, 187–88, 193, 216, 224–25, 227,
    235, 237, 239–40, 247, 320, 326;
    death of, 17–18, 250–51, 261–66;
    described, 78–79, 130–31; and
    democracy, 79; and Indians, 81,
    168–71; addresses legislature,
    141–46; proclamation of, 145;
    and Amherstburg defence, 151,
    166–68; and Tecumseh, 168–69,
    188; and capture of Detroit,
    174, 178–81, 219–20; ultimatum
    of, 175–76; forces on Niagara
    of, 213, 221, 231; and armistice,
    218–19; family of, 219; and Battle
    of Queenston Heights, 247–50;
    funeral of, 263–64; myth of, 188,
    264–66
Brock, Savery, 224
Brock, William, 219
Brock monument, 265–66
Brown, William, 71
Brown's Point, 242
Brownstown, Michigan Terr., 118,
    123, 148, 306; Battle of, 148, 333
Brownstown Creek, 148
Brush, Elijah, 21, 173, 182, 186
Brush, Capt. Henry, 146–47, 165,
    173, 186
Buffalo, N.Y., 213, 231
Buffalo Gazette, 273
Bullock, Capt. Richard, 258
Burlington, Vt., 156, 320
Burns, Sgt. Thomas, 200
Butler, Ens. William O., 311–12
Byfield, Shadrach, 192–93, 308–9

Calais, Me., 21
Caldwell, Col. William, 296, 309
Caledonia, 107, 233–35, 238, 322
Calhoun, John C., 83, 88, 95, 98
Cameron, Capt., 251
Campbell, Lt.-Col. John, 290
Cass, Col. Lewis, 92, 121, 125, 136,
    138, 140, 152–53, 173, 176, 182, 184,
    186; described, 92, 171; and plot
    against Hull, 172–73
Caughnawaga Indians, 329
Chapin, Luther, 114
Châteauguay, 330
Chauncey, Capt. Isaac, 216, 321
Cheeseekau, 55, 57
Chesapeake, 28; incident, 28–32, 40,
    41, 105
Chevalier, Amable, 108

886
—

Chicago, 203. *See also* Fort
  Dearborn
Chippawa, U.C., 248, 252, 258, 272;
  Battle of, 330
Chippewa, 218
Chippewa Indians, 12, 105, 108, 110,
  140
Chrystie, Lt.-Col. John, 237, 241,
  243, 259
Cicely (servant), 199
Clark, Gen. William, 76
Clarke, Maj., 156
Claus, Supt. William, 42, 44,
  62–63, 222, 296
Clay, Henry, 83–84, 88, 95, 187, 276,
  277, 321; described, 95–96; and
  war fever, 96–97; and Harrison,
  280–81
Cleveland, O., 119
Clibborn (soldier), 262
Combs, Leslie, 299
Constitution, 224, 322
Corbin, Mrs., 199
Craig, Sir James, 44, 63–64, 84, 131
Crawford, Lewis, 106
Crawford, Col. William, 34
Crillon, Comte Edouard de, 84
Crooks, Capt. James, 255–57,
  258–59, 261
Crysler's Farm, 330
Cuyahoga Packet, 112–13, 120, 194
Cuyler, Maj., 234

Dalliba, Lt. James, 161, 174, 176–77
Darnell, Allen, 319
Darnell, Elias, 291, 292, 300, 304
Darragh, Lt. Archibald, 12
Davenport, John, 331
Daviess, Joseph, 68–70, 74, 298
Day, Isaac, 297

Day, Sylvester, 12
Deaf Chief, 66
Dean, John, 136, 137, 188
Dearborn, Maj.-Gen. Henry,
  85, 138, 155, 158, 193, 207, 210,
  228, 230, 274, 322; plan of, 87;
  described, 154; and armistice,
  157–58, 212; and attack on
  Montreal, 274
De Boucherville, Thomas
  Verchères, 149, 160–61, 164, 178;
  at Battle of Maguaga, 162–63
Delaware Indians, 34, 35–36, 45, 46
Denison, George, 266
Dennis, Capt. James, 237–38, 243,
  244–45, 249, 252, 258
Detroit, 21, 119, 120, 181, 202, 289,
  305, 321, 325, 328; surrender of,
  185–86, 192, 227, 326
Detroit, 235, 238
Dewar, Lt. Edward, 117
Dickson, Robert, 77, 80, 81–82, 100,
  107–8, 110, 136, 200, 239; and
  Indians, 102–5
Dickson, Thomas, 238–39
Dickson, Mrs. Thomas, 239
Dixon (artillery commander), 184
Dolsen, Matthew, 134
Dominica, 129
Donovan, Sarah, 62
Dousman, Michael, 108, 111
Driscoll, Lt., 261
Dudley, Thomas P., 313
Du Pin (trader), 201

Edwards, Gov. Ninian, 295
Eel Indians, 45
Egmont-op-Zee, 146
Elliott, Alexander, 148, 150, 294
Elliott, Lt. Jesse, 233–36, 322

Elliott, Matthew, 33–34, 42–45, 60–64, 123, 135, 147, 168, 185–86, 222, 233

Elliott, William, 189, 315, 318

Embargo, U.S., 32

England, Joseph, 94

Erie, Pa., 322, 324

Eustis, William, 68, 86–87, 94, 113, 138, 194, 207, 274, 291, 321

Evans, Maj. Thomas, 215, 216, 237–41

Fallen Timbers, Battle of, 32, 37, 57, 197, 209

Family Compact, 265, 266

Federalists, 41, 84–85, 208–9

Fenwick, Lt.-Col. John, 236, 241, 244

Findlay, Col. James, 93, 172, 182, 184–85, 190, 194

1st Lincoln Militia, 255

Forsyth, William, 181

Fort Amherstburg, 80, 121, 122, 133, 136, 144, 150, 166, 305, 330; council at, 1808, 41–45; council at, 1810, 60–67; council at, 1812, 124

Fort Dearborn, 100, 196–97

Fort Defiance, 285

Fort Detroit, 181, 182, 184, 187

Fort Erie, 144, 213, 233, 322; siege of, 330–31

Fort George, 18, 144, 211, 221, 232, 240, 247, 248, 255, 322, 329

Fort Grey, 242

Fort Harrison, 69, 192, 289

Fort McArthur, 93–94

Fort Madison, 192

Fort Malden, 113, 126, 140. See also Fort Amherstburg

Fort Meigs, 202, 320, 322, 328

Fort Miami, 45

Fort Michilimackinac, see Michilimackinac

Fort Necessity, 94

Fort Niagara, N.Y., 213, 229, 231, 270

Fort Stephenson, 329

Fort Wayne, Indiana Terr., 37, 192, 196, 222, 282–83, 294; council at, 1809, 45–49; land purchase at, 45–49, 53, 65, 68; council at, 1812, 123

Fort Winchester, 286

41st Regiment (British), 149, 180, 192, 224, 257

49th Regiment (British), 130, 146, 224–25, 248, 251, 261–62, 264–65

Foster, Augustus John, 38–40, 83–85, 88, 95, 97, 153

Fourneaux, Jean-Baptiste, 134

4th U.S. Infantry Regt., 69–70, 92, 187, 190, 220

Fox Indians, 60

Frenchman's Creek, attack at, 270

Frenchtown, Michigan Terr., 297, 298, 301–3; Battle of, 306–13; massacre at, 314–17, 323–27

Frolic, 264

Galloway, Rebecca, 58

Garrett, Lt. Ashton, 310

Gates (grenadier), 306

Gaylor (quartermaster general), 173

Ghent, Treaty of, 16

Gibson, John, 53–54, 289

Ginac, Jean-Baptiste, 134

Girty, James, 60

Girty, Simon, 33, 62

888

Glegg, Maj. J.B., 168, 175, 185, 220, 262

Gooding, Lt. George, 114, 117

Gore, Francis, 41–45, 63, 143

Goya, Francisco, 146

Goyeau, Jean-Baptiste, 135

Graves, Maj. Benjamin, 301

Great Britain, American policy of, 40–41

Green Bay, 201

Greenville, O., 37, 320; treaty of, 32

Grouseland, 37, 49, 64, 76

Grundy, Felix, 96, 98–99

Guerrière, 223

Hamilton, Alexander, 238, 257

Hamilton, Robert, 238

Hampton Roads, Va., 28, 29

Hancock, James, 136, 137

Hanks, Lt. Porter, 11–12, 109–10, 140, 174, 182

Harrison, William Henry, 60, 67, 197, 230, 298–99, 303, 313–14, 320, 330; speech to legislature of, 33–35; described, 36; and land purchase, 45–49; at council, 1810, 49–54; at council, 1811, 64–66; and Tippecanoe, 67–76; and Winchester, 280–81; Indian policy of, 282–83, 290; appointed commander, Army of Northwest, 285; strategy of, 285–86; and relief of Detroit, 289, 291–92.

Harmar, Josiah, 197

Hart, Anna, 323

Hart, Captain Nathaniel, 278, 303, 314–16, 319

Hayes, Sgt., 199

Heald, Capt. Nathan, 100, 198, 200

Heald, Rebekah, 198, 199, 200

Henry, John, 84

Hickman, Mrs., 315

Hickman, Capt. Paschal, 315, 319

Holcroft, Capt. William, 255, 257

Hopkins, Maj.-Gen. Samuel, 278, 288–89

Howard, Gov., 76

Hull, Abraham, 91, 92, 115, 176, 184, 186

Hull, Isaac, 224

Hull, William, 85–87, 89, 90–94, 112, 119, 120, 121, 123, 135, 147, 158, 160, 166, 170–71, 173, 175, 190, 196, 198, 320; advice of, 86; described, 90; and invasion of Canada, 124, 125; proclamation of, 125–28, 184; at Sandwich, 138–40, 150–53; plot against, 173; and defence of Detroit, 176, 177, 180; mental state of, 182–84; and surrender of Detroit, 184–85, 191; court martial of, 193–94

Hunter, 180

Ilbert, Anne, 263

Impressment, 22, 30–31, 84, 323

Indiana Territory, 35

Indian confederacy, 45, 52, 58, 65, 66–67, 75–76, 170, 294, 326; Indians, 25–26, 30, 35–38, 70–75, 90, 101–2, 105, 110, 117–18, 122, 123, 127–28, 139, 158, 168, 183, 187, 222, 282, 288, 314–18, 325–26; U.S. policy toward, 23, 25–26, 34, 80–81, 85–86, 95; British policy toward, 33–34, 42–45, 60–64, 325; and captives, 149, 200–2, 331; and capture of Detroit, 178

Ironsides, George, 60

Iroquois Indians, 55, 140, 141, 145, 169. *See also* Mohawks
Irvine, 2d Lt. Robert, 234, 308

Jacob, Frederick, 287–88
Jackson, Stonewall, 183
Jarvis, George, 250
Jarvis, Samuel Peters, 186, 247, 260, 262
Java, 322
Jefferson, Thomas, 22, 25, 99; quoted, 13, 34
Jerome, Jean-Baptiste, 314
Jennings, Lt. Jesse, 53–54
Jessamine Blues, 300
Jesup, Maj. Thomas, 177, 183, 184
Johnson, Richard M., 280
Johnson, Samuel (quoted), 31
Jordan, Walter, 199–200
Judy, Capt., 295

Kentuckians, 286, 301, 330, 331; character of, 278–80, 281
Kentucky, 22, 276, 324; volunteers, 69, 276–77, 288, 320
Kingsbury, Col. Jacob, 87
Kingston, 221, 321, 322
Kinzie, John, 199

Lachine, 129
Lady Prevost, 218
Lake Champlain, 158, 274, 331; invasion route of, 87, 129
Lake Erie, 112, 233–34; and American strategy, 86–87; Battle of, 329
Lake Ontario, 215, 216, 230, 321, 322
Langdon, Augustus, 177
La Salle, "Jocko," 304
Lauewausika, *see* The Prophet

Lee, Mrs., 201
Leopard, 29
Lett, Benjamin, 265
Lewis, Morgan, 229
Lewis, Lt.-Col. William, 299–300, 301–2, 304, 310
Lewiston, N.Y., 205, 207, 212, 231
Little Turtle, 37, 44, 197
Long Point, 141
Lower Sandusky, O., 298
Loyal and Patriotic Society of Upper Canada, 327
Lovett, Maj. John, 205, 206, 209–11, 212, 215, 226, 227, 239, 242, 261; described, 211
Lovett, Nancy, 210
Loyalists, 26, 143
Lucas, Robert, 133–34, 136, 146, 151, 153, 172, 190; at Brownstown, 147–48
Lundy's Lane, Battle of, 330

MacArthur, Douglas, 183
McArthur, Col. Duncan, 89, 91–94, 133, 134–35, 150, 152, 165, 172, 173, 182, 194; described, 91
McCay, William, 180
McClanahan, Maj., 309, 313
McCullough, Capt. William, 139, 146, 147, 161
Macdonell, Lt.-Col. John, 175, 185, 186, 247, 251
Macedonian, 322
McGregor, John, 134
Mackinac Island, *see* Michilimackinac
McKee, Alexander, 43–45, 62
McKee, Capt. Sam, 285
McKee, Thomas, 33, 43, 139, 222, 296

McKee's Point, 178
McLean, Lt. Archibald, 251, 266
McLean, Capt. Hector, 43
Madison, Dolley, 85–86, 88
Madison, Maj. George, 301, 311, 312
Madison, James, 22, 32, 45, 97, 98,
    153, 216, 264, 321, 322
Maguaga, 147, 161; Battle of,
    162–65, 326
Maitland, Gen. Alexander, 220
Mallory, Timothy, 331
Manete, 58
Mars, Stephen, 72
Martin, Capt., 118
Martin, Daniel, 28
Mascotapah, see Dickson, Robert
Maumee River, 94; rapids of, 189,
    286–87, 289, 292, 296, 297
Meigs, Gov. Return, 90, 120, 172,
    295
Melampus, 28
Menominee Indians, 12, 104, 108,
    136, 138
Merritt, William Hamilton, 263
Miami Indians, 45, 46, 55, 197, 283,
    289, 296, 305
Michilimackinac, 81, 173, 202, 321;
    capture of, 11–13, 107–11, 140, 326
Milbanke, Annabella, 83
Militia, 19, 20, 92–93, 99, 121;
    Canadian, 19, 80, 121, 128, 129,
    135, 141, 143, 145, 178, 193, 259,
    265; Essex, 124–25; Kent, 124–25;
    Lincoln, 221; Michigan, 182;
    New York, 206; Ohio, 87, 89,
    133, 138, 282; U.S., 20, 123–24,
    156, 159, 207, 225, 240, 252, 258,
    269, 273; York, 221
Miller, Col. James, 92, 136, 161,
    162–63, 172, 182, 185, 194

Miller, John, 177
Mississinewa River, 290, 296
Mohawk Indians, 81, 193, 222, 253,
    257–60, 326
Monroe, James, 280–81, 291
Montreal, 87, 129, 154, 193, 228, 321
Moore, Maj.-Gen., 156
Moravian Town, Battle of, 330
Moscow, 264
Muir, Maj. Adam, 149, 160–61, 163,
    192
Myers, Lt.-Col. Christopher, 215

Nancy, 166
Napoleon, 11, 21–22, 183, 225, 264, 323
Navarre, Col. Francis, 303
Navarre, Peter, 304
Needs, John, 201
Nelson, Horatio, 115, 250
Newark, 213, 255, 263
New England states, 20, 21, 154, 323
New York (city), 31
Niagara frontier, 166, 207, 212–13,
    224, 226
Niagara River, 144, 207, 212, 232, 320
Nichol, Col. Robert, 169, 180
Non-Importation Act, 103
Northcutt, William, 283–84
North West Company, 106, 107, 122
Norton, John, 222, 253–54, 257

Ogdensburg, N.Y., 207
Ohio, 23, 80; volunteers, 89–91, 92,
    298
Ohio River, 193
100th Regiment (British), 60
103rd Regiment (British), 137
Orders in Council, 22, 23, 40, 41, 83,
    84, 95, 323; revoked, 97–98, 153
Orr, Sgt. Montgomery, 72

Osage Indians, 76
Oswego, N.Y., 215, 216
Ottawa Indians, 12, 60, 105, 108,
    110, 140, 148, 296

Peck, Judge, 254
Pennsylvania volunteers, 231, 270,
    272, 320
Perceval, Spencer, 97
Perkins, Gen. Simon, 298, 299, 301
Perry, Oliver Hazard, 322, 329
Petite Coté, 138
Pike, Robert, 135
Pike, Zebulon, 102
Piqua, O., 202, 282; council at,
    193–94
Plattsburg, N.Y., 156, 228, 274
Pope, Sen. John, 279
Port Dover, 166
Port Talbot, 166
Porter, Peter B., 83–84, 209, 213,
    217–18, 227, 229, 270, 272–73
Potawatomi Indians, 45, 46, 53, 60,
    71, 198–99, 283, 296, 305, 310,
    317–18, 325, 326, 328–29, 331
Pothier, Toussaint, 106
Powell, William, 102
Powell, William Dummer, 146, 220
Prescott, 207
Presqu'Isle, O., 300
Prevost, Sir George, 78, 79, 81, 88,
    97, 107, 129, 151, 193–94, 263, 295;
    described, 129–30; policy of,
    129–30, 132, 153, 222–23, 235–36
Price, Capt. James, 300, 319
Prince Regent, 143, 263
Procter, Lt.-Col. Henry, 144,
    163, 168, 169, 173, 188, 190–91,
    220, 221, 222; and Indians,
    293–94, 296, 326; and Battle of

Frenchtown, 305–6, 311, 313; and
    massacre, 323, 324–25
Prophet, the, 35–36, 37, 59–60,
    68–69, 75, 190; land policy of,
    36, 48–49, 55; philosophy of, 59
Prophet's Town, Indiana Terr.,
    48–49, 71, 75

Quebec, 32–33, 78, 193, 324, 330
Queen Charlotte, 177, 180
Queenston (village), 213, 237, 242,
    247, 248; attack on, 242–44
Queenston Heights, Battle of, 16,
    247, 248–52, 257–61, 265, 266,
    312

Randolph, Thomas, 74
Ratford, Jenkin, 29–30
Red-haired Man, see Dickson,
    Robert
Rensselaerwyck, 208
Republicans, 41, 95, 97, 208, 217
Reynolds, Maj. Ebenezer, 296, 297,
    306, 314
Reynolds, Dr. James, 182
Rhea, James, 282
Rheaume, Francis, 100
Richard, Father Gabriel, 190–91
Richardson, Capt. James, 256
Richardson, John, 161, 180, 186, 187,
    305–6, 308; and Indians, 161
Richardson, Robert, 306, 309
Richardson, Dr. Robert, 325
Ridout, George, 262
River aux Canards, 136, 138, 139,
    312
River Raisin, 160, 165, 173, 190, 289,
    297, 301, 309, 318–319. See also
    Frenchtown
Roach, 2d Lt. Isaac, 233–34

Roberts, Capt. Charles, 104–5, 106–8, 140, 173

Robinson, John Beverley, 143, 186, 242, 247, 260

Robinson, Peter, 188

Rocky River, 306

Rolette, Lt. Frederic, 114–15, 234, 306, 307

Rottenburg, Baron Francis de, 132

Roundhead, 124, 187–88, 309, 310

Rouse's Point, N.Y., 274

Royal George, 229

Royal Navy, 22, 29–30

Ruddell, Stephen, 57

Rupes, Capt., 124, 147

Russia, 320

Ryerson, Lt. George, 190

Sackets Harbor, 206, 216, 228, 230, 320, 321

St. Clair, Gen. Arthur, 44, 197

St. George, Lt.-Col. Thomas Bligh, 117, 121, 122, 124–25, 135, 144, 305

St. Joseph's Island, 12, 101, 104

St. Lucia, 129

St. Stephen, N.B., 21

Salina, 140

Sandwich, 21, 121, 122, 124–25

Sandy Creek, 317

Sauk Indians, 59, 76, 118

Scott, Gov. Charles, 277–78, 280

Scott, Dr. John M., 278

Scott, Lt.-Col. Winfield, 225, 233, 234, 241, 252–53, 257, 258, 260

Searls, Pvt. Charles, 317

Secord, Laura, 329

Selkirk, Earl of, 135

Shakers, 35, 59

Shaler, Charles, 119

Shaw, Sophia, 247

Shawnee Indians, 36, 42, 44, 45, 54, 55, 70, 123, 148

Sheaffe, Maj.-Gen. Roger, 18, 132, 215, 238, 263–64; at Queenston Heights, 253, 257–58, 260

Shelby, Gov. Isaac, 280, 288–89, 323

Simcoe, John Graves, 143

Simmons, Mrs. John, 201–3

Simpson, Capt. John, 319

Sims, Lt., 236

Sioux Indians, 12, 103, 104, 107–8, 140

Smilie, John, 96–97

Smith, Gov. John Cotton, 155

Smith, Thomas, 278

Smyth, Brig.-Gen. Alexander, 231, 232–33, 236, 254, 320; proclamation of, 267–68; described, 268–69; invasion attempts of, 270–71

Snelling, Maj. Josiah, 176, 177, 184

Soubiron, *see* Crillon, Comte de

South West Company, 106, 111

Spencer, Capt. Spier, 73

Split Log, 309

Spring Wells, Michigan Terr., 177, 329

Squaw Island, 236

Stoney Creek, 329

Strachan, Dr. John, 26, 265, 327

Strachan, John, 29

Strong, Gov. Caleb, 155

Stubbs, Samuel, 242, 260

Sutherland, Lt. Charles, 163

Talbot, Thomas, 141–42

Taul, Michael, 279

Taylor, Capt. Zachary, 289

894

Tecumseh, 38, 44, 48–49, 59, 60–61,
65–68, 75–76, 123, 140, 149,
161, 165, 169, 173, 178, 179, 187,
190–92, 198, 222, 294, 320, 326,
330; described, 50, 52, 55–59,
96, 168; land policy of, 52–54,
55, 65; advocates war, 123; at
Brownstown, 148; at Maguaga,
162, 163–64; at capture of
Detroit, 179, 181. *See also* Indian
confederacy
Tenskwatawa, *see* The Prophet
10th Royal Veteran Battalion, 104
Thames, 117, 118, 139
Thames River, 134, 144, 322
Thompson, Cpl. David, 72
Thorne, Dr., 261
Tippecanoe River, 48
Tippecanoe, Battle of, 67–75, 170;
effects of, 75–76, 85, 95–96, 117,
279
Tipton, John, 73
Todd, Dr. John, 318
Tomah, 108
Tompkins, Gov. Daniel, 208, 209,
210, 213, 227, 269, 273
To-to-win, 77
Towson, Capt. Nathan, 234
Tupper, Brig.-Gen. Edward,
brigade of, 287
Turkey Creek, 138, 326

United States, strategy of, 86–88,
98, 150, 154, 193
U.S. Army (regulars), 20, 25, 99,
159, 269
U.S. Navy, 22–23, 29
Upper Canada, 64, 98, 113, 129, 134,
327; war in, 16–17; treason in, 20;
American settlers in, 23–26, 118;

disaffection in, 27, 141–42; and
tradition, 26–27; people of, 143,
226; and death of Brock, 261,
262–65
Upper Sandusky, O., 286
Urbana, O., 94, 189

Van Horne, Maj. Thomas, 147, 148
Van Rensselaer, Harriet, 217
Van Rensselaer, Lt.-Col. Solomon,
206, 208, 210, 213, 216–17, 229,
230, 236, 261, 269; described,
209; and armistice, 215; and
attack on Queenston, 241,
242–43, 245
Van Rensselaer, Gen. Stephen,
205, 211–12, 218, 227–28, 230, 231,
269, 274; forces of, 208, 216, 226,
231–32; described, 208–9; attack
plans of, 232–33, 237, 241–42;
and attack on Queenston, 252,
253–54
Van Rensselaer, Van Vechten, 217
Van Vechten, Abraham, 237
Vassar, Peter, 94
Vincennes, Indiana Terr., 33, 48, 49;
council at, 1810, 49–54; council
at, 1811, 64–67
Vincent, Lt.-Col. John, 221
Vrooman, Solomon, 255
Vrooman's Point, 252, 256
Wabasha, 102
Wabash River, 48, 69
Wadsworth, Brig.-Gen. William,
206, 208, 228, 253–55, 258, 259
Walk-in-the-Water, 124, 147, 309
Walworth (postmaster), 119
Ware, William, 28
War Hawks, 22, 25, 41, 84, 95, 280;
strategy of, 95, 99

Washington, George, 183
Washington, D.C., 38–39
Wasp, 264
Watson, Simon Z., 142
Watts, George, 234
Wayne, Gen. Anthony, 37, 45, 197
Wea Indians, 289
Wellington, Duke of, 11, 137, 146
Wells, Billy, 37, 196–99
Wells, Ens. Levi, 319
Wells, Lt.-Col. Samuel, 302, 309
Wellesley, Lord, 83
Westbrook, Andrew, 142
White Horse, 70
White Wing, 58
Wilberforce, William, 258
Williams, John, 135
Williams, Capt. John, 249, 251
Winchester, James, 280, 281, 285,
    286–87, 291, 294, 296, 303, 320;

unpopularity of, 282, 284–85;
    described, 285; army of, 291–92;
    and relief of Frenchtown,
    297–99, 302; and Battle of
    Frenchtown, 304, 309–12
Winemac, 53
Winnebago Indians, 12, 71, 104, 108
Wool, Capt. John, 244–45, 249,
    250, 251
Woolfolk, Capt. John, 319
Wovoka, 59
Wyandot Indians, 42, 123–24, 150,
    296, 305, 309, 326

Yellow Jackets, 73
York, 77–78, 144, 262, 322, 327, 328
York Volunteers, 166, 242, 247, 251,
    256, 264

Adams, John Quincy, 665–66, 667, 670; described, 654–55; in St. Petersburg, 654–56, 659–60; at Ghent, 791, 794–5, 801, 414, 805–8

Adams, Dr. William, 669, 792, 793–4, 801

Alexander I, 654, 658

Alexander, Major, 484

Allan, Maj. William, 411, 420, 423, 425, 426, 432, 470, 471, 473, 817

Allan, Mrs. William, 428

Allcock, Chief Justice Henry, 635

Amherstburg, 403, 527, 529–30, 548, 567, 664, 803, 813

Ancaster, trials at, 665, 681–85

Anderson, Thomas G., 691

Ariel, 535

Armstrong, John, 402, 431–32, 476, 593–96, 603, 608, 632, 674, 702, 757, 773, 802, 817; described, 592–93; quoted, 457, 633, 754

Army, British:
Regulars, 399, 401, 422, 431–32, 619
Centre Division, 434, 510, 558, 588, 631, 642, 663; Right Division, 430, 465, 509, 663;
8th Regiment (King's), 661, 663; at York, 411, 415; at Chippawa, 707, 711–12; at Fort Erie, 738, 741
9th Regiment, 748
41st Regiment, 465, 509, 558, 561, 678; at Fort Meigs, 485, 494–95, 507, 512; at Fort Stephenson, 516–17; at battle of the Thames, 580–87 *passim;* at Fort Niagara, 639; at Lundy's Lane, 724, 727; and raid on Black Rock, 733–34
49th Regiment (Green Tigers), 453, 465; at Stoney Creek, 445–46, 447; at Crysler's Farm, 616–18, 621–23
85th Regiment, at Washington, 750
89th Regiment, 713, 717; at Crysler's Farm, 617, 618, 621, 623; at Lundy's Lane, 719, 727; at Fort Erie, 738, 741

100th Regiment, at Fort Niagara, 638, 641; at Chippawa, 707

103rd Regiment (New South Wales Fencibles), 663, 707; at Lundy's Lane, 725, 727; at Fort Erie, 739

104th Regiment (New Brunswick Regiment), 389–91, 727

Canadian Fencible Regiment, at Châteauguay, 599, 602; at Crysler's Farm, 618

De Watteville Regiment, 738, 740–41, 745

Glengarry Light Infantry (Fencibles), 399, 713–14; at York, 415, 416; at Lundy's Lane, 725, 727

Royal Newfoundland Fencibles, at York, 415; at Michilimackinac, 688, 689

Royal Scots, at Fort Niagara, 639, 642; at Chippawa, 707, 711; at Lundy's Lane, 725, 727

Army, U.S., 398, 399, 400–1; Army of the Center, 402; Army of the North, 402, 674; Army of the Northwest, 402, 474

2nd Artillery, 438

3rd Artillery, 424

9th Battalion, 722

2nd Brigade, 725

3rd Brigade, 622

1st Regiment, 723

4th Regiment, 602, 620

11th Regiment, 611, 711, 721

15th Regiment, 424

16th Regiment, 449

21st Regiment, 704, 710, 723, 730, 740

22nd Regiment, 721, 731

23rd Regiment, 448–49

25th Regiment, 710

Arnold, Capt. Christopher, 572, 573, 586

Askin, John, Sr., 587, 678

Atlantic provinces, 396

Bâby, Lt.-Col. Jacques, 561

Baker, Anthony St. John, 790

Baltimore, Md., 754, 763, 788

Barclay, Capt. Robert Heriot, 509, 523, 524–25, 527, 529–31, 549, 817; strategy of, 532, 538; described, 532–33; at Lake Erie, 538, 543, 545, 546–47

Barney, Commodore Joshua, 759

Barrett, Alfred, 429

Barry, Maj. W.T., 583

Basil, John, 411, 421

Bass Islands, 527

Bathurst, Earl of, 669, 798, 800

Bayard, James Ashton, 665, 666, 667, 669, 670, 817; quoted, 656; at St. Petersburg, 656–57, 658–59, 660; at Ghent, 790, 791–92, 800, 806

Baynes, Col. Edward (later Maj.-Gen.), 770, 787

Beaumont, Dr. William, 426

Beaver Dams, 454; battle of, 459–64

Beman, Joel, 428

Bemis, Asaph, 646, 665

Bemis family, 650

Benedict, Md., 750–51, 763

Bentley, Elijah, 429

Bernadotte, Jean Baptiste, 654

Bidassoa River, 771

Big Sandy Creek, 672

Bisshopp, Lt.-Col. Cecil, 454; at
    Black Rock, 465–69
Black Hawk, 478, 811; quoted, 400
Black Hawk War, 811
Black Rock, N.Y., 403, 464, 504,
    505, 645–47; attack on, 465–66;
    raid on, Aug. 1814, 733–34
Bladensburg, Md., 752, 754–56;
    battle of, 757–59
Blaisdell, Jonathan, 774
Bleecker, Maj., 426
Blockade, British, 398, 667
Bloody Assizes, 681–85
Bloody Boys, 451, 453, 454, 457, 461,
    463, 465
Blücher, Field Marshal Gebhard
    von, 531, 654
Boerstler, Lt.-Col. Charles, 457;
    described, 457; at Beaver Dams,
    460–64
Bois Blanc Island, 553, 559
Bolenstein (soldier), 487–88
Bonaparte, Joseph, 454
Bonaparte, Napoleon, 396, 531, 654,
    668, 770
Bond, Sgt. Elias, 710
Boulton, D'Arcy, 681
Bourne, Lt. Alexander, 484, 487,
    817
Bowles's farm, 569, 571
Boyd, Brig.-Gen. John, 457, 458,
    626, 817; at Fort George, 438,
    441; at Crysler's Farm, 620,
    621, 623
Brady, Col. Hugh, 731
Brevoort, Capt. Henry, 535
Brisbane, Maj.-Gen. Thomas M.,
    770, 787, 788
British Indian Department, 425,
    478, 516, 688, 691, 696

Brock, Maj.-Gen. Sir Isaac, 395,
    407, 414, 453, 554, 558, 636, 661,
    788, 812, 814
Brooks, Lt. John, 538, 539
Brown, Brig.-Gen. Jacob (later
    Maj.-Gen.), 663, 674, 715–17,
    818; on St. Lawrence, 611,
    612–13, 615–16, 620, 626; and
    invasion of Niagara peninsula,
    702–4; described, 704–5, 718; at
    Chippawa, 704–5, 709, 710; at
    Lundy's Lane, 722–23, 724–25,
    726, 728, 729, 731; at Fort Erie,
    746–47
Brown, Rev. James, 405
Brown, Noah, 507, 524, 767
Brown, Samuel, 548
Brown Bess (musket), 401
Brum, Peter, 784
Brush, Elijah, 587, 678
Brush, Henry, 678
Brussells, Belgium, 800
Bryson, Robert (farm), 601
Buchan, Lt. Edward, 541, 546
Buffalo, N.Y., 644, 674, 733; attack
    on, 645–52, 677
Bull, Lt.-Col. John, 709
Bullock, Lt. Richard, 479, 587, 639,
    687n.
Bullock, Capt. Richard, 687
Bunnell, David, 536, 540–41, 542
Burkelon, Isaac, 487
Burlington, Heights, 440, 443, 471,
    472, 587, 628, 685, 716
Burn, Col. James, 440, 449
Burns, John, 629
Burr, Aaron, 591
Byfield, Pte. Shadrach, 735–36; at
    Fort Stephenson, 519–20; at
    battle of Thames, 580–81, 585,

587; at Fort Schlosser, 644; at
    Lundy's Lane, 724; at raid on
    Black Rock, 734

Caldwell, Billy, 573
Caldwell, William, 642
Caledonia, 504, 535, 538, 541, 543
Calloway, Col. John, 579
Campbell, Eliza, 637
Campeaux (scout), 580
Carrol, Mrs., 435
Cassin, Lt. Stephen, 783
Castlereagh, Viscount, 669
Caughnawaga Indians, 454, 455,
    457, 483; at Beaver Dams,
    459–64; at Châteauguay, 606–7
Chambers, Capt. Peter, 488–89,
    495, 517, 580
Champlin, Stephen, 699
Chandler, Brig.-Gen. John, 448–49
Chapin, Dr. Cyrenius, 451, 456, 632,
    633, 644, 645, 818; described, 457;
    at Beaver Dams, 460, 464; at
    Buffalo, 648–49
Chapin children, 648–49, 650
Chatham, 560, 563–64, 571, 664
Châteauguay, battle of, 399,
    602–10, 613
Châteauguay Four Corners, N.Y.,
    596–99, 600, 603, 609–10
Châteauguay River, 596, 597, 600,
    602–3
Chauncey, Commodore Isaac,
    403, 505–6, 511, 522–23, 526,
    551, 671–73, 702, 715–16, 747,
    767, 818; at York, 427, 429,
    431, 471–72; at Fort George,
    439; described, 442; on the St.
    Lawrence, 611, 612
Cheeseekau, 574

Chewett, Lt.-Col. William, 423
Chippawa, 702–3, 715, 717; battle of,
    704–12
Chippawa, 535, 541, 546, 647
Chippawa Creek, 702, 704, 713, 747
Chippewa Indians, 412, 483, 499,
    555, 562, 691
Chittenden, Gov. Martin, 788
Christie, William, 485
Chubb, 779, 781
Church of England, 407
Clark, Gen. George Rogers, 515
Clark, Lt.-Col. John, 462
Clark, Lt.-Col. Thomas, 465
Clark, Gov. William, 515–16
Claus, Col. William, 439
Clay, Cassius Marcellus, 492
Clay, Brig.-Gen. Green, 480, 490,
    492, 500; described, 492; at Fort
    Meigs, 512–13
Clay, Henry, 546, 551, 818; at
    Gothenburg, 665–70; at Ghent,
    791, 796–98, 800–1, 803–4, 805–6
Cleveland, O., 548
Cochrane, Vice-Adm. Alexander,
    677, 752
Cockburn, Rear-Adm. George,
    751–52, 761, 762, 763
Cockrel, Richard, 629
Codd, Lt., 751, 758
Coleman, Capt. Thomas, 582
Combs, Capt. Leslie, 493
Confiance, 767, 773, 778, 779, 780–81
Conner, John, 514
Cook's Point, 616
Cooper, James Fenimore, 552
Corman, Isaac, 444
Corman, Kezia, 444
Covington, Brig.-Gen. Leonard,
    621

Crab Island, 768, 783
Craig, Sir James, 600
Crawford, William H., 669
Croghan, Maj. George (later Lt.-Col.), 818; at Fort Stephenson, 514, 516–22; described, 515; at Michilimackinac, 692–96; at Nottawasaga Bay, 696–97
Crookstown, U.C., 435
Crowther, Capt. William, 564, 569
Crysler, John, 626, 662; farm, battle of, 616–23
Cumberland Head, 768, 779
Cutter, George, 429

Daly, Capt. Charles, 606
Davenport, Ambrose, 694
Davies, Maj. Davis Byron, 641
Dawson, Capt. Thomas, 638, 639
Dearborn, Maj.-Gen. Henry, 402–3, 450, 456–58, 464, 818; described, 410; at York, 425, 427, 430–31; at Fort George, 436, 437–38, 440
De Cew, John, 454; house, 454, 455, 456, 457
Deffield, Mr., 452
Deffield, Mrs., 452
De Haren, Maj. Peter, 454, 459, 460, 461, 462–63
Delaware Indians, 562, 575
De Rottenburg, Maj.-Gen. Francis, 391, 433, 465, 469, 509–10, 559, 563, 587, 770
De Salaberry, Lt.-Col. Charles-Michel d'Irumberry, 814, 822; described, 599–600; at battle of Châteauguay, 599–610
De Salaberry, Ignace, 599
Detour channel, 698, 699

Detroit, Michigan Terr., 395, 559, 561, 566, 568, 588, 687
Detroit, 506, 509, 510, 523, 527, 531, 533; at battle of Lake Erie, 535, 538, 541–43, 545
Devil's Own battalion, see Militia, Canadian: Select Embodied, 5th Battalion
De Watteville, Maj.-Gen. A.L.C., 599, 608, 609
Dick, Lt., 726
Dickson, Robert, 478, 511, 555, 637, 812, 818; at Fort Meigs, 479; at Fort Stephenson, 516; described, 688; at Michilimackinac, 690–91
Dickson, Thomas, 689
Dickson, William, 637, 689
Dickson, Mrs. William, 637
Dixon, Capt. Matthew, 563–64
Dobbins, Daniel, 504, 507–8, 524
Dolsen, Isaac, 662; farm, 570
Don River, 470, 472
Douglass, 2nd-Lt. David Bates, 714–15, 717, 732, 818; at Lundy's Lane, 719, 722, 724; at Fort Erie, 737, 741–42, 743
Dover, U.C., 564, 569
Downie, Capt. George, 768, 773, 777–81, 786
Drummond, Lt.-Gen. Sir Gordon, 631, 661–65, 683, 684, 713, 717, 718, 734, 748, 791, 818; and Fort Niagara, 639–40; described, 661; at Sackets Harbor, 671–73; at Lundy's Lane, 723, 727, 729; quoted, 735, 744–45; at Fort Erie, 736–38, 744, 745, 747
Drummond, Lt.-Col. William, 739, 743, 745

Ducharme, Capt. François
Dominique, 818; at Beaver
Dams, 459–60, 462, 463; at
Châteauguay, 599
Dudley, Lt.-Col. William, 492,
493–94, 495–96, 500
Duke of Gloucester, 423
Dulles, John H., 764–65
Dunlop, Dr. William "Tiger," 626,
732, 743, 746–47, 818; quoted,
399, 816

Eagle, 767, 779, 780–83
Eckford, Henry, 507, 508
Elliott, Lt. Jesse, 504, 507, 526,
549–52, 819; described, 504; at
battle of Lake Erie, 535, 538,
541–42, 544–46
Elliott, Matthew, 498, 505, 555, 688;
at Fort Stephenson, 516, 517;
at battle of Thames, 560–61,
570–71, 576; at Fort Niagara, 642
Ellis, Capt., 623
Empress Mother of Russia, 659
Erie, Pa., 507, 509
Espionage, 396, 596, 600–1, 676, 776
Ewell, Dr. James, 760, 762

Fallen Timbers, Battle of, 481, 556
Family Compact, 815
Farmer's Brother, 468
5th Baltimore Light Dragoons, *see*
Militia, U.S.: Baltimore 5th
Finan, Patrick, 419, 423
Finch, John, 430
Finch, 779, 781, 785
Finnis, Capt. Robert, 538
Fischer, Lt.-Col. Victor, 738, 740, 741
FitzGibbon, Lt. James (later
Capt.), 445, 451, 453–56, 748, 819;

at Stoney Creek, 447; described,
453–54; at Beaver Dams,
460–64; attack on Black Rock,
464–69
Five Mile Meadows, 642
Fontaine, Lt., 729
Forrest, 2nd-Lt. Dulaney, 539, 542,
547
Forsyth, Capt. Benjamin, 416, 425,
436, 614
Fort Amherstburg, 530, 553–54, 557,
558, 559, 588; council at, 1813,
559–60
Fort Covington, N.Y., *see* French
Mills
Fort Erie, 443, 451, 505, 702, 733;
siege of, 736–49
Fort George, U.C., 435, 450, 452,
456–57, 464, 588, 614, 631, 632,
634, 637, 714, 716; attack on,
439–40
Fort Gibson, N.Y., 466
Fort McHenry, Md., 788
Fort Meigs, O., second attack on, 512
Fort Miami, O., 477, 496, 498
Fort Niagara, N.Y., 435, 633, 636,
637, 644, 662–63, 797, 803, 813;
attack on, 639–42
Fort Schlosser, N.Y., 644, 717
Fort Stephenson, O., 472, 513, 514;
attack on, 516–22
Fort Winchester, O., 514
Forty Mile Creek, 443, 444, 451,
630, 631
Francis, William, 802
Frankfort, Ky., 678–81
Fraser, Sgt. Alexander, 447, 449
Fraser, Lt. Donald, 421
French Creek, N.Y., 611
French Mills, N.Y., 625, 663

Frenchtown, Michigan Terr., 564;
    battle of, 395, 397; *see also* River
    Raisin, battle of
Fulford, Henry, 758

Gaines, Brig.-Gen. Edmund P.,
    736–37, 745, 819
Gallatin, Albert, 665, 666, 667, 670,
    761, 819; at St. Petersburg, 656,
    658–59; quoted, 668; at Ghent,
    791, 794, 801, 802, 806
Galloway, Maj., 709, 712, 713
Galloway, Rebecca, 573
Gambier, Vice-Adm. Baron James,
    669, 792, 793, 801, 807
Gamble, Lt. Peter, 781
Garland, John, 545
General Pike, 442, 470
Ghent, Peace of, 807, 810–11;
    results of, 811–12
Gillette, Jervis, 643
Gillette, Miles, 643
Gillette, Orville, 643
Gillette, Solomon, 643
Gillette, Mrs. Solomon, 643
Girty, Simon, 570
Givins, Maj. James, 412, 415
Givins, Mrs. James, 425
Gleig, Lt. George, 750–51, 752, 753,
    758, 759, 761, 763, 819
Gordon, Lt. J.G., 518, 519
Gordon, Lt.-Col. John, 707, 711,
    724
Gothenburg, Sweden, 665–70
    passim
Goulburn, Henry, 669; at Ghent,
    792–93, 795–96, 801, 804, 819;
    quoted, 798–99, 800, 805
Grande Armée, 395
Grand Portage, L.C., 390

Grand River Indians, 636
Great Britain, strategy of, 397, 406,
    510, 772
Green, Billy, 443–46, 450, 819
Green, Levi, 443–44
Green, Tina, 444
Green Tigers, *see* Army, British:
    49th Regiment
Greenville, Treaty of (1795), 794
Grenadier Island, N.Y., 591, 596,
    610–11
Grenadier Pond, 418
Grosvenor, Seth, 648

Halifax, N.S., 598
Hall, Maj.-Gen. Amos, 644, 648, 674
Hall, Capt. John, 462
Hall, Maj. John, 580, 581
Hambleton, Samuel, 525, 528, 537,
    540, 549
Hamilton, Lt.-Col., 641
Hamilton, Capt., 490, 492
Hamilton, 436, 437
Hampton, Maj.-Gen. Wade,
    594–95, 598, 613, 624, 625,
    819; described, 596–97; at
    Châteauguay, 602–10
Hanks, Jarvis, 611, 616, 625, 702–3,
    709, 710, 715, 716–17, 745, 819;
    quoted, 676
Harris, Levitt, 660
Harrison, President Benjamin, 589
Harrison, Maj.-Gen. Henry,
    402, 445, 512, 523, 527, 556, 559,
    567–69, 632, 674, 820; at siege of
    Fort Meigs, 474–87; and attack
    on Fort Stephenson, 513–16; and
    battle of Thames, 577–89 *passim*
Hartwell, Samuel, 683
Hartwell, Stephen, 683

Harvey, Lt.-Col. John, 439, 450, 618, 820; described, 445; at Stoney Creek, 446–47, 449

Hatch, William Stanley, 558

Hawley's Tavern, 446

Hemmingford, L.C., 596

Hickman, Betsey, 679–81

Hickman, Capt. Paschal, 679

Hicks, Lt. William, 782–83, 785

Hinchinbrook, L.C., 596

Hindman, Maj. Jacob, 458, 728–29

Hollenbeck, Sgt., 598, 602

Holmes, Abraham, 572–73

Holmes, Maj. Andrew Hunter, 694, 695–96

Hopkins, Brig.-Gen. Timothy, 644

Hoysington, Job, 646

Hoysington, Mrs. Job, 647

Hughes, Christopher, 669, 810, 811

Hull, William, 788

Hunter, 535, 537, 541, 546

Impressment of seamen, 398, 659, 666, 668, 780, 792

Indians, 398, 484, 552, 589; at York, 415, 416, 418; at Beaver Dams, 462–63; at Fort Meigs, 477, 489, 494, 496–99, 511–13; confederacy, 483, 554, 589; and Procter, 511, 516, 517; at Fort Stephenson, 517–18; and battle of Thames, 575, 577, 582, 583, 585; at Crysler's Farm, 616, 619; at Lewiston, 643; at Buffalo, 646, 649; at Michilimackinac, 690, 691, 693–96; at Chippawa, 705, 709, 712; at Fort Erie, 746; rights of, and peace terms, 793, 794, 795, 797, 799, 805; and results of war, 812–13

Ingersoll, Charles, quoted, 464

Inglis, Lt. George, 545

Iroquois Indians, *see* Caughnawagas, Mohawks, Senecas

Irvine, Lt. Robert, 538, 545

Isaac Brock, 403, 423

Izard, Brig.-Gen. George (later Maj.-Gen.), 598, 626, 674, 747, 773, 775; at Châteauguay, 605–6, 608

Jackson, Andrew, 811

James (Kentuckian), 680

Jesup, Maj. Thomas, 731, 820; at Chippawa, 710; at Lundy's Lane, 720, 725, 728

Johnson, James, 650

Johnson, Lt.-Col. James, 566, 580

Johnson, Levi, 548

Johnson, Col. Richard Mentor, 564–66, 568, 577–78, 582, 583, 586, 820

Jones, William, 547

Jordan's Tavern, 424, 661

Kane, Robert, 648

Keating, Sgt. James, 691

Kelly, Sgt., 466, 469

Kennedy, John Pendleton, 756, 759

Kent, Duke of, 600

Kentucky, 397, 564, 589

Kerby, Mrs. James, 451

Ketcham, Capt., 721

Key, Francis Scott, 788, 802

King, David, 586

King, Maj. William, 424, 425, 427

King, Col. William, 613

King's Regiment, *see* Army, British: 8th Regiment

Kingston, U.C., 391, 595, 597, 611, 625; importance of, 401, 403, 593; and shipbuilding contest, 671–73
Knox, Capt. John, 758

904
—

Lady Prevost, 535, 541, 546
La Fourche, L.C., 601, 608
Lake Champlain, 624–25, 778–86; shipbuilding on, 767
Lake Erie, 472, 510, 556, 687; shipbuilding on, 402, 430, 507–8; battle of, 533–48, 587
Lake Ontario, 442, 470, 510, 523, 702; shipbuilding on, 402, 671–73, 778
Lake Simcoe, 696
Lake Winnebago, 689
Lamb, Henry, 540
Lawrence, James, 528
Lawrence, 507, 524, 526, 528, 532, 550, 692, 696; in battle of Lake Erie, 533–44, 546, 548
Leavenworth, Col. Henry, 718, 727, 728, 731
Le Couteur, Lt. John, 389–91, 744
Leftwich, Brig.-Gen. Joel B., 475
Leonard, Capt. Nathaniel, 640–41, 642
L'Espagnol, 695
Lewis, Meriwether, 515
Lewis, Maj.-Gen. Morgan, 457, 592, 597, 620, 626, 820; at Fort George, 441; described, 450; on St. Lawrence, 613, 614, 619
Lewiston, N.Y., 718; attack on, 642–43
Linnet, 779, 780–85
Little Belt, 535, 541, 546
Liverpool, Earl of, 668, 792, 797–99, 802, 804

Livingston, Robert, 696–700
London, 659, 665, 668, 670
Long Old Fields, Md., 752, 754
Long Point, U.C., 568, 662, 677
Long Sault, 615
Loring, Capt. Robert, 421, 681, 721
Loucks, John, 616–17
Lovejoy, Henry, 647
Lovejoy, Henry, Jr., 647
Lovejoy, Sally, 646, 649
Loyalists, 397, 407, 598, 626, 634
Lundy's Lane, 719; battle of, 719–30
Lyon, John, 429, 471

Macadesh Bay, 692
McAfee, Capt. Robert, 565, 566
McArthur, Brig.-Gen. Duncan, 588
McClay, John, 732
McClure, Brig.-Gen. George, 630, 632–33, 634, 637, 640, 644
Macdonald, Prime Minister John A., 815
Macdonell, Lt.-Col. "Red" George, 601, 605–6, 608
Macdonell, John, 681–82
Macdonough, Commodore Thomas, 764–69, 778, 820; described, 766, 767; at battle of Lake Champlain, 780, 784–86
McDonough, Lt. John, 743
McDouall, Capt. Robert, 509, 686–87, 688, 690, 691, 698, 811; and attack on Michilimackinac, 692–96
McDowell, Capt., 461
McGill, Andrew, 413
McGill, James, 413
McGregor's Creek, 572

McKay, William, 691

McKee, Alexander, 570

McKee, Mrs. Alex, 636

McKee, Thomas, 688

McKenney, Cornet Amos, 628–29

Mackinac Island, *see*
    Michilimackinac Island

McLean, Donald, 411, 418, 425, 428

McMullen, Alexander, 726, 728,
    731–32

MacNab, Allan, 411, 639, 640

McNeale, Capt. Neal, 415, 418

Macomb, Brig.-Gen. Alexander,
    775–76, 788, 820; described, 775

McRee, Col. William, 722–23

Madawaska River, 389

Madison, Dolley, 759, 760, 762

Madison, Maj. George, 679, 681

Madison, President James, 397, 592,
    667, 757, 759, 760, 763

Madison, 410, 416, 422, 427, 436,
    438, 439

Mallory, Benajah, 453, 634, 643,
    645, 664, 820

Manchester, N.Y., 644

Mann, James, 439

Manning, David, 596–98, 602

Manning, Jacob, 596–98

Markle, Abraham, 634, 664–65,
    677, 684, 820

Mascotopah, see Dickson, Robert

May, Wilson, 541

Menominee Indians, 483, 499, 516,
    691, 695

Merritt, Capt. William Hamilton,
    435, 443, 449, 627–32, 638, 639,
    642, 729, 820

Methodism, 407

Métoss, 478–80

Miami Indians, 562, 813

Michilimackinac Island, 396, 588,
    686–87, 690, 698, 700, 811, 813;
    American attack on, 692–96

Militia, Canadian: 398, 407, 412,
    415, 419–20, 432, 443, 455, 661,
    705, 716; Beauharnois, 599, 604,
    607; Canadian Voltigeurs, 399,
    599, at battle of Châteauguay,
    602, 605, 606, at Crysler's Farm,
    616, 619, 620–21; Châteauguay
    Chasseurs, 605; Essex and Kent,
    501; Green Bay Fencibles, 691;
    Incorporated (Upper Canada),
    398; Lincoln, 465, 639; Niagara
    Light Dragoons, 630; Norfolk,
    664; Oxford, 664; Provincial
    Dragoons, 435, 454, 616,
    627–30; Sedentary, 399; Select
    Embodied (Lower Canada),
    399, 601, 605, 5th Battalion, 599;
    York Volunteers, 407; Sedentary
    and Select Embodied at battle
    of Châteauguay, 599–610

Militia, U.S.: 396, 398, 475,
    559, 632–33, 748; Baltimore
    5th, 756–57, 758; Canadian
    Volunteers, 453, 633, 643, 726;
    District of Columbia, 755,
    759; Kentucky, 397, 398, 518,
    527, 564–66, 568, 679, at Fort
    Meigs, 476–77, 491, 493–96, 502,
    at battle of Thames, 578–84;
    Maryland, 755–58; New York,
    396; Pennsylvania, 396, 476–77,
    523, 568, 704–5, 706, 722, 726,
    755; Vermont, 744; Virginia, 475,
    601, 755

Miller, Col. James, 723, 731

Milligan, George, 790

Mississauga Indians, 412

Mississippi River Valley, 690–91
Mitchell, Col. George, 424, 425
Mohawk Indians, 435–36, 454, 455,
    460, 463, 706–7
Monroe, James, 592, 657, 756, 757,
    804; quoted, 666
Montreal, 592–93, 595, 597, 599, 601,
    611, 612, 625
Moose Island, 805, 806
Moraviantown, U.C., 564, 569, 571,
    575, 585–86, 589
Morrison, Capt. John, 493, 496
Morrison, Lt.-Col. Joseph, 616–18,
    621, 727, 821
Morristown, N.Y., 612
Morton, Simeon, 429
Muir, Maj. Adam, 499, 561, 571
Mulcaster, Capt. William, 533, 612,
    615–16, 620
Mulholland, Henry, 430
Murray, Col. John, 630, 631–32, 637,
    638, 642
Myers, Lt.-Col. Christopher, 438

Nancy, 696–97
National Intelligencer, 762
Neill, Garrett, 685
Nelson, Horatio, 768
Newark, U.C., 435, 439; burning of,
    632–34, 636–38, 643, 651, 677
New Brunswick Regiment, see
    Army, British: 104th Regiment
New England states, 396
New Orleans, battle of, 810–11
New South Wales Fencibles, see
    Army, British: 103rd Regiment
Niagara, 507, 524, 526, 528, 532, 692,
    696; at battle of Lake Erie, 535,
    538, 541–46
Nicholas, Col. Robert, 723, 726

Nicholson, Capt. John, 421
Nolan, Lt. Maurice, 641
North West Company, 691, 697
Norton, John, 436, 463, 688, 706–7
Nottawasaga Bay, 304; action at,
    311–12
Nottawasaga River, 696, 697

Odelltown, L.C., 595
Oliver, Capt. William, 480, 489–90
Ottawa Indians, 554, 562
Overholzer, Jacob, 683–84

Pakenham, Sir Edward, 810
Parsons, Dr. Usher, 505, 527,
    548–49, 550, 821; at battle of
    Lake Erie, 534–39 passim
Paulding, Hiram, 783
Peace negotiations (Ghent), 669,
    790–807
Peace terms, British: 792, 794,
    797–98, 801, 804; American:
    657–58, 659, 666, 801–2, 804
Pearce, Col. Cromwell, 427
Perry, Alexander, 527, 548
Perry, Matthew, 505
Perry, Commodore Oliver Hazard,
    436–37, 472, 476, 505–8, 522–29,
    549–52, 569, 577, 583, 587, 767,
    821; described, 503–4, 505–6; at
    battle of Lake Erie, 533–48
Pettigrew (hired man), 650, 651
Pettit, Isaac, 685
Phelps, Samuel Shether, 785
Phillips, Edward, 472
Pike, Brig.-Gen. Zebulon M.,
    408; described, 409–10; at York,
    416–18, 420–22
Plattsburgh, N.Y., 624–25, 626, 768,
    770, 771, 775–77

Playter, Lt. Ely, 411, 412, 414, 418, 420, 421, 423–24, 428, 435, 470, 472

Playter, George, 411, 428, 470, 472

Plenderleath, Maj. Charles, at Stoney Creek, 447–48; at Crysler's Farm, 618, 622–23

Poe, Thomas, 732

Port Dover, U.C., 662, 664, 677

Porter, Col. Moses, 440

Porter, Peter B., 466, 674, 702, 704, 731, 821; quoted, 450; described, 408, 706; at Chippawa, 705–6, 708; at Lundy's Lane, 726

Potawatomi Indians, 489, 499, 813

Powell, Grant, 470

Powell, Mrs. Grant, 410–11, 425–26, 432

Powell, Justice William Dummer, 411, 425, 682

Power, Maj.-Gen. Manley, 770, 788

Prairie du Chien, Illinois Terr., 690, 692

Pratt, Sophia, 650

Pratt's Ferry, 647, 650

Preble, 779, 781

Prescott, U.C., 612–13, 615

Presque Isle, Pa., 403, 472, 504, 506, 510

Prevost, Sir George, 406, 432, 501, 509, 510, 530, 531, 563, 601, 625, 671, 677, 687, 689, 745, 747, 766, 797–98, 821; at Châteauguay, 227–28; quoted, 609, 687, 777; at Plattsburgh, 770–74, 777, 786–89; described, 772

Prince Regent, 671, 672

Pring, Capt. Daniel, 778, 779, 785

Procter, Maj.-Gen. Henry, 397, 477, 509, 510, HO, 523, 530, 554, 556, 557–64, 567, 569, 570, 571, 821;

at Fort Meigs, 483–502 *passim*, 512; at Fort Stephenson, 516–22; and Indians, 516–17, 562–64; and battle of Thames, 574–85, 588–89

Prophet, the, 483, 511, 554, 555, 571, 821

Prophetstown, Indiana Terr., 572

Provincial Corps of Light Infantry, *see* Militia, Canadian: Canadian Voltigeurs

Prussia, 396

Purdy, Col. Robert, 602–9

Put-in Bay, O., 527, 533, 587, 664

Queen Charlotte, 535–38, 545–46

Queenston, U.C., 456, 458, 707, 714–15, 716, 718; battle of, 395, 414, 636, 674

Riall, Maj.-Gen. Phineas, 642, 649, 663, 703, 714, 718, 821; at Chippawa, 706–7, 710, 713; described, 707; at Lundy's Lane, 720–22

Richardson, John, 576, 678–81, 821; at Fort Meigs, 485, 494–95, 499, 512; at Fort Stephenson, 521; at battle of Thames, 581, 584, 585, 587

Richardson, Dr. Robert, 587

Ridout, Thomas, 473

Ripley, Lt.-Col. Eleazar W. (later Brig.-Gen.), 620, 674, 702, 704, 715, 718, 730–31, 746, 748, 821; at Chippawa, 710; at Lundy's Lane, 722, 723–24, 726, 728

River aux Canards, 560

River Raisin, battle of, 462, 489, 491, 518, 558, 679; *see also* Frenchtown

Roach, Capt. Isaac, 458

Roberts, Benjamin, farm, 596

Robertson, James, 780, 784, 785

Robinson, Maj.-Gen. Frederick
Philipse, 770, 773, 776–77, 786,
788, 821; described, 771–72;
quoted, 789

Robinson, John Beverley, 413, 473,
664–65, 772, 822; and Ancaster
trials, 681–85

Robinson, Capt. Peter, 473

Roe, Billy, 428

Rogers, John, 637

Rogers, Pte. Reuben, 390–91

Rolette, Joseph, 691

Romanzoff, Count, 658, 659, 660

Ross, Maj.-Gen. Robert, 751–54,
758, 762, 763, 788

Ross, Dr. William, 594

Rush, Richard, 758

Russell, Jonathan, 822; at
Gothenburg, 665, 666, 667, 670;
at Ghent, 791, 801, 806

Russell, Peter, 635

Sacjaquady Creek, 734

Sackets Harbor, N.Y., 391, 402,
403, 442, 471, 505, 590–91, 592,
626, 663, 674, 797; and shipbuilding contest, 671–73

St. André, L.C., 391

St. Catharines, U.C., see Shipman's
Corners

St. Clair, Maj.-Gen. Arthur, 555–56

St. Davids, U.C., 459, 638, 716

St. John, Margaret, 645, 646, 648,
649, 651

St. John, Margaret (the younger),
650

St. John, Maria, 649

St. John, Martha, 648, 650

St. John, Parnell, 650

St. John, Sarah, 650

St. John family, 649–50, 651

St. Joseph's Island, 692, 696

St. Lawrence River, 597, 599, 602,
610, 612, 625, 626, 674

St. Lawrence, 672, 673, 747, 748

St. Petersburg, Russia, 531, 653–54

St. Regis, N.Y., 624

Sandwich, U.C., 560, 561

San Sebastian, Spain, 761, 772

Saranac River, 771, 787

Saratoga, 767, 768–69, 778, 779,
780–85

Sauk Indians, 483

Saunders, Matthias, 420, 421

Sausamauee, quoted, 812

Schnall, Mrs., 585–86

Scorpion, 535, 537, 692, 696, 697,
698, 699

Scott, Lt.-Col. Hercules, 739, 742,
744

Scott, James, 761

Scott, Chief Justice Thomas, 411,
684

Scott, Col. Winfield (later Brig.-
Gen.), 399, 436–42, 457, 458, 470,
471, 614, 620, 673, 676, 701–2,
713, 718, 822; described, 675; and
invasion of Niagara peninsula,
703–4; at Chippawa, 709–12; at
Lundy's Lane, 719, 720, 721, 727,
729

Secord, Laura (Mrs. James),
455–56, 458–59, 814

Selby, Prideaux, 411, 427

Selby, Mrs. Prideaux, 428

Seneca Indians, 468, 647, 648, 704,
706

908

Seneca Town, O., 513, 515, 519
Sergeant, Hosea, 543
Servos, Daniel, 639
Sewell, Lt. John, 616, 620–21, 623
Shane, Anthony, 586
Shaw, Aeneas, 415
Shawnee Indians, 554, 813
Sheaffe, Maj.-Gen. Sir Roger
    Hale, 406–7, 424, 432, 433,
    636, 661, 822; at York, 412, 415,
    418–19, 420, 422–23; described,
    414
Shelby, Gov. Isaac, 476, 566–67,
    568, 578, 582–83, 585, 586
Sherman, David, 573, 586
Sherman's farm, 571
Shipman's Corners, U.C., 627–28,
    630
Shipp, Lt. Edmund, 517–19
Shortt, Lt.-Col. William, 518, 519
Simmons, William, 757
Sinclair, Capt. Arthur, 692; at
    Michilimackinac, 693–96; at
    Nottawasaga Bay, 696–97
Siousa, John, 760
Sioux Indians, 483, 499, 516, 555,
    688, 691
Sloan, James, 466–67
Smith, Daniel, 496
Smith, Harry, 753, 758
Smith, Brig.-Gen. Walter, 755, 756
Smuggling, 596, 705, 774
Snake Hill, 737, 738, 740, 742
Sodus, N.Y., 471
Somers, 544
Spanish Conspiracy, 591
Spearman, Sgt. Andrew, 640, 641
Spears's farm, 598–99, 602, 605
Stansbury, Brig.-Gen. Tobias, 755
Stone, Col. Isaac, 716, 731

Stoney Creek, U.C., 444; battle of,
    447–49, 450–51, 457, 754
Strachan, Ann McGill, 413
Strachan, Rev. John, 405, 411,
    432–33, 473, 815, 822; convictions
    of, 406–7, 455; character, 413–14;
    at York, 419, 422, 424, 426–27,
    430, 470–71; quoted, 661, 682
Street's Creek, 703, 704, 708, 709, 747
Strong, Samuel, 775
Stucker, Capt. Jacob, 578, 579
Superior, 672
Suter, Barbara, 762
Sutton, Quartermaster, 488

Talbot, Col. Thomas, 564
Tappan, Samuel, 730–31
Taylor, William, 526, 534
Tecumseh, 398, 511, 553–57, 559–60,
    561, 570, 812; described, 483, 555;
    at Fort Meigs, 477, 495, 498, 501,
    512; at Fort Stephenson, 516, 522;
    and mythology, 572–74; at battle
    of Thames, 576, 582, 584; death
    of, 584, 585–86
Tête du Chien, 690
Thames River, 559, 560, 567–68,
    577, 588, 589, 662; battle of,
    574–84, 678; results of, 587–89
Thornton, Col. William, 753, 758
Thorpe, Daniel, 614
Thorpe, Judge Robert, 635
Ticonderoga, 767, 779, 783
Tigress, 692, 696, 697, 698, 699
Toll, Johnny, 572
Tomah, 695
Tonawanda Creek, 644
Towson, Nathan, 709–10, 718; at
    Lundy's Lane, 720; at Fort Erie,
    737, 741

Treat, Capt. Joseph, 704, 710, 718
Trotter, Brig.-Gen. George, 578
Trowbridge, Dr. Josiah, 646
Tucker, Lt.-Col. J.G.P., 733–34
Turner, Daniel, 551
Tweeddale, Marquis of, 707, 711
Twelve Mile Creek, 454, 627, 631,
    722
Twenty Mile Creek, 454, 587, 628,
    631, 633, 716

Underwood, Lt. Joseph, 490–91,
    492–93, 495–96
United States, strategy of, 402–4;
    war purposes of, 397; see also
    Peace terms
Upper Canada, disaffection in, 396,
    423, 429, 471–72, 628, 661–62,
    664; American settlers in, 396,
    407, 683, 815

Vincent, Brig.-Gen. John, 440, 587,
    630, 631, 822; at Fort George,
    434–35, 439; at Stoney Creek,
    446, 449–50
Vitoria, Spain, 454
Volunteers, see Militia, U.S.

Walden, Judge, 650
Walk-in-the-Water, 570
Walmer Castle, 796
Warburton, Lt.-Col. Augustus, 518,
    548, 558, 561, 562, 564, 569–71
War Hawks, 565, 666
Washington, D.C., 638, 800
Washington, George, 391
Wayne, Gen. Anthony, 481, 556,
    591
Weekes, William, 635, 637
Weisinger, Dan, 678

Wellington, Duke of, 454, 654, 802;
    quoted, 804
Wells, Col. Sam, 514
Western Battery (York), 418–20
Wheeler, Timothy, 472
White, Capt. Samuel, 706, 709,
    712–14
Whitley, William, 572, 577, 582, 586
Wickliffe, Pvt. Charles, 584
Wilkinson, Maj.-Gen. James,
    409, 464, 590–96, 601, 608, 822;
    descent of St. Lawrence, 610–26
Willcocks, Joseph, 452–53, 627–28,
    630, 633, 637, 664–65, 677; de-
    scribed, 634–36
Willink, N.Y., 650
Wilson, Mrs., 719
Wilson's Tavern, 718, 722
Winder, Brig.-Gen. William,
    at Stoney Creek, 449; at
    Bladensburg, 754–59
Winnebago Indians, 499, 516, 688,
    689–91, 813
Wood, Calvin, 471–72
Wood, Capt. Eleazer D. (later
    Maj. and Col.), at Fort Meigs,
    477, 482, 487, 488, 493; at battle
    of Thames, 572, 577, 585; at
    Lundy's Lane, 718, 719, 740, 746
Wool, Maj. John E., 770
Worsley, Lt. Miller, 696–99
Wright, Moses, 514
Wyandot Indians, 554, 562

Yarnell, 1st-Lt. John, 537, 542, 543
Yellow Dog, 695
Yeo, Commodore Sir James Lucas,
    442, 450, 471, 510, 522, 523, 530,
    531, 747, 823; and shipbuilding
    contest, 671–673

York, U.C., 402, 403–4, 470–73, 501, 504

Young, Col. Robert, 663

Young King, 468

Youngstown, N.Y., 439, 640, 644